# INSIDERS' GUIDE® TO

# SANTA FE

## HELP US KEEP THIS GUIDE UP TO DATE

We would love to hear from you concerning your experiences with this guide and how you feel it could be improved and kept up to date. Please send your comments and suggestions to:

editorial@GlobePequot.com

Thanks for your input, and happy travels!

INSIDERS' GUIDE® SERIES

# INSIDERS' GUIDE® TO

# SANTA FE

FIFTH EDITION

**NICKY LEACH**

## INSIDERS' GUIDE

GUILFORD, CONNECTICUT
AN IMPRINT OF GLOBE PEQUOT PRESS

All the information in this guidebook is subject to change. We recommend that you call ahead to obtain current information before traveling.

# INSIDERS' GUIDE®

Copyright © 2003, 2005, 2010 Morris Book Publishing, LLC
A previous edition of this book was published by Falcon Publishing, Inc. in 2000.

Project Editor: Lynn Zelem
Layout Artist: Kevin Mak
Text design: Sheryl Kober
Maps: XNR Productions, Inc. © Morris Book Publishing, LLC

ISSN 1525-7959
ISBN 978-0-7627-5346-8

Printed in the United States of America
10 9 8 7 6 5 4 3 2 1

# CONTENTS

## Directory of Maps

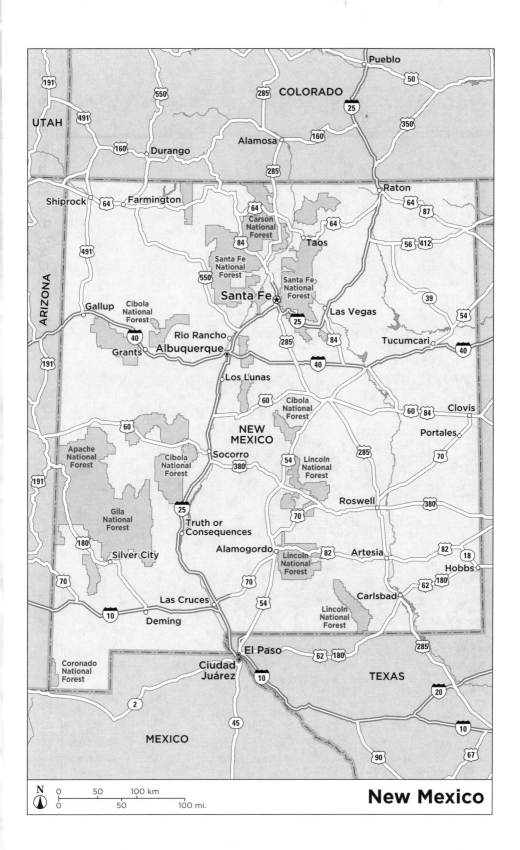

**New Mexico**

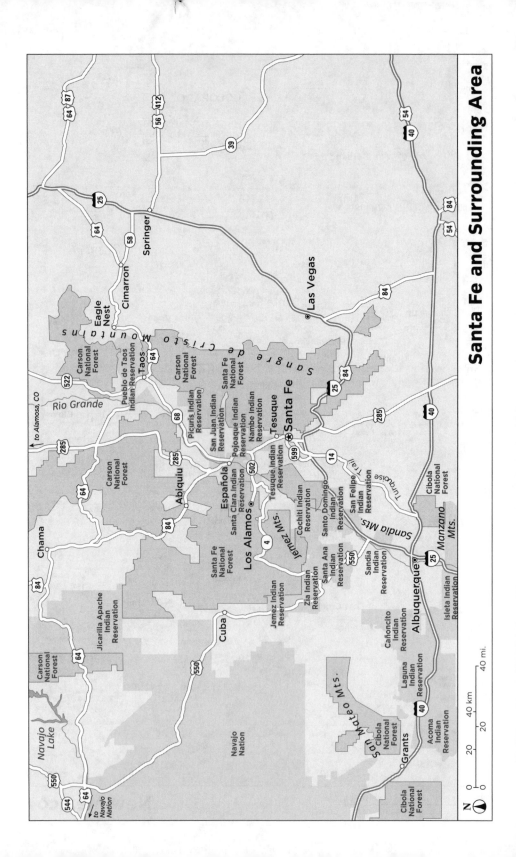

# Santa Fe and Surrounding Area

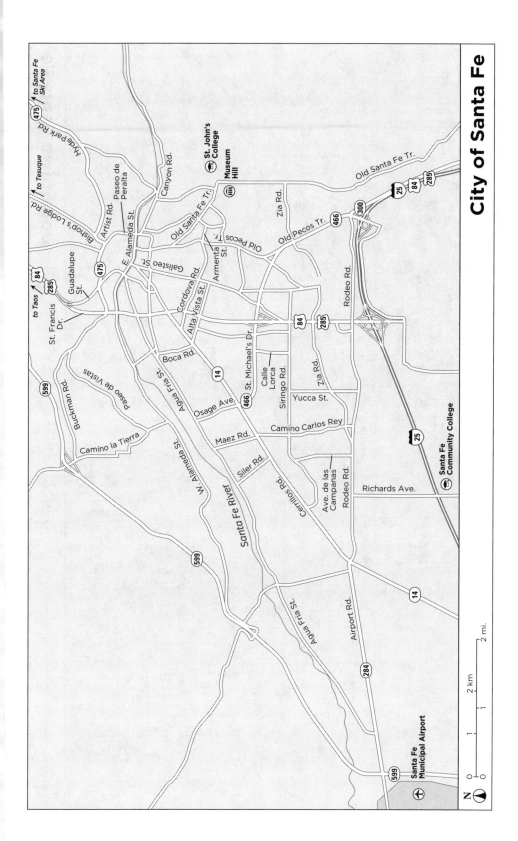

# City of Santa Fe

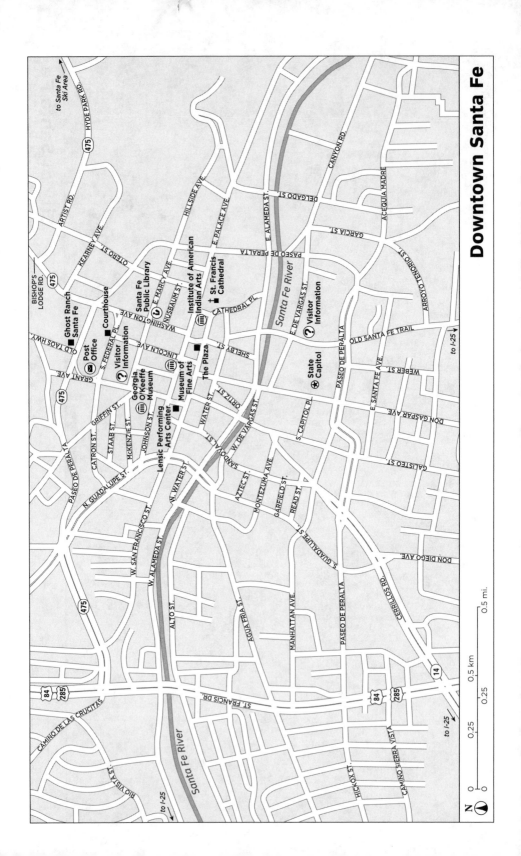

# Downtown Santa Fe

# PREFACE

Santa Fe is a jewel of a city. And like a jewel, either in the rough or finely cut, it has many facets, not all of which present themselves at first glance. All of the writers who have contributed to this guide over the years—Ann Hillerman, Tamar Stieber, Richard Mahler, and Nicky Leach—have probed the city from the outside in and, as residents, explored it from the inside out. We come to this project with different experiences and differing perspectives but with a shared affection and abiding respect for the city we call home. We've tried to impart our knowledge and enjoyment of Santa Fe in an illustrative, entertaining, and thoroughly candid fashion.

This is not meant to be an exhaustive account of what Santa Fe has to offer. That's why we have telephone books. The purpose of the *Insiders' Guide to Santa Fe* is to give you a taste of this extraordinary city, including its natural and cultural history, its physical and spiritual beauty, and, of course, suggestions about where to eat and sleep and what to see and do while you're here. Whether you're staying a couple of days, a couple of weeks, or the rest of your life, we're confident you'll find information in these pages you won't see in other travel guides. Even locals may learn a thing or two, just as we did in the course of our research.

As you can see just from the size of this book, Santa Fe has an enormous variety of attractions—its natural beauty and clean, crisp mountain air being high on the list—and distractions, ranging from the down-home to the urbane. For many visitors to the capital of New Mexico, a "backwater" state that even many Americans don't realize is one of our 50, this is a surprising revelation. But keep in mind that, despite its sophisticated trappings, Santa Fe is really just a small town in size and at heart. You're not going to find the same level of service and efficiency here that you would in, say, San Francisco or Miami. What you will find is a beautiful little city with friendly people and a fascinating history that predates Plymouth Rock. You'll also find a city deeply in touch with its cultural roots and a center of original thought and artistic enterprise. In fact, in July 2005, Santa Fe was honored by the United Nations Education, Scientific, and Cultural Organization (UNESCO) as the first "Creative City" in the United States—one of only three such cities in the world—in recognition of its leading role in promoting folk art and design. Santa Fe's mystery goes far beyond its artistic sensibility, though. There's an ageless mystery here—a magic that has drawn humankind to this place for thousands of years.

Please keep in mind as you read the *Insiders' Guide to Santa Fe* that people and places change, especially in an area undergoing as much metamorphosis as Santa Fe has in recent years and probably will continue doing far into the new millennium. We can't guarantee that the quality—or even the places—we've discovered in our travels will be the same during yours. Please let us know if you've had either a bad experience or a good one. We care.

# ACKNOWLEDGMENTS

I continue to learn more about Santa Fe every time I update this guide. For a town of some 72,000 people, we have an extraordinary number of creative and talented people doing wonderful and worthwhile things. I enjoyed talking to you all. Thanks to Ann Hillerman and Tamar Stieber for doing a superhuman volume of research and writing to create the first and second editions; Richard Mahler, my co-author and photographer on the third edition; and Richard Harris for assistance in updating parts of the Fourth Edition. Any errors in this, the Fifth Edition, are entirely my own. Gracias, Amigos!

—Nicky Leach

# HOW TO USE THIS BOOK

Where you start reading the *Insiders' Guide to Santa Fe* depends on your needs. One of the things we've liked about writing this book, and one of the things we hope you'll appreciate as you read it, is that each chapter is packed with useful information designed to be accessible and, we hope, entertaining. In this edition, we've added new "Close-ups," stories that give you insights into some of the people, places, and events that make our area special. Throughout the text you'll find tips (look for the 🛈) that provide an Insider's look into The City Different.

If you're on the plane heading for New Mexico, you'll probably want to look at the Getting Here, Getting Around chapter to help you figure out the best way to get from the Albuquerque airport to Santa Fe. If you're using the book to plan a vacation, our extensive accommodations chapter offers valuable information for finding a hotel or motel, bed-and-breakfast, deluxe resort, or vacation rental. Use the Annual Events and Festivals chapter to discover if a festival or something special is going on when you plan to be in town. The maps will help you find Santa Fe's sights and attractions.

We've got it covered in terms of what to do and where to go when you get here, too. The Attractions chapter, for example, gives you a comprehensive overview of Santa Fe's historic buildings, museums, and other places of interest. Kidstuff offers an overview of what to do to keep the little ones happy. Add the Parks and Recreation, Nightlife, and The Arts chapters, and you have a cornucopia of ideas, from galleries to golf, from hikes in the mountains to evenings with Mozart, from pottery classes to poetry readings.

To help visitors gain a greater appreciation for our town, the book includes a readable thumbnail history of the city from its prehistoric days as an Indian hunting camp to the present, post-atomic age. You'll find a layman's explanation of the American Indian and Hispanic cultures as reflected in the city's contemporary life and some suggestions on shopping for the handmade arts and crafts famous in both these traditions. Unlike most guidebooks, we include a close look at the diversity of religions and spiritual practices available here, and information on education, mainstream and alternative health services, and child care. If you're considering a move to Santa Fe, be sure to read our Relocation chapter for a comprehensive overview.

We've attempted, above all else, to give you information you can use to enrich your visit here or to help you decide if Santa Fe would be an appropriate place for you to live. If you've used other books in the *Insiders' Guide* series (and if you haven't, we hope you will), you'll find this book similar in terms of content.

Finally, we beg your indulgence if you encounter phone numbers or addresses that have changed since publication. We verified addresses and Web sites—but the currents of change run strongly here. Shops come and go; restaurants change owners, chefs, and focus; hotels move from private ownership to corporate properties; galleries get new artists. This everchanging scene—against the city's historic backdrop—keeps Santa Fe fresh and interesting.

If you'd like to share your own Insider's tips with us, we'd love to hear from you. Please send your comments and suggestions to: editorial@GlobePequot.com.

# AREA OVERVIEW

September 2008. Most of the United States had plunged into deepening recession with the failure of a string of banks and brokerage firms brought down by toxic mortgage loans and Wall Street ambitions. The repercussions were immediately felt worldwide, with worse still to come. Everyone had been affected in one way or another: a home foreclosure, a lost job in a shrinking economy, a tightening of credit and purse strings, and a general mood of apprehension worldwide.

But even in the midst of this crisis, it was not all gloom and doom. In fact, in Santa Fe, New Mexico, they were celebrating what many see as an exciting new milestone in the long, convoluted history of the New Mexico capital: the opening of the long-planned Railyard Park and farmers' market in the historic Guadalupe District and the spectacular new Santa Fe Community Convention Center in downtown. The Railyard and Convention Center were just the first in a string of grand construction and redevelopment projects whose completion coincides with the 400-year anniversary of the founding of the city. By May 2009, other critically acclaimed, multimillion-dollar projects had opened, including the refurbished downtown Plaza and the state-of-the-art New Mexico History Museum. Santa Fe's new attractions were given a big boost by the opening of the New Mexico Rail Runner train service between Albuquerque and Santa Fe on December 17, 2008. In a stroke of amazing serendipity, 60,000 passengers between the two cities rode the train in the first month alone, boosting local businesses even as others went out of business elsewhere in the country.

Over a decade in the planning, these cultural infrastructure projects have begun to fulfill Santa Fe's promise as a cultural capital, a promise given a big boost by the city's designation in 2005 as one of only three UNESCO "creative cities" in the world. For Santa Feans, it confirms what they already know: Santa Fe is unique. Since the late 19th-century, artists, architects, scientists, and thinkers have been attracted to this 7,000-foot-elevation, high-desert town for its glorious mountain setting; healthful air and seductive light; rich mix of Hispanic, Indian, and Anglo cultures; and laid-back lifestyle. Like a spicy salsa, made of native ingredients sparked with unexpected new exotic additions, outsiders have brought with them a variety of skills and institutions, from the Museum of New Mexico to the Santa Fe Institute, cultural events, new markets and businesses, and festivals beloved by locals and tourists alike, as well as new ideas that have become woven into the life of the city.

"These projects have moved us toward creating a slower but more equitable economy that will remain strong," said Santa Fe's hardworking mayor David Coss, a veteran of the exhaustive planning and construction process that led to Santa Fe's redevelopment projects. But that doesn't seem so strange in a city that has always been far removed—both literally and metaphorically—from the rest of the country for centuries. Change comes slowly here, and often painfully, as people with many differing views struggle for consensus. While western towns around it have boomed and bust, Santa Fe has deep roots that have allowed it to endure over generations and ride the swells of passing political and cultural storms elsewhere. That is the true appeal of the City Different.

i New Mexico's official state symbol is the Zia, an ancient sun sign taken from a design seen on a late-19th-century water jar from Zia Pueblo. The New Mexico flag—designed in 1923 by Reba Mera and officially recognized two years later—features a Zia symbol in red on a field of bright gold. Those were the colors of Queen Isabel of Castilla, which the Spanish conquistadores brought with them to the New World.

## TRICULTURAL HARMONY

For those of you who still believe the Pilgrims were the first Europeans to settle in what would become the United States of America, throw away your old Anglo-centric textbooks and ideas and take note: Santa Fe was founded between 1607 and 1610—Historians disagree on the exact date—long before the Pilgrims landed on Plymouth Rock, making Santa Fe America's oldest state capital and its second-oldest city. Only St. Augustine, Florida, founded in 1563, is older. You can almost feel the history buzz beneath your feet as you walk the narrow, winding streets of downtown Santa Fe toward the Plaza—the social, commercial, and historical heart of the city. The Plaza is the site of the original settlement of Santa Fe. It's also where the Santa Fe Trail—the 19th-century trade route that originated in Independence, Missouri—ended and El Camino Real, the 16th-century "Royal Road" or "King's Highway" from Mexico City, began.

A few structures, such as the Palace of the Governors on the Plaza's north side, actually date from the 17th century. But most downtown buildings have been renovated or newly built with facades of adobe-colored stucco designed to blend in with the early-20th-century Spanish-Pueblo revival architecture whose earth tones, flat roofs, small, deeply set windows, and protruding vigas (log beams) and canales (rectangular overhead drainage pipes) imitate construction methods used for centuries by the Pueblo Indians. You'll also see examples of the Territorial

style, a relative of Greek Revival architecture that first came to Santa Fe in 1846 with the U.S. occupation. These buildings, both old and new, are characterized by redbrick facades, slender exterior columns, dentiled cornices, and larger windows and doors than in classical Spanish-Pueblo revival buildings like the Museum of Fine Arts and La Fonda Hotel on the Plaza. Whatever and wherever the architecture, you're likely to find pendulous red *ristras*, or strings of chiles, hanging welcomingly from a viga or *portal* (porch).

Despite its face-lift and a proliferation of tourist-oriented businesses, the Plaza remains the soul of Santa Fe—a meeting place for old-timers and newcomers, for lunch breaks and lovers' trysts, for political rallies and historical festivals, or just to put your feet up and sleep.

Though many ethnic groups coexist in Santa Fe, the three that dominate are Hispanics, Native Americans, and "Anglos"—a category that refers to anyone who's not Hispanic or Native American, including such distinctly non-Anglo ethnicities as Italians, Jews, and Poles, and sometimes even Asians and African Americans! Together they create a fascinating mosaic of cultures and values that overlap and occasionally conflict. Voices are sometimes raised, as are fists—the latter only figuratively as a rule. Much of the tension stems from ethnic and economic reapportionment.

Although it has not been the case for most of Santa Fe's history, Hispanics now comprise a minority of the city's population. According to the 2000 U.S. Census, Hispanics represent 47.8 percent, non-Hispanic Whites 46.0 percent, and other ethnic groups 3.2 percent of the population. Though the margin is tiny, it is hugely symbolic of a growing sense among Hispanics that wealthy Anglos have invaded what was once a tranquil little town and, however unwittingly, overshadowed the traditional culture. To a lesser—or at least less vocal—extent, Santa Fe's Native American community shares many of these sentiments. Though only 3.1 percent of the city's population, Indians exert a far greater influence than their numbers imply.

## GROWING PAINS

Like an adolescent whose emotions can't keep up with his or her physical development, Santa Fe is facing an identity crisis. It's asking itself what it wants to be when it grows up. And growth is definitely a burning issue—perhaps the greatest single issue the city and county face. Santa Fe's beauty, its reputation for tolerance of most lifestyles, and, in recent years, its trendiness have attracted so many new residents that the county's population has tripled over the past 50 years to 143,937 residents. Of those, 72,056 live within the city limits. That's up nearly 50 percent from the 49,299 who called Santa Fe home in 1980.

Unfortunately, income and housing and especially water haven't kept up with the influx of new bodies. In other words, welcome to Santa Fe, but don't count on a job that will leave much spending money after you've paid your rent or mortgage. According to the Santa Fe Living Wage Alliance, the average wage in Santa Fe is roughly 23 percent below the rest of the country while housing costs are roughly 18 percent higher. The minimum wage in Santa Fe is currently at $9.85 per hour. Compared with many other areas of the country, Santa Fe's popularity as a tourist destination and retirement center has helped it weather the current recession, although a number of businesses, large and small, have been forced to close their doors, and employers often have their pick of over-qualified candidates for any job advertised. Salaried full-time jobs are few and far between in this tourism-oriented service economy, and most Santa Feans find themselves doing several part-time jobs to make ends meet generally at or just above minimum wage. In recent years, Santa Fe's tight housing market has loosened slightly, due to new development, primarily on the south side of town, but housing will still take a big bite out of your paycheck.

## QUALITY OF LIFE

Quality of life means different things to different people. In Santa Fe, it almost universally refers to the unique combination of small-town atmosphere in a centrally located, urban setting with access to a wide variety of cultural activities that range from the urbane to the rustic—all this against a backdrop of extraordinary natural beauty and a healthy climate with crisp, clean mountain air.

Undoubtedly the most striking thing about Santa Fe is the loveliness and grandeur of the landscape and its brilliant skies. Artists, particularly painters, have been attracted to northern New Mexico since time immemorial, lured by natural light that is like no other in the world. An hour's drive in any direction will quickly tell you why. The vistas are as fascinating as they are beautiful, changing from minute to minute, mile to mile. A bend or two in the road can take you from gently rolling hills pocked with piñon, juniper, and scrub brush to flat-topped mesas standing dark and aloof against streaky, iridescent blue skies. Another few miles and you're in the forest among white-barked aspen, ponderosa pine, and, depending on the season, snow.

Snow? Seasons? In the desert? Indeed, many visitors come to Santa Fe with the misconception that because it's desert, northern New Mexico is always hot. Wrong! This is high desert; mountain country. That means four distinct seasons, including winters that get an average of 30 to 34 inches of snow each year and attract skiers from around the world. Santa Fe sits in the foothills of the Sangre de Cristo mountain range at an elevation of 7,000 feet. While the mountains are rugged—Santa Fe Baldy reaches more than 12,600 feet, while Wheeler Peak in Taos measures in at 13,161 feet—they also help protect the region below from the elements, affording Santa Fe relatively mild weather conditions.

Still, Mother Nature likes to flex her muscles every once in a while with dry, scorching hot spells or brutally cold winters. So be prepared for all possibilities. Generally, however, the seasons are predictable, each arriving with its distinct brand of beauty—perhaps none more vibrantly than autumn.

In fall the hillsides explode with reds and oranges, pinks and purples, and the shimmering gold of aspen groves that streak through the mountains. The colors compel even the most jaded locals to stare in awe at nature's artistry. Many join the tourists at the Santa Fe Ski Area to take a lift up the mountain and get a bird's-eye view of the autumn leaves.

Springtime in Santa Fe County is also a sight to behold. The high desert virtually comes alive with wildflowers, the winter-barren earth bursting forth in colorful blooms and—allergy sufferers beware—pollen. Do bring plenty of extra-strength Allerest but, whatever else you do, don't hide indoors.

**i** **Don't assume that because you're out of the big city, you're out of the woods when it comes to crime. Santa Fe has a high rate of thefts, especially from automobile break-ins, which account for nearly all property crimes. Lock your car at all times and avoid leaving tempting items in plain view. Try to park in well-trafficked areas or at least well-lighted ones.**

## THINGS TO DO

If you insist on staying indoors, you can choose from a host of activities: world-class museums for art, history, and native culture; historic buildings and churches; and more than 250 art galleries in a city reputed to be the third-largest art market in the country. Classical music lovers can enjoy the Santa Fe Opera, Santa Fe Chamber Music Festival, and Santa Fe Desert Chorale in summer; Santa Fe Pro Musica from September to May; and the Santa Fe Symphony Orchestra and Chorus year-round.

Santa Fe also offers a nightly assortment of live music and dancing from piano bars and cabaret to salsa, jazz, blues, rock, and much, much more. Flamenco fans look forward to summer when the dazzling María Benítez Teatro Flamenco returns. July and August bring Spanish Market, Indian Market, and the new International Folk Art Market on Milner Plaza, which, combined, attract up to 150,000 visitors each year. Equally popular is September's Fiestas de Santa Fe, commemorating Don Diego De Vargas's reconquest of New

Mexico 12 years after the 1680 Pueblo Revolt. Several days of pageantry and parades culminate in the burning of "Zozobra"—a 40-foot-plus effigy of "Old Man Gloom." (See The Arts and Annual Events and Festivals chapters for more about these events.)

Then, of course, there's the real outdoors—camping, hiking, bicycling, swimming, tennis, golf, rock climbing, and horseback riding all within a few miles of town; hunting and fishing, rafting, and hot-air ballooning will require a bit of travel. But few will complain about the scenery along the way. Winter sports include downhill skiing, snowboarding, and even inner tubing down the slopes of the Santa Fe National Forest. Cross-country skiers and snow-shoers can blaze their own trails through the trees.

When all else fails, there's shopping, of course. Whether you're in the market for jewelry, pottery, clothing, or kitsch, you'll be overwhelmed by the number and variety of places to explore.

### The Wily Coyote

Within minutes of arriving in Santa Fe, you are likely to see your first "coyote fence." Made of tall, narrow juniper poles lashed closely together, these traditionally were used by New Mexicans to keep roaming coyotes away from penned livestock. They are still sometimes referred to as "goat fences," even though very few locals raise goats anymore. (Plenty of coyotes roam close to towns, however, including Santa Fe.) Such fences assure privacy and are much cheaper to build than the adobe or faux-adobe walls that are also common in Santa Fe. In fact, some entrepreneurs earn a living building nothing but coyote fences, which can be erected around a single yard in less than a day.

## Santa Fe Vital Statistics

**Capital of New Mexico:** Santa Fe

**Other major cities:** Albuquerque, Las Cruces, Los Alamos, Taos, Roswell, Rio Rancho

**Population (2006 U.S. Census estimates):** Santa Fe 72,056; Santa Fe County 143,937; New Mexico 1,984,356

**Area of Santa Fe:** 37.3 square miles

**Santa Fe's nickname:** The City Different

**Santa Fe's average temperatures:**
　　　July: High 91, Low 57
　　　January: High 40, Low 19

**Average rainfall:** 14 inches

**Average snowfall:** 32 inches

**Average number of sunny days per year:** 300

**Santa Fe founded:** 1607-10

**New Mexico achieved statehood:** 1912

**Major colleges:** St. John's College, Santa Fe Community College

**Major area employers:** Santa Fe Public Schools, U.S. Government, St. Vincent's Hospital, City of Santa Fe, State of New Mexico, Los Alamos National Laboratory

**Major airports:** Albuquerque International, about 60 miles to the south

**Major interstates:** I-25 north-south

## LOCAL COLOR—SANTA FE STYLE

Santa Fe has a unique style that's instantly recognizable. Whether it's art or architecture, food or clothing, home decor or entertainment, it's always colorful, casual, and downright earthy. Architecturally, for example, it doesn't get much earthier than adobe, which after all is mud brick. Even faux-adobe buildings are earth-toned and, like the real thing, often trimmed with turquoise window panes and doorways, rough-hewn vigas (log ceiling beams), and bright red chile ristras. Inside you're likely to find terra-cotta saltillo tile on the floor; handpainted ceramic tile in the kitchen or bathroom; colorful, geometric-designed Navajo rugs on the walls and/or floors; perhaps a wooden santo (religious sculpture) or an Indian pot in a nicho (niche) built right into the wall; maybe even a banco (earthen bench) on either side of a corner kiva or fogón fireplace. Santa Fe also has a distinctive clothing style, conspicuous not only for its color and flair, but also for its casualness. Even in Santa Fe's most expensive restaurants, diners are as likely to be dressed in jeans and fancy cowboy boots as Armani and Donna Karan fashions. Day or night, it's a sure bet you'll see lots of jewelry on both men and women—heavy silver bracelets, watchbands, and rings trimmed with turquoise, onyx, and other stones; concho or silver-buckled leather belts; bolo ties; squash blossom necklaces; big, dangly earrings with crystals and gems on women; men with a small stud or hoop in their ear, even at City Hall. You'll see a variety of cowboy hats, too, but probably not as many as you expected.

**Public transportation:** Santa Fe Trails bus system serves the city of Santa Fe, the New Mexico Rail Runner train runs between Santa Fe and Albuquerque daily and is linked, via free shuttle, to Amtrak rail service at nearby Lamy

**Driving laws:** Seat belts and child restraints are mandatory. If you are taking up residency in New Mexico, you must surrender your license from any other state and apply for a New Mexico license within 30 days of moving to New Mexico. All first-time licensees in New Mexico, ages 18 to 24, inclusive (not required for persons 25 years and older) are required to take the "None for the Road" DWI awareness class. Drivers who are 75 years old or older must renew their licenses yearly, but they are not charged renewal fees.

**Alcohol laws:** You must be 21 to drink in New Mexico, and you can buy alcohol of all sorts after noon in supermarkets and elsewhere. The bars may remain open until 2 a.m. In New Mexico the legal limit for blood-alcohol content is 0.08 for drivers. Administrative license suspension for the first offense is 90 days, with the possibility of restored driving privileges after 30 days of suspension. There is no mandatory jail time or community service for the first DWI offense.

**Daily newspapers:** The Santa Fe *New Mexican, Journal North* edition of the Albuquerque *Journal*

**Sales tax:** Gross receipts tax is 8.0625 percent on all goods and services, including prepared foods, inside the city limits.

**Room tax:** 14.7 percent

**The Chamber of Commerce:** 8380 Cerrillos Rd., Suite 302; (505) 988-3279

**Convention and Visitors Bureau:** 201 West Marcy St.; (505) 995-6200, (800) 777-2489

**Time and temperature:** (505) 473-2211

**Important phone numbers:** 911 emergency; (505) 983-3361 Christus St. Vincent Regional Medical Center

# POLITICS

Stop half a dozen Santa Feans on the street and ask what the favorite local pastime is. They may hesitate for a millisecond before answering, "politics." While this may be less than shocking in a state capital—especially one in which nearly every third worker has a government job—the tremendous interest residents take in local issues is still striking. It helps, of course, to have a high-flying governor like Bill Richardson, a former U.S. ambassador to the United Nations and Energy secretary under President Clinton and presidential candidate himself in 2008. In 2009, Richardson was finishing out his final term as governor, somewhat under a cloud after an ongoing investigation into financial impropriety ended his hopes of confirmation as Commerce Secretary in President Obama's new cabinet. As

governor, though, the energetic Richardson has achieved a remarkable amount for New Mexico. Successful high-profile New Mexico initiatives that have come to fruition in time for Santa Fe's 400th anniversary celebrations include the New Mexico Rail Runner train linking Albuquerque and Santa Fe, the mixed-use Railyard Park in the Historic Guadalupe District, the state-of-the-art History Museum near the Santa Fe Plaza, breaking ground on a new Space Port near Las Cruces where Virgin Air's Richard Branson plans on offering space rides, and Sundance New Mexico partnership with Robert Redford, a new experimental film immersion program aimed at Hispanics and Native Americans, a sign that New Mexico's growing film industry is beginning to pay big dividends.

On your travels in and around Santa Fe, you will occasionally encounter small roadside crosses adorned with plastic flowers, religious icons, and other decorations. These are not gravesites. The cruciforms, known as *descansos,* or resting places, mark a spot where an individual died in a car accident. This tradition goes back at least as far as the beginnings of El Camino Real, along which travelers constructed rough crosses to commemorate the site of a fellow pilgrim's death, and continued two centuries later along the Santa Fe Trail. (The paths eventually merged south of Santa Fe, forming a single trade route connecting Mexico City to Missouri.) These "rustic crosses, held in place by piles of stones, were thickly scattered over the country from one end of it to the other," wrote an engineer with U.S. Army of the West, which Gen. Stephen Kearny led to victory in Mexico at the end of America's two-year war with its southern neighbor.

## FOOD

Eating is another favorite pastime in Santa Fe, especially when it comes to local cuisine. While the ingredients might be the same ones used in other Hispanic cultures—Mexican, Tex-Mex, Spanish, etc.—the food here is a culinary blend of Indian and Mexican influences that's as distinct as the local dialect. This is largely due to the ubiquitous chile pepper. Whether you like it hot or mild, whether you prefer green or red or even "Christmas" (some of each), you're going to encounter New Mexican chile in many different forms, usually in traditional native foods such as enchiladas, tamales, *carne adovada* (marinated and baked pork), or *posole* (stewed hominy), but also in hamburgers, on pizza, and even in apple pie. Regardless of nationality, most of Santa Fe's 375-plus restaurants use local chile in at least one of their dishes whether it's a five-star restaurant— and Santa Fe boasts many—or McDonald's. Don't be shy about using a *sopaipilla*—a hollow, deep-

fried yeast bread eaten with honey—to wipe up that last drop of chile from your plate. Celebrated not only for its fine New Mexican fare, Santa Fe is deservedly famous for the variety and quality of its many other restaurants, from nouvelle cuisine with a Southwestern twist to Chinese, French, Greek, Indian (from India), fine Italian, Japanese, Middle Eastern, Native American, Thai, Tibetan, vegetarian . . . the list goes on.

## LANGUAGE

Spanish is the second official language of Santa Fe—the first language for an estimated 10,000 residents. Some are old-timers. Others are Mexican and Central American immigrants who surprisingly often face similar prejudices in New Mexico, among both Hispanics and Anglos, as they do in other states that share a common border with Mexico. Locals pepper their conversations with colorful Spanish words and phrases interspersed with English (dubbed "Spanglish") that are unique to New Mexico and have no adequate translation in English. Newspapers throughout the state contain liberal sprinklings of Spanish with tildes (~) and accent marks (´) appearing as a matter of course. Many also feature Spanish-language sections.

But don't come to Santa Fe planning to speak Spanish with the natives. While a huge portion of the population speaks Spanish at home—around 35,000, according to the last census—English tends to be the language of choice here. Remember, New Mexico is one of the 50 United States—the 47th, to be precise. Though, apparently enough Americans are unaware of that fact to warrant an anecdotal column in *New Mexico Magazine* called "One of Our Fifty Is Missing."

## TOLERANCE

Santa Fe has long served as a beacon for alternative lifestyles and ideologies, attracting more than its share of Aquarian Age adherents. It began in the 1960s with the hippie movement, which found, if not open arms, at least passive ones in northern New Mexico. Today Santa Fe is filled with old and young flower children as well as aura readers, channelers, Iron Johns, non-native shamans, white Rastafarians, and women who "run with wolves." Once merely the state capital of New Mexico, Santa Fe is now the New Age capital of the United States. Santa Fe's more traditional spiritual community offers options as diverse as they are plentiful, from Assembly of God to Zen Buddhism as well as Baha'i, Hinduism, Islam, Mormonism, Sikh, Sufism, and Unitarian, to name just a few. There's never a moment's doubt, however, as to which religion dominates. One need only look up at the mountain range that reigns regally and protectively over the region—the Sangre de Cristo, or "Blood of Christ," Mountains—to be reminded that Catholicism runs deeply in the veins and the hearts of northern New Mexicans. Running just as deeply is an abiding respect for the traditional herbal medicine of Hispanic healers called *curanderas* and Indian medicine men known as shamans. Perhaps for that reason, Santa Fe has long been a mecca for alternative health care. Even a brief glance in the Yellow Pages offers a mind-boggling array of therapies, including craniosacral therapy, polarity, acupuncture, chiropractic, hypnotism, massage therapy, homeopathy, energy healing, biofeedback, herbs, and spiritual healing.

## BIENVENIDOS

New Agers, old-timers, and trust funders; Hispanics, Native Americans, and Anglos—they're all part of the fabric of Santa Fe, a cloth tightly woven from a variety of belief systems, traditions, and lifestyles. The only way to know it is to experience it—and even then it could take a lifetime.

So *¡Bienvenidos a Santa Fe!* And remember, don't move the furniture.

# GETTING HERE, GETTING AROUND

Four hundred years ago, there was only one way into Santa Fe—El Camino Real (the "Royal Road" or "King's Highway"), an arduous and, for some, fatal network of roads and trails that began in Mexico City. This *camino de tierra adentro,* or "road to the interior," started out as Indian trails and slowly extended northward, segment by segment, throughout the 16th century, as conquistadores and settlers, missionaries and merchants, and seekers of fame, fortune, and adventure all made their way to New Mexico.

More than two centuries later, on September 1, 1821, William Becknell left Franklin, Missouri, with a wagonload of goods to trade with Indians. He never got farther than Santa Fe where, despite Spain's restrictions against Anglo Americans and trade with the eastern United States, colonists eagerly bought all his goods, which were scarce and highly coveted in the territory. This was in November. The following month—on December 26, 1821—word reached Santa Fe that Mexico, and therefore New Mexico, had won independence from Spain. With that news the frontier opened and, with it, so did the Santa Fe Trail. For the next six decades, until the first locomotive steamed through northeastern New Mexico, the 900-mile stretch from Independence, Missouri, to Santa Fe, New Mexico, remained a bustling, if hazardous, trade route that represented profits to businessmen, adventure to mountain men, and converts for Protestant missionaries—all of them willing to risk death by disease, starvation, or hostile Indians to achieve their goals.

Only traces of the original Santa Fe Trail remain in the city, most notably behind the Museum of Indian Arts and Culture, 2 miles southeast of the Plaza, where you can still see the indentation of wagon wheels in the hard, dry dirt. Much of the original trail is now beneath the pavement of the well-traveled Old Santa Fe Trail—a scenic, narrow road wending its way from County Road 67 south of the city to its terminus at the Santa Fe Plaza. El Camino Real, however, is still a vital Santa Fe thoroughfare—at least the part now called Agua Fria ("Cold Water") Street, which begins in the Guadalupe District west of the Plaza and meanders parallel to the Santa Fe River through the west side barrio and the historic village of Agua Fria.

Today, of course, there are a number of ways to get into and out of Santa Fe, as well as around and through it—though never enough for some people and far too many for others. Additional roads naturally translate into more traffic and all its accoutrements: congestion, noise, and the threat of polluting our pristine skies. So far, however, a population painfully aware of this particular downside of growth, as well as city and county governments that for the most part are sympathetic to their constituents' concerns, are trying to find a happy medium that allows for expanding our highways and byways without destroying the aesthetic, cultural, and historic integrity of Santa Fe. Here's what we've got thus far.

## BY AIR

For more than 60 years, Santa Fe's city-owned airport has been popular with privately licensed pilots, though commercial service remains limited. Small commuter airlines have attempted service from time to time and usually given up due to lack of business. In June 2009, American Eagle began service once per day between Dallas/Fort Worth and Santa Fe Municipal Airport; it remains to be seen, however, whether the service will be popular. Most people who come to Santa Fe fly into Albuquerque International Sunport, served by a broad range of airlines. From the Sunport, you can get to Santa Fe by New Mexico Rail Runner train and shuttle, shuttle van, scheduled bus, rental car, taxi, limousine, or pick up by private car. The drive north on I–25 takes about an hour, depending on traffic and your driving speed.

## Albuquerque International Sunport

Located about 60 miles south of Santa Fe, the Albuquerque International Sunport (AIS) is the only airport in New Mexico with full-size jet airline service. Regardless of your specific destination in the state, if you plan to get there via a commercial flight, your visit to the Land of Enchantment will likely begin in Albuquerque, the state's largest city. The airport, which the city shares with Kirtland Air Force Base, lies at the southern end of Albuquerque, approximately 4 miles south of the central business district. It is at the Sunport exit off I-25.

**ALBUQUERQUE INTERNATIONAL SUNPORT**
**2200 Sunport Blvd. SE**
**Albuquerque**
**(505) 244-7700**
**www.cabq.gov/airport**
From the moment you set foot inside the Albuquerque International Sunport's cool, pink and turquoise, adobe-style interior, you know you're in the Southwest. The terminal's ornate, carved beamed ceilings are part of the original building in the current location. Albuquerque architect William Emmett Burk Jr. (1909–88) designed the 20 laminated beams, each about 84 feet long and carved with decorative motifs used by Pueblo and Navajo Indians. The airport's art collection comprises original paintings, weavings, sculpture, photography, and other media—all by New Mexico artists, many of them with national and international reputations. The terminal houses 12 eateries ranging from a full-service restaurant and lounge to delis and snack bars; a microbrewery; a smoke-free sports bar; three gift and news shops;

five cart vendors selling T-shirts, balloons, key chains, and other tchotchkes; a bank and ATM; a barber shop; and a shoeshine stand.

The airport's 574,000-square-foot terminal has come a long way from 1928, when the entire airport was little more than a small adobe building and a dirt runway a few miles southwest of its present location. The first aircraft to land there was a Stearman piloted by Ross Hadley, who was chauffeuring "air tourists" from Hollywood to New Mexico. Other cross-country pilots quickly followed suit, including Charles Lindbergh; Arthur S. Goebel, the 1927 Dole Prize winner for the first flight to Honolulu from the mainland; and air speedster Frank Hawk. The little Albuquerque airport saw its first commercial flights in 1929, when Western Air Express operated one eastbound and one westbound flight per day with radio equipment installed by the U.S. president's son, Herbert Hoover Jr. Two months later, Trans-Continental Air Transport began operating a fleet of 10 Ford tri-motored transports, each accommodating up to 18 passengers.

The airport grew quickly to accommodate newer, faster planes as well as the public's demand for more flights. When wind severely damaged the airport in 1938, the city decided to build a new, larger one on 53 acres nearby. Using Works Progress Administration (WPA) and military funds, it completed construction in 1939, with Kirtland Field and Air Force Base occupying the east end of the airport. By 1945 the property had grown to 223 acres. Five years later, the federal government took possession of the airport. Over the next decade it would expand Kirtland and build what is now Sandia National Laboratories. In 1962 the federal government returned much of the airport to the city, retaining title to the facilities on the air base, paying Albuquerque for continued use of the airfield and providing crash, fire, and rescue services for civilian aircraft. Nine years later the airport began international service. It underwent a major remodeling in 1988, added a new traffic control tower in 1994, and in 1996 underwent a small-scale expansion, including the addition of an observation deck.

Today Albuquerque International Sunport has 23 gates in two concourses. Nine commercial carriers offer nonstop service to 30 cities including Amarillo, Atlanta, Baltimore, Chicago, Cincinnati, Colorado Springs, Dallas, Denver, Houston, Las Vegas, Los Angeles, Minneapolis, Oakland, Orlando, Phoenix, St. Louis, Salt Lake City, San Diego, Seattle, Tampa, and Tucson. There are no direct flights between Albuquerque and Santa Fe. A four-level parking structure and adjacent surface lot accommodate 3,700 vehicles. Short-term parking rates start at $1 per half hour with a maximum of $7 per day for the first 72 hours, $10 per day thereafter. Daily long-term rates are $6 per day for the first three days, then $8 per day. Nearby long-term parking lots served by free shuttles average $5 per day.

AIS is home to two fixed-base operators—Cutter Flying Service, (800) 678-5382, and Atlantic Aviation, (505) 842-4990. Other companies that provide services to business and private fliers include Aircraft Service International, (505) 842-4266; Four Seasons Aviation, (505) 450-4618; RBR Aircraft, (505) 842-6015; Robertson Aircraft, (505) 842-4999; Seven Bar Aviation, (505) 842-4949; and South Aero, (505) 842-4337.

## Commercial Airline Phone Reservation Numbers:

| | |
|---|---|
| Aeromexico Connect | (800) 237-6639 |
| American Airlines | (800) 433-7300 |
| Continental Airlines | (800) 525-0280 |
| Delta Airlines | (800) 221-1212 |
| Frontier Airlines | (800) 432-1359 |
| Northwest Airlines | (800) 225-2525 |
| Southwest Airlines | (800) 435-9792 |
| United Airlines | (800) 241-6522 |

## Commuter Airline Phone Reservation Numbers:

| | |
|---|---|
| Great Lakes Airlines | (800) 554-5111 |
| New Mexico Airlines | (888) 564-6119 |

## Bus Service from AIS to Santa Fe:
### GREYHOUND/TNM&O
**(505) 243-4435, (800) 231-2222**
Greyhound and TNM&O coaches provide bus service between the Albuquerque airport and the Santa Fe Bus Depot at 858 St. Michael's Dr. Call for times and prices.

## Renting a Car at the Albuquerque International Sunport

To get from AIS to Santa Fe, follow the signs to exit the airport, which will put you westbound on Sunport Boulevard. Follow the blue Interstate signs for I-25 North for approximately 1 mile and turn right at the on-ramp for exit 221. Continue on I-25 northbound for about 60 miles and get off at the St. Francis Drive exit for downtown Santa Fe.

Car rental customer service counters and ready/return lots are now located at the Sunport Car Rental Center, 3400 University SE. Car rental shuttles provide transportation between the terminal building and the Car Rental Center. The car rental shuttle is a free service. Shuttles run every five minutes from the commercial lane located outside the first level of the airport terminal building.

## Car Rentals

| | |
|---|---|
| Alamo Rent-A-Car | (800) 462-5266 |
| Avis Rent-A-Car | (800) 331-1212 |
| Budget Car Rental | (800) 527-0700 |
| Enterprise Rent-A-Car | (800) 736-8222 |
| Hertz Rent-A-Car | (800) 654-3131 |
| National Car Rental | (800) 227-7368 |
| Thrifty Car Rental | (800) 847-4389 |

## Shuttle Service

Several companies operate nonstop shuttles between Albuquerque International Sunport and Santa Fe. Fares range from $20 to $25 each way with pickups and dropoffs at various hotels, motels, and bed-and-breakfast inns throughout Santa Fe. Some carriers also stop at St. John's College (see our Education chapter). Be sure to confirm the exact location before buying your ticket. Under normal circumstances, you can figure on a 70-minute commute to or from the airport. The shuttles run from about 5 a.m. to 11 p.m. daily; be ready to depart 10 minutes before scheduled pickup. Most shuttles have ticket counters opposite the east baggage claim area. Although reservations are not required, we strongly advise that you guarantee your seat or you could find yourself left in the dust with your baggage in hand and a useless plane ticket in your pocket. Most shuttles accept traveler's checks and credit cards, though you can only charge your ticket at the time you make your reservations.

## SANDIA SHUTTLE EXPRESS
3600 Cerrillos Rd., Suite 207C
(505) 474-5696 (Santa Fe),
(888) 775-5696
Sandia Shuttle Express makes 26 runs daily to and from the Albuquerque airport for $25 each way, or $45 prepaid with a credit card. The first run of the day is at 5 a.m. out of Santa Fe; the last van leaves the Capital City at 7 p.m. From the airport, you can catch the first shuttle to Santa Fe at 8:45 a.m. and the last at 10:45 p.m. Sandia Shuttle Express picks up and drops off passengers at all Santa Fe hotels, motels, bed-and-breakfast inns, and a number of other locations in and around the Capital City, including retirement homes, Fort Marcy Compound, and St. John's College.

## ROADRUNNER SHUTTLE SERVICES
Albuquerque
(505) 424-3367
Offers door-to-door shuttle service between Albuquerque and various points in Santa Fe between 6 a.m. and 9 p.m. $45 one-way by reservation.

## STAR LIMO SERVICE
1715 57th St. NW
Albuquerque
(505) 848-9999
Limousine and luxury sedan and SUV service between Albuquerque and Santa Fe beginning at $140 one way.

## TWIN HEARTS EXPRESS AND TRANSPORTATION
102 Demus Lane, Taos
(505) 751-1201, (800) 654-9456
Twin Hearts will take you from the Albuquerque airport all the way to south-central Colorado, if

you want, with stops at Santa Fe, Taos, and other points in between. Departures are four times daily and will stop at all Santa Fe hotels, motels, and bed-and-breakfasts on the roughly three-hour journey.

## By Air to Santa Fe
### SANTA FE MUNICIPAL AIRPORT
443 Airport Rd.
(505) 955-2908 (information),
(505) 955-2900 (manager)
Santa Fe Municipal Airport (SFMA), at the southwest corner of the city, provides once-daily commuter service between Santa Fe and Dallas/Fort Worth, and will begin service between Santa Fe and Los Angeles in November 2009. The 2,100-acre airport was established in 1941 as a military airfield during World War II. It became a "commercial" airport—technically a "non-hub primary" airport—in the 1950s when it replaced its tiny terminal with the larger one you see today. Inside you'll find the Santa Fe Airport Grill and Gift Shop, (505) 471-5227, open 7:30 a.m. to 3 p.m.

Airport parking is in an outdoor lot and costs $3 per day. The airport handles about 230 take-offs and landings a day, most of them private corporate aircraft. As of June 2009, American Eagle began providing once-daily service between Santa Fe and Dallas/Fort Worth, departing Dallas/Fort Worth at 10:50 a.m., arriving in Santa Fe at 11:45 a.m., and returning to Dallas/Fort Worth at 12:10 p.m. The flight takes just under an hour. Details of the new service between Santa Fe and Los Angeles, beginning in November 2009, had yet to be announced at press time.

The air traffic control tower, (505) 471-3810, is open between 6:45 a.m. and 9 p.m., though flights can take off and land 24 hours a day. Both the New Mexico State Police and Army National Guard keep aircraft at the SFMA. The airport has two fixed-base operators. Capital Aviation fuels and services private, government, and commuter aircraft, (505) 471-2700, and Santa Fe Air Center, (505) 471-2525 or (800) 263-7695, provides aircraft charters and private aircraft services. For ground transportation, you have a number of choices. Avis, (505) 471-5892, and Hertz, (505) 471-7189, have rental cars at the airport.

To get to the downtown area, head east on Airport Road for about 3 miles. Turn left onto Cerrillos Road and travel approximately 5 miles. It will turn into Galisteo Road as you near downtown and dead-end at San Francisco Street exactly 1 block west of the Plaza. The drive will take about 20 minutes. Or you can take the RoadRunner Shuttle, (505) 424-3367, to or from any hotel in town for $12 one way or $20 round-trip. Road-Runner also shuttles passengers to local Indian casinos and Los Alamos and operates charter buses to the Santa Fe Opera (see The Arts chapter), the ski area (see our Winter Sports chapter), and other local and regional destinations. Capital City Cab Company, Santa Fe's only taxi service, provides service throughout Santa Fe, (505) 438-0000.

## BY LAND

Maybe things in Santa Fe haven't changed that much after all since the days of El Camino Real and the Santa Fe Trail. Here we are, 400-plus years and 150-plus years later, respectively, and there still are only two direct overland routes to the state capital—I-25 northbound from Las Cruces, near New Mexico's southern border, and southbound from Buffalo in north-central Wyoming; US 84/285 south from Taos and Chama. The closest east-west route is I–40, which intersects I-25 in Albuquerque at what's popularly called "The Big I."

Coming from Albuquerque, there are four main off-ramps from I-25, which skirts the southern edge of Santa Fe before continuing south and east toward Colorado. The first of these, State Road 599, is the Santa Fe Bypass. It was designed to make travel easier between I-25 and US 285/68, the main route north from Santa Fe to Española, Los Alamos, and Taos. However, it also provides easy access to the west and north sides of Santa Fe. Next is the Cerrillos Road exit, which puts you on Santa Fe's main drag, a commercial strip that will take you almost to the Plaza. Third

is the St. Francis Drive exit, which is the most convenient route into the heart of the city. Finally, the Old Pecos Trail exit is best for reaching the southeastern portions of Santa Fe.

Getting to Santa Fe is the easy part. It's getting around that's hard, especially in an old downtown filled with narrow, winding, one-way streets that seem to lead everywhere but where you want to go or continually lead you right back from where you came. Even if you manage to navigate the downtown area, at some point you're going to have to find a place to leave your car. And you thought parking was difficult in Manhattan! It's also at a premium in Santa Fe, especially in summer—so much so that a former municipal judge decided it just wasn't cricket to fine locals who parked illegally when legal parking spots were so hard to find. Every year at Thanksgiving, he offered amnesty to parking scofflaws who donated a turkey or two to one of the local homeless shelters in lieu of paying their fines. This wound up costing the city tens of thousands of dollars in lost revenue and eventually cost the judge his robes.

All this is to suggest that if your digs are within walking distance of downtown use shanks' mare to get there. Not only will you work off that extra sopaipilla you had for lunch but you'll also see a lot more of Santa Fe. Beware, however, that Santa Fe is not particularly pedestrian-friendly once you leave downtown. Sidewalks are rare; traffic lights on main drags often don't allow enough time to cross the street without making a run for it; and in wider, more heavily trafficked roads where the speed limits are higher, drivers may not be as aware of pedestrians as they might be in areas with more foot traffic.

If you're too far from the Plaza or just too tired to walk, redevelopment in the downtown now offers eight municipal parking lots, including four parking garages and four surface lots, for a combined total of 2,520 parking spaces. The new parking garages include some 500 spots beneath the new convention center on Federal Place, another 400 surface and subterranean spaces at the new Railyard development, and 500 additional surface spaces. Lot prices vary, but most are 90 cents per half hour up to $9 per day. Street parking downtown comes in two forms: metered at 25 cents for 15 minutes ($1 per hour) Monday through Saturday (Sundays are free); and permit parking for residents. On weekends—except during Indian Market, Spanish Market, and Fiestas (see our Annual Events and Festivals chapter)—you're almost guaranteed a spot in front of the state capitol building, affectionately called the Roundhouse for reasons that will become obvious once you've seen it.

Of course, you can avoid both walking and parking by using public transportation (see entries below) or cycling (see our Parks and Recreation chapter).

**i** Perhaps the most important piece of advice to anyone visiting Santa Fe's downtown is to leave your car at home or in the hotel parking lot. Not only is downtown parking hard to come by but the streets, some of which are 400 years old, are narrow and winding and often congested with cars and sightseers. So put on your walking shoes and stretch those muscles. It's the best way to see the downtown, anyway.

## Bus and Shuttle Service
### GREYHOUND/TNM&O
858 St. Michael's Dr.
(505) 471-0008, (800) 231-2222
Greyhound and TNM&O coaches provide bus service between the Albuquerque airport and the Santa Fe bus station on St. Michael's Drive several times a day. One-way nonrefundable fare is $19.75. Buses also run between Santa Fe and Alamogordo, Carlsbad, Clovis, Gallup, Grants, Las Cruces, Las Vegas (NM), Roswell, and Taos in New Mexico; Alamosa, Colorado Springs, Denver, and Pueblo in Colorado; Amarillo, Dallas, and El Paso in Texas; Flagstaff and Phoenix in Arizona; and New Orleans. Call the bus station for times and fares. The depot is open Monday through Friday from 7 a.m. to 5:30 p.m. and 7:30 to 9:45 p.m. and on weekends when buses arrive and depart.

**i** Santa Feans seem to be allergic to their turn signals. If you stay here long enough, you, too, will find you use your directionals less and less often, though whether it's from spite or assimilation is hard to determine. The reverse, of course, is that you'll often run into (sometimes literally) a car whose turn signal is flashing although the driver has no intention of turning. Maybe it's because drivers here are so unaccustomed to using their signals that they forget to turn them off. In any case, drive defensively.

### LAMY SHUTTLE AND TOURS
1476 North Miracerros Loop
(505) 982-8829
The Lamy shuttle takes passengers with reservations to meet the Amtrak Southwest Chief trains that arrive once a day at the Lamy Depot from Chicago and Los Angeles. For $16 per person—which works out to less than $1 a mile—the shuttle provides door-to-door service from the depot to your hotel or residence and vice versa. As its name implies, the company also offers custom tours. Call for details and prices.

### SANTA FE TRAILS TRANSIT SYSTEM
2931 Rufina St.
(505) 955-2001
The city bus system, Santa Fe Trails, can take you nearly anywhere you want to go within the city limits on any of seven different routes. Buses run Monday through Friday from 6 a.m. to 11 p.m. and Saturday from 8 a.m. to 8 p.m. (Times may vary depending on the route.) There's limited bus service on Sunday and major holidays. You can pick up a bus schedule and information book on board any Santa Fe Trails bus and at more than 75 locations throughout the city, including most public buildings and many stores. Schedules are also available at most hotels, the Sheridan Street Transit Center, and Sweeney Visitor Center. At $1 per ride for adults, including free transfers, Santa Fe Trails is one of the best buys in town. A $2 "day pass" takes you anywhere the system goes for a

full day. Seniors age 60 and older and students age six to 17 pay only 50 cents per ride, including transfers. Children younger than age six ride free when accompanied by an adult. Santa Fe Trails also offers monthly passes for only $20. You can't beat it. The buses have lifts for wheelchair access and bike racks for cyclists who get caught in the rain or just can't bear to ride out that last stretch. For help planning a trip or for answers to any questions, call the customer assistance center, (505) 955-2001, between 7 a.m. and 7 p.m.

**SANDIA SHUTTLE EXPRESS**
**3600 Cerrillos Rd., Suite 207C**
**(505) 474-5696 (Santa Fe),**
**(888) 775-5696**
Sandia Shuttle Express provides nonstop service between Santa Fe and the Albuquerque airport (see listing under Albuquerque International Sunport on page 13).

## Train Service
**NEW MEXICO RAIL RUNNER EXPRESS**
**(866) 795-RAIL**
**www.nmrailrunner.com**
Beginning service in December 2008, the attractive Rail Runner commuter train, the linchpin of New Mexico's new intermodal transportation system, has been a huge hit. The commuter train serves a 100-mile scenic corridor between Santa Fe and various stops in the Albuquerque valley. It operates Monday to Saturday, starting at 6:10 a.m., with the last train at 9:30 p.m., and occasional special service on Sundays and holidays The train departs from stations at the Santa Fe Railyard and the South Capitol/Alta Vista; additional stations in Santa Fe at the corner of St. Francis and Zia and Highway 599 will come online shortly. A free shuttle, the Santa Fe Pickup, meets every train in Santa Fe and drops off riders at hotels and attractions around downtown. In Albuquerque, the No. 350 airport express shuttle leaves from the Alvarado Transportation Center in downtown and provides fast service to Albuquerque International Sunport on a limited schedule during the week only. Leave plenty of time to catch your

flight, if you choose this option. A one-way trip from Santa Fe to downtown Albuquerque is $6; $8 round trip. Monthly passes are $90. Discounts available online.

## Santa Fe's Layout

Learning to navigate the streets of Santa Fe involves trial and error, since the city is not laid out in a grid pattern. Instead, its streets tend to follow old wagon roads (like the Santa Fe and Pecos Trails) and natural features, such as the Santa Fe River and the foothills of the Sangre de Cristo Mountains. Streets are narrow and parking is limited in the heart of the city, which is best explored on foot.

Paseo de Peralta rings Santa Fe's core, beyond which are newer neighborhoods extending as far as 10 miles from the downtown plaza. Spanish street names are the rule here, not the exception. Thus you will encounter *calle, camino, vereda, canjilón, paseo, avenida,* and *sendero.* In asking directions, it is helpful to know the rudiments of Spanish pronunciation. For example, that a double-L is pronounced like the English Y and a double-R is trilled on the tip of the tongue, as in "say-rhee-yoss" (Cerrillos) Road, Santa Fe's main thoroughfare. Also be aware that some streets change their names from one block to the next. Notable examples include Washington Street (which becomes Bishop's Lodge Road) and Artist Road (which becomes Hyde Park Road and the Santa Fe Ski Basin Road, formally known as Highway 475).

**AMTRAK**
County Rd. 33, Lamy
(505) 466-4511, (800) 872-7245
Amtrak's Southwest Chief trains, which run eastbound from Los Angeles and westbound from
Chicago, meet each afternoon at the train depot
in Lamy, located approximately 18 miles southwest of Santa Fe. Call Lamy Shuttle and Tours,
(505) 982-8829 (see entry above), to arrange
transportation to or from the downtown area.
To get to the Lamy Depot from Santa Fe, take
I-25 north to exit 290 (US 285). Go south on US
285 approximately 6 miles to the Lamy turnoff
on the left. Drive a short way to the center of the
village. You'll easily spot the railroad station on
your right.

## Charter Vans and Tours

**CUSTOM TOURS BY CLARICE**
3201 Calle de Molina
(505) 438-7116
www.santafecustomtours.com

**GRAYLINE TOURS OF SANTA FE**
1330 Hickox St.
(505) 983-9491

## Limousines

**CAREY SOUTHWEST LIMOUSINE**
1251 S. St. Francis Dr.
(505) 820-6700

## Rental Car Companies

**ADVANTAGE RENT-A-CAR**
3963 Cerrillos Rd.
(505) 983-9470, (800) 777-5500

**AVIS RENT-A-CAR**
Santa Fe Municipal Airport
443 Airport Rd.
(505) 471-5892, (800) 831-2847

**BUDGET CAR RENTAL**
1946 Cerrillos Rd.
(505) 984-1596, (800) 527-7000

**ENTERPRISE RENT-A-CAR**
2641A Cerrillos Rd.
(505) 473-3600, (800) RENTCAR

**HERTZ RENT-A-CAR**
Santa Fe Municipal Airport
443 Airport Rd. #2
(505) 471-7189, (800) 654-3131

**THRIFTY CAR RENTAL**
2865 Cerrillos Rd.
(505) 474-3365, (800) 847-4389

## Taxi Service

**CAPITAL CITY CAB COMPANY**
2875 Industrial Rd.
(505) 438-0000

# HISTORY

O ne of the things that differentiates Santa Fe from other cities in the United States is its long, rich history. Although some date the city's history from 1608, the date Governor Peralta and the Spanish colonists settled here, the area had seen millennia of human habitation before that. The story of Santa Fe stretches from the nomadic natives who camped here around 10,000 B.C. to modern trailblazers using Santa Fe as a base for their work in human gene research or to develop practical uses for the technology born of the atomic bomb at nearby Los Alamos.

## EARLY INDIAN DAYS

It's difficult to re-create the history of Santa Fe's earliest residents because they left no written records save their carved petroglyphs, which remain an enigma. From archaeological evidence, though, we know that transient Paleo-Indians camped in the Santa Fe area on hunting trips for bison and other animals as long ago as 10,000 B.C., at the end of the Ice Age. By about 5,500 B.C., Archaic era hunters had established permanent annual camps in the area. From the few clues that remain about these early residents, we know they hunted deer and antelope with obsidian points on primitive spears that they threw using atlatls, and they ate piñon nuts and seeds as part of their diet.

Around the start of the Christian era, the Santa Fe area had attracted permanent residents. Archaeologists have found pit houses, cavelike homes built partly underground, along the Santa Fe River and its tributaries. For about eight centuries, Indians lived in what is now known as Santa Fe, first in the dark pit houses and later in organized multistory pueblos, some with hundreds of rooms and community plazas. A suspected 13th-century southeastward migration of the ancestors of today's Pueblo people (once known by their Navajo name of the Anasazi but now usually referred to as the Ancestral Puebloans) from such places as Mesa Verde on the Colorado Plateau temporarily swelled the pueblos along the Río Grande. What brought them here? While

no one knows for sure, drought, overcrowding, resource depletion, and social unrest in earlier lands and the need for more reliable water and farmlands probably attracted these first settlers to what was to become Santa Fe and elsewhere throughout the arid Southwest.

The exact figures aren't known, but the combined population of the pueblos near the current site of Santa Fe may have been several thousand. At least seven major pueblos existed within a 20-minute drive of the spot where the Plaza now stands. Archaeologists gave the pottery made by these communities its own distinctive names, among them Santa Fe Black on White, Agua Fria Glaze on Red, and Cieneguilla Polychrome.

**i** Agua Fria Village, a historic area that has been encompassed by the city's growth, was built on the site of Pindi Pueblo. Indians occupied the pueblo's several hundred rooms between 1250 and 1350. The Laboratory of Anthropology organized its excavation in 1932 and 1933. The ruins of another major pueblo, Arroyo Hondo, lie 8 miles south of Santa Fe and were the focus of extensive archaeological and ecological research by the School of American Research (now the School of Advanced Research) between 1970 and 1974.

Pueblo people speaking the Tano language occupied large villages south of Santa Fe for centuries. Archaeologists have discovered evidence of pueblo communities beneath Agua Fria Village on the west side of Santa Fe, in Arroyo Hondo and Galisteo to the south, Cerrillos to the southwest, and near the current Fort Marcy Park, a few blocks from the Plaza. Another pueblo may have occupied the very site on which the Plaza now stands. Archaeologists speculate that sometime after 900 A.D. Indians built the Pueblo of Ogapoge, on or near the site of Santa Fe's Plaza and spreading south. By the time the first Spanish arrived in the 16th century, however, Ogapoge had been abandoned for more than a century.

Arroyo Hondo Pueblo had 1,000 rooms built around 10 plazas by 1330. The pueblo's population fluctuated, and at one point the Indians moved out, probably because of lack of rainfall, but later reoccupied it. Then the rain stopped again, and the population began to decline. Archaeological evidence shows that in 1410 a fire destroyed the pueblo, and the Indians left Arroyo Hondo for the last time. After many generations of life in and near the present site of Santa Fe, the Pueblo Indians moved away between the years of 1400 and 1425, possibly settling at the villages of Tesuque, Pecos, and Cieneguilla in the Galisteo Basin and along the Río Grande. The clues these people left behind point to drought as the prime motivator for the move. Skeletons of children and young adults buried in the ruins at Arroyo Hondo Pueblo, for example, exhibit evidence of extreme malnutrition. Tree-ring data indicate that this period saw the worst drought in 1,000 years. The settlements of Tesuque, Nambé, and San Juan remained and continue to be occupied to this day.

## THE SPANISH ARRIVE

Historians tracing the story of the early Spanish presence in Santa Fe face a major challenge. The Pueblo Revolt—the only successful native uprising against European settlement in the United States—destroyed the city's official records dating from the early Spanish explorations until 1680. Nonetheless, using copies of some of the documents that survived in the Vatican, in Mexico City, and in Spain, along with archaeological

evidence and the journals and letters of explorers who came later, we have a fairly good idea of what life was like here in the 17th century.

When wealthy and well-placed Juan de Oñate became the first person to receive permission to establish a colony in what is now New Mexico—at his own expense—he was one of many who expected to enjoy some of the riches of the region. For years rumors of cities of gold had spawned Spanish exploration from the capital of New Spain, Mexico City. Wealth, however, provided only part of the motivation. The Spanish explorers and colonists also wanted land of their own, sought to convert more souls to Catholicism, and viewed the new territory as a much-needed buffer against rival Europeans who had settled elsewhere in the vast New World. Oñate, accompanied by 129 soldiers and their families and a small group of friars, arrived near San Juan Pueblo in 1598, approximately 25 miles north of the ruins of Ogapoge. They called their encampment San Juan de los Caballeros. The colonists found life difficult here, but Governor Oñate spent most of his time exploring. By 1600 the Spaniards had moved their capital across the Río Grande, one of the largest rivers in the Southwest, to the confluence of the Río Chama and the Río Grande. The fledgling colony, which they called San Gabriel, struggled to survive and sent no riches back to Spain. Ever optimistic, Oñate and his men rode through much of the rest of New Mexico hunting for gold and demanding submission of the Indians to the Spanish Crown and their conversion to the Christian god.

At Ácoma Pueblo, Indians attacked and killed 13 Spaniards who visited the pueblo in search of provisions. One of those killed was Oñate's nephew. In retaliation, the Spanish military declared a "holy war" on the pueblo based on the assumption that there could be no peace in New Mexico until the Indians either submitted to Spanish dominance or died. At the governor's command (and with the approval of the friars), 70 Spanish soldiers vowed revenge on the Ácoma. Another Oñate nephew, the brother of the killed leader, took Spanish troops to the pueblo. They demanded the surrender of the Indians responsible for the deaths and the Ácomas' acquiescence to the king. The Indians resisted, but the better-armed Spanish defeated them after three days of battle and hundreds of deaths. The conquerors destroyed the pueblo and brought those whom they held responsible for the earlier Spanish deaths to Santo Domingo Pueblo for trial. Oñate met the party there and dealt with the Ácoma prisoners.

The Ácoma and people from other pueblos who may have watched the trial probably didn't comprehend the formality of Spanish law, but they understood the results. The governor sentenced some 20 Ácoma males aged 25 and older to have one foot hacked off. They, along with the captured Ácoma women and young boys, had to serve 20 years as Spanish slaves. Two Hopi Indians caught at Ácoma had their right hands cut off and were set free, "in order that they may convey the news of this punishment," Oñate commanded.

Life in the colony resumed, with Oñate continuing his search for the riches that would repay his personal investment in the settlement and bring honor to Spain. The governor headed west to the Colorado River and then south to the Gulf of California, taking possession of more new land for his king. His efforts left him exhausted and used up his family fortune. Meanwhile, rather than living the easy life as they'd envisioned, the colonists had to work hard to survive in this demanding land. They resented the chronic lack of food and the failure to find gold. The poverty and desolation, the suffering of the women and children, the bugs in summer, cold of the winter, and the sullen looks of the Indians, who resented the Spanish intrusion, disheartened the settlers.

**i** **The Spanish rulers established the Inquisition in New Mexico in 1626. Historians praise its first agent, Fray Alonso de Benavides, as a model of reason and moderation. Benavides's chronicles of New Mexico provide vivid and interesting information about Santa Fe in its early days.**

In his book *Kiva, Cross, and Crown,* historian John Kessell writes that the colonists had a saying about New Mexico: *"Ocho meses de invierno y cuatro de infierno!"* which translates as "Eight months of winter and four months of hell!"

So it was no wonder that when the governor left once again to search for wealth, accompanied by half of the colony's armed men and a couple of friars, those left behind made tracks, too. Most of the colonists, and all but one of the friars, seized the opportunity to desert their wretched settlement and head back to Mexico. Only two dozen settlers and one Franciscan remained. When Oñate and his party returned, the governor ordered the fleeing colonists pursued, but they had too much of a lead to be captured. When the defectors reached Mexico City, they reported the expedition's dismal lack of success in converting the Indians or finding gold. The Viceroy of Mexico, with the concurrence of the king of Spain, decided to abandon the New Mexico experiment.

New Mexico would have been abandoned, except for the problem of what to do with the Christianized Indians there. (While estimates of the number of converts differed considerably, all agreed that some Indians had become Christians.) Rather than abandon these new converts or force them to leave New Mexico, secular and religious authorities decided to keep the new areas as mission territory. The viceroy named a new governor, Pedro de Peralta, but ordered Oñate to remain until Peralta arrived. Embarrassed and disgraced, Oñate resigned in 1607.

When Peralta arrived, Oñate and his son, Cristóbal, left for Mexico City, but on the journey Cristóbal died. The courts charged Oñate with failure to obey royal decrees, lack of respect for the friars, and mistreatment of the Indians, especially of the Ácomas. He was fined, banned perpetually from New Mexico, and returned to Spain in disgrace.

Conventional history places the establishment of Santa Fe, where Peralta moved the capital, at 1608. Some historians say Oñate or his son founded Santa Fe as early as 1605. But even the 1608 date makes Santa Fe the oldest capital city in the United States, predating the establishment of New England's more famous Plymouth

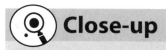 **Close-up**

## A Santa Fe Time Line

**1150-1400:** Pueblo Indian villages thrive along the Santa Fe River.

**Early 15th century:** Indians abandon the villages closest to Santa Fe, such as Pindi, Ogapoge, and Arroyo Hondo Pueblos.

**1598:** Juan de Oñate claims New Mexico for Spain and establishes the first permanent European settlement in New Mexico (the second in the United States) near San Juan Pueblo, northwest of Santa Fe.

**1608-10:** Pedro de Peralta establishes the city of Santa Fe as Spain's northernmost administrative capital in the Southwest. The Palace of the Governors is built. El Camino Real runs from Mexico City to Santa Fe as a supply route for the Spanish missions and colony.

**1680:** The Pueblo Indians drive the Spanish out of Santa Fe and New Mexico in the Pueblo Revolt. The Indians burn Spanish records and remodel the Palace of the Governors to serve their needs.

**1692:** Diego de Vargas brings a Spanish military expedition back to Santa Fe and reclaims Santa Fe for the king of Spain.

**1693-96:** Vargas returns to Santa Fe with a band of settlers. After a fierce battle, the Indians give up the Palace of the Governors. Vargas spends the next few years reconquering the outlying pueblos.

**1712:** Santa Fe celebrates its first official Fiesta in thanksgiving for the reconquest.

**1777:** The first known map of Santa Fe is drawn.

**1778:** Juan Bautista de Anza arrives in Santa Fe as governor and begins making peace with the Comanches of the high plains of eastern New Mexico.

**1792:** Pedro Vial blazes a trail from Santa Fe to St. Louis and returns the following year, making the first complete journey over what will eventually be known as the Santa Fe Trail.

**1807:** American explorer Zebulon Pike and his party are arrested as intruders in Spanish New Mexico. The Spanish government institutes protective trade measures to restrict American influence in New Spain, including Santa Fe.

**1821:** Mexico wins independence from Spain. Trader William Becknell arrives in Santa Fe to do business, opening up the Santa Fe Trail.

**1822:** Wagons roll into the Santa Fe Plaza over the Santa Fe Trail, leading the way for millions of dollars of trade goods and new ideas and cultural influences in Santa Fe.

**1833:** The first gold mines west of the Mississippi open in the Ortíz Mountains between Santa Fe and Albuquerque.

**1834:** New Mexico's first newspaper, *El Crepúsculo de la Libertad,* the *Dawn of Liberty*—is published in Santa Fe.

**1837:** A group of northern New Mexican farmers and Indians band together to protest new taxes imposed by the Mexican government. Governor Albino Pérez is killed. Manuel Armijo resumes his post as governor.

**1846:** The United States declares war on Mexico. U.S. General Stephen W. Kearny occupies Santa Fe without firing a shot after Mexican governor Armijo flees.

**1847:** Territorial governor Charles Bent is assassinated in Taos. U.S. forces quell the rebellion in an attack that seriously damages the mission church at Taos Pueblo.

**1848:** The Treaty of Guadalupe Hidalgo is signed. Mexico cedes New Mexico to the United States.

**(continued)**

**1850:** New Mexico becomes a U.S. territory.

**1851:** The first English language school is founded in Santa Fe by Frenchman Bishop Jean Lamy, founder of St. Francis Cathedral.

**1851:** A territorial library in founded in Santa Fe.

**1861-62:** Confederate soldiers from Texas invade Santa Fe and occupy the Palace of the Governors. The Battle of Glorieta, just southeast of Santa Fe, ends Confederate control in New Mexico and squelches their plan to capture the West.

**1869:** Construction of St. Francis Cathedral begins.

**1870:** The territorial governor disposes of many of the official records of New Mexico. Only about one-fourth are recovered.

**1874:** Workers lay the foundations for Loretto Chapel.

**1879:** Governor Lew Wallace writes a portion of *Ben Hur* in the Palace of the Governors.

**1880:** The Atchison, Topeka & Santa Fe Railroad arrives in Santa Fe over a spur line from the main station in Lamy. Travel along the Santa Fe Trail dies off.

**1881:** Santa Fe installs its first water and telegraph systems.

**1891:** The city of Santa Fe is officially incorporated.

**1892:** New Mexico's new territorial capitol burns in Santa Fe. Arson by Albuquerque boosters who want the seat of government moved south is suspected but never proven.

**1907:** The Palace of the Governors, saved from demolition, becomes a museum.

**1909:** The joint Museum of New Mexico-School of American Archaeology, under the direction of Edgar Lee Hewitt, establishes the criteria for Santa Fe Style.

**1912:** New Mexico becomes the 47th state.

**1913:** The Palace of the Governors is remodeled with a Pueblo Revival-style *portal*. Soon many other buildings receive similar treatment, and new architecture also adopts this look.

**1917:** The Museum of Fine Arts, another example of Pueblo Revival style, is dedicated.

**1922:** The Southwestern Association on Indian Affairs establishes the annual Indian market, a show and sale that remains part of modern Santa Fe's cultural life.

**1926:** The Old Santa Fe Association is formed to help preserve city landmarks.

**1926:** Artist Will Shuster founds a "revolutionary protest fiesta" that includes the ritual burning of the giant puppet Zozobra, or Old Man Gloom. Zozobra quickly become a mainstay of the Santa Fe Fiesta.

**1927:** The Daughters of the American Revolution offer to Santa Fe the *Madonna of the Trail* statue, which depicts a white Madonna pioneer. Writers Frank Applegate and Mary Austin speak out against the statue, noting it does not represent the real pioneers of the region at all. . . the Spanish people. The city ultimately refuses the gift.

**1942:** The federal government selects Los Alamos Boys School site for a secret project to develop an atomic bomb. Scientists and their families begin coming to Santa Fe on their way to the research site.

**1945:** Scientists working in Los Alamos produce the world's first atomic bomb.

**1948:** Indians receive the right to vote.

**1957:** Santa Fe adopts its Historic District Ordinance to help protect landmark buildings.

**1957:** John Crosby founds the Santa Fe Opera.

**1961:** Architect John Gaw Meem and other concerned residents establish The Historic Santa Fe Foundation in response to the demolition of a historic house for a parking lot. The foundation continues to work to promote the preservation of the city's unique architectural character.

**1964:** St. John's College of Annapolis establishes a second campus in Santa Fe.

**1966:** New Mexico's present state capitol, nicknamed the Roundhouse, is dedicated in Santa Fe.

**1975:** Extensive archaeological work begins at the Palace of the Governors.

**1975:** Democrat Jerry Apodaca becomes New Mexico's first Hispanic governor since 1918.

**1975:** The Santa Fe Chamber Music Festival is established.

**1980s:** Celebrities "discover" Santa Fe. The city begins to become trendy; real estate prices start to climb. New Age seekers arrive in Santa Fe, and it becomes a popular spiritual center.

**1983:** Santa Fe Community College is created.

**1987:** The Santa Fe City Council adopts an archaeological review ordinance protecting artifacts older than 75 years.

**1989:** Santa Fe Children's Museum is founded.

**1994:** Debbie Jaramillo becomes Santa Fe's first woman mayor.

**1995:** Landscaping crews remove the last of the trees planted by Archbishop Jean Baptiste Lamy in the St. Francis Cathedral Rectory Garden. The parish replaced the pine, apple, almond, and apricot trees—some dead, some diseased—with new trees and donated the wood to local wood workers.

**2000:** Santa Fe peacefully welcomes the new millennium.

**2002:** The Spanish Colonial Arts Museum opens on Museum Hill, the newly renamed and land-scaped complex containing the Wheelwright and other museums. The Spanish Colonial Arts Museum is housed in a historic adobe building designed by famed Pueblo Revival architect John Gaw Meem.

**2003:** An excavation behind the Palace of the Governors unearths 195,000 artifacts of importance.

**2008:** The new Santa Fe Railyard mixed-use development and adjoining 10-acre park, decades in the planning, and the new 72,000-square-foot Santa Fe Community Convention Center on the site of the former Sweeney Center open in September. The New Mexico Rail Runner commuter train linking Santa Fe and Albuquerque begins service in December.

**2009:** The Santa Fe Plaza is renovated, and the much-anticipated New Mexico History Museum, a state-of-the-art facility behind the Palace of the Governors, opens over Memorial Day weekend with two days of music, dancing, exhibits, and lectures.

colony by more than 10 years. Governor Peralta and settlers from San Gabriel selected a site on the southern end of the Sangre de Cristo Mountains. The new site had a higher elevation, which meant cooler summers, and offered better protection against the attacks of the Apache, Navajo, and Comanche tribes. The Spanish laid out the town, which they called Santa Fe (meaning "Holy Faith"), according to instructions from Spain; modern Santa Fe retains this basic design in its oldest neighborhoods.

The city grew from the mud with small, one-story adobe buildings situated around a rectangular plaza. The original Plaza was at least an additional block larger than today's Plaza. Land for farming lay just beyond this town square and the city spread along the Santa Fe River—a decision the settlers came to regret. The most important building was the Casas Reales, which later became known by its English name, the Palace of the Governors. The governors and their families lived in this adobe compound, with adjoining rooms for municipal offices, meetings of the town council, storage, and a jail. Many settlers moved from San Gabriel to the new city, attracted by the promise of land of their own with water rights if they could survive for 10 years. Other newcomers trickled in over El Camino Real, an important trail into the territory from Mexico City. All roads in the province—and there weren't many—led to the Santa Fe Plaza.

In the early 1600s Santa Fe had approximately 1,000 residents, including Mexican Indians who came to Santa Fe as servants of the Spanish and who lived separately in Barrio Analco across the Santa Fe River. The population included settlers of pure Spanish blood, many *mestizos*—or people of mixed race—and people from France and Portugal. Some were black, and at least one came from Flanders. Santa Fe's early settlers were uniformly Catholic, including some Spaniards of Judaic heritage, or Crypto Jews, whose ancestors chose baptism rather than deportation or death from the Inquisition.

Santa Fe and New Mexico grew slowly as more colonists arrived and babies were born. A statue of the Virgin Mary called La Conquistadora, which ultimately became the city's most revered religious object, arrived in 1625. The economy ran largely on the barter system; by and large, people helped their neighbors. While in some ways life was hard on the frontier, in other ways the settlers were freer than they may have been in Spain or Mexico. People made their own fun, and gambling flourished in the new settlement as it did in most frontier towns.

The arrival of the supply caravan from Mexico City every three years brought village-wide celebration. Although the central purpose of the caravans was to bring supplies for the missions and official correspondence from government headquarters in Mexico City, the wagons also delivered a few precious luxury items such as silver, silk, lace, tobacco, saddles, writing desks, and chocolate. And the visitors had news and gossip from the world outside dusty Santa Fe.

By 1680 three generations of Santa Fe residents had been born, some of whom had Indian mothers. Ninety percent of the city's population was native to the province. As it grew, the village's two major areas of conflict continued to fester. First, ever-present friction between the church and state over who ruled not only the Indians but also the colony as a whole sometimes required settlers to choose between the governor and the friars. Meanwhile, the Pueblo Indians were growing increasingly unhappy with the Spanish for their economic exploitation and periodic attempts to undermine the Indians' spiritual, political, and social way of life. The colony established the *encomienda* system, which granted certain settlers the right to collect tributes from Indians who lived on designed parcels of land.

**i** A projectile point found in northeastern New Mexico, in Folsom, served as a turning point in American archaeology. Radiocarbon dating at the Folsom site showed that people had been in the region beginning 10,900 years ago—near the end of the last ice age. Identical versions of the Folsom point have been found as far east as Iowa, as far west as the Great Basin, and from southern Canada all the way down to northern Mexico.

The *encomienda* system was born of the 1573 colonization laws, which stated that Indians should be persuaded to pay moderate amounts of tribute in local products. In exchange, the Spanish *encomiendero*, or the man who received the tribute, was supposed to protect the colony—including the Pueblo Indians—by answering the governor's call to arms whenever the need arose. And the Indians, whether they liked it or not, received the "benefits" of Christianity and became subjects of the king of Spain.

Spanish law made it clear that Indians had to be paid at least minimum wage if they worked for the colonists. But New Mexico was a long way from Spain and the territory was poor. Pueblo Indians were often forced to labor against their will by the *encomienderos*. Adding to the uproar, raiding Comanche and other nonfarming Indians frequently stole the crops and livestock of both the Pueblo Indians and the Spanish settlers.

But Indian-Spanish relationships weren't exclusively antagonistic. In the worldview of the Franciscans, Indian souls deserved God's salvation, the same as those of the Spanish. In the years since Oñate's arrival, the friars had married many Pueblo Indians and Spanish. The families served as godparents for each other's children and had established friendships based on mutual respect and the need to cooperate. This wasn't enough, however, to stay the building forces of revolution.

In 1675, Spanish officials flogged a large group of Pueblo religious leaders, including Popé from San Juan Pueblo, for practicing witchcraft—a common mischaracterization of Native American religion. This public humiliation, which followed an earlier incident in which 1,600 ceremonial masks, prayer sticks, and fetishes had been burned, brought ramifications for New Mexico for many years to come.

## THE PUEBLO REVOLT

After his flogging, Popé fled to Taos, where he began to work with other Río Grande Pueblo Indian leaders and those in Arizona's Hopi country to organize a sophisticated rebellion. The cau-tious conspiracy went on for five years, hampered by the fact that the Pueblo Indians did not share a common language. (See our Local Cultures chapter.) The Indians agreed to join forces to drive the Spanish invaders out of Santa Fe and the rest of what had been their territory. They timed the rebellion for the year before the supply train arrived so the settlers would be low on food and ammunition. On August 9, 1680, runners with knotted ropes signifying the exact day of the revolt went from pueblo to pueblo, telling the Indian warriors that the time had come. Popé originally planned the uprising to coincide with the Feast of San Lorenzo but changed the date when he realized that the Spanish were on to the plan.

Despite Popé's switch, Santa Fe's Governor Antonio de Otermín discovered the plot two days before the date of the rebellion. Even with the knowledge, the governor failed to marshal any organized defense. The Indians split the scattered Spanish settlements in New Mexico into two groups, one centered in Santa Fe and one in Isleta. They tried to convince each group of settlers that the other had been killed and that their situation was hopeless. The Pueblo warriors rode through the territory, burning and sacking missions, killing priests, attacking settlers, and stealing or stampeding livestock.

When word of the uprising arrived in Santa Fe, Governor Otermín sent messengers to warn all settlers in the outlying districts to defend themselves. Those who lived between Taos and Cochití Pueblo literally ran for their lives to the walled city of Santa Fe. Settlers between Cochití and Socorro sought safety at Isleta Pueblo (near what is now Albuquerque), which remained friendly to the Spanish. Settlers living on the western side of the province, from Ziá and Jémez pueblos across to Zuni and Oraibi, had to fend for themselves. Most were killed.

At the Palace of the Governors, Otermín distributed weapons to the male colonists, and they prepared for a siege. Each new group of refugees brought grim reports of how the murder and rebellion had spread. Otermín sent soldiers to assist settlers who had held out in Los Cerrillos and La Cañada, helping them reach Santa Fe. The Spanish made sure that La Conquistadora, the 3-foot-high image of the Virgin, was safe inside the thick adobe walls.

By August 13 the Indians arrived in Santa Fe, and a nine-day siege began. Some 1,000 men, women, and children, along with a few of their animals, waited inside the palace. The Indians cut off the acequia, an irrigation ditch that supplied water to the palace. To preserve precious food and water, the colonists let their animals die. The Indians burned Santa Fe, and the besieged band watched the glow of flames from their homes and crops in the evening sky. The Pueblo leader sent a delegate to the settlers with a red flag and a white flag. The Spanish could pick the white flag, surrender, and leave. If they picked red and chose to fight, they should prepare to die. Otermín scolded the emissary and gruffly instructed him to tell the Indians to abandon the revolt and ask God to forgive them. The Indians scoffed at the message.

Finally, Otermín had to make a decision. Rather than perish of thirst and starvation, the Spanish decided to attempt to fight their way out of the palace at dawn. Otermín advanced with a small force of handpicked soldiers and caught the Indians by surprise. Although the rebels numbered about 1,500 warriors, the Spanish claimed to have slain 300, captured 47, and temporarily driven away the rest.

During a lull in the battle, the Spanish left their fortification for water and led the weakened livestock out to the ruined fields to scrounge for food. They saw the extent of the devastation the Indians had wrought. With their possessions destroyed, homes burned, and crops ravaged, they knew they could not survive the winter in Santa Fe. On August 21, 1680, Otermín signed an affidavit that he and the remaining Santa Fe settlers would abandon the villa. The party divided all clothing, food, and livestock among the sorrowful families and, in military formation, marched southward down El Camino Real, the route their optimistic ancestors had taken into New Mexico 82 years earlier.

The Spanish had lost 21 clergymen and between 380 and 400 settlers—a devastating blow to the new colony. At least 20 more were missing, either left behind as captives or in hiding from the Indians. Many, including Otermín himself, were wounded. The disheartened band headed downriver toward El Paso, joined on the way by other terrified settlers and Indians who had befriended the Spanish and feared for their lives. Otermín, stunned by the defeat, vowed to reconquer the territory and led two unsuccessful expeditions. In 1683, his term as governor ended.

After Otermín, other Spanish conquistadors attempted to reclaim New Mexico, but the Indians rebuffed them all. Spain viewed the loss of the territory as an embarrassment. The Indians ruled New Mexico for 12 years, during which time they attempted, with wide success, to obliterate all traces of the European settlers and their religion. They destroyed most of the Spanish buildings and replaced them with cornfields, saving only the Casas Reales. (The walls and foundation of San Miguel Mission—New Mexico's oldest church—also remained.) Indians burned the Spanish records, crosses, and other traces of the foreigners. Some moved into the Casas Reales, modifying it to suit their needs. Some historians believe that they also built a pueblo on the Plaza.

When things settled down, many of the Indians left Santa Fe and returned to their home pueblos. The Indian coalition dissolved, despite the efforts of some leaders to keep it together. In 1690, the king of Spain appointed Diego de Vargas to be New Mexico's new governor. Vargas agreed to reclaim the territory for Spain at his own expense. Vargas traced his family back to a famous senator of imperial Rome and believed he had the necessary military and organizational skills, along with the requisite courage, to face the Indians and succeed. He planned a two-stage reconquest: first a military presence and then the return of the settlers.

City workers excavating in the parking lot beside the old Sweeney Convention Center, prior to constructing the new convention center, recently made a surprising find—buried pottery shards and other pre-Columbian artifacts. They suggest that an Ancestral Puebloan pueblo stood in what is now downtown Santa Fe more than 200 years before the first Spanish colonists arrived.

## THE SPANISH RETURN

On September 13, 1692, at 4 a.m., Vargas and a band of 40 Spanish soldiers and 50 Indian allies arrived at the pueblo that had once been Santa Fe. Vargas had given the order: No one was to fire a shot unless and until he himself so signaled. The Spanish approached the palace in the early morning darkness, crying in unison, "Glory to the Blessed Sacrament of the Altar!" With the help of Spanish soldiers who spoke the languages of the different pueblos, Vargas told the Indians that he had come in peace to pardon them and accept their obedience to God and the king of Spain. The Indians initially refused to acquiesce. Vargas instructed his men to encircle the stronghold, positioning himself in front of the main gate. Taking his cue from Otermín's experience, he ordered his men to shut off the acequia that allowed water to flow into the fortification. The Spaniards then brought forward the cannon they'd hauled all the way from El Paso, and pointed it at the pueblo wall. The Indians began to surrender.

As the native leaders tentatively appeared, Vargas climbed down from his horse to embrace them. They invited Vargas and his men inside the palace. The Franciscans celebrated mass, absolved the Indians of their "sins," and baptized the children born since 1680. This is the peaceful reconquest that the historic Santa Fe Fiesta celebrates, a credit to Vargas's faith in God and in himself. However, the story was far from over.

Vargas and his men returned to Mexico and came back with 70 families of settlers, about 800 people. They left El Paso in mid-October 1693 and got to Santa Fe on December 16 after camping in snow and bitter cold for two weeks. With them, they brought the statue of the Virgin, *La Conquistadora*, home to Santa Fe to stay. This time the Indians declined to abandon their home and its food supplies, and a fierce battle ensued. Vargas and his men succeeded in seizing the Casas Reales. Vargas ordered the execution of 70 of the Indian defenders he had captured. Some 400 others became slaves to the Spanish for 10 years. It took the Spanish conquistadors years of battle to subdue the rest of New Mexico, but by 1696 they had reconquered all the pueblos. The longest and most successful uprising of Native Americans against foreign colonists had ended and Spanish rule was reestablished. Twenty-six Spanish governors followed Vargas. Some represented Spain with honor, wisdom, and integrity; others with ignorance and corruption. All faced hardships in managing a poor isolated colony besieged by raids from Apache, Navajo, and other Indians and requiring almost constant support from the mother country.

## 18TH-CENTURY SANTA FE

Although New Mexico's reinstated Spanish government and settlers faced many of the same problems as before, the *encomienda* system never functioned again. New Mexico's new Spanish rulers abandoned attempts to integrate the Pueblo Indians into Spanish society, probably causing relief on both sides. The Indians and the friars made peace; as long as the Indians officially professed to be Christians, the friars generally ignored their ceremonial dances and other non-Christian rituals.

In 1712 the residents of Santa Fe established a fiesta to celebrate Vargas's initial re-entry into the city. Santa Fe's defensive walls came down, and some settlers moved to homes along the Santa Fe River to protect their fields from animals and marauding neighbors. Like most villages in New Spain, Santa Fe struggled to survive during the 18th century, with the settlers fighting poverty, disease, and the whims of the weather. But life wasn't all hard work, even on the frontier. People loved the fandangos, or social dances. Utilitarian folk arts of many kinds flourished, in part because of the colony's isolation from manufactured products. Spain discouraged foreign trade, and as a result, many New Mexicans learned crafts such as folk painting, weaving, and wood carving, which they refined over generations.

Almost continuous raids by the Comanches, Apaches, Navajos, and Utes against both the Pueblo Indians and the Spanish settlements marked life in 18th-century Santa Fe. The Spanish launched frequent campaigns of reprisal and retaliation; their attacks in turn prompted revenge attacks, and the cycle continued. Frontiersman Juan Bautista de Anza, governor of New Mexico from 1778 to 1787, made peace with the Comanches, a happy condition that continued through 1794.

Santa Fe, along with Taos, Pecos, and Abiquiú, hosted annual trade fairs to allow the Spanish and the nomadic Indians to exchange goods. The barter system still ran strong, but by the end of the century money had begun to circulate in New Mexico, and Santa Fe, as the capital, led the trend.

**i** In *Down the Santa Fe Trail and into Mexico,* Susan Shelby Magoffin tells of her experience as the first white American woman to come to Santa Fe. She traveled in a private carriage heavy with books and included two servant boys in her entourage. Less than a dozen American women crossed the trail in its first 25 years of existence.

The Louisiana Purchase in 1803 signaled the beginning of the end of Spanish control over New Mexico. The purchase inspired U.S. residents to move westward. American trappers had trespassed in the territory for decades, but in 1805 Zebulon Pike led a group of explorers westward into New Mexico under direct orders from President Thomas Jefferson. The Spanish authorities arrested Pike and jailed him in Santa Fe. The governor treated Pike to dinner, outfitted him in new clothes, and sent him down to Durango, Mexico,

where he was further questioned and released. He later wrote about his adventures, fueling curiosity about New Mexico and Santa Fe.

For almost 300 years, El Camino Real had been the major thoroughfare for missionaries, colonists, soldiers, and commercial caravans into New Mexico. But that was about to change.

The longest of America's trails, El Camino Real ran 1,200 miles from Santa Fe to Mexico City. Until the opening of the Santa Fe Trail, it was virtually Santa Fe's only link to the outside world. The passage from Mexico to Santa Fe took months and put the travelers in danger; in addition to severe natural forces, the fear of attack by Indians was ever present. Once they arrived in Santa Fe, the Mexican caravans would pause several weeks or months, buying local products with which to return south. Beginning about 1709, the caravans became annual events from Chihuahua, and the northern part of El Camino Real became known as the Camino de Chihuahua.

## THE MEXICAN PERIOD

In the late 18th century, Spain, preoccupied with the Napoleonic War, lost its grip on its New World colonies. In 1821 Mexico gained its independence from Spain, and New Mexico, then part of Mexico, came along with it. Although Mexican independence had little initial effect, the winds of change again swept over Santa Fe with hurricane force.

Santa Fe remained the provincial capital during Mexican rule, as it had during centuries of Spanish authority. With a population of almost 5,100 at the turn of the 19th century, Santa Fe was the official seat of government for a territory that stretched to Arizona and included parts of Colorado and Utah. Conflict with Indians and lack of adequate finances continued, and the understaffed and underfunded Mexican government provided even less to New Mexico than had Spain.

Albuquerque-born Manuel Armijo, who served as New Mexico's governor during most of the Mexican period, became one of the most colorful and controversial figures in the state's history. Some scholars regard him as a cowardly scoundrel; others characterize him as a pragmatic leader and successful administrator.

Armijo acted notoriously independently of the Mexican government, often refusing to enforce Mexican laws he considered inappropriate for the colony. Armijo declined to collect taxes, for example, saying that service in the militia was enough of a burden for New Mexico's poor residents.

In 1835 the Mexican government replaced Armijo with Albino Peréz, a Mexican nobleman with a taste for luxury. In 1837, the residents of New Mexico rebelled against the Mexican rules and Peréz, who personified their resentment. A mob savagely murdered the governor and 16 other civil servants and elected Jose Gonzales, a Taos Indian, to rule them. Gonzales appointed Armijo as part of a delegation to go to Mexico and reassure the Mexican officials that all was under control. But, sensing an opportunity, Armijo instead gathered a small army and marched into Santa Fe to officially "reclaim" the city for Mexico. Gonzales resigned. In 1838 the Mexican government confirmed Armijo as governor once again. In 1844 Armijo resigned and was replaced with a governor from Mexico who re-instigated war with the Utes. The Mexicans removed him from office in 1845, re-installing Manuel Armijo.

Unlike the Spanish governors who preceded him, Armijo welcomed Anglo-American traders, seeing tremendous economic advantage to Santa Fe—and himself—from the caravans. He also realized the United States could pose a threat to Mexican rule and repeatedly pleaded with Mexico for more trained soldiers, weapons, and supplies. Mexico, overwhelmed with its own problems, ignored his requests.

## THE SANTA FE TRAIL

The same year Mexico won its independence, 1821, William Becknell, the man who became known as "The Father of the Old Santa Fe Trail," arrived in Santa Fe on an exploratory mission with pack mules loaded with items for trade. The Mexican governor, Facundo Melgares, encouraged

Becknell to tell other Anglo-Americans that Santa Fe would welcome them. By 1822 caravans were on the move down the Santa Fe Trail. (Although Becknell gets the credit for "founding" the trail, Spanish explorer Pedro Vial originally blazed the route in 1792.)

For decades the arrival of the caravans brought buyers, sellers, animals, and goods of all sorts to the territory. The wagons made a 900-mile trip from central Missouri on the edge of the American frontier to Santa Fe's Plaza. The trail entered and left the Plaza at its southeast corner, near the present intersection of San Francisco and Shelby Streets and La Fonda, the historic inn at the end of the trail. The traders and their merchandise came down what's now Shelby Street with a jog east at the present Water Street, then followed Old Santa Fe Trail south to near the intersection of Old Pecos Trail.

In the early years of the Santa Fe Trail, the travelers did not pass a single permanent settlement between the western boundaries of Missouri and San Miguel del Vado, about 50 miles east of Santa Fe. The trip put them to the test as they faced water and food shortages, Indian attacks, disease, freezing storms, floods, and starvation. The wagons seldom covered more than 15 miles a day.

i An excavation behind the former Woolworth's building just off the Plaza in 1999 uncovered almost 30 boxes of historic debris. The crews found numerous artifacts from the Old Santa Fe Trail days. People who work downtown, visitors, and school groups had an opportunity to watch the urban archaeologists on the job and ask them questions about the dig.

About 100 miles east of Santa Fe, two different routes converged near Fort Union National Monument. The Cimarron Cutoff was a route of the trail that took travelers across the hot, dry desert of eastern New Mexico, frequently at the mercy of Indian attack. The Mountain Route followed a difficult route through the Sangre de Cristo Mountains, which slowed wagons but was somewhat shorter and safer. Beyond Fort Union, soldiers accompanied wagon trains to Santa Fe after New Mexico became a territory. You can see ruts from the trail throughout eastern New Mexico.

Santa Fe's adobe look was strange to the newcomers; many didn't even recognize the small, brown, boxlike buildings as houses at first. Some travelers compared Santa Fe to a prairie dog town, perhaps not realizing that the mud bricks were ideal material for keeping out the day's heat and, once warmed by the fires from wood stoves in the winter, they retained heat far better than a log home. Inside, the homes lacked the furnishings common to the United States. Instead of formal beds, for instance, Santa Fe's practical residents folded their sleeping mattresses to double as couches during the day.

And the differences were more than just superficial. Blacks and Indians living in New Mexico and other Mexican territories had full rights of citizenship, unlike their counterparts in the United States. Also, as specified in the Mexican Constitution, all residents had the right of free speech. The Mexicans abolished the old Spanish caste system, which established rigid social rankings based on a person's degree of Spanish blood. At the Governor's Ball in 1839, for example, an American visitor noted that the poor and rich alike attended and even danced together.

Another strong difference between Mexican Santa Fe and the United States was the status of women. Santa Fe women enjoyed much more freedom than their counterparts in the United States. They retained their maiden names after marriage. They smoked, danced, and enjoyed gambling as much as the men. The women dressed less formally and in styles considerably less confining than those worn by women in the early-19th-century United States. Not only were they not considered their husbands' property, but women in Santa Fe had property rights and legal rights denied their U.S. counterparts. They worked for wages in jobs such as bakers, weavers, card dealers, and, of course, prostitutes. Women could own rental property and flocks and were not legally required to share their money with their husbands. Both wives and husbands could take spouses to court for legal redress of their grievances.

The U.S. travelers also entered a territory that was largely on its own in terms of religion. The Mexican government had offered no financial support to the Catholic Church—the only religion in the territory other than that of the American Indians—and priests were included in Mexico's orders for all Spanish-born citizens to leave the country. Afterwards, historians report, only five to eight priests remained to minister to the far-flung population. As a result of the lack of clergy, lay Catholic orders developed in rural communities to keep the faith alive. These brotherhoods became known as the Penitentes for their severe penance during Holy Week. As another result of the scarcity of priests and the high fee on marriage, more than half of the couples in Santa Fe lived together without the church's blessing.

Commerce and information flowed both ways along the Santa Fe Trail. In addition to selling the American products they brought by the wagonload, caravans returned to the United States with hides, pelts, and Indian weavings from New Mexico. Some Santa Fe merchants journeyed to the United States themselves to make purchases and return with goods that could be sold at a substantial profit. One of Santa Fe's best-known merchants was Gertrudes Barcelo, or "La Tules." La Tules made her money gambling and invested it in American goods, which she had shipped to Santa Fe to sell at a profit. Another trader who profited from the wagons was Governor Manuel Armijo himself. In addition to the benefit of their trade goods, the U.S. merchants paid customs duties on their cargoes, money that supported New Mexico's government, and paid the Santa Fe soldiers' salaries. Some travelers from the United States became citizens and lifelong residents of Santa Fe, holding office and helping the territory in many ways, including fighting Indian raiders as members of the citizen militia. Others were arrogant and lawless, trapping animals illegally, cheating their customers, demeaning the territory's Spanish-speaking people and their culture, and selling guns to hostile Indians.

**New Mexico governor Manuel Armijo rented rooms in the Palace of the Governors to travelers who arrived in Santa Fe along the Santa Fe Trail.**

## SANTA FE, U.S.A.

In June 1846, New Mexico's governor received word that the United States had declared war on Mexico. The war put Armijo in a terrible position. His duty as governor would be to fight the Americans in what was sure to be a doomed effort. After assembling several thousand disheveled troops for battle in Apache Canyon outside Santa Fe, Armijo decided not to fight and fled to Mexico. He was tried and acquitted of treason in Mexico City and returned to New Mexico, where he died under U.S. rule. Questions remain about Armijo's motivation: Was he bribed to leave or did he decide that avoiding bloodshed was in the best interests of New Mexico?

U.S. general Stephen Watts Kearny and his staff rode into Santa Fe unobstructed to meet with New Mexico's acting governor, who greeted them politely and served them dinner complete with wine imported from El Paso over El Camino Real. The next day Kearny made a speech to Santa Fe residents, attempting to alleviate their fears. He promised that their religion and language would be protected, and that all provisions needed by the U.S. soldiers would be purchased, not stolen. He assured Santa Fe residents that they would have a voice in the new government and a role in the area's future. Three years later, in 1850, New Mexico became a U.S. territory and remained so for 62 years before finally achieving statehood.

Kearny and his forces had taken Santa Fe without firing a shot, and the Stars and Stripes now flew over the Plaza. Five days after his arrival, the general instructed the soldiers with him to begin building the garrison of Fort Marcy on a hill overlooking the city. For the next 10 years, until New Mexico became involved in the Civil War, soldiers stationed here spent their time fighting off Apache and other Indian raids and protecting new immigrants along the Santa Fe Trail.

In 1847, however, the soldiers left their Santa Fe base and headed north to quell a revolution after hearing some startling news: The state's first U.S. territorial governor, Charles Bent, had been assassinated in Taos. The conspirators planned to attack and kill all Anglo-Americans in northern New Mexico as well as all New Mexico natives who had accepted positions in the new government. On the night of January 18, conspirators had murdered Bent and five others and paraded Bent's scalp through the town. They continued the rampage, attacking and killing seven other men a few miles north of Taos; more were shot in Mora.

The U.S. forces responded with troops from Albuquerque joining the Santa Fe army. After defeating the rebels in a battle at Embudo, the U.S. forces continued on to Taos. They discovered that the New Mexicans had fortified themselves in the church at Taos Pueblo. Army artillery broke down the church walls, and after 150 rebels died in the fight, the others fled or surrendered. U.S. courts tried the prisoners and hanged six of the leaders for their role in the bloody attempt at revolution.

The Taos rebellion was the last organized revolt against American authority in New Mexico, but raids and uprisings continued through 1847. Meanwhile, the English-speaking soldiers protected the Santa Fe settlers, new and old, from Indian raids. The U.S. government began work on a new state capitol, intended to replace the Spanish Casas Reales (Palace of the Governors). Construction began in 1850, but the money ran out before crews finished the work.

Native Santa Fe residents slowly adjusted to the U.S. presence and the slow but steady influx of Americans. They didn't complain about the establishment of twice-a-month mail service beginning in 1857. Stagecoaches added Santa Fe to their line, and the city enjoyed a temporary economic boom in the 1850s, a period described by historian Marc Simmons as the heyday of the Santa Fe Trail.

As a concession to the ethnic realities of the area, territorial government was conducted in both English and Spanish, and the legislature itself was primarily Hispanic until 1886. Hispanics outnumbered non-Hispanics by about 50 to 1.

Among the new arrivals along the trail was Santa Fe's first bishop, Frenchman Jean Baptiste Lamy. Lamy recruited adventurous priests, nuns, and brothers from Europe to help establish schools, hospitals, and orphanages in New Mexico and to care for the territory's sprawling population of Catholics. Lamy began construction of St. Francis Cathedral and Loretto Chapel. He introduced reform into New Mexico's long-neglected Catholic Church but declined to show what many residents believed was sufficient respect for New Mexico's indigenous religious traditions.

Lamy's imposition of northern European cultural values on New Mexico's Catholics, who had been largely independent of church authority for many decades, led to resentment. His clashes with native clergy and what many considered his disrespect for northern New Mexico's indigenous arts and culture—much of which had been created for the glory of God and the saints—brought conflict that continued throughout his long tenure as bishop and archbishop.

Other settlers came to Santa Fe as traders who wished to establish businesses or as sheep raisers, ranchers, and homesteaders looking for a fresh start. The people of Santa Fe called them "Anglo"—a word used to mean people who were not Spanish or American Indian.

The influx of Anglo settlers was prompted by cheap land and the rumor that the New Mexico climate was good for one's health. Health seekers and artists, who also appreciated Santa Fe's brilliantly clear air and high-country climate, continued to visit and move to Santa Fe off and on throughout the city's history. Many Spanish women married Anglos, but whether they did or not, women lost many of the freedoms they'd enjoyed prior to U.S. occupation.

Despite the area's geographic isolation, the Civil War found New Mexico. In February 1862, a Confederate general leading troops from Texas invaded, won several crucial battles, and took control of Santa Fe. But Confederate rule didn't last long. On March 26, Union and Confederate forces met about 15 miles southwest of Santa Fe, near what is now Pecos National Historical Park. The Union troops destroyed Confederate supplies in the Battle of Glorieta and the Texans went south, abandoning their dreams of capturing the West.

The end of the Civil War brought no peace to the Santa Fe area because the major battles, conflicts with the Plains Indians, increased during U.S. rule. Unlike the Mexicans and Spanish governors, who had recognized Indian rights and lands, the new territorial government took a radically different approach. Reflecting the cultural values of the day, the U.S. government openly suppressed Indian rights and worked to destroy Native American culture. One of the most effective methods was forcing Indian children to leave their homes and go to boarding schools where they were not allowed to speak their native languages, practice their traditional religion, or stay in close touch with their families. As more settlers moved in, the problems worsened.

Conflict between the territorial government and the Spanish citizenry also continued. One governor, William Pile, angered Santa Fe residents when he ordered workers to dispose of all historic documents in a room at the Palace of the Governors, as the Casas Reales was now called. Outraged Hispanic and Anglo residents attempted to recover the priceless papers. Some were found as waste paper or meat wrappers; many were lost forever.

Although the Treaty of Guadalupe Hidalgo specified that Spanish and Mexican land grants in the territories acquired by the United States after the Mexican War would be respected, this was not to be. Differences in the systems of law made it difficult for many land-grant owners to substantiate their land titles. Although some of Santa Fe's prominent longtime families managed to keep their land and their power, most fared badly. Not speaking English or understanding the American legal system, they were easy prey for unscrupulous lawyers and politicians. The Spanish and Mexican judicial system required only that alcaldes, or judges, know how to read and write; the U.S. system called for trained lawyers. Anglo lawyers soon concentrated in Santa Fe, and many grew rich on their clients' misfortune.

One of Santa Fe's most powerful men during this period was Thomas Catron. Catron moved to Santa Fe from Missouri, learned to speak and write Spanish, and amassed more than a million and a half acres of land-grant property. A lawyer, Catron involved himself in local politics, ruled the powerful Republican Party, then worked as an advocate for statehood. He became one of New Mexico's first two senators. During his day and afterward, many accused him of unethical practices; his defenders say he accumulated his fortune and power legally and died bankrupt.

Accusations of fraud, political corruption, and malfeasance flowed freely for years in territorial New Mexico. Finally, the U.S. secretary of the interior suspended New Mexico governor Samuel Axtell and named Lew Wallace in his place. Wallace is the best known of the state's territorial rulers, not so much for his politics, but because he worked on his famous novel, *Ben Hur,* while living at the Palace of the Governors.

In addition to the problems of Spanish families, who felt they were being unjustly deprived of their land, Wallace had to deal with Indian uprisings, raids by Billy the Kid in southeastern New Mexico, and growing conflict between cattle and sheep ranchers. He coined the often-repeated expression: "Every calculation based on experience elsewhere fails in New Mexico." During Wallace's administration, the first successful effort was made to preserve and catalog priceless documents from Santa Fe's Mexican and Spanish periods.

Just as the Santa Fe Trail brought tremendous change to Santa Fe, so did another transportation innovation, the railroad. In 1880 the train made its presence felt and change followed rapidly. Even though it was named Atchison, Topeka & Santa Fe, the company planned to bypass Santa Fe because of engineering problems. A group of city boosters prevailed on the railroad to run an 18-mile spur to serve Santa Fe. Without rail service, they feared that Santa Fe would lose its prominence to rail towns such as Las Vegas and Albuquerque. The locomotives quickly brought the end to the Santa Fe Trail and delivered curious tourists to the city's doorstep. The spur line cut through the western part of town; railyards and depots went up using not adobe but red bricks brought by the trains.

## SANTA FE STYLE

The look of Santa Fe began to change. The railroad delivered building materials not previously available, among them wood for shingles and siding and glass for windows. Santa Fe residents enjoyed these new options; some wished to duplicate the homes they'd known in the East or Midwest; some longtime residents liked the idea of a more modern-looking house.

As Santa Fe's look began to become more like other cities in the United States, preservationists and the city promoters worried that the town would sacrifice its architectural distinctiveness and that the popularity of the new materials would mean the end of adobe and of Santa Fe's unique look. If the city lost its charm, they believed, it would also lose the tourist dollars that had begun to flow into its economy.

These city boosters, among them artists, archaeologists, civic leaders, and merchants, began to develop a plan for Santa Fe's future that included a unique architectural vision. The Pueblo Revival-style, which is also known as Spanish Pueblo style, combined modern convenience with the city's traditional look and ultimately came to be known as "Santa Fe style."

In the 1880s, however, Santa Fe's style was not so tightly defined. A new state capitol and a governor's mansion—neither of them "Santa Fe style"—were constructed on vacant land south of the Santa Fe River. The capitol burned under mysterious circumstances five years later. Some blamed arson by Albuquerque partisans who wanted their town to become the state capital. Another new capitol, complete with pillars and a dome rather than Santa Fe-style vigas and a *portal,* was built in 1900.

But the proponents of Santa Fe's architectural heritage won a larger battle. The city persuaded the territorial legislature to renovate the Palace of the Governors and transform it into a museum instead of demolishing the old building. The Palace and the Fine Arts Museum constructed in the new "Santa Fe" style set the tone for later construction. Hotel La Fonda, the School of Advanced Research, and the old Post Office building across from the Cathedral Place all testify to the early popularity of this look, which was to become an enduring trademark of modern Santa Fe.

Santa Fe's allure began to spread. Governor Lew Wallace wrote enthusiastically about his new home, one of many 19th-century writers and artists who raved about Santa Fe's attractions. Although the territory obviously had its problems, no one wanted to know about that; the city's romanticization had begun. The railroad made it easier to come West, and visitors did.

With wonderful foresight, the territory of New Mexico established the Bureau of Immigration, a precursor to the modern Department of Economic Development, in Santa Fe in 1880. The department offered information to outsiders who hoped to make money here, but also received inquiries from artists, writers, and anthropologists drawn by Santa Fe's physical beauty and Hispanic and Indian cultures. Santa Fe's business community came together in 1882 as the Santa Fe Board of Trade, spearheading the movement that led to the incorporation of the city in 1891. By the end of the 19th century, many community leaders recognized that Santa Fe's economic future hinged on two factors: tourism and government employment. In the decades that followed, their insight continued to ring true.

## STATEHOOD AND BEYOND

When General Kearny first brought U.S. rule to Santa Fe, the city's population was estimated at between 2,000 and 4,000. By 1910 that figure was 5,600, with an additional 9,200 people living outside the city proper. Santa Fe and New Mexico marked the early years of the 20th century with ongoing cries for the rights of statehood. Three attempts at admission to the Union had failed, at least partly because of continuing anti-Catholic, anti-Spanish sentiment in Congress. New Mexico suggested joint statehood with Arizona in 1906, but Arizona rejected the idea. Finally, on January 6, 1912, President William Howard Taft signed the bill making New Mexico the 47th state.

Although it has been amended several times, the state constitution has never been rewritten— but the idea arises frequently. As is still true today, the constitution specified that Spanish was equal to English in both public education and legal discourse, and included a bill of rights that again stressed that the rights provided in the Treaty of Guadalupe Hidalgo must be upheld. William C. MacDonald was New Mexico's first U.S. governor, living and working in Santa Fe, which continued to be the state capital.

**The pen used by President William Howard Taft to sign the document authorizing New Mexico's statehood is on display at the Palace of the Governors, 107 West Palace Ave. New Mexico became the 47th state in 1912.**

In 1916 the old Fort Marcy headquarters were demolished to make way for the construction of the new Fine Arts Museum. A few years later, a group of artists and newcomers resurrected the Santa Fe Fiesta, including secular events and more parties to give the festival additional appeal. The custom of honoring *La Conquistadora* had survived, but when Santa Fe became a Mexican city the community began to celebrate Mexican independence rather than the exploits of Vargas—who became known in Santa Fe as "DeVargas."

In the 1920s, Santa Fe's art colony thrived, and visitors returned to the city seeking to become permanent residents. Painters captured the city's beauty on canvas and spread the word with their work. Before World War I, Sheldon Parsons, Victor Higgins, Gerald Cassidy, William Penhallow Henderson, B. J. O. Nordfeldt, and many more artists enriched the city in many ways. Will Shuster— now best known for creating Zozobra—and four other Santa Fe painters became known as Los

Cinco Pintores and spread the glory of Santa Fe's scenery and people with their art. John Sloan, George Bellows, and Leon Kroll—important names in 20th-century American art—spent time visiting and painting in Santa Fe. Edward Hopper and Marsden Hartley lived here in the 1920s and 1930s, as did Robert Henri and Andrew Dausburg. In 1925 author Mary Austin and a group of artists and collectors founded the Spanish Colonial Arts Society to encourage Hispanic artists to continue working in the traditions of the 18th century and to sell and promote their work. The 1920s also saw Santa Fe's first Indian Market, which became a long-standing community event. Leading southwestern anthropologist Clyde Kluckhohn arrived in Santa Fe in 1925. In addition to "real" art, Santa Fe of this era also was filled with curio shops for tourists, including travelers who came on the Indian Detours circuit, a popular southwestern touring business based in Santa Fe.

In the 1930s Santa Fe architect John Gaw Meem, who had originally moved here to cure his tuberculosis, accelerated the trend to re-create Santa Fe's traditional look. The National Park Service Headquarters on Old Santa Fe Trail, built during the New Deal era, is a beautiful example of Pueblo Revival style. In the 1930s, due partly to the pressure applied to the federal government by some of the city's well-placed Anglo residents and changing cultural views, the repression of Indian culture eased. The U.S. Indian School, a boarding school that brought Indian students to Santa Fe, was allowed to open an art department. The result renewed interest in Indian art among American Indians and the broader culture and led to the founding of the Institute of American Indian Arts in 1962.

## INTO THE NEW MILLENNIUM

In the 1940s, New Mexico became nationally important because of its crucial role in the development of the atomic bomb. The U.S. government took over Los Alamos Ranch School in 1943, transforming the site into a secret center for nuclear research. The project brought a steady stream of scientists and their families through Santa Fe for the clandestine work. By 1945 more than 3,000 civilian and military personnel were living there. Atomic bombs built in Los Alamos were dropped in Nagasaki and Hiroshima, Japan. Los Alamos National Laboratory (LANL), operated by the United States Department of Energy through a contract with the University of California, continues as a major contributor to Santa Fe and northern New Mexico's economy. The lab conducts a variety of scientific and technological research, including work on nuclear weapons. With approximately 7,000 on staff and millions of dollars' worth of contracts with northern New Mexico businesses, LANL's presence is seen by some as a blessing. Others believe that weapons research should have no place in the modern world, much less in northern New Mexico.

**i** **Santa Fe residents had no idea what was going on in the Jémez Mountains at the secret research site that became Los Alamos. As work on the atomic bomb continued, one rumor had it that the crews were building windshield wipers for submarines.**

Through the 1950s, Santa Fe continued to grow, spreading southwest in a pattern that continues to this day. However, during the 1960s and 1970s urban renewal, highway construction, state capitol expansion projects, and the construction of large office buildings for state workers changed the city's urban pattern. The project caused realignment of roads and division of neighborhoods. Shopping centers, which offered lower rents and convenient parking, drew local customers away from downtown; Plaza businesses began to cater more to tourists and art buyers.

The construction of the Santa Fe Opera and its subsequent rise to national prominence helped keep Santa Fe's arts community in the spotlight. Established in 1957, the Opera successfully involved Santa Fe and New Mexico residents and businesses in its fund-raising. The Opera also attracted major corporate and out-of-state donors and now draws an international audience. The establishment of the Santa Fe Chamber Music Festival in 1975 added to Santa Fe's stature as an arts center. (See The Arts chapter.)

In 1957 the city created a historic district encompassing the Plaza and the eastern part of town. After the construction of two large buildings downtown in the 1970s and 1980s, the city again tightened its protection for historic properties. Since then the designations have been expanded, and the rules and regulations for protecting historic properties in other neighborhoods clarified. Excavation at the Palace of the Governors in 1975 uncovered evidence from all periods of the history of the building. Visitors to the Palace today can see storage bins from 1693 in a glass-covered pit beneath the floorboards.

The establishment of St. John's College in 1964 enhanced Santa Fe's status as an educational center. The creation of Santa Fe Community College in 1983 made it possible for Santa Fe students to continue their learning at a public college without leaving home. (See our Education and Child Care chapter.) Beginning in the early 1980s, Hollywood and music celebrities "discovered" Santa Fe, many buying homes in the area and others vacationing here regularly. Their presence and the resulting media attention added to Santa Fe's growing attraction as a place for millionaires to build second homes and others to seek permanent retirement here.

A growing gap between the independently wealthy and working populations now characterizes Santa Fe, resulting in a widely different experience of the town, depending on one's background. This has led to more gourmet restaurants, coffee shops, high-end art galleries, luxury shops, and housing development. It also has led to accelerating rents and real estate prices, higher property taxes, and the dislocation of many longtime residents. Santa Fe attracts many "New Agers" and has become a center for the study and practice of alternative medicine. By the 1990s, Hispanics had become a minority here for the first time in the city's history.

Modern Santa Fe contends with issues that face many cities in the United States: traffic, the need for affordable housing, problems with the public school system, crime, and growing demand for better-paying jobs beyond the service industry, for city and county services, often in remote, difficult terrain where the laying of infrastructure is notoriously difficult. In 1994 Santa Fe elected its first woman mayor, former city councilor Debbie Jaramillo. Jaramillo's anti-tourism comments and the hiring of her brother and brother-in-law in major city jobs led to considerable controversy and brought negative national attention to Santa Fe. But the Jaramillo administration also inaugurated a successful affordable-housing program, purchased the railyard property, and initiated new services for children and teenagers. The voters replaced Jaramillo with a more moderate mayor and also approved a city charter allowing "home rule," which, among other changes, gives Santa Fe voters the right to recall public officials. Under the current mayor, David Coss, a number of projects have come to fruition: the construction of a new convention center, the opening of the new Railyard Park, the return of a living river with seasonal water releases along the Santa Fe River, and an emphasis on improving multimodal transportation, from the new Rail Runner train to free shuttles and better bike lanes.

The city's reputation as an intellectual center was boosted with the opening of the Santa Fe Institute, a high-tech think tank that draws scientists, computer experts, writers, and intellectuals from around the world. By 2009, Santa Fe was also home to more than 50 publishing companies. As the city grows in the new millennium, Santa Fe's economic base remains tourism and government, with a recent influx of small entrepreneurial companies, including spin-offs of technology developed by Los Alamos National Laboratory.

During World War II, the first Japanese detainees arrived in Santa Fe on March 14, 1942, and went to a former Civilian Conservation Corps camp in an area now known as Casa Solana. At peak population, Camp Santa Fe held as many as 2,000 prisoners.

Modern Santa Fe's population reflects the city's deep roots. You'll find American Indian families, the descendants of the founding Spanish immigrants, great-grandchildren of merchants who arrived over the Santa Fe Trail, and new residents from New York, California, Texas, and abroad, who find the city's culture, history, and natural environment irresistible.

Readers of the upscale Condé Nast travel publications consistently rank Santa Fe among their top-10 national and international destinations. The city's visitors bureau estimates that 1.3 million tourists spend time here over the course of a year—with more than half of them arriving in the three months of summer. After an initial falloff in tourism following the September 11 terrorism attacks, the city has largely recovered its main industry and remains a top destination for visitors. Unlike many other cities in the United States, it has weathered the major economic downturn that began in December 2007 quite well, having long planned and raised funds for infrastructure improvements that have suddenly come to fruition all at once, as the city celebrates its 400th anniversary. In many ways, Santa Fe's greatest attraction has always been that it has resisted the superficial rapid boom and bust of other places and continued to march to its own tune. Like its enduring Indian and Hispanic cultures, it has learned the benefits of simply waiting things out and staying true to its own beliefs. It's a tried-and-true approach whose time may have come.

**i** The "Oldest House in the U.S.A.," located at 215 East De Vargas St., was built in the 1700s.

# LOCAL CULTURE

**N**orthern New Mexico is a land of conquest and reconquest, sometimes accomplished by forceful means, other times without a drop of blood spilled. The region has changed hands and complexions many times, starting with the Pueblo Indians, whose agrarian, cliff-dwelling forebears settled the region as far back as the 1st century B.C.

Pueblo culture as we know it today took root at the beginning of the 14th century and flourished—until its first encounter in 1540 with Europeans, who brought guns as well as a new world of diseases against which the natives had no natural defenses. Through force in some cases and friendly but firm persuasion in others, Spanish conquistadores, priests, and settlers claimed the region in the name of the motherland and the Catholic Church, only to lose it in 1680 in the Pueblo Revolt (see our History chapter). Spain reconquered the New Mexico Territory in 1692 and held onto it until 1821, when Mexico won independence from Spain and claimed the territory as its own. But the Mexican flag flew over New Mexico only 27 years, to be replaced by the Stars and Stripes after Mexico lost a two-year war with the United States. It ceded the territory in 1848 to its young northern neighbor in accordance with the terms of the Treaty of Guadalupe Hidalgo.

## HISPANIC CULTURE

The result of this checkered history is a checkerboard of cultures, with Anglo-Americans among the last to arrive. "Anglo" culture is a category that today in New Mexico encompasses everything from white-bred Middle Americans to African Americans, Arabs, Asians, East Indians, Irish, Italians, Jews, Poles, Russians, and anyone else not of Hispanic or Native American origin. Despite the subtle and not-so-subtle encroachment of Anglo culture over the past 150 years, the dominant flavor of northern New Mexico is without a doubt Hispanic. What that means, however, has been an ongoing—and often heated—debate in which many Hispanos have shunned their Mexican roots in favor of their Spanish heritage, while a few have taken the opposite stance.

Today, however, most people agree that local Hispanic culture has its roots in both Spain and Mexico as well as in Native America. Whatever the precise definition, it's a combination unique to New Mexico—one you'll see, hear, and feel the moment you emerge from the airplane into the Albuquerque International Sunport and make your way toward Santa Fe or other points north. It's all around you—in the art and the architecture, the music and the clothing, the food, and the language . . . especially the language.

Here we live in flat-roofed adobe homes on *caminos* and *calles*. Outside, our *portales* (porches) are decorated with strings of bright red chile *ristras*. Inside, our *casas* have corner kiva fireplaces and log beam vigas that hold up *latilla* (latticed) ceilings. Our walls come complete with built-in *nichos* for displaying handcrafted santos—religious images carved by *santeros*—that glorify *Díos*. We wear bolo ties, concho belts, and cowboy boots. We dance to ranchero music, mariachi, or salsa, which is also something we eat with tortilla chips and guacamole before digging into plates filled with enchiladas or burritos with pure red or green chile and perhaps a side of hominy posole or *chicos*. *Chicos* are also children, whom parents affectionately call *mi hijo* or *mi hijita*—elided to *m'ijo* or *m'ijita*—sending them off to *la escuela* (school) where they recite the Pledge of Allegiance first in English, then in Spanish.

That's a far cry from the time between the 19th century and the mid-20th century, when New Mexican children were punished for speaking Español in school. Today, students learn early on that the Spanish arrived in New Mexico years before the real Anglos—the English Puritans—landed at Plymouth Rock. They're fully aware that Santa Fe is the oldest state capital and the second-oldest city in the nation.

In schools and elsewhere throughout New Mexico, there's a pride in *la raza*, which means "the race" but has become synonymous with a Hispanic heritage that locally has produced artists and artisans whose work is recognized throughout the United States and abroad. Traditional or folk artists utilize native materials—wood, tin, silver, straw, etc.—and techniques that in many cases their families have been using for generations. While the Spanish and Mexican influences are apparent in their work, the styles are uniquely New Mexican—and often unique to a particular family. Like their brethren around the world, contemporary Hispano artists work in every imaginable medium. Sculpture, painting, photography, jewelry, and, yes, those elegant, traffic-stopping labors of love called lowriders all play an integral role in the northern New Mexico art scene. So do Hispanic literature, film, theater, dance, music, and lore.

**i** **Lowriders are rebuilt American cars with lowered suspensions and custom paint and interiors. Every Saturday, lowriders adorned with velvet upholstery, chainlink mini–steering wheels, fuzzy dice, TVs, blaring stereos, and custom paintings of saints cruise Espanola's Riverside Drive. They have become an authentic contemporary Hispanic art form, expressing Hispanic values of faith, family, and art, and can even be found in the Smithsonian Institution.**

Of course, Hispanics—who represent nearly half the population of Santa Fe—play major roles in all walks of life, not just the arts. They're accomplished doctors, dentists, lawyers, teachers, priests, and politicians, to name just a few professions. The governor of the state is Hispanic, as are two other powerful men in the State Legislature. The latter each have been in their respective positions—Speaker of the House of Representatives and Senate president pro tem—for a decade and a half.

But *la cultura Hispana* is far more than what people do for a living, the clothes they wear, the food they eat, or even the language they speak, though the latter is closer to the crux of the matter. Here in northern New Mexico, Hispanic culture is la gente (the people), whose first priority generally is la familia followed by la comunidad. Sometimes they're one and the same.

Embedded in the local Hispanic culture is a deep-rooted sense of *hidalguismo*—an aristocratic lineage that hearkens back to the founding of Santa Fe in 1608 by the nobility *(los hidalgos)* in concert with the Catholic Church. While *el hidalguismo* and the entitlement that came with it is today merely a vestige, the Catholic Church has survived intact. Indeed, *el catolicismo* touches all aspects of la vida in northern New Mexico, regardless of one's faith. From the *Sangre de Cristo* (Blood of Christ) Mountains that loom over the northern Río Grande Valley to the myriad churches, missions, and *moradas* (see the Close-up on Penitentes in our Worship and Spirituality chapter) dotting the landscape; from invocations at government functions and school sporting events to Las Fiestas de Santa Fe, which, despite its secular trappings, is Catholic at its core; from the festive *farolitos* that light rooftops and driveways throughout the Christmas season to the annual Easter pilgrimage to the Santuario de Chimayó—there's no question that northern New Mexico, and particularly La Villa Real de Santa Fe (Royal City of the Holy Faith), was founded as a far-reaching bastion of the Spanish Catholic Church. It remains tied to those roots at its deepest levels.

Spain's influence in New Mexico goes beyond religion and art. Spanish colonizers who survived the perilous six-month trek along El Camino Real—the 2,000-mile "Royal Road" or "King's Highway" from Mexico City to Santa Fe—brought with them mining and forging equipment and techniques. They showed the Native Americans how to use metals for weapons, tools, and art. They brought the wheel, introduced horses to the continent, and taught Pueblos how to raise cattle and sheep. They engineered the efficient and esthetic acequia irrigation system still used throughout New Mexico today.

Despite armed conflicts between the two cultures, the settlers in time found they had more in common with their native neighbors than they did with distant Spain, if only because they shared a common enemy in the hostile Plains Indians. Years of commingling among the Spanish, Mexicans, and Indians eventually gave rise in New Mexico to a unique mestizo culture of its own—one rich with tradition, much of it oral. *La curandera* (healer) cures body and mind with unwritten methods passed down to her, and which she will pass on to the next generation; *el mayordomo* consults no manual to direct the annual cleaning of the *acequias* (irrigation ditches); *la cuentista* (storyteller) needs no script to relate *los cuentos* (tales) and *las leyendas* (legends) that hundreds of years of telling and retelling have refined and embellished.

What we've described thus far is a colorful portrait of Hispanic life in northern New Mexico. But this multifaceted culture that has flourished here since the 16th century has of late been confronted by a dark side. In Santa Fe, where until recently Hispanos were in the majority, the unemployment and poverty rates among Hispanics are disproportionately high. Consequently, so are the school dropout rate, teen pregnancies, the homicide rate, and incidents of domestic violence. The powers that be attribute this largely to a movement away from what was once primarily a land-based culture to a free-market, wage-dependent economy where traditional skills such as farming and ranching are no longer marketable. Add to this volatility an invasion of visitors and new, moneyed residents and perhaps you can understand why many in the Hispanic community feel disenfranchised. They sense they're losing their land, their voice, and ultimately their culture to the highest bidder.

For the survival of their rich heritage and a legacy to pass on to future generations, it's vital that Santa Fe cling to its roots. The answer lies not in isolationism, but rather in education, an openness to new ideas rooted in the good of the whole community, and preserving the cultural vitality of the region without exploiting it.

## PUEBLO CULTURE

Centuries before Europeans reached the Americas, New Mexico was home to the thriving Ancestral Puebloan culture, once known as the Anasazi—"the ancient ones," according to the most familiar translation from the Navajo, though the term means "the enemy of my ancestors." At the height of their civilization (approximately 900 to 1350), the ancestors of today's Pueblo people lived in a territory that stretched from central Utah and southern Colorado south to Mexico and from western Arizona into the Texas panhandle. Their abandoned cliff dwellings, multistory villages, pit houses, underground ceremonial kivas, wall paintings, and petroglyphs etched in rock and many material remains are silent testament to the richness and resourcefulness of their culture. Many of New Mexico's 19 existing Indian pueblos—nine of them within 65 miles from Santa Fe—trace their origins directly to Ancestral Puebloan groups such as the Mesa Verde and the Chaco cultures. The Navajo and Jicarilla Apache tribes, located in or near the remote Four Corners region in northeastern New Mexico, and the Mescalero Apaches in south-central New Mexico descended from the nomadic Athapascan tribe that arrived later from northwest Canada. With some notable exceptions—among them the 1680 Pueblo Revolt (see our History chapter) and the current controversy over tribal casinos, tribal golf courses, and other businesses—Native Americans in the Southwest have kept a low profile, both politically and socially. Yet their artistic, architectural, and culinary influence on the region is unmistakable. Native culture permeates all aspects of life here.

It was the Pueblo Indians whom Spanish explorers first encountered when they arrived in

New Mexico in the mid-1600s. They found a flour-ishing, agrarian, and relatively peaceful popula-tion living in compact, apartmentlike dwellings made of stone or adobe. The explorers christened them "pueblo" Indians from the Spanish word for "village"—a term that refers to the entire cul-ture rather than a specific tribe. Spanish settlers adopted the native architecture and adapted the Indians' sophisticated method of underground irrigation to their own acequia system. At the time of the first encounter, between 40,000 and 50,000 Indians lived in more than 100 pueblos. By 1857 they numbered only 7,000. Their civilization had been decimated by disease, starvation, and execution while their culture was dying from assimilation—both forced and voluntary—and intermarriage. Still, the tribes managed to pre-serve many traditions by externally adopting the ways of the various paternalistic governments that occupied their native lands while secretly continuing to practice their own pantheistic religions and customs. Many of the new ways stuck, most notably Catholicism, which is widely practiced on the pueblos, though it has been adapted to native practices. This is particularly evident on feast days, which combine elements of the native religion with commemoration of Catholic saints.

**The ancestors of today's Pueblo people are no longer officially called Anasazi, a Navajo word meaning "Enemy Ancestors," which upsets some Pueblo people. The pref-erable term today is to refer to that culture as Ancestral Puebloan or, better yet, by its specific regional designation—Chaco, Mesa Verde, or Kayenta.**

## MODERN PUEBLO LIFE

Today, New Mexico's 19 pueblos count an esti-mated 40,000 members, many of whom live away from their tribal lands. The pueblos share many characteristics, including similar customs and native languages—Tewa, Tiwa, Towa, and Keresan. (Zuni Indians speak Zunian, which is unrelated to the other four languages.) But each

pueblo is a unique, sovereign entity, as it has been since being accorded these rights by Spanish rule, with individual governmental, religious, and social structure. Every tribe also has a distinctive style in jewelry, weaving, basketry, carving, and especially pottery; pueblo pottery is considered among the finest of all North American tribes. The black-on-black pottery made famous by María Martínez, for example, is recognized inter-nationally as being from San Ildefonso Pueblo, while geometric black-and-white pots are clearly from Ácoma Pueblo, "The City in the Sky" west of Albuquerque.

Underlying the art and the very culture of the Pueblo Indians is a deeply personal and religious connection to the earth. Sometimes this is literal, as in the earth-toned, close-to-the-ground, mud and clay pueblo architecture that inspired the Spanish colonial construction universally recog-nized as "Santa Fe style." Other times it's symbolic, as in dances or other religious ceremonies. In either case, Native culture embraces the notion that one doesn't own the land, one belongs to it. As such, land is not a resource to be exploited but rather one to be respected. The land defines your origins as it defines your destiny. It also provides shelter and food and is the source of native art.

Until recently, land was the basis of the pueb-los' economy—through agriculture, livestock, and the sale of pottery, jewelry, baskets, and other crafts. Today, however, a land-based economy is rapidly being supplanted by casinos, hotels, golf courses, and other commercial businesses as the main sources of income for many pueblos. Casinos, in particular, have stirred a tremendous debate both within and outside the Indian com-munity. Casinos have brought jobs and dollars to communities where unemployment has been as high as 45 percent and where staggering pov-erty and its associated ills—malnutrition, alcohol-ism, poor education, domestic violence, and an alarming increase in violent crimes—have over the years become the norm. With revenue from their casinos, many tribes for the first time can afford to build sorely needed infrastructure and social programs. Fewer young men and women are leaving the pueblos, while many who took off for urban centers are returning home. As a result, tribes are gaining the human and material resources necessary to compete with their non-Indian neighbors on a more level playing field. And, indeed, they're taking a more active role in local, state, and federal policy making.

But many say it's a Faustian bargain that comes with its own set of problems, among them gambling addictions, increased substance abuse, the potential for corruption, and especially a clash of values. In trying to balance culture and tradition with political and economic pragmatism, the pueblos are taking steps to diversify their economies in ways that are both lucrative and in harmony with traditional values. But they're not likely to supplant the casinos, at least not any time soon. That genie has long left the bottle, leaving behind it a colossal political, cultural, social, and economic hot potato with still unimagined implications. A second issue in drought-ridden New Mexico is the building of golf courses at pueblos such as Pojoaque. Indian water rights are generally first in line, but in dry years increased demand on rivers by landscaping such as this has sparked concern.

i The *Eight Northern Pueblos Visitors Guide* is available at the Santa Fe Convention and Visitors Bureau, 201 West Marcy St., (505) 955-6200, (800) 777-2489, or the New Mexico Tourism Department in Santa Fe at the Lamy Building, 491 Old Santa Fe Trail, (505) 827-7336, (800) 545-2040. The booklet includes descriptions and histories of each pueblo and a tentative calendar of events for the year. Or log on to www.eightnorthernpueblos.com.

## DANCES AND FEAST DAYS

There's no doubt that the pueblos are undergoing dramatic change. Through it all, they continue to practice their old and largely secret ways. These include ceremonial dances, which link the pueblo people to their physical and spiritual ancestors and to nature. Although some dances are open to the public, they are not entertainment. Dances

are religious ceremonies, most of which are tied to seasonal or life-cycle events such as hunting, sowing, harvesting, initiations, rites of passage, etc. The pueblos perform dances to sanctify an event, to give thanks or to influence nature—for bountiful crops, for example, or a successful hunt. Non-Indians are privileged to watch selected dances on the pueblos at various times during the year, typically on Christmas Eve, Christmas Day, New Year's Day, Easter, and selected days throughout the year, most in summer. The rest are closed to outsiders—a result, in part, of centuries of persecution by non-Indians who have misunderstood and misinterpreted Native rituals. The tribes believe that secrecy has helped their religion survive. For that reason, you're likely to be met with a stony silence if you ask questions about dances or volunteer comments on their symbolic or spiritual meaning. Please refer to this chapter's Close-up on pueblo etiquette.

Feast days, on the other hand, are a remnant of the pueblos' encounters with Europeans. Yet they're a uniquely Indian event. When Spanish settlers arrived in New Mexico in the late 16th century, missionaries assigned a patron saint to each pueblo in an effort to convert the Indians to Catholicism. In time the saints' days became aligned with the pueblos' Native religion because they coincided with tribal rituals. Today feast days are a time when friends and family gather to eat together and participate in Native ceremonies. They're also a time when tribal members invite complete strangers into their homes for a meal of green or red chile, posole (stewed hominy), fry bread, cookies, or any of a number of other dishes. Forget the diet when you visit a pueblo on a feast day. It's considered impolite to refuse an invitation to eat. By doing so, you will have spurned your host's hospitality and generosity. Once again, we implore you to read the Close-up in this chapter for tips on etiquette.

Feast days are held the same day every year. Dances take place at various times and may be scheduled a year or maybe just a few days ahead of time. We recommend calling the pueblo before visiting to confirm any dates listed here or elsewhere, even in pueblo literature.

Schedule changes are common. The pueblo can also provide you with information about taking photographs or making recordings or drawings, any or all of which may be prohibited or for which there may be a charge.

Following are individual descriptions of what collectively are called the Eight Northern Indian Pueblos, all within an hour and a half's drive north of Santa Fe. Each entry includes a brief history as well as the date of the pueblo's annual feast day. You'll find a complete, tentative schedule of dances and other events in this chapter's Close-up. Most ceremonies begin midmorning and last until shortly after dusk. Again, please be sure to call the pueblo before attending an event to make sure the date and times haven't changed.

## EIGHT NORTHERN INDIAN PUEBLOS COUNCIL

**Oke Owingeh (formerly San Juan Pueblo),
P.O. Box 969, Scenic Route 74,
Santa Fe 87504
(505) 747-1593
www.eightnorthernpueblos.com**

The Eight Northern Indian Pueblos Council is a cooperative group that works to promote joint projects and improve the economy, education, and ceremonial efforts of the eight pueblos located due north of Santa Fe. The council, a consortium of the eight pueblos' governors, sponsors the Eight Northern Indian Arts and Crafts Show, which takes place in July at Oke Owingeh (formerly San Juan Pueblo). The show features Native American arts and crafts, dancing, and traditional food. Unlike Indian Market (see our Annual Events and Festivals chapter), the Eight Northern Indian Arts and Crafts Show is an Indian-run enterprise. The rest of the year you can buy arts and crafts at the Oke Owingeh Arts and Crafts Cooperative (505-852-2372).

**i** Most Pueblo people speak their native language, English, and often some Spanish as well.

## NAMBÉ PUEBLO
**Route 1, Box 117BB, Santa Fe 87747
(505) 455-2036**
Patron saint: San Francisco de Asís (St. Francis of Assisi). Feast day: October 4 with pre-feast celebrations and dances on October 3.

Pronounced Nahm-BEH, the name of this pueblo is Tewa for "Mound of Earth in the Corner"—a poetic and apt description for the 19,076 acres that are home to an estimated 600 tribal members. It is one of the smaller of the northern pueblos. Occupied since 1300, Nambé was a religious and cultural center for Pueblo Indians throughout the region long before the Spanish arrived. As such, it became a target for conquistadores and priests whose mission included converting the natives to Catholicism. The tribe took an active role in the Pueblo Revolt of 1680, when their priest was killed and their church destroyed.

Today the tribe is highly assimilated with the surrounding community, which is primarily Hispanic. Over the past decade, however, members have taken an active interest in reviving traditional arts and crafts—a mainstay of the tribe's economy. You'll find many residents selling pottery, jewelry, and other crafts out of their homes. The pueblo also houses a sculpture gallery and studio displaying both traditional and contemporary art at the pueblo. Nambé Pueblo offers recreational opportunities galore, including camping, fishing, and boating at Nambé Falls Recreation Area. As the name implies, the recreation area affords a close look at three natural waterfalls as well as a lake and stunning views of the Sangre de Cristo Mountains. You might even catch a glimpse of the tribe's buffalo herd. The pueblo holds its annual Nambé Falls Celebration on July 4 with a variety of traditional dances, food vendors, and arts and crafts. The pueblo has an economic development corporation that oversees a 150-acre industrial park, a 410-unit mobile home park, a recycling center, and a number of other enterprises. Directions from Santa Fe: Take US 84/285 16 miles to the junction with Highway 503 north of Pojoaque; then head east 2 miles on Highway 503.

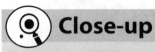 **Close-up**

## Pueblo Annual Events

New Mexico's pueblos hold numerous feasts, dances, and other celebrations throughout the year that are open to non-Indians. We've included below a tentative schedule. Please call the pueblo before attending any event as schedules can—and often do—change with little advance notice. Feast days remain the same from year to year. So do the celebrations for the Transfer of the Canes and All King's Day celebrations, which fall respectively on New Year's Day and January 6, as do the dances on Christmas Eve and Christmas Day. Be sure to check with the individual pueblo, however, to ascertain that the celebrations are open to the public. Please refer to this Close-up's section on pueblo etiquette before your visit.

### JANUARY

January 1: Transfer of the Canes (inauguration of new tribal officials). Various dances. Most pueblos.

January 6: All King's Day celebration in honor of new tribal officials. Most northern pueblos.

January 22-23: Feast day celebrations. Various dances. San Ildefonso Pueblo.

January 25: St. Paul feast day. Various dances. Picurís Pueblo.

Late January: San Juan Cloud or basket dance.

### FEBRUARY

February 2: Candelaria Day celebrations. Various dances. Picurís Pueblo.

Late February: Deer dance. San Juan Pueblo.

### MARCH/APRIL

Easter weekend: Easter dances. Most pueblos.

### MAY

Corn dances. Tesuque Pueblo.

May 3: Santa Cruz feast day. Various dances. Cochiti. Taos Pueblo.

May 4: Corn dances, foot races. Taos Pueblo.

### JUNE

First Saturday: Blessing of the Fields. Various dances. Tesuque Pueblo.

June 13: San Antonio feast day. Various dances. Santa Clara and Taos Pueblos.

June 24: Feast day. Various dances. Corn dances. San Juan and Taos Pueblos.

### JULY

First weekend: Weekend High Country Arts & Crafts Festival. Picurís Pueblo.

July 4: Nambé Falls celebration. Various dances. Nambé Pueblo.

Second weekend: Annual Pow-Wow. Taos Pueblo.

Mid-July: Annual Northern Pueblo Artist & Craftsman Show. San Ildefonso.

July 25: Santiago feast day. Corn dances. Taos Pueblo.

### AUGUST

August 9-10: San Lorenzo feast day. Various dances. Picurís Pueblo.

August 12: Santa Clara feast day. Various dances. Santa Clara Pueblo.

Late August/Early September: Corn dances. San Ildefonso Pueblo.

### SEPTEMBER

TBA: Harvest dance. San Juan Pueblo.

September 28-29: San Geronimo feast day. Various dances. Nambé, Picurís,

San Juan, and Taos Pueblos.

### OCTOBER

October 3-4: St. Francis of Assisi feast day. Various dances. Nambé Pueblo.

### NOVEMBER

TBA: San Diego feast day. Various dances. Tesuque Pueblo.

### DECEMBER

December 12: Guadalupe feast day celebrations. Pojoaque Pueblo.

December 24: Christmas celebrations. Various dances. Most pueblos.

December 26: Turtle dance. San Juan Pueblo.

December 28: Holy Innocents Day. Children's dances. Picuris and Santa Clara Pueblos.

Please call each pueblo for schedule and/or event change.

## PUEBLO ETIQUETTE

Remember that old adage, "When in Rome, do as the Romans do,"? It applies doubly when visiting Indian reservations. Please don't be lulled into a sense of complacency because people on the reservations speak English. The pueblos are sovereign lands with their own culture and a different code of etiquette from the one with which you're most likely familiar. The language may be the same, but it's a completely different culture. Please take to heart the following suggestions for courteous behavior so as not to offend your hosts or make future guests unwelcome. Several dances are now closed to non-Indians due to the poor behavior of outsiders. Be respectful. Please take special note of the rules at the end of this section for taking photographs.

## GENERAL ETIQUETTE

- Every pueblo has its own government and its own set of rules for visitors. Please learn the rules and regulations of each pueblo before entering and obey them during your visit.

- While the pueblos are open to the public during the day, private homes are not. Do not enter anyone's house without permission.

- If you are invited into someone's house on a feast day, don't linger at the table after you've finished eating. Your host will want to serve many guests throughout the day.

- By all means, thank your host, but it is inappropriate to offer any payment or tip.

- Pueblo dances are religious ceremonies, not staged performances. Observe them with the respect and quiet attention you would maintain in a house of worship.

Think of the dances as extended prayers for universal well-being; your role as spectator is to help these prayers succeed. Please don't talk or wave or otherwise disturb nondancers. It's considered impolite to ask questions about dances or make comments about their meaning. Applause is inappropriate.

- Refrain from talking to dancers and don't approach them as they are entering, leaving, or resting near the kiva.

- Kivas and graveyards are sacred places and not to be entered by any non-pueblo person.

- Don't wander beyond areas open to tourists.

- Don't climb walls or other structures. Some are hundreds of years old and fragile.

- Do not take or even pick up artifacts such as broken pottery or other objects.

- Obey all parking and traffic signs, especially speed limits, to keep the pueblo safe for children and the elderly.

- Do not bring in pets.

- Alcohol, weapons, and drugs are strictly forbidden.

- Dress modestly. Revealing clothing, such as shorts and tank tops, is inappropriate.

## PHOTOGRAPHY

- Permits, fees, and restrictions vary from pueblo to pueblo.

- Any photographs you take must be for private use only and may not be reproduced or used for commercial purposes without written permission.

- Please do not photograph any individuals without their express permission.

- Do not attempt to take a photo or make sketches or recordings if you are forbidden to do so.

- A photo permit does not give anyone license to disrupt dances by getting in front of the dancers or spectators.

## OKE OWINGEH (SAN JUAN PUEBLO)

SR 74, P.O. Box 1099,
San Juan Pueblo 87566
(505) 842-4400
www.indianpueblo.org/sanjuan.html
Patron saint: San Juan (St. John the Baptist). Feast day: June 24.

Located 26 miles northwest of Santa Fe along the Río Grande, Oke Owingeh or Ohkay Owingey (formerly known as San Juan Pueblo) is the largest of all the northern pueblos, with 2,500 members and a total population of about 5,300 people. Tribal members share complex and closely guarded social and belief systems based on their traditional clan system.

The tribe's 12,238-acre pueblo sits across the Río Grande from Yunque, the original San Juan Pueblo. In 1598 it was chosen by the Spanish colonists as the site of the first Spanish settlement in New Mexico and renamed San Gabriel. San Juan was also the birthplace of Popé, the man credited with organizing the Pueblo Revolt of 1680 that succeeded in banishing the Spanish from the region for 12 years. San Juan has retained a reputation for leadership among Tewa-speaking people, hence its name, *Oke Owingeh,* "Place of the Strong People." The pueblo is home to the offices of the Eight Northern Indian Pueblos Council (see earlier entry) and the Bureau of Indian Affairs, Northern Pueblos Agency.

San Juan's two central plazas feature rectangular kivas. To the west of the plaza area stands St. John the Baptist Catholic Church, a redbrick building facing Our Lady of Lourdes Chapel, which was built from volcanic rock. Among the pueblo's natural attractions are tribal lakes, a recreation area, and a herd of buffalo, which may be viewed by reservation only. The tribe's Tsay Corporation reopened the Ohkay Casino-Resort, which offers gambling and 100 hotel rooms run by Best Western chain. Those who prefer sleeping a little closer to the great outdoors can stay in the pueblo's top-rated 84-site RV park next to the San Juan Lakes (505-753-5067). Tsay Corporation also operates the Harvest Cafe, located in the casino; the Oke Owingeh Arts and Crafts Cooperative, which displays and sells the pueblo's distinctive red pottery along with wood and stone carvings, weavings, paintings, and jewelry; the Ohkay T'owa Gardens Cooperative, which grows and processes traditional native food products under the Harvest Foods label; a construction company; and a cabinet shop. The tribe's newest venture is the Ohkay Sporting Clays Club. Directions from Santa Fe: Take US 84/285 north 24.3 miles to the junction with Highway 68 in Española; head 4 miles north on Highway 68 to the junction with SR 74. Go 1 mile west on SR 74.

## PICURÍS PUEBLO

off Highway 75, 13 miles east of Dixon
P.O. Box 127, Peñasco 87553
(505) 587-2519 (visitor center)
www.picurispueblo.com
Patron saint: San Lorenzo (St. Lawrence). Feast day: August 10, with pre-feast celebrations and dances on August 9.

Once one of the largest of the northern pueblos, today *Picurís* [pee-kuh-REES]—or We-lai, which means "Those Who Paint" in Tiwa—is among the smallest, with 340 members living in a secluded valley of the Sangre de Cristo Mountains about an hour north of Santa Fe. The Picurís ancestors arrived in the region around 750 A.D., settling first in a larger pueblo called Pot Creek before moving in or around the year 1250 to its current location some 20 miles south of Taos. The Picurís historically were more aggressive than other pueblos, perhaps because of greater contact with Plains Indians. Picurís Indians were deeply involved in the 1680 Pueblo Revolt (see our History chapter), killing their priest and many of the area's Spanish settlers on August 10, 1680, which also happens to be the saint's day for San Lorenzo, for whom the pueblo was named. The Picurís paid a heavy price for their rebellion when the Spanish returned in 1692 and taxed them into starvation.

Picurís was 3,000 members strong when the Spanish arrived. By the end of the 17th century, only 500 were left, and they abandoned their pueblo. They reclaimed their ancestral land in 1706—17,000 acres that today boasts a number of excavated ruins and an aboveground ceremonial kiva that's at least 700 years old.

The pueblo's centerpiece remains the San Lorenzo de Picurís mission, an old adobe church that took 12 years to restore by hand. The tribe operates an on-site museum, gift shop, and restaurant and is the majority owner of the Hotel Santa Fe in the capital city. The pueblo has a small buffalo herd and two well-stocked trout-fishing ponds. Tours are available for Ancestral Pueblo and church ruins. In addition to the Feast of San Lorenzo in August, the pueblo hosts a feast day for St. Paul (San Pablo) on January 25 and another for St. Anthony (San Antonio) in June. On Father's Day weekend, the tribe hosts a Tri-Cultural Arts & Crafts Fair featuring the work of Native Americans, Hispanics, and "Anglos." The pueblo opened a Holistic Healing Center in the summer of 2000. Directions from Santa Fe: Take US 84/285 24.3 miles to the junction with Highway 68 in Española. Go 20 miles north on Highway 68 to the junction with Highway 75 in the vicinity of Dixon, and go 13 miles east on Highway 75.

## POJOAQUE PUEBLO
**17746 US 84/285, Pojoaque**
**(505) 455-3334 (Poeh Cultural Center)**
**www.poehcenter.com**
Patron saint: Our Lady of Guadalupe. Feast day: December 12.

With an estimated 325 members, Pojoaque (po-WAH-keh) is the smallest of all the northern pueblos but is now the second-largest private employer in northern New Mexico due to many business endeavors. Its name is a Spanish derivative of *P'o-Suwae-Geh,* which is Tewa for "Water Drinking Place." Because of its abundance of water, Pojoaque was a major gathering place for Pueblo Indians of the Río Grande prior to the Pueblo Revolt of 1680. The 11,600-acre pueblo sits between Nambé and Tesuque (Teh-SOO-keh) Pueblos along US 84/285, the northbound highway out of Santa Fe. Pojoaque is the site of the first Spanish mission in New Mexico, San Francisco de Pojoaque, founded in the early 1600s. The pueblo is notable for twice rising from near extinction. The first occurrence was in 1706 when five families resettled on tribal lands that had been ravaged during and after the Pueblo Revolt and were completely deserted by the time the Spanish returned in 1692. The second revival was in 1934, when 14 individuals returned from nearby pueblos and states to which the Pojoaque tribe had scattered after a turn-of-the-20th-century smallpox epidemic nearly wiped out all its members. A drought and encroachment by non-Indians added to the pueblo's demise. But like the Phoenix, the pueblo quite literally rose from its ashes, with survivors rebuilding it physically and culturally. Its church, built in 1706, is still used today. Among the pueblo's newer buildings is its 10,000-square-foot Poeh Cultural Center and Museum, built in Ancestral Pueblo style. In addition to showcasing arts and crafts of Tewa-speaking people, the cultural center also offers classes in pottery, sculpture, textiles, and art business management to tribal members and other Indians. The tribe owns and operates the Pueblo Plaza Shopping Center and the Pojoaque Visitor Center, which sells artwork from a variety of Tewa-speaking pueblos. But the pueblo's pride and joy, without a doubt, is its popular new Buffalo Thunder Resort (877-465-3489), northern New Mexico's first Indian-owned luxury resort. The 2,500-square-foot resort offers an art-filled 400-room hotel run by Hilton; concert facilities; 10 restaurants, including Red Sage, chef Mark Miller's newest venture since selling Coyote Cafe; a high-end spa; the Towa golf course; and a casino. Other enterprises include the 79-suite Homewood Suites (505-455-9100); Cities of Gold Casino (505) 455-3313, (800) 455-3313; a 40,000-square-foot gambling hall, which employs about 700 people; the 125-room Cities of Gold Hotel (505) 455-0515, (800) 455-0515; Cities of Gold Sports Bar (505) 455-2072, (800) 455-3313; a wellness center (505) 455-9355; and even a public library (505) 455-7411. The tribe also operates a mobile home park, an apartment complex, a gas station and convenience store, and a nearby industrial park. Directions from Santa Fe: Take US 84/285 north 15 miles.

**i** Pojoaque was the first pueblo to elect a woman as governor, which occurred in 1973.

## SAN ILDEFONSO PUEBLO
Route 5, P.O. Box 315A,
San Ildefonso Pueblo 87506
(505) 455-3549

Patron saint: San Ildefonso (St. Ildefonse). Feast day: January 23. Pre-feast ceremonies are held on January 22.

Named for a seventh-century archbishop from Toledo, San Ildefonso's Tewa name is *Po-Woh-Ge-Oweenge*, or "Where the Water Cuts Down Through." A small pueblo, San Ildefonso is also one of the most beautiful, with 26,198 acres that run from the Río Grande to the upper elevations of the Jémez Mountains near Los Alamos. Cottonwood *(alamo)* trees line the riverbanks, deer and elk roam the land, and from all directions you can see Black Mesa—a dark, lonely hill sacred to the pueblo because it's the site where San Ildefonso and other pueblos valiantly but unsuccessfully defended their lands against the Spanish in 1694.

San Ildefonso people trace their origins to Mesa Verde in southwestern Colorado, where their ancestors built cliff dwellings in the first century, now preserved in a national park. After leaving Mesa Verde, these ancestors settled first in what is now Bandelier National Monument, near Los Alamos. A drought sent them to lower ground at the end of the 13th century, when they settled in their current location 23 miles northwest of Santa Fe.

San Ildefonso is perhaps best known for its striking black-on-black pottery, especially that of the late María Martínez, whose pots today fetch high prices. Martínez and her husband, Julian, are largely responsible for the resurgence in the 1920s of traditional arts and crafts at San Ildefonso and other pueblos. María's son, Popovi Da, and her grandson, Tony Da, continued to break new ground after María's death, setting stones into pots after firing them.

Tewa is still spoken by many of the tribe's 700 members, who strive to preserve their cultural identity by observing ancient traditions and preserving or reconstructing original pueblo architecture. The enclosed central plaza, for example, looks much as it did centuries ago right down to the kiva, which the tribe still uses for ceremonial purposes. The pueblo has also taken pains to preserve more recent history, including rebuilding a 17th-century Catholic church originally erected during the Spanish occupation. Self-guided tours begin at San Ildefonso Visitor and Information Center (505-455-3549). Maria Martinez's work can be seen at the Maria Moveka Martinez Museum. You can fish at San Ildefonso Fishing Lake (505-455-2273). Directions from Santa Fe: Take US 84/285 15 miles to the junction with Highway 502 in Pojoaque; go 6 miles west on Highway 502.

**It is traditional to paint the frames around house windows and doors blue to keep evil spirits out. Although the custom is Spanish in origin, Pueblo Indians—who consider the color blue to be sacred—also practice it.**

## SANTA CLARA PUEBLO
P.O. Box 580, Española 87532
(505) 753-7326

Patron saint: Santa Clara (St. Claire). Feast day: August 12.

With an estimated 2,600 tribal members and 47,000 acres, Santa Clara is the second largest in both population and land of the Eight Northern Indian Pueblos. Located west of the Río Grande and adjacent to San Ildefonso Pueblo, Santa Clara offers majestic landscapes and stunning views. The Santa Clara people trace their ancestors to the Ancestral Pueblo Indians who occupied the Puyé Cliff Dwellings along and beneath the mesa tops that loom above the pueblo. They're believed to have arrived between 1100 and 1300, when they carved cavelike "apartments" into the compacted volcanic ash, or tuff rock, along the *Pajarito* (pa-ha-REE-to, Spanish for "little bird") Plateau at the base of the Jémez Mountains. They later moved to the top of the mesa, where they built adobe structures whose remains extend for more than a mile. A drought forced the people of Puyé to abandon their settlement about 600 years ago. They settled in what is now the Santa Clara Pueblo, or Kha p'o, which is Tewa for "Valley of the Wild Roses." The Puyé ruins are accessible year-round on foot for the hale and hardy or by driving to the top of the mesa. The pueblo also offers guided tours by reservation only.

Another of the pueblo's great attractions is Santa Clara Canyon, a beautiful recreation area that offers trout fishing in several well-stocked lakes and 86 campsites with tables, lean-tos, RV parking, and picnicking. The canyon is open to visitors from April through October. In Spring 2009, Puyé Ruins and Santa Clara Canyon once again welcomed visitors after a nine-year restoration following the 2000 Cerro Grande Fire, which burnt 700 acres of Santa Clara Pueblo land.

Santa Clara Pueblo is justly famous for its lustrous, hand-coiled blackware and redware, both made of clay molded from individual coils and refined by hand, then decorated with carved or painted designs, hand-polished with a smooth stone, and finally finished on an open wood fire. You can buy pottery and other arts and crafts in a number of shops at the pueblo. In addition to its patron saint, Santa Clara commemorates St. Anthony with a feast day on June 13.

Directions from Santa Fe: Take US 84/285 25 miles to the junction with Highway 201 in Española; go 1 mile southwest on Highway 30.

**i** In New Mexico, you will more often hear indigenous people refer to themselves as "Indians" rather than "Native Americans," though the latter is perfectly acceptable.

## TAOS PUEBLO
**P.O. Box 1846, Taos 87571**
**(505) 758-1028**
**www.taospueblo.com**
Patron saint: San Geronimo (St. Jerome). Feast day: September 30 with pre-feast ceremonies on September 29.

The oldest and most well-known of all the existing northern pueblos, Taos (rhymes with "house") is also the most striking primarily because of its multistoried, tiered adobe buildings with jutting log vigas and the rough-hewn wooden ladders residents still use to reach the

upper floors. The five-story pueblo is a national historic landmark and was designated a World Heritage Site in 1992. It is one of the oldest, continuously occupied villages in North America. Although approximately 50 people live in the old pueblo, most residents now live on pueblo land nearby, with modern conveniences. Taos has inspired countless artists to capture the drama of the pueblo at dusk, when it sometimes appears golden. In winter, its graceful, snow-lined walls, rooftops, and hornos (round, outdoor mud ovens pronounced "OR-nose") provide a striking contrast to the deep purple of the Sangre de Cristo Mountains that watch over it.

Taos Pueblo—*Tu-tah* ("Our Village") in the tribe's native Tewa—sits on 105,000 acres in the foothills of the northern Sangre de Cristos. Except for some scattered modern housing, the pueblo probably looks much as it did 450 years ago, when Spain made its first foray into what would become New Mexico. This may be due in part to the northern location, which historically rendered Taos more inaccessible than other pueblos in the territory. It's surely a result of the Taos people's independence and fierce determination to preserve their ancient traditions and culture. The pueblo maintains a strict taboo on intermarriage and forbids plumbing and electricity in some of the oldest structures. These and other restrictions help maintain an air of serenity that belies a turbulent history whose chapters include the Pueblo Revolt of 1680 and the Taos Rebellion against the United States in 1847, when 150 tribal members died.

Although the Taos people have lived in the same location for more than a thousand years, much of their history and culture remains a mystery to the outside world largely because the pueblo bans excavations. Anthropologists believe the estimated 2,200 Taos Indians who live at the pueblo could be related either to the ancestral Mesa Verde or Chaco cultures. They also suspect that the nearby Plains Indians—in particular the Kiowa and Apache with whom the tribe traded—influenced the pueblo to the extent that it added leather craft to an economy once based primarily on farming, raising cattle and horses, and hunting bear, buffalo, deer, elk, and birds. The pueblo's boots, moccasins, clothing, and drums are justly famous. These days, however, the pueblo's primary source of income is Taos Mountain Casino.

Although Taos Pueblo shrouds itself in secrecy, visitors are welcome to enjoy the architecture on almost any day and to observe some of the pueblo's ceremonies and rituals on selected dates. These include traditional foot races in May and the Taos Pueblo Pow-Wow the second weekend in July. Taos Mountain Casino (888-WIN-TAOS; www.taosmountaincasino.com), the state's only nonsmoking casino, is very popular. The pueblo closes to non-Indians for about six weeks starting in February or March for religious activities. Directions from Santa Fe: Take US 84/285 24.3 miles to the junction with Highway 68 in Española; go 48 miles north on Highway 68 to the junction with US 64 in Taos; 1 mile north on US 64.

**i** Santa Fe Indian Market, which takes place each August, is the world's largest American Indian art market.

## TESUQUE PUEBLO
**Route 5, Box 360-T, Tesuque 87574**
**(505) 983-2667**
Patron saint: San Diego (St. James). Feast day: November 12.

Tesuque (teh-SOO-keh) Pueblo—*Te-tsu-geh*, or "The Narrow Place of Cottonwood Trees" in Tewa—encompasses 17,204 acres in the lush foothills of the Sangre de Cristo Mountains, including forestland adjacent to Santa Fe National Forest and farmland near the Río Grande. The Tesuque people settled in this area, located just 9 miles north of Santa Fe, 14 years after the 1680 Pueblo Revolt in which Tesuque Indians struck the first blows against the Spanish and suffered the first casualties. Two members of the pueblo also served as messengers to the other tribes, spreading word of the revolt. An earlier pueblo existed before the 12th century but was abandoned after the revolt.

A relatively small pueblo of about 400 tribal members, Tesuque today is nonetheless among the most traditional of the Tewa-speaking people. Only a very few of its celebrations are open to the public, and the pueblo sometimes closes to outsiders with little or no notice. The pueblo owns and operates Camel Rock Casino, (800) GO–CAMEL), named for the centuries-old, distinctive sandstone formation near the entrance to the pueblo. Inside the casino is Pueblo Artist Cafe, considered the best restaurant among the Eight Northern Indian Pueblos. The tribe also owns Santa Fe Suites, (87-989-3600), on South St. Francis Drive in Santa Fe and took over the famous— and upscale—outdoor flea market on the west side of US 84/285 next to the Santa Fe Opera. At the pueblo itself, visitors may buy permits for fishing and primitive camping at Tesuque's Aspen Ranch. The pueblo also operates Tesuque Natural Farms, an organic produce company that sells at local farmers' markets and to some of Santa Fe's better restaurants. The tribe also sells native arts and crafts, including the brightly colored pottery for which the pueblo has become known, neo-traditional rain god figurines, sculpture, painting, jewelry, and traditional clothing. Directions from Santa Fe: Take US 84/285 9 miles.

**i** Santa Fe, one of the first U.S. communities to welcome Tibetan refugees, has a highly visible Tibetan population today. Tibetans can be found throughout the business community and Tibetan cultural festivals, ceremonies, and concerts take place throughout the year.

## A FOOTNOTE ON ANGLOS

Anglo culture? What's that? If you've seen Woody Allen's 1986 film, *Hannah and Her Sisters,* you might think it's turkey sandwiches on white bread with mayonnaise. In much of the country, it's the short form for "WASP"—White Anglo Saxon Protestant. In Santa Fe, however, "Anglo" takes on a variety of shades, from African American to Asian, Arab to Jew. As we've mentioned elsewhere in this guide, the term as generally used in New Mexico refers to anyone who's not

Hispanic or Native American, regardless of race or heritage. Because that embraces so many cultures, it's difficult to define. But it's fun exploring the stereotypes. They include wealthy retirees or celebrities, perhaps buying their second or third home; trust-fund babies (age is unimportant) who come here to "find themselves"; New Age adherents in search of a mystical experience and hoping to find one by sheer proximity to Native Americans; hippies who arrived in the 1960s and never left—some of them still hippies, others successful professionals or entrepreneurs; artists and writers looking for their muse; and ski bums who work three seasons a year to play on the slopes all winter. We're sure everyone in Santa Fe could come up with a few stereotypes of their own.

Outside the cultural clichés are the "Anglos" who have lived here all their lives, some with roots going back 150 years to the Santa Fe Trail.

Others are regular working stiffs who personally, or whose parents, chose Santa Fe as their home because of its physical beauty and fascinating blend of cultures. In the mix are pockets of ethnic communities including Tibetans, who have strong political support here in their fight to reclaim their homeland from China; Chinese, many of whom arrived here in the 19th century with the railroad; African Americans, who account for 0.6 percent of the population; Ashkenazi Jews, whose ancestors helped blaze the Santa Fe Trail; scientists of all backgrounds who work at Los Alamos National Laboratory; and people of dozens of other ancestries from Afghanistan to Zimbabwe. Santa Fe is its own melting pot and becoming more so every year as people from one end of the country to the other, one end of the world to the other, discover all it has to offer.

# ACCOMMODATIONS

Santa Fe has vast array of lodgings, ranging from ultra luxurious and very expensive to basic and cheap. In this chapter we've presented a cross-section of the area's hotels, motels, bed-and-breakfasts, and vacation rentals in three geographic categories: downtown, which is usually most desirable because of its proximity to the historic districts and the Plaza; Cerrillos Road and environs, which encompass a 6-mile-long commercial (and rather soulless and hotel chain-heavy) strip that runs south from downtown Santa Fe directly into the beautiful Turquoise Trail; and the county, which takes in rural areas both north and south of town. Perhaps the single most important warning for visitors to Santa Fe is this: Make your reservations well in advance if you plan to be here during peak times—primarily in summertime and throughout the ski season—when rooms, especially on weekends, are at or near capacity. Lodgings often are booked up to a year in advance for Indian Market (see our Annual Events and Festivals chapter) in late August and during Christmas—a very special time in Santa Fe, when the nights glow from thousands of *farolitos* burning on balconies and rooftops, driveways and pathways, throughout the city. These times can, and usually do, command higher prices than the rest of the years. Some hotels divide the year up into as many as a half-dozen seasons, when prices on single rooms can fluctuate by as much as $50.

## OVERVIEW

While pricing can be tricky in Santa Fe—rooms range anywhere from $55 a night at the far end of Cerrillos to $1,500 for a grand suite downtown—the general rule is, the closer you are to the Plaza, the more you'll pay. You'll find most lodgings fall in the $80 to $180 range, and many offer discounts for extended stays. Prices quoted do not include taxes. Within the city limits, be prepared to pay 8.0625 percent in gross receipts taxes and a 7 percent lodgers tax. In the county, the lodgers tax is only 4 percent and the gross receipts tax is 6.3125 percent.

Most lodgings pay tribute to Santa Fe style, even if only by the pattern and colors of the bedspread. For descriptions of the Santa Fe-style embellishments you're likely to encounter in our lodgings—kivas, vigas, *latillas,* and *nichos,*

for example—refer to our Santa Fe Style Close-up in the Relocation chapter. If you're bringing your laptop, confirm that in-room phones have dataports or are modem-friendly. High-speed or wireless Internet (WiFi) access is usually available; there's often a hefty charge for in-room Internet access in high-end hotels but you will often be able to get free wireless access in the lobby or at a nearby coffee shop. Flat-screen LCD TVs are becoming more ubiquitous in rooms; all have cable and many have satellite channel lineups. Many also have DVD/VCR players—especially suites, where both DVD/VCR players and CD players are standard issue. With very few exceptions, establishments listed in this section accept most major credit cards. Even if you loathe using plastic, you'd be well-advised to guarantee your reservation with a credit card during peak season. Also be sure to check on cancellation policies, minimum stays, and surcharges, especially for heavily trafficked weekends like the Indian and Spanish Markets or the opening week of the Santa Fe Opera.

ℹ️ Most hotels offer discounts for AAA, AARP, and other organizations. They often don't volunteer this information, so make a point of asking.

Check with the individual establishment for its policies regarding children and additional charges if you bring them. Most inns add $15 or $20 per night for an extra person in the room. Also, be aware that some bed-and-breakfasts require a two-night stay on weekends, though that rule is usually flexible off-season. The City of Santa Fe has passed a law banning smoking in and around public institutions, restaurants, and bars in Santa Fe, and 80 percent of hotel rooms are now required to be designated nonsmoking. As a result, most Santa Fe hotels are now entirely smoke free. One last caveat: although Santa Feans are mad about their dogs, most lodgings do not allow pets (exceptions are noted in the listings here). On the other hand, you may find pets with the run of the house at a number of small bed-and-breakfasts (often mentioned on the Web site). Inquire before booking.

## Price Code

Our legend is based on the lowest rate per night for double occupancy during peak season. Price ratings don't reflect taxes or other surcharges and are subject to change.

$.................less than $100
$$ ...............$100 to $175
$$$ ..............$176 to $275
$$$$..............$276 to $350
$$$$$.............$351 and up

# HOTELS AND MOTELS

## In or Near Downtown

### ELDORADO HOTEL $$$$$
309 West San Francisco St.
(505) 988-4455, (800) 955-4455
www.eldoradohotel.com
A favorite with visiting celebrities, the newly renovated Eldorado is an enormous luxury hotel in the heart of downtown Santa Fe, just 2 blocks from the Plaza. The hotel boasts 219 elegant rooms and suites, many featuring kiva fireplaces and balconies or terraces with views of the Sangre de Cristo Mountains, as well as triple-sheeted

beds, reading chairs, flat screen TVs, and WiFi. The Eldorado pampers guests with plush terry-cloth robes, nightly turndown services, extended room service, and valet parking. It even provides private, English-style butler service with deluxe rooms and suites. Guests have access to a rooftop swimming pool and whirlpool along with a fully equipped fitness center and saunas.

The Nidah Spa offers treatments inspired by the Native American concept of harmonizing seasonally with the four directions, using southwest blue corn, mud, essential oils, and other approaches. The award-winning Old House Restaurant—housed in the historic home around which the hotel was built—was the first four-star restaurant in the state. It offers fine dining seven nights a week featuring creative gourmet dishes with a southwestern touch. Less formal dining is available for breakfast and lunch in the Eldorado Court, which on Sunday serves a lavish prix fixe champagne brunch, buffet style, with prime rib and other meats carved to your liking; bottomless bowls of fresh shrimp; smoked meats and fish; gourmet salads; omelet and waffle stations; and a decadent dessert table. For live nightly entertainment, guests need go no farther than the adjoining lobby lounge. Children under 16 stay free with paying adult.

### GARRETT'S DESERT INN $$
311 Old Santa Fe Trail
(505) 982-1851, (800) 888-2145
www.garrettsdesertinn.com
Family-owned Garrett's offers the most affordable rates in downtown Santa Fe. You won't find vigas, kiva fireplaces, or saltillo tile at this motel. What you will get are unpretentious southwestern rooms and location, location, location. If you're looking for luxury, you can walk across the street to the Inn at Loretto, but be prepared to pay from three to ten times as much, depending on the room. Either way, you're 2 blocks from the Plaza and just footsteps from some of the city's historic landmarks. Garrett's has an authentic French bakery, Le Zodiac Cafe, on the premises and a seasonal outdoor heated swimming pool. It offers 83 standard rooms and seven suites with

small living rooms and kitchenettes furnished with microwaves and small refrigerators. The motel has limited wheelchair access. A parking fee is charged for use of the hotel lot.

## GHOST RANCH IN SANTA FE $$
401 Old Taos Hwy
(505) 982-8539
www.ghostranch.org

Few locals even know that Presbyterian Church-run Ghost Ranch has a retreat and educational center in Santa Fe, 3 short blocks north of the Plaza, let alone that it often has low-cost bed-and-breakfast pension-style adobe rooms available for nonretreat travelers when it's not full. Basic but pleasant rooms have twin or double beds, sinks, toilets, and showers, with full breakfast included for just over $100 per night in summer. An apartment accommodating up to four people is available for $250 per night. A boon if you're traveling solo and want to meet interesting people, strike up intelligent conversations, and walk around downtown, it's one of Santa Fe's best-kept secrets. *NOTE:* The better-known main Ghost Ranch campus in Abiquiú has a full range of very low-cost lodgings, from campground and dorm rooms to private rooms, available about an hour northwest of Santa Fe.

## HILTON OF SANTA FE $$$
100 Sandoval St.
(505) 988-2811, (800) 336-3676
www.hilton.com

Although it looks rather ordinary from the outside, the Hilton of Santa Fe is in fact quite extraordinary in that it was built around a 300-year-old hacienda that belonged to one of Santa Fe's early prominent families. Casa de Ortíz now encompasses the hotel's dining room, as well as three luxurious casitas built into and around what used to be Nicholas Ortíz III's coach houses. Two of the spacious casitas are one-bedroom suites and a third has two bedrooms; each has a "window" from which guests can view the original thick adobe walls that have stood for three centuries. The decor is modern southwestern with such traditional touches as kiva fireplaces, viga ceilings,

and four-poster beds. One casita has a heart-shaped tub. Ask about Internet specials.

Just a few blocks from the Plaza, the hotel has a total of 157 rooms, five suites, and three casitas, including the Casa de Ortíz. It boasts Santa Fe's largest outdoor pool, which has a 6-foot tile bear fetish on the bottom. Other amenities include an outdoor Jacuzzi, a health club, and three restaurants. The award-winning Piñon Grill was built on the site of the Ortíz bedroom. The hotel's 6,000-square-foot meeting space was the Ortízes' private sanctuary. Voice mail and modem ports are standard in all guest rooms. The suites and casitas have kitchens. The hotel is completely nonsmoking.

> **i** If you have friends who live in Santa Fe, ask them to make your reservations. Locals can often get better prices than out-of-town callers.

## HOTEL SANTA FE AND THE HACIENDA AT HOTEL SANTA FE $$$
1501 Paseo de Peralta
(505) 982-1200, (800) 825-9876
www.hotelsantafe.com

The influence of Picurís Pueblo, the majority owners of this lovely property, permeates Hotel Santa Fe—in the Pueblo Revival architecture; the decor; the artwork, which includes three garden sculptures by renowned Apache artist Allan Houser; native foods; and hospitality from a staff that is 25 percent Indian. Entertainment includes Indian dancers, Hispanic and Indian musicians, lectures by local historians, and native storytellers who weave tales in front of the lobby's majestic kiva fireplace. There's also an outdoor heated pool and Jacuzzi and an on-site masseuse. Although there are no sports facilities on the premises, guests can get complimentary passes to the Santa Fe Spa, located a few miles away. The hotel has 128 rooms and suites. A luxury wing, The Hacienda, has 35 rooms and suites and butler service.

The hotel is the closest upmarket hotel to Railyard Park in the heart of the historic Guadalupe district. It's a 10-minute stroll to the Santa Fe Plaza, or you can take the complimentary hotel shuttle (a purple London taxi cab brought over by the hotel's British manager). The top-rated Amaya Restaurant offers contemporary Native American cuisine (see Restaurant listings).

## INN AND SPA AT LORETTO          $$$
**211 Old Santa Fe Trail**
**(505) 988-5531, (800) 727-5531**
**www.innatloretto.com**
Named for the nearby historic Loretto Chapel, whose "miraculous" spiral staircase has no central support, the Inn and Spa at Loretto is located near the end of Old Santa Fe Trail, just 1 block from the Plaza. Its faux-adobe, Pueblo-style architecture is complemented by furniture, doors, windows, corbels, and light fixtures that are 13th-century replicas handcrafted by local artisans. Even the interior wall mural incorporates designs and symbols found in New Mexico's Pueblo and Spanish artistry, as well as in ancient petroglyphs and weavings. The Inn and Spa at Loretto is among the most photographed buildings in Santa Fe during the winter months, when its rooftops and balconies light up with electric *farolitos*—a permanent version of the traditional candle-in-a-paper-bag Christmas decoration that has become an internationally recognized symbol of Santa Fe.

The inn's 129 guest rooms and five suites feature individual climate control, refrigerators, in-room coffee service, speaker phones with data jacks, WiFi, and semiprivate balconies with spectacular sunset and mountain views. The 2,800-square-foot Presidential Suite has wraparound balconies providing a panoramic view of the city and the Sangre de Cristos, a library, fireplace, and even a custom billiard table. The Spa at Loretto offers Balinese and Native American treatments. All guests have access to the hotel's heated outdoor pool. The in-house restaurant, Luminaria, features primarily southwestern and Mediterranean cuisine using locally sourced ingredients. The concierge can arrange golf, rafting, fly fishing, skiing, horseback riding, or any number of other activities. The inn's famous Loretto Tours offers daily tours of downtown in an open-air bus in summer.

## ROSEWOOD INN OF THE ANASAZI       $$$$
**113 Washington Ave.**
**(505) 988-3030, (800) 688-8100**
**www.innoftheanasazi.com**
Just steps from the Plaza stands Inn of the Anasazi, an intimate, elegant luxury boutique hotel named for the ancestors of today's Pueblo Indians. These ancient settlers of the Four Corners Region inhabited the cliff dwellings of Chaco Canyon and Mesa Verde, which served as inspiration for the hotel's architecture and design. The Inn's 58 guest rooms and eight suites have gas-lit kiva fireplaces, four-poster beds, and traditional ceilings with vigas and *latillas*. Authentic regional artwork graces the floors and walls. Every room has a flat screen TV, WiFi, coffeemaker, safe, minibar, stereo, and DVD player. Guests may borrow DVDs from the hotel's extensive collection. Massage and aromatherapy services are also available.

The inn's award-winning, world-class restaurant serves gourmet Native American, northern New Mexican, and American cowboy cuisine. Guests who want a more intimate setting can reserve the wine cellar for a meal for up to 12 people. The hotel also rents out its library/boardroom for private dinners of up to 40 guests as well as for corporate retreats and board meetings. When it's not rented out, the library is open to guests, who may peruse the library's shelves of books on regional indigenous cultures. The inn is a Mobil Four-Star and AAA Four-Diamond hotel.

## THE INN OF THE FIVE GRACES       $$$$$
**147 East De Vargas St.**
**(505) 982-6636, (866) 507-1001**
**www.fivegraces.com**
Just 3 blocks from the Plaza and across the street from a church reputed to be the oldest in the United States, The Inn of the Five Graces is located in a classic Santa Fe compound adjoining the celebrated Pink Adobe restaurant and the narrow, rambling, historic streets for which Santa Fe is famous. The inn's 13 vibrantly colored guest rooms and suites, which date from the 19th century, benefited from the creative vision of traders Ira and Sylvia Seret, who continue to run one of

Santa Fe's most famous import stores. Each has been fitted with centuries-old Spanish colonial handcrafted doors and shutters and furnished with custom-made furniture, exotic vintage weavings from the Near East, and southwestern rugs and pottery. All the suites have fireplaces, full kitchens, cable television with free premium channels and DVD/CD players, WiFi, and access to a private central courtyard, where choice of hot or cold breakfast is served daily.

Among the extras offered to guests are a small sumptuous on-site spa, complimentary wet bar, twice-daily housekeeping, car parking, and a daily historical walking tour followed by wine and cheese. A 10 percent service charge is added to all accommodations; no additional tips are required.

### INN OF THE GOVERNORS $$
101 West Alameda St.
(505) 982-4333, (800) 693-3359
www.innofthegovernors.com

Inn of the Governors is a midsize, deluxe hotel just 2 blocks from the Santa Fe Plaza. Its 100 newly remodeled rooms and suites are decorated in a light, airy southwestern style with handmade furniture, local artwork, and special touches, such as handpainted tin mirrors, turquoise-washed writing desks, wrought-iron wall lamps, and carved headboards with Mexican *trasteros* (cupboards). Some rooms also have wood-burning kiva fireplaces and/or private balconies overlooking the mountains or downtown. Amenities include a heated outdoor swimming pool, open year-round; complimentary newspaper and hot breakfast buffet in the morning, and tea and sherry at 4 p.m.; cable television with in-room movies, WiFi, and a restaurant/piano bar where guests can eat indoors or on the hotel's private patio.

### INN ON THE ALAMEDA $$
303 East Alameda St.
(505) 984-2121, (888) 984-2124
www.innonthealameda.com

Just a five-minute walk from the Plaza, this bed-and-breakfast inn is located adjacent to the Canyon Road arts district. Each of its 59 rooms and 12 suites is individually designed to reflect classic southwestern design. The suites offer private patios or balconies, open courtyards, and kiva fireplaces. There is a complimentary "Breakfast of Enchantment"—a continental breakfast of fresh fruit and juices, pastries and other baked goods, granolas, cereals, Kona coffee, and more—all served buffet style in the hotel's lounge or delivered to your room. A complimentary wine and cheese reception is held each afternoon. Other amenities include an exercise room, on-call massage, two open-air whirlpool spas, same-day dry cleaning and coin-operated laundry, cable, and HBO. All rooms come with luxurious robes and fresh flowers; some also have wet bars and refrigerators.

### LA FONDA HOTEL $$$
100 East San Francisco St.
(505) 982-5511, (800) 523-5002
www.lafondasantafe.com

Located on the southeast corner of the Plaza, the current structure was built in 1923 on the site of previous inns, or fondas, a tradition that stretches back to Santa Fe's founding around 1610. Today, La Fonda's award-winning Spanish Pueblo-style architecture makes it a beacon not only for tourists but also for locals, who meet in the summer at the rooftop Bell Tower bar to watch incredible sunsets over margaritas or gather in La Fiesta Lounge to two-step to the tunes of locally famous Texan country musician Bill Hearne and other popular local musicians. This vibrant, historic landmark is filled with unique paintings; colorful, handpainted and hand-carved wooden furniture, vigas, and corbels; as well as custom paintings and other original artwork. Many of its newly renovated 167 rooms (14 located on the luxury Terraza concierge floor) are uniquely decorated and have balconies and fireplaces. La Fonda also has a heated outdoor pool, hot tubs, massage service, and a multilingual concierge. La Plazuela is a lovely enclosed courtyard restaurant that's open daily.

## LA POSADA DE SANTA FE
## RESORT & SPA $$$$$
**330 East Palace Ave.**
**(505) 986-0000, (866) 331–ROCK**
**www.laposadarockresorts.com**

La Posada is Santa Fe's only hotel with a resident ghost. Employees and guests alike swear they've seen, or at least felt, the presence of the long-deceased Julia Schuster Staab, who died on May 15, 1896. Most encounters have occurred in what was Julia's upstairs bedroom, formerly known simply as Room 256, now called the Victorian Suite and renumbered as room 100. Originally from Germany, Julia married wealthy Santa Fe merchant Abraham Staab, who in 1882 built his young wife the Victorian mansion that is now the main building of La Posada. Although Julia is not the only ghost in Santa Fe, she's certainly the most famous. But her presence, at least in principle, doesn't seem to scare away either tourists or locals, who come in droves to this lovely, serene hotel set among six acres of lawns, trees, and flowers.

Renovated in 2008, many of La Posada's 127 faux- and real-adobe rooms and 30 suites come with kiva fireplaces and patios overlooking the rambling grounds that are a favorite setting for weddings. The romantic Victorian bar, the Staab House Lounge, is popular among locals, as is Fuego Restaurant, which offers four-star dining emphasizing seasonal, locally sourced foods. La Posada's well-regarded spa offers Indigenous-inspired massage, facials, and adobe mud wraps. *NOTE:* there's a $30 daily room fee for use of resort amenities such as WiFi, shuttle, valet parking, and wine tastings.

## HOTEL PLAZA REAL $$$
**125 Washington Ave.**
**(505) 988-4900, (877) 901-7666**
**www.hotelplazareal.com**

The Hotel Plaza Real is a Territorial-style boutique hotel next to the Santa Fe Public Library near the Santa Fe Plaza. Its 56 rooms and suites feature handcrafted furnishings, fireplaces, original artwork, and private patios overlooking a very pretty courtyard. It is part of the Heritage Hotels and

Resorts group, which also owns the Lodge at Santa Fe and Hotel Saint Francis in Santa Fe as well as the Nativo Lodge in Albuquerque. There's live music nightly in Jesse's Lounge, and the hotel is across the street from famed restaurants the Bull Ring and Casa Sena. Or you can mingle with the masses on one of the concierge's complimentary city walking tours. The concierge will also make your restaurant reservations and suggest other outside activities. Rooms come with a complimentary continental breakfast served in the Santa Clara Room, on the patio, or delivered to your room.

## THE LODGE AT SANTA FE $$
**750 North St. Francis Dr.**
**(505) 992-5800, (800) 333-3333**
**www.radisson.com/santafenm**

While not exactly downtown, this reasonably priced hotel is close enough—a five-minute drive to the Plaza—to warrant a listing here. On a hilltop immediately north of Paseo de Peralta, which forms a U around the downtown area, the Lodge has sweeping views of the mountains, lovely perennial gardens, and breathtaking sunsets from its rooms as well as its restaurant and bar, Las Mañanitas. Many of the 127 nicely appointed guest rooms and suites have fireplaces and either microwaves and refrigerators or full kitchens and WiFi. Guests enjoy complimentary workouts in the 20,000-square-foot Santa Fe Spa next door or relax poolside in the hotel's landscaped courtyard. The hotel was bought by Heritage Hotels and Resorts and completely refurbished recently. Its distinctive tower, or torreon, features Ancestral Pueblo-style stonework and is easily visible from the highway. This hotel is most famous locally for its live flamenco shows, which are offered nightly in summer in the small Maria Benitez Theater, named for Santa Fe's most famous flamenco diva.

## SANTA FE MOTEL AND INN $$
**510 Cerrillos Rd.**
**(505) 982-1039, (800) 930-5002**
**www.santafemotel.com**

Located next to Hotel Santa Fe and across the street from Sage Bakehouse, Santa Fe Motel and

Inn has 23 moderately priced rooms with color televisions and HBO and direct-dial telephones. Five standard rooms have kitchenettes equipped with dishes and utensils. Eight rooms are in two renovated adobe houses with viga ceilings and patio entrances. One of these rooms has a fireplace, another a skylight. The motel serves a complimentary hot breakfast and keeps a pot of hot coffee at the ready all day long.

**SANTA FE SAGE INN**                    **$$**
**725 Cerrillos Rd.**
**(505) 820-9341, (866) 433-0355**
**www.santafesageinn.com**
Situated at the busy corner of Cerrillos Road and Guadalupe Street, opposite the new Railyard Park, this budget motel's location and price can't be beat in downtown Santa Fe. The inn was recently completed upgraded and has clean, southwestern rooms with phones, color satellite television with movies, in-room coffeemakers, a heated outdoor swimming pool open during the spring and summer, and plenty of on-site parking. Pets are allowed. For those without a car, a Santa Fe Trails city bus stops in front of the motel. A Whole Foods Market is conveniently located next door. A complimentary breakfast is served in an airy new Santa Fe-style breakfast room across from the office.

## Cerrillos Road and Environs

**LAMPLIGHTER INN**                    **$$**
**2405 Cerrillos Rd.**
**(505) 471-8000, (800) 767-5267**
**www.lamplighterinn.com**
The popular Lamplighter Inn is centrally located just a few blocks from one of the busiest intersections in Santa Fe—Cerrillos Road and St. Michael's Drive. In the heart of the strip-mall district, the Lamplighter is surrounded by dozens of restaurants, from fast food to fine dining in a variety of ethnicities. You can hop in your vehicle and be downtown in 10 or 15 minutes, depending on traffic, or catch a Santa Fe Trails bus (see our Getting Here, Getting Around chapter), which stops 1 block from the hotel.

The Lamplighter bows to Santa Fe style with a large *portal,* complete with wooden pillars, beams, and corbels, while several of its 82 units have high, beamed ceilings. Most rooms, however, are generic but pleasant. Sixteen have kitchenettes; the rest come equipped with a refrigerator and coffeemaker. Suites each have a DVD player and a foldout couch, in addition to one or two beds. All have free WiFi. The inn serves a complimentary hot breakfast from 7 to 11 a.m. Among the most popular features of the Lamplighter is its canopied, 25-yard heated indoor/outdoor lap pool.

**i** The double "L" in Spanish is pronounced like "Y" in English. So Cerrillos Road is pronounced Seh-REE-yose Road.

**COMFORT INN**                    **$$**
**4312 Cerrillos Rd.**
**(505) 474-7330, (877) 424-6243**
**www.comfortinn.com/hotel-santa_fe-new_mexico-NM068**
The 96-room Comfort Inn is located south of the intersection at Cerrillos and Rodeo roads—approximately 6 miles from the Plaza—within walking distance of Santa Fe Place Mall, Santa Fe's largest indoor shopping mall. And while there's no restaurant in the hotel, there are a number of eateries nearby, including several chains and a privately owned, down-home New Mexican restaurant called the Horseman's Haven, renowned for serving the hottest green chile in town. For breakfast, guests needn't leave the inn because an expanded continental breakfast comes with their rooms. The inn features a heated indoor

**i** Consider paying a little more and staying in downtown if you want to understand why so many people fall in love with Santa Fe, especially on a short trip. Lodgings on Cerrillos Road, the town's busy, noisy commercial strip, although cheaper, are usually bland chains, far from the Plaza, and depressingly soulless and devoid of Santa Fe charm.

pool and hot tub, coin-operated laundry, and free local calls in the rooms. Some rooms have whirlpool baths, microwaves, and/or refrigerators. All have hair dryers and coffeemakers and free WiFi. The inn is pet friendly.

## COURTYARD BY MARRIOTT, SANTA FE  $$$
**3347 Cerrillos Rd.**
**(505) 473-4905, (800) 777-3347**
**www.marriott.com**
Although it's located toward the far end of Santa Fe's commercial strip, the Courtyard by Marriott has a distinctly "downtown" feel, with its pueblo-style architecture and handsome southwestern interiors, especially after its $3.5 million renovation. Its spacious, meandering lobby offers a number of attractive and comfortable sitting areas, including one with a large kiva fireplace graced on both sides by neat stacks of logs. The hotel's 209 rooms and suites feature such southwestern touches as natural pine furniture and earth-toned colors. All rooms have pull-out sofa beds and rollaways, refrigerators, coffeemakers, hair dryers, irons and ironing boards, free WiFi, two telephones with data ports and voice mail, and cable color television with free and pay-per-view movie channels. Guests also have access to coin-operated laundry facilities. The three-story hotel has an attractive outdoor courtyard, interior and exterior corridors, a heated indoor pool, two indoor hot tubs, and an exercise room. Guests can ride downtown on the hotel's free shuttle, which runs from 8 a.m. to 9 p.m. The hotel restaurant, Cafe Santa Fe, is open for breakfast and dinner.

## EL REY INN  $
**1862 Cerrillos Rd.**
**(505) 982-1931, (800) 521-1349**
**www.elreyinnsantafe.com**
El Rey Inn is one of Santa Fe's best-kept secrets and one of the only hotels in these listings to squeak under $100 per night during peak season. About 10 minutes by car from the Plaza, El Rey (The King) offers comfort, surprising tranquility, and soulful Santa Fe style. Each of its 86 rooms, including 12 suites, is unique and blends

traditional southwestern decor with modern comforts, including satellite TV with HBO and direct-dial phones with voice mail. High-speed Internet access is available in the lobby. Rooms open onto spacious gardens, patios, tiled walkways, fountains, and tall elms that cover much of the five-acre property. A heated pool for seasonal use and two year-round hot tubs—one indoors, the other outside—occupy one corner of the grounds, while a playground occupies another.

El Rey's overall motif is traditional New Mexican Spanish architecture with wrought iron and whitewashed adobe and stucco. Rooms contain any combination of decorative touches that might include *latillas* held up by rough-hewn vigas, kiva fireplace, *nichos,* and murals as well as tile, wood, and polished brass accents. A number of rooms also have complete kitchens. Rooms come with a complimentary continental breakfast in the inn's spacious, European-style breakfast room or patio, and guests can help themselves to coffee throughout the day. The Pantry, a reasonably priced diner open for breakfast, lunch, and dinner and popular with locals, is next door.

## FAIRFIELD INN–MARRIOTT  $$
**4150 Cerrillos Rd.**
**(505) 474-4442, (800) 758-1128**
**www.marriott.com**
Part of Marriott's economy line, Fairfield Inn provides guests with reasonable prices and a little Santa Fe style. The lobby and entrance have vigas, *saltillo* tile, and a kiva fireplace. Its 57 rooms have southwestern touches, pullout sofa beds, rollaways, and come with a continental breakfast as well as use of the year-round heated indoor pool. They also have microwaves, free wireless Internet access, work desks, data ports, and cable color television with free HBO. Valet laundry is available for a fee.

Located at the south end of town, about 6 miles from the Plaza, the inn is contiguous with Santa Fe Place mall—the largest indoor shopping center in Santa Fe—and across the street from an upscale strip mall. While there's no restaurant on the premises, the inn is within walking distance of several eateries in and around both malls. It's a 15-minute drive to downtown Santa Fe.

## LUXURY INN DE SANTA FE $
3752 Cerrillos Rd.
(505) 474-6709
www.santafeluxuryinn.net

Despite its name, this locally owned motel prides itself on providing a homey atmosphere and rock-bottom rates. Its 51 rooms and five suites, come with color cable television and free movies; suites also have refrigerators, microwaves, and free wireless Internet access. Rooms with three beds are available. There's a seasonal outdoor heated pool and hot tub. Although the hotel is along the bland, busy Cerrillos Road commercial strip, it is near dozens of restaurants, some within walking distance, many a short distance by car. A continental breakfast is free for guests.

## PECOS TRAIL INN $$
2239 Old Pecos Trail
(505) 982-1943
www.thepecostrailinn.com

A former speakeasy, the Pecos Trail Inn is the only motel to be located on Santa Fe's quiet southeast side, at the crossroads of two historic trade routes—the Old Santa Fe Trail and the Old Pecos Trail—near scenic Old Las Vegas Highway. Situated on 3.9 acres of piñon trees, the hotel feels very rural, a benefit for those who enjoy silence and views yet want to be close to town. Guests can visit the park next door, which has a playground, jogging path, and exercise equipment, or enjoy the inn's outdoor heated pool, open from May through September. They also have workout privileges at a local health club for $2.50 a visit. The inn has 23 remodeled rooms, suites, studios, and casitas decorated in authentic Santa Fe style. Studios and casitas have fully equipped kitchens and kitchenettes, making this a pleasant place for a longer stay. The on-site restaurant is Real Burger, a popular family-style restaurant open for breakfast, lunch, and dinner. Its eclectic offerings span traditional New Mexican dishes to famously juicy burgers.

## SANTA FE INTERNATIONAL HOSTEL $
1412 Cerrillos Rd.
(505) 988-1153
www.hostelsantafe.com

The 80-bed hostel was founded in 1983 and caters primarily to people traveling for personal development and self-education. It leans toward members of youth hostelling associations, though any brand of international youth travel card almost guarantees admission. The hostel has five single-sex dorms with enough bunk beds to sleep four to seven people for $18 per night. There are also 25 private rooms for individuals, couples, or families, and one suite that is wheelchair-accessible. Rates for half baths with cold water and shared showers are $25 per night, $35 for rooms with private baths. A fully equipped cook's kitchen rivals those in many restaurants with bread, cereals, pasta, rice, beans, coffee, tea, sugar, spices, and various donated foods, such as meat and cheese, for use by lodgers. Hostellers not only clean up after themselves but must also complete a 15-minute chore they choose themselves every morning. The earlier you get up, the better your choices.

If you call to make reservations, don't be put off if no one answers the phone immediately. In this case, persistence pays off. The hostel offers many amenities you won't find in other places—guitars and other musical instruments; games; pleasant, non-institutional rooms; and lots of information about Santa Fe and its environs. The population tends to be primarily French in August and British in September. The rest of the year you're likely to bump into anyone from anywhere. No credit cards accepted; cash and travelers checks only.

**i** **Like commercial strips everywhere, Cerrillos Road attracts a fair share of burglaries and robberies. Please take all common-sense precautions, such as bringing your belongings from your car into your room at night and locking your vehicle at all times.**

## SILVER SADDLE MOTEL $$
2810 Cerrillos Rd.
(505) 471-7663

Independent film fans may already be familiar with the Silver Saddle from a 1988 German documentary called *Motel*. Filmmaker Christian Blackwood accurately portrayed the motel as an old-fashioned, authentically funky, cowboy-style inn, with a western motif provided primarily by the color scheme and the pictures on the wall. As the owner puts it, "We try to keep it simple and rustic." That may mean a few rough edges on this decidedly different "Cerrillos Road joint." But that's all part of the charm. That's not to say the Silver Saddle has no amenities. Guests get a complimentary continental breakfast that has been known to include biscuits and gravy in the winter. Ten of the motel's 27 rooms have kitchenettes, all have queen-size beds, color cable television with HBO, air-conditioning, and free local calls. Only 4 miles from the Plaza, the Silver Saddle has great shopping right next door at Jackalope (see our Shopping chapter). You can call for reservations or just ride up on your horse.

## County

### THE BISHOP'S LODGE RANCH
### RESORT AND SPA $$$$
Bishop's Lodge Rd.
(505) 983-6377, (800) 419-0492
www.bishopslodge.com

Once the private retreat of Territorial-era Bishop Jean Baptiste Lamy, Bishop's Lodge has been operating as a resort since 1918, when the family of James R. Thorpe bought the property from the Pulitzer publishing family of St. Louis. Although management has changed, the hotel property hasn't. The Bishop's own chapel, which is listed on the National Register of Historic Places, still sits in his original garden among fruit trees planted by 17th-century Franciscan priests.

The lodge is nestled in the lush foothills of the Sangre de Cristo Mountains, outside the village of Tesuque, and, though only 5 miles from the Santa Fe Plaza, feels like another world entirely. That's because the resort is secluded in a private valley covering 450 acres of landscaped property and natural piñon-juniper forest. The hotel's 111 rooms and 16 suites are divided among 15 distinctive "lodges." The North and South lodges are the oldest and were once grand summer homes before World War I. Among the newest is the Chamisa Lodge, which contains 14 deluxe accommodations above the banks of the Little Tesuque Creek. There are now also 18 deluxe rooms with fireplaces, a 3,500-square-foot conference center, and the award-winning full-service ShaNah Spa and Wellness Center. The Hills and Lodges at Bishop's Lodge, a new residential community, has recently been constructed above the resort. Hotel accommodations include high-speed Internet access, voice-mail telephone with modem jacks; cable color television with HBO; private heat and air-conditioning controls; morning local paper delivery; plush bathrobes; hair dryers; evening turndown service; and in-room safes. Deluxe rooms and suites also have a kiva fireplace, a refrigerator, an iron and ironing board, and a private balcony or patio. Las Fuentes, the popular on-site restaurant, serves a prix fixe Sunday brunch that's popular among locals as well as hotel guests.

There is a popular summertime program for children under age 12. Additional activities include horseback riding, hiking, nature walks, tennis, skeet-shooting, an outdoor pool, an indoor Jacuzzi, and an exercise area. Off-site, but still nearby, are golf, rafting, fishing, and skiing.

### THE HILTON SANTA FE GOLF AND SPA
### RESORT AT BUFFALO THUNDER $$$$
30 Buffalo Thunder Trail
(505) 455-5555
www.buffalothunderresort.com

Opened in 2008, this new luxury casino resort is the showcase property developed and owned by Pojoaque Pueblo, just north of Santa Fe, off US 285. The hotel operation, managed by Hilton, offers 395 spacious suites with gorgeous southwestern furnishings. Indian art is found throughout the property, including a large statue of Buffalo Thunder created by the young pueblo governor, a well-known artist, and a selection of winners from Indian Market through a special arrangement with the organizers of Santa Fe's famous Indian Market. In addition to the professionally designed Towa Golf Course, there are a 61,000-square-foot casino, a large theater offering world-class entertainment, a 16,000-square-foot spa, and 13,000 square feet of high-end shops. Among the 10 restaurants is Red Sage, the latest restaurant from chef-owner Mark Miller, former owner of Coyote Cafe in Santa Fe. Homewood Suites, another Hilton-managed property, is located nearby on pueblo land and offers reasonably priced rooms.

### TEN THOUSAND WAVES      $$$$
**3451 Hyde Park Rd.**
**(505) 992-5003**
**www.tenthousandwaves.com**
Ten Thousand Waves is a Japanese-style health spa built directly into 20 acres of the Sangre de Cristo foothills. It has added lodgings called Houses of the Moon to its list of offerings. The Houses of the Moon consist of 11 guest suites—Crescent Moon, Full Moon, Rising Moon, Blue Moon, New Moon, Luna, Tsuki, Suigetsu, Yado, Sailor Moon, and Moonlit—and Silver Moon, an inexpensive Japanese-style capsule lodging with built-in basics in an Airstream trailer. All are located at the end of a path through a grove of piñon trees. The suites range in size from a 1,000-square-foot space with a Japanese courtyard garden, two fireplaces and a wood-burning stove, a full kitchen and separate bedroom, living room, and dining room to a cozy, rustic studio casita with a kiva fireplace and a small private courtyard. All have kimonos and Japanese-style furnishings, such as tatami mats, shoji screens, and futon beds, as well as TVs, DVD players, private phones with voice messaging, minirefrigerators or full kitchens, coffeemakers with a supply of gourmet coffees and teas, and access to laundry facilities. Lodging guests receive complimentary access to the Waves' communal coed and women's tubs and to the saunas, as well as preferential treatment for private tubs, which often are booked a week in advance. In-room massage by Santa Fe's best therapists is available.

# BED-AND-BREAKFASTS

## Santa Fe

### ADOBE ABODE BED-AND-BREAKFAST    $$$
**202 Chapelle St.**
**(505) 983-3133**
**www.adobeabode.com**
No two rooms at the perennially popular six-room Adobe Inn in downtown Santa Fe are the same. Bloomsbury, for example, is done in rose and celadon with an Out of Africa feeling while Cabin-in-the-Woods is decorated in a woodsy Adirondack-lodge style. Looking exactly as it sounds is Bronco, a rustic, western-style room with cowboy hats on the wall, a saddle and riatas on the bedposts, a private covered porch, and a brick patio with twig furniture. Cactus has a distinctly south-of-the-border flavor with hand-loomed fabrics from Oaxaca, whitewashed vigas, and a kiva fireplace, while Casita de Corazon, or "Little House of the Heart," features Santa Fe-style decor, including custom-designed twin beds finished with aspen poles lashed together. Provence Suite contains a full living room and separate bedroom with a queen-size, whitewashed lodgepole bed and French designer linens that highlight the blue and yellow color scheme so reminiscent of southern France. Breakfasts are hearty and imaginative and feature a different southwestern-style entree every day.

**i**   Prices in Santa Fe's hotels, motels, and inns are often negotiable, especially during the off-season, which may vary from one establishment to another. Also check the hotel's Web site; discounted rates are often offered on the Internet.

### CASA DE LA CUMA BED & BREAKFAST    $$
**105 Paseo de la Cuma**
**(505) 983-1717, (877) 741-7928**
**www.casacuma.com**
Located at the bottom of a narrow, winding street in the convenient historic residential Fort Marcy district just north of Paseo de Peralta, Casa

de la Cuma is a pleasant stroll to downtown Santa Fe and the Plaza. This southwestern-style inn offers eight beautifully decorated artistic rooms and suites that share an outdoor patio with a Jacuzzi and mountain views. All rooms have air-conditioning, free WiFi, and cable TV. The common room has a cozy fireplace in front of which guests can browse through books and magazines scattered on several coffee tables or simply sit back and enjoy the 1940s Chinle rug on the wall. There's off-street parking for guests, a blessing on the narrow street. There's a full gourmet breakfast, including stuffed toast, burritos, quiche, and other delicacies.

## CASA DEL TORO                    $$$
**326 Staab St.**
**(505) 995-9689, (866) 277-1002**
**www.casadeltoro.com**
Casa del Toro sits right around the corner from the Georgia O'Keeffe Museum and has 30 bed-and-breakfast and breakfast-optional vacation rental rooms sprinkled around this quaint neighborhood. The adobe-style furnishings include viga ceilings, kiva fireplaces, Mexican tile, skylights, and southwestern art and knickknacks throughout. Guests rave about Casa del Toro's laid-back, unpretentious atmosphere and gourmet breakfasts, which always include a hot entree such as a quiche or soufflé with artichoke hearts, spinach, and white chiles. Sometimes there's more traditional fare—breakfast burritos, huevos rancheros, waffles, or pancakes—but always with a gourmet touch such as homemade chorizo or fresh organic fruit from the local farmers' market. Breakfast also includes fresh fruit and juice, homemade breads and muffins (chile cheese corn muffins are a favorite), fresh coffee, and a variety of dark and herbal teas.

**i** The city of Santa Fe has more than 5,000 rooms in hotels, motels, and bed-and-breakfasts.

## DON GASPAR INN                    $$$
**623 Don Gaspar Ave.**
**(505) 986-8664, (888) 986-8664**
**www.dongaspar.com**
Located in the peaceful South Capital district, Don Gaspar Inn welcomes you with the spreading arms of an old peach tree and a tranquil, adobe-walled garden courtyard where heirloom flowers and the trickle of water from a central fountain soothe the soul. The inn is a classic example of mission and adobe architecture, with brick paths and distressed wooden gates. There are eight large suites and two casitas, for long- or short-term stays, and a sunny, beautifully appointed bungalow overlooking the gardens that features two wood-burning fireplaces, three bedrooms, two baths, and a fully equipped kitchen. All accommodations have private bathrooms, televisions, and private phones. Those without kitchens have kitchenettes with refrigerators, microwaves, coffeemakers, toasters, and some utensils. The refrigerators are stocked with fresh coffee beans, spring water, and Blue Sky natural sodas. A hot gourmet breakfast is served daily and includes New Mexico favorites such as Huevos Rancheros and Santa Fe Sausage and Biscuits.

## EL FAROLITO BED & BREAKFAST INN    $$$
**514 Galisteo St.**
**(505) 988-1631, (888) 634-8782**
**www.farolito.com**
A few short blocks from the Plaza and around the corner from the state capitol, El Farolito is located in an off-street compound in the city's oldest district. The award-winning inn features five guest rooms and a suite in three buildings, two private casitas, and a main house with a dining room and lounge/library. A number of the buildings are adobe and all have been decorated in traditional southwestern style. The owners display paintings, pottery, kachinas, weavings, and other items from their private art collection throughout the inn. (They also own the nearby Four Kachinas Inn.) Each room has its own private entrance and outdoor patio as well as a private, hand-tiled bath, brick or tile floors, wood-beamed ceiling, hand-carved furniture, and a kiva fireplace as well as

color cable television and a private phone. Some rooms also have wet bars with small refrigerators. The inn reflects Santa Fe's tricultural heritage of Pueblo Indian, Spanish colonial, and Pioneer Anglo settlers. The breakfast room is sunny and bright, with a fireplace and tables for two, four, and eight. The "expanded" continental breakfast buffet includes a hot entree.

## EL PARADERO BED & BREAKFAST INN $$
220 West Manhattan Ave.
(505) 988-1177
www.elparadero.com
Built between 1800 and 1820, El Paradero was originally a Spanish farmhouse. Territorial touches were added in the late 19th century, and in 1912, the main house was completely remodeled with Victorian doors and windows. The house became Santa Fe's second bed-and-breakfast inn in 1980. A further remodel has added modern architectural touches while maintaining the eccentric, rambling character of the old farmhouse—from its thick adobe walls to its high ceilings, kiva fireplaces, vigas, *bancos* (benches built into the walls), and *nichos* (small niches in the wall to place religious icons or decorations). El Paradero has 15 rooms. Each room is furnished with southwestern-style furniture, hand-woven textiles, and folk art; many have fireplaces and skylights or mountain-view balconies. Breakfasts are hearty. They include a gourmet entree, home-baked bread, fresh fruit, and juice. Sundays bring lighter-than-air pancakes, a tradition of the innkeepers, who will meet special dietary needs. They serve tea—either hot or iced, hot cider, homemade baked goods, and chips and salsa—every afternoon. A warning for those with allergies: A cat and dog live on the premises.

## HACIENDA NICHOLAS $$$
320 East Marcy St.
(505) 992-8385, (888) 284-3170
www.haciendanicholas.com
Under the same family ownership as the Madeleine Inn, Hacienda Nicholas matches its sister bed-and-breakfast property in tasteful decor, scrumptious food, and lush gardens. Originally

the hacienda of Antonio Abelard Rodriguez, who built it in 1910 as a loving gesture to his wife, Isabella, the adobe home now has seven guest rooms, each with a queen- or king-size bed and private bath. Several suites have fireplaces and all guests have access to a communal great room, with 20-foot ceilings, chiseled vigas, and hand-troweled plaster walls. The current name honors the owner's eldest son.

## INN OF THE TURQUOISE BEAR $$
342 East Buena Vista St.
(505) 983-0798, (800) 396-4104
www.turquoisebear.net
This award-winning historic bed-and-breakfast on the Old Santa Fe Trail occupies the former home of poet Witter Bynner (1881-1968), for decades a prominent citizen of Santa Fe who, in recent years, has slipped into obscurity. During his day, Bynner was a leading figure of Santa Fe's flourishing writer's colony—a noted poet, translator, and essayist who staunchly advocated human rights for women, Native Americans, gays, and other minorities. Bynner's rambling adobe is built in the Spanish Pueblo Revival style around a core of rooms that date from the mid-1800s and glorious gardens. The interior contains 11 southwestern guest rooms, with kiva fireplaces, viga ceilings, *saltillo* tile, private entrances, and brick

**i** In the early 1900s, poet Witter Bynner was Santa Fe's answer to famed Taos salon hostess Mabel Dodge Luhan. Bynner loved a good party, hosting with Robert Hunt, his companion of more than 30 years, many a "Bynner's bash," as photographer Ansel Adams described their riotous soirees. Among their guests were D. H. Lawrence, who spent his first night in an American home here and eventually settled near Taos; Willa Cather, whose classic novel, *Death Comes for the Archbishop,* has been for many readers their first introduction to Santa Fe; and Robert Oppenheimer, under whose leadership Los Alamos Scientific Laboratory built the world's first atomic bomb.

or wooden floors. Most have private baths and sitting areas; all have phones, cable televisions, and DVD players. The inn has an impressive video library and, as you might expect, an extensive book collection. Hosts Ralph Bolton and Robert Frost serve complimentary wine and cheese at sunset and an expanded continental breakfast that includes fresh-squeezed orange juice, cereals, seasonal fruit, a variety of home-baked pastries and breads, and coffee from a roaster down the street. The inn is 6 blocks from the Plaza and a pleasant stroll to Canyon Road. Inn of the Turquoise Bear is "gay and lesbian friendly"; pet friendly in select rooms.

## LAS PALOMAS $$$–$$$$$
### 460 West San Francisco St.
### (877) 982-5560
### www.laspalomas.com

Only 3 blocks from the Plaza, in two tree-covered compounds with rambling courtyards, Las Palomas offers the charm, elegance, and ambience of a country inn in the heart of the city. And because of its affiliation with the Hotel Santa Fe and contemporary southwestern Inn on the Paseo, Las Palomas can provide its guests with the best of both worlds—the intimacy of a small bed-and-breakfast and the amenities of a world-class hotel. It's a great value. Las Palomas was built sometime around the turn of the 20th century. In restoring these 39 casitas, the owners have kept the style and feel of the adobe structures while adding the comforts of modern life. The odd-size doorways, uneven adobe walls, and individual kiva fireplaces combine with air-conditioning, cable television, WiFi, DVD players, stereos with CD players, and modern kitchens to strike this aesthetic balance. Each adobe casita has a living room, dining area, kitchen, private bath, and kiva fireplace. A deluxe just-baked continental breakfast is served in the bistro each morning. Pets are allowed for an additional charge. Families will appreciate the kid-friendly amenities, including games, toys, videos, night-lights, cribs, high chairs, and a children's playground. Nonsmoking throughout.

## THE MADELEINE INN $$
### 106 Faithway St.
### (505) 982-3465, (888) 877-7622
### www.madeleineinn.com

Formerly the Preston House—Santa Fe's first bed-and-breakfast inn—the eco-friendly Madeleine Inn sits tucked at the end of a street that even many Santa Feans don't know exists. (It is named after the owner's daughter.) Obscured by ancient elms in summer and open to the sun in winter, this lovely 1886 Queen Anne-style house now bears a historical plaque. A charming garden winds its way throughout the property, offering guests a colorful display of seasonal blooms and an inviting patio on which to enjoy reading and afternoon tea and pastries. The Victorian-style guest rooms are fantasies in linen and lace, stained glass, antique armoires, delicate floral wall coverings, and ornately carved fireplaces. All seven rooms have a telephone and cable television. All but two have private baths. Guests breakfast in a big country kitchen where there's always a hot entree—frittata, perhaps, or pancakes or quiche—accompanied by freshly squeezed orange juice, coffee or tea, and breads and pastries baked daily on the premises. Absolute Nirvana, the inn's gorgeous Balinese-style spa, offers the most decadent massages in Santa Fe. The signature Royal Lular treatment is a relaxing combination of body masque using sandalwood, rice powder, and other ingredients; massage using aromatherapy oils; and rose petal bath.

## WATER STREET INN $$$
### 427 West Water St.
### (505) 984-1193, (800) 646-6752
### www.waterstreetinn.com

An award-winning adobe restoration earned Water Street Inn a rightful place among Santa Fe's more luxurious bed-and-breakfasts. Its 11 spacious rooms and suites all have private baths, cable TV, WiFi, and a kiva, antique fireplace, or woodstove. The decor is refined southwestern and varies from room to room with details such as brick floors, beamed ceilings, and built-in sleeping *bancos* in addition to beds of varying styles, including New Mexico pine, four-posters, pediment, or sleigh. One room boasts a spiral staircase and a private deck, another features a private patio with a *portal*. A number of rooms open onto a fountained courtyard. One room is wheelchair-accessible. The four suites are located in a separate building; three feature private, partially enclosed patios, two with their own fountains. The largest suite, Tesuque, is big enough to sleep five in two separate rooms. Breakfast includes fresh pastries, cereals, fruit, juices, coffees, and a morning paper. The inn also hosts an evening happy hour when it serves New Mexican wines and hot hors d'oeuvres. The Plaza is just 3 blocks away.

## Santa Fe County

### CRYSTAL MESA FARM BED-AND-BREAKFAST $$
3547 Hwy. 14, Building B
(505) 474-5224
www.crystalmesafarm.com
Built near the ancient site of San Marcos Pueblo on the historic Turquoise Trail, this bed-and-breakfast inn is located on a farm filled with kid-friendly critters, from potbellied pigs to goats. Each of the four guest rooms has a private bath and entrance, cable television, a VCR, and a phone. In one, an Apache ladder leads to a meditation loft with breathtaking views of the sunset and starry night skies. The Lookout Room boasts a bed designed by famous Santa Fe "cowboy artist" L. D. Burke, a kitchen, and a private deck with its own panoramic view. The more adventurous can follow the Tipi Trail to the inn's Sioux tepee. It contains a platform futon, flagstone floor, sheepskins, and a central fire pit to warm up winter nights. The inn is filled with stained-glass windows, including one called the "star of summer," which focuses the light of sunset during the summer solstice through a central prism onto a *nicho* across the room, bathing it and the statue it holds in a rainbow of light. A gourmet continental breakfast is served, and there is an extensive library with books on local natural and cultural history. A two-day minimum stay is required.

i If you're counting your pennies, staying in the county could save you some money—up to 4 percent or more in taxes alone. Santa Fe County charges only 6.3125 percent in gross receipts tax and 4 percent in lodgers tax compared to the city, where you'll now pay a 8.0625 percent gross receipts plus 7 percent lodgers tax.

### OPEN SKY BED-AND-BREAKFAST $$
134 Turquoise Trail
(505) 471-3475, (800) 244-3475
www.inntravels.com/usa/nm/opensky
This is a true country B&B located 10 minutes south of Santa Fe off the historic Turquoise Trail. The inn offers spectacular 360-degree views and Southwest elegance from its adobe architecture to its brick floors and high viga ceilings. Guests can choose from three guest rooms. The largest, in a separate building, is 350 square feet with a private entrance, king-size bed, shower and bath, fireplace, sitting area, patio, and privacy. The next-largest is half the size with a king-size bed and a full private bath that has both a tub and a shower as well as double sinks. The smallest room has a queen-size bed and a large private bath next door with a shower and an antique tub. All rooms offer northern views that show the Santa Fe skyline to advantage at night. Open Sky serves a continental breakfast of fresh breads, cereals, fruit, juice, and a hot beverage of your choice at private tables facing a garden courtyard. The inn also has an outdoor Jacuzzi, a large lounge with a fireplace, and a number of private patios. There are four pets on the premises.

### THE TRIANGLE INN—SANTA FE $
14 Arroyo Cuyamungue,
Cuyamungue
(505) 455-3375
www.triangleinn.com
The Triangle Inn is a beautifully rustic country bed-and-breakfast that caters to the lesbian and gay community. Located on an old adobe compound surrounded by Tesuque, Nambé, and Pojoaque pueblos, the inn is just 15 minutes north of downtown Santa Fe and convenient to all that north-

ern New Mexico has to offer. There are seven guest rooms, all in private casitas, which range in size from a cozy studio to a large, two-bedroom house. Each is unique and features southwestern decor and an attention to detail complemented by Mexican and other handcrafted furnishings, fireplaces, viga ceilings, and private courtyards. All rooms have kitchenettes and either king- or queen-size beds with down bedding. Additional amenities include stereos with CD players, color televisions and VCRs, telephones, hair dryers, and gourmet coffees and teas in the room. The hosts even provide you with terry robes and spa towels for use in the bath or the twenty-four-hour hot tub in the main courtyard, which also has a large deck and sunbathing area. The Hacienda Courtyard has extensive gardens, an orchard, and a large freestanding *portal* with an outdoor fireplace. Your hosts serve refreshments here in warmer months. A hearty continental breakfast of muffins, a fruit platter, yogurt, oatmeal, juice, coffee, and tea is included.

## VACATION RENTALS

### Downtown

#### ADELANTE CASITAS                      $–$$$$$
326 Staab St.
(866) 476-1091
www.santafecasitas.com
Just a few blocks from the Plaza and around the corner from the Georgia O'Keeffe Museum, Adelante Casitas consists of four one- and two-bedroom units with large backyards suitable for children and pets—both of which are welcome. Done up in southwestern style, three of the casitas have queen beds and sleeper sofas, fireplaces, beamed ceilings, skylights, full kitchens, and washers and dryers; one is a suite with two twin beds and a separate breakfast area. Under the same ownership as Casa del Toro bed-and-breakfast, Adelante has many other interesting casitas for rent around Santa Fe. If you're on a budget and not fussy about which neighborhood you stay in, ask about new unremodeled properties. They can cost below $100 per night.

#### FORT MARCY HOTEL SUITES               $$$
321 Kearney Rd.
(888) 570-2775
www.allseasonsresortlodging.com
Named for an 1846 military outpost, Fort Marcy Hotel Suites is located on nine landscaped acres in a quiet residential neighborhood only 4 blocks north of the Santa Fe Plaza, just off the road to the Santa Fe Ski Basin. There are 83 elegant Santa Fe-style one-, two-, and three-bedroom suites with fireplaces, full kitchens, air-conditioning, DVD players, WiFi, and cable color television with premium channels. Guests have access to a hot tub, an indoor pool, coin-operated laundry facilities, and a free downtown shuttle in summer.

#### LAS BRISAS DE SANTA FE                 $$$
624 Galisteo St.
(800) 449-6231
www.lasbrisasdesantafe.com
Las Brisas is a compound of 20 one-, two-, and three-bedroom condominiums—10 time-shares, the rest owner-occupied or rentals, and all of them pure Santa Fe: exposed adobe walls, *saltillo* tile floors, viga ceilings, kiva fireplaces, enclosed courtyards or patios, punched tin decorations, and other southwestern touches. For the truly decadent, there's even one with a whirlpool bath and an enclosed atrium with a skylight. All units are fully furnished and include dishwashers, microwaves, cooking and eating utensils, linens, stackable washers and dryers, and queen-size sleeper sofas in the living rooms. They do not include daily maid service. Las Brisas is around the corner from the state capitol and 6 blocks from the Plaza. Guests can rent by the night, the week, or the month, based on availability. No pets allowed.

#### OTRA VEZ EN SANTA FE                   $$$
202 Galisteo St.
(505) 988-2244, (800) 536-6488
www.otravezensantafe.com
At the corner of Galisteo and Water streets, above two narrow intersecting roads in the heart of historic downtown Santa Fe, sits an elegant time-share that few locals even know exists. Otra Vez—

which means "once again" in Spanish—occupies the second and third floors of a relatively "new" Santa Fe building, ca. 1923, above Harry's, a chic men's store, and Foreign Traders, which sells high-quality Mexican furniture, collectibles, and accessories. Otra Vez doesn't have to advertise. It fills up its 18 one- and two-bedroom units by word of mouth. Among the attractions are a sun terrace with a year-round, outdoor hot tub and barbecues. The apartments are elegantly decorated in modern southwestern style with handcrafted furniture and some have fireplaces. Each has a full kitchen with microwave, dishwasher, and cooking and eating utensils. The rates include daily maid service, access to free laundry facilities, and parking in a lot behind the building.

## ZONA ROSA SUITES                    $$
429 West San Francisco St.
(505) 988-4455, (800) 955-4455
www.laspalomas.com
Zona Rosa Suites is an independently owned complex of 10 luxury condominiums managed by Hotel Santa Fe. Each one-, two-, and three-bedroom suite features southwestern furnishings, kiva fireplaces *saltillo* tile floors, rustic viga ceilings, and Native American artwork. All contain a fireplace, full kitchen, living room, a balcony or patio, separate entrance, and off-street parking. The two- and three-bedroom units each have two full bathrooms. Flat-screen TVs, DVD players, and WiFi

**i** Dogs are welcome in Santa Fe. In fact, they're about as ubiquitous as the kitschy bandana-clad howling coyote you'll see everywhere. Keep in mind, however, that a city ordinance requires all dogs to be leashed in public, even in parks and on trails. The sole exception is Ortíz Park, where dogs may run without a leash. In the county, your pooch must be within voice command. For energetic canines, this could present a real hardship. Please consider this before taking Rufus with you to see—and, of course, smell—The City Different. He may be happier at home with a dog sitter or staying with a neighbor.

are in every room. Guests at Zona Rosa may use all the Hotel Santa Fe facilities. Complimentary continental breakfast served daily at the sister property of Las Palomas Bed and Breakfast across the street. Make reservations through Las Palomas.

**i** Check out ski vacation amenities. Ask the rental management about ski area shuttles, ski equipment lockers on-site, and special ticket discounts.

## County
### RANCHO JACONA CASITAS          $$
Route 5, Box 250, Pojoaque,
Santa Fe 87506
(505) 455-7948
www.ranchojacona.com
The name of this vacation rental/farm in the country north of Santa Fe, comes from the Tewa Indian word Saconai—"the cliffs where the tobacco grows." Although tobacco no longer grows here, lots of critters do—rabbits, sheep, goats, burros, and birds. Kids love it. This is without a doubt a child-friendly place with lots to offer adults, too, including beauty, quiet, relaxation, and close proximity to the Santa Fe Opera (see our The Arts chapter), Bandelier National Monument, and a number of Indian pueblos, all within a half hour of town. The farm's 11 self-catering casitas—Coyote, Frog, Lizard, Parrot, Piglet, Owl, Rabbit, Raccoon, Rooster, Butterfly, and Turtle—are cheerfully furnished, pueblo-style adobe houses with one or two bathrooms and from one to three bedrooms with a king- or queen-size bed. All the casitas have fireplaces in addition to central heating; *portals* or patios for sitting, sunning, or barbecuing; fully equipped kitchens, including garbage disposals; washers and dryers; cable television; and private phones. The grounds feature a 60-foot heated outdoor pool set among lawns and trees, a pond, barn, and lots of pastureland. Rancho Jacona requires a three-night minimum stay. Prices drop between $10 and $25 per night for stays of one week or more. Seniors are eligible for discounts from November through March except during certain holidays.

## Agencies

**KOKOPELLI PROPERTY MANAGEMENT**
**607 Old Santa Fe Trail**
**(505) 988-7244**
**www.kokoproperty.com**
Kokopelli can match you up with a condo, casita, private home, or guesthouse with Santa Fe charm and modern conveniences. Homes, many built of adobe and featuring patios or decks, come with fully equipped kitchens, laundry facilities, linens, televisions, WiFi, and DVD/VCRs. The agency will even provide wood for the fireplace. The 103 rentals are available for long-term stays or outings as short as a single day.

# RESTAURANTS

People who live in Santa Fe are spoiled when it comes to good food. This community of 72,000 has more than 375 restaurants. Among them are many that have received national acclaim—Coyote Cafe, SantaCafe, Cafe Pasqual, La Casa Sena, Inn of the Anasazi Restaurant, Geronimo, and The Compound. Santa Fe consistently ranks in the top 25 culinary destinations in the United States as selected by both *Playboy* and *Money* magazines. Variety marks Santa Fe's restaurant scene. You'll find many places that specialize in the tasty regional cuisine, ranging from Tia Sophia's, popular with politicos, and Maria's New Mexico Kitchen, famous for its specialty tequila, to the Salvadoran-owned Tune Up Cafe, an authentic neighborhood restaurant whose unique stuffed pupusas and chile rellenos immediately won over die-hard fans of Dave's Not Here, a longtime legendary restaurant at this location. If you decide you'd like to eat something that doesn't have chile in it, Santa Fe can accommodate you with first-rate American cuisine from such deluxe dining places as The Old House to laid-back all-American joints as Zia Diner, Cowgirl Hall of Fame, and Josh's Barbecue. A number of Santa Fe chefs, such as Geronimo's Eric Distefano and Martin Rios and The Compound's Mark Kiffin, are nationally recognized for their talent. It's not unusual for top hotels and restaurants in Santa Fe to hire away the best-known chefs to reinvigorate the menu at newly refurbished dining rooms so frequently, it can seem like musical chairs. A handful, such as Boca's James Caruso, formerly of El Farol, and David Sellars of Amavi, open their own establishments and succeed in creating eateries that outlast fickle Santa Fe tastes and the ups and downs of the tourism economy.

Santa Fe's luster as a food town is reflected in the city's many food-centered benefits and special events. The Wine and Chile Fiesta, a citywide celebration each September, brings nationally and internationally acclaimed chefs to town, along with thousands of eager gourmands (see our Annual Events and Festivals chapter). The city has a long-established, well-regarded cooking school, the Santa Fe School of Cooking, which frequently hosts guest chefs from around the country. The Taste of Santa Fe benefit honors local restaurants for the best selection in several categories.

## OVERVIEW

This chapter offers some suggestions on where to eat. We mention only places unique to the area, figuring that you already know what to expect at the chains. We've organized the listings by style of food served. If you're unfamiliar with the New Mexican style of cuisine, see our Close-up in this chapter, which explains and defines many of the foods and terms you'll encounter when dining out in Santa Fe. And we've separated "Mexican and Latin American" and "New Mexican" because these cuisines are different.

Our advice on reservations is simple—make them whenever you can. Some places—like the perennially popular Tomasita's and breakfast at Cafe Pasqual's—don't take reservations. Others take them only for large parties. If you call these places ahead of time, they will gladly give you an idea of when to come to minimize your wait. After all, it's their business to make you happy.

Dress is casual here, although diners tend to dress better when they go to more expensive places. Nowhere in Santa Fe, however, is a coat and/or tie required for men. And if you want to eat outside in the summer—we recommend it—remember that you're at 7,000 feet and the air cools when the sun sets. Even if the day's high temperature has been in the 90s, you'll probably welcome a jacket or sweater in the evening.

Unless otherwise noted, restaurants listed in this chapter accept major credit cards and are open daily. However, many restaurants close for Christmas, Thanksgiving, New Year's Day, and other holidays—if you want to dine out on those days, please call ahead. Keep in mind that some places expand their hours during the summer or cut back during the winter.

### Price Code

The dollar signs after each restaurant's name refer to the average price of a dinner entree—no appetizers, desserts, side orders, wine, not even a Diet Coke. We also did not factor in tax or gratuity. If a restaurant is open only for breakfast and lunch, we made adjustments accordingly. And, of course, prices can change. If you're concerned, call to verify.

Our scale for dinner entree:

$................. less than $10
$$ .................. $10 to $20
$$$ ................. $21 to $30
$$$$ ............... $31 and up

## AMERICAN (FINE DINING)

### ANASAZI RESTAURANT                $$$$
Inn of the Anasazi
113 Washington Ave.
(505) 988-3030
www.innoftheanasazi.com
This award-winning restaurant prides itself on food that is a feast for the eyes as well as the palate. British-born chef Oliver Ridgeway's light flavorful Contemporary Southwest cuisine features organic poultry, game meats, and sustainably sourced fish flown in fresh daily. To start try duck enchilada mole or heirloom beets with aged goat cheese salad followed by an entree of Hatch chile-crusted tuna with New Mexico ratatouille or chile-mustard braised rabbit with spring pea fettuccine. The Anasazi serves breakfast, lunch,

Sunday brunch, and dinner and also has a bar menu served after the dining room closes. Private dinners can be arranged in the hotel's wine cellar and its library.

### THE COMPOUND                $$$$
653 Canyon Rd.
(505) 982-4353
www.compoundrestaurant.com
The Compound's chef-owner Mark Kiffin was named "Best Chef of the Southwest" by the James Beard Foundation in 2005. Eat in this classic New Mexico adobe compound and you'll find out why. Kiffin's New American cuisine is fun, inventive, and satisfying, never more than it needs to be. Try water-seared rare tuna salad with avocado, radish, mango, and sesame to start, followed by seared Alaskan halibut with crab and Yukon gold potatoes or braised veal osso bucco. A great place for a special night out. Open Monday through Friday for lunch, and nightly for dinner. Indoor and outdoor seating. Opt for the lovely patio in warm weather for a romantic meal.

### COYOTE CAFE                $$$$
132 West Water St.
(505) 983-1615
www.coyotecafe.com
In 2007, when legendary chef-owner Mark Miller decided to sell Santa Fe's most famous restaurant to concentrate on a new venture, he left the Coyote in the capable hands of one of Santa Fe's most acclaimed new generation of chefs, Eric DiStefano, who with partners has taken over ownership. DiStefano has reinvigorated the Coyote's menu while still retaining the novel mix of Tex-Mex, Pueblo Indian, and Hispanic–New Mexican that put Coyote on the culinary map. You can still find the Coyote's trademark 24-ounce New Mexico Cowboy Rib Chop and Mexican white shrimp "short stack," with corn-griddled cakes. But also look for a buttermilk pan-fried organic chicken from local producer Pollo Real, pan-seared sea bass, salmon Napoleon, and sashimi grade walu. Eating here is pricey, but the four-course prix-fixe tasting menu at $85 per head ($40 extra for paired

wines) is a good deal. There's also an extensive cocktail and wine list. Dinner only. Reserve ahead.

## FUEGO RESTAURANT $$$$
**(La Posada de Santa Fe Resort and Spa)**
**330 East Palace Ave.**
**(505) 986-0000**
**www.laposadarockresorts.com**
This resort restaurant offers pleasant patio dining as well as a European-style dining room with roaring wood fires in winter. Sample dishes include the pan-fried grouper and Caribbean spice tenderloin with venison medaillons to start and a rich chocolate molten cake for dessert or well-chosen cheese plate. Fuego serves dinner only, Wednesday to Sunday. Its famous Rancher's Brunch on Sundays is one of the best in town.

## GERONIMO $$$$
**724 Canyon Rd.**
**(505) 982-1500**
**www.geronimorestaurant.com**
It's for good reason that any list of Santa Fe's top-10 restaurants includes this Canyon Road eatery, which has received the Mobil Four-Star rating. Housed in a landmark adobe with a long *portal* for outside dining, Geronimo carries on a fine tradition of good restaurants in this lovely site. Inside you'll find three fireplaces, gleaming, brass-plated tabletops, 24-inch-thick adobe walls, and huge beams high overhead. In mid-2009, Geronimo's renowned former executive chef Eric DiStefano, new chef-owner of Coyote Cafe, took over ownership of Geronimo and was busy developing a new Asian- and French-themed menu at press time. One popular dish locals hope will return is elk tenderloin, ranch-raised in Texas, and fish dishes such as potato-crusted sea scallops with tatsoi salad and caviar sauce. You can sit on the patio in the summer or request a table near the lovely fireplace in the winter. Currently only open for dinner (closed Sunday). Full bar.

## LA CASA SENA $$$
**Sena Plaza, 125 East Palace Ave.**
**(505) 988-9232**
**www.lacasasena.com**

Historic Santa Fe ambience combined with a creative approach to food makes La Casa Sena a longtime favorite place to celebrate special occasions. To start, try chef Patrick Gharrity's flash-fried goat cheese with adobe chile cajeta and wonton chips. An entree of trout cooked in adobe offers a wonderfully succulent and unique dish; meat lovers will enjoy the Sitka venison and wild boar duo. The shady courtyard of this historic hacienda complex is one of Santa Fe's nicest. The restaurant has a full bar and a huge, award-winning wine selection. It is open for dinner daily, lunch Monday to Saturday, and brunch on Sundays.

## THE OLD HOUSE $$$$
**Eldorado Hotel**
**309 West San Francisco St.**
**(505) 995-4530**
One of New Mexico's top restaurants, the Old House's food is both beautiful and original; the atmosphere upscale and peaceful. Under former executive chef Martin Rios, this award-winning hotel restaurant's contemporary southwestern cooking scaled new heights; new chef Eugene Staples continues that tradition and has added global touches to some old favorites. Try his unusual warm Brussels sprout salad with caramelized pear, radicchio, and bacon vinaigrette or sautéed scallops with saffron velouté and prickly pear. Popular entrees include rack of lamb with roasted spaghetti squash and rosemary jus and buffalo strip with cowboy beans, sautéed spinach, and crispy onions. Locally sourced beef and free-range chicken and organic produce are on the menu. The Old House, which offers a full bar, is open for dinner only. Private dinners can be arranged in the Wine Room. You can also eat at the Eldorado Court, which serves breakfast, lunch, and dinner and offers a less-gourmet, less-expensive menu. It adjoins a sometimes-lively cocktail lounge.

## THE PINK ADOBE $$$
**406 Old Santa Fe Trail**
**(505) 983-7712**
**www.thepinkadobe.com**
Opened in 1944 by Santa Fe artist Rosalea Murphy, this family-owned restaurant is one of Santa

Fe's most popular local restaurants, as much for its beautiful Santa Fe-style dining room as for the consistent quality of its food and service. Housed in a centuries-old building with 36-inch-thick walls and six fireplaces, the restaurant is named for its characteristic pink stucco exterior. At lunch, try the signature Gypsy Stew, a wonderful, comforting concoction of chicken, green chile, tomatoes, and onions in a rich sherry-flavored broth, served with fresh hot corn bread. At dinner, the combination of juicy beef and the pep of green chile in Steak Dunnigan is one of the Pink's signature dishes. Save room for a piece of the famous apple pie with hot rum sauce (it's available to take out, too). The Pink Adobe is open for lunch Monday through Friday and dinner daily. The always popular Dragon Room bar serves a limited menu and is frequently standing-room only. The Pink adjoins the luxurious Inn of the Five Graces in the Barrio del Analco, Santa Fe's oldest district.

### SANTACAFE $$$
231 Washington Ave.
(505) 984-1788
www.santacafe.com

This casually elegant bistro has a creative Southwest-meets-French approach to food and fine service and is one of Santa Fe's best-known and loved restaurants. Lunch is a bargain at $10 a plate and includes green chile meatloaf, succulent calamari (also available at dinner), and an omelet of the day. The red chile onion rings served with Judy's house-made ketchup and filet burger draw rave reviews. At night, listen for the fish specials or try the grilled Black Angus filet mignon with pommes frites and red chile béarnaise. Vegetarians will be delighted by the Roasted Poblano Relleno with Three-Mushroom Quinoa and Chipotle Cream. The SantaCafe occupies part of a restored hacienda, and its white walls, fresh flowers, and warming fireplaces add to the dining experience. It also has a lovely patio for quiet summer dining. SantaCafe serves lunch Monday through Saturday, dinner daily, and Sunday brunch from Mother's Day to Labor Day. Early-evening prix-fixe dinners are sometimes offered. The restaurant has a full bar.

## AMERICAN FOOD (CASUAL DINING)

### BACK STREET BISTRO $
513 Camino de los Marquez
(505) 982-3500

Just off the beaten track, this informal cafe serves first-rate soup, with 10 choices featured daily. Owner David Jacoby consistently wins Best Soup and Best Presentation at the Annual Souper Bowl fund-raiser. Try the sweet pepper bisque or the Hungarian mushroom. The hot or cold sandwiches, including New York corned beef, can be ordered by the half, so you'll have room for the top-notch pies and desserts. Daily soups are posted on white boards. The restaurant does not allow smoking or cell phones. An art exhibit that changes regularly adds to the ambience. Expect to wait if you come at the height of noon-hour business. There's ample parking along the street or in the lot behind the restaurant. Closed Sundays. No credit cards accepted.

**i** If a restaurant advertises that it serves beer and wine, that means it doesn't have a full liquor license.

### BOBCAT BITE $-$$
420 Old Las Vegas Hwy.
(505) 983-5319

The winner of Bon Appetit magazine's best burger in the United States, this classic old roadhouse out the southeast side of town, off I-25, attracts fans from across the country for its huge freshly ground burgers loaded up with green chile and the fixin's. The teeny counter next to the 55-year-old cast-iron griddle offers a ringside seat, but expect a wait. This place is tiny. Open for lunch and dinner, Wednesday to Saturday. No alcohol.

### CHOCOLATE MAVEN $-$$
821 West San Mateo
(505) 984-1980

It's almost a shame to spill the beans about this excellent European-style bakery but, tucked away as it is in the slowly gentrifying Second Street arts

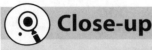 **Close-up**

## A Beginner's Guide to Santa Fe Dining

**Biscochito:** An anise-flavored cookie.

**Burrito:** A flour tortilla rolled to enclose meats, beans, cheese, or a combination of these and often served smothered with chile sauce and melted cheese. Breakfast burritos may be filled with scrambled eggs, potatoes, and bacon.

**Carne adovada:** Cubes of marinated meat, usually pork, cooked in red chile, garlic, and oregano.

**Chalupas:** Corn tortillas fried into a bowl shape, filled with shredded chicken, beef, and/or beans, usually topped with guacamole and salsa.

**Chile:** The vegetable that puts the fire in traditional New Mexican cooking. Green chile is the fresh vegetable, which is roasted, chopped, and thickened to produce a sauce. Red chiles are mature green chiles, which are dried and used as seasoning or for a sauce. While red may look hotter, the spiciness depends not on the color, but on where the chile was grown and the weather conditions during the growing season. Note the Spanish spelling of chilli.

**Chile con queso:** Green chile and melted cheese mixed together into a dip.

**Chile relleno:** A whole green chile roasted, peeled, and stuffed (usually with cheese), then dipped in a batter and fried.

**Chorizo:** A spicy pork sausage seasoned with garlic and red chile.

**Christmas:** The phrase that means you'd like to try both red and green chile on your dish.

**Empanada:** A turnover usually filled with a sweetened meat mixture or fruit.

**Enchiladas:** Corn tortillas filled with chicken, ground meat, or cheese and covered with chile sauce and cheese, often topped with shredded lettuce and tomato. The tortillas may be rolled with the filling inside or stacked with the filling in between. Either yellow-corn or blue-corn tortillas—made from a special variety of corn with blue kernels—are used. Enchiladas may be served topped with sour cream or a fried egg, a New Mexico tradition.

**Fajitas:** Strips of grilled steak, chicken, or sometimes shrimp with sautéed peppers and onions, often served still sizzling in a metal fry pan. Warm tortillas and side dishes of salsa, cheese, sour cream, and guacamole are served alongside so you can make your own burritos.

**Flan:** Caramel custard dessert similar to crème caramel, the French dish from which flan originated.

**Flauta:** Tightly rolled corn tortillas filled with meat and fried to a crunch, usually served with salsa and guacamole for dipping.

district, you'd never find it on your own. Daram Andrew Segal, the Sikh owner of Española's Love and Company Bakery, bought what was then a popular bakery on Guadalupe Street in 1995 and moved it to San Mateo. Now the soulful brownies, green chile scones, German chocolate and carrot cakes, and other delectable baked items share retail space with one of Santa Fe's most popular eateries. Breakfasts are served daily from 7:30 to 10:30 a.m. and feature a variety of egg dishes, waffles, pancakes, and a homemade granola and hot chocolate that drew raves from Food Network's Giada DeLaurentis. The weekend brunch also includes specials such as buckwheat napoleon with smoked trout and crepes. At lunchtime, try the Indian Red Lentil Soup, the Baja wrap, or wild mushroom and goat cheese sandwich. Tip: If you want to sample Chocolate Maven but prefer to avoid the lunch rush, come for the elegant afternoon tea between 3 and 5 p.m. and linger over tiny open-faced sandwiches, scones with cream and jam, and an assortment of cakes all presented on a silver platter and served on bone china.

**Frijoles:** Beans, usually pinto beans; frijoles negros are black beans.

**Guacamole:** Mashed avocado, usually seasoned with chopped onion, garlic, lime juice, and chile powder. Served as a dip, a topping for some dishes, or even a filling for tacos.

**Huevos rancheros:** Eggs, usually fried, served atop corn tortillas and smothered with chile and cheese. A popular Santa Fe breakfast.

**Menudo:** A soup made with tripe and chiles. (It's known as the "breakfast of champions.")

**Nachos:** Corn chips topped with refried beans, melted cheese, and sliced jalapeños. If served "grande" they will probably include ground beef or shredded chicken, guacamole, and sour cream. Olives, fresh tomatoes, and onions may be added.

**Natilla:** Soft custard dessert.

**Pico de gallo:** Salsa with chopped fresh chiles, tomatoes, onions, and cilantro. It's usually spicier than traditional salsa and very fresh-tasting.

**Posole:** Hominy stew, usually made with pork, onions, and oregano and served with chile sauce on top or on the side.

**Quesadilla:** A turnover made of a flour tortilla filled with cheese and sometimes beef, chicken, or other ingredients, then toasted, fried, or baked.

**Refritos:** Beans, usually pintos, mashed and fried.

**Ristra:** A string of chiles, usually red, hung to dry or for decoration.

**Salsa:** An uncooked mixture of chile, tomatoes, onions, cilantro, and other spices. Usually eaten as a dip.

**Sopaipilla:** Puffed, fried yeast bread served hot with honey or honey butter and eaten with the meal.

**Taco:** A folded corn tortilla either fried crisp or soft and usually filled with meat or chicken and garnished with cheese, fresh chopped lettuce, onions, and tomatoes.

**Tostadas:** Corn tortilla chips. This term also means an open-faced fried corn tortilla covered with refried beans, salsa, cheese, and chopped lettuce and tomato.

**Tortilla:** An unleavened bread made of corn or wheat. Flour tortillas may be served with the meal in New Mexican cooking; corn tortillas tend to be incorporated in dishes and baked with sauce.

**HARRY'S ROADHOUSE**  $$
96 Old Las Vegas Hwy.
(505) 989-4629

There are bachelors in Santa Fe (you know who you are!) who eat almost every meal at Harry's. It's that kind of home-away-from-home place. The extensive, well-executed, and reasonably priced menu has something for everyone—egg dishes such as migas and just-baked cinnamon rolls at breakfast, and barbecue, New Mexican food, blackened catfish, pizza, salads, juicy burgers (include buffalo) with all the toppings, Moroccan couscous, and fish tacos for lunch and dinner. In the hands of Harry's wife Peyton, desserts here are in a class of their own. Everything is made from scratch. Strawberry rhubarb pie and apricot crisp groan with fresh fruit and are garnished with real whipped cream or premium or homemade ice cream. The banana cream pie with white chocolate comes in a crust so tender it's amazing it doesn't crumble before you can eat it. Unless you come mid-afternoon, you will probably have to wait, but the service is professional and quick once you're seated. You'll get seated quicker if you sit at the counter, but the lovely landscaped patio is worth the wait in summer. There's a full bar. Open daily for breakfast, lunch, and dinner.

## PLAZA RESTAURANT                    $–$$
54 Lincoln Ave.
(505) 982-1664

Location and history give this high-decibel diner a definite edge on the competition. You'll find hefty, Santa Fe-style breakfasts, as well as lunch and dinner. The menu includes burgers and salads, enchiladas, burritos, and tacos, and some Greek dishes, a nod to the owners' Greek heritage. Try the Gyro Sandwich served with hot thick fries or the vegetable moussaka. Daily specials may include a Mediterranean plate or a chicken mole tamale. The atmosphere is reminiscent of the fifties, complete with some interesting old photos on the walls. The Plaza offers a kid's menu and beer and wine are available with meals for the parents. If you're lucky enough to get a window seat, you can watch life on the Plaza as you enjoy your food. Open every day.

## ZIA DINER                    $–$$
326 South Guadalupe St.
(505) 988-7008

Now that the Rail Runner train brings visitors directly to its door, it's a fair bet that more people are going to discover what Santa Feans already know: this contemporary diner is one of the most consistently good family restaurants in town. Zia specializes in comfort food—potatoes and gravy, fish and chips, piñon meat loaf, an open-faced turkey sandwich with all the trimmings, cherry and other homemade pies, and ice-cream drinks. But there's also hummus with pita, Greek salads, spaghetti, enchiladas, Asiago cheese pie, and, on some days, Asian specials. Fish dishes tend to be creative and delicious and include a delicious Snapper Veracruzana, reminiscent of Mexico. Pies are the real deal. Save room for a slice. The Zia serves breakfast, lunch, and dinner daily and offers patio dining in the summer. You can also eat at the bar or the kitchen counter.

# ASIAN

## CHOW'S                    $$
720 St. Michael's Dr.
(505) 471-7120
www.mychows.com

Even though it looks like a shopping center storefront, Chow's offers gourmet Chinese food in a calm, upscale setting. The contemporary, eclectic Chinese cuisine is a long way from steam-tray chow mein. Appetizers include firecracker dumplings filled with vegetables, ground turkey, and chile, served with a pesto dipping sauce and wonderful barbecued ribs. The Santa Fe Won Ton Soup features turkey dumplings, sliced chicken breast, wild mushrooms, and fresh spinach in a light chicken vegetable broth. The Pearl River Splash, a steamed whole boneless trout in a delicate ginger and scallion sauce, makes a light healthy choice. The noodle dishes satisfy the appetite and the eye, and interesting vegetarian choices are available. Chow's makes everything without MSG. It's open Monday through Saturday for lunch and dinner. Beer and wine are available with meals in this smoke-free restaurant. Credit cards are accepted only for meals that cost more than $20.

## JINJA ASIAN CAFE                    $$
510 North Guadalupe St., Suite P
(505) 982-4321
www.jinjabistro.com

This contemporary Asian restaurant features a very attractive retro-Polynesian 1950s-style dining room offering South Seas cocktails and a varied menu for both carnivores and vegetarians. Seating is in booths, where you can linger over cocktails and enjoy a night out with friends. Try the Tokyo Tofu appetizer, a crispy fried tofu dish with mild soy-scallion sauce that even tofu-haters will enjoy. For dinner, the Ten Tigers shrimp, 10 large shrimp marinated in lemongrass and served with mango vinaigrette and cucumber salad, is a winner. Shanghai pork is another good bet. The kava rum drink for two is festive. Hawaiian beers and Thai iced tea are also good.

## SAIGON CAFE $
501 West Cordova Rd.
(505) 988-4951

The Saigon offers an interesting variety of noodle dishes, some unusual cold salads with noodles, and a few other Vietnamese specials. The soups, including many varieties of rice noodle, egg noodle, vermicelli, and wonton, come to the table steaming hot and a feast for the eyes as well as the palate. The atmosphere is basic storefront Asian and the service informed and efficient. The servings are generous—if you invite a moderately hungry friend to join you for lunch and order two dishes to share, you'll both have something to take home. You can order beer and wine to go with your meals. The Saigon is closed on Sundays.

## SHOHKO-CAFE $$-$$$$
321 Johnson St.
(505) 982-9708
www.shohkocafe.com

Japanese food is the house specialty. Look on the board for the daily appetizer specials, which may include wonderful steamed dumplings. The sushi bar has a half-dozen tables in addition to counter seats, where you can watch chefs roll your sushi. There are two other dining rooms in this lovely old adobe where you can order yakitori, superb sukiyaki, or even sushi made with green chile or green chile tempura. Try the Bento Box lunch. Beer and wine are available with meals. Shohko is open Monday to Saturday for dinner, Monday to Friday for lunch, and closed Sundays.

> **i** At last count, Santa Fe had about 375 sit-down restaurants, not counting fast-food operations.

## THAI CAFE $-$$
329 West San Francisco St.
(505) 982-3886

Thai Cafe has kept the old vigas, hardwood floors, and southwestern touches of the old adobe building it's housed in but infused the space with hot tropical colors that provide a perfect backdrop for equally invigorating dishes. The best deals are at lunchtime, when 12 different specials

are served with a complexly flavored vegetable tofu soup and a large side order of coconut-milk, brown, or steamed rice. Popular entrees are the Basil-Lemongrass Chicken, Red Curry Beef, and Pad Thai. Things can get pretty spicy here, so instruct your server accordingly. Thai iced coffee is a good way to cool down. Allow time for parking; the restaurant's own lot is tiny.

# BREAKFAST

## AZTEC STREET COFFEE HOUSE $
317 Aztec St.
(505) 983-9464

The Aztec serves locally sourced and beautifully executed vegetarian food. At breakfast, there are fresh breakfast burritos, bagels, pastries, and granola to accompany excellent coffee. At lunch, try homemade soup, stew, bruschetta (open-faced grilled sandwich), hummus, and hot vegetarian entrees such as quiche. Aztec's homemade ice cream is worth a special trip. Flavors include a delicious green chile-pistachio. Weekend evenings at the Aztec feature open-mike sessions for music, poetry, performance, or any other variation of the spoken word. The cafe runs a revolving art show on its adobe walls, showing the work of local artists and changing the exhibit monthly. Free WiFi.

## DOWNTOWN SUBSCRIPTION $
376 Galisteo St.
(505) 983-3085

Downtown Subscription is an airy neighborhood cafe and international newsstand near Canyon Road. The food and drink are sophisticated and include excellent tea and coffee drinks and hot Mexican mocha made with ground Ibarra chocolate. Choose from a variety of delicious homemade baked goods, such as lime bar, rugelah, or Aunt Helen's sour cream coffee cake. Sandwiches made by local maker Purple Onion are available. Downtown Subscription is popular with New Yorkers and other urbanites as well as east-side residents, who enjoy sitting in the sunny garden and reading in summer. Open from 7 a.m. to 7 p.m. daily.

## MISSION CAFE AND SWEET SHOP $
239 E. De Vargas St.
(505) 983-3033
Located in the lovely old Valdes Home behind Santa Fe's Oldest House, this rambling adobe has finally attracted a restaurant that really works here. The local owners are on a "mission" to offer local and organic foods at reasonable prices for the average joe. Popular with government workers for breakfast burritos, huevos rancheros, and other New Mexico specialties, and for those with a sweet tooth that can only be satisfied with a slice of pie accompanied by a scoop of locally made Tara's organic ice cream, which comes in unusual flavors such as lemongrass. Open for breakfast and lunch daily. Its shady courtyard is perfect in summer.

## SANTA FE BAKING COMPANY $
504 West Cordova Rd.
(505) 988-4292
www.santafebakingcompanycafe.com
This cheery, unpretentious cafe is a comfortable arty community meeting place for Santa Feans of all classes, cultures, and inclinations—from street Rastas and journaling writers to bankers and government workers. Presiding over the dining room is owner Eric Struck, who, along with brothers Kevin and Steve, greets regulars by name, banters in "Spanglish" with a loyal Mexican kitchen staff, and seriously hustles a dizzying array of egg dishes, quesadillas, burritos, and daily specials to a hungry crowd. Try the Cowboy Bowl, a soothing stew of black beans, home fries, green and red chile, fried egg, and sour cream served with tortillas, or a slice of homemade pueblo pie or turkey-chile croissant. All orders are taken at the counter and brought to your table. Community radio station KSFR broadcasts a weekday morning talk show from one corner of the room. Live music at brunch on weekends. Open for breakfast, lunch, and dinner. Free WiFi.

## TECOLOTE CAFE $
1203 Cerrillos Rd.
(505) 988-1362
Tecolote—it means "owl"—specializes in good food and quick service. They keep your coffee cup full while you wait for French toast made from a variety of breads or a simple order of fresh fruit you can enjoy by itself or add to your breakfast order. The chile is wonderful here, but not for the faint of heart. Pancakes—including the Tollhouse, with walnuts and chocolate chips—are another specialty. A basket of homemade sweet breads comes with your egg meal. You can also order any of the sandwiches, burgers, or other lunch items throughout the day—the enchiladas and black bean soup are worth a try.

## TREE HOUSE BAKERY $
1600 Lena St.
(505) 474-5543
www.treehousepastry.com
In early 2009, this all-organic bakery moved from a rustic adobe barn in a nursery in far-west Santa Fe to the gentrifying Second Street arts district. The new space is contemporary, light, relaxed, and filled with art but still offers an open kitchen where you can watch the owners work their magic to create featherweight, naturally sweetened muffins, scones, and cakes, from wedding cakes to their signature cup cakes. There's a chalkboard of daily hot dishes, including frittata with farmers' market salad, squash blossom quesadillas with local goat cheese, brown rice croquettes, and vegetarian sandwiches on homemade bread. Portions are on the small side for the price, but the owner's dedication to offering clean, delicious, locally sourced food has built a loyal clientele. Open for breakfast and lunch, Monday to Saturday, and brunch on Sundays. Free WiFi.

## CONTINENTAL/FRENCH

## RISTRA $$$$
548 Agua Fria St.
(505) 982-8608
www.ristrarestaurant.com
Xavier Grenier's Guadalupe-district restaurant is housed in an unassumingly plain bungalow. All the better for showcasing the exceptional food: a heady Southwest variation on French cuisine. House specialties include grilled foie gras, black

Mediterranean mussels in aromatic chipotle and mint. The knowledgeable staff will expertly help with selections from an extensive wine list. Reservations recommended. Ristra is open daily for dinner only.

## 315 $$$$

315 Old Santa Fe Trail
(505) 986-9190
www.315santafe.com

This small French restaurant, owned by executive chef, Louis Moskow, is big on imagination and service. The specials change daily and seasonally with usually eight to 10 entrees offered at lunch and dinner. 315 serves a wonderful bouillabaisse soup and a grilled Bibb salad with smoked salmon. Entrees might include pan-fried sage-dusted Texas quail, sliced duck breast with dried cherries, braised Galisteo lamb shank with walnut sage pesto sauce, or roasted beet and goat cheese tart. 315 may have Santa Fe's best crème brûlée, finished at your table with a blowtorch! It's open for lunch and dinner. Moskow also owns the Railyard Restaurant, housed in a converted warehouse in the Guadalupe District, a good place for American classics like burgers.

# IN A CLASS OF THEIR OWN

## AMAYA RESTAURANT AT THE HOTEL SANTA FE $$$

1501 Paseo de Peralta
(505) 982-1200
www.hotelsantafe.com

One of the first restaurants in the country serving Native American cuisine, Hotel Santa Fe's consistently excellent Amaya Restaurant is still Number One in Santa Fe for gourmet Native cuisine. The signature Picurís Mixed Grill—named for the hotel's majority owners, Picuris Pueblo—includes tender elk tenderloin, lamb chop, and rabbit sausage with butternut squash flan and caramelized new vegetables in a thyme reduction and is more than enough for two. The Wild Boar Tenderloin with apple-Bourbon red chile reduction and Lemon-Thyme Chilean sea bass are also popular choices. At lunch, a buffalo burger, made from

Picuris reared bison, or the Amaya salmon wrap with crème fraîche make a good lighter meal at reasonable prices. Artisan bread is from Sage Bakehouse across the street.

**i** Eating in Santa Fe can get pretty pricey. Never fear, help is on the way, in the form of a new online discount dining program. Log on to the http://999dine .com Web site for discounts of 30, 40, 50, sometimes 60 percent off full price at favorite local establishments, including Tree House Bakery and The Compound. Plan ahead and buy certificates for $10, $20, and $50, depending on the restaurant. They're good for three months and have minimally restrictive blackout dates and times.

## CAFE PASQUAL'S $$$

121 Don Gaspar Ave.
(505) 983-9340, (800) 722-7672
www.pasquals.com

Tiny Cafe Pasqual's has been serving original cuisine inspired by the culinary traditions of New Mexico, Old Mexico, and Asia, using fresh, seasonal, organic, and naturally raised foods, for more than two decades. Owner Katherine Kagel has been honored with the James Beard America's Regional Cooking Classics Award. Pasqual's serves memorable lunches and dinners, but breakfast is where it truly shines. Try the chorizo burritos or huevos motuleños, a breakfast classic from Yucatán, Mexico. There's even trout, either grilled or served as smoked trout hash. To beat the line (no reservations taken at breakfast), sit at the large community table and join the conversation. You can order beer and wine, but just looking at this pretty room, decorated with Mexican garlands and homages to San Pasqual, the patron of the kitchen, lifts your spirits.

## INDIA PALACE $$

227 Don Gaspar Ave.
(505) 986-5859
www.indiapalace.com

This may be the only East Indian restaurant in the country to be housed in an adobe building with Santa Fe charm inside and a mural of India on the outside. India Palace sits on the edge of a city parking lot across from the Hotel St. Francis. From certain tables, you can watch what's happening in the kitchen through a window. The food includes all the Indian specialties you'd expect, well flavored with garlic, ginger, cardamom, cloves, saffron, and other spices. You can also order well-prepared tandoori meats and succulent lamb as well as vegetarian choices. The hearty luncheon buffet is a good value. Beer and wine are available with lunch and dinner, and you can dine on the patio in the summer.

## THE TEA HOUSE $
821 Canyon Rd.
(505) 992-0972
www.teahousesantafe.com

This European-style teahouse on arty Canyon Road has a Bohemian vibe in keeping with owner Dionne Christian's eclectic background as an interior designer, accomplished cook, and world traveler. Dionne custom blends all 100 imported teas she serves, including 10 varieties of South African Rooibos; home-brewed Indian chais; pure green matcha from Japan that will blow your head off; flavored tea blends; and tisanes. With your cuppa, try an airy almond-flavored homemade scone with homemade clotted cream, a real show-stopper. If you're hungry, order a bowl of homemade soup, rice or polenta and veggies, baguette sandwich with natural meats, salad, or a cheese plate for two. At breakfast, the inventive Eggs Confetti, a light egg dish scrambled using the steam from the espresso machine and strewn with pepper strips, is terrific. Coffee drinks, wine, sake, champagne, and margaritas are available. Nightly entertainment. Open 8:30 a.m. to 9 p.m.; closed Tuesdays.

## ITALIAN

### AMAVI $$$$
221 Shelby St.
(505) 988-2355
www.amavirestaurant.com

Ex-SantaCafe chef David Sellers and his wife Heather opened this romantic restaurant (Amavi

means "love of life") at the site of the former Julian's in 2008. Dishes from France, Spain, and Italy are listed on the creative menu, which might include Spanish tapas or tuna Nicoise to start, followed by pan-seared Alaskan halibut, elk tenderloin, or homemade linguine with heirloom tomatoes. Open for dinner nightly.

### ANDIAMO! $$$
322 Garfield St.
(505) 995-9595
www.andiamoonline.com

Andiamo!, which means "let's go!," offers good, fresh food prepared with panache. The menu changes daily and may include an antipasto, such as freshly made mozzarella with appropriate accompaniments or crispy polenta set off with a creamy topping of rosemary and Gorgonzola. Each evening features a pasta special and desserts that are beautiful as well as flavor-packed. The Caesar salad is one of the city's best, filled with flavor but not overpowering with either garlic or anchovies. The restaurant operates from an old bungalow in the Railyard district redone in rich Tuscan yellows and reds and crammed full of tables—eating outside will give you more space and privacy. Open for dinner daily. Beer and wine are available and reservations recommended.

### OSTERIA D'ASSISI $$$
58 South Federal Place
(505) 986-5858
www.osteriadassisi.net

You'll find good pasta at this north Italian restaurant as well as nicely presented grilled dishes. The Mediterranean menu changes daily. Typical appetizers include rolled eggplant with ricotta, tomato, parmesan, and fresh herbs and fresh ravioli. House specialties include pizza fruitti di mare (seafood pizza), cioppino (seafood soup), and Osso Buco. The two-story restaurant has a bright, open feel to it and offers patio dining when the weather permits. Osteria also does take-out orders for sandwiches, entrees, pasta, sauces, and salads. Located across from the federal courthouse, downtown. Open Monday to Saturday for lunch, daily for dinner.

## PRANZO ITALIAN GRILL                $$$
**Sanbusco Center, 540 Montezuma Ave.**
**(505) 984-2645**

Service at Pranzo is consistently professional, a skillful blend of friendliness and knowledge. The menu offers a nice selection of starters, pizza, delicious pasta, and original entrees to keep locals and visitors happy. In fact, Pranzo is consistently selected as the city's best Italian restaurant by readers of the Santa Fe Reporter. A good opener is the Antipasto Misto, a sampler plate that includes a head of roasted garlic, a grilled portobello mushroom, salmon, prosciutto, fontina cheese, and more. Salads are great here; we recommend the Gorgonzola dressing. The restaurant is nicely appointed, comfortable, and classy—a very "in" place for lunch. The staff happily accommodates special food requests. Pranzo serves lunch Monday through Saturday and dinner nightly. You can order off the full menu at the bar.

# MEXICAN & LATIN AMERICAN

## EL TESORO IN THE SANBUSCO CENTER   $
**500 Montezuma Ave.**
**(505) 988-3886**

This tiny cafe inside the upmarket Sanbusco Center offers a fabulous Salvadoran twist on the usual New Mexican fare. Try the Tesoro Tamal, a moist tamale filled with lots of roasted chicken and steamed inside banana leaves, or the Sanbusco Burrito, which is bursting with flank steak, cheese, and Tesoro's own uniquely spiced salsa. Save room for the yummy fried plantains with cream. Everything is super fresh and homemade (check out the cooks in the open kitchen making tortillas)—muy sabroso. Open for breakfast and lunch daily.

## LA BOCA                             $-$$
**22 West Marcy St.**
**(505) 982-3433**

When chef James Campbell Caruso left El Farol to open his own Spanish tapas restaurant in the former Paul's in downtown Santa Fe, he dedicated himself to celebrating the concept of "small is beautiful," including the size of this tiny restaurant where dining is a casual, intimate affair. Small plates feature inspired combinations of the fresh, unadulterated ingredients at the heart of Mediterranean cuisine. Try the smoky grilled eggplant with creamy manchego cheese, honey, and capers or perhaps a plate of tuna carpaccio and olives drizzled with blood-orange aioli and sea salt. The menu is only limited by the chef's daily creativity.

**i** Chile sparks New Mexico's regional cuisine. Some are harvested green—usually beginning in September—roasted until the skin blisters, then peeled. Chile enthusiasts claim that chopped green chile, sometimes thickened with a bit of flour to make a sauce, goes well with meat, fish, fowl, eggs, cheese, and vegetables. No one will think it unusual if you ask for a side of green chile with just about anything—even hash browns.

## LOS MAYAS                          $$$
**409 West Water St.**
**(505) 986-9930**
**www.losmayas.com**

Eating here is fun, especially in the summer when you and your family can be outside on the large patio. This is Latin American food and both tortilla dishes and seafood are well represented on the extensive menu. The restaurant's slogan is "Cuisine of the Americas." Try the enchiladas banana appetizer—two rolled tortillas stuffed with fried plantains topped with a nicely spiced mole sauce and Mexican cheese. Entrees include choose-your-own combination plates, Mayan fajitas, and grilled items. The Santo Domingo is a warm plate filled with skirt steak and jumbo shrimp split, grilled, and served in the shell, with rice and beans. Beer and wine, including sangria, add to the fun. You'll find live music nightly. Los Mayas serves lunch and dinner seven days a week.

## MARISCOS "LA PLAYA"                    $$
537 Cordova Rd.
(505) 982-2790

## LA PLAYA 2                             $$
2875 Cerrillos Rd.
(505) 473-4594

These simple little eateries have an authentic, south-of-the-border feel. At the Cordova location, you can imagine you're on the beach as you look at the mural of white sand, waves, and parasailers while you wait for your meal. Chances are the wait will be a quick one—the kitchen runs efficiently. You can choose cold selections, such as seafood cocktails or ceviche, or hot fish and shellfish entrees fixed many ways. The soups are filled with fish and vegetables, and the grilled platters are served hot and well seasoned. You can get fish tacos and shrimp burritos, along with soft, fresh corn tortillas. Try the Filete a la Plancha, baked snapper stuffed with shellfish, octopus, and cheese. The restaurants serve lunch and dinner daily except Tuesday. You can order beer—Mexican or from the good ol' U.S.A.—with your meal. Reservations are accepted at the Cerrillos Road location, which sometimes has live music.

## TUNE UP CAFE                          $
1115 Hickox St.
(505) 983-7060
www.tuneupcafe.com

In 2008, Cafe Pasqual veterans Charlotte and Jesus Rivera took over what was a perennially popular tiny neighborhood hole-in-the-wall eatery on a side street and, in true tune-up tradition, made it run even better. The menu is still recognizably New Mexican, but the couple has added several dishes that pay homage to Jesus' El Salvadoran roots and Charlotte's southern upbringing. Enjoy corn-masa pupusas (deep-fried tortillas stuffed with flank steak or refried beans), the national dish of El Salvador; pressed-meat cubano sandwiches on ciabatta bread; and New Orleans-style fresh fruit French toast. The Dave Was Here burger recalls the original neighborhood restaurant (Dave's Not Here) that lived at this locale for a quarter-century. Portions are enormous. Open 7 a.m. to 10 p.m.

# NEW MEXICAN

## LA PLAZUELA RESTAURANT                 $$$
La Fonda Hotel
100 East San Francisco St.
(505) 982-5511
www.lafondasantafe.com

La Plazuela is one of the loveliest dining rooms in Santa Fe. The bright courtyard dining room, with its colorful handpainted windows, mural of New Mexico pueblo life, and welcoming fireplace, could be anywhere in Mexico. The bright table settings and waitresses, attractively dressed in flowing skirts and Santa Fe-style blouses, add to the ambience. Salmon, chicken, and other dishes are great here, but chef Lane Warner's Nuevo Latino offerings are real standouts. A hearty combination plate, first-rate chile rellenos, and pork or vegetarian tamales topped with red or green chile are popular. For vegetarians, the eggplant sandwich gets a gold star—grilled eggplant and a hint of pesto. Produce is locally sourced and sparkling fresh. Don't miss La Plazuela's most enjoyable offerings: homemade guacamole made tableside by your waiter. Open for breakfast, lunch, and dinner. Full bar.

## MARIA'S NEW MEXICAN KITCHEN           $$
555 West Cordova Rd.
(505) 983-7929
www.marias-santafe.com

Maria's is known for great luncheon specials, one of Santa Fe's best margarita menus, and murals in the cantina by artist Alfred Morang, which the artist traded for food and drink. You can order dozens of types of margaritas, made with different tequilas and complementary liquors, each served with panache. The food is tasty and affordable, and Maria's uses local chile and produce whenever possible. For a change, try the Green Chile Philly at lunch, a variation of a tradition Philly sandwich served on a flour tortilla with the spice of green chile as a special addition. You can watch the tortillas being made so you know they're fresh. Strolling musicians add to the ambience in the evenings. Flan is the recommended dessert. Reservations are welcome—and a good idea. Lunch and dinner daily.

## RESTAURANTE RANCHO DE CHIMAYÓ    $$
**3 miles from the Highway 76 intersection with Highway 520, on County Rd. 98, 32 miles north of Santa Fe, Chimayó**
**(505) 984-2100, (505) 351-4444**
**www.ranchodechimayo.com**
The drive from Santa Fe is part of the pleasure of dining in this touristy but worthwhile New Mexican mainstay. Plan your reservations for just after sunset and you'll have a chance to see the Jémez Mountains against a wonderful golden, crimson, or peach-colored sky. Housed in a sprawling old hacienda, the restaurant sits near apple orchards and the Santuario de Chimayó. It offers patio dining and a lovely bar with a fireplace. You'll find strolling musicians here most weekends. The fare is New Mexican with a few other choices for nonchile eaters, such as steak and trout. The sopaipillas here are light and crisp and they refill the basket as often as you ask. From mid-May through October, the restaurant is open daily for lunch and dinner; otherwise it's closed Monday. Breakfast is served only on weekends.

> **i** Al Lucero, co-owner of Maria's New Mexican Kitchen with his wife, Lori, is also an author. His *The Great Margarita Book,* published by Ten Speed Press, includes some 90 recipes and is available in local and national bookstores. Robert Redford wrote the introduction.

## THE SHED    $$
**113½ East Palace Ave.**
**(505) 982-9030**
The Shed is housed in a part of Sena Plaza, a historic hacienda a block off the Plaza. The small rooms give you a feeling of Santa Fe ambience, and the food will kindle your inner fire. Established in 1954, The Shed's signature dish is red-chile enchiladas, served with a piece of garlic bread. Other specialties include green-chile stew with potatoes and pork and charbroiled "Shedburg-

ers." The homemade desserts are fabulous—save room for the mocha cake. The Shed is open for lunch and dinner daily except Sunday. The same folks run La Choza restaurant, an old hacienda with more room for diners near Railyard Park.

> **i** Alex Maryol, Santa Fe's most popular young blues musician, is the son of the owners of Tomasita's and Tia Sophia's restaurants. He often can be found playing at Cowgirl Hall of Fame Restaurant and Bar.

## TÍA SOPHIA'S    $
**210 West San Francisco St.**
**(505) 983-9880**
Come to Tía Sophia's for breakfast or lunch and experience good, well-priced New Mexican food in an unpretentious atmosphere. You may have a short wait to get seated at one of the old wooden booths or a table. The green-chile stew and daily blue-plate specials are ever popular, and the sopaipillas are some of Santa Fe's best. The servers are good-natured and efficient, and when you're finished you can walk to the Plaza, enjoying the shops and galleries on the way. No alcohol is available. The Maryols also own Tomasita's, (505-983-5721), next to the Santa Fe Southern Railway in the Railyard, probably Santa Fe's most popular New Mexican restaurant. The red and green chile at both restaurants are excellent, the sopaipillas light and tender, and the sangria and margaritas exceptional. No reservations taken at Tomasita's. Open daily.

# PIZZA

## BACK ROAD PIZZA    $
**1807 Second St.**
**(505) 955-9055**
**www.backroadpizza.com**
Located in a mixed-use complex in the increasingly hip Second Street arts district, across from Second Street Brewery, Back Road dishes up good New York-style thin-crust pizza with a Santa Fe twist. This is a great place to mingle with the community with live music, a jukebox, pool tables, courtyard seating, and a balcony. There's

a second location south of town off Highway 14. Open daily until 9 p.m.

**i** Tomasita's, Santa Fe's most popular New Mexican restaurant, purchases 120,000 pounds of chile annually.

### IL VICINO $
**321 West San Francisco St.**
**(505) 986-8700,**
**(505) 820-0524 (order fax)**
**www.ilvicino.com**
When you've had enough chile or too many fancy dinners, the casual, comfortable Il Vicino will fill the bill. Order at the counter, choosing among wood-fired pizzas, salads, soups, calzones, sandwiches, and lasagna. The chicken pizza is a favorite here. You'll have to stand in line to order during busy times; phone or fax in your order to speed pickup if you want pizza to go. You can select a beer—including their own microbrew—or wine from their extensive list. Smoking is allowed on the patio only. This chain has eight locations in the western United States. It is open late.

### PIZZA ETC. $
**De Vargas Center, 151 Paseo de Peralta**
**(505) 986-1500,**
**www.pizzaetc.com**
You might not expect to find gourmet fare in this shopping mall, but chef-owner Roland Richter's eatery is first rate, perfect for a bite before catching a movie at the adjoining theater. Try the special pizzas, like the Greek with feta cheese, Kalamata olives, sun-dried tomatoes, fresh roasted garlic, and fresh cucumbers. Yummy. We like the Pontchartrain, complete with shrimp and andouille sausage and the sweetness of caramelized onions. In addition to the standards, toppings you can add include soy cheese, ground buffalo meat, pine nuts, and shrimp. You'll also find pizza by the slice here. This little place does a good carry-out business and has some tables for din-

ing in. It's open for lunch and dinner daily and is smoke-free. They'll deliver for free within a 2-mile radius, which includes most downtown hotels. Open daily.

### UPPER CRUST PIZZA $
**329 Old Santa Fe Trail**
**(505) 982-0000**
**www.uppercrustpizza.com**
Upper Crust is a Santa Fe tradition. The food is served hot and fresh, and you can order pizza with whole-wheat crust. The Grecian Gourmet, a succulent combination of feta cheese, Kalamata olives, mushrooms, garlic, and other pizza magic, is a good choice. Toppings available include green chile and chorizo, a spicy Mexican sausage. We love the whole-wheat crust. In addition to pizza, Upper Crust serves meallike salads, several sandwiches, and calzones. You can get a glass of wine with your meal or order from their interesting selection of microbrews. In the summer, after you order at the counter, you can eat on the front porch and watch the crowds stroll by. Free delivery.

## STEAKS

### BULL RING $$$$
**150 Washington Ave.**
**(505) 983-3328**
**www.santafebullring.com**
The Bull Ring steak house and lounge is the place to go if you like rubbing elbows with politicians. It's the "other" State Capitol, a second office of sorts for lawmakers when the state legislature is in session. Many New Mexico politicians and lobbyists head to the Bull Ring at the end of the legislative day to hang out, chill out, and sometimes strike political deals. With its leather booths and masculine dark green-and-wood decor, the upscale restaurant and lounge attracts a variety of primarily male professionals, many of whom mingle at the oaken and brass-railed bar until closing at 10:30 or 11 p.m. The Bull Ring serves only USDA prime, corn-fed steaks from Chicago.

## EL NIDO $$$–$$$$

County Rd. 73 at Bishop's Lodge Rd.,
Tesuque
(505) 988-4340
www.nmrestaurants.com/elnido

A former dance hall and trading post, El Nido (The Nest) offers choice aged beef, fresh seafood, and a few local specialties. Only a five-minute drive from the Santa Fe Opera in the village of Tesuque, El Nido is a summer favorite of opera fans. Consistency throughout the years has given El Nido a cadre of loyal customers. The small, lively bar adds to the restaurant's ambience, as does the adobe building, complete with fireplaces. The menu is built on choice aged meat— prime rib, sirloin, lamb chops—plus fresh seafood and some other choices, such as duck breast and a New Mexican green-chile enchilada. You'll also find several nightly specials—braised lamb shanks, perhaps—and some Cajun touches. El Nido is open for dinner every day except Monday. It's 2.5 miles from the US 84/285 Tesuque exit and 7 miles from the Santa Fe Plaza.

## RÍO CHAMA STEAKHOUSE $$$–$$$$

414 Old Santa Fe Trail
(505) 955-0765

Located in a tastefully remodeled and expanded adobe house in the historic Barrio de Analco, Río Chama Steakhouse offers elegant dining and a sumptuous bar in surroundings decorated with world-class art collected by owner/art dealer Gerald Peters, whose gallery is 2 blocks away. As the name suggests, steaks and chops are the featured attraction here, with prime, dry-aged cuts cooked to your order. Seafood and vegetarian items are also on the menu and you can dine in secluded courtyard patios during warm weather. Old-timers will remember this as the original site of The Bull Ring, long popular with legislators because of its proximity to the New Mexico state capitol.

## STEAKSMITH AT EL GANCHO $$$

104 Old Las Vegas Hwy.
1 mile from I–25 exit 387
(505) 988-3333
www.santafesteaksmith.com

This spacious restaurant, a Santa Fe standby since 1973, is well known for its 17 appetizers, including spinach-cheese balls and deep-fried avocado. The bar, with a fireplace and TVs, is a lovely spot to relax. Steaks and seafood are the rule here, and dinners are served with a choice of salads and homemade soup. You can order green chile, piñon chile, or other sauces on the side. For dessert, try the sour cream apple walnut pie or ask if they have the fresh raspberry pie. The Steaksmith is open for dinner every night. The view, which you'll notice from the parking lot, is one of Santa Fe's nicest vistas, and it puts the sparkling lights of the city on display each evening.

# NIGHTLIFE

If you're in search of a nonstop, highly varied nightlife, you'd best catch the next flight to Los Angeles, Miami, or New York. It's not that commercial nighttime entertainment doesn't exist in Santa Fe. In fact The City Different boasts a thriving nightlife. You just have to look a little harder for it than you would in other, larger cities. It's also somewhat limited in scope, especially as evening turns into night and night turns into morning. Except for bars, dance concerts at the two microbreweries, and a handful of cafes, Santa Fe rolls up the sidewalks after 10 p.m. Many bars close at 11:30 or midnight during the week, some even on weekends.

Locals are resourceful, however. They create their own nightlife, much of which consists of meeting friends at favorite restaurants or bars which, like their denizens, have distinct personalities. For those who live to dance, the choices have narrowed in recent years, but you'll find special salsa evenings sometimes advertised, deejayed by local aficionados. Many hotels also offer live entertainment, much of it homegrown—though that by no means rules out the occasional big-name act. Thanks to Santa Fe's magnetic attraction for artists, musicians, and celebrities of all ilk and fame, local talent is excellent and plentiful here.

For detailed information about how to fill your evenings in Santa Fe, check the Pasatiempo, the arts and entertainment supplement of the local daily newspaper, the Santa Fe *New Mexican*, published every Friday. The Albuquerque *Journal* offers nightlife suggestions in "Revue," which comes out on Fridays, and daily in *Journal North*. The free, weekly Santa Fe *Reporter* also contains day-by-day listings of nighttime entertainment in the "Arts and Culture" section.

## LA CASA SENA CANTINA
**Sena Plaza, 125 East Palace Ave.**
**(505) 988-9232**

You're just about to bite into your almond-crusted salmon while your partner is slicing into honey-glazed New Mexico pork loin. Suddenly your waiter breaks into song. It must be La Casa Sena Cantina, a dinner club where the wait staff doubles as musical comedy performers usually after, though sometimes during, your meal. In summer, there are two seatings nightly—at 5:30 p.m. and again at 8 p.m. In winter, one seating a night takes place at 6:30 p.m. The performance begins an hour or so after you arrive, probably about the time you're having dessert and coffee, and lasts approximately one hour. Prior to the show, live piano music plays in the background as you dine on any of a variety of innovative New Mexican and southwestern entrees, which

range in price from $18 to $30 a la carte. There's no additional charge for the entertainment; it's included with your dinner. But do leave some extra cash in the tip bowl for the performers in addition to a gratuity for serving your dinner. They heartily deserve it. La Casa Sena Cantina is open seven nights a week, 364 days a year, closing only on Christmas Day. Walk-ins are welcome, but we strongly recommend you make reservations, especially during the summer and on holidays. For Indian Market weekend (see our Annual Events and Festivals chapter), people often book months in advance.

**i** Santa Fe restaurants and bars that participate in the county's Designated Driver program will provide soft drinks on the house to a table's designated driver. Some establishments even offer the entire table free snacks.

## CATAMOUNT BAR & GRILLE
**125 East Water St.**
**(505) 988-7222**
The Catamount Bar & Grille is a lively stomping ground for the 20- to 30-year-old set who come to dance, dine, and maybe meet the love of their lives in an Irish tavernlike atmosphere. The Catamount features live music on weekends, primarily rock, blues, and jazz, mostly by local talent and occasionally a national band on tour. There's a small cover charge, then it's up to you to find space on the small dance floor. The grill offers standard pub fare, including chicken breast, hamburgers, buffalo wings, and nachos, while the bar bills its margaritas as a specialty and carries locally made microbrews. Upstairs, the billiards room features six 9-foot Brunswick pool tables for rent. The bar is open 11 a.m. to 2 a.m. Monday to Saturday; noon until midnight, Sunday.

## COWGIRL HALL OF FAME BBQ
**319 South Guadalupe St.**
**(505) 982-2565**
**www.cowgirlsantafe.com**
The Cowgirl is Santa Fe's most visible happening spot, no matter what time of day. It combines a reasonably priced restaurant, bar, and mini-museum as well as an entertainment space for music, comedy, and improv theater. The walls and mantels of the front room are filled with all sorts of western knick knacks and memorabilia. The bar itself is a copper-topped half-rectangle made from barn-board planking with some barstools constructed from tractor seats. Resting their boots on the iron footrest are real cowboys, urban cowboys, artists, bankers, cooks, doctors, EMTs, farriers, furriers, good ol' boys, and jus' plain folks. This room also serves as the stage for live music that might be blues, folk, country and western, or rock 'n' roll. You can hear the music in the large dining room in the back whose glittered walls feature dozens of black-and-white archive photos of honorees inducted into the original Cowgirl Hall of Fame. In summertime, musicians play daily on the spacious, attractive front patio from 9 p.m. to 1 a.m. Cowgirl specializes in "deep Southwestern barbecue with a twist," served up by waitresses in full cowgirl regalia. Signature dishes are Texas mesquite-smoked barbecue, although you can find char-grilled fish and veggie offerings here, too, as well as traditional New Mexican chile-based food and a butternut squash casserole. The menu also offers chicken-fried steak, burgers, jerked chicken salad, and other Louisiana specialties. Ranch breakfasts are served on weekends, and include steak and eggs, smoked salmon Benedict, and French toast. In winter, the restaurant opens its Mustang Room—reserved for private parties in the summer—to diners looking for a tonier atmosphere. There's also a billiards room. The Cowgirl is open Monday through Friday 11 a.m. until 2 a.m. (midnight on Sundays); it opens at 8:30 a.m. for breakfast on weekends. No checks.

## EL FAROL
**808 Canyon Rd.**
**(505) 983-9912**
**www.elfarolsf.com**
El Farol consistently runs neck and neck with the Pink Adobe Dragon Room Bar (see entry in this section) as the "friendliest bar" in the Santa Fe Reporter's "Best of Santa Fe." Some people come to drink and socialize, others to listen to music that's as eclectic as the patrons, including blues, country, flamenco, folk, jazz, klezmer, and even belly-dancing acts. The front of the building is framed by an inviting old porch with pillars and vigas and, in summer, spills over with patrons. The inside is dominated by the murals of Alfred Morang, who traded artwork for drinks at La Cantina del Cañon as well as other Santa Fe bars. You'll find well-known artists, actors, and other luminaries drinking with carpenters, secretaries, and CEOs, and all variety of wannabes. The bar is relatively small, but that has never stopped patrons from wearing out the floor from dancing. There's a cover charge for live entertainment. Sunday, Monday, and Tuesday shows are free. Don't miss the flamenco dinner show every Wednesday at 8 p.m. until 10 p.m. Cost is $35 per person, with dinner; $5 for show only. The sounds tend to spill into El Farol's adjacent restaurant, famous for its tapas and Spanish cuisine. El Farol

also has an extensive list of wines, sherries, ports, and brandies from the Iberian Peninsula and elsewhere. The bar is open daily until 2 a.m. except Sunday, when it closes at midnight.

> **i** Too tipsy to drive home from a restaurant or bar? Ask the manager or bartender about Safe Ride Home. He or she will call a taxi to deliver you safely anywhere in Santa Fe County at no charge.

## EL MESÓN AND ¡CHISPA! TAPAS BAR
213 Washington Ave.
(505) 983-6756
www.elmeson-santafe.com
Open for lunch, dinner, and Sunday buffet brunch, chef-owner David Huertas' Spanish restaurant and adjoining tapas bar serves tapas, paella, and a few other entrees. The house special tapas include shrimp in garlic sauce, fried calamari, spicy lamb brochettes, and manchego cheese in olive oil. Ask about the nightly specials, too, such as a wonderful stew of summer squash served with crisp toast for dipping. The saffron-infused Spanish paellas are available with seafood, chicken, sausage, or vegetarian and serve two. On a cold day, try the thick Spanish hot chocolate. And leave a little room for the creamy orange flan. You can get a beer or glass of wine with your meal, and patio seating is available. The restaurant is nicely appointed inside, with lace curtains and solid wooden furniture set off by the light walls. There's a full bar and sometimes live music and tango dancing.

## EVANGELO'S COCKTAIL LOUNGE
200 West San Francisco St.
(505) 982-9014
Evangelo's first opened its doors in 1971 when Evangelo Klonis, a Greek immigrant and American World War II hero, decided to branch out from his restaurant business on the Plaza. Today his son, Nick Klonis, runs the bar. He attributes the popularity of Evangelo's to its being "the only bar left in Santa Fe where you can go have a drink, meet friends, have a good time, and not be pretentious." Only 1 block west of the Plaza, Evangelo's practically owns the corner of West San Francisco and Galisteo Streets, if only because of the volume of its live blues, Latin, and rock 'n' roll blasting out through the open windows. You could almost be on Bourbon Street in New Orleans, so authentic and insistent is the music and the sense of celebration. Weekends at Evangelo's are always a fun, happening time with live rock 'n' roll. A cover is rarely charged. The interior has an odd mixture of Polynesian, Greek, and Santa Fe decor. But it works, lending a unique personality to the bar, which offers 60 different types of beer and has been featured in the *New York Times* and other national dailies as well as in newspapers and magazines in Sweden, Norway, and Japan. Evangelo's is open until 2 a.m. Monday through Saturday and until midnight on Sunday.

## GIG
1808 Second St.
www.gigsantafe.com
GIG is one of Santa Fe's hidden gems for inexpensive live music. It's the brainchild of well-known local jazz guitarist and musical promoter Bruce Dunlap who has been responsible for the Jazz and International Music Festival in the past but now focuses exclusively on promoting informal concerts at this small, friendly venue on Second Street. Dunlap himself performs regularly, along with talented local bands such as world music–influenced Round Mountain, flamenco guitarist Chuscales, and a long list of virtuoso musicians, from Iraqi oud player Rahim Al Haj to Brazilian guitarist Richard Boukas. Tickets at the door.

## LA FIESTA LOUNGE
La Fonda Hotel
100 East San Francisco St.
(505) 982-5511
www.lafondasantafe.com
Located in the lovely Pueblo Revival lobby of Santa Fe's most historic hotel—legend has it that a fonda, or inn, has existed on that same corner since 1610—La Fiesta Lounge is a welcome haven for both the weary and the wired, a place to relax over a beer or a margarita or to dance 'til you drop. Whether you lean toward country

and western, ranchero, swing, blues, or Latin jazz, La Fiesta offers Santa Fe's consistently best live entertainment nightly, usually at no charge. Regular musicians include Bill Hearne, a local country and western singer transplanted from Austin who has achieved national prominence; the Bert Dalton Trio, a jazz outfit; country swing by Syd Masters and the Swing Riders; and blues by Fat Tuesday and Night Train. La Fiesta Lounge is open Monday through Thursday until 11 p.m., Friday and Saturday until midnight; Sunday from noon until 11:30 p.m. A tasty New Mexico buffet is available. From May to October, take time to sip a summer cocktail and view incredible sunsets in La Fonda's outdoor Bell Tower Bar on the hotel's fifth-floor roof.

## DEL CHARRO SALOON
**Inn of the Governors,**
**Alameda St. at Don Gaspar Ave.**
**(505) 982-4333**
Located off the lobby of the Inn of the Governors, one of downtown Santa Fe's best-priced lodgings, a few blocks south of the Plaza, Del Charro is popular among locals, tourists, and hotel guests for its central location and lovely fireside patio, just the place to enjoy one of the saloon's famous margaritas. Its horseshoe bar, copper-topped tables, and southwestern-style decor create a warm ambience enhanced in winter with a crackling fire in a large kiva fireplace, perfect after a day on the slopes, especially with a hot toddy or coffee drink. The bar menu at Del Charro is an astonishing value for a downtown eatery; the average price for the popular Chef Burger, a substantial chef salad, or Tortilla Club is just $6 per item. Del Charro attracts primarily the

**i** You're considered legally drunk in New Mexico if your blood-alcohol level is 0.08 percent or greater for adults. New Mexico is coming down hard on people who drink and drive. Weekend and holiday drivers have a good chance of encountering unannounced police checkpoints, where officers may test a driver's alcohol level if they suspect drunkenness.

over-30 set, including lots of professionals and a fair share of lawmakers during the legislative session. Del Charro is open daily from 11:30 a.m. until midnight.

## MINE SHAFT TAVERN
**2846 Hwy. 14, Madrid**
**(505) 473-0743**
**www.themineshafttavern.com**
The Mine Shaft Tavern in Madrid, about 25 miles south of town off Highway 14, is an authentic tavern in the once-booming coal-mining village of Madrid (pronounced MAA-drid, oddly enough). Madrid turned into a ghost town after it fell on hard times in the 1950s but was reborn in the 1970s, when it began attracting artists who converted many of the old buildings into galleries and shops. New owners bought the tavern in 2007, but it is almost unchanged from when it was built in 1946 by Madrid founder Oscar Huber for his coal miners. The rustic room has a 40-foot lodgepole-pine bar—the longest stand-up bar in New Mexico. The clientele is as eclectic as the decor. You'll find everyone from artists and old hippies to cowboys and Indians, Vietnam vets and yuppies, tourists and commuters, skiers and couch potatoes, and even a few ghosts. Except for the ghosts, they come to drink, to eat what the owners claim is the best burger west of the Mississippi, and to dance to live music on the weekends. Open until 11 p.m. on weeknights and until midnight on weekends.

## THE ORE HOUSE ON THE PLAZA
**40 Lincoln Ave.**
**(505) 983-8687**
**www.orehouseontheplaza.com**
The Ore House restaurant and cantina is popular, not only because of its location but also because of its large, heated balcony overlooking the Plaza. It is one of the locations used for Las Posadas performances, the annual Christmas retelling of the Christ child's birth. The Ore House offers free live music on the weekends. There's no official dance floor, however, customers occasionally annex the balcony for dancing. Cantina patrons can order from a bar menu or from the restaurant's main menu,

which features steak, seafood, and southwestern specialties. If you have a favorite wine, it's a good bet you'll find it among the Ore House's award-winning selection. The bar mixes more than 40 different margaritas with a variety of tequilas. For the connoisseur, the bar serves a $100 shot of tequila, though you'd probably want to drink that one straight. The Ore House closes anywhere from 11 p.m. to 2 a.m., depending on how busy they are.

## PINK ADOBE DRAGON ROOM BAR
406 Old Santa Fe Trail
(505) 983-7712
www.thepinkadobe.com

The atmospheric Dragon Room, the bar portion of the late artist Rosalea Murphy's famous Pink Adobe restaurant, has gained a reputation as one of the best bars in the world. In winter, fires burn in two fireplaces, one each in the front and back rooms, making it a cozy place for a beer or a bourbon. There's still more fire on Christmas Eve when a traditional luminaria (bonfire) burns on the sidewalk in front of the bar for Canyon Road farolito (lantern) viewers and passersby to warm themselves. The lounge features live music until 9 or 10 p.m. While you're listening to the music, glance around the room at the paintings by Rosalea Murphy, who also handpainted the tables. The bar menu includes the famous gypsy stew, a hearty one-dish meal made with chicken, tomatoes, onions, and peppers. Open Monday through Saturday until anywhere between midnight and 2 a.m. and Sunday until midnight. *NOTE:* Parking is limited in the lot behind the bar. We recommend you park in the state office building lot across the street, although that, too gets full when the legislature is in session in January.

## THE PUB AND GRILL AT THE SANTA FE BREWING COMPANY
37 Fire Place (off Highway 14)
(505) 424-9637
www.santafebrewing.com/pubgrill.com

Tour Santa Fe's oldest microbrewery, then stroll next door for a burger and sweet potato fries, a salad, sandwich, followed by homemade apple pie with local Taos Cow ice cream. Fiesta IPA,

Santa Fe Pale Ale, Chicken Killer Barley Wine, and other beers are on tap, and you can sample New Mexican wines. The Pub and Grill is turning into one of Santa Fe's most popular and happening places for nightly live music and let-your-hair-down dancing. The 2009 lineup featured such homegrown acts such as The Gumbo Project and The Heartless Bastards and repeat performances from internationally known The English Beat, Acoustic Alchemy, Gregory Isaacs, and Thomas Mapfumo. Open for breakfast, lunch, and dinner 7 a.m. to 10 p.m. Music nightly.

**i** Until just a few years ago, Santa Fe still had "blue laws" on the books, which banned sales of packaged liquor on Sundays, certain holidays, and Election Day until after the polls closed. Although most of the arcane liquor laws have been taken off the books, the Election Day prohibition still stands. Nor can you buy packaged liquor on Christmas or Thanksgiving, so plan ahead if you're hosting a party or plan to bring wine to one you're attending. With those exceptions, you may buy packaged liquor every day, supermarkets included, between 7 a.m. and midnight Monday through Saturday and noon to midnight on Sunday.

## SECOND STREET BREWERY
1814 Second St.
(505) 982-3030
www.secondstreetbrewery.com

Second Street Brewery is a locally owned brewpub with some of the best beer in Santa Fe. The brewmaster, originally from Oregon, has won numerous awards at the Great American Beer Festival in Denver—the Superbowl of beer festivals in the United States. The food is darned good, too, with such traditional English pub fare as fish and chips (the real thing, served with malt vinegar), shepherd's pie, chicken potpie, and London broil, as well as classic American dishes, including burgers, Philadelphia cheese steaks, Reuben sandwiches, and a number of creative vegetarian offerings. Second Street offers some of the interesting and seductive global music in town, including Alex Maryol blues; Jaka, a marimba band; and Wagogo, fusing Zimbabwean and New Mexican music. The pub is open daily until midnight. The kitchen serves food until 10 p.m.

## THE STAAB HOUSE LOUNGE
La Posada de Santa Fe
330 East Palace Ave.
(505) 986-0000

Locals consider the Staab House Lounge the perfect rendezvous, in part because it's remarkably unpretentious despite its rarefied Victorian decor. Some of the parlors feel like smoking rooms, others like a maiden aunt's sitting room. You'd feel just as comfortable drinking tea as tequila there. The latter is in good supply in the bar, whose centerpiece is a graceful Victorian cherrywood bar with a brass foot rail. La Posada still receives visits from Julia Staab, wife of the original owner of the house, whose presence manifests itself fairly frequently in and around the bar with flying glasses, swinging chandeliers, banging in the lounge bathroom, and even curling smoke by a particular chair, as if someone were sitting there holding a lighted cigarette. The extensive lounge menu features tapas, salads, and sandwiches as well as larger entrees such as steak, shrimp tacos, and veal. Live music Thursday through Saturday. Open daily from 11 a.m. until late.

## SUMMER BANDSTAND SERIES
Santa Fe Plaza
www.outsideinproductions.org

During the summer, some of Santa Fe's most popular and accessible nightlife is on the Plaza—and it's free. Produced by Santa Fe nonprofit Outside In Productions, this community program is partially funded by the City of Santa Fe Arts Commission. People of all ages are welcome to dance under the stars to everything from bluegrass to opera. Performances take place in the gazebo on the Plaza on Monday, Tuesday, Wednesday, and Thursday from 6 to 8:30 p.m. and from noon to 1:30 p.m. on Monday and Wednesday beginning the second week in July and continuing

through the third week in August. The Plaza was refurbished with new stone and landscaping in 2009 and has never been more inviting. We recommend you dine alfresco with a picnic lunch or supper.

## TINY'S RESTAURANT & LOUNGE
1015 Pen Rd.
(505) 983-9817

Located in an unassuming little strip mall that also houses a cafe, a grocery store, and a photo shop, Tiny's isn't merely an old-school dining and drinking establishment, it's an experience—especially in the lounge. As the restaurant nears closing, the lounge takes on a life of its own with an older crowd that really knows how to cut a rug, whether they're listening to country and western or old standards. The atmosphere is, well, kind of bare bones, with bright lighting, Formica tables, a television set over the bar and another above the dance floor. Above the bar are hundreds of novelty decanters that once belonged to Tiny Moore, who opened the restaurant and nightclub in 1950. Tiny's son-in-law, Jimmie Palermo, has been running the restaurant since 1959, but he's kept the restaurant in Tiny's name—and kept the decanters, too—as a tribute to his father-in-law, who died in 1984. Open until 2 a.m. Monday through Saturday. Sunday hours are from 11 a.m. to 6 p.m. You can hear live music Wednesday, Friday, and Saturday nights.

## VANESSIE OF SANTA FE RESTAURANT AND PIANO BAR
434 West San Francisco St.
(505) 982-9966
www.vanessiesantafe.com

Vanessie is a sophisticated, upscale, and surprisingly comfortable place to have a cocktail, whether you're ensconced at the bar watching the bartender mix magic, or sitting around the grand piano singing to timeless standards. New Year's Eve is an elegant gala affair for which people fly in from around the world to listen to music, drink champagne, and dine on Texas-size servings of prime rib. All of Vanessie's classic American cuisine—steak and seafood, salads,

**i** Concerts in Santa Fe are almost all produced by Fan Man Productions. Venues include Paolo Soleri Amphitheater, the Lensic Center for Performing Arts, Santa Fe Brewing Company, and, occasionally, the Santa Fe Opera. You can check Fan Man's Web site at www.fanmanproductions.com for more information or Pasatiempo (see the Santa Fe New Mexican in our Media chapter) for performers, times, and prices.

baked potatoes, its famous onion loaf, cheesecake, etc.—come in obscenely large portions, beautifully presented. The bar keeps a computer file of hundreds of drink recipes, many with creative—and occasionally risqué—names such as a "slippery nipple" made from Bailey's Irish Cream and butterscotch liqueur. Open nightly until 2 a.m., except Sunday and winter weekdays, when it closes at midnight.

# SHOPPING

The most difficult decision about shopping in Santa Fe is where to start. The clusters of stores and the shopping plazas in the downtown area can lure even the most shopping-resistant travelers. The city's unique shops delight visitors and draw return local business. Often located in former homes, many of the specialty shops downtown and on Canyon Road are built around pleasant courtyards with fountains and well-tended gardens. Of course, like Any Town, U.S.A., Santa Fe also has malls, chain stores, a flea market, and outlets to fill all kinds of shopping needs.

In this chapter we describe Santa Fe's main shopping areas, followed by a listing of specialty stores. We couldn't possibly list all of the fine places to shop, but we've done our best to include a representative sample. Santa Fe has such an eclectic and plentiful arts-and-crafts market that we've included those types of stores in their own chapter, Regional Arts, and in the "Visual Arts" section of our The Arts chapter. Retail businesses can change quickly, so don't be shy about checking out a shop or boutique that may have opened since this guide was updated.

Cash, credit cards, and traveler's checks are welcome in most of the area's specialty shops, malls, plazas, boutiques, and shopping centers. Most shops are open from 9 or 10 a.m. until 5 or 6 p.m. Monday through Saturday, and some are open Sunday afternoons.

Santa Fe is a great place to find items you might not be able to buy at home—locally made crafts, chile-based products, or cookbooks that specialize in the cuisine of the region. The city is an active artistic community, and many shops, including those in museums, carry handmade work at affordable prices.

## SHOPPING AREAS

### Downtown/the Plaza

The Plaza sits between San Francisco Street, Old Santa Fe Trail, Palace Avenue, and Lincoln Avenue, and the Downtown area stretches 2 or 3 blocks from the Plaza in all directions. You'll find city-owned parking lots on Water, San Francisco, and Marcy Streets. There's limited on-street parking, and some private lots are available for shoppers.

As the last stop along both El Camino Real and the better-known Santa Fe Trail, the Plaza has been a shopping paradise since the days when wagons unloaded their imported treasures here. If you time your visit right, you can still shop here on days when the city hosts outdoor arts-and-crafts shows or during Spanish or Indian Market (see our Annual Events and Festivals chapter).

The Plaza pulses with activity, especially in the summer, hosting community events of all shapes and sizes, some with parades and music. And the Plaza's shady benches offer an ideal place to take a break while shopping.

The overall tenor of Santa Fe's downtown area is galleries, American Indian goods, and tourist souvenirs such as T-shirts and coffee mugs, but you'll discover an interesting variety of upscale merchandise here. The best place to start your downtown shopping expedition is the Plaza area itself.

If you want American Indian wares, the most intriguing spot for buying is under the *portal* of the **Palace of the Governors on Palace Avenue** (see our Attractions chapter). Here you can purchase directly from the Indian artists. Another first-rate place for Indian merchandise is **Packard's Indian Trading Co.,** on the corner of Old

Santa Fe Trail and San Francisco Street. The sales staff at this long-established business can give you a great education in Indian-made items.

Next to American Indian treasures and souvenirs, clothing stores dominate downtown. You'll find many chic and original clothing stores as well as Santa Fe representatives of national chains. For an idea of the variety, look for casual **Chico's,** 122 West San Francisco St. (and a second location at 328 South Guadalupe St.), and **Mimosa,** at 52 Lincoln Ave., which sells elegant Santa Fe-style clothing.

**Santa Fe Dry Goods,** 53 Old Santa Fe Trail, has been a steady fixture in downtown merchandizing, and features tasteful shoes, scarves, and clothing for men and women. A few nationally known stores usually found in malls add to the downtown. In Lincoln Place, a shopping complex at 130 Lincoln Ave., you'll find **Talbots** for the stylish look and **J.Crew** for the sporty look. If you're in the market for souvenirs, visit **Dressman's Gift Shop,** in Plaza West, just across the Plaza from Packard's. This longtime business is geared for the tourist who wants to take back some inexpensive reminders of Santa Fe. You'll find Indian jewelry, a large selection of T-shirts, and some items you probably weren't expecting.

Just down the street, **Ortega's on the Plaza** has sold fine Indian jewelry since 1975. You may find a pot by the famous San Ildefonso Pueblo potter Mariá Martinez here. Other downtown shops with Indian goods are the **Eagle Dancer, Virginia Trading Post, Pueblo Trading Post.**

As an example of what shopping downtown is all about, let's take an imaginary walk west from the Plaza on West San Francisco Street. You'll pass coffee shops, galleries, small boutiques, and major retail businesses.

You'll find the **Plaza Mercado Shopping Plaza** at 112 West San Francisco St. This complex spans a solid half-block and includes an interesting variety of shops and restaurants arranged over three stories. **Nambé Foundry** has a shop here selling the beautiful, silver-colored metalware they've been designing and manufacturing since 1951. You'll find everything from heavy baking dishes to Christmas ornaments, and you can

also buy seconds. The Mercado complex includes the top-rated **Santa Fe School of Cooking and Market,** with a shop that has all you need to make your own New Mexican recipes. The **White House-Black Market,** 112 West San Francisco St., is an intimate women's shop with sleek dresses, blazers, and slacks all in white or light beige.

Just east of Plaza Mercado, in the old Woolworth's, is **Santa Fe Arcade,** an upmarket mall anchoring the south side of the Plaza. Opened in March 2004, the three-story, Pueblo-style mini-mall is already home to a variety of small art galleries and jewelry stores selling Southwest items.

Just off West San Francisco Street, you'll find **Collected Works Bookstore,** one of Santa Fe's last independent bookstores. Don't forget to say hello to Kitty Carson, the ginger store cat. Nearby is the renovated **Lensic Performing Arts Center,** a lively community-oriented performing arts center offering daily entertainment, from concerts and readings to ballet and opera.

**Origins,** 135 West San Francisco St., feels a little like a folk-art/textile museum, showing dolls, puppets, jewelry, and wearable art from around the world. You'll find clothing from Africa, Pakistan, India, and Thailand as well as creations by local designers. Just walking in makes you feel elegant.

Around the corner, on Don Gaspar Avenue, you'll find more shops, including **Spirit of the Earth,** 108 Don Gaspar, which features jewelry by Tony Malmed, clothing, and collectibles. And don't miss the eclectic **Doodlet's Shop,** 120 Don Gaspar. This longtime local business has wonderful gifts collected from around the world.

More surprises await you the next street over, on Galisteo Street, which runs parallel to Don Gaspar to the west. At 223 Galisteo St. you'll find **Lucille's,** a store packed full of those long flowing skirts you see Santa Fe women wearing, with blouses, vests, jackets, and more to mix and match. **Harry's,** 202 Galisteo St., carries fine men's clothing and shoes as well as some great items for the ladies.

Shady Marcy Street, a block north of the Plaza, has numerous attractions. At 101 West Marcy St., the **Design Warehouse** offers comfortable and affordable home furnishings and kitchenware. At the **Marcy Street Card Shop,** 75 West Marcy St., you can choose from more than 500 postcards and then move on to unusual cards for birthdays, anniversaries, getting well, first communions, retirements, and more. **Gloriana's Fine Crafts,** 55 West Marcy St., delights bead lovers with jars and bags and strands of every shape, size, and color.

For a look at wonderful hand-carved folk-art animals, step into **Davis Mather Folk Art Gallery** on 141 Lincoln Ave. Be cautious: The fanciful wooden snakes beg to go home with you!

## Sena Plaza

Although it's downtown, Sena Plaza (121-135 Palace Ave.; no central phone) deserves a listing all its own because of its special shopping ambience. This former family hacienda, 1 block east of the Plaza on Palace Avenue, offers a variety of shops as well as a first-class restaurant. There is limited complimentary parking available behind the building. It's easy to find Sena Plaza: A photogenic wooden *portal* covers the sidewalk running in front. Originally part of a 1697 land grant, the place still has that old Spanish ambience. The two-story Territorial building was once the gracious home of the Senas, a prominent family. Myriad rooms run under long *portals,* all facing an enclosed, beautifully landscaped patio.

The original adobe rooms now house galleries and specialty shops with a diversity that can keep you browsing for hours. **Goler Fine Imported Shoes** tempts the most sophisticated feet with snazzy shoe styles, and **Taos Mountain Candles De Santa Fe** offers an array of shaped, colored, and scented candles. The cleverly named **Soap Opera** carries a wide range of fragrances, lotions, massage oils, and items for the bath. **Gusterman Silversmiths** shows a fine collection of original affordable jewelry. The long-established women's clothing store **Zephyr** specializes in unique, contemporary fashions.

Tiny **Todos Santos,** one of the top artisan chocolate makers in the country, is a must-see. Owned by an artist from New Orleans, just walking into this colorful shop is enough to lift the

spirits. It's loaded to the vigas with imported sweets, Hayward Simoneaux's antique French molds, and unusual chocolate combinations featuring chile, lavender, and other treats. For a unique gift from Santa Fe, buy a handmade chocolate milagro, or traditional Mexican religious charm, made entirely from dark chocolate and covered in edible gold leaf. The creative packaging is worth the price alone.

**Susan's Christmas Shop** has ornaments from around the world with a nice selection of handmade southwestern items. The shop changes its name to suit the season, with merchandise appropriate to the coming holiday.

> **i** Santa Fe shopping trips can be difficult to end. If you are planning a day out shopping with small children, plan on bringing strollers, backpacks, and plenty of items to entertain.

## Canyon Road

Arty Canyon Road begins just east of Paseo de Peralta and runs roughly parallel to Alameda Street. You can walk from downtown hotels. Historically important and currently quaint, the road began as a trail down from the mountains. People would lead their burros this way into town to sell or trade their wares.

The area teems with Santa Fe charm: thick adobe walls draped with vines, sidewalks shaded from large cottonwood trees, lovely gardens, and a mix of residential and commercial uses—shops, restaurants, and galleries. You can easily spend a day moseying along the road, taking your time, learning how to slow down, southwestern style.

Canyon Road is famous for its galleries. They line the street for blocks and blocks (see our The Arts chapter). Interspersed, you'll discover clothing, jewelry, leather, and other specialty stores. Most of the retail shops cluster near the intersection of Camino del Monte Sol. A walk of just a few blocks on either side of this corner will take you to most of the stores.

**Gypsy Alley,** 708 Canyon Rd., can lure even the most footsore tourist. This once dusty place, now lined with flower beds brimming with color in summer, has been renovated into a row of shops (and of course more galleries).

**Desert Son,** 725 Canyon Rd., has been selling belts, buckles, hats, and silver buttons for more than 30 years. Its custom boots are snazzy to say the least. Wind down a path and find **Canyon Road Pottery,** 821 Canyon Rd., a store filled with handsome glazed and originally designed contemporary pots.

If you can't walk from your hotel to shop Canyon Road, first try parking along the main road and side streets. A few stores have small lots for patrons, and a public lot is available at the intersection of Canyon Road and Camino del Monte Sol across the street from El Farol.

## Guadalupe Street

This shopping area, between Agua Fria and Garfield Street, near the new Railyard Park in the historic warehouse district, is also an easy walk from downtown, and is Santa Fe's most interesting new shopping and eating area.

i Looking for well-made, comfortable shoes that (surprise!) also look good? Walking on Water, 207 West Water St., a locally owned, one-of-a-kind store, specializes in fine shoes for women and men. At this family-operated store you can find clogs, slippers, and shoes from Canada, England, Switzerland, France, and the good ol' U.S.A.

In the 1970s, Guadalupe Street was the place where several counterculture types tried their hand at retail—often selling their own arts and crafts—fitting their shops in among the garages and upholstery shops. Renovation has been extensive, and Guadalupe is now a street of the modern commercial age. You'll find restaurants, vintage clothing stores, a historic church, and a train station. The **Santa Fe Farmers' Market** (see our Attractions chapter) now operates year-round from a beautiful new green-

built warehouse in the newly opened **Railyard Park,** which includes the Southern Railway/New Mexico Road Runner train station, a 10-acre park, live-work lofts, Warehouse 21 Teen Center, SITE Santa Fe contemporary art museum, the Railyard Performance Space, El Museo Cultural Hispanic cultural museum, REI, Flying Star Cafe, and the Ark spiritual bookstore. A multiplex movie theater is due to be built shortly. The renovated **Gross-Kelley Almacen** (grocery), designed by Santa Fe-style architect Isaac Rapp, now houses upscale businesses, including imported furniture stores, Station coffeehouse, and the Santa Fe Railyard Restaurant, under the same ownership as 315 restaurant on Agua Fria.

For a decade, the **Rio Bravo Trading Co.,** 411 South Guadalupe, has specialized in "American Indian and Western relics—collectible cowboy stuff," to use the words of the owner. Saddles, spurs, hats, chaps, Indian jewelry, and Old West posters abound. The shopping compound at the corner of Guadalupe and Montezuma Avenue, 328 South Guadalupe St., has several stores of interest. **Paper Unlimited** offers a rich supply of cards, ribbons, gift boxes, and bags. And be sure to be lured into **Allure,** a high-end lingerie shop with an interesting variety of the feminine and sensuous. Chico's clothing has another outlet here, and the well-appointed windows tempt you inside. It's next door to the **Peruvian Connection,** featuring brightly woven alpaca wool women's clothing. Le Bon Voyage, whose owners advertise themselves as "the Bag Ladies," has a great assortment of travel accessories—portable alarm clocks and coffee warmers and the like in addition to luggage.

Limited metered parking is available along Guadalupe Street. You'll find a parking garage and more metered parking in the new Railyard development. Expect to pay $1/hour. On Saturdays and Sundays, parking is $1 for the whole day.

## Sanbusco Market Center

From Guadalupe Street, **Sanbusco Market Center** (500 Montezuma Ave.; 505-989-9390; www

.sanbusco.com) is just a block to the west, adjoining the railroad tracks. The building that now houses these shops originated in 1882 as part of Santa Fe's warehouse district. Renovation in the 1980s made it a bright addition to Santa Fe's shopping options. Complete with restaurants and a spacious across-the-street parking lot, Sanbusco is home to professional offices, small, upscale shops, and the very popular World Market. You can also get a bite to eat here or nearby at restaurants such as Pranzo and Zia Diner, which share the parking lot.

Boutiques come and go here, but **Bodhi Bazaar** is a long-standing tenant. This women's store offers natural fiber clothing, and the linen and cotton attracts a strong local clientele. Another local favorite is **Teca Tu,** a store for pets. The owner is fond of both cats and dogs, and her array of bowls and brushes, beds, collars, fancy dog blankets, and leashes gives you plenty of choice for your pet. There's also a small collection of books and cards and soft, cuddly stuffed animals and cute dog vests.

**On Your Feet** is *the* store in Santa Fe to shop for good-quality shoes. They carry Wolky, Dansko, Sebago, and other name-brand European footwear. **The Reel Life/Orvis Outfitter** sells fly-fishing supplies, and also offers classes. **Borders Books** anchors the south side of Sanbusco and has become quite a social center, with readings, concerts, and other events in its cafe. It has one of the city's best selections of books, magazines, music, and videos.

## MALLS

While some longtime locals may complain that malls lack Santa Fe style, they have to acknowledge the convenience malls offer. Parking is no problem here, and you'll find specialty shops with Santa Fe style as well as national chains. At all three of Santa Fe's major malls, you can buy New Mexican foods, spices, and other treats as well as American Indian arts to remind you of your Santa Fe vacation. In addition to these, the city has other shopping centers, usually anchored by a grocery store, with auxiliary shops mostly geared toward local business, offering those who live nearby convenience and a chance to chat with their neighbors over the produce.

ℹ️ For unique candy, visit Señor Murphy Candymaker in Santa Fe Place mall and at the La Fonda hotel. The piñon concoctions, including piñon brittle, piñon fudge, and a piñon log, are hard to find outside of Santa Fe. For a special, nonmelting treat, try the red chile peanut brittle or the chile jelly. The candy is made at the Santa Fe factory at 1904 Chamisa St., but the candymaker will gladly ship it for you as long as the weather isn't too hot. Order online at www.senormurphy.com.

## DE VARGAS CENTER MALL
**564 North Guadalupe St.**
**(505) 982-2655**
**www.devargascenter.com**
At the corner of Guadalupe Street and Paseo de Peralta, De Vargas Center is Santa Fe's oldest and most attractive mall. Relatively small at 246,000 square feet and easy to negotiate, at this mall you'll find a post office, movie theaters, a pizza joint, a candy shop, restaurants, antiques stores, pharmacies, shoe stores, jewelry stores, and women's clothing boutiques.

**Las Cosas Kitchen Shoppe** offers top-of-the-line, restaurant-quality cookware and popular cooking classes with Santa Fe chef Jon Vollertson. Opposite, you'll find **Santa Fe Beeswax Candle Company,** featuring lovely locally made beeswax candles in all shapes and sizes and Buddhist and Hindu paraphernalia, from tankas to statues of Quan Yin. **Radio Shack, Ross Dress for Less,** and **Christine's** bridal and tuxedo shop are in the center of the mall, along with **CVS Pharmacy.** You can shop for jewelry at **Zales** or **Chavez Fine Jewelers. Gameco** offers a place for people, mostly teens, to play "Magic" and other games and to buy game cards and supplies. **Hastings** has a wide selection of music, magazines, books, and videos, and a coffee bar. Sunflower Market, a discount natural food market, opened in the mall

SHOPPING

in the summer of 2009. For a sweet treat, head to **Starbucks** or **Baskin Robbins 31 Flavors** ice-cream and yogurt store. On the north end of the mall, you'll find **Albertson's** supermarket, **Java Joe's** coffeehouse, and **Jinja,** one of Santa Fe's most popular new Asian restaurants.

## SANTA FE PREMIUM OUTLETS
**8380 Cerrillos Rd. (at I–25)**
**(505) 474-4000**
This out-of-the-way outlet center offers about 40 factory stores selling a wide variety of name-brand merchandise at a discount. You'll find clothing, shoes, luggage, gifts, and housewares. There are also some purely local shops. The stores all open onto a central outdoor patio and are all on one level. You can get a bite to eat at the cafe here, too.

Some of the name-brand stores are **OshKosh b'Gosh, Brooks Brothers, Jones New York, Eddie Bauer,** and **Liz Claiborne.** The clothing available ranges from casual to professional to conservative for both men and women. Tastefully displayed items make it hard to resist the deals. You'll also find clothing for children.

**Sissel's—Fine Indian Jewelry, Pottery and Kachinas** carries just what the sign says and lots of it. With a sharp eye you can get some good buys. Try **Zales** jewelers for diamonds. The **Peruvian Connection** sells textiles from that South American country.

For home furnishings, among the stores you'll find are **Dansk, Springmaid, Wamsutta,** and **Harry and David.** Looking for shoes? Try on

i Santa Fe is a good place to find Nambé ware—beautiful, practical, and decorative items that have won awards for their design. Made from a metal alloy containing no silver, lead, or pewter, Nambé possesses the beauty of sterling combined with the striking durability of iron. The lustrous alloy does not crack, chip, peel, or tarnish and can retain heat and cold for hours. Nambé has outlets at 924 Paseo de Peralta and 104 West San Francisco St. and a Web site, www.nambe.com.

styles from **Bass, Nine West,** and **Factory Brand Shoes.** Top-quality luggage and leather goods are available at Coach and Samsonite. Santa Fe Chamber of Commerce is located here, too.

## SANTA FE PLACE
**4250 Cerrillos Rd.**
**(505) 473-4253**
**www.shopsantafeplace.com**
With more than 80 shops, this is Santa Fe's largest and most mainstream mall, the place where teens hang with their friends and folks buy their back-to-school clothes. South of town, at the corner of Rodeo and Cerrillos roads, Santa Fe Place is a great central place to get all those normal, necessary things. Of course some fun, unnecessary things can be found here, too. Santa Fe Place has a food court, a reduced-admission movie theater, and a video arcade.

Anchors include **Sears** on the southwest end, **JCPenney** on the east, and **Dillard's** on the north. Between the big department stores, scores of shops offer accessories, jewelry, shoes, sports equipment, software, home furnishings, gifts, and books.

Clothing stores are scattered throughout the mall. You can walk into **Victoria's Secret** and fulfill that slinky fantasy. **Western Warehouse** carries clothing with a cowboy touch for men and women. It's a store to help you dude up with pearl-button vests, jeans, shirts with fringe, fancy skirts, and boots. **Sports Authority** has sports gear and equipment. There are several shoe stores, including **Payless ShoeSource, Lady Foot Locker, Foot Locker,** and **Footaction USA.**

An interesting accessories shop in the mall is **Claire's Boutique,** which carries a delightful array of inexpensive things for the hair and ears. For more jewelry, try **Zales** and **Kay's.**

In the center of the promenade running the length of the mall are booths, carts, and islands, those pagodas that offer everything from seasonal specialties like Christmas ornaments or Halloween costumes to fancy reading glasses, lighters, knives, massage, and specialty foods.

Tuesday Morning has a variety of housewares on sale, including Portmeirion pottery from England. One interesting addition is a store with a Tibetan Buddhist focus called Heart of the Lotus. It specializes in sacred art from bronze Buddhas to painted tankas. The **U.S. Post Office** has a substation in the mall that makes mailing all your packages easy. The **General Nutrition Center,** for all your health needs, sells supplements and supplies. Like malls everywhere, Santa Fe Place also has a food court with a variety of offerings, from Italian to New Mexican. A large parking lot surrounds the entire mall, and security officers are always on duty.

## SPECIALTY SHOPS

Here's a brief introduction to some of Santa Fe's more interesting shops.

### Antiques and Home-Decorator Items

ANTIQUE WAREHOUSE
**530 South Guadalupe St.**
**#B at the Railyard**
**(505) 984-1159**
**www.antiquewarehouse-santafe.com**
This store's name isn't trendy. It really is a warehouse in Santa Fe's original warehouse district. You'll find more than 600 sets of doors and shutters, along with gates and windows from Mexico. Telephone inquiries are welcome, but it's fun to come and look. It's closed on Sunday.

ARTESANOS IMPORTS CO.
**1414 Maclovia St.**
**(505) 471-8020**
**www.artesanos.com**
Mexican imports are the specialty in this store, which recently closed its downtown retail store and moved operations to the second location, off Cerrillos Road. Artesanos has lights, tile, glass, and pottery items, some stored in a large outdoor lot. You'll find genuine pigskin equipale furniture as well as hundreds of types of tile for the floor, bath, or countertop. Artesanos says it is the largest distributor of Mexican tile in the United States. It's closed on Sunday.

EL PASO IMPORT COMPANY
**Design Center, 418 Cerrillos Rd.**
**(505) 982-5698**
**www.elpasoimportco.com**
This business has been around many years, carrying an extensive selection of old and new furniture shipped in from Mexico. Tables, wardrobes, bed frames, and other large items are a specialty.

JACKALOPE POTTERY
**2820 Cerrillos Rd.**
**(505) 471-8539**
**www.jackalope.com**
You can spend hours here poking around and looking at all the imported pots, figurines, weavings, clothing, and decorations. Jackalope's international collection of goodies occupies several large buildings, including one that looks like an old church. "Folk art by the truckload" is their motto! You may find music on the patio in the summer and you can get a bite to eat at the Jackalope cafe. There's a small zoo and prairie dog town for the kids. This company, which began in Santa Fe in 1975, has several other outlets and a catalog business.

SOUTHWEST SPANISH CRAFTSMAN
**328 South Guadalupe St.**
**(505) 982-1767**
**www.southwestspanishcraftsmen.com**
In business since 1927, this store specializes in heavy southwestern carved chairs, tables, beds, and sofas. The look that characterizes the selection is one of carefully constructed solidity. You'll also find southwestern tinwork here. It's closed on Sunday.

STEPHEN'S, A CONSIGNMENT GALLERY
**2701 Cerrillos Rd.**
**(505) 471-0802**
**www.stephensconsignment.com**
One of the best places to buy used furniture, Stephen's includes antiques and art among its treasures. The large store is packed with all sorts of items, from mirrors and dressers to knick knacks of every type imaginable. They also will appraise and buy either single items or estates.

## The Santa Fe Look— Women's Apparel

The following list of shops, by no means complete, provides a few places where you can find the items you might need to complete your Santa Fe look—broomstick skirts, concho belts, boots, velvet or satin blouses, and turquoise jewelry. Also included are some places that sell wearable art. If your favorite isn't here, just let us know, and we'll try to include it the next time.

### BACK AT THE RANCH
**209 East Marcy St.**
**(505) 989-8110**
**www.backattheranch.com**
Satisfy your passion for unique cowboy boots at this downtown store. In business 13 years, this shop carries beautiful handmade boots by Rocketbusters, Stallion, and Lucheesi. If you don't see a design that grabs you, you can order custom-made boots to express your own style. You can also find "Santa Kleese" Christmas boots (they're really stockings) by Rocketbusters, in a variety of designs. Our favorites are Day of the Dead and the Virgin of Guadalupe.

**i** Seattle-based membership cooperative REI is the flagship store in the new warehouse-style Railyard Park trackside development in the historic Guadalupe District of Sante Fe. Now aficionados of this popular outdoor store no longer have to trek to Albuquerque to buy tents, hiking boots, and other gear.

### HOP A LONG BOOT COMPANY
**3908 Rodeo Rd.**
**just west of Richards Ave.**
**(505) 471-5570**
This place, off the beaten track and out of the high-rent district, bills itself as "A First-Class Second-Hand" Western Shop—where you'll find "broken-in" cowboy boots, vintage clothing, and collectibles. Hop A Long has something for cowgirls and cowboys of all ages. Look for the big purple double gates with the rabbit mural; you

can't miss it! Open 10 a.m. to 4 p.m., Monday through Saturday.

### LUCILLE'S
**223 Galisteo St.**
**(505) 983-6331**
A front-porch sale rack welcomes shoppers here. Lucille's specializes in Santa Fe style and its creative variations, with plenty of flowing skirts, dresses, silk T-shirts, blouses, and tops. Natural fibers are the rule, with merchandise imported from India and elsewhere. Shoppers like the ranges of styles, colors, and sizes—including clothing that looks great on full-figured women. Lucille's also has a tempting collection of earrings and fanciful necklaces from Africa and India. The shop carries sweaters all year long.

### MAYA CLOTHING—SACRED ART
**108 Galisteo St.**
**(505) 989-7590**
If you're shopping for something different, the fashions hanging outside this downtown store are sure to catch your eye. Indoors, you'll discover two stories packed with folk art and fashion. In addition to easy-to-wear blouses, pants, skirts, dresses, and vests imported from around the world, you'll find all sorts of jewelry, belts, and hats. This eclectic shop also offers international folk art, including carvings from India, milagros—charms from Latin America that are said to aid in healing—and a wonderful assortment of Day of the Dead figures from Mexico.

### ORIGINS
**135 West San Francisco St.**
**(505) 988-2323**
**www.originssantafe.com**
This is one of those stores that compels you to go inside—even if there's absolutely nothing you think you need. For starters, the windows skillfully combine art and marketing, displaying the clothing and accessories in combination with folk art for eye-catching results. Among the plentiful merchandise are creations especially designed for this shop, wearable art by local and world-renowned artists from elsewhere in the United

States and Europe. Evening wear and the more casual fashions include styles and sizes that look great on every woman, not just the size twos. The jewelry, including 18- and 24-karat gold, and objects from around the world will demand your attention. Watch for sales!

## PURPLE SAGE
**110 Don Gaspar Ave.**
**(505) 984-0600**
**www.purplesage-santafe.com**
Handwoven clothing is a specialty here, and you'll find styles from Santa Fe chic to elegant silks. Ask about the sueded rayons, designed and handmade by a local fabric artist. Be sure to take a look at the nice assortment of handbags. Contemporary handwoven jackets and shawls in rayon chenille are Purple Sage's trademarks. Another is the colorful handblown glass that makes this store not just another fashion shop. More than 35 glassblowers show their wares, including many perfume bottles, platters, and vases. You'll also find gift items along with an impressive assortment of kaleidoscopes. For non-shoppers, Purple Sage has couches, magazines, TV, and candy. Can't decide? Take home a catalog for phone orders.

**i** Shopping for folk art? Don't overlook the Tesuque Flea Market, situated just north of the Santa Fe Opera off US 84/285. Adventurous importers travel the world in the winter buying up collectibles and then sell their wares at the flea market on summer weekends.

## SIGN OF THE PAMPERED MAIDEN
**205 East Water St.**
**(505) 982-5948**
In business since 1968, this tasteful women's clothing and accessory store moved away from downtown briefly but has recently returned to the other side of Water Street. It specializes in what the owner aptly describes as comfortable, beautiful clothing you can wear every day. You'll find her inventory on the romantic side, with plenty of velvet, lace, and silk. Granddaughters,

moms, and grandmothers can shop together here—and each take home something they'll like. In addition to clothing, this downtown shop also offers a variety of accessories to complement the fashions.

## SPIRIT OF THE EARTH
**108 Don Gaspar Ave.**
**(505) 988-9558**
**www.spiritoftheearth.com**
Spirit of the Earth sells clothing that could be described as wearable art and jewelry by designer Tony Malmed in gold with precious stones and festive opals. Malmed's bracelets, rings, necklaces, earrings, and the like are one-of-a-kind pieces, which means if you like it and it fits your budget, take it home because you'll never find it again. The fashions are soft and sensual in cut velvets, lace, and sueded rayons with a feminine flowing look. You'll find an abundance of color and luscious tactile fabrics. The sales staff knows how to be helpful without being pushy and are happy to help you make the right choice to complement your figure and coloring.

# BARGAIN SHOPPING
## ACT 2
**839 Paseo de Peralta, Suite A**
**(505) 983-8585**
At Act 2 you'll discover vintage and modern clothing, jewelry, and accessories. You might have to hunt for this shop—it's slightly off the beaten path—but it's worth the search. A consignment business, Act 2 has great clearance sales.

## DOUBLE TAKE
**320 Aztec St.**
**(505) 989-8886**
This popular consignment shop, just off Guadalupe Street, labels itself as "eclectic," with styles for men, women, and children. The items are carefully chosen and well displayed—you don't have to wade through junk. The management mixes a few new items with the old, and the layout makes going through the racks exciting. You'll also find shoes and other accessories. Next door, Double

Take at the Ranch features classic cowboy clothes and other western items, Encore at Double Take has upscale consignment clothing, and Double Take Hacienda upstairs has furniture and home accessories. Colored-label discounts daily.

## HOSPICE CENTER THRIFT STORE
1303 Cerrillos Rd.
(505) 995-9901

Santa Fe Hospice Center originally established its thrift store as a fund-raising/community service program in 1993. The store's bright, big space features clothing, furniture, artwork, housewares, appliances, and more. You find all sorts of second-hand treasures—some of the nicest things you'll see in the recycled world. Items for sale have been appraised, so you know you're getting your money's worth. The funds raised help the nonprofit Hospice Center continue its highly respected work with the terminally ill and their families.

## OPEN HANDS THRIFT STORE
851 West San Mateo Rd. and
1836 Cerrillos Rd.
(505) 986-1077

Open Hands' two well-stocked stores (one is next to El Rey Inn on Cerrillos, the other is a stone's throw from Yoga Source and Chocolate Maven in the Second Street arts district) have lots of choices in clothing and household goods at good prices. The donations and sales receipts go for an important and worthy cause—operation of adult day care, wheelchair loans, and other programs for the elderly.

## PUEBLO OF TESUQUE FLEA MARKET
US 84/285
7 miles north of Santa Fe
(505) 995-8626

This huge flea market sits on 12 acres of Tesuque Pueblo land northwest of Santa Fe, right next to the Santa Fe Opera, in one of those wonderful Santa Fe juxtapositions. Connoisseurs say this is one of the best markets of its kind around. You'll find whole sections of antiques; imports from Africa, Bali, South and Central America; vintage

and handmade clothing; and more. Depending on the season, you might be able to take home watermelons, apples from northern New Mexico orchards, or fresh flowers. You'll see tables by commercial dealers who specialize in Indian jewelry, rainsticks, or collectible fishing tackle, as well as neighbors who've pooled their junk and brought it here rather than having a yard sale. Nonprofit agencies rent space to sell donated treasures and raise a few bucks. It's easy to spend hours and money as you amble among the stalls. If you get hungry or thirsty, you can buy what you need from the concession stand. Parking and admission are free. *NOTE:* Be careful arriving and leaving, as US 285 traffic is fast and heavy here. Open weekends 8 a.m. to 5 p.m. April to October.

## ST. VINCENT DE PAUL LA TIENDITA
1088 Early St.
(505) 988-4308

At this granddaddy of an operation, you'll find racks and racks of goodies, all at low prices. Operated by a Catholic auxiliary, money raised through this business benefits Santa Fe's poor.

## ST. VINCENT DE PAWS BARKIN' BOUTIQUE
1107 Pen Rd.
(505) 986-0699

"It's all going to the dogs . . . and the cats, too," is the slogan of this resale clothing store benefiting Española Animal Shelter, just off Cordova Road. For anyone with Champagne clothing tastes on a lemonade budget, not only is this cleverly named store a wonderful find but every dollar you spend here benefits one of the area's best no-kill animal shelters. Barkin' Boutique offers a large and changing selection of donated preworn women's designer clothing. Brands commonly found here are Chico's, Ann Taylor, Banana Republic, Eddie Bauer, Ann Klein, and Ralph Lauren, among others. Also on sale is a wide variety of unique home accessories, antiques, books, artwork, and vintage clothing; some of the best pieces are auctioned on eBay. Colored-label discounts are offered daily. The shelter also runs the Española Thrift Store.

# YARD SALES

Santa Fe residents love their yard sales. If you read the *New Mexican* any weekend during the summer, you're likely to find scores of yard sales, estate sales, multifamily sales, garage sales—junk and treasure recycling opportunities by any name you can think of. Clothing, toys, furniture, books, treats, and necessities for baby, exercise bikes, antiques, plants, knick knacks, and all those things you don't know how you managed to live without await you. Saturday is the big sale day, but some folks extend to buyers the opportunity to visit Sunday as well.

**i** **If you run out of shopping opportunities in Santa Fe, Taos is only 65 miles away. If you travel from Santa Fe to Taos in the summer or fall, you'll notice roadside produce vendors selling farm-grown fruits and vegetables from the backs of their trucks or fruit stands. Stop and see what's for sale. You might find ristras (bunches of chiles strung together), honey, apples, and other treats.**

The best selection goes to those who arrive early, but please respect the "no early birds" advisory. Real bargains can come to those who shop late, waiting until the seller would rather make a sweet deal than repack his or her items to save them for another sale or donate them to Salvation Army or Open Hands. While May through September is Santa Fe's prime yard sale season, you'll find a sprinkling of sales sooner and later in the year, depending on the weather. Take small bills and change; the seller will smile at you. Be sure to poke through boxes and bags—while families tend to display their best stuff, taste varies. And if you see something you like that you think is overpriced, make an offer. If the seller refuses, you can leave your phone number for him or her to call later if the item hasn't sold.

# BOOKSTORES—NEW BOOKS

## ARK BOOKS
**133 Romero St.**
**(505) 988-3709**
**www.arkbooks.com**
Ark Books is a mainstay for esoteric and New Age books and tapes, but the store has a good selection of material on self-improvement, anthropology, cultural studies, women's issues, and more. You'll find nice jewelry and stones as well as drums and tarot cards. Authors sometimes come here to speak and sign. The Ark, operating out of a converted home in a largely residential area, opened in 1980, survived a fire, and came back bigger than ever. It has now been absorbed into the new Railyard Park in the Guadalupe Historic District and has a bit more visibility.

## BORDERS BOOKS & MORE
**500 Montezuma in the Sanbusco Center**
**(505) 954-4707**
Like its sister stores, this Borders offers a lot of everything. You'll find a selection of fiction and nonfiction of the Southwest. You'll also find bilingual selections (English and Spanish predominate) and an assortment of periodicals. The store hosts a variety of special events, author talks and signings, weekend programs for children, and evenings with local musicians. You can get coffee and snacks in the cafe. There's a second branch on Zafarano, off Cerrillos, on the south side of town.

## THE COLLECTED WORKS BOOKSTORE
**202 Galisteo St.**
**(505) 988-4226**
On June 1, 2009, this downtown Santa Fe literary landmark moved from its original location on West San Francisco Street to a larger 4,000-square-foot building around the corner. Supporters helped owner Dorothy Massey move the books by forming a chain round the block and passing them hand to hand. The new location will allow for the expansion of several book

categories and additional space for hosting its popular author readings, fund-raisers and book clubs, and possibly serving food and coffee. The store is strong in its southwestern and Indian sections as well as nature, travel, and children's books and is a popular browsing spot before concerts at the nearby Lensic theater. The staff is great with special orders and will ship your books.

### GARCIA STREET BOOKS
**376 Garcia St.**
**(505) 986-0151**

This locally owned and operated bookstore has a wide variety of books, particularly art and literature, and a great computer system that helps you find what you need. Book people work here, and they can answer your questions and recommend titles. The store is an easy stroll from Canyon Road, next to Downtown Subscription Cafe. Garcia often hosts autograph parties and has discount items out front. You'll also find them selling books in the lobby during author readings at the Lensic.

### HORIZONS—THE DISCOVERY STORE
**328 South Guadalupe St.**
**(505) 983-1554**

Peruse an outstanding collection of nature books for children and adults in this science store. You'll find guidebooks galore, along with a nice assortment of globes, atlases, binoculars, and gifts for children and adults with an interest in the natural world around them.

### LA FONDA NEWSSTAND
**La Fonda Hotel**
**100 East San Francisco St.**
**(505) 988-1404**

How do they pack so much interesting stuff into such a small space? Especially designed for tourists, La Fonda has a collection of southwestern fiction and nonfiction books covering the most often requested titles as well as folk art and other interesting collectibles. You'll also discover some unusual magazines as well as old favorites.

### ST. JOHN'S COLLEGE BOOKSTORE
**1160 Camino de la Cruz Blanca**
**(505) 984-6056**
**www.stjohnscollege.edu**

This store is a wonderful place to browse. As one would expect from a college that focuses on the "great books," you'll discover an excellent selection of the classics here as well as mainstream titles and more experimental literary offerings. While you're here, take a look at St. John's College's attractive campus or go for a hike on the steep but scenic Atalaya Trail into the foothills.

### TRAVEL BUG
**839 Paseo de Peralta**
**(505) 992-0418**
**www.mapsofnewmexico.com**

This excellent little specialty bookstore has Santa Fe's best selection of travel books, maps, guides, and travel journals, and the complete USGS map series for New Mexico and Colorado. The store also has all the topographic maps of New Mexico on CD-ROM. Travel Bug regularly schedules slide shows and talks by travel writers and photographers, usually Saturdays at 5 p.m. The store serves espresso bar, teas, cold drinks, and light snacks. The helpful staff can assist you in trip planning. Look for the flags of several nations and the carving of the Patron Saint of Espresso.

## BOOKS—USED, RARE, AND HARD TO FIND

### BLUE MOON BOOKS AND VINTAGE VIDEO
**329 Garfield St.**
**(505) 982-3035**

In an old house turned bookstore, Blue Moon's books and rooms seem to go on and on—it's easy to lose yourself in the stacks. Not only will you find your way out again, but you'll also discover a great selection of videos to rent or buy, and a staff that knows the inventory. Spiritual traditions of the East and West, books on the occult, and books about film are among their specialties.

## BOOK MOUNTAIN
Used Paperback Exchange
2101 Cerrillos Rd.
(505) 471-2625

This one-room space is crammed with paperbacks of all kinds, including some books you probably never heard of. You'll find a good selection of mysteries and romances as well as best sellers, Westerns, and even comic books. You can pick up some inexpensive vacation reading and trade them in for something else when you're done. Closed Sundays.

**i** Lavender thrives in the semiarid, sandy soil of northern New Mexico, and it has become a cash crop for many specialty farmers. Look for it at the farmers' market and the flea market in such forms as sachets, lotions, soaps, and even fudge.

## BOOKS AND MORE BOOKS
1341 Cerrillos Rd.
(505) 983-5438

A well-stocked, well-organized bookstore, Books and More Books offers pre-owned treasures in categories ranging from art to science. You can browse to your heart's content or ask the owners, a poet and his wife, for their recommendations on a specific topic.

## NICHOLAS POTTER BOOKSELLER
211 East Palace Ave.
(505) 983-5434
www.tibetan-mastiffs.com

Proprietor and owner Potter has made use of all the available space—and then some—to the delight of his established customers and newcomers who might chance on the store. A selective and savvy book dealer, Potter has been in the book business for more than 40 years. Located in an old house on historic Palace Avenue, the store is inviting—a great place to spend a quiet afternoon.

# SPECIALTY FOODS AND HEALTH PRODUCTS

Santa Fe is fortunate to have several natural foods stores, Whole Foods Market, Wild Oats, Vitamin Cottage, and Sunflower Market, the newest of the crop, which is due to open in De Vargas Mall in the summer of 2009, with a second location due to open on Zafarano on the south side in 2010. **Whole Foods Market** (753 Cerrillos Rd., 505-992-1700) is one of the largest national retailers of organic foods and its friendly, well-trained staff make shopping here a real pleasure. It has liquor, including some hard-to-find microbrewed beers, as well as produce, meats, non-animal-tested cosmetics and skin-care items, and bulk foods. After a remodel, it now has expanded deli options, including espresso, pizza, sandwich, sushi, soup, hot entree, and salad bars. You'll also find vitamins, hair products, dairy products and dairy alternatives, fresh flowers, gift items, and chair massage booths. Wine tasting, food samples, and special food-fair tastings are a feature of Whole Foods. **Wild Oats** (1090 St. Francis Dr., 505-983-5333), which was bought by Whole Foods Market recently and may eventually be closed, is a smaller, quieter version of Whole Foods that many locals prefer. Colorado-based **Vitamin Cottage** (3328 Cerrillos Rd., 505-474-0111) is the only natural foods supermarket to serve the South Side right now. It's set up warehouse-style with bright lights and little ambience, but it runs monthly specials that are frequently the cheapest natural-food, vitamin, and bulk buys in town, making it worth the effort to schlep to that end of town. **Sunflower Market,** founded by the original owner of Wild Oats, already has a popular store in Albuquerque. Its slogan is "Serious Food—Silly Prices." It generally occupies the middle ground between "whole-paycheck" Whole Foods and specialty discount gourmet grocer Trader Joe's. It is particularly strong in well-priced organic produce and carryout food sections. Like the other natural foods stores, it frequently hosts workshops on various aspects of health and nutrition and offers a health newsletter. Also check out the following local and specialty stores.

## HERBS ETC.
**1345 Cerrillos Rd.**
**(505) 982-1265**

Jars of dried leaves, stems, and flowers cover the shelves at Herbs Etc. You can find tinctures, oils, and infusions as well as herbs packed in capsules just like Tylenol. The people who work here can answer health questions from an alternative health-care perspective.

## KAUNE FOOD TOWN
**511 Old Santa Fe Trail**
**(505) 982-2629**

This is a great place for the gourmet shopper and is within walking distance for Canyon Road and Old Santa Fe Trail shoppers. You'll find out-of-the-ordinary sauces and mustards and imported crackers and caviar to spread on them. Kaune's carries jars and cans of everything you need to fix that unique Asian, Italian, or otherwise one-of-a-kind meal. This locally owned grocery is packed with the unusual and exotic, but you can also buy milk, eggs, and, if you must, sliced white bread. It carries a fine selection of fresh meat and welcomes holiday orders.

## LA MONTANITA CO-OP MARKETPLACE GROCERY
**627 West Alameda St. in the Solana Center**
**(505) 984-3852**
**www.lamontanita.coop**

Santa Fe's oldest health-food store, La Montanita Co-op Marketplace Grocery, was purchased from the longtime owner by La Montanita Co-op in Albuquerque in January 2005. In 2008, it completed a major remodel that expanded the square footage of the store and made it much more inviting. It added a branch of New Mexico Educators Credit Union, the only one in Santa Fe, a massage booth, a flower stand, and increased space to eat in. Although by far the most expensive of the natural food stores, due to its mission to purchase from local farmers whenever possible, the coop offers weekly specials and the option to become a member for greater discounts. The laid-back staff offers good personal service. This is a popular neighborhood place to eat lunch. The expanded deli features two daily soups; fresh local Aroma coffee; natural meat and vegetarian sandwiches, entrees, and salads; and a good selection of pastries from Chocolate Maven and Sage Bakehouse. The meat and fish department and cheese counter are very good and the staff is very knowledgeable.

## TRADER JOE'S
**530 West Cordova Rd.**
**(505) 995-8145**

It took 10 years of begging by Santa Feans who had shopped at its stores in California, Arizona, and elsewhere, but finally Trader Joe's Grocery came to Santa Fe in August 2004, and things haven't been the same since. The California-based discount gourmet grocery, known for carefully selected prepared foods, a large discount wine and liquor section, and natural personal items has been a hit from Day One. The store has taken a big bite out of the business of other markets, with inexpensive natural and organic proprietary products, such as salads, juices, dips, international cheeses, teas, coffees, meats, dairy products, snacks, and frozen entrees. The locally baked breads and pastries are from Sage Bakehouse and Chocolate Maven (with Trader Joe's own label on them) and are less expensive here. The famous "Two Buck Chuck" Charles Shaw wine is a roaring deal, even at the slightly more pricey $3. TJ's own label vitamins are also an excellent buy. With the arrival of Trader Joe's, other grocers have refined their own strategies: a win-win for them and for Santa Fe.

# REGIONAL ARTS

In addition to its deserved reputation as one of the best cities in the nation to buy fine art, Santa Fe also offers a host of wonderful places to purchase work by American Indian and Hispanic artists. There are many ways to approach this kind of shopping, and they're all fun.

Some visitors spend time learning as much as they can about such things as traditional Indian jewelry, pottery, kachinas, baskets, and weaving. Others, fascinated by the city's Spanish heritage, gravitate toward the Hispanic santos, tinwork, and straw inlay. These savvy shoppers try to find out who are the best among the modern practitioners of these indigenous crafts and then search Santa Fe's shops for their work.

Other shoppers just follow their eyes to bracelets, earrings, bolo ties, pots of all sizes, shapes, and design, and masterful handwoven rugs. They discover a wealth of other American Indian arts and Hispanic treasures.

Whatever method you pick, you'll find that Santa Fe offers dozens of attractive options. There's no problem finding beautiful shops that sell first-quality Indian-made items; places to buy traditional Hispanic arts are harder to come by but worth the search.

## OVERVIEW

Among the best places to shop for American Indian items is the Native American Vendors Program beneath the portal of the Palace of the Governors, 107 West Palace Ave., and the shop operated by the Museum of New Mexico Foundation inside—where you may also find some Hispanic art. You can see and buy interesting Indian jewelry, pottery, and weavings as well as a fine selection of books at the shop at the Museum of Indian Arts and Culture, 710 Camino Lejo. The shops at the Institute of American Indian Arts Museum, 108 Cathedral Place, and the Wheelwright Museum, 704 Camino Lejo, also offer authentic handmade Indian items. You'll find Hispanic arts and crafts and other interesting items at the shops at the Museum of International Folk Art (MOIFA) and at El Rancho de las Golondrinas a few miles out of town in La Cienega. MOIFA expanded its book selections with a lobby and shop renovation several years ago. A percentage of the sales at all these interesting little stores benefits the respective museums. The knowledgeable staff knows about the artists

and their works. (See our Attractions and The Arts chapters for more about these museums.)

If your timing is right, you'll enjoy shopping at Indian Market in August or at the Spanish Market and the International Folk Art Market and the Eight Northern Pueblos Arts and Crafts Show in July (see our Annual Events and Festivals chapter). At any of these shows, you can get an education while you make a purchase. Ask the artists about their work; the more you understand, the more you'll appreciate these long-standing traditional art forms.

You can see excellent examples of early New Mexican Spanish arts at the Museum of International Folk Art. Indian arts and artifacts are exhibited and explained at the Museum of Indian Arts and Culture and elsewhere. (See our Attractions chapter.) Scholars have written shelves full of books about Indian arts and crafts—their origins, the interconnectedness of themes and materials, the evolution of certain designs, family heritage in various arts, use of native or commercial materials, innovation in design, and much more. Although less has been written on the traditional Spanish colonial art forms, there are several fine published sources of information available. Our purpose in this chapter is to provide a basic overview of the local artistic styles and forms to help visitors encountering them for the first time.

# AMERICAN INDIAN ART

## Jewelry

Much of the jewelry you'll see for sale in Santa Fe comes from the surrounding pueblos, including Santo Domingo, San Felipe, Cochití, and San Juan. You'll also find work by Navajo and Hopi artists. The Navajo learned to work silver from Mexican silversmiths in the second half of the 19th century. The concho belt, named after the Spanish word for shell, is among their best-known designs. The belts are a collection of silver discs (today's version of the silver coins that Navajos shipped off to pay for things), sometimes with inset stones, connected on a leather belt.

Authentic American Indian jewelry is crafted by hand and is usually one of a kind. The jeweler normally begins with metal. While silver is the most common metal used, you'll also see American Indians working in gold.

i Be alert for fake turquoise, which has recently flooded the market. All vendors in the vendors market at the Palace of Governors must guarantee that they are using authentic materials and that family members are making the pieces.

Jewelers create through cutting, shaping, hammering, soldering, texturing, stamping, roller printing, and embossing metal. Stamping involves using a steel tool to press a decoration into the surfaces of metal. Casting is a metalsmithing method that gives the jewelry both surface texture and shape. Molten metal is poured into a mold and hardened to make a jewelry form. Jewelers use both tufa casting, which employs porous rock made of volcanic ash, and the lost-wax method to make their creations.

During an early exploration of Chaco Canyon's Pueblo Bonito—one of the world's most extensive American Indian ruins—workers found 56,000 pieces of turquoise, mostly beads and pendants. The turquoise found at Chaco came from the mines in Cerrillos just outside Santa Fe. The Pueblo Indians mined turquoise long before the Spanish arrived. They used the stone as currency, as a valuable trade item, in sacred ceremonies, and in all sorts of jewelry. Because New Mexico's native supplies of turquoise were largely depleted in the 1980s, most jewelers now get their stones from traders who buy it in Arizona, Colorado, Nevada, or even China. Turquoise comes in a variety of colors, from intense blue to pale green.

But you'll find more than turquoise in Indian jewelry. During your exploration of Santa Fe, you're likely to see Indian jewelry made with lapis, diamonds, rubies, ironwood, opal, jet, and about any other stone you can think of.

In addition to setting them in metal, jewelers may use turquoise, coral, and shell as the basis for lapidary work, shaping the raw materials into beads, some so delicate they seem fragile. Beads may be formed and smoothed using a hand drill; other jewelers tool them on machines. Indian jewelers also incorporate stones, coral, and shell for inlay work, setting a decorative pattern of various colors into a base of silver or other material.

Silver overlay, a technique developed in the 1940s, is a distinctive southwestern procedure used by the Hopi people of Arizona and other American Indians. The jeweler cuts a design into a sheet of silver, then places the design over a solid layer of silver. The jeweler then solders the pieces together and allows oxidation to darken the bottom layer that shows through to make the design more pronounced.

Here are a few tips for jewelry shopping:

Look at the craftsmanship. Check to see that the edges are smooth and the stones securely fastened, that the stamp work is deep, sharp, and even, and that the finish is consistent.

Try on the bracelet, necklace, or bolo before you buy it. Make sure it's comfortable to wear and of the appropriate size and weight for you. Look at it in a mirror; get a friend to give you an opinion.

Ask about the materials and techniques the jeweler used.

Fine jewelry will have the stamp or signature of its creator.

ℹ️ Interested in American Indian jewelry? The Indian Arts and Crafts Association offers buying tips: Look for the artists' hallmark stamped on jewelry. If you're considering silver, look for a stamp that says "sterling." Ask the seller to certify that the item was Indian made. By law, a member of a state or federally recognized tribe or an artist who is tribally certified must create any item sold as such. Genuine handmade Indian jewelry is often expensive. If the price seems too good to be true, it probably is.

## Pottery

A generation ago it was easy to tell where a potter came from because the pottery from one pueblo differed sometimes markedly from another in color and design. Today the definitions are less rigid, but pueblo potters still follow their ancestors' traditions in the type of clay they use, the symbols incorporated in the design, and in many other ways. But each potter also is an individual, and the final work reflects this artist's creativity, inspiration, and even sense of humor.

Picurís, Isleta, and Taos Pueblos specialize in micaceous ware. They make it using local clay that has bits of mica in it, which gives the finished pots a lovely sparkle. Potters may add relief bands, handles, and lids. They commonly make large jars and pots, along with animal figures. These tribes also make storytellers—ceramic figurines that feature a central character such as a grandmother covered with smaller characters, like grandchildren, listening to a story. These pueblos also make undecorated ceramics.

Ácoma, Cochití, Laguna, Santo Domingo, Santa Ana, and Ziá pueblos traditionally make white- or buff-slipped vessels with black- and brick-colored motifs, usually with a reddish-brown base. Larger, earth-tone vessels are also popular. Their design elements may include stylized rain, lightning and clouds, humans and animals as well as crosshatching and geometric patterns. Ácoma is famous for its black-on-white fine-line pots. You'll find storytellers and animal figurines there as well as at Cochití.

Nambé, Pojoaque, San Ildefonso, San Juan, Santa Clara, and Tesuque traditionally make black or red polished jars, wedding vases—tall pots with two spouts—water and storage jars, nativity scenes, and bowls. They carve, etch, or paint the finished pot, which tends to be black, red, or a combination of both colors. These pueblos also make some micaceous ware. Tesuque is also beginning to revive its painted rain god figurines, popular with tourists in the early 1900s.

Jémez, a pueblo in the Jémez Mountains between Santa Fe and Albuquerque, is known for buff- or red-slipped wares with buff, white, or red designs. Storytellers, clowns, and animal figures are among the pueblo's specialties.

Hopi pottery, made by the Pueblo people of the Arizona mesa land, tends to be warm amber colored with designs that include stylized birds, kiva steps, and rain symbols.

Zuni Pueblo traditionally makes large bowls and jars with brownish, black, and red designs painted on a white or buff slip. The rain bird, plants, and animals form the basic designs. Owl effigies and designs created by adding clay relief figures to the surface of the vessel are also common.

Although best known for their weaving and jewelry, the Navajo also make some pottery. It tends to be dark with a shiny piñon pitch finish and is usually unpainted.

ℹ️ Several regional publishers publish books on New Mexico arts and crafts. Some of the best are Museum of New Mexico Press, University of New Mexico Press, School of American Research Press, and Northland Publishing, in Flagstaff, Arizona.

Just like jewelers, potters approach their craft with tremendous variation and innovation within their tribal tradition. You'll find vessels inlaid with turquoise, exquisite miniatures, and carved

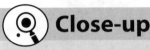 **Close-up**

## Contemporary Art in Santa Fe

If it's been a while since you've taken a good look at the Santa Fe art scene, chances are you'll find that it holds some surprises. As Michael Carroll, president of the Santa Fe Gallery Association, points out, as recently as 1990 only about 10 percent of the city's galleries represented contemporary artists. Today, contemporary art galleries make up fully half of the association's membership.

Of course, Santa Fe has been a haven for "modern" artists since the early years of the 20th century, when such artists as John Sloan, a leading figure in New York's Ashcan school of painting, came to town and inspired other artists such as Santa Fe's legendary Cinco Pintores to bring an array of Modernist and experimental elements into their work. At the same time, as an exhibit entitled "Women Artists of Santa Fe" at West Texas A&M University's Panhandle-Plains Historical Museum revealed, dozens of women painters and sculptors joined the city's burgeoning art colony and "were far bolder and more avant-garde than their male counterparts."

Yet the present boom in Santa Fe's contemporary art scene is unprecedented. It has been brought about by several cultural and market factors. Its seeds can probably be traced back to the 1970s, when Abstract Expressionist turned postmodernist painter Fritz Scholder taught at the Institute of American Indian Arts (IAIA). Scholder is credited with introducing modern art into the school curriculum and inspiring the first generation of Native American contemporary artists. Among the IAIA graduates Scholder taught were such now-famous names as Dan Naminga, Doug Hyde, and T. C. Cannon. The acceptance of their work in Santa Fe galleries both paved the way for more daring works by non-Indians and attracted collectors whose interest focused on modern art, which in turn opened the door to more contemporary galleries.

Topping the list of "third-generation" modern Indian artists, Apache painter Darren Vigil Gray was mentored by the now-legendary T. C. Cannon. A creator of nonliteral portraits and surrealistic "dreamscapes," Gray speaks for many Native American artists when he says, "As a modern Indian and a modern painter my greatest challenge is to straddle the two worlds in

and etched pots. Indian artists make all sorts of animals and figures and decorate their work, large and small, with everything from geometric designs to kachina figures to acrobats. Traditional Pueblo artists fire their pots in shallow pits. After they place the pots inside and cover them with wood bark and animal dung, they ignite the fuels, and the vessels smolder. Some set the pottery on a metal crate atop stones or old cans rather than in a fire pit. Fire clouds, or dark spots on the surface, are a result of these firing methods. In traditional firings as much as 25 percent of the pottery can break. Other potters use kiln firing, a sometimes controversial innovation, which reduces the breakage but also changes the finish of the pot.

### Basketry

Archaeologists have found evidence that Indians were making baskets as early as 9,000 B.C. Baskets traditionally had many functions, and the variety of the modern craft reflects this heritage. Tribes with strong hunter-gatherer roots, such as the Apache, Navajo, and Southern Paiute, are particularly renowned for their baskets.

Indians coiled or twined large cylindrical baskets for carrying food and fuel. They used broad, shallow trays to help winnow seeds. Basket bowls of many depths and shapes were used for food preparation and eating. Large, lidded baskets stored food; open baskets were used for washing corn. Baskets covered with piñon pitch waterproofed the vessel for water use and boiling water by placing hot stones inside. Tribes also which I exist . . . keeping one foot in the modern world, without compromising the elements of the natural world that feed and nurture my spirit."

Hispanic artists and artisans in Santa Fe have also felt the pull of postmodernism on traditional art forms. The city's twice-a-year Spanish Markets originated as a showplace for old-fashioned crafts like tinwork, *santo* carving, and wool weaving that remain alive in the small villages to the north. But each year more of the market is taken up by a separate Contemporary Spanish Market featuring painting, sculpture, photography, and abstract wood carving and wrought-iron work.

Nicholas Herrera, who lives beyond the outskirts of the city in the small village of his birth, typifies the new breed of contemporary Hispanic artist. His paintings, done on slabs of wood using natural pigments—the materials that have been used by northern New Mexico artisans for centuries to make religious *retablos* or religious paintings—often use familiar Catholic imagery for humorous or satirical effect. Herrera points out that not long ago most folk art was anonymous, but today the heirs to traditional craft skills are developing their own unique styles, and their work is being accepted into fine-arts museums on its own merits.

Museums, such as the Georgia O'Keeffe Museum and especially SITE Santa Fe, have undoubtedly played a key role in both inspiring local avante-garde artists and attracting modern art collectors to Santa Fe. Charles Stainback, former director of SITE Santa Fe, knows that "contemporary" art means more than that the artist is still alive. He was quoted in a Santa Fe *New Mexican* article as saying: "Contemporary art can be perplexing, but at the same time it can be quite wonderful. It does take patience . . . When you're in the first grade, you weren't reading Kafka, you were reading Dick and Jane."

Translation: It's looking at modern art that makes both modern artists and modern art buyers. Today, whether you're gallery hopping or just driving along Paseo de Peralta past dozens of large outdoor sculptures, Santa Fe provides plenty of opportunities to feast your eyes on contemporary art.

made basket cradles to carry their babies. Other baskets had special ceremonial uses.

Baskets can be woven from many different materials, but American Indian baskets are usually crafted from plant stems, either whole or split. The materials produce an interesting range of natural color, and some basketmakers also use dyes, both commercial and vegetable, to enhance their work. Basketmakers use three basic techniques to make their art: twining, plaiting, and coiling. Because of the hundreds of hours involved in creating the basket—a good one can take five months—a beautiful, well-made piece will demand a high price.

Among the Pueblo people, the Hopi are the best-known basketmakers, with different colors and designs reflecting the artistry of each village.

Flat plaques and shallow bowls as well as deep containers characterize this work. The coiling is done from right to left. The Hopi also make some plaited wicker baskets. The design may include kachina or spirit figures, traditional abstractions, or birds.

The Jicarilla Apaches, whose reservation is in northern New Mexico near Chama, have been known for their superbly crafted baskets for centuries. The term *jicarilla* means finely made baskets. Their cylindrical and hamper-shaped baskets, which they tend to decorate with geometric forms, catch collectors' eyes and get top dollar.

Navajo basketmaking underwent a renaissance in the 1970s, with more practitioners taking up the craft and more commercial-quality baskets created. Navajo baskets come in many sizes and shapes in both new, original designs and in the historic tradition. The most famous of their baskets—The Navajo Wedding Basket—is made by both Navajo and Southern Paiute artisans, many of whom live on the Shonto Plateau of northern Arizona and the Four Corners region.

## Weaving

While most people think "Navajo" when they think of American Indian weaving, the Pueblo people, including the Hopi of Arizona, also create fine textiles. Early evidence of pueblo weaving dates from turkey feather and fur blankets and from items of clothing made from the native cotton that grew in the Río Grande Valley and in irrigated fields in Arizona. An early account of the Spanish encounters with the Hopi mentions their cotton dresses.

The arrival of the Spanish meant the arrival of sheep's wool, looms, and a new approach to an old craft. By the 18th century, wool weaving was an established pueblo tradition. When commercial cloth became available with the opening of the Santa Fe Trail, the pueblos near Santa Fe de-emphasized weaving, but in the more isolated Hopi country the tradition continued. The Hopi helped supply the woven articles other pueblo people needed.

Pueblo men traditionally are the weavers, although women also weave. Handwoven tunics and belts are used in pueblo dances and also sold commercially.

When the Navajo people migrated into the Southwest from northwest Canada, they learned weaving from the agricultural Pueblo Indians. The Navajo soon became sheepherders, a livelihood ideally adapted to their seminomadic way of life. They transferred the skills they had acquired with cotton to the working and weaving of wool. By 1800 they were masters of the craft and had moved away from the pueblo tradition to create their own patterns and designs. They made blankets, sashes, and even bridles for their horses. Weavers created items for their family's own use and for trade. The Navajo weavers, who were usu-ally women, dyed the wool with natural dyes as well as chemicals. Their work utilized traditional designs and colors, creating textile styles that were influential in the development of weaving in the American Southwest.

Navajo weaving became widespread in popularity following the arrival of such important traders as Lorenzo Hubbell to the newly created Navajo Reservation after 1868. Hubbell, C. N. Cotton, and others worked with the Navajo to create more marketable heavy rugs for markets back East opened up by the arrival of the railroad in 1880 and hotelier Fred Harvey.

By the early 20th century, Navajo weaving had become so famous and important that museums were collecting samples and working with weavers to ensure quality work. Designs are traditionally associated with different areas of the reservation and range from geometric patterns of all styles to depiction of Navajo figures or Yeis, to pictorial weaving, which might have trains, trucks, or whatever else catches the weaver's fancy. There are no machine-made Navajo or pueblo weavings—all the work is done by hand on an upright loom that holds spiritual significance for the weaver.

## Kachinas

Ceremonially costumed carved figurines known as kachinas were originally an element used in the Pueblo peoples' complex and private religion. They are most common among the Hopi people and are also known as *katsinas*. For the Hopi, kachinas are sacred religious objects modeled after tribal deities. They were traditionally carved by Hopi men to give to women or children to remind them of what the deities looked like during the time of year when no ceremonies are performed. Traditionally children were encouraged to believe that the kachina spirits themselves made the dolls.

The kachinas offer a way to represent forces outside human control, to maintain the balance between the natural world and human world. They help the people learn about a hierarchy of power and responsibility but are not similar to Christian icons.

Kachinas come in a range of forms, colors, costumes, and attitudes. Some represent creation and life; death and war; lightning and storms; stars and planets; water and air; mountain peaks; the important foods of corn, squash, and beans; other tribes; and animals, birds, and insects. There may be various depictions of the same kachina. Carvers generally craft kachinas from cottonwood roots and dress them with feathers, animal hides, and handwoven fabric.

The oldest dolls were simple, with painted faces and uncomplicated bodies. Hopi and Zuni kachinas were known for the most figurative detail. Earliest kachinas hung on walls, but after World War II, collectors sought figures that showed more action, and the carvers responded with kachinas that could stand on flat surfaces. Kachina art has become a source of income for tribal artists as the market for the carvings has grown among collectors. Hopi work can be recognized by its meticulous attention to detail. The figures have passed from religious icons to fine art.

Each kachina is unique; buyers should make sure they know who the artist is and that the work is guaranteed as Indian-made and made by hand. The name of the artist and the kachina should be on the piece. In buying kachinas, look for an active stance and graceful positioning of the body, attention to details in the carving, and skilled use of paint and costuming. The price, as with all American Indian art, depends on the age and quality of the piece and the renown of the artist.

Although they were not part of the Navajo tradition, the Navajos make "kachinas" today. The Navajo carvings, which some collectors and dealers prefer to call dolls, are inspired by traditional and contemporary Pueblo kachinas but, because they are do not have religious significance to the Navajo artist, may include colors, costumes, or poses that are particular to the individual artist. The Navajo work tends to be less expensive than the Hopi, and of poorer quality.

## Pricing

As you shop for jewelry, pottery, textiles, baskets, kachinas, and other American Indian arts and crafts, you'll probably notice a tremendous variety of prices. Some of the differences may be due to the quality of materials used, the artist's skill in design, or the artist's reputation and popularity. If a piece seems too inexpensive to be authentic, ask where it came from and how it was made. Likewise, if the price seems excessive, ask why. A reputable dealer or legitimate artist will be delighted to tell you.

**The nonprofit Spanish Colonial Arts Society, the group that presents the Traditional Spanish Market, maintains one of the largest and most comprehensive collections of Spanish colonial art in the world. The society's long-held goal of having a facility in which to display its 2,500-item collection became a reality in July 2002, when its 4,600-square-foot Spanish Colonial Arts Museum opened.**

## TRADITIONAL SPANISH ART

Although not as well known as American Indian art forms, the northern New Mexico Hispanic tradition of handmade items, many of them religious, has a special place in Santa Fe.

In the centuries before New Mexico became part of the United States, the settlers here had to use their own resourcefulness and creativity to produce what they needed for daily life. In addition to useful items, this included images of Jesus and the saints to be used on household altars. The traditions of wood carving, straw inlay, embroidery, and weaving that were brought from Spain and Mexico grew into a unique indigenous art form. The Museum of International Folk Art has one of the most important collections of Spanish colonial art, with pieces dating from the late 1700s to the present.

Among the Spanish colonial arts you may find in Santa Fe or elsewhere in northern New Mexico are religious figures carved from wood or painted on wooden panels; loom weavings from hand-spun, vegetable-dyed yarn; decorative and utilitarian furniture usually made from pine; and wheat-straw and corn-husk appliqué, applied to wood in intricate designs. Other artists work in metal: tin that they have cut, punched, and worked into useful and/or decorative objects; forged iron used for tools and household objects; and gold and silver filigree jewelry.

**i** You'll find wonderful handmade American Indian and Hispanic arts in many of the museum shops. Not only are you assured of quality here, part of your shopping dollar goes to support the museums. The Museum of New Mexico has a consolidated shopping Web site for your convenience: www.shopmuseum.com.

As you shop for traditional northern New Mexican Spanish items, you may come across these terms:

*Bulto:* A statue or three-dimensional image of a saint

*Colcha:* A distinctive embroidery style

*Reredos:* An altar screen. (This is actually a French term—in Spanish they were called retablo mayor for the main screen and retablo collateral for the side screens.)

*Retablo:* A painting of a saint on a wooden panel

*Santo:* A saint image

A final word of advice: Follow your heart. If you love it and can afford it, buy it. If you don't, someone else probably will and chances are you may never see its likes again. These are unique folk-art items.

Santa Fe has dozens of wonderful commercial shops in addition to the nonprofit museum shops mentioned in the introduction to this chapter. The following selection, which also includes places to buy Hispanic arts and crafts, is provided for your convenience. Unless otherwise noted, these places accept credit cards. Most shops are open from 9 or 10 a.m. until 5 or 6 p.m. Monday through Saturday. Some may be open on Sunday, especially during the summer.

# SHOPPING GUIDE

## ANDREA FISHER FINE POTTERY
100 West San Francisco St.
(505) 986-1234
www.andreafisherpottery.com

This classy shop specializes in just one thing: southwestern Indian pottery. You'll see fine examples from New Mexico's pueblos, including historic work by María Martínez, and exquisite work by contemporary potters. Fisher arranges her contemporary and historic pieces by area. They're also grouped according to age and then by families, sometimes showing seven generations of pots by one family. The owner says a visit is an educational experience—we wish education was always this much fun!

## THE CLAY ANGEL
125 Lincoln Ave.
(505) 988-4800

This downtown shop presents work by New Mexico Hispanic artists, along with imports from around the world. You'll find aspen, pine, and cottonwood bultos, painted retablos, and altar screens by Anita Romero-Jones. Just a short walk from the Plaza, the store specializes in ceramics, glassware, and flatware, but you'll find a variety of other fine crafts here, too.

**i** The popular Santa Fe International Folk Art Market was born from a small folk art exhibition, "Focus Folk Art," at The Clay Angel pottery store in Santa Fe in 2003. Clay Angel owner Judith Espinar and Museum of New Mexico Foundation Executive Director Tom Aageson believed the exhibit's success would translate to a larger, community-based folk art event. It is now one of Santa Fe's best-attended festivals.

## DAVIS MATHER FOLK ART GALLERY
141 Lincoln Ave.
(505) 983-1660
www.santafefolkartgallery.com

This tiny gallery is packed full of wonderful animal wood carvings by New Mexican Hispanic artists and American Indians from instate and elsewhere. Among the craftspeople featured are Josefina Aguilar, Ron Rodriguez, Paul Lutonsky, David Alvarez, Doreen Herbert, and Joe Ortega. The gallery has been in business since 1975 and is open daily.

## HELEN HARDIN ESTATE/SILVER SUN
656 Canyon Rd.
(505) 983-0553

Santa Clara Pueblo artist Helen Hardin, who died in 1984, left a wonderful legacy of artwork, which is featured in this gallery, along with the sculpture of Gerard Tsonakwa and delicate Ácoma and Mata Ortíz pottery from near historic Casas Grandes in Chihuahua, Mexico. You'll also find Indian jewelry at a wide range of prices. The shop's jewelry specialty is high-quality, natural American turquoise stones in custom-designed silver and gold settings, created by their own Navajo silversmiths. It also sells pottery by Jacquie Stevens, rugs, fetishes, and carvings.

## KESHI—THE ZUNI CONNECTION
Santa Fe Village Mall
227 Don Gaspar
(505) 989-8728

This shop, originally started by Zuni Indians, has been in business for decades and is a direct outlet for the Zuni Pueblo. You'll find Zuni jewelry exclusively and the largest collection of authentic Zuni fetishes in the Santa Fe area. The prices are good and the staff can answer your questions. They're open seven days a week.

## KIVA CONTEMPORARY GALLERY
El Centro Mall
102 East Water St.
(505) 820-7413
www.kivaindianart.com

This shop may be off the beaten path, but it's well worth the visit. In business for near 20 years, it specializes in contemporary Native American art, including sculpture, paintings, textiles, pottery, and kachinas. Some of their many artists include C. S. Tarpley, Yellowman, Benjamin Nelson, and David K. John. You'll also find a display of old

studio art from 1930 to about 1960, along with vintage rugs and jewelry.

## LA FONDA INDIAN SHOP AND GALLERY
La Fonda Hotel
100 East San Francisco St.
(505) 988-2488
www.lafonda.com

This gallery features fine art by American Indians from throughout the Southwest. La Fonda acquires private estates and collections on a consignment basis. You may find beautiful etched miniature pots or Indian jewelry made from gold and opals as well as silver and turquoise.

## MONTEZ GALLERY
125 East Palace Ave., # 33
(505) 982-1828
www.montezsantafe.com

Traditional-style arts and crafts by New Mexico's leading Hispanic artists are on display in this gallery, including both contemporary and antique items. The owner, from a family of *santeros* himself, knows his business. You'll find wood carvings of the saints, tin work, santos, and other lovely and unusual items. The shop is in Sena Plaza near the northwest corner.

## MORNING STAR GALLERY, LTD.
513 Canyon Rd.
(505) 982-8187
www.morningstargallery.com

Morning Star promotes itself as the largest gallery in the country devoted exclusively to antique Native American art. The gallery occupies an old Canyon Road hacienda. The inventory includes a variety of material from the major cultural areas of North America. The emphasis is on Plains beadwork, quill work, ledger drawings, and parfleche, southwestern pottery, baskets, textiles, and jewelry.

## ORTEGA'S ON THE PLAZA
101 West San Francisco St.
(505) 988-1866.

Ortega's sells fine Indian jewelry from all the pueblos. You'll also find Pendleton blankets, old

Navajo rugs, baskets, and even a pot by the famous San Ildefonso Pueblo potter María Martínez. The merchandise is beautifully presented, and the staff is knowledgeable. The gallery is open seven days a week.

## PACKARD'S ON THE PLAZA
61 Old Santa Fe Trail
(505) 983-9241
www.packards-santafe.com
On the Plaza since 1920, Packard's offers the finest Native American art and crafts, including exquisite jewelry, katsinas (also known as kachinas), weavings, pottery, evening bags, and gift items. To learn more about katsinas, attend one of their popular one-hour educational seminars at noon each Tuesday during the summer. Packard's is open daily.

## THE RAINBOW MAN
107 East Palace Ave.
(505) 982-8706
www.therainbowman.com
At The Rainbow Man you'll find works by regional Hispanic and Navajo folk artists, including some of the people who show at Santa Fe's annual Spanish and International Folk Art Markets. Don't miss the wood carvings with nice touches of fantasy. The shop also has an interesting selection of early Chimayó and Río Grande Weavings, as well as an extensive collection of Native American arts and crafts—including miniature kachinas. All the way to the back of the shop you'll find an enormous selection of historic Edward Curtis photographs of American Indians. The store is open daily.

## RELICS OF THE OLD WEST
402 Old Santa Fe Trail
(505) 989-7663
In business since 1959, this shop carries top-quality antique American Indian art and sells baskets, rugs, and other items to collectors and museums. You'll find exceptional Two Grey Hills weavings

from Toadlena Trading Post on the Navajo Reservation. It also carries Spanish colonial items as well as Egyptian, Greek, and Roman treasures.

## ROBERT F. NICHOLS GALLERY
Contemporary Clay
419 Canyon Rd.
(505) 982-2145
www.robertnicholsgallery.com
Open nearly 30 years on Canyon Road, this gallery's primary emphasis is contemporary work in clay by Native American artists of the American Southwest. Artists represented are Diego Romero, Les Namingha, Bill Glass, Nathan Begay, and the Ortíz family. This is a destination for established collectors, with a broad enough price range to include those just starting out.

## SHERWOOD'S SPIRIT OF AMERICA
1005 Paseo de Peralta
(505) 988-1776
www.sherwoodsspirit.com
Located next to the Pueblo Mission Revival-style Gerald Peters Gallery, in a beautifully restored hacienda once occupied by archaeologist Adolph Bandelier, this purveyor of antique American Indian arts and crafts is well worth a look. Tribes represented include Lakota and non-Southwest groups as well as regional artists. Open 10 a.m. to 6 p.m. Monday through Saturday.

## SUN COUNTRY TRADERS
123 East Water St.
(505) 982-0467
www.suncountrysantafe.com
Open since 1979, this lovely shop offers a beautiful selection of Native American jewelry and is well known for its large display of Taos drums as well as drums from the Cochití and Santo Domingo Pueblos, and even some from the Sioux tribe. Look for the bright yellow awning at the east end of Water Street.

# ATTRACTIONS

W e're the first to admit it. Santa Fe thrives on its contradictions, and one of the most basic is this: Why is it that a town that prides itself on its mañana attitude offers more things to do than a place three or four times its size? Don't worry if Santa Fe's many options to spend your time seem overwhelming—they are!

The diversity of attractions here, coupled with the community's natural beauty, bring visitors back year after year. Between 1.2 and 1.4 million visitors come to Santa Fe annually.

As you explore Santa Fe, you'll find many superlatives: the biggest adobe office building, the oldest bell, the largest sculpture garden in New Mexico, the largest collection of contemporary American Indian art, the only museum dedicated to a woman artist of international stature . . . and that's just for starters.

Santa Fe offers so much that if you're making your first trip, we recommend that you take a city tour. You can take walking tours of all sorts, ride an open-air tram, or climb aboard a big bus. A few hours with a well-trained guide will not only give you a better appreciation for the tremendous historic and cultural riches you'll find here, but it can also help you avoid spending any of your precious vacation time getting lost or searching for a parking place. Attractions are divided into logical categories: churches, museums, historic buildings and districts, other attractions, tours, and visitor information.

In addition to information here, please see our Kidstuff chapter for information on family-friendly museums in Albuquerque and Los Alamos. Parks and national forests near Santa Fe are covered in the Parks and Recreation chapter. Special events at listed attractions are listed by month in the Calendar of Events chapter.

We've done our best to include up-to-the-minute information about hours and admission fees of the attractions we list, but if you're on a limited budget or a tight schedule, please call to see if anything has changed since our book was published.

## Price Code

The following price code is based on the cost for general admission for one adult. Most sites offer considerably discounted tickets for seniors and children, and some allow discounts or even free entry for employees, members of the military, and certain organizations.

| | |
|---|---|
| $ | $5 and under |
| $$ | $6 to $15 |
| $$$ | $16 to $30 |
| $$$$ | $31 and up |

## HISTORIC BUILDINGS

### LAMY BUILDING
(State of New Mexico
Santa Fe Welcome Center)
491 Old Santa Fe Trail
(505) 827-7336
vcenter@state.nm.us

Visitors who stop here for information are literally stepping into history. Named after Archbishop Jean Lamy, the building was erected in 1878 as part of St. Michael's College, the oldest private school in New Mexico. (See our Education and Child Care chapter.) With its tower, portico, galleries, veranda, and mansard roof, the building is typical of many 19th-century New Mexico buildings, most of which have now disappeared. In 1926 fire almost completely destroyed it, but the students saved the day by forming a fire brigade. The visitor center is open from 8 a.m. to 5 p.m. daily with very few exceptions, but your best view of the building is from outside.

ℹ️ Santa Fe's many historic districts and neighborhoods contain more than 100 individual sites that are recognized on the National Register of Historic Places and the State Register of Cultural Properties. As you explore these areas, you may notice plaques installed by the Historic Santa Fe Foundation. The foundation has selected more than 50 Santa Fe buildings the group judges to be worthy of preservation. Most of these structures are included in the New Mexico State Register of Cultural Properties.

## NEW MEXICO STATE CAPITOL
Paseo Peralta at Old Santa Fe Trail
(505) 986-4589
www.legis.state.nm.us (legislature)

The New Mexico State Capitol, nicknamed the Roundhouse for its circular shape, was built in 1966 and remodeled at a cost of $34 million in 1992. The architectural design comes from the Ziá Pueblo sun sign or circle of life, the same symbol you'll notice on New Mexico's red-and-yellow state flag. The current capitol is New Mexico's fourth, following the Palace of the Governors and a downtown building constructed in 1887 and reconstructed in 1890 after it burned.

The capitol has four levels, three above ground. In the basement (not open to the public) are the House and Senate chambers. The second floor, at ground level, contains a visitor information office and the rotunda, where visitors find changing art exhibits. The floor of the rotunda displays the state seal. All of the semiprecious stones decorating the seal and the marble of the surrounding walls and floor were mined in New Mexico. Old photographs of past legislators line the walls of the third-floor House and Senate galleries, the area where visitors may watch laws

being made. During the legislative sessions—the 30-day financial session and 60-day general session in alternating years—the Roundhouse is filled with students on field trips, lobbyists, and interested residents who come to observe their elected representatives in action. The legislature convenes beginning at noon on the second Tuesday in January.

On the fourth floor, the Governor's Gallery features art by New Mexicans in exhibits that rotate often. Walls elsewhere in the building display paintings, photographs, weaving, and mixed-media work by some of New Mexico's best-known artists. On the capitol grounds, you'll find monumental sculptures by Allan Houser, Glenna Goodacre, and others. Docents offer free guided tours by appointment; call (505) 986-4589. The capitol is open from 7 a.m. to 6 p.m. Monday through Friday.

## EL ZAGUAN
545 Canyon Rd.
(505) 983-2567 (Historic Santa Fe Foundation)
www.historicsantafe.org

This long, rambling Territorial-style hacienda, with its lovely garden, was named El Zaguan, "the passageway," because of the long hall running from the patio to the garden. Early floor plans show two patios, a central patio that served as the entry from the street with larger, more formal rooms opening onto it, and an east patio, which was the center of household activities. The house, today with 14 rooms, once had 24 rooms, including a chapel, a "chocolate room," and a library that once housed the largest collection of books in the Territory. The property was bought by Adolph Bandelier—the anthropologist for whom Bandelier National Monument is named—in 1890. It was converted to apartments in the 1920s by two artist sisters. In 1962, preservationists purchased the property, and today one of its apartments is an office shared by the Historic Santa Fe Foundation and the Old Santa Fe Association. El Zaguan remains a thriving artist community, with six small low-cost apartments available for rent by artists and writers annually. The Historic Santa Fe office is open 9 a.m. to noon and 1:30 to 5 p.m., Monday through Friday; the garden, which may be rented for events, is open Monday through Saturday, 9 a.m. to 5 p.m. Admission is free.

## HISTORIC CHURCHES

### ARCHBISHOP LAMY'S CHAPEL
Bishop's Lodge Resort
1292 Bishop's Lodge Rd. North
(505) 983-6377
www.bishopslodge.com

Santa Fe's remarkable Archbishop Jean Baptiste Lamy prayed in this lovely little chapel that he built as a retreat beginning in the late 1860s. The building, about 5 miles north of the Plaza on Bishop's Lodge Road, reflects both European and traditional Hispanic New Mexico architectural styles. The walls are adobe, but the spire looks like something from New England. In addition to his role as religious leader and promoter of education (see our Education and Child Care chapter), Lamy attempted to transform Santa Fe from an adobe village to a more European-looking city. He contracted stone masons and artisans from France and Italy who, in 1869, began to build the St. Francis Cathedral. He also guided the construction of Loretto Chapel. Today the Bishop's chapel is surrounded by Bishop's Lodge Resort. The chapel is open during daylight hours free of charge. Visitors can arrange for weddings, baptisms, and other religious ceremonies in the chapel.

### THE CATHEDRAL BASILICA OF ST. FRANCIS OF ASSISI
213 Cathedral Place
(505) 982-5619
www.cbsfa.org

Constructed from New Mexico sandstone, St. Francis Cathedral was the first church between Durango, Mexico, and St. Louis, Missouri, to be designated a cathedral, built directly over an earlier church on the same site. Archbishop Jean Lamy supervised its construction in 1869, recruiting artisans from Europe and working on the plans himself. Lamy died before the workers fin-

ished. (He is buried beneath the cathedral's altar.) The cathedral's Romanesque-style stained glass imported from Clermont, France, and never-finished dual bell towers stand in sharp contrast to New Mexico's simple adobe churches. The exterior was completed in 1884, but work went on inside for many years after that. The builders erected Corinthian columns leading to a ribbed vaulted ceiling. Frosted glass chandeliers illuminate the sanctuary. The windows depict the 12 apostles; today, painted stations of the cross

## La Conquistadora

In a small chapel—all that remains of the original church on this site—the Basilica Cathedral of St. Francis in Santa Fe shelters a religious icon greatly revered by New Mexico's Hispanic Catholics and others who treasure the state's religious history. This small wooden statue of the Virgin Mary was for years known as La Conquistadora and now is also called Nuestra Señora de la Paz, or Our Lady of Peace. It is the oldest representation of the Madonna in the United States. Spanish friars brought the image from Mexico City to Santa Fe and carefully took it out of New Mexico again when they fled during the Pueblo Revolt. La Conquistadora returned to Santa Fe with Don Diego de Vargas during the reconquest and is carried in procession as part of the religious commemorations of the Santa Fe Fiesta. When you visit the cathedral, it's hard to overlook the massive bronze double doors out front. They chronicle more than four centuries of the Roman Catholic religion in New Mexico. Each panel weighs 25 pounds. Notice La Conquistadora in the "1680" panel.

in the New Mexican folk-art santero style hang on the wall beneath them, a fitting reminder that this is Santa Fe, after all. The cathedral was elevated to the designation of basilica by Pope Benedict XVI in 2005, signifying its global importance in spreading the Catholic faith. In 2009, the cathedral participated in the city's 400th anniversary celebrations by completely cleaning the exterior stonework and installing four bells in the long-vacant South Tower. A PBS documentary about the cathedral, *El Corazon de Santa Fe*, premiered in July 2009. The cathedral is open to visitors from 6 a.m. to 5:45 p.m. Admission is free. Mass is celebrated daily.

## CRISTO REY CHURCH
**1120 Canyon Rd.**
**(505) 983-8528**
**www.santafeparishesonline.com**
The Catholic parish of Cristo Rey uses this church, America's largest adobe building, for regular worship, but visitors are welcome. A classic example of New Mexico mission architecture, Cristo Rey was designed by Santa Fe-style architect John Gaw Meem and built of 200,000 adobe bricks made from soil at the church's site. The 1940 construction commemorated the 400th anniversary of Coronado's exploration of the Southwest, which led, of course, to the founding of Santa Fe. In addition to the architecture, the church's principal attraction is its gorgeous restored painted stone reredos, a sculpted Spanish colonial-style altar screen with images of the saints. Crafted in 1760, the 18- by 40-foot screen was originally installed in the old military chapel situated near the Plaza. Admission is free. The church is open to visitors from 8 a.m. to 7 p.m. daily.

**i** If you don't want to sound like a tourist, please call the Plaza, "The Plaza," not "The Town Square."

## LORETTO CHAPEL $
**211 Old Santa Fe Trail**
**(505) 982-0092**
**www.lorettochapel.com**

This chapel, dedicated to Our Lady of Light, was the first Gothic structure west of the Mississippi. Today the chapel is one of Santa Fe's top visitor attractions and a popular place for weddings and concerts. Built for the Sisters of Loretto, the style of this jewellike chapel testifies to the influence of Santa Fe's first bishop, Frenchman Jean Baptiste Lamy. The Sisters came to Santa Fe at the request of Lamy to establish a school for young women downtown. Their Loretto Academy occupied the site upon which the neighboring Inn at Loretto now stands. The French influence includes the white altar, beautifully adorned sanctuary, rose windows, and architectural beauty modeled after Paris's Sainte Chapelle. The chapel's claim to fame, however, is a graceful spiral staircase that winds to the choir loft with no center support and not a single nail. Legend has it that work on the chapel was nearly done when the Sisters realized no room remained for a traditional staircase. They prayed to St. Joseph for guidance and believed he answered their novena when a carpenter arrived. He agreed to build the staircase. Using only a saw, a carpenter's square, and tubs of hot water to soften and shape the wood, he crafted a beautiful circular staircase. He then disappeared before he could be paid. The story was featured on television's *Unsolved Mysteries* in the late 1990s. The chapel is administered by the Sisters of Loretto but maintained by the Historic Santa Fe Foundation. The chapel is open from 9 a.m. to 6 p.m. Monday through Saturday, and from 10:30 a.m. to 5 p.m. Sunday.

## SAN MIGUEL MISSION $
**401 Old Santa Fe Trail**
**(505) 983-3974**
Many people believe this mission is the oldest church in the United States. Construction began in 1610 by the Tlaxcalan Indians who came from Mexico as servants of the Spanish soldiers and missionaries. The job was completed in 1625. When the Pueblo Indians drove the Spanish from New Mexico in 1680, they nearly destroyed the mission and burned all records of its early history. The sturdy adobe walls remained unharmed, however. When the Spanish returned,

they ordered the church rebuilt and construction was finished in 1710. For many years it served the surrounding Barrio Analco, one of Santa Fe's most historic neighborhoods. Inside you can see traditional religious images crafted by Hispanic artists. The wooden reredos, or altar screen, dates from 1798 and holds paintings from the early 18th century. You'll see rare and ancient images of Jesus on buffalo and deer hides, testimony to the faith and ingenuity of frontier artists. Among the chapel's drawing cards is the San Jose bell, cast of silver, copper, iron, and gold. Touted as the oldest bell in America, some historians date its fabrication to 1356. Spanish churches used it before it was shipped to Mexico and then hauled to Santa Fe by oxcart in the 19th century. A helpful staff of Christian brothers and a six-minute audio presentation that runs continuously as a recorded tour will help orient you to the mission. It's open Monday through Saturday from 9 a.m. to 5 p.m. and Sunday from 10 a.m. to 4 p.m. Mass is celebrated here Sunday at 5 p.m.

## SANTUARIO DE GUADALUPE
**100 Guadalupe St.**
**(505) 988-2027**
Over the centuries, this beautiful former church has gone from Spanish adobe to colonial New England to California Mission in appearance. Today it looks much like it did when it was first built, between 1776 and 1796. The lintels above the windows and the front door are original. The ceiling includes some original beams, but the building's roof, brick parapets, and bell are new. Among the Santuario's art is a 1783 oil-on-canvas altar painting of Our Lady of Guadalupe by Mexican baroque artist José de Alzibar, a renowned Mexican painter. It is one of the finest and largest oil paintings of the Spanish Southwest. The Santuario is the oldest United States shrine to Our Lady of Guadalupe, the name given by the Catholic Church to the apparition of the Virgin to the Indian Juan Diego outside Mexico City on December 12, 1531, which is credited with spreading the Catholic faith to native people of the Americas. A beautiful new statue of Our Lady of Guadalupe has been erected outside the church and serves

as a shrine for those making pilgrimages here. The nonprofit, nonsectarian Guadalupe Historic Foundation operates the Santuario as a museum, performing arts center, and occasional art gallery. Santa Fe Desert Chorale has performed most of its summer and Christmas concerts here since 1982. Visit the Santuario Monday through Friday from 9 a.m. to 4 p.m., 10 a.m. to 4 p.m. on Saturdays in summer. It's closed weekends from November through April. Admission is free. Mass is celebrated here once a month.

**Southwest Seminars (505-466-2775),** a nonprofit educational group headed by Alan Osborne, a local college professor, offers public talks and slide shows on Southwest culture and natural history at 6 p.m. Mondays at Hotel Santa Fe. Experts present Spanish colonial history, geology, archaeology, ethnomusicology, and other topics in a light and fun way. A fee is charged.

# HISTORIC DISTRICTS

### BARRIO ANALCO
**East De Vargas St. between Don**
**Gaspar Ave. and Old Santa Fe Trail**
Believed to have been one of the first parts of Santa Fe to be settled by the Spanish, this area was named "analco" or "other side of the river" because it sits across the Santa Fe River from the Palace of the Governors. The early residents were Mexican Indians, who came to Santa Fe in the early 1600s with the Spanish settlers, missionaries, and soldiers. Spanish colonists lived closer to the thick-walled haven of the Palace of the Governors. Because of its vulnerability, angry Pueblo Indians were able to totally destroy this area during the revolt of 1680. The neighborhood was rebuilt when the Spanish returned and, as years went by, became a more class-inclusive kind of place. Today state buildings dominate this area, but some of the old charm remains. The homes are privately owned and not open to visitors, but a stroll along East De Vargas Street gives you a sense of Santa Fe in its early days.

i One of the best free things to do in Santa Fe is to stroll Canyon Road on a Friday evening in summer and attend openings at the various art galleries. There is often food, drink, and entertainment. This is a tradition for longtime Santa Feans, as well as visitors.

## CANYON ROAD
### from Paseo De Peralta to Camino Cabra, roughly parallel to East Alameda and Acequia Madre

The best way to explore Canyon Road, Santa Fe's famous historic art district, is on foot. Don't worry if you get hungry, there are restaurants here, too. If art interests you, you'll discover a variety of styles, media, and prices here. Many of the road's galleries and shops occupy former homes. Several nearby streets—Camino del Monte Sol, García Street, and Acequia Madre—are also worth a look. Primarily residential, they offer another glimpse of Santa Fe's classic beauty. In the spring and early summer, the lilacs and fruit trees here are spectacular. Acequia Madre means "mother ditch," a name that comes from the irrigation ditch that runs along the street. In pre-Spanish times, Indians used this footpath to travel between the Santa Fe River valley and Pecos Pueblo. Later it was the conduit for haulers bringing their loads of firewood from the mountains to sell in town. Farmers grew chiles, beans, and peaches, drawing the water for irrigation from acequias, or communal ditches. Sheep and goats grazed on the nearby hillsides.

Canyon Road owes part of its fame to a group of artists who came to Santa Fe in the 1920s. They called themselves "Los Cinco Pintores" (The Five Painters) and built homes along Camino del Monte Sol, just off Canyon Road. Their paintings often reflected a romantic Santa Fe. (See our The Arts chapter.) The artists became neighbors of Canyon Road's long-established Hispanic families. The cultures intermixed, and the area saw little visible change until recent years, when some longtime residents began selling their land, in part because of rising taxes. Today this area, known as the East Side, is one of Santa Fe's most desirable and pricey neighborhoods. (See our Relocation chapter.)

Artist Olive Rush, said to be the first female Anglo artist to move to Santa Fe, lived and worked in a studio at 630 Canyon Rd. for 40 years. A Quaker, Rush left her home to the Santa Fe Society of Friends at her death, and it is still used for Quaker meetings. El Zaguan, 545 Canyon Rd., is among the street's historic buildings. (See separate write-up in this chapter.)

Parking in the Canyon Road area is a challenge, especially in the summer. Look for parking places along the street or in the city lot, 225 Canyon Rd., near the corner of Canyon Road and Camino del Monte Sol.

## THE PLAZA/DOWNTOWN

Directly across from the Palace of the Governors, the Plaza is bordered by Lincoln Avenue to the west, Washington Avenue to the east, San Francisco Street to the south, and Palace Avenue to the north. The downtown area extends several blocks from the Plaza in all directions.

The Plaza, a shady expanse of trees, grass, benches, and monuments, is the core of old Santa Fe, the city's "Central Park." It's one of four sites in Santa Fe listed on the National Register of Historic Places. (The others are the Palace of the Governors, the National Park Service Southwest Headquarters, and the Barrio Analco near the San Miguel Mission.) To many residents, despite all the changes during the past decades, the Plaza is still the community's sentimental place of the heart. A few years ago the city sponsored a program of free entertainment on the Plaza appropriately called "El Corazón de Santa Fe" (The Heart of Santa Fe).

For many visitors, time spent exploring the Plaza and downtown Santa Fe, with its museums, shops, restaurants, and historic attractions, forms one of their most vivid memories of this unusual city. The Plaza is Santa Fe's favorite place for festivals and fairs. You'll find Spanish Market, Indian Market, Fiesta de Santa Fe, the Christmas drama Las Posadas, and many other events here. They fill the Plaza and spread into the surrounding streets, bringing Santa Fe residents and visitors downtown. In the summer the city traditionally blocks traffic on San Francisco Street and Lincoln Avenue to make the area more pedestrian friendly.

The small stone marker on the north side, just across the street from the Palace of the Governors, notes the arrival of Gen. Stephen Watts Kearny with the Army of the West in 1846 during the war between Mexico and the United States. Kearny claimed Santa Fe for the U.S. government without firing a shot. The monument on the south side of the Plaza marks the end of the Old Santa Fe Trail The 900-milelong Santa Fe Trail from Independence, Missouri to Santa Fe. The Plaza also marks the end of an older commercially important trail, El Camino Real, the trade route to Santa Fe from Mexico City. At the center of the Plaza, the obelisk commemorates Civil War battles in the area. Surrounding the Plaza are narrow streets and distinctive buildings that represent three and a half centuries of continuous civilization, beginning with the 1610 establishment of the city as the seat of the government of Spain's northern frontier. Architectural styles range from Spanish Pueblo to Territorial and European. Strict building codes govern what you can design, erect, or demolish. Rents are high, and as a result, in addition to museums, you'll find shops that handle exclusive and expensive merchandise and shops that make their money on heavy sales of less expensive items. Parking in the Plaza area is not allowed. The city operates several downtown lots (see our Getting Here, Getting Around chapter), and some private businesses offer limited parking. There also are a few spaces along side streets. Your best bet, if you're staying downtown, is to walk from your hotel. If you're outside the downtown area, you can take a city bus, a free shuttle, or a taxi.

## MUSEUMS

### ARCHDIOCESE OF SANTA FE MUSEUM
223 Cathedral Place
(505) 982-5619
www.archdiocesesantafe.org

### The Civil War in New Mexico

Although most visitors may not realize it, the Civil War reached New Mexico in 1861. The Confederacy, in an effort to take the West, sent soldiers from Texas up the Río Grande to capture New Mexico's Fort Union, the garrison established by the U.S. Army to protect wagons along the Santa Fe Trail from Indian marauders. The Confederacy controlled both Albuquerque and Santa Fe by 1862, setting up headquarters in the Palace of the Governors. The rebel plan would have succeeded except for the pivotal Battle of Glorieta on March 28. Major John Chivington took some Union soldiers and destroyed the Confederates' central supply base, leaving them with no support and no choice except to abandon the area. A plaque on the Plaza commemorates the Battle of Glorieta. The battlefield is part of Pecos National Historical Park, east of Santa Fe.

Because the Spanish government wanted converts as well as gold from New Mexico, the Catholic faith played a vital role in the area's history (see our Worship and Spirituality chapter). This unimposing little museum features historic documents, photographs, and artifacts that trace the development and role of the Catholic Church in New Mexico. You can see the beautiful chalice used by Archbishop Jean Lamy when he said mass more than a century ago and the proclamation formally re-establishing the Spanish presence and Catholicism in Santa Fe, dated June 20, 1692, and signed by Don Diego de Vargas. The museum is open from 9 a.m. to 4 p.m. Monday through Friday. Admission is by donation.

## BATAAN MEMORIAL MILITARY MUSEUM AND LIBRARY
**1050 Old Pecos Trail**
**(505) 474-1670**
**bataanmm@cs.com**
Organized through the efforts of the New Mexico National Guard, the Bataan Veterans Organization, and many other interested parties, this museum displays artifacts collected by the state's military veterans and honors all New Mexicans who have done military service. The museum occupies an old armory and displays items dating from World War I through the Gulf War. The highlight is a tribute to the Bataan veterans, the 200th Coast Artillery Regiment that was sent to the Philippine Islands to furnish anti-aircraft support. The regiment was later divided to form the 515th Coast Artillery Regiment. The men saw enemy action on Bataan when the Japanese overran the Philippines in 1942. The 200th is officially credited with firing the first shot and being the last to surrender to the armies of Japan. The 200th consisted of 1,800 men when deployed. After three and a half years of brutal captivity, fewer than 900 men returned to their families in New Mexico. The state has a government office building named in honor of these brave fighters, and a perpetual flame burns for them just outside it.

The museum has 30,000 artifacts, an extensive research library, and an archive of military documents relating to New Mexico's history. It's open Tuesday, Wednesday, and Friday from 9 a.m. to 4 p.m., and Saturday from 9 a.m. to 1 p.m., but hours can change with seasonal visitors and tour groups. There is no admission charge.

## GEORGIA O'KEEFFE MUSEUM     $$
**217 Johnson St.**
**(505) 995-0785**
**www.okeeffemuseum.org**
The Georgia O'Keeffe Museum is America's first museum dedicated to the work of a woman artist of international stature. O'Keeffe visited New Mexico in 1917 and came here permanently in 1949, settling in an old adobe home in the small village of Abiquiú. She lived there, inspired by the landscape and the light, for nearly 40 years before

moving to Santa Fe in 1986, a few years before her death at age 98.

This small museum houses the world's largest permanent collection of Georgia O'Keeffe's work, including many pieces the artist kept for herself that have never been previously exhibited. At the museum, you'll see revolving exhibitions of work O'Keeffe produced between 1916 and 1980. Flowers and bleached desert bones, abstractions, nudes, landscapes, cityscapes, and still lifes are all here. The museum's galleries trace O'Keeffe's artistic evolution, tracing the depth and breadth of her long, productive career.

As a secondary goal, the museum collects and hosts guest exhibits of works by contemporaries of O'Keeffe who were part of her artistic community. Philanthropists Anne and John Marion endowed the 13,000-square-foot museum, whose 10 galleries are simple and unpretentious, just as O'Keeffe would have liked. The museum offers guided tours, educational programming, and special events. Don't miss the short video featuring O'Keefe discussing her life and work as you enter the galleries.

The Georgia O'Keeffe Museum is open 10 a.m. to 5 p.m. Tuesday through Sunday and 10 a.m. to 8 p.m. Friday. It is closed Monday, New Year's Day, Easter, Thanksgiving, Christmas, and on Wednesday from November through June. Free admission is offered daily to ages 16 and younger and on Friday evenings.

## INSTITUTE OF AMERICAN INDIAN ARTS MUSEUM     $
**108 Cathedral Place**
**(505) 983-8900**
**www.iaiancad.org/museum/museum.html**
If you're interested in contemporary American Indian art, be sure to visit this downtown museum housed in the old Santa Fe-style post office designed by Isaac Rapp. The museum is affiliated with the Institute of American Indian Arts, which has long been one of America's leading schools for Indian arts. Among the teachers and students whose work has put the IAIA on the national map are Allan Houser, Dan Namingha, Estella Loretto,

Linda Lomahaftewa, and T. C. Cannon. With more than 7,000 pieces in the collection representing 3,000 artists, the museum is the largest repository of contemporary Indian art in the world. Painting and sculpture and traditional crafts such as beadwork, pottery, weaving, and basketry are displayed in the museum's five galleries. The museum offers educational programming and the outdoor Allan Houser Art Park for large sculpture. On April 21, Children's Day is held at the museum, and includes dancing, weaving, art, and puppets. The IAIA Museum is open 10 a.m. to 5 p.m., Monday through Saturday; Sunday, noon to 5 p.m. Closed Tuesdays November through May. Admission is free for IAIA members and children younger than age 16.

## SCHOOL OF ADVANCED RESEARCH, INDIAN ARTS RESEARCH CENTER $$

660 Garcia St.
(505) 954-7205
www.sarweb.org

Although not, strictly speaking, a public museum, the public can view this anthropology research center's extensive collection of American Indian art of the Southwest, including textiles, pottery, basketry, and jewelry, once a week on a special tour. Docents will explain SAR's fascinating history and role in American archaeology in addition to offering insights into the beautiful objects you'll see. Tours, by advance reservation only, are available every Friday at 2 p.m. Free to SAR members.

## WHEELWRIGHT MUSEUM OF THE AMERICAN INDIAN

704 Camino Lejo
(505) 982-4636, (800) 607-4636
www.wheelwright.org

New Englander Mary Cabot Wheelwright founded this private museum in 1937 with Hastiin Klah, an esteemed and influential Navajo singer, or "medicine man." The pair were introduced by traders Frances "Franc" and Arthur Newcomb and became close friends, dedicated to creating a permanent record of Klah's and other singers'

ritual knowledge. By the early 1930s it was clear to Wheelwright and Klah that a museum would be needed as a repository and to give the public an opportunity to sense the beauty, dignity, and profound logic of the Navajo religion. The architect they chose, William Penhallow Henderson, based his design for the building on the hogan—the traditional eight-sided Navajo home and the setting for Navajo ceremonies. The museum's earliest names were the Navajo House of Prayer and House of Navajo Religion, but soon after it opened its official name became the Museum of Navajo Ceremonial Art.

Times changed, and the resilient Navajo culture proved that the apprehension Wheelwright and Klah shared about the death of the Navajo religion was unfounded. In the 1960s and 1970s, the Navajo Nation exerted its independence in a number of ways, including the establishment of its own community college system. Also at that time, Navajo singers founded the Navajo Medicine Men's Association. The teaching of traditional Navajo religion enjoyed a revival, and its practitioners began to express their concerns about the sacred items and information in museums throughout the country.

In 1977 the Navajo Museum's board of trustees voted to repatriate several Navajo medicine bundles and other items sacred to the Navajo people. The museum' name was changed to the Wheelwright Museum of the American Indian to reflect an expanded focus on contemporary American Indian art.

The Wheelwright maintains world-renowned collections and archives that document Navajo art and culture from 1850 to the present. Exhibitions in the main gallery include contemporary and traditional American Indian art with an emphasis on the Southwest. A second gallery presents one-person exhibitions. The entrance displays outdoor sculptures by Allan Houser and others. Case Trading Post has an exceptional selection of artwork, jewelry, pottery, books, and increasingly collectable Navajo folk art. Some of the most famous folk artists visit the trading post during the popular International Folk Art Festival in July.

The Indian-themed children's programs at the Wheelwright are one of the museum's main selling points. A Children's Intertribal Pow Wow, with dancing contests, is held every October (see Annual Events and Festivals chapter). For 25 years, storytellers at the Wheelwright Museum have been entertaining Santa Fe kids every Saturday and Sunday, July through August, with Storytelling in the Tipi, when storytellers like Joe Hayes tell tales drawn from Hispanic, American Indian, and Wild West traditions. Even the tiniest kids stay still for these dramatic stories. Especially popular are traditional northern New Mexico *cuentos,* or stories, about La Llorana, the legendary Weeping Woman, and funny tales about Coyote the Trickster. In addition, a Children's Reading Hour takes place at 11 a.m. on the second Saturday of the month, featuring a story combined with a related art project. Juice and animal crackers are served.

The museum is open from 10 a.m. to 5 p.m. Monday through Saturday and 1 to 5 p.m. on Sunday. Admission is free.

**i** The Santa Fe Pickup, a new free shuttle, meets every Rail Runner train at Montezuma Street, just north of the Santa Fe Depot, starting at 6:30 a.m. and ending at 6:30 p.m. weekdays, and 7:30 a.m. to 4:30 p.m. Saturdays. It drops passengers off at the PERA Building, the Cathedral Basilica of St. Francis of Assisi, City Hall, the Plaza, and the Hilton and El Dorado hotels.

## MUSEUM OF NEW MEXICO                 $$
Administrative offices, Camino Lejo
(505) 827-6451
www.museumofnewmexico.org

Headquartered on Museum Hill in Santa Fe, the state's museum system includes research libraries; artifact conservation; archaeological research; education programs; traveling exhibits; the American Indian *portal* vendors' "living exhibit;" Museum of New Mexico Press; *El Palacio* magazine; Fray Angelico History Library and Photo Archives; and six state monuments. Operated with state funding, private grants, and money earned though admission fees, the museum

system is managed as part of the New Mexico Office of Cultural Affairs. The four Santa Fe-based museums are the Palace of the Governors and newly opened adjoining New Mexico History Museum, the New Mexico Museum of Art (formerly the Museum of Fine Arts), the Museum of International Folk Art, and the Museum of Indian Arts and Culture/Laboratory of Anthropology. The Palace/History Museum and the Fine Arts Museum are downtown. Museum of Indian Arts and Culture, the Museum of International Folk Art is about 2 miles from the Plaza on Camino Lejo, just off the Old Santa Fe Trail.

Admission is charged at all four museums. A discount four-day pass, which offers admission to all Museum of New Mexico locations plus the Spanish Colonial Arts Museum on Museum Hill is available. Admission is free to all on Friday nights between 5 and 8 p.m. and all day Sunday for New Mexico residents. Wednesday is free to New Mexico seniors with ID. Free admission is offered daily to youth age 17 and younger. All branches of the Museum of New Mexico are open from 10 a.m. to 5 p.m., Tuesday through Sunday (daily in summer). The Palace of the Governors and the Museum of Fine Arts are also open from 5 to 8 p.m. for Free Friday Evenings. The museums are closed Monday (except summer), New Year's Day, Easter, Thanksgiving, and Christmas. For information about the Museum of New Mexico's events and attractions, call the twenty-four-hour information line, (505) 827-6463.

## NEW MEXICO MUSEUM OF ART         $$
107 West Palace Ave.
(505) 476-5072
www.nmartmuseum.org

The New Mexico Museum of Art (formerly the Museum of Fine Arts) is easy to find once you're on the Plaza. It's right across the street from the Palace of the Governors, at the corner of Lincoln and Palace avenues. Like its sister, the Palace of the Governors, this museum attracts attention for its architecture as well as its archives. Completed in 1917, the museum is a beautiful example of the Pueblo Revival style of construction, complete with split cedar *latillas* (roof supporters), hand-hewn vigas (log roof beams) and carved corbels. The gracious style reflected in the thick walls, pleasantly landscaped central courtyard, smooth interior plaster, and other finishing touches became synonymous with "Santa Fe Style."

The collections focus mainly on art from New Mexico and include both traditional and contemporary work in a variety of media. The museum owns and displays creations by many well-known artists, including the Santa Fe and Taos master painters who first brought the art world's attention to New Mexico as well as Georgia O'Keeffe and Peter Hurd. (See our The Arts chapter.) The museum's galleries change exhibits fairly frequently and usually include cutting-edge work by living artists as well as shows that draw on the museum's 20,000-strong collections. In 2009, the museum opened its new long-term exhibit "How the West Is One: The Art of New Mexico," drawing on 70 pieces in the permanent collections to create an intercultural time line from the arrival of the railroad in 1879 to the present.

The New Mexico Museum of Art offers art classes for kids, an extensive program of lectures, and gallery talks. The Santa Fe Chamber Music Festival makes its home in the museum's St. Francis Auditorium during the summer. Rehearsals are free to the public.

## MUSEUM OF INDIAN ARTS
## AND CULTURE                                    $$
710 Camino Lejo
(505) 476-1250
**www.indianartsandculture.org**
This museum's pride and joy is its permanent exhibit, "Here, Now and Always," which opened with tremendous fanfare and blessings from Indian leaders in August 1997. The exhibit goes on the must-see list for anyone interested in American Indians and their arts, culture, and history. Housed in a large wing, "Here, Now and Always" tells the story of the Native American presence in the Southwest with more than 1,300 objects and a multimedia production created during the eight-year period the museum spent in collaboration with Native American elders, artists, scholars, teachers, builders, and writers. These consultants worked with a team of Indian

and non-Indian museum curators and designers to develop an exhibit that combines the actual voices of contemporary American Indians with ancient artifacts. The architectural design helps bring centuries of culture and tradition to life.

The exhibit uses stone and silver, clay and wool, feast days, fairs, and family stories to tell of the enduring communities of the Southwest. To orient visitors, it incorporates the landscape itself, mesas and settlements, plazas, and sacred peaks. Visitors proceed by theme through the galleries. You can visit a pueblo kitchen, an Apache wickiup, a Navajo hogan, a 1930s trading post, and a contemporary vendor's booth at a tribal feast day celebration. The stories in "Here, Now and Always" are told on videotape by 50 American Indians.

The Museum of Indian Arts and Culture was established in 1987 next to its adjoining research facility, the Laboratory of Anthropology, on Museum Hill. In addition to exhibits, the museum has a resource center with looms, magazines, books, maps, and other useful tools. The museum is noted for its prehistoric and historic pottery, basketry, woven fabrics, and jewelry. The museum offers a "Breakfast with the Curators" program, day trips, and other special events.

## MUSEUM OF INTERNATIONAL
## FOLK ART                                        $$
706 Camino Lejo
(505) 476-1200
**www.internationalfolkart.org**
Just as the Museum of Indian Arts and Culture provides a fascinating and informative orientation to the American Indian cultures of the Southwest, the Folk Art Museum does the same for New Mexico's Hispanic culture. And that's just one of its exhibits! The Hispanic Heritage Wing, under reconstruction at press time in 2009, features Spanish colonial folk art in finely crafted displays that delineate the central position of extended family relationships and the Catholic faith in northern New Mexico's Hispanic culture. On display is the resourcefulness of the pioneer families who lived for more than a century in tremendous isolation from manufactured goods, European medicine, and formal education.

In addition to insight into New Mexico's Hispanic past, museum visitors can come away with a better sense of the world as a whole. This museum is the repository for the world's largest collection of international folk art. In the "Multiple Visions: A Common Bond" exhibit, for example, you'll find objects from more than 100 countries displayed in fascinating dioramas. Toys from 19th-century Europe, Chinese prints, embroidered Indian mandalas, Mexican Day of the Dead mementos, and examples of early 20th-century Americana are among the treasures. This exhibit alone includes more than 10,000 pieces of folk art, all donated by the Girard Foundation Collection.

Opened in 1998, the Neutrogena Wing houses an impressive array of textiles, costumes, and masks donated by Lloyd Cotsen and the Neutrogena Corporation. Get an up-close look at riches from the collection with a visit to "Lloyd's Treasure Chest," where you will have an opportunity to examine cherished objects and watch the collection's staff as they work behind the scenes.

The museum hosts changing exhibits and a variety of special events, some ready-made for children and families. Check with the museum about docent-guided tours, which are free with admission.

**i** Looking for a sweet deal? At all Santa Fe branches of the Museum of New Mexico admission is free on Sundays for New Mexico residents with ID. Free admission is offered daily to those ages 16 and younger. Wednesday is a free day for New Mexico seniors (age 60 and older with an ID to prove it). And Friday from 5 to 8 p.m. everyone gets in free!

## MUSEUM OF SPANISH COLONIAL ARTS $$
750 Camino Lejo
(505) 982-2226
www.spanishcolonial.org
Dedicated to preserving and promoting the Spanish influence on New Mexico's art, the Museum of Spanish Colonial Arts showcases about 3,000 arti-

facts from the collection of the Spanish Colonial Arts Society. See our The Arts chapter for more information.

## NEW MEXICO HISTORY MUSEUM $$
113 Lincoln Ave.
(505) 476-5200
www.nmhistorymuseum.org
Begun in 2006 behind the Palace of the Governors, with which it shares a campus, the 96,000-square-foot New Mexico History Museum, a state-of-the-art interpretive museum, was opened on Memorial Day 2009 by Governor Bill Richardson. It attracted 7,000 visitors on the first day alone, and two days of partying on the Plaza that included music, food, dancing, and author signings. The new museum is modern and elegant. It has storytelling and hands-on exhibits on three and a half floors that celebrate the state's diverse history and teach by engaging the senses. The core exhibit, "Telling New Mexico: Stories from Then and Now," presents New Mexico history through six periods: early Native American, Spanish, Mexican, Territorial, Statehood, and Present. When touched, petroglyph-style Indian handprints recount Indian history from the Apache, Navajo, and Pueblo speakers. Touch-screen replicas of the famous Segesser Hide Paintings detail daily life in Spanish colonial times. And a touch-screen bilingual wall-size version of the Treaty of Guadalupe Hidalgo allows visitors to choose a linear or self-directed timeline of history using its pages and listen to scholars discussing its importance as the oldest U.S. treaty. The Palace of the Governors (see entry below) remains the core artifact of the history museum, displaying original treasures, such as the Segesser Hides, along with the Native American Artisans Program under the *portal*, Fray Angelico Chavez History Library and Photo Archives, and the Palace Press. There is a new cafe above the courtyard. Open daily in summer.

## PALACE OF THE GOVERNORS
105 East Palace Ave.
(505) 476-5100
www.palaceofthegovernors.org

Despite the name, this 400-year-old building—the oldest public building in continuous use in the United States—doesn't look much like a storybook palace or the grand structures of Europe. Santa Fe's Palace, a single-storied, earth-colored building with a long front *portal* and a shady interior courtyard, speaks more of early New Mexico's entrepreneurial, frontier style than the glory of Mother Spain. The Spanish used the Palace until the Pueblo Revolt of 1680, when consolidated forces of Pueblo Indians seized the building and drove the Europeans out of New Mexico. (See our History chapter.) The Indians remained in control for 12 years; then the Spanish returned and the Palace again became their Territorial headquarters. When Mexico won its independence, taking New Mexico with it, the Mexican flag flew here. The United States government seized control during the Mexican-American War. Confederate forces occupied the Palace during their attempt to win the West. Territorial Governor Lew Wallace wrote part of *Ben Hur* here.

The building was replaced as a governmental seat in 1909 after it had housed 60 New Mexico governors. It then became Santa Fe's first museum, the Museum of New Mexico and the original home of the School of American Research founded by archaeologist Edgar Lee Hewett. The building itself is rich with history because of the many events and decisions crucial to the history of New Mexico that were born inside these thick mud walls. Whenever changes to the building that are more than superficial are made, archaeologists discover more treasures and historic tidbits beneath its floors. With the opening of the New Mexico History Museum in 2009, marking the centennial of the Museum of New Mexico, Palace exhibits will be changing but will continue to house the original artifacts interpreted next door at the new History Museum. These include the Segesser Hides depicting Spanish and Native contacts, Spanish colonial treasures, a roomful of sacred devotional artifacts, and an original Mexican-era chapel, or capilla, with traditional dirt floors cured with oxblood.

# OTHER ATTRACTIONS

## THE CROSS OF THE MARTYRS AND COMMEMORATIVE WALKWAY
**Paseo de Peralta at Otero St.**
**No phone**
You feel like you're walking through history as you climb the winding brick path that takes you to the Cross of the Martyrs. Informative plaques line the walkway, summarizing the city's early history and the events that led to the deaths of the Franciscan missionaries who are commemorated by a 20-foot white metal cross at the path's end. From the top of the hill, you get a lovely view of the city and a panorama of the Sangre de Cristo, Jémez, and Sandía mountains—a reward for your energetic effort. Santa Fe's annual Fiesta ends with a candlelight procession from the cathedral to the cross. And on Christmas Eve, bright bonfires, or luminarias, surround it. There are no official visiting hours, and no fees are charged.

## SANTA FE BOTANICAL GARDEN $
**1213 Mercantile, Suite A**
**(505) 471-9103**
**www.santafebotanicalgarden.com**
Santa Fe Botanical Garden manages two main botanical areas—the Leonora Curtin Natural History Area and the Ortiz Mountains Educational Preserve—and is at work on a third site, a demonstration xeriscape (dry) garden on Museum Hill. Leonora Curtin Natural History Area, a 35-acre wetland area south of Santa Fe, is open to the public Saturdays 9 a.m. until noon and Sundays 1 until 4 p.m. May through October. Visitors may walk a nature trail, and there are docent-led walks at 10 a.m. on Saturday mornings. A working preserve and outdoor laboratory overseen by the Garden, Leonora Curtin is a sanctuary for native plant and animal species that affords birders and nature lovers a unique experience. Tours of the 1,350-acre wilderness preserve in the Ortíz Mountains, 28 miles south of Santa Fe off Highway 14 in Cerrillos, are available on weekends by reservation. SFBG offers regular programs and classes on gardening and horticulture, tours of private gardens in and around Santa Fe, and numerous other events

throughout the year. A quarterly newsletter and reduced event fees are among member benefits.

## SANTA FE FARMERS' MARKET
**1607 Paseo de Peralta, Suite A**
**(505) 983-4098**
**www.santafefarmersmarket.com**

After a historic fundraising campaign, Santa Fe Farmers' Market, one of the nation's top farmers' markets, moved into a permanent, year-round home in an attractive, purpose-built green building in the new Railyard Park in September 2008. The new indoor-outdoor market has plenty of room to expand, with 100 outdoor trackside covered spaces and 50 indoor spaces. Currently, 100 vendors from throughout central and northern New Mexico, sell at the market, which attracts thousands of visitors each year and is a major tourist draw. On sale are homemade salsa, baked goods, herbal remedies, garlic oil, goat cheeses and soaps, organic meats and produce, fragrant cut flowers, native plants for landscaping, handmade sweaters, and lavender items. When you buy here, you not only get delicious locally grown food but you also know who is growing your food and support the future of family farms, restaurant farm to table programs, school programs, food-stamp programs, and small local businesses. Music, free samples, coffee, and food demonstrations by notable cooks such as Deborah Madison mark most markets. The summer outdoor market begins at the end of April and continues until the end of October. The main market is Saturday from 7 a.m. to noon, with a smaller Tuesday morning market running the same hours. In winter, the market moves indoors and offers a cozy setting and a more limited selection from 9 a.m. to 1 p.m. on Saturdays only. A Community Fair selling arts and crafts as well as select foods takes place every Sunday, 11 a.m. to 4 p.m. A southside market takes place every Thursday in the Santa Fe Place parking lot from 3 to 6 p.m. in summer.

## SANTA FE SOUTHERN RAILWAY    $$–$$$$
**410 South Guadalupe St.**
**(505) 989-8600, (888) 989-8600**
**www.thetraininsantafe.com**

Santa Fe Southern Railway is a great day out for the whole family. Passengers travel on a working freight train between Santa Fe and Lamy, some 18 miles away. You can watch the high-desert scenery through the windows of restored vintage coaches as well as open-air flat cars. Daily year-round freight-train trips between the Santa Fe Railyard and Lamy leave the depot at 11 a.m. and return at 3 p.m. From April through October you can enjoy New Mexico's spectacular sunsets and clear, starlit skies on the Friday evening "High Desert Highball" trip. Departure is timed for sunset. Call the depot for departure times. On Saturday nights you can join fellow passengers for a campfire barbecue, April through October; the train leaves at 5 p.m. and returns at 9:30 p.m. Depot hours are 9 a.m. to 5 p.m. Monday through Saturday, 11 a.m. to 5 p.m. on Sunday. Bring a picnic or dine at the Lamy Station Cafe (505-466-1904), a new gourmet cafe in a converted Pullman carriage. Catering is available on the train on some days; call ahead.

## SHIDONI FOUNDRY AND GALLERY
**P.O. Box 250, Bishop's Lodge Rd.**
**Tesuque 87574**
**(505) 988-8001**
**www.shidoni.com**

Established in 1971, Shidoni is one of the world's leading fine-art casting facilities and showplaces. Sculpture produced here represents leading artists from throughout the world. On Saturday afternoons (times vary, please call), you can watch 2,000-degree molten bronze as it's poured into ceramic shell molds for casting. The foundry is open for visitors who'd like to walk through from noon to 1 p.m. Monday to Friday and 9 a.m. to 5 p.m. Saturday. The self-guided tours are free. Shidoni also offers an eight-acre sculpture garden with 500 works, the largest outdoor sculpture display in New Mexico. You can stroll among monumental sculptures in a variety of styles and media year-round during daylight hours. Shidoni makes its grounds available for private parties and fundraising events. Two contemporary art galleries are located on the property. One features painting and crafts and the other highlights sculpture. The galleries are open from 9 a.m. to 5 p.m. Monday through Saturday. Shidoni is in Tesuque, about 7 miles north of the Plaza.

**i** The best place from which to watch— and photograph—Santa Fe's spectacular sunsets is Old Fort Marcy Park above the Cross of the Martyrs.

# TOURS

### ACCESS/ABOOT ABOUT SANTA FE
624 Galisteo St., No. 32
(505) 988-2774
www.accesssantafe.com
This company offers walking tours with guides who are archaeologists, artists, and anthropologists. In addition to the popular Santa Fe orientation tour, the company offers ghost and mystery walks, literary walking tours, artist and gallery tours, and a full range of half- and full-day adventures throughout New Mexico. The basic historic walking tour is a 2¼-hour stroll to Santa Fe's significant sites. Tours leave daily at 9:30 a.m. and 1:30 p.m. from the El Dorado Hotel lobby and 9:45 a.m. Saturday and Monday from La Posada Resort and Spa. Children under age six go along free if accompanied by an adult. You can park in city lots across the street from the hotels.

### AFOOT IN SANTA FE WALKING TOURS AND THE LORETTO LINE TRAM TOURS      $$
211 Old Santa Fe Trail at the Inn at Loretto
(505) 983-3701
In business since 1990, this tour company prides itself on hiring guides who know their history and have a good sense of humor. Owner Charles Porter has conducted tours for groups from the National Parks Foundation and the Smithsonian. The walking tours are heavy on history; the driving tours on the Loretto Line trolley cover more sightseeing territory. The walking tour, which encompasses about 2 miles of the city's nooks and crannies and takes about two hours, leaves daily year-round at 9:30 a.m. Free for children younger than age 16 with a parent. The open-air trolley tours operate between 10 a.m. and 4 p.m.

May to October and last 1½ hours. No reservations are needed for either tour. All tours depart from the Inn at Loretto. Pay parking for tour guests is usually available at the hotel.

### ART WALKING TOURS      $$
New Mexico Museum of Art
107 West Palace Ave.
(505) 476-5041
www.mfasantafe.org
Every Monday at 10 a.m. in the summer, you can join trained docents on an interactive walking tour of downtown Santa Fe. Learn about Santa Fe's outdoor sculptures, Frederico Vigil's mural in the County Courthouse, WPA murals in the Federal Building, and the art collection at La Fonda Hotel. Children aged 18 years and under are free. Proceeds support the Museum of Fine Arts Library and Education Department. Tour participants meet at the Museum of Fine Arts Shop steps.

### GREAT SOUTHWEST ADVENTURES      $$$$
P.O. Box 31151, Santa Fe 87594
(505) 455-2700
www.swadventures.com
Great Southwest Adventures specializes in customized, small group tours of Santa Fe, Taos, Los Alamos, Abiquiú, Bandelier National Monument, Pecos National Historical Park, and other areas of northern New Mexico. Co-owner Tom Ribe grew up here and is the author of a unique guidebook focusing on the Los Alamos area. He brings a strong outdoors and cultural focus to his tours. In addition to the Opera, Balloon Fiesta, Pueblo dances, and other special-event tours, clients can choose from a variety of special tours providing a close-up look at the area's geology, anthropology, and archaeology. All guides have strong backgrounds in these topics. Custom backpacking and cross-country ski tours are a specialty.

### HISTORIC WALKS OF SANTA FE      $$–$$$$
608 E. Palace
(505) 986-8388
www.historicwalksofsantafe.com

These walking tours give visitors a chance to learn local history, shop, or discover Santa Fe's art scene. The history tours depart mornings and afternoons daily and include admission to the Miraculous Staircase. No reservations are required. The company's other tours do require reservations and may require minimum numbers. The shopping tour includes lunch and the gallery tour includes refreshments. The "Ghostwalker" tour presents ghost lore with good-humored guides who take these hair-raising legends just seriously enough to make the tours fun. The deluxe ghost walk takes you down to the Santa Fe River, where, if you're lucky (and every group seems to be) you might see La Llorona, northern New Mexico's infamous weeping woman who haunts riverbeds looking for her lost children. Bring your cameras. Ghostwalker tours are held on Friday evenings. Tours depart from La Fonda lobby at 9:45 a.m. and 1:15 p.m. daily; from the Plaza Galeria at 10 a.m. and 1:30 p.m.; and from Hilton Santa Fe/Historic Plaza at 10:15 a.m. and 1:45 p.m.

### PALACE WALKS HISTORY TOURS          $$
**Palace of the Governors**
**105 East Palace Ave.**
**(505) 476-5100**
**www.palaceofthegovernors.org**
During the summer and fall, the Palace of the Governors hosts tours of historic downtown Santa Fe. Each walk is personalized by a specially trained guide and reflects his/her particular area of interest. The walk covers history beginning in the 17th century and ending with current assessment of contemporary life in Santa Fe. The tour takes about 1¾ hours and departs from the Blue Gate on Lincoln Avenue at 10:15 a.m., Monday through Saturday, April through October. Accompanied children younger than age 17 are free. All proceeds benefit the museum.

### ROJO TOURS          $$$$
**2408 Calle Bella**
**(505) 474-8333**
**www.rojotours.com**

Isabelle Rojo arranges customized tours for groups and individuals and packages for convention and meeting planners that range from visits to private artist studios, O'Keeffe Country, Chaco Canyon, Taos Pueblo, and Pueblo dances to gallery tours, cooking classes, and western barbecues.

### SANTA FE DETOURS          $$-$$$$
**54 East San Francisco St.**
**(505) 983-6565, (800) DETOURS**
**www.sfdetours.com**
In town or out of town, by foot, raft, or railroad, Santa Fe Detours has served visitors and residents for more than 20 years. This locally owned and operated company will also arrange horseback riding, private guides for hiking and biking, Grayline bus tours, and even help find tickets to popular performances. Their central reservation service can also help with accommodations from luxury suites to cozy vacation rentals.

### SOUTHWEST SAFARIS          $$$$
**P.O. Box 945, Santa Fe 87504**
**(505) 988-4246, (800) 842-4246**
**www.southwestsafaris.com**
These unique air/land tours take visitors by aircraft and land vehicle to some of the Southwest's most magnificent landmarks and ruins, providing a detailed look at the area's geology, archaeology, and natural history. One-day expeditions are offered from Santa Fe to the Grand Canyon, Monument Valley, Canyon de Chelly, Mesa Verde, and Arches. On the one-day trip to Canyon de Chelly, for example, safari travelers fly over the Río Grande and the Jémez Mountains. They see the San Juan Basin, the rugged Chuska Mountains, and picturesque Canyon de Chelly before landing in the heart of the Navajo Reservation. Passengers rendezvous with a ground tour and Navajo driver for exploration of the canyon, famous for its cliff dwellings and sheer sandstone walls. The trip departs Santa Fe Airport at 7 a.m. and returns by 3:30 p.m.

Want a shorter tour? Try a half-day safari to Aztec Ruins National Monument. After a one-hour flight over the enchanted vistas of northern New Mexico, travelers land and are met by an archaeologist/anthropologist who serves as personal guide through the pueblo ruins of the monument. The trip leaves Santa Fe at 7 a.m., returning by 12:30 p.m. Pilot/guide Bruce Adams will also arrange custom trips, such as Chaco Canyon. All trips are by reservation, with a two-fare minimum.

**WINGSWEST BIRDING TOURS** $$$$
**2599 Camino Chueco**
**(505) 473-2780, (800) 583-6928**
**www.collectorsguide.com/wingswest**
WingsWest Birding Tours offers customized trips throughout the northern half of New Mexico. Bird-watchers select from four-hour, seven-hour, or sunrise-to-sunset expeditions. Company founder Bill West, an avid birder, has spent the last two decades in New Mexico. Because of the diversity of habitat and the change of seasons found in the Land of Enchantment, visitors can enjoy northern New Mexico's birds year-round. West and company welcome beginners as well as experienced birders on the excursions and provide loaner binoculars. Rates are the same for one or two visitors. There is a small per person charge for groups bigger than two.

# VISITOR INFORMATION

## BIENVENIDOS PLAZA INFORMATION BOOTH
**62 Lincoln Ave. in the *portal* window**
**of the First National Bank on the Plaza**
**No phone**
Volunteers from the Santa Fe Chamber of Commerce staff the Plaza Information Booth as a service to Santa Fe's multitude of visitors during the peak of the tourist season. You'll find brochures of all kinds and free copies of locally published visitor guides. They can give you a list of restaurants and lodging possibilities. Even better, you'll find people who live here and can answer your questions. Mid-May through mid-October, the booth is open from 9 a.m. to 4 p.m. Monday through Friday.

## LA BAJADA VISITOR CENTER
**I-25 at the La Bajada exit 268,**
**17 miles south of Santa Fe**
**(505) 424-0823**
La Bajada, Spanish for "the descent," was clearly named by travelers heading south to Río Abajo or the lower Río Grande country—rather than those making the arduous climb uphill from Albuquerque. The newly renovated La Bajada Visitor Center, serving more than 140,000 travelers a year, offers the largest assortment of free publications about Santa Fe and northern New Mexico and the state of New Mexico's comprehensive free vacation guide. Located 17 miles south of Santa Fe, it's a logical first stop for travelers arriving from Albuquerque. For added comfort, the center has public restrooms and telephones maintained by the state highway department and serves free coffee until 4 p.m. daily. Take an extra minute here and enjoy the view of glittering Santa Fe above you with the blue Sangre de Cristo Mountains towering in the background. The center is open from 7:30 a.m. to 5:30 p.m. daily from Memorial Day to the end of October and from 8 a.m. to 5 p.m. the rest of the year. It's closed on Thanksgiving, Christmas, and New Year's Day.

## SANTA FE VISITOR INFORMATION CENTER
**Lamy Building**
**491 Old Santa Fe Trail**
**(505) 827-7336, (800) 545-2040**
**www.newmexico.org**
Conveniently located near the corner of Old Santa Fe Trail and Paseo de Peralta, right across the street from the State Capitol, this is one of Santa Fe and New Mexico's most comprehensive sources for visitor information. The free maps, brochures, and visitor guides are arranged by county. The friendly and knowledgeable staff can answer your questions, or at the very least, refer you to someone else who can. And if you time it right, you might be able to find a shady parking place for your RV while you gather the information you need. Best of all, this center is open from 8 a.m. to 5 p.m. (until 7 p.m. after Memorial Day) seven days a week! The center occupies the historic Lamy Building (see the listing in this chapter).

## NEW MEXICO PUBLIC LANDS INFORMATION CENTER
1474 Rodeo Rd.
(505) 438–PLIC
www.publiclands.org
This interagency program offers books, maps, permits, and licenses for people interested in outdoor activities and audiovisual information about recreational opportunities on all of the state's public lands. A partnership between the Bureau of Land Management and the Public Lands Interpretive Association established and maintains the center. PLIC offers a wonderful source of information on public lands in New Mexico, along with BLM, USFS, and NPS maps, hiking books, and fun things for kids. Center manager Richard is a mine of information. Open 8 a.m. to 5 p.m. Monday to Friday.

## SANTA FE CONVENTION AND VISITORS BUREAU
Santa Fe Community Convention Center
201 West Marcy St.
(505) 955-6200, (800) 777-2489
www.santafe.org
You'll find a variety of information about Santa Fe here along with a schedule of events for the newly opened Santa Fe Community Convention Center, a 72,000-square-foot Santa Fe-style building that replaced the Sweeney Center in September 2008 as one of Santa Fe's most popular spots for conferences, conventions, trade shows, and public events. Public parking in a purpose-built parking structure is available behind the convention center or at meters on neighboring streets. The bureau is an easy walk from the Plaza and downtown hotels. You can pick up information between 8 a.m. and 5 p.m. Monday through Friday.

## SANTA FE COUNTY CHAMBER OF COMMERCE INFORMATION CENTER
8380 Cerrillos Rd.
(505) 988-3279
www.santafechamber.com
If you're considering a move to Santa Fe, stop here for information about real estate, taxes,

the business climate, and more. The chamber of commerce has a separate room devoted to all kinds of free material provided by members. You can order a comprehensive relocation packet online or by phone for $29.95 including shipping. A Santa Fe Membership and Business Directory is available free online. The center is open Monday through Friday 8 a.m. to 5 p.m. at the Santa Fe Premium Outlets Mall on the south side of Santa Fe, off Highway 14.

# WORTH THE TRIP

## Albuquerque

(also see Kidstuff chapter)

## NATIONAL HISPANIC CULTURAL CENTER                        $–$$$$
1701 4th St. SW,
Albuquerque
(505) 246-2261
www.nationalhispaniccenter.org
The National Hispanic Cultural Center (NHCC) is one of Albuquerque's new cultural crown jewels. Opened in 2000, it is dedicated to the preservation, promotion, and advancement of Hispanic culture, arts, and humanities. The center conducts ever-changing programs in the visual arts, performing arts, history and literary arts, media arts, and education. In 2009, for example, its art museum featured selections from its large collection of contemporary and traditional Latino art and a temporary special exhibit showcasing the monumental blown-glass and mixed-media Border Baroque art of Einar and Jamex de la Torre. The center is an extraordinary venue for performing arts. Its outdoor Plaza Mayor can hold 2,500 for summer performances of dance and theater. Indoor performances are held the rest of the year in the center's main 691-seat proscenium theater, the Roy E. Disney Center for Performing Arts, an award-winning building designed as a stylized Mayan pyramid with Romanesque interior features. The smaller Wells Fargo Auditorium, Bank of America Theatre, and Albuquerque Journal Theatre are used for more intimate performances.

The on-site restaurant, La Fonda del Bosque, serves Hispanic breakfast and lunch menus. The store, La Tiendita, sells New Mexican and Latin American arts and crafts.

Since its grand opening, it has staged more than 25 art exhibitions and 500 programs in the visual, performing, and literary arts. The center, located in the historic Albuquerque neighborhood of Barelas along the banks of the Río Grande, provides venues for visitors to learn about Hispanic culture throughout the world. Opening hours are Tuesday to Friday, 8:30 a.m. to 5:30 p.m. Admission to the art museum is modest and free for children under 16 and everyone on Sunday.

**i** A call from Santa Fe to most other New Mexico communities—Albuquerque, Pecos, Las Vegas, or Española for example—is long distance. A call to Los Alamos is not.

## Abiquiú

### THE GEORGIA O'KEEFFE HOUSE $$$
P.O. Box 40, Abiquiú 87510
(505) 685-4539
www.okeeffemuseum.org

If homes reflect the personalities of their owners, you won't find a better example than the Abiquiú house of the late painter Georgia O'Keeffe. Like the artist herself, the 7,000-square-foot adobe is strikingly beautiful yet austere and even aloof. Despite its cool, almost disengaging personality, the residence reveals magnitudes about O'Keeffe and her work. Once off-limits to the public, the mesa-top home and its magnificent views are now available by appointment only. The artist's Ghost Ranch home remains off-limits. Thousands of O'Keeffe admirers have visited the artist's house and studio since the Santa Fe-based Georgia O'Keeffe Foundation began giving tours in 1994. Few are disappointed with the four-bedroom, three-bath residence, which remains essentially as O'Keeffe left it in 1984 when she moved to Santa Fe—and nearer to medical care—for the last two years of her life. One certainly comes

away from the house understanding O'Keeffe's keen sense of simplicity, balance, and focus. Her home inspires a soothing, inviting calm with clean, simple lines and muted colors that draw in and celebrate the glorious southwestern panorama that so captivated O'Keeffe. Tours are by reservation only, and you should make reservations well in advance. The foundation limits interior tours to 12 people at a time, but may accommodate larger groups with advance notice. No backpacks or totes are allowed. You will need to lock these in your car in front of the inn. Tours take place Tuesday, Thursday, and Friday, March 15 to Thanksgiving. Visitors meet at an office next to the Abiquiú Inn and are bused to the house. Proceeds benefit the Georgia O'Keeffe Foundation and are tax deductible. Abiquiú is approximately one hour northwest of Santa Fe.

## La Cienega

### EL RANCHO DE LAS GOLONDRINAS $$
334 Los Pinos Rd.,
La Cienega
(505) 471-2261
www.golondrinas.org

It's easy to imagine the relief of the tired travelers along the famous El Camino Real, the main trade route connecting New Mexico to Mexico, when they reached this shady oasis. The ranch was the last stop before Santa Fe on the grueling journey from Mexico City to the northernmost province of New Spain. Centuries later the natural beauty remains.

Approximately 15 miles southwest of Santa Fe, El Rancho de las Golondrinas, "the Ranch of the Swallows," offers a vivid re-creation of the area's 18th- and 19th-century history. The restored buildings—built on original foundations—have been furnished as appropriate to the period. You can visit an 18th-century placita, a home built around a patio with thick walls and defensive towers. You can see a water-powered mill, feel the heat in a blacksmith shop, visit a schoolhouse, hike through the mountain village, and notice the solemnity in the morada, a chapel/meetinghouse used by the Penitentes. El

Rancho de las Golondrinas presents theme weekends throughout the summer, focusing on topics such as arts, oral history and storytelling, colonial traditions, the Catholic faith as it shaped the area's arts, and the animals the Spanish brought with them.

For kids, goats, burros, sheep and other animals are a big attraction of this living ranch and museum, where hands-on activities such as baking bread, weaving, and grinding corn are encouraged. The museum's self-guided tour involves about a 1.5-mile hike over roads and trails that are sometimes steep and rocky. Little kids may find this tiring. You should allow at least an hour and a half for the tour. On festival days, volunteers demonstrate many of the skills early settlers needed to survive on the frontier. Lively dancing, foot-stomping music, and scrumptious food add to the fun.

The ranch is open for self-guided tours Wednesday through Sunday, 10 a.m. to 4 p.m. Guided tours are available Wednesday through Friday at 9:30 a.m. from June to September. Food is available most weekends, but during the week you'll need to bring a picnic. Popular themed weekends (see Annual Events and Festivals chapter) include the Civil War weekend (May), the Spring Fair (June), the Wine Festival (July), the Summer Festival and Frontier Market (August), and the Harvest Festival (October).

To reach the ranch from Santa Fe, take I-25 to exit 276 and bear right onto Highway 599. Turn left at the traffic light onto the frontage road and right just before the racetrack on Los Piños Road. The museum is 3 miles from this intersection.

# KIDSTUFF

**D**espite its reputation as a cultural mecca and town of retirees, Santa Fe also welcomes kids with all sorts of fun things to do. Not only will they be busy but they'll also learn something here, too!

Like adult visitors, children have two basic sets of options: things to see and to do in town and attractions and adventures in the big outdoors surrounding Santa Fe. Among the highlights of the city is a museum designed and constructed just for kids, complete with a special child-size door. Santa Fe has a river to walk along, parks to explore, an Audubon Center, scenic railroad tours, the new high-tech New Mexico History Museum, swimming pools, an ice-skating rink that's open year-round, places to in-line skate and skateboard, and a bowling alley. The Genoveva Chávez Center on Rodeo Road offers lots of family fun—swimming, diving, a big-screen TV, the above-mentioned ice rink, and classes galore. The mountains and foothills surrounding Santa Fe are rich with opportunities for family picnics, hiking, skiing, and mountain biking. If you didn't bring bikes, you can rent them in town. And don't forget the sunscreen!

In the spring and summer, parents and kids can take a raft trip, spending a day on the Río Grande or Río Chama having fun and getting wet. Many commercial rafting companies are based in Santa Fe and offer a variety of options from gentle floats to white-water excitement. Please call first and ask if there are age requirements; some trips don't accept the youngest children. (See our Parks and Recreation chapter for more on rafting.) Horseback riding is another popular option. Trail rides through a variety of terrains, breakfast trips, and campfire rides are available from several businesses and resorts in the area for children more than seven years of age. Many stables also offer riding lessons for children.

Fishing, surprisingly to some people, is as much a part of summer here as it is anywhere in the United States. Children younger than age 12 can fish for free in New Mexico. In the Santa Fe area, opportunities for lake fishing—which is often easier for young children—include the Cochití, Abiquiú, Santa Cruz, and Monastery Lakes. Nambé, Santa Clara, and San Juan Pueblos have public fishing lakes. If you want your kids to try stream or river fishing, the Río Grande between Santa Fe and Taos, off Highway 68—especially near Pilar—is worth a visit. Or cast your lines into the Pecos River and streams that flow into it in the Santa Fe National Forest outside the community of Pecos, off I–25 on Highway 63, about 30 miles east of Santa Fe.

In the winter you and your kids can have fun together at the Santa Fe Ski Area, which offers an extensive program of classes for children, or along cross-country trails in Santa Fe National Forest and elsewhere. You can go sledding or tubing in Hyde Park, north of Santa Fe on Highway 475. Take a look at our Parks and Recreation chapter for other activities and destinations that are ideal for children.

As you might expect in this community of artists, art activities are a big draw. Kids can study everything from painting and pottery to drama and dance. We mention a few of these schools in this chapter, but be sure to check the phone book or specialized publications for children for more suggestions. Santa Fe children can put on their own shows or go to professional theater, opera, and music productions. Some groups offer special free concerts just for children. Many of the city's events include children in wonderful ways. The Fiesta de Santa Fe, a community celebration each

September, invites kids to walk in their own parade. Both the Spanish and Indian Markets, major summer arts-and-crafts shows, have exhibitor spaces dedicated to children who are also artists.

And, if Santa Fe seems a little too different at times, don't worry: Our community has the comfortable old standbys—movie theaters, video arcades, and malls where teens can meet their friends. For more information, the Santa Fe *New Mexican*, (505) 995-3839, offers a "Family Attractions" category in its *Pasatiempo* calendar each Friday and "Best Bets for Kids," on Thursdays. A special *Kids Summer* edition is published in April. Two specialized free publications, *New Mexico Kids!* and *Tumbleweeds*, present pages of ideas, suggestions, and insights into services and activities for children in the Santa Fe areas. (See our Media chapter.) We've done our best to make sure all information in this chapter is current, but the phone numbers are listed for your convenience if you wish to double-check any information. In addition to the information here and in our Parks and Recreation chapter, you'll find more suggestions in our Attractions and The Arts chapters. Have a good time and remember: Before you know it, your little ones will be all grown-up.

## BE A HAPPY CAMPER

In addition to the programs listed here, many of the agencies listed under our "Get Arty" section offer summer programs.

### BIG SKY SUMMER OF SCIENCE $$$$
1114 Hickox St., Unit G
(505) 428-7575
www.bigskylearning.com
Kids with a love of science will enjoy this half- and full-day science camp for ages five through 13. Director Michael Sheppard offers children the opportunity to design and build robots, lie detectors, and many other gadgets.

### BRUSH RANCH CAMP $$$$
HC 73, Box 32, Terrero 87573
(505) 757-8821, (800) 722-2843
www.brushranchcamps.com

This long-established camp along the Pecos River in the Sangre de Cristo Mountains, 35 miles northeast of Santa Fe, offers an assortment of programs: all sorts of kids' camps for ages six to 15 and camps kids and parents can attend together. You'll find traditional camp and adventure camp for older children, Mountaineers sessions for nine- to 12-year-olds, Trailblazers for six- to eight-year-old first-time campers and Family Camp for all ages from grandparents on down. The setting amid the ponderosa pines is beautiful and convenient to Santa Fe. Sessions run one to eight weeks from mid-June through mid-August.

### CAMP ELLIOTT BARKER $$$$
Girl Scouts—Sangre de Cristo Council
450 St. Michael's Dr.
(505) 983-6339, (877) 983-6339
www.nmgirlscouts.org
The Sangre de Cristo Girl Scouts council, which serves 13 counties in northern New Mexico and one in Colorado, does a lot more than sell cookies. One of the most popular scouting activities is also open to nonscout girls—camping at Camp Elliott Barker near Angel Fire. The camp offers one- and two-week sessions for girls from age seven through 17. The camp also hosts family weekends and sessions for mothers and daughters and dads and daughters. Here, in the cool and beautiful Sangre de Cristo Mountains, girls can ride horses, try their skill in a ropes challenge course, backpack, learn New Mexico crafts and culture, build rockets, and, most importantly, have fun. Camping experience is available in three-, six-, or 10-day sessions.

### CHALLENGE NEW MEXICO $$-$$$$
74 Caja del Rio Rd.
(505) 988-7621
www.challengenewmexico.com
An organization aimed at children ages 10 through 18 with disabilities. Activities include dance, therapeutic horseback riding, swimming, baseball, fishing, and bowling. Fees are based on a sliding scale.

**CHILDREN'S ADVENTURE COMPANY    $$$$**
935 Alto St.
(505) 988-7201
www.childrensadventurecompany.org
This popular program offers an extensive summer camp, overnight camping, and after-school programs for children ages five up through the 9th grade. Summer day camps include nature trips, cooking, swimming, and art with field trips to Albuquerque every Friday. The company also offers enriched after-school programs for kindergarteners through 6th graders, with price adjustments for children who don't attend every day. Call for prices.

**WISE FOOL NEW MEXICO    $$–$$$$**
2778 Agua Fria #BB
(505) 992-2558
www.wisefoolnewmexico.com
Wise Fool, Santa Fe's own performing arts circus, offers a six-week workshop year-round that allows kids ages seven through 14 to learn acrobatics, walk on stilts, and swing on the trapeze. Programs geared toward adults are also scheduled.

# BE DRAMATIC/GET ARTY!

## Classes and Workshops

**ART ACADEMY DE LOS NIÑOS    $$$$**
2504 Calle de los Niños
(505) 473-3003
The August through May after-school programs here focus on many different art media. Private sessions can also be arranged. The teacher is Sandi Wright, M.A., a longtime art educator who works with students to help develop and release their innate creativity. Media range from drawing and painting to sculpture and pottery. Fees paid monthly for weekly 90-minute classes including materials.

**CHILDREN'S DANCE PROGRAM    $$–$$$$**
2536 Camino Entrada
(505) 982-1662
Pearl Potts offers a range of year-round dance classes for kids, teens, and adults, including ballet, modern dance, tap, jazz, Irish, and creative movement. Seven- to 12-year-olds may attend her two-week summer workshops consisting of four-hour classes; two-hour classes are offered for kids ages five to seven on Tuesdays and Thursdays. Potts also offers creative movement classes for children ages two through seven.

**i** You'll notice murals throughout the city created by the Santa Fe Youth Mural project. The program teaches teenagers the basics of art, teams them with professional artists, and decorates walls and utility boxes with a variety of paintings. Buses and even garbage trucks have been painted as part of the project.

**FINE ARTS FOR CHILDREN AND TEENS (FACT)    $$$$**
1516 Pacheco St.
(505) 992-2787
www.FACTsantafe.org
Aimed at kids ages four through 18, this arts program is hosted by the ARTbarn, a 15-year-old organization aiming to pick up the shortfall in arts education in the schools. Programs take place at the ARTbarn building behind the Pink Church on Pacheco Street, at venues around town, and as after-school programs. Once-a-week sessions last six weeks and include art supplies and nutritious snacks. Kids learn to draw, paint, sculpt, make papier-mâché masks, and other skills, as well as learn art history. Field trips to Shidoni Foundry in Tesuque, the Museum of Fine Arts, and other arts venues are offered. Scholarships are available, and no child is turned away for lack of funds.

**GEORGIA O'KEEFFE MUSEUM ART AND LEADERSHIP PROGRAM FOR GIRLS**
123 Grant Ave.
(505) 946-1012
The O'Keeffe Art and Leadership Program for Girls, an interactive program for preteen and adolescent girls, incorporates skill building and problem solving in the areas of identity, creativity, and self-esteem. Every summer more than 100 girls participate in the intensive sessions. Open-

ing circles provided the time to share ideas, feelings, and dreams as explored in independently completed home assignments. The late artist and New Mexico resident Georgia O'Keeffe and several contemporary women artists function as strong role models. The three- to six-day education programs have included a hike in O'Keeffe's Ghost Ranch country followed by an overnight stay in Ojo Caliente, New Mexico. Participants' artwork is displayed in a public exhibition at the end of the program. Participants are nominated through their schools. There are also programs for boys.

## NATIONAL DANCE INSTITUTE OF NEW MEXICO
P.O. Box 22988, Santa Fe 87502
(505) 795-7088
www.ndi-nm.org

This exceptional program works with 39 northern New Mexico public elementary schools each year to offer the students an introduction to movement and dance held at the attractive Dance Barns facility near the Santa Fe River on Alto Street. Lessons culminate with a public performance at the Lensic Performing Arts Center for parents, friends, and the community in general. The National Dance Institute of New Mexico was founded to help children develop discipline, a standard of excellence, and a belief in themselves that will carry over to other aspects of their lives. Participation is free thanks to grants and volunteers.

## SCHOOL OF ASPEN SANTA FE BALLET                    $$–$$$$
550B St. Michael's Dr.
(505) 983-5591
www.aspensantafeballet.com

Children ages three through their teens can study ballet, modern dance, creative movement, and jazz here. Adult classes are also available. The students dance in at least one annual public performance at the Lensic Performing Arts Center. An annual performance of *The Nutcracker* and a spring recital give the students on-stage experience. The school also offers a summer intensive in June.

# CATCH SOME CULTURE

## LENSIC PERFORMING ARTS CENTER
211 West San Francisco St.
(505) 988-1234
www.lensic.com

Free daytime family events, youth performances, and school programs are integral to the Lensic's ambitious Community Outreach program. Among those participating are Santa Fe Opera (see entry below), which works with 2,000 local school children in its Apprenticeship program, and Santa Fe Symphony, where musicians offer special youth performances and conductors teach kids about instruments in the orchestra. The Lensic offers a regular Partners in Learning program that busses in local school kids throughout the year for performances of traditional New Mexican music, circus artists, classical concerts, and the *Nutcracker Ballet* at Christmas. The high-school Technical Apprenticeship Program offers internships to students whereby they apprentice with the theater's technical director to learn all aspects of lighting, sound, and stagecraft.

**i** The Santa Fe Children's Museum hosts an annual birthday party each February, with free admission and a big birthday cake to thank everyone who makes it the city's most popular museum among the younger set. The night before the family party, the museum hosts a benefit dinner and auction to raise some of the money needed to keep its doors open.

## SANTA FE CHAMBER MUSIC FESTIVAL YOUTH CONCERTS
St. Francis Auditorium
Museum of Fine Arts
(505) 983-2075
www.santafechambermusic.org/SFCMF.html

The festival's youth concerts, founded in 1993, bring music to children in five performances during July and August. Past programs have included jazzy string music, a presentation about violin making, a flamenco-inspired piece for chamber ensemble and dancers, and a program that high-lighted young musicians. The concerts are free thanks to private foundations and support from the city of Santa Fe and the state.

## SANTA FE OPERA YOUTH NIGHT
## AND BACKSTAGE TOURS $$
Santa Fe Opera Theater,
7 miles north of Santa Fe on US 84/285
(505) 986-5900
www.santafeopera.org
Youth Night at the Opera provides children and young adults an opportunity to attend dress rehearsals of the opera productions at low cost. In 2009, the operas included La Traviata and Don Giovanni. A special adjunct, the Pueblo Opera Program, reaches more than 2,000 pueblo children and their parents. (For more information on the opera, see our The Arts chapter.) The kids see a real opera—not a watered-down production. Most youth night performances sell out early. Children younger than age 18 can accompany a parent free of charge on Opera Day, in early May. Docents show visitors costumes, sets, scenery, and props and explain how the opera makes them.

## SANTA FE PERFORMING ARTS
## SCHOOL & THEATRE $$-$$$$
Armory for the Arts
1050 Old Pecos Trail
(505) 984-1370
www.sfperformingarts.org
These after-school and summer programs pro-vide training in music, dance, and drama for Santa Fe kids ages six through 18. Company members use the skills and techniques they learn in the workshops to present four annual produc-tions, two designed for and acted by younger children and two for older company members. Watch the newspapers for a schedule.

## SOUTHWEST CHILDREN'S
## THEATRE $$-$$$$
Santa Fe Playhouse
142 East De Vargas St.
(505) 984-3055
www.southwestchildrenstheatre.com

Quality children's plays and theater education are offered by this nonprofit group, founded in January 1988. Children learn improvisation, creative dramatics, voice and body training, and characterization. Adult professionals join the students for two main-stage productions each year, one in the spring and one in the fall. Each summer the company presents an all-student production—written by, produced by, and star-ring the summer theater students. After-school programs welcome kindergartners through 8th graders, and outreach to area schools offers even greater access to the theater arts for all of Santa Fe's youth.

# GET MOVING!

## BODY OF SANTA FE $$
333 Cordova Rd.
(505) 986-0362
www.bodyofsantafe.com
This community-oriented day spa, natural cloth-ing store, and raw-foods cafe offers a full array of yoga classes. A yoga class for children four to nine years of age is offered on Wednesdays at 4:15 p.m., and a Family Nia movement class is offered on Thursdays at 3:15 p.m.

## SANTA FE CITY PARKS AND
## RECREATION DEPARTMENT $-$$$
1142 Siler Rd.
(505) 955-2100 for park/program information
www.santafenm.gov
The city of Santa Fe offers an extensive summer recreation program and an assortment of other events during the year. Children can learn to swim and play tennis or spend the day in a park with a program of sports, games, and arts and crafts. All offerings are free or inexpensive. Kids also can compete in basketball and football con-tests, races, and fun walks. The city sponsors sum-mer gymnastics, cheerleading camps, a diaper bash, pumpkin-carving contests, and an Easter egg hunt. When it comes to parks, Santa Fe had 50 at last count, and all of them welcome kids. Many have swings, slides, tot equipment, tennis courts, basketball hoops, and fields for sports.

Salvador Pérez, 610 Alta Vista St., (505) 955-2604, provides a fine, fenced tot lot where toddlers can swing, slide, play in the sand, and explore to their hearts content. The park, next to the Salvador Pérez Pool, has a train locomotive engine (fenced for safety) as its centerpiece. The Santa Fe Place Park, 4250 Cerrillos Rd., offers swings, slides, and climbing bars as well as a picnic area and a multipurpose field that's perfect for Frisbees. Fort Marcy Complex, 490 Washington Ave., (505) 955-2500, has a gym for basketball, fitness classes, a weight room, and outdoor fields for soccer, baseball, and other sports in addition to an indoor pool. Genoveva Chávez Community Center, 3321 Rodeo Rd., (505) 955-4001, includes Santa Fe's first public indoor ice rink along with an Olympic-sized swimming pool and toddler's pool, a fully equipped gymnasium, fitness classrooms, racquetball courts, and more. (Please see our Parks and Recreation chapter for all the details.)

For a different kind of park, visit the Arroyo Chamisa Trail. The paved path stretches from Yucca Road to Santa Fe Place Mall. The trail meanders along the Arroyo Chamisa, a major wash that is dry 99 percent of the year, and past a colorful mural painted by Santa Fe youth. The trail draws families from all over town. The route can be used by strollers and tricycles and is especially inviting at sunset. And don't forget Frenchy's Field Park, Agua Fria Street and Osage Avenue, a passive park with historic structures, walking trails, a labyrinth, picnic areas, and its own pond.

For more detailed information, look in the Parks and Recreation chapter.

## JOIN THE CLUB

### GIRLS INC.                                $$
301 Hillside Ave.
(505) 982-2042
www.girlsincofsantafe.org
Part of a national organization to help girls, Girls Inc. offers after-school programs, a summer camp, and special camps during the schools' winter holidays and spring break. Programs are designed for girls ages six through 12 and include arts and crafts, sports, cooking, field trips, guest speakers,

community service projects, and more. Programs offered are designed to increase girls' self-esteem and confidence in many areas, from financial and media literacy to leadership and community action, violence and pregnancy prevention. The summer and holiday camps work with girls from 7:30 a.m. until 6 p.m. Monday through Friday and are popular among parents who work at the State Capitol or City Hall because of the club's downtown location near Hillside Park. The camps are offered on a sliding-fee scale.

**i** If your child is interested in organized sports, Santa Fe is filled with opportunities. Here are some resources for you:

Little League Baseball, ages five through 18, Toni Chávez, (505) 466-7543.

Northern Soccer Club, (505) 982-0878.

Basketball offered through the Boys and Girls Club, (505) 983-6632.

Hockey, Santa Fe Trailrunners Youth Hockey Program, (505) 986-1552.

### SANTA FE BOYS AND GIRLS CLUB        $$$
730 Alto St.
(505) 983-6632
www.santafebgc.org
Established in 1938, the club now serves about 5,300 Santa Fe county children and teens with special events and activities. Programs include basketball, music, dancing, photography, boxing, computer labs, tutoring of all sorts, and job training. The club staff also works with members on substance-abuse prevention and personal and social skills, including conflict management. Children and teens can study for scholarships and college placement tests or prepare for their high-school diplomas. In addition to the main building on Alto Street, the club offers programs at five other locations in Santa Fe county. The members are ages six through 17. The club is open Monday through Thursday 2 to 7 p.m., Friday noon to 6 p.m., and Saturday 10 a.m. to 2 p.m. during spring and winter break and during the summer. Membership is on a sliding fee scale.

## WAREHOUSE 21 SANTA FE TEEN
## ARTS CENTER                              $$
**1614 Paseo de Peralta**
**(505) 989-4423**
**https://sites.google.com/a/warehouse21**
**.org/home/**
The closest thing Santa Fe has to a teen hangout, Warehouse 21 offers teens mentorship programs that allow them to learn about photography, flamenco, music recording, radio announcing, various forms of theater, and more. Programs are open to young people ages 12 through 21. Friday evenings bring comedy or music from local acts or touring bands. Classes, some of which are free and others low cost, vary with the season and availability of teachers, and have included paper making, swing dance, beading, guitar, and computer graphics. Warehouse 21, with typical teen bravado, bills itself as "The Future of Art in Santa Fe." Artists-in-Residence workshops give interested teens a chance to work with a professional artist. Warehouse 21 receives funding from the city of Santa Fe, the Santa Fe Arts Commission, the Rotary Foundation, and several private nonprofit foundations with a special interest in kids. It has a national reputation for its work promoting small-label and college bands. The center is now housed in a beautiful new building in Railyard Park and is usually open at noon, closing between 7 p.m. and 10 p.m. depending on day. Closed Mondays.

## JUST FOR FUN

### SANTA FE CHILDREN'S MUSEUM          $
**1050 Old Pecos Trail**
**(505) 989-8359**
**www.santafechildrensmuseum.org**
Founded in 1989, this excellent museum is aimed at kids age 12 and younger. Activities involve water, magnets, live snakes and giant cockroaches, bubbles you can stand inside, a climbing wall, microscopes, magnets, pulleys, beading and weaving looms, and a place outside to make bread in *hornos*. Environmental educators offer garden-based biology and environmental education projects such as making miniature gardens,

including a "pizza garden," nature prints, and seasonal wreaths made from natural materials. There's even a special garden planted with flowers that attract hummingbirds! Time is set aside time each week for toddlers and their parents to have the place all to themselves; there's a special climbing structure for toddlers on the property. On Sunday, visiting scientists introduce astronomy, physics, electricity, and biology in fun ways, and there are afternoon performances for families that include puppet shows, clowning, drumming, magicians, storytelling, and actors. The museum invites guest artists to lead children in a variety of hands-on activities every day. For parents and teachers, there are free topical workshops on child development to answer common parenting questions.

Open Tuesday through Sunday in summer; Wednesday to Sunday the rest of the year. Hours vary from 10 a.m. to 5 p.m. Tuesday, Wednesday, and Saturday; 9 a.m. to 5 p.m. Friday; noon to 8 p.m. Thursday; and noon to 5 p.m. Sunday. Please call for special holiday hours and programs. Kids younger than age 12 must be accompanied by an adult.

**i** Originally started as part of a museum exhibit, the All Children's Powwow has taken on a life of its own, and now draws participants between the ages of two and 15 to Santa Fe from Arizona, Colorado, Oklahoma, and Wyoming. In addition to dancing, children make their own costumes. The event, held in September, is sponsored by the Wheelwright Museum.

### SANTA FE KIDZ ZONE                     $$
**3005 S. St. Francis Dr. # 2B**
**(505) 988-KIDZ**
**www.kidzzonesantafe.com**
Even the parents get in on the fun at this new kids park, which includes an indoor tree house, a two-story padded maze, comfy couches, WiFi, party rooms, and cafe serving healthy food. Games include Guitar Hero and Dance Dance Revolution. There's a separate infant and toddler zone. Free admission for anyone under two or

over 16. Open Wednesday to Saturday 10 a.m. to 8 p.m. and Sunday 10 a.m. to 5 p.m. Closed Monday and Tuesday.

## QUIGGY'S PUTT AND PLAY                    $$
**6700 Cerrillos Rd.**
**(505) 424-6200**
A combination restaurant, playground, and PGMA-designed 18-hole miniature golf course, Quiggy's is just south of the Auto Park and is aimed at family fun. The restaurant has a loose Australian theme and serves pizza; the golf course features a replica of Ayers Rock, Australia's most famous attraction.

## SANTA FE PUBLIC LIBRARY
**145 Washington Ave.**
**(505) 955-6780**
**www.santafelibrary.org**
Free programs targeting babies and toddlers are held at the Main and satellite branches of the library weekly. Fridays at 10:30 a.m. at the main library, there is a preschool story time. Books and Babies is aimed at babies 6 to 24 months by introducing books, songs, and finger puppets. There is also a reading and writing club for teens called Teen Poetry Cafe.

> **i** The New Mexico Children's Foundation is a nonprofit, charitable organization that makes grants to other nonprofit agencies that serve children and families in Santa Fe and throughout the state. For more information, call (505) 986-2043.

# NATURE, ANYONE?

## CHAIRLIFT RIDES SANTA FE SKI AREA      $
**16 miles northeast of Santa Fe on**
**Highway 475**
**(505) 983-9155, (505) 982-4429**
Kids feel all grown-up when they ride to the top of the mountain on this comfy, four-person chairlift. The lift, which is also great for anyone else who might enjoy the chance to see a magnificent view without a big hike in the fall, takes passengers to the top of Aspen Peak at an elevation of

11,000 feet. If you're energetic, you can continue hiking through the spruce and fir forest. You may see marmots, bushy-tailed woodchucklike creatures also known as "whistle pigs" for their high-pitched barks. You'll find dozens of different wildflowers and colorful mushrooms. When you're ready, you can ride the lift back down.

The chairlift operates from 10 a.m. to 3 p.m. on weekends and holidays in the fall for aspen viewing, with the dates determined annually based on the weather. Children shorter than 46 inches may ride for free accompanied by a paying adult; seniors age 72 or older may ride for free.

## THE PLANETARIUM                          $
**Santa Fe Community College**
**6401 Richards Ave.**
**(505) 428-1677**
**www.sfccnm.edu/planetarium**
One of Santa Fe's favorite attractions for children and families, The Planetarium offers a changing schedule of productions intended to give the audience a better knowledge of the night sky. Each month's programs explore a new theme that includes history, cultural aspects, astronomy news, and maybe even some physics. Shows take place about four times monthly beginning at 8 p.m. About 10,000 children visit The Planetarium for free each year through a special arrangement with the Santa Fe Public Schools. Tickets go on sale a half hour before show time. No latecomers admitted. Children must be accompanied.

## SANTA FE FARMERS' MARKET
**Santa Fe Railyard**
**(505) 983-4098**
If your kids think peas come from a can and carrots from a bag, a trip to farmers' market in the new Railyard Park will open their eyes and please their taste buds. You can see and buy fresh area produce, colorful cut flowers, and freshly baked treats here on Tuesdays and Saturdays, from late April to late October, then on Saturdays in winter. You'll find live music at the market most mornings, sometimes with children as part of the performance, and storytelling with a fairy

story lady. The market hosts special demonstrations and events and sponsors an annual tour of working farms. It's open from 7 a.m. to noon on Tuesday and Saturday in summer, and 9 a.m. to 1 p.m. in winter. There's a southside market in the summer on Thursday afternoons in the Santa Fe Place parking lot from 3 to 6 p.m.

# ON THE ROAD

## Albuquerque

### THE ANDERSON-ABRUZZO ALBUQUERQUE INTERNATIONAL BALLOON MUSEUM    $
9201 Balloon Museum Dr. NE
(505) 768-6020
www.cabq.gov/balloon
Opened in 2005, the long-awaited Balloon Museum occupies a beautiful new facility that has been purpose-built to celebrate all aspects of ballooning, from scientific experiments and space exploration to spying and adventure. It traces the development of ballooning around the world from 1783 to the present day using films, exhibits that include the Soukup and Thomas International Balloon and Airship Collection, and hands-on scientific experiments that will appeal to kids. Of particular note are 50 historic balloon gondolas, a number of which were involved in record-setting flights such as the Kitty Hawk in which Maxie Anderson and Kristian Anderson crossed North America in 1980. The museum is named for two pioneers of ballooning—Ben Abruzzo and Maxie Anderson—and is co-managed with the City of Albuquerque. The new Balloon Museum is decidedly kid-friendly, with all kinds of exhibits on ballooning history, hands-on exhibits on the art and science of ballooning, a film that offers a unique aerial ballooner's perspective of the activity, and replicas of the balloon gondolas used by the pioneers of the sport. There's storytelling for the very young on Wednesday morning. This is a great place to watch balloon activities on the adjoining Balloon Fiesta Field during the October Fiesta. Open 9 a.m. to 5 p.m. Tuesday to Sunday year-round, closed Mondays and major holidays. Toddlers three and under are free.

### ALBUQUERQUE AQUARIUM AND BOTANIC GARDEN    $$
2601 West Central Ave. NW
(505) 768-2000
www.cabq.gov/biopark/aquarium
www.cabq.gov/biopark/garden
This desert aquarium has been a huge hit since it opened in 1996. You'll get a kick out of the eel cave, with its large population of scary-looking moray eels. But the aquarium's most popular attraction is the 285,000-gallon shark tank, where about 20 sand, tiger, brown, and nurse sharks circle and watch the people who've come to watch them. One exhibit features highly endangered and fascinating seahorses and seadragons. The newest exhibit is the Shark and Ray Encounter featuring bambook sharks and stingrays. Try to time your visit to watch the divers cleaning the tank between 2 and 3 p.m. daily. Children can have an encounter of the skin-to-skin kind with whelks, sea urchins, sea stars, and other invertebrates at the education station, the marine equivalent of a petting zoo. The Río Grande Botanic Garden is across the plaza; in summer, the two facilities often share live performances in the evening, free with the price of admission. Open from 9 a.m. to 5 p.m. daily, to 6 p.m. on summer weekends. Kids younger than age two are admitted free.

Altitude can have an effect on children, too. Make sure that your kids get plenty of sleep—or at least rest—during your visit to Santa Fe. They'll need their energy to handle the 7,000-foot elevation, not to mention all the things you'll want to do.

### EXPLORA! SCIENCE CENTER AND CHILDREN'S MUSEUM    $
1701 Mountain Rd. NW,
Albuquerque
(505) 224-8300
www.explora.us
There's something for kids of all ages at the spectacular new Explora! Children's Museum, which

now occupies an attractive, brand-new two-story building opposite Tiguex Park in Albuquerque's Museum Row. Experiment with motion, force, and energy at stations set up throughout the museum and explore the properties of electricity, light, gravity, and water through fun exhibits, including a miniature working power station. More than 250 exhibits explore the properties of electricity, light, gravity, and water. Highlights include a kinetic sculpture and a series of exhibits where kids can experiment with motion, force, and energy as well as the human body. The entry hall offers a lesson in acoustics. The museum is open 10 a.m. to 6 p.m. Monday through Saturday and noon to 6 p.m. on Sunday. Admission is free for children younger than age two.

## INDIAN PUEBLO CULTURAL CENTER $
2401 12th St. NW
(505) 843-7270, (800) 766-4405
www.indianpueblo.org
If you don't have time to go to the pueblos, this Indian-owned cultural center is the next-best thing, especially if you have kids. A 10,000-square-foot museum traces the beginning of the Pueblo Indians through modern times, focusing on New Mexico's 19 pueblos. Particularly interesting is the Indians' own version of the Spanish Conquest. You'll also find a children's center with hands-on activities. The cultural center's biggest draw is its dances, held every Saturday and Sunday (and some other days) between 11 a.m. and 4 p.m. Crafts demonstrations take place at 10 a.m. At the gift shop you can shop for jewelry from the various pueblos as well as pottery, rugs, and books. The newly expanded Pueblo Harvest Cafe and Bakery offers authentic American Indian and Southwest meals such as buffalo tenderloin and free baked bread made in two *horno* ovens. Center open from 9 a.m. to 5:30 p.m. daily. Cafe is open 8 a.m. to 8 p.m. Tuesday to Thursday, until 9 p.m. weekends. Museum admission is free for those age four and younger.

## NATIONAL MUSEUM OF NUCLEAR SCIENCE AND HISTORY $
601 Eubank SE
www.nuclearmuseum.org
A Smithsonian affiliate, the newly renamed National Museum of Nuclear Science and History is the only museum in Albuquerque to be Congressionally chartered and now has its own purpose-built warehouse-style building in Albuquerque. The museum not only serves as a readily accessible repository of educational materials and information about the Atomic Age but also does a fine job of interpreting and exhibiting its collections in an educational and entertaining way. As America's museum resource for nuclear history and science, the museum's exhibits tell the story of the people behind the science that led not only to the development of the atomic bomb but also to nuclear medicine. Exhibits include the development of x-rays, radiation, Hiroshima and Nagasaki, the Cold War, the Uranium Cycle, and the development of nuclear bomb technology. The museum's collection of nuclear hardware is on display in Heritage Park, and includes planes, rockets, missiles, cannons, and a nuclear subsail.

## NEW MEXICO MUSEUM OF NATURAL HISTORY AND SCIENCE $$
1801 Mountain Rd. NW
(505) 841-2800
www.nmnaturalhistory.org
From the life-size sculptures of Spike the Pentaceratops and Alberta the Albertosaurus to the FossilWorks Laboratory where kids can watch scientists extract real dinosaur bones from rock, this is New Mexico's version of dinosaur heaven. Stand next to the skeletons of real dinosaurs that actually lived in what is now New Mexico and see casts of their footprints, view a replica of New Mexico's ancient seashore, walk through a simulated volcano, and ride in an "Evolator," which takes you back to the days when arid Albuquerque was a rain forest. Other attractions include the newly opened Space Frontiers exhibit tracing

New Mexico's important role in space exploration and STARTUP, an exhibit detailing Albuquerque's important role in personal computer technology (Microsoft's Bill Gates got his start in a garage here). The planetarium uses high-definition digital video imaging over a 55-foot-diameter domed projection screen. The Lockheed Martin Dynatheater presents large-screen movies hourly from 10 a.m. until 5 p.m. Recent topics include river rafting through Arizona's Grand Canyon. The museum is open 9 a.m. to 5 p.m. daily except Christmas and nonholiday Mondays in January and September. Tickets to the Dynatheater and planetarium are extra.

**RÍO GRANDE ZOOLOGICAL PARK**    **$–$$**
903 10th St. SW
(505) 768-2000
www.cabq.gov/biopark/zoo/
Part of the Río Grande Biopark, the zoo's beautifully landscaped grounds include an aviary, elephants, petting zoo, and reptile house with 6-foot cobras, 20-foot pythons, and Komodo dragons. The zoo has a $2.2 million exhibit where polar bears cavort in an 11-foot-deep pool, lounge by a stream, play under four waterfalls, slip down a waterslide, and enjoy an air-conditioned ice cave. Australian animals, Mexican wolves, a primate area, a Tropical America exhibit, and a 6-acre Africa exhibit have expanded the zoo's attractions. Try to time a visit to coincide with animal feeding times: 2:30 daily for the polar bears, 10:30 and 3:30 p.m. daily for the seals and sea lions. Thursday to Sunday in summer, you can purchase food and help feed the lorikeets (9:30 to 11 a.m. and 1 to 3 p.m.) and giraffes (11 a.m. to

1 p.m.) A three-quarter-scale train runs on a loop throughout the grounds from 10 a.m. to 4 p.m. daily. The zoo raises money with special events, where contests, face-painting, international food, musicians, puppets, clowns, and music add to the fun. You can picnic here or eat at the on-site Cottonwood Cafe. Open from 9 a.m. to 5 p.m. daily. Children ages 12 and younger must be accompanied by an adult. A combined Biopark pass is available.

## Los Alamos
**BRADBURY SCIENCE MUSEUM**
15th St. at Central Ave.
(505) 667-4444
www.lanl.gov/museum
The development of the atomic bomb and the role Los Alamos National Laboratory played in the process is a key focus here. The museum offers visitors the opportunity to play with a laser, see Fat Man and Little Boy atomic bombs, learn about DNA fingerprinting, work with computers and interactive video, and watch a 20-minute movie about the development of the atomic bomb. Operated by Los Alamos National Laboratories, the museum shows the role Los Alamos played in the atomic bomb's creation and offers interactive exhibits explaining the scope of its nuclear research today. Even if you're not especially interested in the nuclear weapons world, anyone curious about science will enjoy the hands-on displays and lively demonstrations and shows. Open daily except Thanksgiving, Christmas, and New Year's Day. Hours are 10 a.m. to 5 p.m. Tuesday through Saturday and 1 to 5 p.m. Sunday and Monday. Admission is free.

# ANNUAL EVENTS AND FESTIVALS

**A**rts festivals, celebrations deeply rooted in the area's history and traditions, family events: Santa Fe's schedule of special events is unmatched in communities twice its size. As is true in most places, summer means more activities. But there's something to do year-round. Many events here are benefits for one good cause or another, a testament to Santa Fe's generosity.

August brings Santa Fe's most popular event, Indian Market. The two-day show and sale, the largest in the country, highlights the best in American Indian arts. It packs Santa Fe's hotels and restaurants, and sends some locals packing, too! Galleries around town honor their best and best-selling artists on market weekend with exhibits and gala openings. Indian Market includes a growing performing-arts component, offering a chance for American Indian musicians, storytellers, and dancers to perform before an appreciative audience.

While Indian Market draws the most visitors, Fiesta wins hands-down as Santa Fe's oldest celebration and takes the honors as a favorite with residents. Held the weekend following Labor Day, Fiesta commemorates Santa Fe's Spanish heritage with parades and pageants, music, dancing, and food galore. Fiesta also has a strong religious element, celebrating the contribution of the Franciscan missionaries and the city's deeply rooted Catholic heritage.

Christmas in Santa Fe showcases the community's rich traditions in the most enchanting way. *Farolitos*—little bags filled with sand and lit with a small candle—and luminarias, or bonfires, line the streets and light the way for the Christ child and for neighbors and churchgoers on Christmas Eve. A troupe of Spanish-speaking actors reenacts Mary and Joseph's search for an inn as an ancient Christmas pageant, *Las Posadas,* each December on the Santa Fe Plaza.

Spring brings the annual Easter pilgrimage to the historic Santuario de Chimayó Church, about 40 miles north of Santa Fe. Pilgrims from throughout New Mexico walk to the shrine on Good Friday as a testimony to their faith or to ask for divine blessings.

Summer offers a full schedule of performing- and visual-arts events—too many to list separately in this chapter. From June through August the city buzzes with choices ranging from storytelling in a tepee to lectures on culture and history, and from ballet to flamenco performances. The visual-arts scene sparkles with gallery openings and outdoor art shows and fairs. Please see our The Arts chapter for more specific information about the Santa Fe Opera and classical music concerts. And whenever you're planning to visit, check the local papers to see if a big-name jazz artist, a reggae concert, or who-knows-what-else has arrived for the weekend.

## OVERVIEW

We've organized this list of highlights based on when the event usually occurs. Unless otherwise noted, prices are per adult ticket, and parking is free. (During Indian Market, Fiesta, and other big celebrations some entrepreneurs and nonprofit groups may set up lots and charge for parking. If you don't want to pay, you can park elsewhere for free, but you'll have a longer walk.) You'll notice that many events happen on the Plaza. You'll find the Plaza downtown at the northern end of Old Santa Fe Trail, at the corner of Lincoln and Palace avenues. In addition to this calendar, don't forget the public events at the Indian pueblos near Santa Fe, which are listed in the Pueblo Culture section of our Local Culture chapter.

Santa Fe has a lively schedule of concerts, plays, and art show openings yearlong. For information please see our The Arts chapter, or check the local newspapers when you're in town.

## JANUARY

### SOUPER BOWL SUNDAY $–$$
Sweeney Convention Center
sponsored by the Food Depot
1222 Siler Rd.
(505) 471-1633

Timed to coincide with the real Super Bowl, this event combines fun and fund-raising. Those who attend have an opportunity to sample soups from more than 35 of Santa Fe's finest restaurants and vote for their favorites. Best soups usually end up on the restaurant's menu. Proceeds benefit the Food Depot, Santa Fe's local food bank, which provides food to more than 60 nonprofit agencies in northern New Mexico.

## FEBRUARY

### ART FEAST $$$
Santa Fe art galleries and studios
(505) 603-4643
www.artfeast.com

The Santa Fe Gallery Association and ARTsmart combine efforts for this event, a fund-raiser for ARTsmart's work in the Santa Fe schools. You can celebrate the art of food and food as art. Some of Santa Fe's top chefs are paired with galleries to create beautiful, edible art. Begun in 1998, the tour grows more popular every year. The offerings in prior years have included venison gumbo, miniature sweet potato pies, and homemade sausage.

## MARCH

### JEFF GLADFELTER MEMORIAL
### BUMP RUN $$
Santa Fe Ski Area, 16 miles northeast
of Santa Fe on Highway 475
(505) 982-4429
www.skisantafe.com

The area's best mogul skiers and snowboarders compete for glory and prizes in the annual Gladfelter competition named for the late photographer who enjoyed building caves on ridges in the ski area. The Snowboard Championships include jumps, half-pipes, and a slalom course and draw snowboarders from throughout the region. The event is held in March, depending on snow conditions. Spectators are welcome, but you have to be able to ski or snowboard to get to the course, and you'll need a lift ticket.

## APRIL

### CHIMAYÓ PILGRIMAGE
Santuario de Chimayó, Chimayó
no phone

Every Holy Week beginning on Thursday, thousands of pilgrims walk to the Santuario de Chimayó, about 40 miles north of Santa Fe. Christians, a few of them carrying wooden crosses, walk to this beautiful adobe church to repay a solemn vow or to ask for Christ's blessings. Pilgrims travel along US 84/285 through Santa Fe to the Nambé junction at Highway 503 and then on to Chimayó on Highway 76. The majority of the devout walk late on Holy Thursday and on Good Friday. Area law enforcement pays close attention to traffic to keep the pilgrims safe. If you're driving this route, please slow down and be careful. If you'd like to join the pilgrims for your own spiritual reasons, by all means do so. People walking at night should bring a flashlight and wear light-colored clothes. Day or night, carry plenty of water, wear sturdy shoes, and watch for cars.

The Wheelwright Museum offers its "Looking at Indian Art" series every Saturday morning at 10:15 a.m. The program, which varies weekly, talks about techniques used in making Indian jewelry, how to identify different styles of pottery, the meanings behind traditional designs and symbols, and more. The program is free at the museum, 704 Camino Lejo.

## MAY

### BACH FESTIVAL $$$
Loretto Chapel
(505) 988-4640
www.santafepromusica.com

Santa Fe Pro Musica treats Santa Fe residents and visitors to several evenings of the music of J. S. Bach and his talented sons. A past program featured performers on instruments from Bach's time presenting St. Matthew's Passion. Santa Fe Pro Musica musicians were joined for the performance by the Smithsonian Chamber Players. Chamber music and cantatas are among the festival's highlights, along with sonatas and concertos of all sorts.

### BATTLEFIELD NEW MEXICO: THE CIVIL WAR AND MORE $-$$
El Rancho de las Golondrinas
334 Los Pinos Rd., La Cienega
(505) 471-2261
www.golondrinas.org

The first weekend of May, families can step back in time to the days of the Civil War and New Mexico's Battle of Glorieta at the annual Civil War Weekend festival at this living-history museum just south of Santa Fe. (See our Attractions chapter for more information on the museum.) Between 10 a.m. and 4 p.m. both days, you'll have an opportunity to watch artillery and marching demonstrations, experience camp life, and see reenactments of the historic 1862 battles around Glorieta, New Mexico, between Union and Confederate troops. At noon, the New Mexico Territorial Brass Band plays period songs. This event is co-sponsored by the New Mexico Civil War Commemorative Congress. Food is available. Children younger than age five always get in free.

### NATIVE TREASURES INDIAN ARTS FESTIVAL $
Museum of Indian Arts and Culture
Santa Fe Community Convention Center
(505) 827-6344
www.nativetreasuressantafe.org

Celebrate the work of 180 traditional and contemporary Indian artisans at this Memorial Day weekend festival at Santa Fe's new convention center. Meet the artist, purchase unique items, and support MIAC programs.

### THE SANTA FE CENTURY BICYCLE RIDE $$$-$$$$
ride begins at Christus St. Vincent Memorial Hospital
Hospital Drive/St. Michael's Drive
(505) 982-1282
www.santafecentury.com

More than 2,600 bicyclists pedal down the Turquoise Trail, through the old mining towns of Madrid and Golden, across the Estancia Valley to the villages of Cedar Grove, Stanley, and Galisteo, and back into Santa Fe. You also can sign on for 25-, 50-, or 75-mile loops. The idea here is to have fun, and toward that end, organizers offer detailed maps, sag wagons (vans to pick up tired riders), and a van with a bike mechanic. You can stop for snacks and water along the route and purchase a blue-corn pancake breakfast in the Christus St. Vincent Hospital parking lot at the start of the trail. The ride traditionally happens on the third Sunday of May. Entry fees benefit the Leukemia Society of America. A strong rider completes the trip in four or five hours, to the cheers of friends and family who may be waiting at the finish line.

## JUNE

### ANNUAL PLAZA ARTS AND CRAFTS FESTIVAL
(505) 988-7621

Challenge New Mexico, a group that works with people with disabilities and sponsors a popular and a successful horseback therapy program, benefits from this show. You'll find arts and crafts from all disciplines. Everything is handmade by professional artists. You can chat with the artisans, and food and live music add to the weekend's festivities. The mid-month event attracts artists from throughout the region. Admission is free.

## BUCKAROO BALL $$$$
Eaves Movie Ranch, near Cerrillos
(505) 992-3700
www.buckarooball.com

Buckaroo Ball takes the honors as Santa Fe's single most profitable fund-raising event. Loosely modeled after the Cattle Baron's Ball in Dallas, the Buckaroo Ball is an upscale gala evening with first-rate food, exotic auction items, and stunning entertainment. Recent events, for example, have featured singer Patty Loveless and Asleep at the Wheel. A casually glitzy/western-looking crowd of about 1,200 enjoys spectacular hors d'oeuvres from Santa Fe's finest restaurants, dinner, and a fabulous silent and live auction including such things as trips to Bali, France, Tuscany, and Africa, and television guest spots. A committee disperses the money as grants to nonprofit groups working with children in Santa Fe and Northern New Mexico. As of 2009, $6.8 million has been awarded in grants. Despite the stratospheric purchase price, tickets sell quickly and usually disappear long before party night.

## JUAN SIDDI FLAMENCO THEATRE COMPANY $$$–$$$$
Benítez Cabaret Theater at The Lodge at Santa Fe
750 North Francis Dr.
(505) 988-1234, Lensic box office
www.ticketssantafe.org
www.juansiddiflamenco.com

In 2008, internationally acclaimed local flamenco legend María Benítez and her dance group officially retired from nightly summer performances in the hotel theater named for her after many years entertaining Santa Feans and visitors. In 2009, the Juan Siddi Flamenco group stepped into Ms. Benitez's famous shoes. The world-renowned ensemble of leading dancers, singers, and guitarists from the United States and Spain reflects the passionate and dramatic world of Spanish dance. The season runs from late June through Labor Day Weekend and includes six performances per week at 8:30 p.m. nightly except Tuesday.

## OPENING NIGHT, SANTA FE OPERA $$$–$$$$
Santa Fe Opera Theater
US 84/285,
7 miles north of Santa Fe
(505) 986-5900, (800) 280-4654
www.santafeopera.org

Opening night at The Santa Fe Opera means tails and tailgate parties, black ties and caviar. For the most part, Santa Fe isn't a dress-up town, but you'd never know it tonight. Denim with diamond studs, velvet capes, lace and satin, cowboy boots shined to a high polish, the latest New York fashions, and thousands of pounds of turquoise come out for the occasion. The glitter of the audience rivals that on stage. A variety of public and private parties precede the night's operatic performance—watch the papers or call the opera to find out what's on the schedule. After the opening night soiree (which is either the last Friday in June or the first Friday in July), the opera season continues through late August with five productions in repertory and some special concerts by apprentice artists. (See our The Arts chapter.)

## PRIDE ON THE RAILYARD PLAZA
www.santahra.org
www.gaysantafe.org

Santa Fe has a very large and visible gay community, never more so than during this pull-out-the-stops gay pride celebration the last week in June. In 2009, events included art exhibits at local gay-owned restaurants, a Pride Train to Lamy for sightseeing and campfire barbecue, a Swim and Spin pool disco at The Lodge at Santa Fe's pool, live performances of favorite Golden Girls episodes, and a comedy evening featuring a top-ranked comedian at the St. Francis Auditorium. The centerpiece is the outrageous Quirky Parade and Festival on the Saturday. The parade has floats, costumed and painted divas, and other frivolities to enjoy as it winds its way from the P.E.R.A. Building parking lot on Paseo de Peralta a short way west to the new Railyard Park Plaza near the water tower and farmers' market for an afternoon of food and beverage booths, a beer garden, a Kid's Korner, and nonstop entertainment.

**RODEO DE SANTA FE**                    $$–$$$
Santa Fe Rodeo Grounds
Rodeo Rd. at Richards Ave.
(505) 471-4300
www.rodeodesantafe.org

Begun in 1949 this PRCA rodeo runs for four days in late June, usually including the third weekend. You'll find all the required competitions here—bareback and saddle bronc riding, steer wrestling, barrel racing, and the ever-popular bull riding. More than 600 cowboys and cowgirls come from throughout the Southwest to test their skill, and the rodeo also attracts a fair share of local talent. Unlike most professional sports, the cowboys aren't paid. Not only do they have to come up with their own entry fees but they also cover the cost of transporting and feeding their horses, overnight rooms, medical and rehab bills, and all other expenses. For some, a good year is breaking even. Those who don't place in the money go home with only their memories— and the appreciation of the Santa Fe audience.

The rodeo features evening shows and a matinee. A rodeo queen and princess are crowned one evening, and the royalty from Fiesta de Santa Fe are featured guests at another performance (see the Fiesta listing under September in this chapter). Rodeo de Santa Fe has always welcomed families. Some little buckaroos watch from right behind the fence. Kids can compete in mutton busting, which gives them a chance to ride a bucking sheep. Or they can join a calf scramble, the goal of which is to capture a red ribbon from the tail of an uncooperative calf.

Before the rodeo starts, there's live entertainment on the grounds, and you can buy the food that goes with the fun—a complete chuck wagon dinner, burgers, hot dogs, popcorn, cotton candy, cold drinks, and hot coffee. There are a limited number of box seats available. Kids get a discount and can attend Saturday's matinee free with a paid adult. Parking is free.

**SANTA FE BOTANICAL
GARDEN'S GARDEN TOURS**             $$$$
Various locations
(505) 988-1234, Lensic box office
www.ticketssantafe.org

From Memorial Day through Labor Day, Santa Fe's nonprofit Botanical Garden offers glimpses of some of the most interesting and beautiful private gardens in Santa Fe and other nearby communities. Scheduled tours might include artists' gardens or xeric sites, which use drought-tolerant plants to great advantage. The tours are self-guided and, due to their popularity, have been known to sell out, so book early. Advance tickets are discounted to members. A tour of fall garden gems is often offered as well.

**SANTA FE DESERT CHORALE**        $$$–$$$$
Various venues
(505) 988-2282, (800) 244-4011
www.desertchorale.org

The Desert Chorale, New Mexico's only professional vocal ensemble, offers more than 25 performances of four separate concert repertoires throughout July and early August. Since its inception in 1983, the Desert Chorale has been noted for its effective programming and virtuoso performances. Critics and audience members have consistently praised the chorale for presenting some of the world's most significant and engaging repertoire—from the ancient to the modern. Summer concerts begin at 8 p.m. except Sunday, when the ensemble performs at 4 p.m. The company also offers a winter season and a Christmas holiday series. The Desert Chorale performs its concerts at the Santuario de Guadalupe, the Loretto Chapel, and the Cathedral Basilica of St. Francis, settings as beautiful as the music.

**SANTA FE RIVER FESTIVAL AND FISHING
DERBY**
De Vargas Park
(505) 820-1696
www.santafewatershed.org

Inaugurated in 2006 to celebrate renewed flows in the Santa Fe River, this fun community event brings parents and kids together along downtown Santa Fe's riverside Alameda Street for river activities, live animals, games, arts and crafts, live music, and booths. Kids 11 years of age and under are invited to participate in a fishing derby to hook stocked rainbow trout. Admission is free.

**SPRING FESTIVAL** $–$$
El Rancho de las Golondrinas
15 miles south of Santa Fe in La Cienega
at 334 Los Pinos Rd.
Take exit 276 off I-25
(505) 471-2261
www.golondrinas.org

During this two-day celebration on a weekend in early June, the old ranch comes to life with dancing, music, and demonstrations of the skills necessary for successful living in early New Mexico. Among the things you'll see are hand shearing of the curly-horned churro sheep; a procession honoring San Isidro, the patron of New Mexico farmers; a working blacksmith shop; and bread baking in traditional outdoor ovens. Music, dance, art, and entertainment add to the fun. Children younger than age five always get in free.

**i** The Santa Fe Opera offers a variety of programs designed to strengthen its ties with Santa Feans and broaden the local base of its audience. During fall, usually around Thanksgiving, a light opera is produced and presented—with full costuming and a live orchestra—at prices far below those charged during the summer season. These programs are popular, so get your tickets early.

## JULY

**CONTEMPORARY HISPANIC MARKET**
On the Plaza
(505) 992-0591
www.elmuseocultural.org

Running simultaneously with the Traditional Spanish Market (see later listing) this contempo-rary art show features a wide range of styles and media by artists from Santa Fe and elsewhere. First organized in 1986, this continues as the largest annual exhibit of contemporary Hispanic work in the Southwest. Expect to see the works of some 80 artists. It's a diverse show in terms of sophistication and content, with works in watercolor, photography, silkscreen, jewelry, sculpture, drawing, lithography, and more. Admission is free and El Museo Cultural sponsors the show.

**FOURTH OF JULY PANCAKE**
**BREAKFAST** $
On the Plaza
(505) 982-2002
www.uwsfc.org/pancakes

Food is the centerpiece of this day of community fun, a fund-raiser for United Way of Santa Fe County. Hundreds of community volunteers cook pancakes and ham; serve coffee, orange juice, and milk; and chat with the crowd. On the bandstand, entertainment ranges from mariachi music to flamenco dancing. A vintage car show presented by Santa Fe Vintage Car Club lines the streets. You can even sleep late if you want; the grills stay hot, and the pancakes keep coming until noon, or as long as the batter lasts.

**NEW MEXICO WINE FESTIVAL** $$
El Rancho de las Golondrinas
334 Los Pinos Rd., La Cienega,
15 miles south of Santa Fe on I-25
Take exit 276 to La Cienega and
follow the signs
(505) 471-2261, (888) 888-0882
www.santafewinefestival.com

Believe it or not, New Mexico has 21 wineries producing about 350,000 gallons of wine a year. Between noon and 6 p.m. on a Saturday and Sunday on the first weekend in July, you can sample some of these New Mexico wines while enjoying a variety of food and entertainment. The event, sponsored by the New Mexico Wine Growers' Association, also includes continuous live entertainment and agricultural product tastings and sales. Children age 12 and younger are free.

## SANTA FE CHAMBER MUSIC FESTIVAL $$-$$$$
St. Francis Auditorium in the
Museum of Fine Arts,
107 East Palace Ave.
(505) 983-2075, (888) 221-9836
www.santafechambermusic.org

The terrific Santa Fe Chamber Music Festival was founded in 1972 and is now one of the leading performance organizations of its kind in the United States. During the first season, 14 artists performed six Sunday concerts in Santa Fe and toured to several New Mexico and eastern Arizona communities. That season, Pablo Casals served as the Festival's honorary president, and a 20-year series of Georgia O'Keeffe posters and program covers began. Today the Festival presents more than 80 events during its annual summer season—including concerts, adult and youth education/outreach presentations, free open rehearsals, concert previews, and roundtable discussions with composers and musicians. The season runs from mid-July through the third week in August. In addition to what most people think of as "chamber music," the season features jazz and world music performed by musicians from the world's stages. Guest musicians have included Pinchas Zukerman, Jaime Laredo, Herbie Mann, Eddie Daniels, R. Carlos Nakai, and many more. Purchase tickets early; many concerts sell out. Venues include St. Francis Auditorium and the Lensic Performing Arts Center in Santa Fe and the KiMo Theatre in Albuquerque.

## SANTA FE INTERNATIONAL FOLK ART MARKET $-$$
Milner Plaza, Museum Hill
(505) 476-1203
www.folkartmarket.org

Santa Fe's first International Folk Art Market took place on Museum Hill the weekend following the Fourth of July in 2004. The event was such an immediate success, the only question in many globe-trotting Santa Feans' minds was: What took so long? Today, the market is the largest folk art market in the world and one of Santa Fe's most beloved festivals. Visitors stroll among scores of artisans from Latin America, Africa, Eastern Europe, and Asia in colorful booths laid out around Milner Plaza. Ethnic foods offered by some of Santa Fe's best restaurants and a varied roster of exciting onstage world music and dance add to the upbeat ambience. Attendees seize the opportunity to converse with vendors from around the world and purchase unique arts and crafts. A small sampling of their wares includes brightly colored textiles from Bangladesh, India, Ecuador, Bolivia, Lithuania, Madagascar, Mexico, Nigeria, Thailand, Cambodia, and Uzbekistan; *thanka* paintings from Tibet; exotic basketry from the Amazon rain forest; clever gourd arts from Peru decorated with intricate burnt designs; wood-fired ceramics from Japan; wood-block prints from Brazil; and a variety of ceramic and painted wooden sculptures from Mexico. Among the special events are artist panel discussions, hands-on children's activities, behind-the-scenes collection tours at the Museum of International Folk Art; an international folk-art dealer showcase; special Santa Fe home tours of private folk-art collections; and exciting stage performances from around the world organized by FanMan productions, Santa Fe's premier concert promoter. Tickets are half-price on Sunday "family days."

## THE SANTA FE OPERA
Community Concerts
Cathedral Basilica of Saint Francis,
131 Cathedral Place
(505) 986-5955
www.santafeopera.org

Each summer, The Santa Fe Opera and cooperating sponsors present free public concerts in Santa Fe and Albuquerque featuring apprentice artists from The Santa Fe Opera. The concerts, about an hour of arias, duets, and sacred music, offer a no-risk introduction to operatic music—and you don't even have to drive to the theater. The project started as a way to reach the elderly, disadvantaged, and children. Everyone is welcome. Admission is free. The Santa Fe performance is usually held late morning during the week in late July.

ℹ️ At Spanish Market and Indian Market, award-winning work tends to sell quickly. If you want to see the winners, come early.

## TRADITIONAL SPANISH MARKET
On the Plaza
(505) 982-2226
www.spanishcolonial.org
Unique work in the Spanish colonial tradition fills the Plaza for the last weekend in July. Much is religious—carved and painted images of the saints that reflect New Mexico's long isolation from the religious art of Mexico and Spain. Some 200 artists also display handsome tinwork, silver filigree jewelry, wood carvings, weaving, straw inlay, and embroidery. A special youth division showcases the creative efforts of more than 100 children and teens. Many of the artists featured here don't show in galleries; the Spanish Market and the Winter Market in December offer two of the few opportunities to see and purchase their work. Prizes go to the best entries in each medium. Music, dance, food, and pageantry add to the fun. Artists' demonstrations continue throughout both days. Admission is free.

# AUGUST

## ARTS AND CRAFTS FAIR
On the Plaza
(505) 982-2042
www.girlsincofsantafe.org
From early morning to dusk on the first weekend in August, the Plaza is filled with all sorts of arts and crafts from more than 275 exhibitors who come to Santa Fe from throughout the country. Girls Incorporated of Santa Fe, a nonprofit organization that offers programs for girls during the school year and throughout the summer, benefits from the booth fees. Santa Fe residents and visitors can see and buy paintings, handmade clothing, original toys, jewelry of all sorts, stained glass, and more. Admission is free.

## FIESTA MELODRAMA                    $$
Santa Fe Playhouse
142 East De Vargas St.
(505) 988-4262
www.santafeplayhouse.org
This funny, spunky show has a different plot each year but always features the same general tone—poking fun at Santa Fe's foibles. An anonymous committee puts together an original script about contemporary Santa Fe, structuring the show to resemble an old-time melodrama. The villain is always terrible, the heroine always in big trouble, and the good guys always win. The story itself draws on the city's freshest controversies and might include contentiousness among city, county, and state officials, Santa Fe's ongoing saga of street repair and crazy traffic, the water situation, the latest uproar in the arts, school politics, or New Age hype as subjects of its comic ridicule. The show usually opens in late August and runs through the Santa Fe Fiesta weekend in mid-September. Although some of the jokes might be rated PG-13, children are welcome.

## HACIENDAS—A PARADE OF HOMES
Various locations
(505) 982-1774
www.sfahba.com
The Santa Fe Area Home Builders Association offers this tour of more than a dozen new homes to showcase their members' most professional and creative work. A map guides visitors to the homes, built in various Santa Fe neighborhoods, from working class to millionaire territory. The tour features homes representing many varieties of building products as well as new styles. Green-built homes are of particular interest. You can pick the winners of juried competitions for Best Floor Plan, Best Kitchen, Best Craftsmanship, and other categories in each price range. The association also awards a "Best of Show" prize in each price category and an overall winner, the "Grand Hacienda." After you've seen the homes, vote for your favorite. You might even want to buy it! Tours are free.

## ICE CREAM SUNDAY $

Santa Fe Children's Museum
1050 Old Pecos Trail
(505) 989-8359

If there's any better way to sweeten a summer afternoon than with a bowl of ice cream, it involves adding the goodies you need to turn your vanilla into a sundae or even a banana split. The museum goes all out for this annual family-style fund-raiser. The sticky fun begins at noon, traditionally on the first Sunday in August, and continues until 5 p.m. or until the ice cream runs out. Santa Fe celebrities, including the mayor, the superintendent of schools, and chief of police, have helped with the scooping. Some years, a big red fire truck is on hand and the firefighters offer the little ones an up-close look. You'll also find music and performances by children throughout the day. Kids can also get their faces painted, ride donkeys, or jump themselves silly in the bounce-a-matic, one of those rubber rooms filled with balls. All the money goes directly for new exhibits at the museum, the only one in Santa Fe dedicated to kids. Admission fee includes ice cream.

## MOUNTAIN MAN RENDEZVOUS AND TRADE FAIR

Palace of the Governors
105 East Palace Ave.
(505) 476-5100
www.palaceofthegovernors.org

The Palace of the Governors, once the center of New Mexico's political life and now the main artifact of the newly opened adjoining New Mexico History Museum, hosts this colorful fair as a tribute to Santa Fe's history as a trade center. Demonstrations of mountain man skills and other events that may change from year to year are part of the event. The Mountain Men—contemporary versions of the original mountain men who lived off their wits and the bounty of the Western mountains as trappers, guides, hunters, and traders—display a variety of handmade items. You'll find examples of the goods their counterparts traded a century ago. And, yes, Mountain Women are also represented. Free.

## SANTA FE BLUEGRASS AND OLD TIME MUSIC FESTIVAL $$–$$$$

Santa Fe Rodeo Grounds,
Rodeo Rd. at Richards Ave.
(505) 385-4815
www.southwestpickers.org

For 35 years, folks who enjoy banjo and fiddle music and other traditional fare have gathered at the Rodeo Grounds for three days of great music in late August or early September. A series of Friday evening concerts opens the festival, followed by two days of workshops, band scrambles, jam sessions, and contests on Saturday and Sunday. The festival is a labor of love for the Southwest Traditional and Bluegrass Music Association AKA the Southwest Pickers. Among the highlights are original song-writing performances and concerts by the prior year's winners in the Bluegrass Band and Old Time Band contests. Don't miss the children's fiddle contest, which is usually held on Saturday morning. As part of the multistage event, the grounds are open to "rough" camping (no hookups). Children younger than age 12 are free and those older than age 65 receive a $2 discount. You can buy food and beverages.

## SANTA FE COUNTY FAIR $$

Santa Fe County Fair Grounds
Rodeo Rd. at Richards Ave.
(505) 471-4711
www.santafeextension.nmsu.edu/santa-fe-county-fair

Santa Fe County 4-H plays a major role in this three-day event, which draws produce, livestock, and other entries from throughout rural Santa Fe County. Among the highlights are the frog-jumping contest, a llama show, a herding-dog exhibition, and, of course, the livestock auction. Kiddie rides, entertainment, and concessions sold by bright-eyed 4-H'ers add to the fun. Don't miss the music and Western dancing or the chile challenge and salsa cook-off. Watch for it in the first two weeks of August. Admission is free, but there is a small parking charge.

## SANTA FE INDIAN MARKET
On and around the Plaza
(505) 983-5220
www.swaia.org

Serious collectors and the curious flock to Santa Fe for this show and sale, always held the weekend following the third Thursday of the month. One of Santa Fe's most famous and popular events, the market features a wide selection of the finest American Indian art from about 1,200 Indian artisans from 100 different tribes exhibit their work at more than 600 booths. Dancing, food sales (including favorites such as mutton stew), and demonstrations of various craft techniques add to the market's attraction. Indian Market includes a Fashion Showcase, a juried clothing show open to artists working in wearable art, sewing, weaving, and beadwork. A youth market occupies nearby Cathedral Park. Admission to the market is free.

The Southwestern Association for Indian Arts Inc. has presented Indian Market since 1922. It is the largest contemporary American Indian art event in the world, generating some $130 million in revenue for artists, galleries, and the tourism industry. (The average amount spent on Indian arts and crafts during the market is about $735 per visitor, organizers say.) The market has become a driving force in setting prices and standards for first-class American Indian art. Indian Market's awards program distributes more than $60,000 in prizes in numerous juried categories. Artists cherish the awards for the prestige they carry. There's a long waiting list of artists to join the market; these folks may have a chance if the artists first chosen sell out early during the market.

To make the market less overwhelming, SWAIA publishes a guide that lists every artist by name and category and includes a map of booth locations. You can pick them up at the SWAIA office, 125 East Palace Ave., Suite 65. Since the market draws more than 100,000 visitors, expect crowds.

Serious collectors become members of SWAIA for a chance to preview the prize-winning works before they go on sale the next morning. Memberships can be purchased at the new Santa Fe Community Convention Center, 210 West Marcy St., on Friday night before the preview. Having seen what they want, collectors line up long before the booths open for a chance to purchase the winning pieces.

During Indian Market, parking downtown is at a premium, and the city runs shuttles from outlying lots to reduce downtown congestion and frustration. Special shows and gala openings in most of Santa Fe's galleries, a concurrent Native film showcase at the CCA, and exhibits in the Convention Center and many area hotels also are part of Indian Market weekend. Speaking of hotels, make reservations early—some 70 percent of those in attendance come from outside New Mexico; the majority of these visitors say that Indian Market was the primary reason for their visit.

## SUMMER FESTIVAL, FRONTIER DAYS, AND HORSES OF THE WEST $$
El Rancho de las Golondrinas
334 Los Pinos Rd., La Cienega
(505) 471-2261
www.golondrinas.org

This outdoor museum comes to life the first weekend in August with an old-fashioned Mountain Man market and a festival celebrating the bounty of summer. Events include characters dressed as mountain men, soldiers, traders, and gunfighters, as well as music, dance, art, and fun for the whole family. Events run from 10 a.m. to 4 p.m. both days. Children younger than age five always get in free.

## WHEELWRIGHT MUSEUM AUCTION $$
Wheelwright Museum, 704 Camino Lejo
(505) 982-4636
www.wheelwright.org

Jewelry, paintings, and pottery by contemporary Native American artists will be on the auction block here, along with dinners donated by some of Santa Fe's finest restaurants. Art appraisals, spa treatments, or tax advice also are offered. But the real reason this event attracts a crowd is the high-quality Indian art sold to benefit the museum, one of Santa Fe's favorite institutions. The Wheelwright, a small, private museum devoted to Indian art, uses the auction as its main money-making event. The sale opens with a preview party on Thursday evening and a silent auction. The live auction usually begins on Friday about 1 p.m. Some 80 lots of antique and contemporary pottery, jewelry, Navajo textiles, kachina dolls, beaded goods, paintings, baskets, and more are featured. The auction audience gathers in a big tent on the museum grounds, usually the Thursday before Indian Market. You can meet the artists and authors and watch demonstrations.

## SEPTEMBER

### ASPEN VIEWING $$
**Santa Fe Ski Area, 16 miles northeast of Santa Fe on Highway 475**
**(505) 982-4429 in season,**
**(505) 983-9155 off season**
**www.skisantafe.com**
Ride the chairlift (from 10 a.m. to 3 p.m.) to enjoy shimmering golden aspen, fall wildflowers, and a stunning view. The aspen schedule depends on the weather; some years the viewing lasts from mid-September through mid-October. You can, of course, also see the aspen from your car and from other spots along Highway 475, including the well-named Aspen Vista hiking and picnic area. From the chairlift, however, you get an eagle's-eye look at the trees and panoramic views of mountains as far away as the Colorado border. You can purchase a one-way ticket and hike down through the spruce, aspen, and wildflowers or ride both ways. Lunch and snacks are served at the outdoor grill on the Ski Area deck near the chairlift. Bring a jacket—it's cool up here at 12,000 feet! Children shorter than 46 inches will ride for free if accompanied by a paying adult.

### FIESTA DE SANTA FE $$
**On the Plaza and other locations**
**(505) 988-7575**
**www.santafefiesta.org**
Fiesta is one of Santa Fe's favorite parties. Held the weekend following Labor Day, Fiesta commemorates the Spanish resettlement in Santa Fe after the Pueblo Revolt chased the conquistadores back to Mexico (see our History chapter). It's the oldest continuous community celebration in the United States.

Each year at the Santa Fe Fiesta, the city remembers the contribution of Don Diego de Vargas and the Catholic Church to the community's survival. The Fiesta began as a religious commemoration, but parties, parades, a fashion show, and Zozobra, a giant puppet that is burned with great fanfare, were added as the community changed and grew.

Even before Fiesta officially begins, Santa Fe starts celebrating. The Fiesta Melodrama (see August events), appearances by the Fiesta Queen and the Caballeros de Vargas, pre-Fiesta shows, and mariachi concerts are part of the fun. Throughout Fiesta weekend, the Plaza is alive with free entertainment provided by a variety of local and area music and dance groups. The Gran Baile de la Fiesta, or Fiesta Ball, a show of historic fashions, and a commercially operated carnival at the Rodeo Grounds add to the merriment. Admission is charged for the ball and fashion show, but Plaza events are free.

For most revelers, Fiesta begins with the burning of Zozobra on Thursday night. You'll pay to watch from the field, which is usually very crowded. Santa Fe artist Will Shuster created Zozobra, a 44-foot-tall puppet with glowing eyes and a gravelly voice, to personify the disappointments and mistakes of the year. (His nickname is Old Man Gloom.) Crews of volunteers build Zozobra the week before Fiesta and erect the big white puppet on a huge pole at Fort Marcy Park, 490 Washington Ave. As the sky grows dark, the puppet comes to life, moaning, growling, and waving his hands. (Very young children may be scared.) Finally, after a performance by the Fire Dancers and children dressed as Little Glooms, Zozobra disappears in flames to a rowdy chorus of cheers.

One of Fiesta's most charming events, the Pet Parade, or *Desfile de los Niños*, begins around 10 a.m. on Saturday. Children, parents, and pets ranging from cats and dogs to llamas and snakes circle the Plaza and walk along downtown streets. Many of the humans wear real or imaginary animal costumes, and many of the animals are dressed up, too. Watch from the shade of the Plaza or from in front of the Palace of the Governors, 105 East Palace Ave., just across from the Plaza bandstand. Arrive early for a good curbside seat.

Among Sunday's highlights is the Historical/Hysterical parade. The parade, which features floats, marching bands, horses, and politicians, begins at 2 p.m. It starts in the parking lots at DeVargas Mall, North Guadalupe at Paseo de Peralta, continues to the Plaza, and returns using a different downtown route.

A final review of Fiesta celebrities—Don Diego de Vargas, his court, and the Fiesta Queen—follows the parade. At 7 p.m. comes the Fiesta Mass of Thanksgiving at the Cathedral Basilica of St. Francis, 213 Cathedral Place, followed by a candlelight procession from the church to Cross of the Martyrs, north of Palace Avenue off of Paseo de Peralta. The soft light of hundreds of candles as the procession makes its way up the hill is a beautiful sight and an appropriate ending to the weekend's events. Viva la Fiesta!

## LABOR DAY ARTS AND CRAFTS MARKET
On the Plaza
(505) 988-7575 (number also includes Santa Fe Fiesta information)
Jewelry of all styles and materials—from delicate silver earrings to bolo ties like the ones cowboys wear—is one of the highlights at this end-of-summer show on Labor Day Weekend. You'll also find oil and watercolor paintings, sculptures, ceramics both useful and decorative, one-of-a-kind clothing, and more. Proceeds from the Plaza booth rentals benefit the Santa Fe Fiesta Council, the volunteer group who presents the community's biggest party, La Fiesta de Santa Fe. As with all Plaza art shows, artists have to submit their work to a jury and may sit on the waiting list before they get one of the coveted spaces to show and sell their creations. Since Labor Day brings a fresh wave of visitors to town, this show is especially popular.

## NEW MEXICO STATE FAIR $
State Fair Grounds,
300 San Pedro Blvd. NE, Albuquerque
(505) 265-1791, (800) 867–FAIR
www.nmstatefair.com
The New Mexico State Fair is one of the state's most popular events, and the fair's attendance records usually top all but two other shows in the West. (It's exceeded by the Texas State Fair and the Houston Livestock Show and Rodeo.)

The State Fair runs from early to mid-September. You'll find free schedules of each day's events and a map of the grounds at the information booth. Kids flock to the midway; the cowboy crowd loves the rodeo and accompanying country music concerts in Tingley Coliseum; and the cultured set is drawn to several galleries. Everyone likes the food, dished out by more than 100 vendors in virtually every corner of the fair grounds. Don't miss Indian Village, African American Pavilion, Villa Hispaña, and Pioneer Village, all of which serve up tasty ethnic dishes and pleasing entertainment. The fair also offers a day of bull riding and daily horse shows.

Animal exhibits include a large petting farm for the little ones. At the Creative and Home Arts exhibits, you'll find everything from dolls to homemade donuts. The Kid's Park midway for ages 12 and younger features its own gentler rides and two stages for performances, including a magic show and puppet theater. Children age two and younger are free.

## SANTA FE WINE AND CHILE FIESTA $$$$
Various venues
551 West Cordova Rd., Suite 723
(505) 438-8060
www.santafewineandchile.org
Food and wine tastings featuring Santa Fe's finest restaurants and dozens of the world's best vineyards, cooking demonstrations, food tours, a wine auction, seminars, and even golf and horseback riding—what more could you want in a gastronomic extravaganza? The annual Santa Fe Wine and Chile Fiesta has grown in size and stature since its founding in 1990. Highlights include demonstrations by chefs from Santa Fe's

top restaurants, a Georgia O'Keeffe country tour and wine luncheon, and a golf tour sponsored by Gruet Winery. The Big Event, subtitled The Grand Food and Wine Tasting, includes more than 200 varietals produced by 90 wineries to complement the chile-inspired cuisine prepared by some 60 of Santa Fe's best restaurants. Usually held over a five-day period in late September, the festival's smaller events (those limited to 25 guests) sell out quickly, and even the Big Event closes some two weeks before showtime. Reservations are usually due three weeks in advance. No one younger than age 21 is admitted.

**i** Change happens, even in a town as filled with tradition as Santa Fe. If you'd like to plan your vacation around a specific event, please call the sponsor or the Santa Fe Convention and Visitors Bureau, (800) 777-2489, or consult www .santafe.org to double-check dates and other specifics.

## OCTOBER

**ALBUQUERQUE INTERNATIONAL
BALLOON FIESTA**                                    **$$–$$$**
Balloon Fiesta Park
between Alameda and Tramway NE,
west of I-25, Albuquerque
(505) 821-1000, (888) 422-7277
www.balloonfiesta.com
If you're anywhere near New Mexico during the first two weeks of October, make it a point to visit this spectacular event. Not only is the Albuquerque International Balloon Fiesta worth the 60-mile drive from Santa Fe, it's also worth getting up before dawn to get there! The world's largest ballooning event, the Balloon Fiesta drew 621 balloons from around the world in 2008—and plenty of eager spectators. Pilots compete for prizes in precision events and fly for fun.

The nine-day festival includes mass ascensions held on the four weekend mornings and gala events that fill the sky with balloons of every shape, size, and color. The ascension begins at dawn—other attractions are even earlier. The

mass ascensions are the festival's most popular draws among spectators and you can usually see balloons as late as 10 a.m. Festival vendors peddle coffee, hot chocolate, breakfast burritos, and other morning treats to help you enjoy the show wide-eyed. As many as 800,000 people attend this event during its nine-day run. In addition to the balloons, the Fiesta presents live music, including jazz, country-western, and mariachi.

If dawn is too early for you, don't despair. You can get a taste of the Fiesta at the evening balloon glows. The enormous colorful balloons lit by the flame of their propane burners against the dark sky resemble oversized light bulbs lined up on the launch field.

Everyone loves the special-shape balloons so much that the balloons have been given events all their own—a special-shape mass ascension and a balloon glow "rodeo." Dinosaurs and dragons, flying shoes and bottles, fantasy castles, and a cow jumping over the moon delight the audience during each Fiesta.

Albuquerque hosts the Balloon Fiesta from the first Saturday through the second Sunday of October at the Balloon Fiesta Park near Osuna Road and west of I-25. Don't worry about getting lost if you're coming from Santa Fe—signs, the steady flow of vehicles, and traffic cops will help you find the field. Kids younger than age 12 get in free.

**i** If you go to Albuquerque for the International Balloon Fiesta—and you should—take a jacket or sweater. October mornings are warmer in Albuquerque than in Santa Fe, but you can still expect temperatures in the 40s. Don't complain: Balloons can stay afloat longer in the cool air.

**ANNUAL ALL CHILDREN'S POWWOW**
Wheelwright Museum
704 Camino Lejo
(505) 982-4636, (800) 607-4636
www.wheelwright.org
The oldest children's powwow in the country, this event attracts more than a hundred young American Indians who perform intertribal, blan-

ket, and social dances on either the first or second Saturday of the month. Prizes go to the winners in different age groups, and spectators are welcome to take pictures. Public events usually begin at 11 a.m. and run until dusk. If you can't stay the whole time, the Grand Entry that opens the powwow is especially colorful and photogenic. An all-volunteer staff does the organizing. Please call for current site information. The event is free. You'll also find American Indian crafts and food sales.

## ARTISTS' STUDIO TOURS
**Many northern New Mexico communities (see area newspapers for details)**
Fall is a wonderful time to visit Santa Fe and the surrounding communities, not only for the scenery but also for the visual-arts celebrations throughout the area. The dates and itineraries change from year to year, but you can usually expect El Rito/Ojo Caliente, Taos, Los Alamos, Madrid/Cerrillos, Abiquiú, Galisteo, Dixon, Chimayó, and other communities to participate. Artists open their studios to visitors, sometimes offering refreshments as well as an opportunity to buy work directly from the maker. You might discover the next star; and at the very least you'll have a chance to see some beautiful things and enjoy some of the wonderful landscape beyond the city limits.

## BARKIN' BALL $$$$
**Santa Fe Community Convention Center**
**210 West Marcy St.**
**(505) 983-4309**
**www.sfhumanesociety.org**
Barkin' Ball is *the* annual fund-raising event for the Santa Fe Animal Shelter and Humane Society, usually held the second week of October. Any well-behaved dog is welcome to attend. The event includes cocktails, dinner, dancing (with or without your dog), best look-alikes, canine costume contests, the shelter store, door prizes, and more. Human attire ranges from black tie to blue jeans, and costumes are encouraged (for both two- and four-legged attendees). Tickets are available at the shelter, on Santa Fe's northwest

side, off Highway 599, at 100 Caja del Rio Rd. They always sell out quickly.

## HARVEST FESTIVAL $-$$
**El Rancho de las Golondrinas**
**334 Los Pinos Rd., La Cienega**
**(505) 471-2261**
**www.golondrinas.org**
The Harvest Festival gives modern visitors a chance to see what the harvest season of the Spanish colonial era was like. Harvest meant hard work in early New Mexico, but the visitors at the reenactment get to have fun. Special events for this weekend in late September or early October depict life on an old ranch using volunteers in the costumes of the time. Music and dancing, artists, and craftspeople selling their work, and the baking and sampling of bread and biscochitos, New Mexico's famous anise and sugar cookies, add to the fun. Visitors can see a wheelwright at work, attend an outdoor mass, and join a procession in honor of San Ysidro. Adding to the harvest ambience, volunteers demonstrate techniques for stringing chiles into *ristras*, preparing fruits and vegetables for drying, making sorghum molasses, shelling corn and making *chicos* (dried corn to last the winter), crushing grapes for wine, and threshing wheat. The farm's animals—burros, horses, goats, sheep, turkeys, geese, ducks, and chickens—are always popular with children. Events run from 10 a.m. to 4 p.m. and food is available! Children younger than age five always get in free.

## SPANISH COLONIAL ARTS MARKET AND MEEM LIBRARY BOOK SALE
**St. John's College Great Hall**
**1160 Camino Cruz Blanca**
**(505) 984-6104**
**www.stjohnscollege.edu**
This market, not to be confused with the Spanish Market held in downtown Santa Fe in July, features some 20 of the area's best-known Hispanic artists working in the traditional style. The art sale, often accompanied by Spanish guitar music, is held on a Saturday mid-month from 10 a.m. to 3 p.m. The book sale, hosted by the college's Meem

Library, is also that Saturday and Sunday from 10 a.m. to 5 p.m. Admission is free, but bring your checkbook!

## TASTE OF SANTA FE $$$
**Santa Fe Community Convention Center**
**201 West Marcy St.**
**(505) 982-6366**
**www.tasteofsantafe.com**
More than two dozen Santa Fe restaurants strut their stuff, competing for attractive plaques and the bragging rights that go to the winners. But the real winners are Santa Fe's foodies and the New Mexico History Museum/Palace of the Governors, which receives the proceeds. Ticket holders sample and vote on everything from appetizers to desserts. Chefs go all-out for this event, and the food ranges from simple New Mexican dishes—Santa Fe's comfort food—to the fancy, exotic, and sublime, with an emphasis on locally sourced foods. A no-host bar and a coffee booth are part of the evening's festivities. A "nonessential auction," which usually includes trips and meals in private homes, is part of the evening's fun.

## NOVEMBER

### AID AND COMFORT GALA $$$$
**Eldorado Hotel**
**309 West San Francisco St.**
**(505) 989-8132**
**www.southwestcare.org**
Santa Fe gets into the holiday spirit with this festive, big-hearted event, always held the Saturday after Thanksgiving. In addition to fabulous buffets of tasty finger foods, AID and Comfort features a glittering assortment of entertainment, music for dancing, an auction of Christmas wreaths and other wonderful things, and a sale of Christmas trees decorated for the occasion. This is one of the few occasions when Santa Fe folks dress up grandly, and it's one of the favorite social events of the season. Tickets are available from Southwest Care Center, which offers one-stop specialized health care, social services, HIV testing, and advocacy to people with AIDS and their loved

ones and is the direct beneficiary of proceeds from the gala.

## OPEN HANDS BENEFIT AUCTION $$$$
**Nussbaumer Fine Art Gallery**
**314 S. Guadalupe**
**(505) 428-2346**
**www.openhands.org**
Open Hands serves nearly 10,000 elderly people in Santa Fe and is one of the city's most important nonprofit service organizations. The auction usually gathers great donations and a friendly crowd of bidders. Items available are primarily artworks by well-known local artists, meals at some of the city's nicest restaurants, weekend getaways, private concerts, and other pleasures for the mind and body. In addition to a live and silent auction, the afternoon includes refreshments, wine, and entertainment.

## OPENING DAY AT THE SANTA FE SKI AREA
**Santa Fe Ski Area, 16 miles northeast of**
**Santa Fe on Highway 475**
**(505) 982-4429**
**www.skisantafe.com**
If the snow gods smile on us, the ski area opens Thanksgiving Day. In good years, the lifts might start a little sooner; in snow-free seasons the opening is delayed. Sometimes just the beginner slopes are in good shape; some years the whole mountain is gloriously covered in sweet powder. Santa Fe's snow pattern differs from that of Colorado or Taos Ski Valley. The skiers usually frolic through mid-April. (See our Winter Sports chapter for other details.)

## SKI SWAP $-$$$
**Genoveva Chavez Community Center**
**Rodeo Road**
**(505) 955-4000**
The Santa Fe Ski Team, kids who like to ski race, sponsors this event to raise the money they need to travel from Santa Fe for races during the year. You'll find great buys on used, and some new, equipment here. You can recycle your outgrown, unneeded skis, boots, and whatever else in good cause. Volunteers include people who work in the

ski business. They can give you advice on how to buy boots and skis that suit your style. This is also a good place to find children's equipment. Admission charge is negligible during regular hours Saturday and Sunday, but quite a bit more for the preview on Friday evening before the sale officially begins.

# DECEMBER

## ANNUAL BAUMANN MARIONETTE PERFORMANCES
New Mexico Museum of Art
107 West Palace Ave.
(505) 476-5041
www.nmartmuseum.org
Created by well-known Santa Fe artist Gus Baumann, these puppets gave their inaugural performance in 1932. The ancient marionettes come out on stage only once a year to entertain children and their parents in St. Francis auditorium at the Museum of Fine Arts. The free shows, usually one on Friday night and a second on Saturday afternoon the week before Christmas, are part of the museum's holiday presentation, which is also held at the Palace of the Governors.

ⓘ Christmas Eve on Canyon Road is one of Santa Fe's biggest community events. As many as 10,000 people promenade up the narrow road lined with *farolitos* (brown-bag candle lanterns) and pause to sing carols around luminarias (bonfires) before warming up with a cup of hot cider from one of the art galleries along the way.

## CHRISTMAS AT THE PALACE
Palace of the Governors
105 East Palace Ave.
(505) 476-5100
www.palaceofthegovernors.org
Usually held on a Thursday and Friday evening in mid-December, Christmas at the Palace draws hundreds of Santa Fe families and lucky visitors. This annual community celebration brings the Palace of the Governors museum to life with music, stories, dance, puppet shows, a visit from

Santa, and more. Volunteers serve hot cider and biscochitos, New Mexico's traditional anise sugar cookies. The museum sparkles with *farolitos* and other decorations. Although the party is free, donations of nonperishable food for the poor are welcome.

## CHRISTMAS EVE FAROLITO WALK
Hillside Ave., Acequia Madre,
Cross of the Martyrs and elsewhere
in the downtown/Canyon Rd. area
no phone
On Christmas Eve, old Santa Fe twinkles with the light of thousands of tiny candles. The city's ancient neighborhoods are decorated with *farolitos*, little paper bags weighted with sand and lit with a candle. They line sidewalks and the tops of adobe walls. Neighbors and neighborhoods join to create the subtle, beautiful reminder of the days when Santa Fe was primarily a Catholic town where residents lit the way for Baby Jesus. Luminarias, or bonfires, stand on corners to warm the walkers. Because of the number of pedestrians along Garcia Street and Acequia Madre, the city closes roads in this area to all but resident traffic. The closure means that you don't have to walk through gasoline fumes and suffer bright car lights to enjoy the sights—but be sure to dress warmly. Some households or merchants along the way serve hot cider to passersby. Strangers often congregate to sing Christmas carols next to warm bonfires.

The Cross of the Martyrs, at the top of the hill just off Paseo Peralta near Marcy Street, is another fine place to see luminaries and *farolitos*. In addition, many churches decorate with *farolitos* for the Christmas Eve services, and private homes throughout the city keep the tradition alive.

While you're cruising, don't forget to take a look at the Plaza, which has an annual holiday ice sculpture carved by the kitchen staff at nearby La Fonda hotel in addition to its *farolitos* and other decorations. And the Inn at Loretto, a downtown hotel designed to resemble an Indian Pueblo, does Christmas up right with electric *farolitos* to highlight its many levels. All sights are free.

## HOLIDAY CONCERTS
**Various venues**
**(see the local papers for details)**
December is a wonderful month for music in Santa Fe, with nearly every performance group offering something to make your holiday season brighter. The Santa Fe Symphony and Chorus, Desert Chorale, Santa Fe Pro Musica Chamber Orchestra, and the Santa Fe Women's Ensemble offer performances to warm your December evenings. New Mexico Pro Coro, Sangre de Cristo Choral, Santa Fe Opera, and Music One (Santa Fe Concert Association) also usually schedule special performances for the holidays. For more information, please check the newspapers or see our The Arts chapter.

## LAS POSADAS
**On the Plaza**
**(505) 476-5100**
Wear your hat and gloves when you come to see this traditional New Mexican folk drama, which presents the story of Joseph and Mary and their search for shelter. (La posada means "the inn" in Spanish.) A troupe of costumed, bilingual actors performs this ancient play in original archaic Spanish beneath the stars, or amid snowflakes, usually on the second Sunday of December. The pageant concludes in the courtyard of the Palace of Governors with hot chocolate for everyone. Spectators are asked to bring a candle or a flashlight. No flash photography is allowed. The event is free.

## SANTA FE FILM FESTIVAL @ THE JEAN COCTEAU THEATER    $$–$$$$
**418 Montezuma Ave.**
**(505) 988-7414**
**www.santafefilmfestival.com**
Founded in 2000, the Santa Fe Film Festival has become a popular winter festival, taking place the first week of December, in the lull between Thanksgiving and Christmas. As many as 9,000 cinephiles, movie producers, directors, and actors have viewed all kinds of movies screened during the festival, from big mainstream feature premieres to quirky independent shorts, Southwest-themed movies, documentaries, films about the arts, and international films. The festival is guided by local film aficionados, including a local movie critic and several prominent producers and directors who make Santa Fe their home. Events include gala awards ceremonies, panel discussions, and retrospectives, which are usually held at the Lensic Performing Arts Center as well as SIFF's new year-round venue at the Jean Cocteau Theater in the Guadalupe District.

## VAMOS TODOS A BELEN (LET'S ALL GO TO BETHLEHEM)
**New Mexico Museum of Art**
**(505) 471-5041**
This well-loved Hispanic holiday celebration, sponsored by the Museum of Fine Arts and Rancho de las Golondrinas, kicks off the Christmas season in Santa Fe with a rousing selection of traditional Spanish and New Mexican carols and performances onstage in the beautiful St. Francis Auditorium. Everyone joins in with the better-known songs—all sung in Spanish on old instruments—and enjoys a miniature version of the longer Las Posadas performed on the Plaza, a reenactment of Joseph and Mary's search for an inn where Baby Jesus can be born. Hot chocolate, cider, and biscochito cookies afterward.

## WINTER SPANISH MARKET
**Santa Fe Community Convention Center, 201 West Marcy St.**
**(505) 922-2226**
**www.spanishcolonial.org**
Like its sister event, the Traditional Spanish Market in July, Winter Market showcases work in the Spanish colonial tradition by artisans from throughout New Mexico and southern Colorado. You'll find holiday gifts you can't buy anywhere else and a special booth of work by children. When they're not making sales, most of the artists are happy to explain the history behind their art. The Spanish Colonial Arts Society sponsors this event, which is usually held the first weekend of the month. Admission is free and the show runs from 9 a.m. to 4 p.m. each day.

# THE ARTS

Long before "cultural tourism" became a catch phrase, the arts and culture drew tourists to Santa Fe. Although the city is best known for its visual arts, as reflected in its nationally recognized museums and some 200 galleries, you'll also find opera, chamber music of all sorts, and vocal music. You'll discover theater, both homegrown and imported, and quite a bit of dance, including world-famous flamenco by Juan Siddi Flamenco Theater, in residence at a local hotel all summer. Since 2000, an international film festival has attracted movie fans from throughout the world. Santa Fe has everything from free performances to $100-a-ticket extravaganzas.

The arts here encompass the traditional and the modern. The prehistoric petroglyphs in the Galisteo Basin area and along the rock canyons of the Santa Fe River south of the city reflect the antiquity of Santa Fe's attraction as an arts center. The descendants of the city's founding families set the stage for Santa Fe's development as an art mecca with their indigenous arts—the colcha embroidery, delicate straw inlay, painting, and carving. The Spanish brought the arts of silversmithing, ironsmithing, and weaving to New Mexico. These early Europeans, who used their skills to create religious images and beautiful, practical items for the home and ranch, must have been inspired, as visitors are today, by the pottery and jewelry created at the nearby Indian pueblos.

## OVERVIEW

Santa Fe's blue skies, incredible light, and diverse landscape began to draw painters and photographers from the east at the start of the 20th century, first to Taos then to Santa Fe. The artists found plenty to inspire them—buildings that seemed to grow from the earth itself, narrow twisting streets, the blue bulk of the mountains and foothills framing the city to the east, and the fiery sunsets against the Jémez Mountains to the west.

Many of the earliest artists came seeking better health. The same sunshine and dry air that made them feel better also captured their eyes and imaginations. Carlos Vierra, for example, came for his health and made Santa Fe his permanent home. Vierra, a painter and photographer, worked with the School of American Archaeology (now the School of Advanced Research) and helped develop a unique style of architecture drawn from Santa Fe's antiquity and practical use of available materials. Vierra and other artists also pushed for the restoration of historical buildings.

He painted some of the murals that you can still see on the walls of St. Francis Auditorium at the New Mexico Museum of Art. Before World War I, Sheldon Parsons, Victor Higgins, Gerald Cassidy, William Penhallow Henderson and his poet wife, Alice Corbin Henderson, B. J. O'Nordfeldt, and many more artists came to Santa Fe, enriching the city with their art and energy.

The establishment of the Museum of Fine Arts (now the New Mexico Museum of Art) in 1907 gave Santa Fe artists a boost, helping them financially by making studios available and professionally by displaying their work. The new museum opened with an exhibit of art by Santa Fe and Taos painters. The artists donated paintings to the museum, forming the basis of its now expansive permanent collection. Many of those featured, including Pojoaque potter Maria Martinez who regularly demonstrated her artistry at the museum, are regarded as the most important U.S. artists of their time.

In the 1920s, Will Shuster—best known for creating Zozobra, a giant puppet that is burned as part of the Santa Fe Fiesta—and four other

Santa Fe painters moved to adobes off Canyon Road and became known as Los Cinco Pintores (The Five Painters). They spread the glory of Santa Fe's scenery and people with their art. Even earlier, John Sloan, George Bellows, and Leon Kroll—important names in the rebellious early 20th-century Ashcan School of American art—had visited and painted in Santa Fe. Edward Hopper and Marsden Hartley lived here in the 1920s and 1930s, as did Robert Henri and Andrew Dausburg. Writers "discovered" Santa Fe, too. Mary Austin, Willa Cather, Jack London, H.L. Mencken, Ezra Pound, Witter Brynner, and many others either lived here or were frequent visitors.

The Santa Fe Concert Band, which traces its founding to 1869, is the community's oldest performing organization still in existence. The all-volunteer band includes amateurs and some retired professional performers who still get a kick out of playing before an audience. The group performs several times a year, usually in public parks or on the Plaza, and all concerts are free. (Call 505-471-4865 for information.) Santa Fe Playhouse, formerly Santa Fe Community Theater, is another long-established amateur company, founded in 1922, just 10 years after statehood. Music One/Santa Fe Concert Association has brought classical music to Santa Fe audiences for more than 70 years.

Santa Fe's arts community took a step into the national spotlight in 1957, when the Santa Fe Opera staged its first performances. The Santa Fe Opera, with its commitment to nurturing American talent and offering a venue for new works, is a major player in the operatic world and draws opera fans and the curious from throughout the world for its summer season. Composer Igor Stravinsky spent more than 10 summers here, in part because of his affection for the outdoor Santa Fe Opera. (Please see our Close-up in this chapter.) The Opera's success inspired other performance companies, with the Santa Fe Chamber Music Festival, the Santa Fe Desert Chorale, and Santa Fe Pro Musica adding to Santa Fe's artistic reputation. María Benítez, one of the nation's best-known flamenco dancers and choreographers and a New Mexico native, singlehandedly promoted Spanish dance in New Mexico, through her flamenco school and by mentoring visiting dancers from Spain and across the United States. In 2008, she officially retired from offering nightly summerlong Spanish dance performances in Santa Fe at a local hotel in order to focus on teaching. In 2009, another excellent company with ties to Benitez, the Juan Siddi Flamenco Theater, took over summer residence at the Benitez Theater at the Lodge at Santa Fe.

St. Francis Auditorium, an attractive, shoebox-shaped hall, is a popular venue for musical groups. Acoustics are good here, but some audience members may have trouble seeing. The same is true for the beautiful but small Loretto Chapel and the Santuario de Guadalupe, a former church that serves as a museum, art gallery, and performance venue. The beautiful new Santa Fe-style Santa Fe Community Convention Center, which in September 2008 replaced the old Sweeney Center as the city's main all-purpose public space, can seat large crowds and offers convenient parking. The James A. Little Theater at the New Mexico School for the Deaf is among Santa Fe's most frequently used venues, in part because it was actually built to be a theater! In recent years the Santa Fe cultural scene has expanded with the addition of the downtown Lensic Performing Arts Center, El Museo Cultural (for Hispanic-related arts events) and SITE Santa Fe and other contemporary art galleries in the new Railyard Park, as well as the Spanish Colonial Arts Museum, located in the existing museum cluster at Museum Hill on Camino Lejo.

New Mexico's best-known painter, Georgia O'Keeffe, lived in Santa Fe in the years immediately preceding her death in 1986 and is honored with her own museum. O'Keeffe followed a long tradition of artists from the east migrating to Santa Fe, Taos, and nearby communities. Now, by some estimates, more than a thousand artists—some famous, some unknown but hopeful—live in Santa Fe and the surrounding area.

The New Mexico Museum of Art, The Georgia O'Keeffe Museum, and the exhibits at SITE Santa Fe add to the city's standing as a visual-arts center. The city estimates there are more than 200 art galleries here, making Santa Fe one of the nation's leading places to buy and sell art. Among the galleries are those that show work by well-known national and international artists, those that look for emerging artists and cutting-edge work, and some that strive to display paintings and drawings that average buyers can afford. From traditional cowboy paintings and sculpture to work by Santa Fe and Taos painters of the 1920s and 1930s to contemporary art and even some avant garde creations—if it calls itself art, you probably can buy it here.

But galleries don't have a monopoly on art. The long-established Indian Market brings leading American Indian artists and craftspeople from throughout the country to Santa Fe each August. Spanish Market, held in July and December, offers a rare occasion to see work patterned after traditional Spanish colonial arts created with fresh inspiration by living Hispanic artists. Santa Fe's Plaza hosts a parade of summer arts-and-crafts shows, which make shopping for art—or just looking—accessible to the whole family. (See our Annual Events and Festivals chapter for more information on seasonal art fairs.)

The city of Santa Fe's mural program has resulted in murals at City Hall, on street corner signal boxes, municipal buses, and even on garbage trucks. Aspen Santa Fe Ballet launched its first season in 2000. Arts of all sorts intermingle as part of the fabric of contemporary Santa Fe. From subtle chamber music to lively bilingual theater, it's hard to find a weekend without a concert, lecture, film, or recital to entice you. Enjoy!

The following listings offer a look at some Santa Fe arts organizations. For logical use, it is arranged alphabetically. Where possible we've given addresses for performance locations.

# COMMUNITY ARTS CENTERS

### CENTER FOR CONTEMPORARY
### ARTS (CCA)                                  $$
**1050 Old Pecos Trail**
**(505) 982-1338**
**www.ccasantafe.org**
CCA is an all-purpose arts center, providing the Santa Fe community with a movie theater featur-

ing foreign and art films, a performance stage dedicated to new and exciting dance and theater projects, and visual-arts galleries that feature emerging as well as internationally recognized artists. CCA is passionate about presenting cutting-edge, experimental, and simply beautiful art. You'll find detailed descriptions of all CCA's events on its Web site. There's plenty of free parking.

### EL MUSEO CULTURAL
### DE SANTA FE                             $–$$$$
**1615-B Paseo de Peralta**
**(505) 992-0591**
**www.elmuseocultural.org**
This mixed-use museum and cultural center, in the Railyard art district off Paseo de Peralta, occupies an old warehouse with a new artist-created front. Dedicated to the preservation and support of Hispanic history, traditions, culture, language, and art, the facility's offerings run the gamut. There are classes, seminars, and workshops for every age group and spanning a wide range of disciplines, along with visual-arts shows, theater, literary readings, dance recitals, lectures, music events, and other attractions, even including light opera. The museum also sponsors in-school education programs, field trips, scholarships, and conferences. Fees vary, although many events are free. Call for hours.

### LENSIC PERFORMING
### ARTS CENTER                             $–$$$$
**211 West San Francisco St.**
**(505) 988-1234**
**www.lensic.com**
Opened in early 2001 after an $8.2 million upgrading of a movie theater built 70 years earlier, the Lensic Performing Arts Center is the premier showcase for the offerings of Santa Fe's top performing-arts organizations, including the Santa Fe Symphony, Santa Fe Opera, Santa Fe Chamber Music Festival, Santa Fe Pro Musica, and others. Although these groups still use other venues for performances, at least some of their events are presented here each season. The Lensic management also schedules many of its own events, striving for both breadth and quality, and has an extensive community out-

reach program. In the course of a typical month, one might choose from a lineup that includes a classic movie, modern dance, traditional northern New Mexico music, a poetry reading, light opera, experimental theater, and an orchestra performance. The Lensic is also booked by groups and individuals touring nationally so its calendar is evolving constantly. Check local newspapers for listings or visit the Lensic's Web site. Tickets to all events are generally available at the theater box office; prices vary.

**SITE SANTA FE**                              $–$$
1606 Paseo de Peralta
(505) 989-1199
www.sitesantafe.org

SITE Santa Fe is a private, not-for-profit contemporary-arts organization committed to providing an ongoing venue for regional, national, and international exhibitions and interdisciplinary programs. Although best known as a visual-arts space in the Railyard district, SITE Santa Fe also hosts lectures and literary programs, sometimes in association with other arts groups. The Web site offers a useful calendar of events to keep you up-to-date on pending activities. The art space is open Thursday and Saturday 10 a.m. to 5 p.m., Friday 10 a.m. to 7 p.m., and Sunday noon to 5 p.m. Admission is free on Fridays. Individual events are separately priced.

**i** The $25 annual New Mexico Culture Pass offers one admission to the MNM museums as well as the New Mexico State Monument system and museums in Alamogordo, Albuquerque, and Las Cruces, a total of 14 in all. It's a good deal if you're traveling around the state.

# DANCE

**ASPEN SANTA FE BALLET**
**COMPANY**                              $$$–$$$$
550-B St. Michael's Dr.
(505) 983-5591
(505) 988-1234 for tickets
www.ticketssantafe.org
www.aspensantafeballet.com

The only professional dance company in New Mexico, the Aspen Santa Fe Ballet started in 1996 and has slowly grown. Ballet classes are offered for children and adults, including intensive training programs each summer. The students also participate with professional dancers in an annual holiday performance of The Nutcracker, presented by the Aspen Ballet. The company, with administrative headquarters in Aspen, Colorado, presents three productions each season, from August through March. The 2009 programs included A Gala Evening of Stars, Parsons Dance, and Mixed Repertory, premiering the humorous Sechs Tänze by Jiri Kylian. All performances are at the Lensic Performing Arts Center.

**MARÍA BENÍTEZ TEATRO FLAMENCO/**
**INSTITUTE FOR SPANISH ARTS**            $$
Bataan Memorial Complex
1050 Old Pecos Trail
www.mariabenitez.com

The Institute for Spanish Arts, the nonprofit organization that Benítez co-directs with her husband, Cecilio, presents workshops and classes in Spanish dance and music for adults and children. Offerings include flamenco, tango, cajon, martinete, bata de cola, and alegrias. Youngsters in Flamenco's Next Generation dance troupe perform on the Plaza stage during Fiesta and Spanish Market and in the Benitez Theater at the Lodge at Santa Fe on Sunday matinees.

**MOVING PEOPLE DANCE THEATER**
1583 Pacheco St.
(505) 438-9180
www.movingpeopledance.org

Founded in 2001, Moving People is the only home-based contemporary dance theater in Santa Fe. The spring Louder Than Words performance and holiday Swingin' Suites are popular annual events. The dance school also puts on an annual summer dance festival with specially choreographed performances at the Lensic Theater and a two-week dance intensive for serious students.

## NATIONAL DANCE INSTITUTE OF NEW MEXICO
1140 Alto St.
(505) 983-7646
www.ndi-nm.org

The National Dance Institute of New Mexico was founded in 1994 with the knowledge that the arts have a unique power to engage and motivate children. The purpose of the organization's distinctive dance programs is to help children develop discipline, a standard of excellence, and a belief in themselves that will carry over into all aspects of their lives. Dance educators teach a free-form jazz dance style to about 5,000 children in 72 public schools in New Mexico through the NDI Outreach program. Subsequent performances then are viewed by about 52,000 parents, teachers, and fellow students. In addition, NDI offers After School Advanced Training Programs for children who wish to make dance their career, and a Teaching Excellence Program for those who wish to become dance educators.

In 2000, in an unprecedented action, the Santa Fe School Board voted to lease NDI-NM three and a half acres of school land on the south bank of the Santa Fe River, near Alto Bicentennial Pool, at $1 a year for 50 years with an option to purchase. The NDI-NM Board of Directors initiated a capital campaign to build a 33,000-square-foot facility, the Dance Barns, and the beginnings of an endowment to ensure the future of our program. The performance space has allowed NDI to reach an expanded audience, and the facility is increasingly becoming a popular community center.

## RAILYARD PERFORMANCE CENTER
1611 Paseo de Peralta
(505) 982-8309
www.therailyardblogspot.com

Although privately owned and operated, this venue serves as an educational, cross-cultural meeting ground through the guise of classes, workshops, dances, and performances offered at modest prices—and sometimes free. Particularly popular are Saturday morning African dance and drumming classes, which have attracted scores of enthusiasts for years, and regular yoga classes.

Check local listings for one-time-only appearances by World Beat performers and members of Santa Fe's burgeoning marimba community. The space is large, with one of the finest hardwood dance floors in town, and located in the fast-emerging Railyard Park opposite the tracks from the new farmers' market.

## FILM

### CINEMATHEQUE PROGRAM                    $$
CCA, 1050 Old Pecos Trail
(505) 982-1338
www.ccasantafe.org

The Center for Contemporary Arts' Cinematheque is regularly voted Santa Fe's Favorite Art Film Theater in the annual *Reporter*'s Reader's Poll and screens some of the world's best movies, including classic black-and-white films, beautiful foreign films, and mind-blowing documentaries. Recent offerings include films from Africa, China, Israel, Iran, India, France, and Britain. Popular series include the annual Film Noir festival in July and the Santa Fe Film Festival in late November. The theater sells fresh popcorn with a variety of interesting seasonings, including curry, Parmesan cheese, and nutritional yeast. A new film opens every Friday and runs at least one week. Call for a schedule and show times or check the Web site. CCA has plenty of parking.

**More than 400 feature films have been shot in New Mexico, starting with silent pictures in 1898. The diverse landscape, incredible light, and rich blue skies top the list of why the state was chosen. Santa Fe and northern New Mexico have long been popular with moviemakers—more than half of the state's movies have been shot within the city's mountain and mesa vistas.**

### SANTA FE FILM FESTIVAL @ THE JEAN COCTEAU THEATER              $$–$$$$
418 Montezuma Ave.
(505) 988-7414
www.santafefilmfestival.com

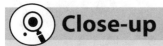 **Close-up**

## Tamalewood: New Mexico's Film Industry

Film makers have been making movies in New Mexico since 1898, and the state is well known as a retreat for actors such as Gene Hackman, Val Kilmer, Shirley McLaine, and Ali McGraw. But in recent years, the film industry has grown in leaps and bounds, backed by generous incentives from the New Mexico Film Office that have made the state attractive to Hollywood. It seems to be working. Since 2002, the state has hosted more than 115 feature films and television projects, 45 films in 2008 alone, that have benefited New Mexico to the tune of $1.2 billion dollars and counting. Of these, 22 projects to date have been backed by the state's loan participation program. A total of 3,829 new in-state jobs in film and related industries was created in 2007, and the number of trained in-state film technicians has swelled to 1,400 from just 60 in 2003, helped by the state's Pre-Employment Training Program.

Much of the success in attracting film makers can be laid at the door of New Mexico Governor Bill Richardson. Elected in 2002, after a campaign that emphasized growing new industries in this economically struggling state, Richardson immediately began working with the State Legislature to offer a series of initiatives to attract film makers. Generous benefits include a 50 percent reimbursement of wages for on-the-job training of state residents, a tax rebate of 25 percent on all direct costs and labor, and no-interest loans to approved film makers (i.e., those with large enough projects to already have distribution) of up to $15 million. "It was natural for us," Governor Richardson says. "We're close to Hollywood, so logistically and cost-wise it's easy for productions to be here. We have a tremendous climate and natural beauty, rich cultural traditions, and the most progressive production incentive program in the country. What's not to love?"

These days, it has become commonplace to run into movies being made on sets in scenic backcountry locations in New Mexico, such as Madrid, Galisteo, and the Jémez Mountains. The state is also investing in permanent studios to attract more than passing location shoots. Albuquerque Studios, a 500,000-square-foot, state-of-the-art facility in Albuquerque, opened in 2008, while Sony Pictures Imageworks recently announced the construction of 100,000-square-foot digital studio in cooperation with Albuquerque Studios, creating another 300 jobs for the state.

In a sign that New Mexico film making has reached a new level of maturity, in May 2009, Governor Richardson and actor/director Robert Redford announced a state-funded initiative to create Sundance in New Mexico, a program modeled on but separate from Redford's nonprofit Sundance Institute in Utah aimed at helping American Indian and Hispanic film makers develop programs in film, arts, and the environment. Sundance in New Mexico will be based at the historic Los Luceros ranch in Alcalde, north of Santa Fe, which was purchased from relatives of Mary Cabot Wheelwright in 2008. Redford has long been associated with New Mexico, after directing a film version of John Nichols' *The Milagro Bean Field War* in Truchas in 1988. For more information, contact the New Mexico Film Office, (505) 476-5600; www.nmfilm.com.

The Santa Fe Film Festival has grown to become a major ingredient in the city's cultural milieu. Organizers of the festival say the event is committed to "championing the power of film to span different cultures." The annual roster of films, videos, awards, and panel discussions reflects this vision, with an emphasis on cinema from a wide range of countries, viewpoints, formats, and styles, including a significant percentage from New Mexico. Some of the greatest living directors, producers, screenwriters, and actors (many of whom now live here full or part time or pass through often to film movies in New Mexico) are honored with awards at the festival, yielding opportunities to see some of their newest and most-classic work. Several world and/or U.S. premieres are also usually screened. The Film Center at Cinemacafe had spent several years ensconced year-round on St. Michael's Drive, a venue where the festival regularly screened independent and art films. In 2009 SIFF moved to temporary quarters in the old Jean Cocteau Theater near the Railyard, the future home of the state-supported Santa Fe Film Museum and New Mexico Film Office (see this chapter's Close-up: Tamalewood: Film in New Mexico). Films will be shown here irregularly. During the annual film festival, movies are shown at several venues around town, including the Jean Cocteau, Cinemacafe, and the Lensic theater.

Santa Fe is a hot market for art films—some studies have shown that the percentage of Santa Fe residents who attend these movies is the highest in the country. Many of those featured are regarded as the most important U.S. films of their time. Art films usually cost theaters less and build an audience over several weeks through word of mouth; blockbusters, in contrast, peak in their first week. Some 90 percent of films that are nationally distributed eventually come to Santa Fe.

## United Artists Theaters

**REGAL SANTA FE STADIUM 14**
3474 Zafarano Dr.
(505) 424-0799

**UA DE VARGAS 6**
De Vargas Center,
562 North Guadalupe St.
(Guadalupe St. at Paseo de Peralta)
(505) 988-2775

**UA NORTH 6, 4250 CERRILLOS RD. (SANTA FE PLACE)**
(505) 471-3377
United Artists is the central force in Santa Fe commercial cinema, with as many as 26 Hollywood

products on display—the movies that get the expensive TV commercials and whose stars are interviewed on talk shows and profiled in *People* magazine. The most luxurious of the multiplexes is the new Regal Stadium 14 theater, off Zafarano, near Santa Fe Place, which has stadium seating, state-of-the-art screens and surround-sound, and expanded concessions. United Artists North, now operating as a discount cinema, is at Santa Fe Place. The De Vargas theaters, specializing in art films as well as mainstream movies, allow people who live on the north side of town and visitors staying in the downtown hotels to not have to drive south to Cerrillos and Rodeo roads to catch a commercial hit. Parking can get very tight at De Vargas Center—especially in the evenings. Come early.

## LITERATURE

### Book Signings

Santa Fe is a literary center and has hosted such writers as Willa Cather, Carl Sandburg, Tony Hillerman, Vachel Lindsay, Robinson Jeffers, Thornton Wilder, Evan Connell, Robert Frost, and many more. Some only visited, some stayed for years, others live here still. Most weekends at least one author, either local or visiting, is celebrating the long-awaited arrival of a new book with an autograph party at any one of the local bookstores. Author talks and signings are also a favorite fund-raising tool. Santa Fe newspapers publish author interviews and information about signings. Sometimes in addition to signings, authors will read from their new works. Please see our Shopping chapter for the addresses and phone numbers of the bookstores.

Santa Fe is becoming increasingly known as a literary mecca. The city has 25 or so publishers and more than a dozen general-interest bookstores. The Lannan Foundation, which moved to Santa Fe from Los Angeles in 1997, offers grants and fellowships to writers.

## LANNAN FOUNDATION $
313 Read St.
(505) 986-8160
www.lannan.org
From September through May, the Santa Fe-based Lannan Foundation presents a series of "Readings & Conversations" featuring appearances at the Lensic Performing Arts Center by critically acclaimed authors and poets from throughout the world. The roughly once-each-month format usually includes the writer reading from his or her own work, followed by an on-stage interview by a distinguished guest. Those appearing have ranged from the famous—including Amy Tan, Peter Matthieson, Jamaica Kincaid, Eduardo Galeano, and Jim Harrison—to the less-well-known but comparably talented from countries around the world. Live radio simulcasts of events can be heard on KUNM-FM and again on Sunday afternoons on KSFR-FM. Videotapes of the series are available. Lannan also sponsors other literary events in Santa Fe from time to time, including appearances by writers and journalists in local schools, museums, and other venues.

## NEW MEXICO BOOK ASSOCIATION (NMBA)
Southwest Literary Center
826 Camino del Monte Rey
(505) 231-1755
www.nmbook.org
This Santa Fe-based organization works to nurture the growing literary and publishing scene throughout New Mexico. In recent years many small presses publishing fine works by local writers have emerged, tested their dreams against reality, and survived in pleasingly strong numbers. NMBA publishes a lively newsletter, *Libro Monthly*, with plenty of news from writers and publishers in Santa Fe, in New Mexico, and even out of state. The group hosts monthly luncheons for publishers, writers, and readers. It also publishes New Mexico's *Book World: A Resource Guide*, a directory of book people and services in the state.

## PEN NEW MEXICO
Southwest Literary Center
826 Camino del Monte Rey
(505) 983-9607
www.pennm.org
Chartered under the U.S.A. PEN Los Angeles Chapter, this group of local authors, poets, and translators started in 1991. A nonprofit professional organization, PEN sponsors local readings, seminars, regional conferences, and other events relevant to writers and the literary world.

## RECURSOS DE SANTA FE
Southwest Literary Center
826 Camino de Monte Rey
(505) 982-9301
www.recursos.org
Founded in 1984, Recursos is a nonprofit educational organization that includes among its missions the encouragement of good writing. To this end, Recursos Southwest Literary Center presents seminars, conferences, expositions, study tours, and academic and artistic projects. The Writers Reading Series in the Writers Room of the Southwest Literary Center gives Santa Fe a regular opportunity to hear poets, novelists, and nonfiction writers read from their works. Sponsored by grants, including support from the Witter Brynner Foundation for Poetry, a national organization based here, the free programs bring writers and readers together twice a month. A Discovery Reading presents less-familiar voices, winners of the national Discovery Writing Competition that Recursos sponsors annually.

In addition, each year the nonprofit organization conducts about six writers' workshops, which draw attendees from throughout the country. Topics have included Writing Women's Lives with Western States Book Award novelist Demetria Martinez, and Pam Houston, who won the same award for her short-story collection. George Johnson, former editor of the *New York Times* News of the Week in Review, joined other top writers for Writing Science Today, a seminar for professional science writers. Recursos also brings many major writers to Santa Fe each summer for its annual Santa Fe Writers Conference.

Student participants are selected based on written submissions; attendance is limited to allow for more individual attention at this popular and successful series. Faculty members have included Natalie Goldberg, E. Annie Proulx, Tony Hillerman, John Nichols, and many other published writers of national and international reputation.

## MUSIC

(In addition to the musical organizations listed here, please see our Nightlife chapter for more information on popular performance venues. Area casinos frequently host musical acts as part of their entertainment. Check the newspapers to find out who may be in town or our Attractions chapter for additional information.)

### Collaborations

**MUSICONE: SANTA FE CONCERT
ASSOCIATION** $$$-$$$$
**210 East Marcy St.**
**(505) 988-1234**
**www.ticketssantafe.org**
Since 1937 Santa Fe Concert Association has made Santa Fe a more cultured place to live by bringing in nationally known artists. Before the Opera and the Chamber Music Festival, the top-quality musicians who came to town under this nonprofit group's sponsorship offered city residents their only chance to hear national artists without a road trip. This group's impressive performance list draws the best musicians and singers from around the world. The association arranges a dozen or more events from September to May with performances ranging from soloists to string quartets, trios to chamber orchestras. In the 2009-10 season, guests included Anonymous 4; the Academy of St. Martins in the Fields, London; Chanticleer; Midori; Sarah Chang; and Dionne Warwick. The Concert Association's Christmas Eve and New Year's Eve concerts presented by local and visiting musicians have been a regular and very popular addition to Santa Fe's musical life since 1981. Performances take place at St. Francis Auditorium, the Lensic theater, the United Church of Santa Fe, and Cristo Rey Catholic Church.

**PAOLO SOLERI AMPHITHEATER**
**Santa Fe Indian School**
**1501 Cerrillos Rd.**
**(505) 474-4043**
**www.ticketssantafe.org**
Designed by and named for the famed Italian architect who apprenticed under Frank Lloyd Wright, Paolo Soleri is an open-air amphitheater tucked into the historic Santa Fe Indian School that's as popular among performers— Tracy Chapman, B. B. King, k. d. lang, Lyle Lovett, Ziggy Marley, the Neville Brothers, Steel Pulse, and James Taylor, to name just a few—as it is among audience members, who get to listen to world-class music under the Santa Fe stars. Tickets are available through the Lensic Performing Arts Center box office (See Catch Some Culture in Kidstuff chapter), (505) 988-1234 or www.ticketssantafe.org. They can be pricey—usually in the $30 to $50 range—but it's worth it for the experience.

**ST. JOHN'S COLLEGE CONCERT SERIES/
MUSIC ON THE HILL**
**St. John's College**
**1160 Camino Cruz Blanca**
**(505) 984-6104**
**www.sjcsf.edu**
Concerts here tend to stress piano music. Musician-in-residence Peter Pesic offers informal free noon performances in the spring and fall in the Junior Common Room of the Peterson Student Center with commentary about the music. During the summer, the college's athletic field serves as a popular sunset picnic spot for popular free Wednesday evening Music on the Hill concerts. Featured are local talent such as jazz musicians the Bert Dalton Trio, Michael Herndon, and Nacha Mendez and world beat by Wagogo.

**SANGRE DE CRISTO CHORALE** $$
**P.O. Box 4462,**
**Santa Fe 87502**
**www.sdcchorale.org**
The Sangre de Cristo Chorale is a volunteer choral ensemble established in 1978 to provide high-quality vocal ensemble music for the northern

New Mexico community. The 30-member group, whose members come from Santa Fe, Albuquerque, and Los Alamos, has been under the artistic direction of Dr. Doyle Preheim. Since its inception, the Chorale has presented hundreds of low-cost or free performances in the three communities. The chorale usually performs in December, March, and May; one holiday performance is free to the public to offer access to low-income patrons. The December concert in Santa Fe includes a holiday dinner. (It sells out in November.) Recordings of the chorale are available; call for information or visit their Web site.

## SANTA FE CHAMBER MUSIC
## FESTIVAL                                   $$–$$$$
239 Johnson St.
(505) 983-2075 office
(505) 982–1890 ext. 102
(888) 221-9836 (tickets)
www.santafechambermusic.org

One of Santa Fe's most esteemed musical groups, the Chamber Music Festival began in the summer of 1973 and has grown into an event with an international following. The Festival draws consistent critical acclaim for the depth of its programming and its vision in commissioning new pieces and presenting seldom-heard works. Each summer, performers at the Festival include established musicians and up-and-comers. A typical season features more than 30 concerts, composers-in-residence, emphasis on American music, and attention to masterworks. Jazz continues to play a major role, but the classics, performed by such musicians as Ani Kavafian, The Orion String Quartet, Leon Fleisher, and Pinchas Zukerman, form the festival's lifeblood. Repertoire ranges from the works of J. S. Bach to the world premiere of Bright Sheng's Festival commission, *The Silver River*. The Festival offers master classes each season with musicians such as Leon Fleisher, Ralph Kirshbaum, Michael Tree, and Pincas Zukerman.

The Festival arranges its programming in separate series to make it easier for patrons to hear the music they like best. The music is taped and often broadcast over public radio and on classical stations.

To help inform the audience and allow those who can't afford the high cost of tickets to attend, the Festival presents free concert previews about the music and artists. Immediately before the concerts, these discussions feature guest composers, artists, and musicologists reviewing the day's repertoire. The public can sit in on selected daytime rehearsals free of charge. As another part of its outreach, the Festival's musicians often give free concerts to senior citizens, residents of rehabilitation centers, schools, and hospitals. The Chamber Music Festival offers a special series for children, also free, and low-cost noon concerts.

Concerts are rehearsed and performed in St. Francis Auditorium and the Lensic Performing Arts Center. The season runs from the second weekend in July through mid-August. Seating is reserved; half-price tickets are offered a half hour before the concert, subject to availability (don't count on this; the Chamber is very popular). You may also order tickets through the Web site.

## SANTA FE DESERT CHORALE           $$–$$$
(505) 988-2282 (box office)
(800) 905-3315 (Tickets.com)
www.desertchorale.org

The Santa Fe Desert Chorale, a fully professional a capella chamber chorus, presents two seasons each year. The summer season offers more than 25 performances of four separate concert repertoires June through August. The Winter Season offers performances of "A Merry New Mexico Christmas" during the week before Christmas and "A Baroque Treasury" during the week following Christmas. The chorale performs in some of the most beautiful and historic sites of Santa Fe and Albuquerque, including the Cathedral Basilica of St. Francis, Loretto Chapel, Santuario de Guadalupe, and the Scottish Rite Temple. Since its inception in 1983, the Desert Chorale has been noted for its effectiveness of programming and virtuosity of performance. Critics and audience members alike have consistently praised the Chorale for presenting some of the world's most significant and engaging repertoire—from the ancient to the modern.

The Chorale has many recordings, including numerous American and world premieres, for sale at retail outlets and through its Web site. Summer concerts begin at 8 p.m. nightly, except Sunday, when the ensemble performs at 4 p.m. Call for information about the winter season and Christmas holiday series. A 50 percent student discount is available for all single-ticket and subscription orders.

ℹ **Many showbiz personalities have first or second homes in or near Santa Fe and many occasionally perform in local venues, often in support of the city's charities. Check local newspapers for information about such events. Names include guitarist Ottmar Liebert, singer Randy Travis, and actors Gene Hackman, Ali McGraw, Shirley McLaine, and Marsha Mason.**

### THE SANTA FE OPERA $$–$$$$
Santa Fe Opera Theater
7 miles NW of Santa Fe on
US 84/285
(505) 986-5955, (800) 280-4654 (box office)
www.santafeopera.org

The Santa Fe Opera presents five operas during its summer season, a combination of classics, rarely heard works, and American or world premieres in beautiful productions that attract opera lovers from around the world. The theater sits atop a hillside in the Sangre de Cristo foothills with a stunning view of the Jémez mountain range. Performances begin just after sunset so you can enjoy the natural light show first.

The Opera operated on a budget of $110,000 its first season; for the 2004 season, the budget was approximately $14 million. The Santa Fe Opera makes its musical magic with the assistance of more than 600 company members at the height of its summer season. Since the 1957 debut season, The Santa Fe Opera has presented more than 1,600 performances of 140 different operas. Forty were world premieres, and of that number, nine were American premieres, including Thomas Ades' The Tempest in 2006. Friday and Saturday performances frequently sell out

in advance. Normal repertoire includes familiar operas such as La Traviata and Don Giovanni in 2009; an older, seldom-heard work, such as Handel's Semele; and an American or world premiere such as 2009's The Letter by Paul Moravec.

In addition to its willingness to take a chance on a new work, the Santa Fe Opera also takes a chance on new talent with its extensive apprentice singer and technician programs. Apprentices, chosen by audition, appear in the productions as chorus members and understudies for major roles. They learn the many facets of opera from some of the world's best conductors, directors, and coaches. Well-known singers, including Samuel Ramey, Ashley Putnam, and James Morris, are among the program's graduates. Kiri te Kanawa made her American debut here, as did Bryn Terfel. Each August the Opera gives the apprentices the stage on their own, in two performances that showcase their talents with a variety of opera vignettes. Technical apprentices learn lighting, costumes, sets, wigs, makeup, and more.

Backstage tours through the costume shop and production area continue late June through August, Monday through Saturday at 9 a.m.; reservations are not required. Since the company makes most of its own sets, props, and costumes, there's plenty to see. The company offers elegant pre-performance buffets with guest speakers. The theater has two bars that serve light fare and libations. At the gift shop you can buy tote bags, sweatshirts, and other merchandise with the distinctive SFO logo, and a portion of the sales benefits the company. Both merchandise and tickets are sold online. The season runs from late June or early July through the last week in August.

ℹ **The Santa Fe Opera was founded in 1957 by John Crosby, a young conductor from New York. He stepped down as general director at the end of the 2000 season—the longest-tenured operative in such a role in America, and was succeeded by Englishman Richard Gaddes, who introduced a more community-oriented expanded program. In 2008, Charles MacKay succeeded Gaddes as director, only the third director in the Opera's history.**

## THE OPERA BUILDING

The Santa Fe Opera completely rebuilt its theater beginning in the fall of 1997 to preserve the open-air ambience while offering the audience more protection from the elements. The new theater, designed by Polshek Partnership of New York, has won a number of important awards for its design. The redesign completely roofed the audience seating area and extended the roofline farther on the sides. The new theater seats 2,128 patrons with additional standing-room designation. The remodeling added 37 lavatory fixtures, five drinking fountains, and three public telephones. The reconstruction, a $19.5 million project, also included better wheelchair accessibility and an electronic libretto system, which provides an English and Spanish translation of the dialogue on stage on a small screen located directly in the front of each seat. Patrons can turn the screen on or off as they wish. Behind the scenes, the Santa Fe Opera has a wetlands sewage treatment and water reclamation system to harvest rainwater from summer thunderstorms.

### SANTA FE PRO MUSICA CHAMBER
### ORCHESTRA AND ENSEMBLE        $$$–$$$$
(505) 988-4640, (800) 960-6680
www.santafepromusica.com
This group consists of a 35-member chamber orchestra and a more intimate chamber ensemble series. The orchestra performs without a conductor in a long-standing tradition of chamber orchestras of the 18th century. Pro Musica presents concerts from October through May and offers an annual Mozart & Haydn Festival,

Santa Fe Bach Festival, and popular Baroque Christmas Concerts in the historic Loretto Chapel. The ensemble presents Santa Fe Bach Festival performances on period instruments—wooden rather than metal flutes, string instruments using gut strings rather than steel. Pro Musica engages some of the world's leading soloists, including Ani Kavafian, David Jolley, John Elwes, Allan Vogel, Kurt Ollmann, Rachel Podger, and Van Cliburn piano competition winner José Feghali. The group covers an impressive repertoire, with works from Beethoven and Vivaldi as well as contemporary masters who celebrate the concerto and symphonic forms. Pop music stars play benefits as well. Tickets for full-time students are half price. Concerts are held at the Lensic Performing Arts Center and Loretto Chapel.

### SANTA FE SYMPHONY AND
### CHORUS        $$–$$$$
(505) 983-1414; (800) 480-1319 (tickets)
www.sf-symphony.org
Since its founding in 1984, the symphony has become known for its outstanding performances by New Mexican musicians and has featured such guest artists as Andre Watts, Elmer Bernstein, Marilyn Horne, and Dave Grusin. The symphony has been heard nationwide on National Public Radio's Performance Today series. The group won Santa Fe's appreciation for presenting the inaugural local performances of such masterpieces as Berlioz's L'Enfance du Christ, the complete Brandenburg Concerti by J. S. Bach, and Handel's Messiah. Premieres, including Mark O'Connor's Fiddle Concerto, are also part of the repertory. The season runs from October through June with nine concerts, including such annual favorites as Holiday Traditions and the Beethoven Festival, as well as new presentations such as The Music of Spain and Mexico and an expanded Beethoven Festival spotlighting talented local soloists. Concerts are held at the Lensic Performing Arts Center.

### SANTA FE WOMEN'S ENSEMBLE        $$
(505) 954-4922
www.sfwe.org

This 12-voice group has delighted Santa Fe audiences since 1980 and attracts an enthusiastic audience. The women sing two concerts a year, their Spring Offering and a Christmas Offering. Past concerts have included Gerald Near's The Storke and Gyorgy Orban's Mass #6. Performances are held at Christmas in the jewellike Loretto Chapel, which sets off the voices in splendor; the Spring Offering is performed at the historic Santuario de Guadalupe. Compact discs of the Ensemble are sold at its concerts and Web site.

**SERENATA OF SANTA FE**          **$$**
**P.O. Box 8410, Santa Fe 87504**
**(505) 989-7988**
Another of Santa Fe's long-established musical groups, the Serenata has two goals: to present chamber music to audiences of all economic resources in an informal, friendly way and to provide an opportunity for musicians to get together to perform pieces they love. All programs are presented in the Santuario de Guadalupe and range from solo music to octets. Ensemble members may chat with the audience about the music and composer prior to concerts. The ensemble's players change, and guest performers may be added depending on the pieces in rehearsal for any of their four or more annual concerts. But the group prides itself on not compromising on rehearsal time and not shying away from challenging works.

## THEATER

(Companies that offer performances and classes for children are featured in our Kidstuff chapter.)

**ENGINE HOUSE THEATRE**          **$–$$**
**Melodrama Company**
**2846 Hwy. 14, Madrid**
**(505) 438-3780**
For unadulterated fun, it's hard to top the Madrid melodrama. Since 1982, the company based in the old theater next to the Mine Shaft Tavern has drawn enthusiastic crowds to cheer for the heroes and hiss at the bad guys. Bags of marshmallows to toss at the villain are included with admission.

The plays are 1800s-style melodramas that fit in well with this old one-time mining town. The season runs weekends from Memorial Day through Columbus Day. Curtain time is 3 and 8 p.m. on Saturday and 3 p.m. on Sunday and Monday holidays, with matinees only during October. Allow at least a half hour to get to the theater from Santa Fe. The drive from Santa Fe, along what's known as the Turquoise Trail because of the historic turquoise mines here, will take you past the village of Cerrillos. Madrid, an old mining town, is now rich with unique shops and galleries. Leave early and poke around a little.

**LENSIC PERFORMING ARTS CENTER**
**225 West San Francisco St.**
**(505) 988-1234 (box office)**
**www.lensic.com (general info)**
**www.ticketssantafe.org (tickets)**
Virtually all of the city's major performing arts organizations now use the world-class Lensic for at least some of their performances. The list includes the Santa Fe Desert Chorale, Santa Fe Pro Musica, Santa Fe Symphony, Santa Fe Chamber Music Festival, Santa Fe Opera, and Lannan Foundation (for readings and talks by distinguished authors and poets). Situated in the heart of downtown and across the street from an ample parking garage, the Lensic is an architectural gem that offers a state-of-the-art acoustic system, comfortable seating, excellent sight lines, and other amenities. The center's schedule is posted on its Web site and updated daily. Even if you are in Santa Fe for only a few days, an evening at the Lensic is highly recommended. For more information, see Community Arts Centers listing above.

**SANTA FE PLAYHOUSE**          **$$**
**142 East De Vargas St.**
**(505) 988-4262 (box office)**
**www.santafeplayhouse.org**
The oldest continuously running theater company west of the Mississippi, the tiny Santa Fe Playhouse was founded in 1922 by famed writer Mary Austin. The company dedicates itself to presenting works that give voice to New Mexico's varied cultures and communities. The Playhouse

offers year-round theater with musicals, comedies, dramas, murder-mysteries, and classics in the mix, usually five or six each year. Located 3 blocks from the Plaza in Santa Fe's ancient Barrio de Analco—one of the oldest neighborhoods in America—the Playhouse theater is an intimate 99-seat historic adobe building. The Santa Fe Fiesta Melodrama, which pokes fun at the city's events, politicians, celebrities, and quirks in the guise of an old-time melodrama, is the group's best-known production, running late August through Fiesta. Other theater groups frequently use this space as well; the Southwest Children's Theatre (www.santafechildrenstheatre.com) is a popular branch of the theater that focuses on getting children involved in theater in their own productions. On Sundays, the theater offers a popular "pay what you wish" option.

## THEATER GROTTESCO                    $$
(505) 474-8400
www.theatergrottesco.org

Founded in Paris in 1983, Theater Grottesco began as a touring company and moved to Santa Fe in 1996. They've been busy ever since. In addition to continuing their national tours, the company has become an active player in the city's theatrical world. During their May through June season, Grottesco has produced original full-length plays and short pieces, presenting its work in various performance spaces around town. The company focuses on homegrown talent in terms of writers, actors, and designers and has plans for an expanded season. Performances take place at various venues. In 2009, the company performed *The Richest Dead Man Alive!* at the Stieren Theater at the Santa Fe Opera.

## THEATERWORK                          $$
1336 Rufina Circle
(505) 471-1799
www.theaterwork.org

Theaterwork is a nonprofit theater company that offers a season from September through June. Since 1996, the company has presented nearly 90 full-length productions ranging from the classics and operas to original new works by local play-

wrights. The theater also hosts play and poetry readings of area writers. The company members offer classes in acting, design, play writing, and story collecting for children and adults. Theaterwork also has a conservatory program for teens who are interested in learning about all aspects of theater. Theaterwork presented Moliere's *Le Malade Imaginaire (The Imaginary Invalid)* at the James A. Little Theater on the New Mexico School for the Deaf campus at 1060 Cerrillos Rd. in 2009. Performances take place Friday and Saturday evenings and Sunday matinees.

## WISE FOOL PUPPET THEATER
2778 Agua Fria, Unit BB
(505) 992-2588
www.wisefoolnewmexico.org

Wise Fool New Mexico is a nonprofit theater-arts project created and staffed by four women artists of diverse backgrounds (Chicana, Native, Anglo, and Jewish) who are dedicated to art as a means of changing our world. In the folk traditions of storytelling, puppetry, circus arts, and public spectacle, they create accessible, highly visual, and participatory performances and lead hands-on workshops in such popular activities as stilt walking and trapeze. Wise Fool encourages dialogue and cooperation through shared creative process, using imagery, music, and theater arts to empower people to become larger than life, speak out, listen, and find common ground. Founded in 1993, Wise Fool has been creating original works for theaters, schools, libraries, and parks to rave reviews and sell-out audiences for 16 years.

# VISUAL ARTS

## Noncommercial Galleries

(For information about Santa Fe's main art museums please see our Attractions chapter.)

## THE GOVERNOR'S GALLERY
New Mexico State Capitol, Fourth Floor,
Old Santa Fe Trail at Paseo de Peralta
(505) 827-3028

Exhibits here feature New Mexico artists and change with some frequency. Receptions for the artists are always open to the public. These exhibits bring people to the State Capitol and introduce the many Roundhouse visitors and state workers to a wide assortment of visual art. The gallery also hosts an annual exhibit of work by the winners of the Governor's Awards for Excellence in the Arts, a program to recognize New Mexican painters, writers, musicians, dancers, and others whose creative work makes the state a better place to live. An outreach of the Museum of Fine Arts, the gallery is open 8 a.m. to 5 p.m. Monday through Friday. Admission is free. Check local newspaper listings for occasional openings and receptions; the governor may even attend!

## ST. JOHN'S COLLEGE GALLERY
**Second Floor, Peterson Student Center**
**1160 Camino de la Cruz Blanca**
**(505) 984-6199**
**www.stjohnscollege.edu**
This small exhibit space hosts shows from faculty members and artists of national reputation and also promotes local artists. There's an annual student show, judged by members of the college's Fine Arts Guild, as well as an annual juried faculty-and-staff show. The hours fluctuate, but the gallery is normally open from 5 to 8 p.m. Friday and Saturday and from 1 to 5 p.m. on Sunday and by appointment. Admission is free.

**i** **Though best known for artists and movie stars, Santa Fe also has more than its share of authors. Among them are best-selling mystery writers Sarah Lovett and Michael McGarrity, New Western writer Cormac McCarthy, and thriller novelist David Morrell.**

## Private Galleries

Santa Fe has more than 200 private galleries, where you'll discover an exciting variety of visual arts. What we offer here is just a small sampling of them. Many of the galleries listed here are members of the Santa Fe Gallery Association. Galleries

that feature predominately American Indian and/or Hispanic arts are featured in the Regional Arts chapter.

## THE ALLAN HOUSER COMPOUND $$
**P.O. Box 5217, Santa Fe 87502**
**(505) 471-1528**
**www.allanhouser.com**
The Allan Houser Compound, located 20 minutes south of Santa Fe, features gardens devoted to the presentation of the sculpture of Apache artist Allan Houser, one of the best-known American Indian artists in the world. Before his death in 1994, Houser constructed a sculpture studio, visitor center, exhibition gallery, and sculpture garden. The project has grown and the studio expanded into a complete bronze foundry. The sculpture garden now displays both the family collection of Houser's work and available bronze editions. Tours of the 110-acre sculpture walk, private family collection, and showroom are available to individuals and groups by advance appointment only.

## ANDREW SMITH GALLERY INC.
**122 Grant Ave.**
**(505) 984-1234**
**www.andrewsmithgallery.com**
Andrew Smith Gallery has an exclusive focus on fine American photography and has been in business since 1974. You'll discover a broad and deep selection of work by the major photographers of the 19th and 20th centuries. The gallery carries original classic photography of the American West by E. S. Curtis, Charles Lummis, and others—along with work by Ansel Adams, Eliot Porter, Edward Weston, and more. The gallery is open Monday through Saturday from 10 a.m. to 5:30 p.m. and Sunday from noon to 4 p.m.

## CHARLOTTE JACKSON FINE ART
**200 West Marcy St., Suite 101**
**(505) 989-8688**
**www.charlottejackson.com**
Carving her own niche in Santa Fe's diverse art market, Charlotte Jackson represents "concrete" and radical painters from the United States and

Europe. These large monochromatic works are seldom seen in the United States. Sculpture and paintings that focus on the exploration of light and surface are also in the collection. Exhibits rotate throughout the year. The gallery also hosts lectures and sponsors publications. It is open Monday through Friday from 10 a.m. to 5 p.m. and Saturday from 11 a.m. to 4 p.m.

## EVO GALLERY
**554 South Guadalupe**
**(505) 982-4610**
**www.evogallery.com**
Located in an attractive, airy, purpose-built warehouse-style building across from SITE Santa Fe in the new Railyard Park, EVO specializes in innovative global art. It represents emerging artists such as Luke Dorman, Dana Chodzko, and Richard Serra as well as established contemporary masters such as Agnes Martin, Jasper Johns, and Jenny Holzer. It's open 10 a.m. to 3 p.m. Tuesday to Friday and 10 a.m. to 5 p.m. Saturday.

## GERALD PETERS GALLERY
**1011 Paseo de Peralta**
**(505) 954-5700**
**www.gpgallery.com**
For 30 years the Gerald Peters Gallery has been a must-see destination for serious art lovers, first in its historic Camino de Monte Sol home and now in larger, grander headquarters. Dedicated to the research, exhibition, and sale of important American paintings of the 19th and 20th centuries, Peters's well-designed 8,500-square-foot gallery space puts many museums to shame.

When it opened in August 1998, Gerald Peters Gallery was heralded by the Dallas Morning News as a symbol of new vitality in the Santa Fe art world. More than 9,000 people passed through opening weekend. Located downtown near Canyon Road, the gallery was designed in traditional Pueblo style, with a lush sculpture garden, attractive landscaping, and museum-quality exhibition space. Beginning with his interest in art of the American West, Peters built a collection centered around the Taos Founders and the Santa Fe art

colony and included the artists of classic Western painting and sculpture. In addition to these works, the gallery also displays American Impressionists, American Modernists (including Georgia O'Keeffe), abstract expressionists, contemporary realists, contemporary sculpture, and vintage and contemporary photography.

The gallery is open Tuesday through Saturday, 10 a.m. to 5 p.m. The adjoining lot offers ample parking.

**i** The McCune Charitable Foundation, the second-largest grant-making institution in New Mexico, is based in Santa Fe and supports many local arts groups, including the International Folk Art Foundation.

## LEWALLEN CONTEMPORARY
**129 West Palace Ave.**
**(505) 988-8997**
**1613 Paseo de Peralta**
**(505) 988-3250**
**Satellite: Encantado Resort**
**(505) 946-5778**
**www.lewallengalleries.com**
One of the largest contemporary galleries in the Southwest, with more than 11,000 square feet of exhibit space downtown, LewAllen was founded by the legendary Elaine Horwitch and has since been expanded by subsequent owners. It hosts monthly rotating exhibitions of contemporary artworks in all media by regionally, nationally, and internationally celebrated artists. You'll see artworks by Forest Moses, John Fincher, Emmi Whitehorse, and Judy Chicago. The gallery has been in Santa Fe for more than 30 years and has recently added a second downtown branch in a purpose-built warehouse-style building in the new Railyard Park, opposite Warehouse 21. There is also a small satellite branch at the Auberge Encantado Resort off State Route 592. The downtown galleries are open Monday through Saturday from 10 a.m. to 6 p.m. and Sunday 11 to 5 p.m. The Encantado branch is open 10 a.m. to 6 p.m. daily.

## LINDA DURHAM CONTEMPORARY ART
1101 Paseo de Peralta
(505) 466-6600
www.lindadurham.com

Located in an attractive building opposite the P.E.R.A. parking lot on Paseo de Peralta, this gallery shows serious, abstract contemporary New Mexico-based artists. The owner has been in business since 1977, knows her stuff, and is considered a forerunner of contemporary art in New Mexico. She represents such interesting local artists as sculptors Erika Wanenmaker and Stacey Neff. Durham's stated mission is nothing less than the "pursuit of truth and beauty" through art. The gallery has a strong community focus. Opening hours are Tuesday through Saturday 10 a.m. to 5 p.m.

## NEDRA MATTEUCCI GALLERIES
1075 Paseo de Peralta
(505) 982-4631
www.matteucci.com

Nedra Matteucci Galleries on Paseo de Peralta, formerly Fenn Gallery, has been in business since 1988, and specializes in 19th- and 20th-century art masters. The gallery features paintings from California regionalists and work by the Hudson River, Ashcan, and Brandywine Schools. And New Mexico isn't ignored; you'll find first-rate, museum-quality bronzes and paintings by the Santa Fe and Taos artists who put New Mexico on the cultural map more than 55 years ago. The gallery displays work by Joseph H. Sharp, E. Martin Hennings, Walter Ufer, Victor Higgins, Nicolai Fechin, Leon Gaspard, and Fremont Ellis. Outside, monumental sculpture by Dan Ostermiller, Glenna Goodacre, and many others is featured in the gallery's beautifully landscaped garden, complete with a large pond. The gallery is open Monday through Saturday from 8:30 a.m. to 5 p.m.

## PEYTON WRIGHT GALLERY
237 East Palace Ave.
(505) 989-9888, (800) 879-8898
www.peytonwright.com

Peyton Wright Gallery, located in the historic Spiegelberg house at the corner of Palace Avenue at Paseo de Peralta, features both contemporary and historic works of art. You can find extensive offerings of Spanish colonial, African, Russian, Native American, and Pre-Columbian art and antiquities in an ambience of museum quality. Exhibitions change monthly and include contemporary painting, sculpture, and works on paper by emerging, mid- and late-career artists of both national and international repute. Established in 1989, the gallery is open Monday through Saturday from 10 a.m. to 5 p.m. and Sunday by appointment.

## REFLECTION GALLERY
201 Canyon Rd.
(505) 995-9795
www.reflectiongallery.com

This gallery is at the base of Canyon Road in a 78-year-old adobe home. It features traditional, realist, and impressionist works by artists such as Vladimir Nasonov, Robert Cook, Jan Saia, Yuri Novikov, and Jei Wei Zhou. Patrons can park in the rear. The gallery is open daily from 10 a.m. to 5:30 p.m.

## VICTORIA PRICE CONTEMPORARY
1512 Pacheco St.,
Building B, Suite 102
(505) 982-8632
www.victoriaprice.com

Victoria Price Art & Design purchased the former Dewey Galleries in 2003, well known for its historic Native American art. Today, its offerings include fine art, contemporary home furnishings, Navajo textiles, tableware, contemporary art jewelry, art consultation, interior design services, and custom furniture design. It's a great one-stop shop for unique, functional but beautiful items for the home that have oodles of style. The owner is a down-to-earth New Mexico native and has an eclectic background as an art historian, writer, screenwriter, designer, and business owner. She is the daughter of the late actor Vincent Price.

# SUPPORT ORGANIZATIONS

## NEW MEXICO ARTS
La Villa Rivera Building
228 East Palace Ave.
(505) 827-6490, (800) 879-4278
www.nmarts.org

New Mexico Arts, an arm of state government through the Office of Cultural Affairs, offers many resources for artists and arts organizations, from grants to tips on networking and other types of technical assistance. The division supports programs throughout New Mexico and has been zealous in its determination to spread the state's artistic wealth among smaller communities. Major programs include Arts in Public Places, which allocates 1 percent of building funds for public art in public buildings, and programs that use artists, musicians, writers, and actors to teach art, music, writing, and drama in New Mexico schools. The agency also administers The Governor's Awards for Excellence in the Arts, a tradition since 1974. Awards have gone to New Mexico artists working in all media and honorees include painter Georgia O'Keeffe, potter María Martínez, playwright Mark Medoff, author Tony Hillerman, and visual artists Fritz Scholder, Luis Jiménez, and Allan Houser.

## SANTA FE ARTS COMMISSION
125 Lincoln Ave., Suite 100
(505) 955-6707
www.santafenm.gov

This arm of city government administers grants to local nonprofit arts and cultural groups, commissions artworks for city-owned facilities, and advocates for arts education in the public schools. In collaboration with local arts organizations, it also offers professional development for teachers. The Commission provides general information on Santa Fe-area arts activities and publishes a good list of arts-and-crafts shows. It has a Community Art Gallery at 201 West Marcy St. that offers artist demonstrations. Call for more information.

## NEW MEXICO CULTURE NET
913 Placita Chaco
(505) 474-8500
www.nmculturenet.org

The mission of the artist-organized New Mexico Culture Net is to promote the understanding and appreciation of the diverse cultures of New Mexico by connecting people, ideas, and resources. This cultural portal offers many useful resources for artists and art lovers. Culture Net partners with Santa Fe Public Schools to produce the Poets in the Schools program, the two-day spring Poetry Jam, an online poetry contest, and a publication with locally owned Sunstone Press of a book of teen poetry. The Santa Fe Arts and Culture Portal, operated in cooperation with the City of Santa Fe, is Santa Fe's most exhaustive list of festivals, events, and art organizations and also includes a 950-member list-serve. NMCN has also produced three short films about American Indian artists Lonnie Vigil, Roxanne Swentzell, and Beverly Singer.

## SANTA FE GALLERY ASSOCIATION
400 Canyon Rd.
(505) 982-1648
www.santafegalleries.net

The Santa Fe Gallery Association is dedicated to supporting the artistic and cultural heritage of the greater Santa Fe area by striving to improve the business conditions for Santa Fe galleries and art dealers. The association provides a forum for communication between galleries and art dealers and supports charitable organizations and causes directly related to the arts. The Association's primary charity, ARTsmart, raises funds for art supplies for Santa Fe's elementary-school children. In 2009, 103 local galleries were members of the SFGA.

# THE NATURAL ENVIRONMENT

Santa Fe's charm begins with the sky. On a July afternoon, for instance, you can watch the thunderheads build, a symphony of towering cumulonimbus clouds sometimes accompanied by a wispy chorus of higher, drier formations.

The billowing clouds that create Santa Fe's summer thunderstorms also bring incredibly rich sunsets. It's not unusual to see cars pull to the side of US 84/285 near the Old Taos Highway or along Artist Road, park, and their passengers climb out and look westward, watching the sky change minute by minute. It is no accident that our local mountains have names that evoke their vivid sunset hues: Sangre de Cristo (Blood of Christ) and Sandía (watermelon).

Winter skies can be equally startling. After a February snowstorm, for instance, the intense cyan blue of the heavens seems to echo the turquoise Pueblo Indians sell under the *portal* along the Plaza. The snow glistens like spun glass in the intensity of the sun's light. To the east the snow-flocked Sangre de Cristos are a shock of white against a cloudless blue backdrop.

The night sky weaves its own magic. Go outside on a moonless evening and look up. When your eyes adjust, you'll see layer on layer of sparkling stars, planets, and constellations. Almost every night, you'll see meteors, passing satellites, and the blinking red lights of planes on their way to Los Angeles or Denver. These are some of the best star-gazing skies in the United States.

## CLIMATE AND WEATHER

At an elevation of 7,000 feet, Santa Fe is the highest state capital in the United States. The air remains unpolluted by industry (Santa Fe's economic base is tourism and state government). And, yes, it's true. The sun really does shine here 300 days of the year.

Average temperatures range from a low of 4 degrees Fahrenheit in January to a high of 91 degrees Fahrenheit in July and August. It's not uncommon for evening temperatures to drop below zero Fahrenheit in the winter and for the heat to soar into the mid-90s in the summer, but such extremes tend to last only a day or two. Traditional Santa Fe adobe homes do not need air-conditioning. Adobe walls are 3 feet thick, so buildings stay cool in summer, warm in winter. Keep the windows closed during the heat of the day and let the cool evening air come in, and you'll be comfortable. Even in summer, nighttime temperatures here in the mountains may dip into

the 40s. The dryness makes summer's warm days easier to take. Humidity usually hovers between 10 and 20 percent. Use plenty of moisturizer and drink lots of water.

Summer "monsoon" thunderstorms begin around the Fourth of July (although storms in May and early June have been bringing spring moisture in recent years, too, much to the delight of Santa Fe gardeners). Daily summer monsoons usually last through August. The clouds start to build in late morning, clumps of thunderheads piling like cotton candy atop the Sangre de Cristos and Jémez Mountains. By late afternoon, lightning may bounce from one cloud to the next, making them glow as if under strobe lights. New Mexico and Florida lead the nation as lightning centers, but this is a dangerous beauty. Lightning strikes start forest fires near Santa Fe each summer and occasionally kill hikers on exposed promontories.

As the storm cell builds, the temperature can drop 30 degrees in seconds. Rain, when it finally comes, sluices from the sky and very quickly saturates the sandy soil. Flash flooding is a very real and present danger along dry wash beds in narrow canyons. Don't hike here on summer afternoons. Flash floods easily outmaneuver humans and even vehicles.

In an average year, Santa Fe gets about 14 inches of rain—as much as might fall in Houston in a single stormy weekend. Some of Santa Fe's precipitation comes in six or eight major winter snowstorms. Average total snowfall in town is 1 to 2 feet, although in particularly heavy years, such as the winter of 2006-07, one snowstorm dumped three feet of snow in one two-day storm that paralyzed the city for days between Christmas and New Year's Day. The snow usually melts fast (10 inches of snow equals about 1 inch of water) but accumulates to greater depths in the mountains. The Santa Fe Ski Area reports an average snowfall of 210 inches a year. Much to the delight of skiers, snow here tends to be light powder (see our chapter on Winter Sports).

**i** **Whether hiking or just shopping and sightseeing, always carry along an extra layer of clothing. Though Santa Fe's climate is mild, the weather can change quickly. Afternoon storms in the summer can drop the temperature by 30 degrees in minutes.**

New Mexico is one of the nation's driest states because of its location between major western mountain ranges that cast a rain shadow, creating deserts. Due to jet-stream changes, many storms come in from the Pacific Northwest in winter, bringing cold wet weather and snow. In summer, storms arrive from the Gulf of California, hence the warm, tropical "monsoon" effect.

Santa Fe is colder in the winter and cooler in summer than one might expect because of the influence of elevation on temperature in this unmoderated high-desert region. Hotel concierges tell stories of January visitors who drive from southern Arizona with shorts and tennis rackets instead of the appropriate skis and parkas, forgetting that the Santa Fe high desert is quite

different from the Phoenix low desert. Typically, nighttime temperatures go down into the 20s or lower in the winter, sometimes reaching a shivery 0 degree, and rarely go above freezing during the day until well into March.

As the snow melts in the mountains, the Santa Fe River (misnamed, it's more of a large stream, really) and other equally small but important tributaries of the Río Grande, usually a tiny trickle, becomes rushing torrents. The Santa Fe River is stocked with rainbow trout in early June for the annual kid's fishing derby, to the delight of local children and their parents, many of whom remember fishing in the Santa Fe River as youngsters. In May 2009, the City Council passed a popular River Flow Resolution to release water from the upstream dams to mimic heavy spring runoff and lower flows in summer. The flows will return this small beautiful river to its rightful place at the heart of Santa Fe life and assure a more natural recharge of the watershed. New Mexico's famous historic acequias, a system of irrigation ditches that date from Spanish times, flow with springtime water that residents who have access divert to their gardens.

## THE LANDSCAPE

Technically, Santa Fe sits on the edge of the Transition or Mountain life zone and the Upper Sonoran life zone. "Life zones" describe variations in living conditions caused by different elevations, temperatures, moisture, and exposure. Each zone has distinctive plants and animals. New Mexico has six of the seven recognized life zones, missing only the lowest tropical zone.

The Sangre de Cristo Mountain Range, which rises from Santa Fe's backyard, is the southernmost portion of the Rocky Mountains. The mountains lie to the northeast of town, providing a good point of orientation. The name Sangre de Cristo means "Blood of Christ."

First-time visitors, especially those who expected Santa Fe to resemble the prairie, find the mountains something to write home about. Artists often delight in the contrast between the blue-green slopes of the Sangres and the dusty tan look of the town. The collection at the Museum of Fine Arts includes many paintings that depict the Sangre de Cristos and their gentle foothills.

If you drive up into the Sangres and ride the chairlift to the top of Aspen Peak, you'll look out on a panoramic view with the town of Santa Fe far below. The Sandía Mountains near Albuquerque, the Ortíz Range with their gold-mining scars, and the gentle Cerrillos Hills rise to the southwest. To the north you can see San Antonio Peak, a rounded volcanic mass near the Colorado border.

To the west, on a clear day, you can see the ancient volcanic Mount Taylor rising to 11,300 feet. This mountain plays a major role in the origin stories of the Navajo, whose reservation spans northwestern New Mexico and northeastern Arizona. Northwest of Santa Fe is another volcanic range, the Jémez Mountains, home to the ancestors of Jémez, Cochití, and other Pueblo Indians. Volcanic Black Mesa, a striking, square-shaped formation beloved by many of the Río Grande Pueblo people, stands in dark contrast to the reddish hues of the Río Grande Valley in the Española area.

**i** In August, Santa Fe Greenhouses sponsors the annual Hummingbird and Butterfly Festival. As part of the festival, the nursery spotlights those plants that attract these visitors. Common hummingbirds in northern New Mexico include the rufous and the blackchin.

## VEGETATION

At the ski area, besides the stunning views, you'll notice fir, spruce, aspen, columbine, wild strawberries, and other plants suited to the cooler, damper climate at 12,000 feet. As you head down toward Santa Fe through Santa Fe National Forest and Hyde Memorial State Park, the vegetation changes. In less than 20 minutes, you pass through ponderosa pine and gambel oak forest into the warmer, drier piñon/juniper zone. Natural vegetation throughout most of the county includes ricegrass, sagebrush, and west-

ern wheatgrass. You don't have to be a botanist to notice that all the plants here are not cactus!

Piñon, a small pine tree, produces edible nuts popular among both animals and humans. Junipers have shaggy bark and purple berries that attract birds. Common in the Santa Fe area, they are tough, slow-growing evergreens that tolerate heat and below-freezing temperatures and, once established, survive in a climate where rain is always a blessing. A 12-foot piñon tree may be 100 years old; piñon can live up to 400 years. A few piñon trees alive today were growing when the Spanish occupied the city of Santa Fe. Piñon and juniper are commonly burned in Santa Fe fireplaces, giving the city its characteristic fragrant aroma.

Because of the elevation, wildflowers of the Santa Fe area have more in common with those of southern Colorado than with their Albuquerque cousins just 60 miles south. You'll find airy sky-blue flax; deep-red Indian paintbrush; magenta verbena and vetch; lavender-hued Russian sage; deep purple, scarlet, and pale pink penstemon; the white blooms and feathery seeds of Apache plume; and cheery orange-and-red firewheels. In the fall, watch for the brilliant yellow of rabbitbrush, or chamisa, framed by purple wild asters. The aspen trees in the Sangres and the Jémez mountains put on a wonderful golden show beginning in mid to late September, along with burnished-copper oak trees.

Santa Fe is a four-season city. You can feel the stirring of spring as early as February, even though the last snowstorm often comes in May, burying the daffodils and covering the apricot blossoms. If the snow has been deep or the city gets spring rain, tulips and hyacinth, fruit trees, lilacs, and iris bloom in abundance. New Mexico's state flower, the yucca, grows in and around Santa Fe. Yuccas generally begin to bloom in May. The large stalks of bell-shaped flowers rise in magnificent showy overstatement. You may notice the cream-colored display as you drive along I–25 between Santa Fe and Albuquerque.

Just before summer hits in full force comes the sweet smell of Russian olive blossoms, tiny yellow flowers among greenish-gray leaves.

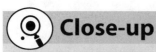 **Close-up**

## Don't Let Altitude and Allergies Get You Down

When some people talk about how Santa Fe takes their breath away, they mean it literally.

Because Santa Fe is perched at 7,000 feet, the air is thinner here. Your lungs and heart have to work harder to do their jobs, and the result can be headaches, lack of energy, nausea, nosebleeds, and other uncomfortable symptoms. People with chronic illnesses such as heart disease or high blood pressure need to pay close attention to how they feel here; if you have any questions about the effect altitude may have on your health, ask your doctor.

Another thing that may leave you breathless is allergies. While Santa Fe ranks low in visible air pollution, the pollen from native plants such as juniper, elms, sage, and cottonwood can make your throat scratch, your eyes itch, and your nose run.

Since more visitors are likely to notice the altitude, we'll talk about that first.

### ALTITUDE

Altitude sickness is odd in its unpredictability. A healthy 20-something person may be slowed down here for a few days; another who might be older and not in the best of shape could notice nothing. Travelers who live at an elevation of 3,000 feet or lower may be listless and headachy, dizzy or light-headed, and have trouble falling asleep or staying that way. More serious symptoms of altitude sickness include appetite loss, nausea, vomiting, heart palpitations or a pounding pulse, congested lungs, and trouble breathing. All this signifies that your body hasn't adjusted to life in the high country. There are some things you can do:

Before you come, get enough rest, drink plenty of water, and eat a diet higher in protein.

Give your body extra time to adjust. If you're flying to New Mexico from Los Angeles or Houston, you might consider spending a night in Albuquerque. At roughly 5,000 feet, the "Duke City" is a good place to let your system begin to adapt.

Take it easy. Don't exercise vigorously until you've adjusted to the altitude. If you feel like a nap in the afternoon, indulge yourself.

Drink plenty of water. Beside being thin, the air here is dry. Dehydration will only add to your discomfort. Cut down on both caffeine and alcohol, though. Both dehydrate you.

Stay at this elevation until you feel better instead of going higher. If you leave Santa Fe for a drive to see the aspens or go skiing, expect the symptoms to worsen.

Wisteria flourish, and migrating hummingbirds return. Native grasses turn green. The cholla cactus explodes with magenta blossoms.

Santa Fe does have big trees like cities elsewhere. Walk along the Santa Fe River, for instance, and you'll see towering cottonwoods, the signature tree of southwestern waterways, which thrive on riverbanks where they get their feet wet and offer shelter for humans and other animals. Fruit trees, especially those bred to bloom late, thrive in backyards and in orchards where they get the water they need. Water always makes the difference.

Landscaping designed to conserve water by using drought-tolerant native plants is called xeriscaping. You'll see many lovely examples of it in Santa Fe. While gardeners may not be able to grow the same things they did in Topeka or San Diego, native plantings are very diverse and thrive even with low rainfall and the city's restrictions on watering.

If you're interested in native plants and how to grow them, visit a Santa Fe nursery. You can also take a look at the xeriscape demonstration gardens at Santa Fe Greenhouses, 2904 Rufina St., (505) 473-2700. Santa Fe Botanical Gardens,

In addition to altitude sickness, higher altitudes also mean more solar radiation and a decreased tolerance for alcohol. People who study these things say one drink at 7,000 feet is the equivalent of three at sea level. So remember your hat and sunscreen when you sit on the patio, and slowly sip your afternoon margarita.

Most people adjust to the altitude in a few days. If you stay in Santa Fe long enough, you'll notice a pleasant side effect when you return to sea level. You may have more energy for a day or two.

## ALLERGIES

The body's reaction to pollen is just as unpredictable as its response to altitude. About one in 20 people is allergic to pollen of some sort. If you move to a different climate, doctors say it usually takes about two years to develop new sensitivity to native plants. Many people who are not initially allergic find they develop allergies after living here a while—sometimes after 20 or 25 years.

A person who's allergic responds to pollen by acting as if the pollen were a virus. Juniper, one of the area's most annoying pollens, usually begins to bother people in February and continues for a couple of months. Other pollens that aggravate come from elm and cottonwood trees, ragweed, and native grass. The good news? Most people are not allergic to the flowers here. And Santa Fe usually ranks low in mold spores because of our dry climate.

If pollen here catches you off guard, there are things you can do besides reach for the anti-histamines:

Most pollen is released in the morning. If you can plan your activities so you aren't outside early, you'll lessen your exposure. It's a great excuse to sleep late, but it does mean you'll miss cooler hiking temperatures in summer.

Wind is the enemy. Stay out of it.

Besides giving you shade from Santa Fe's intense sun, sunglasses help keep pollen out of your eyes.

A change in elevation may help. The plants that grow near the ski area differ from those you'll find at the rodeo grounds.

Santa Fe has a wealth of natural foods stores that sell locally made herbal remedies. There are some effective custom blends. "Allertonic" by Herbs, Etc. is one good choice.

with offices at the Community College, (505) 438-1684, offers tours of established gardens and workshops for gardeners from beginners to experts. The Santa Fe Botanical Garden's Leonora Curtin Natural History Area, south of Santa Fe in La Cienega, is a 35-acre preserve and one of the few relatively intact examples of riparian vegetation left in New Mexico. The area's bird list includes 128 species; you might see red-tailed hawks, wintering duck, crows, piñon and Steller's jays, magpies, northern flickers, ladder-backed woodpeckers, black-capped chickadees, bushtits, towhees, juncos, evening and black-headed grosbeaks, house finches, and various sparrows. Some 34 species of butterfly have been spotted there along with 200 different plants. Please call (505) 428-1684 for information.

ℹ️ Rattlesnakes, common in some rural areas of New Mexico, are virtually nonexistent in Santa Fe, which has been populated for so long that the snakes have all been driven out or exterminated. Both bears and mountain lions are occasionally seen in the heart of the city, though, and coyotes inhabit arroyos all over town. Keep small pets in at night or they'll disappear.

# BIRDS AND ANIMALS

One of your best resources for learning about the birds and animals that live here is the Randall Davey Audubon Center, less than 4 miles from the Plaza (see our Parks and Recreation chapter). While hiking along the center's trails, bird-watchers have identified more than 140 species of birds, ranging from hawks to hummingbirds.

The big, noisy birds with gray-blue wings that you'll see commonly in Santa Fe are piñon jays (they are often mistaken for bluebirds, which also live in these mountains but are smaller and have a more iridescent plumage). In the fall, jays scout the foothills in noisy flocks, looking for their favorite meal, the rich nuts of the piñon trees. Colorful northern flickers, several types of swallows, desert ravens, mountain chickadees, house finches, curve-billed thrashers, towhees, robins, and migratory warblers all are common here. You'll find cottontail rabbits, jackrabbits, coyotes, squirrels, skunks, and several kinds of lizards, too. You probably won't see a rattlesnake, unless you're hiking outside of town in rocky areas. (Despite their reputation, rattlers tend to be shy creatures. If you leave them alone, they'll return the favor and continue to do their part to keep the rodent population in check.)

The Public Service Company of New Mexico (PNM) gave the Randall Davey Audubon Center and the people of the Southwest a wonderful gift in 1999—the 190-acre Santa Fe Canyon Preserve, adjacent to the Audubon Center. The preserve, part of the Santa Fe River watershed, opened in April 2002, for hiking, bird-watching, and other activities. It is administered by The Nature Conservancy of New Mexico (see our Parks and Recreation chapter).

You won't have to look far in Santa Fe to find one animal you may not be used to seeing—the prairie dog. Related to ground squirrels and marmots, prairie dogs eat roots and seeds and live in burrows underground in vacant lots around Santa Fe. The sentry dogs stand on their hind feet at the edge of the burrows, watching for danger or, maybe, enjoying the view. Prairie dogs communicate with different barks and warn each other of an advancing owl or a coyote. When a person approaches, the little tan creatures disappear with a flick of their short black tails.

A large colony of prairie dogs lives near the railroad tracks just west of Cerrillos Road between Guadalupe Street and St. Francis Drive. The Jackalope store, 2820 Cerrillos Rd., (505) 471-8539, has a Prairie Dog Village on its grounds (see our Shopping chapter). A few years ago, the animals claimed squatters' rights to the DeVargas Junior High School athletic field. Volunteers from Prairie Dog Rescue relocated as many of the critters as they could catch and the holes were filled, saving students from the possibility of broken legs. A prairie dog is depicted as part of the statue honoring St. Francis, the patron saint of animals and Santa Fe, downtown in front of City Hall.

# PARKS AND RECREATION

From birding to white-water rafting, baseball to volleyball, disc golf to Ultimate Frisbee, Santa Fe either has it or is close to it. Santa Fe city and county are veritable playgrounds for the young and the old, the rich and the poor, the active and the sedentary. You'll find an abundance of city parks here, many with athletic fields, some just for sitting back and taking in the sunshine. We have mountains and a national forest in our backyard with dozens of hiking trails, ranging from easy to strenuous. And there's biking galore, each hairpin turn yielding magnificent vistas. Santa Fe is a gateway to world-class hunting and trout-filled streams in pristine high country. If hot-air ballooning is your passion, you're just an hour away from one of the best places in the world to do it—Albuquerque, home of the International Balloon Fiesta.

From A to Z—well, okay, B to W—we've included in this chapter a good-sized sampling of what Santa Fe and environs have to offer in the way of public lands as well as indoor and outdoor recreation. A mere glance through this chapter ought to convince even the most die-hard couch potatoes to put down the television remote and explore Santa Fe's recreational bounty.

## GENERAL OUTDOOR TOURS

**KNOWN WORLD GUIDES**                    **$$$$**
Highway 582, No. 702, Lyden
(505) 983-7756, (800) 983-7756
www.knownworldguides.com
Known World offers a variety of outdoor sports adventures. Choose from mountain biking, fishing, and other adventures. The company will arrange summer mountain bike tours for all ages and skill levels—from gradual climbs on logging or ranch roads for beginners to steep, gnarly trails for experts, provide the backup van, bicycle, helmet, water, and healthy gourmet food, and can also arrange custom tours and/ or custom catering. Fly-fishing trips on many of northern New Mexico's best trout waters include the Pecos, Río Grande, Río Chama, and Red Rivers as well as high alpine lakes and smaller creeks. Guides try to avoid crowds and provide personalized service. Most trips last all day and sometimes into the night. Full-day trips include a hearty lunch. Known World also offers a variety of rafting excursions in northern New Mexico, including custom trips and moonlight floats. Your rafting trip can last anywhere from a half day in

the Racecourse, for example, to a week in the upper Río Grande from the Colorado border to the Lower Gorge. Or perhaps you'd prefer to float with your kids through White Rock Canyon, New Mexico's deepest canyon, which borders Bandelier National Monument (see the Parks section in this chapter) and offers up-close sightings of Ancestral Puebloan petroglyphs. Prices include all food and equipment except clothing and sleeping gear. Ask about group rates and multiple-day discounts.

## CITY PARKS

The city of Santa Fe maintains 74 developed parks, six recreational and swimming pool facilities, and 29 miles of trails on more than 350 acres. Some city parks offer extensive facilities and organized activities such as sports, community events, and holiday festivities. Others offer little more than a bench or two, some grass, perhaps a sculpture, and a quiet, restful place to eat lunch, paint a picture, or contemplate your navel. For a list of all city parks, call the City of Santa Fe Parks and Recreation Department, Parks Division, at (505) 955-2106. Superintendent Leroy Apodaca

(505-955-2107) can help you with any detailed questions you may have about sports leagues and facilities.

## FORT MARCY COMPLEX
**490 Washington Ave.**
**(505) 955-2500**
Among the most heavily frequented parks in Santa Fe, after the Plaza Park, is Fort Marcy Complex. Located in downtown Santa Fe just a few blocks north of the Plaza, Fort Marcy features a large indoor/outdoor recreation center with a ballpark and other outdoor fields, an indoor heated pool, a gym and weight room, racquetball courts, and a jogging/walking path. It also offers a variety of classes from swimming and aerobics to dancing and martial arts. The complex is open weekdays from 6 a.m. to 8:30 p.m., 8 a.m. to 6:30 p.m. on Saturday, and noon to 5:30 p.m. on Sunday. Fort Marcy is also the site of the burning of Zozobra—"Old Man Gloom"—at the end of fiestas in September. (See our Annual Events and Festivals chapter for details.)

**i** Although more and more states are banning mountain bikes from all but a few designated trails, New Mexico is bucking that trend and will likely continue to do so provided cyclists respect trail etiquette, i.e., yield to hikers, horseback riders, and uphill traffic; practice low-impact cycling by treading lightly and remembering that "skids are for squids;" and avoid getting so terribly lost that a search and rescue team is required. Do note, however, that all designated wilderness areas—the Pecos near Santa Fe, Taos County's Wheeler Peak, or Sandía Peak east of Albuquerque, for example—and the trails leading to them are always off-limits to mountain bikes. If you violate the rules, you risk losing your wheels. For more information on New Mexico's bicycle laws, contact the New Mexico Highway and Transportation Department (NMDOT), 1120 Cerrillos Rd., (505) 827-5100.

**i** Travelers with canine companions will want to search out Frank Ortiz Park, located on the north side of town off Camino de las Crucitas. Here dogs can romp without their leashes, chase tennis balls on a large, bare field, socialize with local dogs, or hike with their owners on miles of scenic trails through juniper-covered hills.

## FRANKLIN E. MILES PARK
**1027 Camino Carlos Rey at Siringo Rd.**
The city's largest park, General Franklin E. Miles Park offers a variety of facilities, including softball fields, soccer fields, basketball and volleyball courts, an enormous playground, barbecue grills, picnic tables, good lighting at night, and even a skateboard park.

## HERB MARTÍNEZ PARK
**2240 Camino Carlos Rey**
Herb Martínez is another well-used park with good sports facilities. Its soccer fields serve school and youth leagues from March through November. The park also features a ball field, four lighted tennis courts, six lighted basketball courts, a small playground, barbecue grills, and picnic tables.

## PLAZA PARK
**63 Lincoln Ave.**
With the historic Palace of the Governors on its north side, the Plaza is the heart of downtown Santa Fe. Without a doubt, it's the most popular of all city parks. Adult readers of the Santa Fe Reporter have consistently voted the Plaza the best place to bring visitors, walk dogs, people-watch, spot celebrities, or simply "hang out." It's also the choice spot to begin and/or end parades, make speeches, hold community festivals and dances, play Hacky Sack, or take a noontime snooze, if you can wrangle one of the white-painted wrought-iron benches for yourself.

## RAGLE PARK
**Zia Rd. and Yucca St.**
Ragle Park, in a residential area near Santa Fe High School, has the largest adult softball complex in Santa Fe. The park also contains a decent lighted

playground, perfect for softball players with little ones in tow.

### SALVADOR PÓREZ PARK
**601 Alta Vista St.**
**(505) 955-2604**
Kids have voted Salvador Pérez their favorite city park in the Santa Fe Reporter's annual "Best of Santa Fe" survey. Maybe it's the imposing, authentic locomotive car on the centrally located property. Perhaps it's the recently renovated indoor heated pool and new gym equipment. Or it could be the park's cool new playground with equipment made from recyclables. There's also a Little League field with tons of room to run and jump—enough even for grown-ups, who borrow the field in summer for mushball. With tennis courts, volleyball courts, barbecue grills, and lots of picnic tables, Salvador Pérez is an ideal spot for a family outing.

## Passive Parks
### AMELIA E. WHITE PARK
**981 Old Santa Fe Trail**
Sitting prettily at the crossroads of Camino Corrales and Old Santa Fe Trail—mere blocks from the Wheelwright Museum of the American Indian, the Museum of Indian Arts and Culture, and the Museum of International Folk Art—three-acre Amelia E. White Park is an ideal spot for a picnic lunch or simply to relax and enjoy its featured native plants. You might even catch a painter in action as you sit under a grape arbor admiring the sky.

### CORNELL PARK/ROSE GARDEN
**1203 Galisteo Parkway**
While you can find an appropriate spot in any park to celebrate a quiet moment, some are more conducive than others to meditation and aloneness. Among them is Cornell Park, a lovely refuge from the world located a couple of miles south of downtown Santa Fe. A small park—it's about as wide and as long as a city block—in a residential neighborhood, the Rose Garden is aptly named for the rose bushes that come to life

in spring and summer, scenting the air with their fragrant blossoms. The promenade is lined with old trees, making it a favorite among dogs and their owners. Volunteer gardeners maintain the rose bushes, irises, and spring bulb display.

### EAST SANTA FE RIVER PARK
**726 East Alameda St.**
Located only a few blocks south of the Plaza, East Santa Fe River Park is a lovely, narrow stretch of land that begins in front of the Supreme Court Building at Don Gaspar Avenue and continues for about a mile to East Palace Avenue. The park offers shaded, tree-lined walkways and picnic tables along the banks of the Santa Fe River, attracting brown-bag diners when the weather permits. The 19-acre park also continues west over St. Francis Drive along Alameda.

### TOM MACAIONE (HILLSIDE) PARK
**301 East Marcy St.**
Despite its location along heavily trafficked Paseo de Peralta, Tom Macaione Park is a little oasis of greenery among a long line of low-slung adobe or faux-adobe buildings. If you're willing to walk the 3 short blocks northeast of the Plaza, you're likely to have this tiny park, also called Hillside Park, all to yourself—or nearly almost any time of year except summer. Then it's put to good use by Girls Inc. (see our Kidstuff chapter) next door. Otherwise, you'll probably share it only with a bronze sculpture of the much-loved, eccentric, impressionist painter for whom the park is named.

## NATIONAL FOREST
### SANTA FE NATIONAL FOREST
**Highway 475**
**(505) 753-7331**
The million-plus-acre Santa Fe National Forest is Santa Fe's favorite outdoor playground with hiking trails along the stream, a ski basin, and a scenic drive. It has two campgrounds close to Santa Fe, both located off Highway 475 on the way to the Santa Fe Ski Basin. In the order in which you'll first encounter them—they are: **Big Tesuque, 9,700 feet.** The absence of trailer parking makes

the Big Tesuque a particularly pleasant place to pitch one's tent, despite a lack of drinking water. The seven campsites here are available free of charge for 14-day maximum stays between May and October. **Aspen Basin, 10,300 feet.** For the truly hardy, Aspen Basin has six no-fee campsites open year-round with restrooms, drinking water, and picnic tables. Maximum stay is 14 days.

## STATE PARK

### HYDE MEMORIAL STATE PARK
740 Hyde Park Rd.
(505) 983-7175

Located 8 miles northeast of Santa Fe and a mere 3 miles below the Santa Fe Ski Basin, Hyde Memorial State Park contains 350 beautiful acres filled with ponderosa pine, aspen, and meadows at an elevation of 8,500 feet. It's a favorite among locals for hiking and picnicking and a popular base for backpackers heading into the Pecos Wilderness. The park's year-round campground has 50 sites, including seven with hookups, that accommodate both RVs and tents and provides drinking water and toilet facilities, but not showers.

## NATIONAL PARKS

New Mexico has stunningly beautiful public lands, many of them wild and remote, some of them tame and comfortable. Santa Fe, which is surrounded by more than 3 million acres of public forest, is a doorway to many of these. In fact, nearly half the state's national wilderness areas are in north-central New Mexico. These include the popular Pecos Wilderness—223,333 scenic acres featuring some of the state's highest peaks, glacial lakes, waterfalls, and 150 miles of rivers and streams; the 5,200-acre Dome Wilderness adjacent to the Bandelier Wilderness in Bandelier National Monument (see entry below) and providing access to Jémez Mountain canyons as well as 8,200-foot-high St. Peter's Dome; and the lesser known—and lesser used—San Pedro Parks Wilderness northeast of Cuba, New Mexico, with 41,132 spectacular acres of aspen, evergreen forest, and alpine meadows and altitudes reaching

into the 10,000-foot range. Sadly, all are recovering from devastating wildfires that burned more than 300,000 acres of New Mexico public land in 2002. Call or visit the Public Lands Information Center, 1474 Rodeo Rd., (505) 438-7542, for information about conditions, closures, and fire regulations.

These and a fourth wilderness area—50,300-acre Chama River Canyon Wilderness—are located within Santa Fe National Forest, whose more than 1.5 million acres comprise some of the finest mountain scenery in the Southwest. They offer 1,000 miles of mapped trails, 620 miles of trout streams, abundant hunting, camping, picnicking, skiing, and scenic drives where you'll experience mile after mile of breathtaking beauty. The Río Grande divides Santa Fe National Forest into two distinct sections. To the west lie the Jémez Mountains, a canyon- and mesa-filled range with elevations from 5,300 feet in White Rock Canyon to 12,000 feet at the summit of Chicoma Peak. It's in this section that you'll find the Dome and San Pedro Parks wilderness areas as well as Valle Grande—an immense grassy depression that represents a portion of the 14-mile-wide Valles Caldera (now a 90,000-acre national preserve) formed a million years ago by a volcanic eruption. Also within these mountains are the ancient Indian ruins and cliff dwellings at Bandelier National Monument and the high-tech think tank Los Alamos National Laboratory.

East of the Río Grande, the rugged Sangre de Cristo Mountains loom watchfully over Santa Fe—topped by Truchas Peak, whose summit reaches a magnificent 13,101 feet. The Sangres have one of the largest aspen forests in the Southwest, splendid canyons, trout-filled streams and rivers, crystal-clear glacial lakes, a huge variety of wildlife, and recreational opportunities galore.

### BANDELIER NATIONAL MONUMENT    $$
HCR1, Box 1, Suite 15,
Los Alamos 87544
(505) 672-3861
www.nps.gov/band

Located along Highway 4 on the Pajarito Plateau of the Jémez Mountains, near the towns of Los Alamos and White Rock, Bandelier National Monument encompasses 32,737 acres of scenic wilderness and striking land formations that contain prehistoric cliff houses and the ruins of multistoried, pueblo-style dwellings inhabited between the 12th and 16th centuries by the ancestors of today's Pueblo Indians. Although the 47,000-acre Cerro Grande fire began here in May 2000, only a couple hundred acres of Bandelier burned.

Wander the main trail exploring ruins, kivas (round, underground ceremonial rooms), and Ceremonial Cave, which is accessible only by two long, steep ladders that are not recommended for those with a fear of heights or for young children. Some 75 percent of Bandelier is wilderness. You can hike 70-plus miles of pet-free backcountry trails. (Be sure to get a free backcountry pass at the visitor center, if you are planning on spending the night in the wilderness; day hiking does not require a pass.) Located at the bottom of 6,000-foot Frijoles Canyon, where a creek by the same name provided water to the Ancestral Puebloans who lived and farmed there, the visitor center is open year-round except for Christmas and New Year's days. It features exhibits on Pueblo culture and information on the monument and nearby attractions. Visitor center hours are 8 a.m. to 6 p.m. in summer, 9 a.m. to 5:30 p.m. in fall and spring, and 9 a.m. to 4:30 p.m. in winter. Frijoles Canyon itself and the nearby discontinuous unit of Tsankawi are open 7 a.m. to 7 p.m. daily; backcountry areas are open from dawn to dusk. Juniper Campground has 95 campsites and stays open from March through November. It accommodates RVs and tents. During the summer the park offers regularly scheduled guided walks, evening programs and lectures, and "interpretive" talks. To get to Bandelier from Santa Fe, take I–25 north to US 84/285, head west in Pojoaque to Highway 502, and cross the Río Grande to Highway 4. From there, follow the signs to Bandelier.

**KASHA-KATUWE TENT ROCKS NATIONAL MONUMENT** $
**Rio Puerco Field Office**
**435 Montano Rd. NE, Albuquerque**
**505-761-8700**
**www.nm.blm.gov**
New Mexico's youngest national monument, Kasha-Katuwe Tent Rocks was set aside in 2001 as part of the National Landscape Conservation System administered by the Bureau of Land Management. It preserves 4,100 acres of eerie minaret-shaped cones of pale volcanic tuff at the base of the Jémez Mountains, 25 miles southwest of Santa Fe. To get there, drive south on I-25, take Highway 22 west past Cochití Reservoir and Pueblo, then 3 miles on graded FR 266/Tribal Road 92. Park and hike the 2-mile loop through the silent formations, which lure photographers all year but are particularly spectacular in winter when decorated with snow. Continue onto the adjoining promontory for 360-degree views of the Sandía, Sangre de Cristo, and Jémez mountains. Scan the ground for tiny pearls of obsidian, known as Apache Tears, a reminder that Indian people have used this site for thousands of years. The monument is only open in daytime. There are primitive restrooms, information boards, picnic tables, and a parking lot, but no visitor center or campground. *NOTE:* No dogs, mountain bikes, or motorized vehicles are permitted in the monument. From April 1 to October 31, monument hours are 7 a.m. to 6 p.m.; 8 a.m. to 5 p.m. the rest of the year. Occasional ceremonial closures by the Cochití tribe are posted.

**i** It's unlawful and disrespectful to remove pottery shards, arrowheads, or other artifacts from public lands. You can look at them, but don't pocket them.

**PECOS NATIONAL HISTORICAL PARK** $
**P.O. Box 418, Pecos 87552**
**(505) 757-7200 (visitor center)**
**(505) 757-7212 (tours and special-use permits)**
Just 25 miles east of Santa Fe, 6,000-acre Pecos National Historical Park embraces 12,000 years of

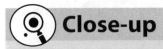 Close-up

## Valles Caldera National Preserve

For New Mexico outdoors enthusiasts, one of the most exciting events of the decade has been the opening of the Valles Caldera National Preserve, an hour's drive northwest of Santa Fe in the mountains above Bandelier National Monument. The 89,000-acre volcano caldera had been off-limits to the public for more than 100 years.

Valles Caldera is one of the best examples anywhere of a caldera complex volcano. It differs from most volcanoes because the eruptions that caused it to form were infrequent but huge. Valles Caldera was formed about 1 million years ago when gas-rich magma quickly erupted from depths of about 3 miles, creating a vast dome that burst like a bubble, covering the surrounding plateau with cinders, ash, lava, and obsidian. The material spewed by the eruption formed the entire circular-shaped Jémez Mountain Range on Santa Fe's western horizon. Since then, volcanic activity on a smaller scale has caused volcanic cones to form inside the huge crater, along with hot springs, fumaroles, and cold acid springs.

Valles Caldera and the surrounding tuff canyonlands of the Pajarito Plateau have been nominated for national park status three times, but because it was a private ranch, each attempt by the park service to acquire it was foiled by logging and grazing interests. The first time it was considered as a potential national park, in 1919, the government actually reached an agreement to purchase the land—but the ranch owners cut down all the big timber before turning it over, and the government backed out of the deal. (The mixed ponderosa pine, aspen, and Douglas fir forest has since grown back.)

The federal government finally bought the Valles Caldera in 2000 for $101 million and designated it as a national preserve. It is not overseen by either the park service or the forest service. Instead, Congress has decided to try something new in public land management, putting administration of the land in the hands of a nine-member board of trustees appointed by the President of the United States, including ranchers, forestry experts, government officials, and environmentalists. The trustees are charged with operating the reserve for the benefit of recreational users and to pay all costs of operating the preserve through grazing, timber sales, and public-use fees. This calls for a delicate balancing of rival interests. Currently, about 700 cattle wander the grassy valleys of the preserve. Scientists study the streams, meadows, forests, and wildlife to gather data for future decisions about use of the land. And the trustees permit limited hiking, skiing, snowshoeing, and hunting. Recreational reservations must be made by calling (877) 382-5537. A use fee is charged.

Valles Caldera National Preserve is a 70-minute drive from Santa Fe, taking US 84/285 north to Pojoaque, Highway 502 west to Los Alamos, and Highway 4 past Bandelier National Monument to the preserve boundary and parking area. No pets are permitted at the preserve. For further information, call (505) 661-3331, www.vallescaldera.gov.

history. Among the highlights are ancient Pecos Pueblo, originally known as Cicuye, a major trading pueblo on an important pass in the Sangre de Cristo Mountains; two ruined Spanish colonial missions; visible trail ruts of the original Santa Fe Trail; the 20th-century Forked Lightning Ranch (formerly the home of actress Greer Garson and her husband E. E. Fogelson, who donated the ranch and land to the National Park Service); and the Glorieta Battlefield, the site of New Mexico's most important Civil War action: the Battle of Glorieta Pass. Visitors may take a 1¼-mile self-guided tour through the remnants of Pecos Pueblo and the mission ruins. Groups can arrange guided tours in advance. The visitor center contains exhibits in both English and Spanish, and offers an excellent 10-minute introductory film. Special weekend cultural demonstrations and night tours take place in summer and include an annual Feast Day Mass the first Sunday in August commemorating the original Indian inhabitants who eventually moved to Cochiti Pueblo. Picnicking is permitted but no camping. The USDA Forest Service operates six campgrounds within a 20-mile radius of the park. The park is open all year except Christmas and New Year's Days. Hours are 8 a.m. to 6 p.m. Memorial Day to Labor Day for the visitor center and Ruins Trail, and 8 a.m. to 5 p.m. from Labor Day to Memorial Day for the Ruins Trail, 8 a.m. to 4:30 p.m. in winter. To get there from Santa Fe, take I-25 to exit 299 (Pecos Village) and continue south for 2 miles.

# RECREATION

What Santa Fe lacks in spectator sports, it more than makes up for in recreation and participatory sports. You could come to Santa Fe and do nothing but play—outdoors, indoors, solo, or on teams. In addition to participatory sports, this section will also deal with a host of other recreational activities, from hiking, biking, and horseback riding to flying, rock climbing, and scuba.

## Baseball

**SANTA FE PARKS AND RECREATION DEPARTMENT**
**Parks Division**
**Municipal Recreation Complex**
**205 Caja Del Rio**
**(505) 955-2102**
**www.santafenm.gov**
Although Santa Fe has no city-sponsored baseball teams, its parks and recreation divisions can point you in the right direction for youth and Little League, semipro, and seniors' baseball. Be prepared, however, to do some legwork on your own to find a team.

For Little League, that will depend upon where the child lives. Eastside kids play on Santa Fe American Little League, (505-986-5004), westsiders on the Santa Fe Metro Little League, (505-986-9802), and south-central children on the National Little League team, (505-474-0131). Kids under nine play in the Santa Fe Mad Dogs, the state champion of the Santa Fe American Amateur Baseball Congress, (505-699-8463). Teens

play in the Santa Fe Amateur Baseball Congress, (505-699-8463), comprising four divisions—Connie Mack for ages 17 and 18, Mickey Mantle for teens ages 15 and 16, Sandy Koufax for ages 13 and 14, and PeeWee Reese for ages 10, 11, and 12—with a Willie Mays division in the works for kids younger than age 10. Teams play at Ragle, Fort Marcy, and Franklin E. Miles ballparks and occasionally use the high schools (Capital, Santa Fe, or St. Michael's) as backup fields.

Santa Fe baseballers age 28 and older play for the semipro Mens' Senior Baseball League part of the American Amateur Baseball Congress, (505-699-8463). The team plays 30 games a season on Sundays, mostly at Fort Marcy Ballpark (Fort Marcy Complex), adjacent to but not part of Fort Marcy, 490 Washington Ave., (505) 955-2500. Away games are almost always at one of the Albuquerque public high schools, though the University of New Mexico occasionally hosts a game at Lobo Field, a NCAA-quality ballpark. The Santa Fe Softball Association, (505-955-4465), also organizes a team that plays on the Municipal Recreation Complex facility on the northwest side of Santa Fe, on Caja del Rio Road.

## Basketball

Twelve of the city's 74 parks have outdoor basketball courts. You can get a list from the Parks and Recreation Department by calling (505) 955-2100.

**CITY OF SANTA FE PARKS AND RECREATION DEPARTMENT**
**125 Lincoln Ave.**
**(505) 955-2508**
The city of Santa Fe sponsors a number of basketball-related activities throughout the year, including men's and women's summer and winter basketball leagues; girls' and boys' basketball leagues and clinics; basketball camp; and such special events as the Hot-Shot competition, in which participants ages seven through 12 try to make as many baskets as possible from various hot spots on the court, and Free-Throw, in which seven- to 12-year-olds attempt 25 shots in each

of two rounds. The city also sponsors several adult basketball tournaments, including 3-on-3 and 5-on-5 competitions. For information on girls' and boy's basketball leagues, log on to the Santa Fe Independent Youth Basketball Association Web site at www.santafeyouthsports.org. For information on the Men's and Women's Baseball Leagues, call (505) 955-2507.

## Biking

Half of New Mexico is public land—thousands of acres crisscrossed with thousands of miles of trails, many of them open to mountain bikers. A locally popular and scenic route for both mountain and touring bikes goes straight up Highway 475—variously called Artist Road, Hyde Park Road, or Ski Basin Road, depending on the particular section—to the Santa Fe Ski Area. Starting at the Fort Marcy Complex, it's a 15-mile uphill ride to the ski basin—or 8 miles to Black Canyon, a nice midway stopping point. The road gets quite narrow and practically shoulderless as you near the ski slopes and you'll encounter numerous hairpin turns and sometimes-heavy traffic. Bring warm clothing and rain gear, in case of a sudden thunderstorm, and eat high-energy snacks whenever you sip water to keep your body balanced in this arid climate. Plan on drinking a gallon of water per day per person when you're active in the desert.

**i** For a fun hike or bike ride on the outskirts of the city, try the Dale Ball Trails. The 22-mile network of hilly loop trails, accessible from Hyde Park Road or Cerro Gordo Road, has grand vistas and hidden glades but also runs practically through the backyards of some of Santa Fe's priciest homes.

A comfortable ride for beginners is the Santa Fe Rail Trail, which runs between Santa Fe and the Lamy railroad depot. The 11.5-mile dirt trail runs alongside the train tracks originally laid by the Atchison, Topeka, & Santa Fe Railway in 1880. It is used today by the Santa Fe Southern Railway,

which runs between the downtown Santa Fe and Lamy depots, and the new Rail Runner train, which runs on segments of the rails between Albuquerque and Santa Fe. From St. Francis Drive, head south until it turns into Frontage Road. Continue southbound to the train tracks and follow them to Lamy. Along the way, you'll pass over a trestle bridge that one devotee happily describes as "pretty scary." If you plan it right, you might even meet up with a train. From Lamy you can either bike back to town or catch the Santa Fe Southern Railway and ride back in style in a restored 1920s passenger coach.

The Jémez Mountains provide spectacular scenery for cyclists, both on- and off-road. One of the more popular loops begins at Highway 501—about 35 miles northwest of Santa Fe—in the parking lot of Los Alamos National Laboratory. Continue south along Highway 4 to the Los Alamos "Truck Route,"—an otherwise unnamed road belonging to LANL's overseer, the U.S. Department of Energy—and finally back to the Lab. The 26-mile trek will take you past the ancient pueblo ruins at Bandelier National Monument and Tsankawi and open up to remarkable high-country vistas.

If you choose to go south, the Turquoise Trail to Albuquerque via the Sandía Crest Scenic Byway offers a route as rich in history as it is in scenery. The 52-mile journey begins on Highway 14, called the Turquoise Trail because of the turquoise mined in the Ortíz Mountains. You'll pass through a number of old mining villages, some of them long-deserted ghost towns while others, such as Madrid and Cerrillos, are thriving artist communities. Just before reaching Albuquerque, go the extra 12 miles to Sandía Crest, a 3,700-foot climb along the Sandía Crest Scenic Byway (Highway 536), to an elevation of 10,678 feet at the summit. On the way up, pay attention to how the piñon-juniper woodland changes to ponderosa pine forest because you'll be too busy catching your breath on the way down to notice.

If you're here the third Sunday in May, you might want to try your hand—er, feet—at the 100-mile Santa Fe Century, or the 75-mile route to Stanley and back, 50 miles to Galisteo, and 25 miles to Eldorado. The Century is a challenging, scenic ride that starts at the Christus St. Vincent Reginal Medical Center parking lot, on the corner of Hospital Road and St. Michael's Drive, and heads south down Highway 14 along the Turquoise Trail to Golden. If you survive "Heartbreak Hill"—a half-mile killer climb between Golden and Edgewood that's steep enough to force many cyclists to walk their bikes—you'll head west toward Stanley, then north through the villages of Galisteo and Lamy to Eldorado, returning to Santa Fe via I-25. The Century will take you anywhere from five to eight hours, depending on your stamina, strength, and skill. Or you could take one of the shorter routes for 25, 50, or 75 miles. The Century, which the National Leukemia Society has adopted as a nationwide fund-raiser, drew 2,612 riders in 2009, with an extraordinary more than half of the riders from out of state. Many of the outings we've suggested here are geared toward off-road vehicles. For information about on-road biking, call Sangre de Cristo Cycling Club at (505) 995-2026. Otherwise, you can get information on trails and tours as well as rent bikes and other equipment from most bike rental shops in town. Some specialize in guided tours, including the following:

**NEW MEXICO BIKE N' SPORT**          $$–$$$
524 West Cordova Rd., Suite C
(505) 820-0809
www.nmbikensport.com
New Mexico Bike N' Sport rents front-suspension mountain and road bikes. The staff stays "mum" about their favorite trails, no doubt in hopes of keeping them from becoming overpopulated. Perhaps that's why lots of hard-core mountain bikers frequent the store, which boasts its own 10-person racing team sponsored by local businesses and national bike manufacturers.

**ROB & CHARLIE'S BIKE SHOP**
St. Michael's Village West
1632 St. Michael's Dr.
(505) 471-9119
In business since 1979, Rob & Charlie's has earned a reputation for being friendly, helpful, and, most

important, knowledgeable about all aspects of bicycles—from buying one to riding one and, inevitably, repairing one. The store carries a large selection of mountain bikes, road bikes, BMX bikes, and kids' bikes from Giant, Raleigh, Redline, S E Racing, and Trek, to name just a few brands. It also sells roof racks, parts, and all manner of accessories and accoutrements from clothing, shoes, and water bottles to books, magazines, and maps. Priceless to those who don't have it, yet free for the asking at Rob & Charlie's, is the skinny on bitchin' biking trails from the most popular to the lesser known. Rob & Charlie's is open Monday through Saturday from 9:30 a.m. to 6 p.m.

## Birding

New Mexico is home to a number of bird sanctuaries, including one right here in Santa Fe and several within a few hours' drive. But you need only venture to any open space outside the city limits to observe hawks soaring in search of prey or, if you're especially lucky, a bald eagle either in flight or repose. In spring and autumn, Santa Fe hosts an astounding number of migrating birds because of its location along a major migratory pathway. For more information, contact the New Mexico Audubon Society, (505) 983-4609.

**BOSQUE DEL APACHE NATIONAL**
**WILDLIFE REFUGE**          $$
P.O. Box 1246, Socorro 87801
(505) 835-1828
www.fws.gov/southwest/refuges/newmex/bosque
One of the top birding sites in the United States, Bosque del Apache ("woods of the Apache") is well worth the 2½-hour drive south from Santa Fe, even if you're not a card-carrying birder. Within the 57,191-acre Bosque are 13,000 acres of moist bottomland at a wide spot of the Río Grande hosting 500 bird species. Tens of thousands of birds gather each autumn and stay through the winter. At dusk you can witness flocks of snow and Arctic geese, eagles, sandhill cranes, and even very rare whooping cranes—

one of a number of endangered species that winter at Bosque del Apache—returning to roost in the marshes. The popular Festival of the Cranes, held the weekend before Thanksgiving, offers tours, talks, and superb birding at peak migration time. During the spring and fall, you'll see migrant warblers, flycatchers, and shorebirds. In summer—the season for nesting songbirds, waders, shorebirds, and ducks—the Bosque returns to its quiet existence as an oasis of ponds, marsh, riparian cottonwood, willow, and tamarisk on the northern edge of the Chihuahuan Desert. Year-round residents include mule deer, coyote, porcupine, muskrat, Canada goose, coot, pheasant, turkey, quail, and New Mexico's state bird, the roadrunner.

To get to Bosque del Apache from Santa Fe, take I-25 south to exit 139 at San Antonio. Head east on US 380 for a half mile, then take Highway 1 south another 8 miles to the refuge. Visitor center hours are 7:30 a.m. to 4 p.m. weekdays and 8 a.m. to 4:30 p.m. weekends; you can drive the 12-mile auto loop from one hour before sunrise to one hour after sunset. Admission.

**i** The annual Audubon Christmas count, begun in 1900, uses volunteers to estimate how many birds are seen in one day. Call the Randall Davey Audubon Center (505-983-4609) for information.

**LAS VEGAS NATIONAL WILDLIFE REFUGE**
Route 1, Box 399, Las Vegas 87701
(505) 425-3581
www.fws.gov/southwest/refuges/newmex/
lasvegas
Located about 70 miles east of Santa Fe, Las Vegas National Wildlife Refuge consists of 8,672 acres of marsh and water, native grasslands, cropland, timbered canyons, and streams providing habitat for a wide variety of plant and animal life—up to 271 species observed since 1966, when the refuge had only been in official existence for a year. Among its feathered visitors are neotropical migrants, species that nest in the United States or Canada, spending the winter primarily south in Mexico, Central or South America,

or the Caribbean. They include colorful hawks, hummingbirds, warblers, and orioles, as well as shorebirds, flycatchers, and thrushes. The existence of the refuge helps preserve their habitat, which is essential to the survival of many of these birds. The refuge is open daily, dawn to dusk; the refuge headquarters is open 8 a.m. to 4:30 p.m. Monday to Friday.

**MAXWELL NATIONAL WILDLIFE REFUGE**
P.O. Box 276, Maxwell 87728
(505) 375-2331
www.fws.gov/southwest/refuges/newmex/
maxwell
With 200 species of birds observed over the years around its largest compound, Maxwell National Wildlife Refuge is the winter home to large concentrations of ducks and geese and to the burrowing owl in summer. Migrating birds are attracted to the many irrigation impoundments that serve this agricultural and ranching area in the northeastern corner of the state. To get to the refuge, take I-25 due north for about 150 miles and get off at the Maxwell exit, between the towns of Springer and Ratón.

**RANDALL DAVEY AUDUBON CENTER** $
1800 Upper Canyon Rd.
(505) 983-4609
www.nm.audubon.org
The Audubon Society acquired this 135-acre former sawmill, farm, and artist's home as its New Mexico headquarters in the mid-1980s and operates it as a nature center, just 10 minutes from the Plaza. Enjoy birdwatching in the garden or hike an easy 0.5-mile loop that begins in piñon-juniper woodlands and meadows and ascends a rocky trail to cool ponderosa pine forest. Other trails connect with those in The Nature Conservancy's Santa Fe Canyon Preserve in the Santa Fe River watershed. You may spot coyote, black bear, mule deer, and, occasionally, mountain lions and bobcats here, as well as some of the more than 100 species of birds that use these foothills. Look for piñon and Steller's jays, chickadees, and hummingbirds in summer. Popular one-hour bird walks are offered every Saturday at 8:30 a.m. (9

a.m. November to February), along with birding trips to surrounding refuges, such as Bosque del Apache and Las Vegas Wildlife Refuge.

The visitor center and store sells bird seed, binoculars, books, trail maps, and other nature goodies. There is a small amphitheater and class-room, used by local schools for nature study, summer camps, and other programs. The popu-lar summer nature programs fill up quickly. Kids ages 5 to 11 get to spend time outside learning about such things as animal camouflage and dis-guises, nocturnal creatures, tracking, and native birds. Themes include nature detectives, flight, water, maps, and treasure hunts as well as stories, art, and games with an Audubon focus. Sessions are held mornings and afternoons, with lunch provided for full-time campers. Sessions usually run from early June to early August. Family activ-ity evenings take place on Saturdays throughout the summer and include astronomy programs and treasure hunts.

The 1920 Randall Davey Home is in the con-verted mill. Randall Davey owned this property from 1920 to 1964. He used the old Martínez hacienda for his studio. It contains a representa-tive sample of the artist's work and furnishings. Tour it on Fridays in summer; by appointment the rest of the year. Call for hours.

The Randall Davey Audubon Center is one of the few Audubon-sponsored bird sanctuaries in the West. To reach the center, follow Canyon Road past the intersection of Camino Cabra at Cristo Rey Church to Upper Canyon Road. The center is open from 10 a.m. to 4 p.m. daily. The grounds are also available for rent for outdoor weddings.

### SANTA FE CANYON PRESERVE
**The Nature Conservancy of New Mexico**
**212 East Marcy St.**
**(505) 988-3867**
**www.nature.org/wherewework/north**
**america/states/newmexico/preserves**
Opened in April 2002 with much fanfare, 190-acre Santa Fe Canyon Preserve is Santa Fe's newest nature preserve, a gift of Public Service Company of New Mexico (PNM). People in Santa Fe now have daily access to a thriving bosque

(bottomlands) of cottonwood and willow trees, a pond, the ruins of a Victorian-era dam, hiking trails, and more than 140 species of birds along the original route of the Santa Fe River. This little jewel is located 2.5 miles from downtown, on Upper Canyon Road next to Randall Davey Audubon Center. One of the best things about it is the impact that the new preserve has on the Santa Fe foothills open-space program. Hikers are now able to hike nonstop between the popular Atalaya Trail to the south and the 25-mile Dale Ball Trail System to the north.

## Boating/Canoeing

New Mexico may be desert, but there's still plenty of recreational water on which to play. Getting there from Santa Fe, however, will take a bit of traveling. Nearest to Santa Fe are Cochití Lake, (505-465-0307), 26 miles southwest of the city; and Abiquiú Lake, (505) 685-4371, a beautiful, winding 45 miles northwest of Santa Fe—both managed by the U.S. Army Corps of Engineers. Cochití—one of the world's largest earthen dams—is a no-charge, no-wake lake with paved boat ramps and a no-frills slip-rental marina man-aged by Cochití Pueblo, (505) 465-2224. There are no boat rentals at the lake itself, but you can rent a craft in Santa Fe and take it with you. Among the most popular water sports at Cochití are sail-ing, fishing, windsurfing, and, in summer, swim-ming. To get there, take I-25 south to the turnoff for Highway 16, which is near the bottom of a long and notoriously steep hill called La Bajada ("the descent"). From Highway 16, turn right on Highway 22, which will take you directly to the lake. While you're in the vicinity, be sure to check out Kasha Katuwe Tent Rocks National Monu-ment (see entry above), which has hiking amid strange and wonderful geological formations.

Abiquiú Lake, located in Georgia O'Keeffe country about 7 miles northwest of the village of Abiquiú, is a stunning sight from US 84, its shim-mering aqua color a lovely contrast to the red hills that surround it. The lake, which has two paved boat ramps on its north side, is a popular site for waterskiing, fishing, Jet Skiing, and simply cruising. Swimmers also take advantage of the lake in summer, despite its lack of developed swimming areas. From Santa Fe, take US 84/285 north to Española. Turn left at Dandy Burger, where the highway splits. Follow US 84 for 18 miles to Abiquiú and another 7 miles to the turnoff for Abiquiú Dam, which is on your left. To rent a kayak, call Sangre de Cristo Mountain Works, 328 South Guadalupe Ave., Santa Fe, (505) 984-8221, open Monday through Friday 10 a.m. to 7 p.m., Saturday 10 a.m. to 6 p.m., and Sunday noon to 5 p.m. There is an inexpensive 54-site campground at the lake with electrical hookups, showers, and toilets. For reservations, contact www.reserve america.com at least four days ahead of time.

## Bowling

### BIG ROCK CASINO AND
### BOWLING CENTER $
Big Rock Shopping Center, Highway 68
460A North Riverside Dr., Española
(505) 747-2695
www.bigrockcasino.com
About half an hour north of Santa Fe, in Española, Santa Clara Pueblo operates a state-of-the-art 24-lane bowling center on pueblo land in its Big Rock Casino, right in downtown Española. The bowling center is open daily 10 a.m. to midnight and at present has five different leagues, bowling weekday evenings. The bowling center is open 10 a.m. to 10 p.m. Sunday to Thursday, until midnight on Friday and Saturday. In the center of the bowling alley is O's, an upmarket tapas bar. Other eating options include a fine-dining restaurant, Black Mesa Steakhouse, and casual dining at BRCS sports bar and cafe grill.

### STRIKE GOLD BOWLING CENTER
Cities of Gold Casino
10 Cities of Gold Rd., Pojoaque
(505) 455-4262
www.citiesofgold.com/bowling
Another casino bowling center, this time with 16 lanes and all-you-can-bowl Sundays, as well as leagues and lessons. Check out the New Mexico Bowling Association (www.nmusbc.com) for tournaments in New Mexico.

## Camping

Most of New Mexico's national and state parks, monuments, and forests have campsites ranging from primitive to developed sites with running water and restrooms. Some also have RV hookups, occasionally even with cable television! Public campsites are usually open from May through October on a first-come, first-served basis and cost $12 and up. You don't need a permit for dispersed camping in national forest, but you do in national parks and monuments where dispersed backcountry camping is permitted. They're available free from park visitor centers, so make sure you stop in to register. Check with the National Park Service—Southwest Office, 1100 Old Santa Fe Trail, (505) 988-6100, for additional information about permits.

### In Town
### LOS CAMPOS DE SANTA FE RV
### RESORT $$$$
3574 Cerrillos Rd.
(505) 473-1949, (800) 852-8160
www.loscamposrv.com
Five miles southwest of the Plaza on Cerrillos Road, Los Campos offers 30-amp and 50-amp service for extra-large RVs. The 11-acre, year-round trailer park has 95 sites, a coin laundry, free WiFi, a heated pool, and a playground. Weekly and monthly rates and AAA, Good Sam, and AARP discounts are available.

### TRAILER RANCH $$$$
3471 Cerrillos Rd.
(505) 471-9970
www.trailerranch.com
This is a combination RV and senior mobile home park, with the first third of the park reserved for up to 50 RVs with full hookups, including cable television, free WiFi, public showers, coin laundry, a heated, seasonal swimming pool, and a community house with a pool table, library, card tables, and a laundry. The back two-thirds of Trailer Ranch is a seniors-only mobile home park with a minimum age of 55. Discounts for senior citizens, Good Sam, and AAA.

## Out of Town

**RANCHEROS DE SANTA FE**      **$$$$**
736 Old Las Vegas Hwy.
(505) 466-3482, (800) 426-9259
www.rancheros.com

With 131 campsites on 22 wooded acres, including 30 sites for tents only, RV hookups, and camping cabins, Rancheros de Santa Fe is the largest camping facility in the area. Amenities include a swimming pool, free WiFi, a recreation room with nightly movies, a game room, a hiking trail, coin laundry, and a playground. Guests can buy groceries, gifts, and propane on-site. Be sure to ask about available discounts. Located 10.5 miles southeast of the Plaza on Frontage Road, in lovely Apache Canyon, the campgrounds are open March 15 through October 31.

**i**   **Each year people die of exposure in the mountains. Don't be one of them. Wear layers of warm, waterproof clothing and a hat, even if you're just going out for a couple of hours. The mountains here are unpredictable and unforgiving. A few hundred feet could mean a sudden and unexpected snow storm—even in late spring or early fall—so be prepared. You should also take some sort of shelter (a space blanket), a gallon of water per day, matches, high-energy food, and a topo map. This is not being alarmist—it's being safe.**

**SANTA FE KOA**      **$$$$**
934 Old Las Vegas Hwy.
(505) 466-1419, (800) 562-1514
www.santafekoa.com

This KOA offers 23 tent sites, 51 RV hookups, and 10 "Kamping Kabins" on 8½ wooded acres in lovely Apache Canyon, located 11 miles southeast of Santa Fe. Campers have access to a coin laundry, free WiFi, free cable TV, a recreation room with nightly movies during the summer, convenience store, upscale gift shop, and a playground. Propane is also available on-site. The camp is open March 1 through November 15.

## Disc Golf

**ASHBAUGH AND MONICA LUCERO PARKS, ST. JOHN'S COLLEGE, ARROYO CHAMISO**
Cerrillos Rd. and Fourth St.
(505) 982-8079 (c/o Ace Mountain Wear)

Disc golf, or Frolf, involves a Frisbeelike disc tossed from tee boxes into 22 stationary metal baskets configured according to Professional Disc Golf Association (PDGA) regulations. The sport, which originated in California (of course), has gained tremendous popularity over the last few decades and is still growing. You can catch disc golf players in action in Ashbaugh Park (Cerrillos Road and Fourth Street), usually on Sunday starting between 9:30 and 11 a.m. Members (and we use the term loosely) also play doubles on Wednesday night starting at about 5 p.m. The times fluctuate with the season—and that includes winter, when players swap their sneakers for Sorels. Even in winter, you'll find anywhere from 10 to 40 people tossing around those little gray discs. Many golfers also play disc golf, though being good at traditional golf doesn't necessarily mean you'll be good at disc golf, which requires an athletic throwing arm. But don't be intimidated. Players, including first-timers, are all welcome; you'll be handicapped according to experience.

## Fishing

New Mexico rivers and lakes are home to a variety of coveted freshwater game fish, including Río Grande cutthroat trout—the state fish, and one for which New Mexico is rightly famous—as well as brown trout, rainbow trout, brook trout, and lake trout. You can also fish for Kokanee salmon, black bass, white bass, and striped bass; largemouth, smallmouth, and spotted bass; panfish, catfish, walleye, bluegill, black crappie, and carp.

While there's little fishing to speak of in Santa Fe—though it's not unheard of to catch a stocked rainbow trout or two in the pretty-but-piddling Santa Fe River—the county is a gateway to superb fishing. Only 35 minutes southeast of Santa Fe, the Pecos River offers fine trout fishing, especially upstream from the village of Pecos or in Villanueva State Park south of I-25. If you're willing to hike, you might venture into the Pecos Wilderness, where the Pecos River originates. You'll find that native cutthroat and rainbow trout thrive in streams such as the Río del Medio near Pecos Baldy. If you plan to fish in this area after September, be prepared for severe winter weather, which can hit with little warning at any time.

The Río Grande, which starts in Colorado and heads south and east to the Gulf of Mexico, is your other choice if you want to stick close to Santa Fe. Take note, however, that it's a temperamental river where fishing is a delight one day and impossible the next. We don't recommend you even attempt fishing the Río Grande during spring runoff, when the water is far too swift and muddy. On a good day, Orilla Verde Recreation Area at Pilar, off Highway 68, which heads to Taos, offers some fine fishing about two hours north of Santa Fe, though you're likely to find yourself competing with whitewater rafters there.

If you're willing to travel a couple of hours or more, the northern part of the state has some of the best trout fishing in New Mexico. In the northwest region, the San Juan River below Navajo Dam offers excellent trout fishing year-round, often yielding trout longer than 20 inches. The most fished part of the San Juan is designated as a "special trout" or "quality" (protected) water with restrictions that limit anglers to artificial flies and lures; single, barbless hooks; and bag and possession limits. In northeastern New Mexico near the Colorado border, the Valle Vidal unit of Carson National Forest—open for fishing from July 1 through December 31 only— offers outstanding trout fishing, as does the Red River south of Questa, part of which is designated as quality water with special restrictions. La Junta, the confluence of the Red River and the Río Grande in the Upper Taos Box, has some of the best fishing on the Río Grande, though its swift and wild waters are recommended for experienced anglers only. Be warned that it will take some serious hiking to get down to the river and even more serious hiking to get back to your car. For anglers with an eye for luxury, Ted Turner's luxury private Vermejo Park Ranch,

(575) 445-3097, located immediately adjacent to Valle Vidal, charges $550 per person per day for a minimum two-night stay to fish in any of its 23 lakes and 20-plus miles of streams between April and September. The American Plan pricing includes lodging, meals, horseback riding, and skeet shooting.

Perhaps the single most important piece of advice before dropping your line in the water is to get a copy of the state fishing proclamation wherever you pick up your license. You can buy a license at the New Mexico Department of Game and Fish or at any of more than 200 vendors statewide, including outfitters, some hardware and grocery stores, and Wal-Mart. An annual fishing license costs $25 for residents, $56 for nonresidents. A one-day license is $12 for everyone, while a 5-day permit costs $24. Seniors and juniors are eligible for discounts. We strongly recommend you pay the extra $5 for a wildlife habitat improvement stamp that allows you to fish on federal lands. Be prepared to pay a $1 vendor fee. If you have any questions about the rules and regulations, call or visit the New Mexico Department of Game and Fish, Wildlife Way, Santa Fe 87507, (505) 476-8000. The department can also provide you with a copy of New Mexico Public Fishing Waters, which includes a map as well as a comprehensive description of streams and lakes throughout New Mexico. You can also call the department's toll-free, twenty-four-hour telephone number—(800) ASK-FISH (275-3474)—for up-to-date fishing and stocking reports and information on regulations, special waters, boat access, etc. For additional information on stocking, call (505) 476-8055 or visit the Web site, www.wildlife.state.nm.us, updated each Friday afternoon for the previous week.

If you're interested in looking at fish but not catching them, the Department of Game and Fish operates seven fish hatcheries that are open for touring. They include Lisboa Springs at Pecos, Red River near Questa, Seven Springs near Jémez Springs, and Parkview near Chama in the northern part of the state. South of Santa Fe you can tour the Glenwood hatchery near the Gila Wilderness and Rock Lake in Santa Rosa, which is the nearer of the two. Call the Fisheries Division at (505) 476-8055 for additional information.

A number of local operators offer guided fishing trips.

## HIGH DESERT ANGLER
### 453 South Cerrillos
### (505) 98–TROUT (988-7688)
### www.highdesertangler.com
In business since 1987, High Desert Angler was Santa Fe's first full-service fly-fishing shop. It sells high-quality fly-fishing equipment and supplies, including popular site-specific fly patterns. It also offers guided fly-fishing trips throughout northern New Mexico and rents all manner of fly-fishing gear, including Sage rods and a variety of reels, waders, and pontoon boats. High Desert Angler can supply you with maps, guidebooks, licenses, and the latest fishing reports, including some that are first-hand.

## THE REEL LIFE
### Sanbusco Market Center,
### 500 Montezuma St.
### (505) 995-8114, (888) 268–FISH (3474)
### www.thereellife.com
The Reel Life, which has stores in Santa Fe and Albuquerque, is an outfitter endorsed by the Orvis Company to guide fishing trips and sell Orvis's high-quality fishing and outdoor gear. It also carries other brands and stocks hundreds of patterns and sizes of flies for freshwater and salt-water fishing as well as material and instructions to tie your own. The store offers guided fishing trips to many of the fine waters of New Mexico including the San Juan River, Taos-area streams, and private lakes and streams in Chama.

## Football
### SANTA FE PARKS AND RECREATION
### DEPARTMENT $$–$$$$
### Parks Department
### Municipal Recreation Complex
### 205 Caja del Río Rd.
### (505) 955-4470
The city of Santa Fe sponsors an annual men's flag football league that plays at the MRC on Caja del Rio Road. The league has 17 teams that play against each other on two football fields Sundays during a season that runs from September through November.

### SANTA FE YOUNG AMERICA FOOTBALL
### LEAGUE $$$$
### 1750 Cerrillos Rd.
### (505) 820-0775
### www.santafeyafl.org
This private coed league is part of a statewide organization for young footballers from ages five through 12. Four hundred youths, the vast majority of them boys, participate in the Santa Fe league, which sponsors 14 teams that play in the city's Franklin E. Miles Park (Siringo Road and Camino Carlos Rey) and Ashbaugh Park (Cerrillos Road and Fourth Street) from August through October. Registration cost is $115. The season starts with four weeks of rigorous conditioning and practice before players are allowed to have physical contact with each other. After that, teams rotate practice Monday through Friday between 5:30 and 7 p.m. They play two games per night on Tuesday, Wednesday, and Thursday from about 6 to 9 p.m. and three games on Saturday between 9 a.m. and 1 p.m. A two-day Cowboy Football Camp is offered in July for K-8 and 9-12. The league discourages stardom and a "winning is everything" mentality. Instead, it concentrates on teaching kids the rules of the game and sportsmanship.

## Golf
Not only do Santa Fe golf courses offer lots of hills, varied terrain, and spectacular scenery but they have a unique feature that any golfer has to love: the high elevation drives the ball farther than the same effort would get you at sea level. Combine that with the high-quality bluegrass and bent grass that local courses use on their greens and fairways—not to mention relatively mild weather that allows you to play golf somewhere nearby yearlong—and you can see why Santa Fe attracts golfers of all stripes.

## MARTY SÁNCHEZ LINKS DE
## SANTA FE                          $$$$
Recreation Complex, 205 Caja del Río Rd.
(505) 955-4400
www.linksdesantafe.com

Named for a young Santa Fe golf champion who died of cancer at age 25, Marty Sánchez Links de Santa Fe is only 20 minutes from the Santa Fe Plaza and offers some of the best golfing in northern New Mexico, with stunning backdrops on every tee. It features an 18-hole/par 72 championship links course with five tee-box locations measuring between 7,415 yards from the championship tees to 5,045 yards from the front tee boxes. It also has a 9-hole/par 3 course called a "Great 28." Green fees cost $35 for 18 holes, $25.50 afternoon/weekend rate, $14.75 junior rate, and $24 senior rate. The cart fee is $15 ($8 afternoon rate). Purchase of a $125 Players Club Card includes the one-time green fee, balls, food/beverage, and offers discounted green fees for a year. There are a variety of other discounts available.

## PUEBLO DE COCHITÍ GOLF COURSE
5200 Cochití Hwy., Cochití Lake
(505) 465-2239
www.golfcochiti.com

Located in the scenic volcanic foothills of the Jémez Mountains, this 18-hole, par 72 course designed by Robert Trent Jones Jr. ranks in the top 50 nationwide among public golf courses. Golfers play roughly 50,000 rounds a year here on scenic bluegrass fairways and bent-grass greens and tees. In July 2000, major renovations on and off the green, including a new three-level clubhouse with restaurant and full-service pro shop, were made by Jones. Championship tees now play at 6,805 yards, back tees at 6,429 yards, and middle tees at 5,932 yards. Guests pay a $29 to $60 greens fee. Pueblo de Cochití Golf Course is open sunup to sundown year-round, weather permitting.

## QUAIL RUN GOLF COURSE
3101 Old Pecos Trail
(505) 986-2255, (800) 548-6990
www.quailrunsantafe.com

Quail Run is a luxury, gated community with a private 9-hole/par 32 golf course that's open year-round, weather permitting, to guests from reciprocating country clubs with prior approval of the golf pro. The Arthur Jack Snyder-designed course, opened in 1986, features native grasses, bluegrass fairways, and tees measuring between 2,600 yards and 1,800 yards. Visitors pay $60 for 18 holes, including cart fees, to golf at Quail Run, where some 9,000 holes are played each year. The club has a pro shop that offers lessons as well as food and beverages. Hours are Tuesday through Sunday from 7 a.m. to 7 p.m.

## SANTA FE COUNTRY CLUB
4360 Airport Rd.
(505) 471-0601
www.santafecountryclub.com

Founded in 1946, this is a wide-open, 18-hole/par 72 public golf course. Golfers play about 30,000 rounds here each season, which runs from February through December. The course measures between 7,098 yards from the championship tees to 5,862 yards at the forward tees and offers a putting green, pitching green, and practice range. State residents pay between $100 per month for a social membership to $280 per month for a full membership. Nonresidents can join for a flat $212 per month. All players pay $33 for 18 holes to golf during the week, $44 a day on weekends, plus a $16 cart fee. Seniors pay $24 a day during the week and $34 on the weekend. The club is open Tuesday through Sunday from dawn to dusk.

## SUN COUNTRY AMATEUR GOLF
## ASSOCIATION
1440 Rio Rancho Blvd., Albuquerque
(505) 897-0864, (800) 346-5319
www.newmexicogolf.org

This is the governing body of amateur golf in New Mexico and can provide suggestions about where to play and how.

## Hiking

The city of Santa Fe and the surrounding mountains and basins offer a beautiful maze of trails, some paved and meandering through neighborhoods in town; others linking the foothills of the Sangre de Cristo, from north to south; and others forging deep into the mountains following stream courses through canyons to grassy, flower-filled meadows and peaks in the adjoining Pecos Wilderness. A network of urban trails includes Arroyo Chamisa in south Santa Fe and the Railyard Park in downtown. Atalaya Mountain, starting at St. John's College on the East Side (see our Education and Child Care chapter), leaves directly from the visitor's parking lot, follows an arroyo and eventually ascends a pretty steep hillside leading to a private road. There you'll begin your ascent of Atalaya Mountain, which starts off gently only to become quite steep in the middle and at the end of the trail. You'll be rewarded with magnificent, sweeping views of the entire city. Watch out for scree on the downhill portion of your hike. The trail is part of the Dale Ball Trail system, which includes Dale Ball and Santa Fe Canyon Preserve trails on Upper Canyon Road and Ski Basin trails, such as those in Hyde Memorial State Park, reachable by car minutes from downtown Santa Fe.

i The unwritten code of the West is to leave things as you found them. If you open a gate, close it behind you. If the previous "tenant" left a pile of deadwood at your campsite, leave some for the next camper. Of course, if you find garbage or other unwanted remnants at your camp or on a trail, by all means tote it out along with your own.

Hyde Memorial State Park in the nearby Santa Fe National Forest offers a variety of woodsy streamside trails, some easy, others strenuous. Among the most popular is the Winsor Trail, which follows Big Tesuque Creek up into the Pecos Wilderness. You can also leave one car in Big Tesuque Canyon, a mile past Bishops Lodge on Bishop's Lodge Road, on the south side of Tesuque, and one car at the Big Tesuque/Borrego trailhead on Hyde Park Road, and hike between the two. Don't attempt to do the round trip in one day: it's 17 miles with numerous stream crossings! Big Tesuque Creek shares a mid-level trailhead with the Borrego Trail, a very easy 4-mile hike that takes you through rolling meadows and forested hills. Simply follow Highway 475 about 8.5 miles north to a parking lot where you'll find the trailhead. In late September/early October, when the aspens are changing, the classic family outing is a walk along Aspen Vista Trail near the Ski Basin surrounded by the golden shimmer of the largest aspen forest in the West.

If you're looking for a strenuous hike, the trail to Lake Katherine will give you spectacular views of Santa Fe Baldy, Penitente Peak, the upper Pecos Basin, the Río Grande Valley, and the Jémez Mountains. This 14.5-mile hike requires seven to eight hours of hiking plus additional time to rest and eat. In that time, you will climb 3,200 feet. It's essential to wear solid hiking shoes with good tread and, due to high-desert conditions, carry high-energy food and a gallon of water per person per day; at least one liter of water on even the shortest hikes.

For more information on trails and conditions, call or visit the New Mexico Public Lands Information Center, 1474 Rodeo Rd., (505) 438-7542. Or contact the Santa Fe chapter of the Sierra Club, 1807 Second St., #45, (505) 983-2703, www.riograndesierraclub.org. You might also check the Outdoors section of Thursday's Santa Fe New Mexican, which lists Sierra Club outings for the upcoming weekend and phone numbers of the group leaders. If you're a serious hiker, buy a copy of the local Sierra Club group's self-published Day Hikes in the Santa Fe Area. This 228-page paperback describes in delightful detail 45 hikes ranging from easy to strenuous, some in Santa Fe, others up to 85 miles away. If you're not the do-it-yourself type, there are numerous guides in Santa Fe who will be happy to guide you on half-day to multiple-day hikes.

## Horseback Riding

**THE BISHOP'S LODGE STABLE AND WRANGLER'S STORE** $$$$
North Bishop's Lodge Rd.
(505) 819-4103
www.bishopslodge.com

Just 3 miles north of the Plaza, historic Bishop's Lodge Resort sits on 500 piñon-and-juniper-forested acres in the lush Big Tesuque Creek valley at the foot of the Sangre de Cristo Mountains, with miles of trails perfect for private and group horseback rides. Daily private rides may be scheduled all year with lodge wranglers. In addition, the Lodge stables offers kids, barbecue, cowboy breakfast, and sunset rides. No riders younger than eight years old are permitted. The weight limit is 225 pounds. No exceptions. The stables are open from 8 a.m. to 5 p.m.

### BROKEN SADDLE RIDING COMPANY   $$$$
**Vicksville Rd., Cerrillos**
**(505) 424-7774**
**www.brokensaddle.com**
South of Santa Fe, about 26 miles from the Plaza, Broken Saddle is the only stable in the state that offers smooth-riding, gaited horses like Tennessee Walkers and Missouri Fox Trotters that use all four legs for power. With horses like these, it goes without saying that, unlike many stables, Broken Saddle allows riders to trot, canter, and even gallop. That's a big draw, especially for experienced riders who want to feel the wind in their face. With 5,500 acres in the Cerrillos Hills south of Santa Fe, Broken Saddle is instantly familiar with dozens of beautiful trails in juniper and piñon country you'll recognize from classic Western movies. Perhaps you'll ride to Devil's Canyon with its beautiful rock formations or to one of the 221 old mines in the Cerrillos Hills—maybe even Old Grand Central Silver Mine, one of the bigger ones. Or you might wend your way up to the Madrid (emphasis on the first syllable) Overlook with 360-degree views of five mountain ranges. Beginners below 220 pounds and kids eight years old and older are welcome. The stable is open for business year-round. Summertime is especially busy, so call two to three days in advance. Closed Saturday.

### MAKARIOS RANCH   $$$$
**190 Camino Querencia, Cerrillos**
**(505) 473-1038**
In the old mining town of Cerrillos, Makarios caters primarily to experienced riders of all ages who are looking for adventure on the back of a horse. Be warned: This is not easy riding. You'll be traveling on rough, mountain terrain to easy valleys, on one of five horses belonging to the ranch. Your journey may take you into the lovely Galisteo Basin area or deep into the Cerrillos Hills or the Ortíz Mountains. This is wild country with Indian ruins and old mines, some of which you might want to stop and explore. Rides are by appointment only.

## Hot-Air Ballooning

An abundance of crosswinds, not to mention city ordinances, make hot-air ballooning in Santa Fe an iffy proposition at best. Most ballooning takes place in Albuquerque, where the skies are calmer, but one balloon company has found that Las Barrancas, north of Santa Fe, offers a safe and scenic place for ballooning, and is now offering rides there in summer.

### SANTA FE BALLOONS
**(505) 699-7555**
**www.santafeballoons.com**
Johnny Lewis, a colorful and respected Texas balloon pilot with 6,000 hours of piloting balloons over three decades, offers one-hour balloon rides over the starkly beautiful Las Barrancas area of Pojoaque north of Santa Fe from May to October. Lewis picks up passengers from Santa Fe hotels in the early morning hours and drives them out to the launch site in Las Barrancas for breakfast while the balloon is prepared for flight. You can't miss Johnny. He's the one with the cowboy boots and hat and grizzled y'all charm.

### SANTA FE DETOURS
**54½ East San Francisco St.**
**(505) 983-6565, (800) DETOURS (338-6877)**
**www.sfdetours.com.**
Santa Fe Detours will be happy to arrange a ballooning adventure in Albuquerque. In summer you'll probably be aloft by early morning when the air is still cool enough to ensure the balloon will rise. In cooler seasons, you're likely to be in the air by noon, so pack a lunch if one hasn't

been provided for you. Santa Fe Detours traditionally celebrates landings with a champagne toast and presents guests with a souvenir pen and, when appropriate, a first-flight certificate.

## Hunting

### NM DEPT. OF GAME AND FISH
1 Wildlife Way
(505) 476-8000
www.wildlife.state.nm.us

Northern New Mexico offers excellent trophy hunting for elk, deer, antelope, and limited bighorn sheep on state, federal, Indian, and private land. Any would-be hunter's first step should be to get a copy of the New Mexico Game and Fish Department's annual *Big Game Proclamation,* which comes out in mid-winter. *NOTE:* Hunters should be aware that the application deadline for special hunts, which include most big game, is in early spring, and before applying you must get a customer ID number from either the Web site or in person at Fish and Wildlife offices before applying. The one-time application fee is $9 for New Mexico residents and $12 for nonresidents. Guides and outfitters must have permits from the appropriate agency if they will be guiding on federal (national forest, BLM) or State Trust lands. Insist that any outfitter provide names of prior customers and should follow-up by checking all references. Also get additional information from the New Mexico Council of Outfitters and Guides (P.O. Box 11816, Albuquerque 87192, 505-977-5926; www.ethics.sos.state.nm.us).

Elk is historically a subsistence food for the state's native populations who rely on the fall hunt to stock the freezer for the winter. The Valle Vidal Unit of the Carson National Forest in northeastern New Mexico is about as good as it gets on public land anywhere in the United States. The Sargent and Humphries wildlife areas near Chama, in northwestern New Mexico, also offer record-book heads. Competition is fierce in both areas for limited slots. If you don't mind paying to hunt on private land, Vermejo Park Ranch, (505) 445-3097—contiguous with the Valle Vidal and owned by media magnate Ted Turner—has one

of the finest elk herds in the country, second, perhaps, only to the national elk refuge in Jackson, Wyoming. Vermejo Park's is a natural herd managed for even age distribution, which allows elks to reach maturity. The ranch also offers world-class accommodations and is priced accordingly. Weeklong guided rifle hunts for mature bulls can cost up to $13,000, including lodging and food. That compares to $772 for nonresident hunters going after trophy elk on public land, such as the already mentioned Valle Vidal unit or, farther south (and much closer to Santa Fe), the Pecos Wilderness, which offers good hunting for those willing to hire a guide with the necessary horseback transportation. Please see the paragraph above regarding outfitters.

On the other side of the Río Grande, hunters are finding increasing success in the Jémez Mountains, northwest of Santa Fe, as the state elk herd continues to expand. Valles Caldera National Preserve offers limited elk hunting by lottery, for $30 per mature bull, closing April 8 each year. Call (866) 382-5537 for more information or log on to www.vallescaldera.gov. On the same side of the Río Grande, north of Dulce near the Colorado border, the Jicarilla Apache tribe (505-759-3255; www.jicarillahunt.com) offers trophy animals and very high success rates. Some 4,000-plus elk, one of the largest herds in New Mexico, are spread out on 850,000 acres in the beautiful Four Corners. The tribe offers guided hunting trips as well as fishing trips on well-stocked private lakes.

Compared to elk, hunting mule deer on New Mexico's public lands is an iffy proposition. Many experts say increasing numbers of elk have pushed out their smaller brethren. Hunters seeking trophies can expect to work hard for them, climbing high, rough country far from paved roads. You may not come home with a trophy—or even a nontrophy animal, for that matter—but you'll see some stunning country. Farmington, in the northeast corner of the state, is among the better deer-hunting areas in New Mexico. The terrain may not be the only challenge deer hunters face in New Mexico. While they may still purchase licenses over the counter, New Mexico is increasingly going to a system requiring hunters to apply through a lottery system for a limited number of permits. Again, applications for drawings are due in early spring. Check the proclamation for the exact dates.

If it's bighorn sheep you're after, the odds of drawing a license are precipitously against you. If you manage to land a permit, do yourself a favor and hire a good outfitter to make the most of a rare opportunity. A handful of hunters each year is lucky enough to get licenses for bighorn sheep in the Pecos Wilderness. These animals, frequently so tame as to eat snacks from the hands of passing backpackers, may offer their biggest challenge in the drawing of the permit. Similarly, would-be pronghorn hunters have the option of facing long odds in public drawings or paying ranchers, who often advertise in local newspapers. Eastern New Mexico on both sides of I–40 offers trophy heads of the keen-sighted animals, mistakenly called antelope.

Spring and fall are hunting seasons for wild turkey, designated as big game in New Mexico. Locals addicted to this challenging—many say impossible—pastime find some success in the lower hills of the Pecos Wilderness and in the northern mountains.

Small-game season varies according to the species. September, when hunting season opens for a number of small-game species, is a perfect time for those who want to combine a lovely hike in the autumn woods with bringing home supper—perhaps a squirrel or grouse.

**i** Remember, this is high desert, and the climate is extremely dry. Make sure you build fires only in designated fire pits and thoroughly douse them with water or a combination of water and dirt before you leave. In an emergency, build fires away from trees and shrubbery that could easily ignite.

## Martial Arts

Santa Fe is a beacon for alternative lifestyles, so it's not surprising that the city has an enormous selection of martial-arts studios to appeal to those with eastern sensibilities. You'll find Aikido in styles ranging from soft to stringent; aikikai, aikido, Brazilian jiu-jitsu, chi kung, judo, karate, kenpo, kung fu, tae kwon do, tai chi, tang soo, and a variety of others in the telephone book listed under "martial arts" or the specific activity.

## Racquetball

A number of gyms in town have racquetball courts and offer lessons. These include the Genoveva Chávez Community Center, 3321 Rodeo Rd., (505) 955-4001; William C. Witter Fitness Education Center at Santa Fe Community College, 6401 Richards Ave., (505) 428-1615; Club International Family Fitness Center, 1931 Warner Ave., (505) 473-9807; and El Gancho Fitness, Swim and Racquet Club, Old Las Vegas Hwy., (505) 988-5000.

### FORT MARCY COMPLEX
**490 Washington Ave.**
**(505) 955-2500**
Two racquetball courts are available at Fort Marcy/Mager's Field Sports Complex. Call Fort Marcy for more information.

## Rock Climbing

One of New Mexico's best-kept secrets is that it is a mecca for rock climbers, with climbing available on lava, tuff, granite, sandstone, and limestone. The state has 25 major crags, offering good climbing. More than 10 sites are within a 1 ½-hour drive of Santa Fe and offer a well-rounded selection of "sport," "traditional," as well as multipitch climbs and places for bouldering, such as the Sandía Mountains, Socorro, and Pecos. White Rock/Los Alamos, in the Jémez Mountains, northwest of Santa Fe, boasts more than 100 climbs alone and is the most popular local climbing spot.

### SANTA FE CLIMBING CENTER     $$–$$$$
**825 Early St., Suite A**
**(505) 986-8944**
**www.climbsantafe.com**
This popular climbing gym, a block east of St. Francis Drive, has a large climbing wall and offers

many different climbing classes, as well as a variety of guided trips, climbing clubs, and teams. The After School Climbing program, offered daily Monday to Friday 3:30 to 5 p.m. for kids age five and up, teaches rock climbing safety, leadership, confidence, and teamwork. A Home School class on Tuesdays 1 to 2:30 p.m. is also offered for the same age group. Single day pass or eight-class discount punch cards are available. Five-day Summer Adventure Camps are offered between June and August. Half-day, full-day, and three-day trips are available. Other outdoor trips can be arranged. The gym can be rented for birthday parties and other events. It is open 5 to 10 p.m. Monday, Wednesday, and Friday; 4 to 10 p.m. Tuesday and Thursday; 1 to 8 p.m. on Saturday; and 1 to 6 p.m. on Sunday.

## Rollerskating

**ROCKIN' ROLLERS EVENT ARENA**　　　**$**
**2915 Agua Fria St.**
**(505) 473-7755**
This 3,500-square-foot purple skating rink, just south of Siler Road, is a favorite with Santa Fe youngsters. It is open to public skating for only limited hours in summer; the rest of the time, the rink may be hired for private parties and events. Kids can skate here between June and August, Monday to Friday, from 1 to 3 p.m. and 3 to 5 p.m. Teen dances with live bands and deejays take place every Friday from 7:30 to 11:30 p.m.

## Rugby

**RÍO GRANDE RUGBY UNION**
**Santa Fe Club**
**1216 Parkway Dr.**
**(505) 231-3374**
**www.santaferugby.com**
Santa Fe has a very active all-male rugby club, the Santos, which celebrated its 37th anniversary in 2009. A member of the Río Grande Rugby Union—which encompasses the area from El Paso, Texas, to Durango, Colorado, and takes in all of New Mexico—the Santos have hosted a number of international clubs and many of its members have ventured abroad themselves to England, Ireland, New Zealand, and Vancouver. The 23-man club boasts a number of high-profile members. Most team mates are age 35 and younger; older members are called the Anasazi after the ancestors of the Pueblo Indians. While it doesn't have the depth of many clubs—some of its members have been playing rugby only five years, though they have backgrounds in football, soccer, wrestling, and other aggressive sports—the Santos' overall athleticism is on par with any rugby club in the country. They have two full regulation pitches at the Municipal Recreation Complex, 205 Caja del Río Rd., (505) 955-4470, and play home games on Saturday starting at 1 p.m. Members practice Tuesday and Thursday starting at 5:30 or 6 p.m. The Santos play primarily in fall and spring, though the club won't say no to summer games in the Colorado Rockies, where the weather is still comfortably cool. The spring season starts in early March, weather permitting, and continues through mid-May. The fall season begins in September and goes through November. The club sponsors an annual Labor Day weekend rugby tournament, which begins at 9 a.m. on Sunday with finals at about 5 p.m. Santa Fe High School Rugby is coached by the president of the New Mexico Athletic Association at the MRC facility. For more information, call (505) 469-9417.

## Running/Walking

If you're lucky enough to be in a relatively undeveloped part of town, or if you don't mind driving to your run or your walk, Santa Fe offers umpteen unpaved roads and trails, some in town, others in the county; some with respectable inclines, others downright intimidating. And practically anywhere you go, you'll find beautiful scenery and attractive architecture—unless, of course, you hate either real or faux adobe.

Santa Fe offers nearly ideal weather for running and walking—even in the winter for zealots who won't let a little snow or slush stop them. There's nothing quite as beautiful as getting out first thing in the morning after a night's snowfall when the trees and adobe walls are outlined in soft shelves of white snow that muffle all sounds, including those of your shoes hitting the ground. Do be careful about slipping, however. The snow may cushion the thud, but it probably won't provide adequate cushioning for your back or hips.

The downside of running or walking in Santa Fe is that it's not a particularly pedestrian-friendly town, except perhaps for the area in and around the Plaza. The city has a dearth of sidewalks, so you'll find yourself sharing the road with cars and bicycles or treading on terribly uneven shoulders that threaten twisted ankles or worse. The best defense is a pair of off-road running or walking shoes that provide lots of ankle support. For runners and walkers both, it's always a good idea to run facing traffic, especially on Santa Fe's many curving roads. Ideally, you want to find a place that has very little car traffic. That way you avoid carbon monoxide as well as possible accidents. If you run or walk at night, wear something reflective and be sure to ask around to make sure the area you choose is safe. Running or walking in groups certainly lessens the odds of being a crime victim, though for some it defeats the purpose entirely. If you prefer to run or walk in company, we've included a few suggestions here.

## SANTA FE PARKS AND RECREATION DEPARTMENT
**Parks Department**
**1142 Siler Rd.**
**(505) 955-2509**
The city sponsors a number of races throughout the year including the Santa Fe Run-Around in June, a 5k run and 1-mile walk co-sponsored by the Santa Fe Striders (see entry below), and the annual Sylvia Pulliam Memorial "Hot Chili Run" in August, a 5k and 10k run starting at Salvador Pérez Park, 601 Alto St.

## SANTA FE STRIDERS      $$
**P.O. 1818, Santa Fe 87504**
**www.santafestriders.org**
Affiliated with Road Runners Club of America, Santa Fe Striders is a local running club for everyone from the casual runner to 100-mile ultra-marathoners. The club has approximately 70 members

of varying ages, from their 20s to their 70s, who promote running, sponsor races, and gather for informal runs open to anybody who's interested. Competitive runners meet Tuesday nights at the Santa Fe High School track for speed workouts. On Thursdays, runners meet at the Runner's Hub, 527B West Cordova, for a tempo run. Trail runs begin on Sundays at 8 a.m. Details for the weekly run are posted on the group's Web site. The club organizes other informal runs, often followed by a picnic, a potluck, or dinner at a restaurant.

The Santa Fe Striders sponsor several 5k and/ or 10k races a year, including the club's flagship event, the Santa Fe Run-Around on the last weekend in May, a charitable 5k run to benefit the Salvation Army; and the Corrida de Los Locos ("Run of the Crazies") in February, an unsanctioned 5-mile race for which contestants pray for the worst weather possible. For the truly loco, there's even a snowshoe race in mid-January. Those who prefer less inclement weather might consider joining the club's Big Tesuque run in early October, an 12-mile mountain run from Aspen Vista to the radio towers at the top of Tesuque Peak and back down again—great training for endurance runners. All races are advertised on the Web site and in the club's newsletter as well as in an annual calendar available from New Mexico USA Track and Field, 31 Sandhill Rd., Los Lunas 87031, (505) 865-8612.

For visitors the club often recommends running around St. John's College, which sits directly in the foothills of the Sangre de Cristo Mountains. It also sends runners up Hyde Park Road (aka Artist Road), the beginning of a long uphill stretch that ends up at the ski slopes; along winding, scenic Bishop's Lodge Road; or up Atalaya Mountain—a 3.5-mile run with an elevation increase of 1,780 feet—for some "light" spring, summer, and autumn running.

## Skateboarding
Located downtown in West De Vargas Park, at De Vargas and Guadalupe Streets, Skateboard Park has concrete ramps and culverts galore, making it a popular destination for skaters as well as cyclists and rollerskaters. Skaters once practiced in and

around the Plaza—to the consternation of many and the fascination of a few. Now, however, they'll have two parks from which to choose. Franklin E. Miles Skateboard Park (see our write-up in the Parks section of this chapter) opened in 2000. With 13,000 square feet, the skateboard park is two-and-a-half times the size of its older sibling. It has plenty of bowls and even a street plaza, giving park habitués a birds-eye view of the talent. As in all city parks, skaters must observe the 10 p.m. curfew. This seems to pose few hardships— except, of course, in summer when avid skaters can never get enough of their favorite pastime. To find other good skateboard locations, ask any skater or just follow the rail marks.

## BEYOND WAVES MOUNTAIN SURF SHOP
**1428 Cerrillos Rd.**
**(505) 988-2240**
**www.beyondwaves.com**
When they're not in Skateboard Park, you're likely to find skaters in Beyond Waves Mountain Surf Shop. It's the only specialty store in Santa Fe that sells skateboards and accessories, including apparel. On rainy days, you're likely to see groups of kids just hanging out at Beyond Waves, conveniently located down the street from Skateboard Park. You'll find some watching any of the store's more than 150 skating or snowboarding videos, others listening to music, and some exploring the wares. The store sponsors an annual summer skateboard contest in which participants in various age groups are judged for ability, and it organizes its own skateboard and snowboard teams. Winners receive trophies, skateboards, T-shirts, and other goodies. Everyone gets a free bumper sticker. The event usually gets some radio and television coverage. Beyond Waves is open seven days a week, 10 a.m. to 7 p.m. in summer with an 8 a.m. opening time in winter to rent out snowboards. During the winter, the store closes Sundays at 6 p.m.

## Soccer

America has long played catch-up with Europe in its appreciation for the game of soccer (known in Europe as football). In Santa Fe, as elsewhere in the country, the sport is rapidly gaining popularity with more than 2,000 local kids and adults playing the game. Along with this popularity have come increasingly more vocal demands for equal time—and equal playing fields—with other sports. Accused for years of treating soccer players like second-class citizens, the city of Santa Fe has finally risen to the challenge with five adult soccer fields at the Municipal Recreation Complex (MRC). Men and women can play in the Santa Fe Adult Soccer League, (505) 204-3329, www.sfasl.org. The club has 500 members and 36 teams. Youth soccer games for boys and girls aged 5 through 16, are played under the auspices of the American Youth Soccer Organization, 1704-B Llano St., #222, (505) 466-3542, www.ayso.org. Matches take place at MRC on Saturdays 8 a.m. to noon, mid-June to early August.

## Softball
### SANTA FE SOFTBALL ASSOCIATION
**3238 Nizhoni Dr.**
**(505) 955-4465**
The Greater Santa Fe Softball Association is a private organization with registered players from age 15 (with parental consent) to 67 in women's, men's, and coed leagues. Teams start practice in March with games beginning in April and continuing through September five nights a week. Tournaments take place on the weekend at the Municipal Recreation Complex, where there are six softball fields, four with lights. For information about joining the Adult Softball League, call (505) 470-2737.

## Swimming

The city of Santa Fe has five indoor heated swimming pools with schedules, classes, and prices unique to each facility. Call the individual pool or pick up a copy of the City of Santa Fe Parks and Recreation Department's annual Activity Guide, which has a complete schedule for each pool. Check with the Recreation Division (505-955-2503; www.nm-santafe.civicplus.com) for special programs and teams.

## BICENTENNIAL POOL
1121 Alto St., (505) 955-2650
(open summers only)

## FORT MARCY SWIMMING POOL
490 Washington Ave., (505) 955-2500

## GENOVEVA CHÁVEZ COMMUNITY CENTER
3321 Rodeo Rd., (505) 955-4000

## SALVADOR PÉREZ PARK AND POOL
601 Alta Vista St., (505) 955-2604

## TINO GRIEGO POOL
1730 Llano St., (505) 955-2660

# Tennis

Santa Fe has public tennis courts throughout the city, all of them outdoors. Call the individual facility, if possible, or the City of Santa Fe Parks Division, (505) 955-2106, for hours, lighting, rules, etc., as well as for information about instruction for children and adults. There is no charge to use the courts, which are available on a first-come, first-served basis only.

## ALTO PARK & BICENTENNIAL POOL
1043 Alto St., (505) 984-6773

## ATALAYA PARK
717 Camino Cabra

## CHAMISA TENNIS COURTS
Dr. Richard Angle Park, Calle Medico

## FORT MARCY/MAGER'S FIELD SPORTS COMPLEX
490 Washington Ave., (505) 955-2500

## GALISTEO TENNIS COURTS
2721 Galisteo St.

## HERB MARTÍNEZ/LA RESOLANA
2240 Camino Carlos Rey

## LARRAGOITE PARK
Agua Fría Street and Avenida Cristobal Colon

## SALVADOR PÉREZ PARK AND POOL
601 Alta Vista St., (505) 955-2604

## *Private Courts*
## EL GANCHO FITNESS, SWIM AND RACQUET CLUB
Old Las Vegas Hwy.
(505) 988-5000

El Gancho is a members-only club with the largest tennis facilities in Santa Fe. They include seven outdoor courts, of which two are clay and three are lighted, and two permanent indoor courts. El Gancho has four on-site tennis pros, leagues, and tournaments.

## SANGRE DE CRISTO RACQUET CLUB
1755 Camino Corrales
(505) 983-7978

Sangre de Cristo Racquet Club is a private tennis club with five outdoor courts—including one clay court and another with lights and heat—and an indoor court in a fabric "bubble." The club also has an outdoor heated swimming pool for seasonal use only. Sangre de Cristo has two tennis pros, a full-service pro shop, and two sanctioned tournaments.

## SANTA FE COUNTRY CLUB
Airport Rd.
(505) 471-3378, ext. 22
www.santafecountryclub.com

The Santa Fe Country Club offers three outdoor courts in a beautiful setting surrounded by trees. The club has a full-service pro shop on the premises and one U.S. Professional Tennis Association–certified pro. Every summer the country club hosts an adult tournament and a junior tournament, both open to the public. The country club is closed on Monday. See the entry under this chapter's Golf section for membership fees.

# Ultimate Frisbee
## SANTA FE ULTIMATE
P.O. Box 23103, Santa Fe 87505
(505) 988-4005
www.santafeultimate.com

There are only two requirements to play for Santa

Fe Ultimate, the only Ultimate Frisbee team in Santa Fe: lots of enthusiasm and an ability to run. Of course a strong, controlled throwing arm won't hurt, either. But mostly the idea is to have fun at the game, which is like a blend of football and soccer using a Frisbee instead of a ball. There's no tackle in this game, nor can you run with the disc. The goal is to get the Frisbee from one end of the field to another by tossing it from player to player. Santa Fe Ultimate is sanctioned by the Ultimate Players Association, based out of Colorado. The team has a roster of about 15 steady players, most of them outdoor sports enthusiasts (rock climbers, mountain bikers, etc.) who show up regularly at St. John's College for pickup games on Tuesdays and Thursdays from 6 p.m. to dark. There are also pickup games in Los Alamos, Albuquerque, and Espanola. The Savage Seven Tournament is played the first weekend of September at the polo grounds at the Santa Fe Horse Park.

## Volleyball

### SANTA FE PARKS AND RECREATION DEPARTMENT
**1142 Siler Rd.**
**(505) 955-2506**
The city of Santa Fe sponsors both a coed and an all-women's volleyball team in a season that begins in early October and ends in early March with tournaments. Register early because the Parks and Recreation Division has only 200 slots and they fill up early.

## White-water Rafting, Kayaking, Canoeing, and Floating

Right here in the high desert of northern New Mexico, you'll experience some of the finest white-water rafting in the West. Come spring, with the melting of winter's snowpack, the Río Grande, Red River, and Río Chama swell their banks with churning, fast-moving water that makes for some mighty hairy rapids. Even the most jaded rafter will get a thrill—and some astoundingly beautiful scenery along the way. Try it for yourself and see why Congress officially designated these magnificent rivers as "wild and

scenic." Among the more popular rafting spots is the Taos Box of the Río Grande, so-called because you'll pass through Class IV rapids boxed in by the sheer cliffs—some of them 1,000 feet high—of the Río Grande Gorge. For a somewhat more sedate ride—and we do mean "somewhat" because you'll still run into several rapids—head northeast for El Vado and float down the Río Chama through canyons of pink, red, and mauve sandstone or ponderosa pine.

Because of the unpredictability of the rivers, you're advised to do some careful research and advanced scouting should you decide to venture out on your own—and even then, you should do so only if you're highly experienced. The Río Grande has some dangerous and, in certain sections, impassible stretches of water. You'd be wise to buy the state Parks and Recreation Division's *New Mexico Whitewater: A Guide to River Trips*. Or hire a professional outfitter, whose business it is to know the rivers and equip you with good gear and knowledgeable guides. You can choose trips lasting from a half day to five days, from flat-out easy to downright dangerous. Call the BLM for a list of New Mexico white-water touring companies or try any of the local outfits listed below:

### KOKOPELLI RAFTING ADVENTURES
**551 Cordova Rd., #541**
**(505) 983-3734, (800) 879-9035**
**www.kokopelliraft.com**
Kokopelli Rafting Adventures' menu of river trips has something for everyone—from folks looking to kick back and relax to adrenaline junkies who can't get enough of those Class IV rapids. You could spend anywhere from a half day to eight days navigating the Río Chama, Río Grande, or other New Mexico rivers. Among Kokopelli's offerings is a two-day float down a rarely traveled portion of the upper Río Grande. Starting at Ute Mountain located about 150 miles north of Santa Fe near the New Mexico–Colorado border, you'll experience 25 miles of a designated wild and scenic section of the river before winding up at Lee Trail after a night under the stars at Costilla Creek. Call Kokopelli for information about longer

trips. And let them worry about things like camping equipment, meals, soft drinks, and water. The company will provide them on day trips and snacks for half-day trips.

## SANTA FE RAFTING COMPANY
**1000 Cerrillos Rd.**
**(505) 988-4914, (888) 988-4914**
**www.santaferafting.com**
Santa Fe Rafting Company provides a variety of trips to make everyone from families to white-water enthusiasts happy. Certified guides not only lead you through rapids but also identify the flora, fauna, and geological attractions along the way. You can paddle yourself or let your guides do the rowing.

## SOUTHWEST WILDERNESS ADVENTURES
**Buckman Rd.**
**(505) 983-7262**
Enjoy the thrill of white-water or the serenity of a float on a half-day, full-day, or overnight trip with Southwest Wilderness Adventures. Southwest offers trips in the Río Grande Gorge, including the exciting Taos Box, in White Rock Canyon, which is suitable for the whole family; and down the "wild and scenic" Río Chama. Quality meals are included with your trip. Discounts are available for groups of 10 or more.

# WINTER SPORTS

For some, the idea of "winter" in Santa Fe may stir images of short-sleeved golfing and tennis. After all, this is the Southwest isn't it? Well, yes—but we're not Phoenix. Santa Fe is at 7,000 feet in elevation and gets a real winter, complete with snow and frigid temperatures. Winter usually begins in late October, settles in to stay in January—the coldest month of the year here—and disappears sometime in March or April. In good snow years, you can still see patches of snow on the Sangre de Cristo Mountains above Santa Fe on the Fourth of July. Thanks to our elevation and the surrounding mountains, snow on Memorial Day is not unheard of. And due to our relatively southerly location, neither is sweatshirt weather in March. Even in winter, some 70 percent of the days here are sunny. A normal winter brings nightly temperatures averaging in the 20s (°F), sometimes plummeting into the single digits, even as low as 0°. Days are often bright and sunny but very cold, frequently below freezing. Beware: "sunny" doesn't necessarily mean "warm."

Ski Apache, in the Sacramento Mountains near Cloudcroft in southern New Mexico, is one of the southernmost ski resorts in the country, with terrific skiing on the Apache reservation. But, since it has more snow and mountains, northern New Mexico boasts the lion's share of the state's ski areas. Old-timers say that running a ski area is like running a farm. In the end, your success depends on the weather. After several winters of drought conditions and little snow, Santa Fe hit the jackpot in the winter of 2006-07, with record-breaking snowstorms over the winter holidays dumping many feet of snow on the mountains, paralyzing the town for days but creating exceptional conditions for skiing. Subsequent winters have seen above-average snowfalls, with adequate snowpack in the mountains to recharge reservoirs and please ski bunnies on the slopes.

Within a three-hour drive from Santa Fe, you have access to the Santa Fe Ski Area, Taos Ski Valley, Angel Fire Ski Resort, Red River Ski Area, Sipapu Ski Area, and Sandía Peak Ski Area. You'll also find The Enchanted Forest cross-country ski area and many places to head off on your own for Nordic skiing, snowshoeing, or winter hiking.

You can bring your sled or inner tubes up to Hyde State Park, just outside Santa Fe on Highway 475. If you don't want the drive on a snowy road, try city parks such as Patrick Smith Park at 1001 Canyon Rd., or Herb Martinez Park, 2240 Camino Carlos Rey, which have hills that make good tubing runs. Note that ski areas in the region often offer warm-weather activities, such as chairlift rides, mountain biking, and disc golf.

## SAFETY TIPS AND PLANNING

Before you go off skiing, snowshoeing, or winter hiking, please keep these tips in mind:

You're at a high altitude here, which affects your heart, lungs, and overall energy. Give yourself time to adjust before you do anything excessively strenuous. Santa Fe sits at 7,000 feet—the top of the Santa Fe Ski Area is 12,000 feet above sea level.

The weather can be volatile. Never assume that the clear, sunny early morning conditions will remain. Be prepared for weather changes, especially if you're headed for the backcountry. Tell people where you're going and when you plan to be back. Take a backpack with extra warm clothing, waterproof matches, space blanket, flashlight, food, water, and whatever else you'll need if you have to spend the night in subfreezing temperatures.

The sun shines brightly here, even in winter. Wear high-SPF sunscreen and reapply at midday. Protect your eyes from the intense glare with polarized sunglasses.

Northern New Mexico's air is dry, and winter exertion can require a lot from your body. Keep a full water bottle with you at all times and drink from it. And remember, alcohol, caffeine, and sugar have stronger effects at higher altitudes and can contribute to dehydration.

If you want to ski during the Christmas holidays or spring break, plan ahead. New Mexico's ski areas are popular and, like ski resorts everywhere, tend to attract more visitors these times of year.

Need to rent equipment? Renting at the ski areas is the most convenient, but on busy days you may have to wait and occasionally—say during the Christmas holidays or over spring break—all the rentals in your size may be gone before you get there. Our advice: Arrive early during peak ski times (it makes parking easier, too) or rent ahead of time at an in-town ski shop. Most will let you rent your equipment the night before at no additional charge. Some will even loan you a ski rack to take it up to the mountain. What a deal!

Driving can be treacherous after a winter storm. Although all the ski areas and the state highway department do their best to keep roads clear, some days you'll be happier with chains on your tires or four-wheel-drive vehicles.

If you plan on snowshoeing or cross-country skiing, dress in layers. Begin with long underwear that will wick perspiration away from your body, then continue with light, comfortable, insulated clothing that will move with you. Top it all off with a breathable waterproof shell or sleeveless vest. And don't forget a hat and gloves.

## DOWNHILL SKIING

Skiing is big business here and an important boost to the state's economy during the off-season, visitor-wise, for all concerned. (Except the town of Taos Ski Valley, which is busiest when the skiers come.) On average, more than a million skiers a year explore the pleasures of the state's generally uncrowded slopes, sunny winters, and abundant snow. According to Ski New Mexico, the sport had an economic impact of $480 million on New Mexico in the 2008–09 season, counting everything from lift tickets and lunches to gasoline and hotel rooms.

New Mexico has had above-normal precipitation in recent winters—the 2008–09 ski season saw an average 153" of snow—which allowed the ski industry here to rebound from several years of very low precipitation and poor ski conditions. In 2008–09, New Mexico had 795,416 skier days, and resorts were open an average of 103 days. Weather patterns in the state are fickle, however, and a drought can follow a heavy snow year. Your best bet is to call or check a ski area's Web site to find out what the situation is at the time you are ready to go.

Santa Fe makes an excellent base for a ski vacation. The southern Rocky Mountain extension surrounding Santa Fe and Taos known as the Sangre de Cristos and the Jémez Mountains, and the Sandía Mountains of Albuquerque are our playground. You can spend a day at any of the state's seven northern ski areas or head to Sandía Peak Ski Area outside Albuquerque and easily accessible to the south. After a day of fun on the slopes, come back to Santa Fe for lodging and dining.

In most years the downhill ski areas open around Thanksgiving and close in early April. Most operate from 9 a.m. to 4 p.m. daily during the ski season and offer food and snacks, lockers, emergency first aid, and a shop where you can buy sunscreen, goggles, and whatever else you need for a day of skiing or snowboarding. All the areas have rental shops with a variety of equipment for children and adults, and offer instruction. To rent equipment you usually need to leave a deposit on a credit card and perhaps a driver's license.

Most areas offer morning and afternoon lessons, and private and semiprivate sessions can be arranged on request. Some ski areas promote bargain weeks, early- or late-season discounts, special deals for first-time skiers, multiday discounts, and other enticements to persuade you to come. Children and older skiers usually get a break on ticket prices. Don't be shy—ask about discounts when you call to make your reservations.

If you've never skied or tried a snowboard before, be sure to inquire about beginner packages. The ski areas encourage people to take up the sport by offering the lessons, rentals, and lift tickets at a good price. And if you don't have clothes for skiing and don't want to make a big investment, check around. Some ski shops will also rent you a ski bib, insulated ski pants, and a jacket. You can also outfit yourself and your kids inexpensively by shopping at resale stores, of which Santa Fe has several.

In this section, we offer you a glimpse of the ski areas near Santa Fe.

## SANTA FE SKI AREA
**16 miles northeast of Santa Fe on Hyde Park Rd. (Highway 475)**
**(505) 982-4429 (ski area)**
**(505) 983-9155 (snow information line and offseason phone)**
**(877) 737-7366 (lodging)**
**www.skisantafe.com**

Santa Fe Ski Area offers visitors the chance to ski one of the 10 highest ski peaks in the United States. From the wide slopes of "Broadway" to the challenging, tree-studded "Dr. Rich," Santa Fe has terrain to please skiers and snowboarders of all abilities. The area's variety keeps strong intermediate and advanced skiers interested and gentle trails are perfect for beginners.

Part of Santa Fe Ski Area's appeal lies in its convenience. The slopes are an easy (most of the time) 45-minute drive from the Santa Fe Plaza. Skiers from Santa Fe, Albuquerque, and elsewhere in New Mexico, as well as visitors from Texas, Oklahoma, California, other states, and even other countries, enjoy themselves here. It's not unusual for conventioneers who come to town between Thanksgiving and Easter to stay an extra day just for the skiing.

**i** **Never tried downhill skiing before? Not to worry. Your best bet is to take a lesson (preferably more than one) from a certified instructor. All New Mexico areas offer ski schools that welcome beginners of all ages. Unlike your friends or spouse, these instructors have worked with countless newbies, helping them master the sport safely and have fun while learning. They won't lose their temper or laugh at you. Go for it!**

The ski area covers 660 acres of Santa Fe National Forest. It averages 225 inches of snow seasonally, with 50 percent snowmaking. There are 69 named trails: 20 percent "beginner," 40 percent "intermediate," and 40 percent "expert." It has seven lifts plus the Millennium Triple Chairlift. Lift capacity is 9,350 skiers per hour. There are no lift lines here.

One of Santa Fe Ski Area's strengths is its family focus. The youngest children head for Chipmunk Corner Children's Center, a safe and convenient place to learn the sport or to be cared for while their parents ski. For children too young to ski, the area offers a nursery with day care and snow play. Day-care slots are limited, so be sure to make reservations at (505) 988-9636. When they graduate from Chipmunk Corner, children can try Adventure Land, a ski playground complete with roller-coaster bumps, an obstacle course, and the opportunity to "ski the trees." Finally, serious young skiers over eight years of age who are of intermediate ability or better can join the Santa Fe Ski Team (505-986-1230). A board of parents and community volunteers handles the team's business, and their financial support comes from training fees, race revenue, and fund-raising events such as Santa Fe Ski Swap each November. (See our Annual Events and Festivals chapter.)

To get skiers to the mountaintop, the area offers a quad chairlift, two triple chairlifts, two double chairs, a poma, and two "mighty mite" surface lifts for beginners. Many skiers are surprised to learn that the top of the new Millennium Triple Chairlift unloads at the state's highest elevation for skiing—12,075 feet. If you ski a short way from the apex, you'll find one of several stunning views. Look down toward Santa Fe, west to Mount Taylor, and north toward the Colorado border. The vista of mountains and valleys, mesas, and riverbeds weaves together, sometimes with a band of low-lying fog or misty clouds, in blues and tans, reds, pinks, and warm beige.

Santa Fe Ski Area frequently receives overnight storms that drop light powder snow. If you want to make first tracks in the powder, leave extra early. The new snow delights skiers—but not drivers. At the other end of snow scale, the area is known for its grooming, a way that Santa Fe makes the most of the snow it gets in limited snow years.

If you break a ski or need advice while you're on the mountain, members of Santa Fe's professional ski patrol can help. For more serious situations, they can use their extensive knowledge of first aid, CPR, mountain rescue, and other emergency skills. Patrol members also enforce safety rules and have been known to pull lift tickets from out-of-control skiers.

If you get hungry while you're on the mountain, you can grab a bowl of soup, a burger, the daily special, or a plate of pasta at La Casa Cafe Grill at the base area. The restaurant is open from 9 a.m. to 4 p.m. and serves a variety of hot and cold snacks as well as full meals. Totemoff's Bar/Grill at mid-mountain offers an outdoor grill with burgers and other ski fare from 11 a.m. to 2 p.m. Totemoff's also is the only place to buy beer or wine at the ski area.

Need a trail map or have questions? Skier Service personnel are usually available near the lockers in the main building and at the stone hut near the base of the quad lift. They'll help with lost-and-found items, distribute maps, and even offer sunscreen to those who came unprepared. You can buy sunscreen, extra socks, or a stylish new ski outfit at the Wintermill in the main La Casa building.

For rental equipment, the Santa Fe Ski Area's rental shop offers an inventory of 1,400 skis and 75 snowboards from beginner to high-performance and demo models. Skis, poles, boots, and

bindings are available. The shop opens at 8 a.m.

How about a lesson? The Santa Fe Ski Area has more than 100 ski and snowboard instructors, all professionally certified. Lessons for beginners, intermediate, and advanced skiers generally take place from 9 a.m. to noon. Or you can work with a private instructor; private lessons can be arranged hourly, and reservations are required. Santa Fe Ski Area offers special ski programs for women with women instructors, classes designed to help people who want to race, classes just for older skiers, and more. Inquire at the ski school.

Depending on the weather and the amount of snow, Santa Fe Ski Area builds a snowboard park with jumps, bowls, half-pipes, and all the other attractions boarders love. More often than not, Santa Fe's black diamond runs develop respectable moguls for those who want to try their skill in the bumps. Santa Fe Ski Area has recreational racing on a coin-op course, which is normally open Thursday through Sunday. Recreational racers may be pre-empted for special events.

The Santa Fe Ski Area is strictly a day resort with no slope-side lodging. If you're staying at a hotel, ask if it has a ski shuttle. Ski tickets and rentals may be purchased online at www.skisantafe.com/lifttickets.html, or in person at Santa Fe Ski Area's in-town office at 2209 Brothers Rd., Suite 220, (505) 982-4429, ext. 4200.

Here's a look at other New Mexico ski areas easily accessible from Santa Fe:

## ANGEL FIRE RESORT
**95 miles north of Santa Fe,**
**22 miles east of Taos,**
**Highway 434, Angel Fire**
**(575) 377-6401,**
**(800) 633-7463 (information and snow report)**
**www.angelfireresort.com**
Established in 1966, Angel Fire is a year-round resort offering skiing, golf, fishing, mountain biking, tennis, boating, and a range of special events in the summer. New Mexico residents and visitors delight in the broad runs and relaxed atmosphere of this popular ski resort. Legend (perhaps

invented by a shrewd PR person) has it that the name comes from the way the mountain looks in a certain light—as if the angels had set them ablaze.

The resort is the only ski area in the state, and one of just a select few in the country, to offer a money-back guarantee to skiers for both lift tickets and lessons. If you don't like the condition of the runs on any given day, report back to the ticket office within an hour of buying your ticket, and you'll get a free ticket to return another time. If you're disappointed in your ski lesson, the area promises to give you another, free of charge, no questions asked.

Angel Fire also attracts visitors with major investments in improvements over the years, and the effort shows. The resort has 74 runs and expanded snowmaking to cover 52 percent of the mountain. There are seven lifts, including two high-speed detachable quad chairlifts, the fastest in all of New Mexico. The resort has a summit terrain park for skiers and snowboarders as well as the state's only half-pipe. The Summit Haus restaurant on top of the mountain has burgers, sandwiches, ice cream, and beverages, and there are two restaurants in the upgraded Lodge: Caliente Grill, which features Mexican and Southwestern food, and the Lazy Lizard cantina, which serves a limited bar menu. The Lodge is open year-round.

**i** For information on ski conditions at all New Mexico resorts, call the Ski New Mexico Snow Phone, (505) 984-0606. For winter road conditions throughout New Mexico, call (800) 432-4269. Also check out Ski New Mexico's Web site at www.skinew mexico.com.

Snowbikes, an Austrian invention, are available. Instead of wheels, these pedal machines run on skis. The instructors will reassure you that the sport is easy to master with just a few hours of practice. All bike rentals include a lesson on how to ride safely without looking foolish or taking too many spills. Accomplished snow bikers can tackle the moguls or plunge into powder.

Beginners, be they skiers, tubers, snowboarders, or snowbikers, especially love Angel Fire because they have their own easy slope and their own chairlift. For those just finding their snow legs or adjusting to the altitude, the poetically named Dreamcatcher lift offers a slow-moving ride that reduces anxiety and makes learning easier. Beginners can get a feeling for the snow and the equipment at their own pace, without pressure from more advanced skiers.

Angel Fire Resort Day Camp Program offers structured, supervised, creative activities for non-skiing kids and accepts infants as young as six weeks of age and children as old as age 11. The Children's Ski and Snowboard Center offers classes for ages three through 12. The area groups youngsters by age and ability. Older children can join the Mountain Adventures Program or, if they want to snowboard, the Angel Fire Riders.

Angel Fire is a fine place for adults to learn to ski, too. The ski school has between 70 and 85 instructors. You can take a group lesson with people of your same ability level or request a private class. Angel Fire also offers equipment and instruction to accommodate skiers with physical and mental challenges, and the staff includes instructors who can teach in languages other than English.

For skiers and snowboarders of all ages, Angel Fire's biggest claim to fame is New Mexico's first and only high-speed detachable quad lifts, the four-person Chile Express and the Southwest Flyer. The Express, installed for the 1996-1997 season, whisks you up the mountain in nine minutes. The Flyer, installed during the summer of 1999, unloads at the highest point on the mountain, offering access to all the area's runs. Less time on the lift, of course, means more time on the snow.

Angel Fire Mountain offers a nice mix of skiing challenges. You can cruise more than 10 miles of skiable terrain, including smooth broad slopes, bumps, and steeps. Of the area's 74 named runs, 26 percent are suitable for beginners, 50 percent for intermediate skiers, and 24 percent for more advanced skiers or boarders. The resort has three double chairs and two surface lifts in addition to the high-speed quads. Angel Fire has a vertical drop of 2,077 feet, with a base elevation of 8,600 feet. Annual snowfall is 210 inches on average.

When the lifts close, you can still have fun on the slope-side tubing run. Between 5 and 7 p.m. you can rent a tube and slip and slide beneath the lights to your heart's content. (You have to be age six or older to join the fun.) The tubing hill is open from mid-December through mid-March.

The resort also offers snowmobiling, ice fishing, sleigh rides, helicopter rides, hot-air balloon rides, and more. At the base of the ski mountain, facilities include the ticket sales office, a rental and repair shop, the ski school and ski patrol offices, retail shops, and the Angel Fire Resort Hotel. You can ride the town shuttle to other businesses and lodgings.

## PAJARITO MOUNTAIN SKI AREA

**45 miles from Santa Fe,**
**7 miles from Los Alamos off**
**Highway 501 on Camp May Rd.**
**(505) 662-5725 (office)**
**(888) 662–SNOW (snow conditions and**
**general information)**
**www.skipajarito.com**

The nonprofit tax-exempt Los Alamos Ski Club, a venerable and enthusiastic group of men and women, runs the Pajarito Ski Area. The club began in the late 1950s to enliven the winter for the scientists and GIs working on the atomic bomb in Los Alamos, a beautiful, isolated spot in the Jémez Mountains. The club moved from an earlier site in search of better snow and came to Pajarito Mountain in the early 1960s. Volunteers cleared trees for the runs, built a cozy lodge, and installed the first lift. Today, volunteers still play a key role here, and the ski area is known for having the only completely volunteer ski patrol in the state.

The club now has more than 4,000 members who elect a board of directors that hires the general manager and other paid staff. To be a member you must live or work in Los Alamos, but to ski here you just need the price of a ticket. The area is not a resort, but a ski hill. You won't find overnight accommodations, valet parking, ski

shuttles, hot tubs, massages, day care, or après-ski activities here—or even a beer to go with your lunch at the Pajarito Mountain Cafe. You will discover a challenging mountain with enough cruiser runs to keep intermediates and beginners happy, too. Perched on a ridge above Los Alamos National Laboratory, the area receives an average snowfall of 250 inches. There's no snowmaking equipment here. Since the area depends totally on the natural stuff, Pajarito is usually among the last of New Mexico's ski areas to open, normally getting sufficient snow by mid-December. Pajarito usually closes some time in April. The lifts operate only on Friday, Saturday, Sunday, and federal holidays except Christmas Day.

The mountain has a peak elevation of 10,441 feet, a vertical drop of 1,400 feet, and 40 trails, of which 80 percent are rated either "intermediate" or "advanced." Pajarito's skiers ride their choice of seven lifts—three doubles, a triple, a quad, and two surface—to the mountaintop. The views are wonderful. From the top of the Aspen chairlift, skiers can see part of the Valle Grande, a huge volcanic crater that now forms an expansive valley. The lifts can accommodate 6,500 skiers per hour, but don't except to see that kind of crowd except, perhaps, during Christmas vacation.

The area's cafeteria and ski school occupy a 13,000-square-foot lodge, and the ski patrol office is nearby in a separate building. Pajarito is one of the few mountains that still uses an all-volunteer ski patrol.

You can get lessons in telemark skiing, cross-country skiing, and snowboarding as well as alpine skiing here. The area has private lessons and group classes for children and adults. On Wednesday you'll find lots of children here taking advantage of the area's classes for school groups from Española, Pojoaque, and the Jémez Valley. Los Alamos Ski Racing Club operates a youth racing program. Challenge New Mexico uses Pajarito to introduce disabled children and adults to the world of skiing. The area does not offer an inclusive children's ski school package, but lessons for children are available. Please check with the area for updated prices. Seniors age 75 and older and skiers age six and younger ski for free.

## RED RIVER SKI AREA

106 miles from Santa Fe,
Highway 38, Red River
(505) 754-2223
(505) 754-2220 (snow phone)
(800) 331–SNOW (reservations)
www.redriverskiarea.com

There aren't many ski towns where you'll find old mines on the slopes—and that's only one of the things that makes Red River Ski Area special. Established in 1959, this family-oriented area has been compared to a dude ranch for skiers. The ski mountain towers above a town settled more than 100 years ago by hardy souls in search of gold. The setting gives Red River its Old West flavor. Some visitors have compared a visit to Red River to a trip back in history, to the simpler days when everything you needed was on Main Street.

Red River has 57 trails, evenly divided among expert, intermediate, and beginner, and three mountain restaurants. The trails are served by seven lifts—four doubles, two triples, and a surface tow. Lift capacity is 7,920 per hour, second only to Taos, so skiers hardly ever have to wait. To supplement the average snowfall of 218 inches, snowmaking covers about 87 percent of the Red River mountain. The area has a vertical drop of 1,600 feet and a peak elevation of 10,350 feet. Before you ski down, you can stop at the Ski Tip Restaurant on top of the mountain for hot chocolate, lunch, or a snack. From there beginners can ski easy runs all the way to the base area. Advanced hot doggers can take the more challenging runs.

Another place that adds to Red River's charm is the Moon-Star Mining Camp, an attraction that's especially popular with children. You can ski right up to an old miner's cabin and through a tipi. The camp stands in an aspen grove, and the terrain is flat enough that even the most novice skiers usually have little trouble. The camp adds to Red River's extensive beginner area—some might call it beginner paradise. The Red River Willows welcomes snowboarders and offers a terrain park.

Need a ride to the Santa Fe Ski Area? Check at your hotel—some offer ski shuttles. The trip takes 3 hours. The Chile Line offers a public transportation van from Taos to the Taos Ski Valley several times a day. The fare is just $1 round trip. For shuttle service from Albuquerque to Taos Ski Valley, try Twin Hearts Express, (575) 751-1201, or Faust's Transportation, (575) 758-3410. The trip takes three hours.

You can take lessons at Red River, choosing from a range of classes for children and adults. Red River's adult programs include all the basics as well as specialty workshops for bumps, powder snow, and racing. The area offers recreational racing on the NASTAR course. To make it less expensive for families to enjoy the sport, many hotels and lodges participate in the Kids Ski Free/Stay Free program. For each paying parent who stays a minimum of three nights and purchases at least a three-day lift ticket, one child stays for free and receives free lift tickets for the same number of days.

While there are more challenge places for experts to ski, visitors appreciate Red River for its convenience. To start with, you won't have to hunt for a parking place because 90 percent of the lodges sit within walking distance of the slopes. Two of the seven chairlifts rise directly from town. If you need rental equipment, the ski area itself operates two rental shops, one on Main Street and one in the Ski Chalet at the area's base. You can book packages of lessons and lift tickets there and rent what you need for skiing, including high-performance packages that include the latest ski designs.

The area hosts some 500,000 people during the summer and about 200,000 in the winter. As a popular summer destination, Red River offers scenic chairlift rides, jeep tours, horseback riding, camping, hiking, biking, fishing, and more.

## SANDÍA PEAK SKI AREA

35 miles from Santa Fe via Highway 14, then
Highway 536
(505) 242-9052
(505) 857-8977 (snow report)
www.sandiapeak.com

Albuquerque skiers appreciate the convenience of this area, and most of the folks who ski here are from "just down the hill." You can make the ride to Sandía Peak unique if you forego the twisting Crest Highway scenic road to the ski slopes on the eastern side of the mountain, and instead take the Sandía Peak Tramway, a spectacular trip up the face of the Sandía Mountains to Sandía Crest on its west side, via I–25. The tram is the longest aerial tram in the world and offers fabulous views of the surrounding Río Grande basin. This is prime hiking terrain in summer, when the temperatures reach the 90s in the valley below. The tram has a ski history museum. At the top of the tram are two eateries: High Finance Restaurant and Sandiago's Mexican Grill.

Located in Cibola National Forest, about 45 minutes from Albuquerque, via I–40 and Highway 14, Sandía Peak has 35 runs, 35 percent of them for beginners, 55 percent for intermediates, and 10 percent expert trails. Skiers choose from 6 lifts—four doubles and two tows. Capacity is 4,500 skiers per hour. Vertical drop is 1,700 feet. The area encompasses 200 acres and has snowmaking equipment for 30 acres of the runs. The base elevation here is 8,678 feet, and the peak is 10,378 feet. Though Sandía Peak is high, it is farther south and it tends to have a shorter season, generally opening in mid-December and closing in March, depending on the snow. New for 2009 is the Scrapyard terrain park, with funboxes, rails, and jumps.

Double Eagle Day Lodge at the base of the ski area offers rental service and a cafe serving breakfast, lunch, and snacks. Kids have their own warming hut and a separate area in which to learn to ski safely. Sandía also offers a package of lessons for senior skiers. The staff teaches all types of lessons through the Snows Sports School, usually 10 a.m. and 1 p.m. daily. There is no on-site day care. Your best bet is to make arrangements for babysitting in Santa Fe or Albuquerque.

## SIPAPU SKI AREA

65 miles north of Santa Fe, 22 miles
southeast of Taos on Highway 518
(505) 587-2240 (snow conditions and
information)
(800) 587-2240 (reservations)
www.sipapunm.com

This little skiing village hidden in a canyon in the Sangre de Cristo Mountains near Taos exudes a woodsy, family-friendly atmosphere. Telemarkers have discovered Sipapu with a passion and love its trails cut through the trees and uncrowded conditions. They share the slopes with skiers and snowboarders.

Owned and operated by the Bolander family, who founded it in 1952, Sipapu caters to folks looking for value and a noncommercial skiing experience. Tired of over-marketed glitzy areas? Sipapu may be just your ticket.

The area's 41 runs offer something for everyone: 20 percent are classified beginner; 50 percent are intermediate; and 30 percent are advanced. Skiers can ride four lifts, including a triple chair and two tows, with a capacity of 2,900 skiers an hour. There are two terrain parks offering beginner and advanced lines, rails and boxes, jumps, and a huge Teeter-Totter.

Sipapu's base elevation is 8,200 feet, and its peak is at 9,255 feet. There are 200 skiable acres here. The season usually opens in November and closes in April. Average snowfall is 190 inches, supplemented with snowmaking on 70 percent of the trails. This ski resort's big selling point is that it has the longest season in New Mexico.

If you're a novice and want to improve more quickly, classes here tend to be very small and offer an opportunity for personalized learning— even in a group setting. The first three lessons are free if you're new to the resort. Sipapu guarantees that you'll be able to accomplish your skiing goals at the end of the lesson or you get another lesson for free. In addition to traditional downhill classes, the area offers telemark and cross-country skiing and snowboard classes near the resort. Because of the area's small staff, day care is available only through prior arrangement.

Anyone who can prove he or she is president of something skis free on President's Day at Sipapu.

Among the special ski events, Sipapu goes all out for Presidents' Day in February Fun Fest, featuring races, games, music, a costume contest, and Clowns Day. A huge castle built completely of snow provides a centerpiece for the event.

At the base area you'll find a folksy lodge with a big fireplace, a riverside cafe that serves New Mexican food as well as standard American offerings, a lounge, a shop for equipment rental, a gift shop, and a place to buy groceries and gasoline. The area has a wide array of accommodations at the lodge, a motel, mobile homes, duplexes, apartments, guest suites and in family-style cabins and a dormitory.

## TAOS SKI VALLEY

**80 miles north of Santa Fe on**
**Highway 150, 18 miles northeast of Taos**
**(866) 968-7386 (information)**
**(505) 776-2916 (snow conditions)**
**(866) 968-7386, ext. 1262 (tickets)**
**www.skitaos.org**

When visitors think of skiing in New Mexico, they usually think of Taos, the state's most famous ski resort. *Outside Magazine* ranks Taos Ski Valley as one of the top 15 resorts in North America, with references to fun in the steeps and thrills on the bump runs.

Visitors return year after year, in part because of the resort's well-regarded Ernie Blake Ski School and its popular learn-to-ski week. Taos also attracts many first-time visitors who learn about it through the area's extensive national marketing program, ads in major ski publications, an active group sales program, and through the area's sophisticated Web site.

Founded in 1956 by Swiss skier and entrepreneur Ernie Blake and now run by his family, Taos Ski Valley established its fame on the challenge of its terrain and the European quality of the resort itself. With a base elevation of 9,207 feet and a peak elevation of 11,819 feet, Taos has a vertical drop of 2,612 feet. The longest run is more than 5 miles.

## Taos and the Summer of Love

Taos, a tiny mountain town of just 8,000, isn't just known for its famous ski valley, Indian pueblo, galleries, and museums. It played a major role in the 1960s counter-culture explosion by hosting hippie communes like the New Buffalo, one of the most successful collectives in America at that time. In 2009, the town kicked off a yearlong celebration of the 40th anniversary of the Summer of Love. In addition to the usual interesting roster of Taos events, such as the popular acoustic Solar Music Festival and Taos Pueblo Pow Wow, the Harwood Museum highlighted the contributions of actor and former Taos resident Dennis Hopper with an exhibit of Hopper's own photographs and an art show curated by Hopper himself including artists Larry Bell, Robert Dean Stockwell, and Ken Price among other contemporaries. Hopper is best known for writing, directing, and starring (with Peter Fonda) in the ultra-cool back-to-the-land movie *Easy Rider*, shot in and around Taos in 1969. The movie was the highlight of celebrations in 2009, including special showings and appearances by the stars.

Taos boasts 321 inches of snow in an average year and is famous for its light, dry powder. The area can supplement nature's efforts with snowmaking on 100 percent of the beginner and intermediate terrain.

To reach the slopes, the area offers skiers four quad lifts, a triple, five doubles, and three surface lifts. The 13 lifts can handle 15,300 skiers per hour—the largest skier capacity of any New Mexico ski area. Al's Run, directly under the No. 1 lift, is a marathon of bumps where you'll find hard-core, hard-muscled mogul hounds. Taos offers chutes, bowls, and cruising runs. Experts who enjoy a challenge love to ski the ridge, an area above the named runs that involves a strenuous climb before you start to ski. Previously prohibited, snowboarding is now permitted at Taos Ski Valley. The Out to Launch terrain park has two huge airs, a hip, a quarter pipe, and rails and is groomed nightly.

Although the mountain is a skilled skier's paradise, there's more than enough terrain here for beginners and intermediates. Of the 110 named runs, 24 percent are beginner, 25 percent intermediate, and 51 percent advanced.

While some who ski here go home with stories of the steep High Traverse or the powder challenge on Lower Stauffenberg, others can speak of their skiing breakthroughs during the Learn to Ski and Learn to Ski Better weeks. *Ski Magazine* has ranked Taos' Ernie Blake Ski School as one of the best in the United States. The Ski Week programs, offered throughout the season, match students of similar ability with a teacher who can help them move on to the next level of skiing. Taos also offers special programs for women, older skiers, telemarkers, and teens. Super Ski Weeks welcome intermediate or advanced skiers who want intensive drills and exercises and specific instructions in racing, moguls, and adventure skiing. You can also take a single class or a workshop in racing or mogul skiing. For the novice, Taos' traditional Yellowbird Programs cater to first- and second-day skiers with morning and afternoon lessons, a lift ticket, and rentals. Private and group lessons are available.

Taos Kinderkäfig Children's Center provides a safe atmosphere for children ages six weeks to three years of age. The Junior Elite ski program teaches youngsters ages three to 12 how to ski. The children's programs have an 18,000-square-foot center with its own ticket counter, ski rental and accessory shop, and cafeteria.

Recent improvements at the area include reshaping and recontouring some runs to improve skiing and reduce congestion. But what hasn't changed here is the prohibition of snowboarders. Taos is one of the few areas in the country where skiers don't have to share the slopes. The resort has an independent, noncorporate spirit. In addition to the Blake family, other skiing families own the lodges in the valley, and there's not a franchise outfit among them. Most of the innkeepers, not surprisingly, are skiers themselves who found the valley's conditions irresistible.

At the Resort Center, you'll find places to purchase equipment and sportswear and to rent skis, boots, and poles, including high-performance and demo models. You can eat at Tenderfoot Katie's Cafeteria or Rhoda's Restaurant. At the Martini Tree Bar you can have a cocktail and listen to live music. You can also eat at two on-mountain restaurants, The Phoenix and Whistlestop Cafe.

Want to spend the night instead of driving back to Santa Fe? You can stay in slope-side accommodations within walking distance of the lifts or elsewhere in the valley. You'll find about 20 lodges, but no high-rises. Most lodges have their own restaurants and offer après-ski and evening entertainment. There are also bed-and-breakfasts and condominiums. Be advised, however, they tend to fill up fast, especially over the holidays. Another popular option is to stay in the town of Taos and ride the shuttle to the ski valley and back.

With more than 80 galleries, seven museums, and numerous restaurants serving traditional northern New Mexican cuisine and gourmet fare, the nearby town of Taos certainly adds to the skier's overall experience—and gives nonskiers plenty to do. The shops here offer high-quality weaving, furniture, pottery, jewelry, and more. And historic Taos Pueblo, which provides guided tours, is just a short drive away. Taos sits on the Río Grande Plateau at 8,000 feet, 1,000 feet higher than Santa Fe, and is much colder in winter, averaging 10° Fahrenheit at night. Be sure to come prepared for the cold.

# CROSS-COUNTRY SKIING, SNOWSHOEING, AND SNOWPLAY

You can snowshoe and cross-country ski on many hiking trails in the Santa Fe area and throughout northern New Mexico. For novice cross-country skiers or families with small children, the Black Canyon Trail in Hyde Park near Santa Fe may provide an enjoyable outing. This 1-mile round-trip route offers nice scenery, gentle to moderate slopes, and picnic tables where you can enjoy lunch. Slightly more experienced skiers head for the Aspen Vista Road, just past Hyde Park on Highway 475 on the way to the Santa Fe Ski Area. You'll get to practice your uphill technique as you climb from 10,000 to 12,000 feet in about 6 miles. Coming back can be a fast trip!

Due to improvements in equipment and a growing desire to get away from it all in the winter, snowshoeing has become increasingly popular. Snowshoe construction has improved, resulting in lighter shoes with curled toes that don't get buried in the powder. Aluminum and synthetic decking has improved flotation over the snow. Sporting-goods stores that sell or rent this equipment—and who may carry state-of-the-art demo models—probably can give you advice on where to go. That technician or salesperson may be a ski fanatic supporting his or her outdoor habit. Don't hesitate to ask them for their suggestions and their favorite runs. You'll also find several guidebooks to cross-country skiing available locally. Santa Fe Community College offers classes that will teach you Nordic skiing and show you some good places to try your new skills.

### ENCHANTED FOREST CROSS COUNTRY SKI AND SNOWSHOE AREA

**106 miles north of Santa Fe,**
**3.5 miles east of Red River on Highway 38**
**(575) 754-2374**
**(800) 966-9381 (Miller's Crossing ski store)**
**www.enchantedforestxc.com**
You'll find 33 kilometers of 12-foot-wide trails at Enchanted Forest, a 5-minute drive from the heart of the village of Red River. New Mexico's largest full-service cross-country ski area, it offers groomed and natural trails through 500 acres of aspen groves in Carson National Forest. The area usually opens before Thanksgiving and serves skiers into April, depending on the weather. Hours are 9 a.m. to 4:30 p.m.

Skiers can explore trails that wind through the trees. The system is groomed with one side tracked for diagonal stride (the more conventional cross-country skiing) and the other side smooth for snowshoeing and freestyle or skate-skiing. You'll cruise on trails such as Northwest Passage and Jabberwocky. The alpine vistas and the solitude of the Rocky Mountain forest are truly spectacular. Bring your camera. The Enchanted Forest receives an average of 240 inches of snow a year—about 2 feet more than the Red River Ski Area. The ski area elevation ranges from 9,800 to 10,030 feet.

Owners John and Judy Miller opened the area in 1985 with a special-use permit from the Carson National Forest and have been catering to cross-country skiers and their families ever since. They added to the warming hut at the base area and offer a nice menu including pizza and chimichangas in addition to snacks. In addition to Nordic skiing, Enchanted Forest also has snowshoeing, and has added an additional 15 kilometers of trails for showshoers only.

## SKI AND SNOWBOARD SHOPS

In addition to these shops, all in Santa Fe, you can rent equipment at all New Mexico ski areas. You'll also find private ski shops in Taos, Angel Fire, Los Alamos, Albuquerque, and elsewhere.

### ALPINE SPORTS

**121 Sandoval St. #B**
**(505) 983-5155**
**www.alpinesports-santafe.com**
In business since 1964, Alpine Sports is a full-service sporting-goods store. Upstairs you'll discover a fine selection of new, top-of-the-line equipment, ski wear, sportswear, and accessories. Downstairs in the rental department, you'll find

all kinds of winter-sports equipment—Nordic and alpine skis, snowboards, and snowshoes. Ask about group rates. Alpine's staff includes seasoned skiers who know how to match customers to equipment. The shop has skilled boot fitters at your service. Another benefit—plenty of free parking in the lot right behind the store, or you can walk from any downtown hotel.

## BEYOND WAVES MOUNTAIN SURF SHOP
**1428 Cerrillos Rd.**
**(505) 988-2240**
**www.beyondwaves.com**
This store caters to snowboarders and skateboarders. You can rent or buy Avalanche boards as well as cool outerwear and boots, hats, sunglasses, and other accessories. The shop will also wax, base, tune, and repair your snowboard.

## NEW MEXICO BIKE N' SPORT
**524 West Cordova Rd., Suite C**
**(505) 820-0809**
**www.nmbikensport.com**
This year-round shop, in the Coronado Mall with Trader Joe's, spreads its business between winter and summer sports enthusiasts. Snowshoes are a winter specialty here, with many different types available for rent or sale. You'll also find a nice selection of cross-country skis, telemark equipment, and snowboards with the latest in bindings and boots. Bike n' Sport, a full-line mountain bike shop in the summer, also carries clothing and accessories. The staff can offer you plenty of sug-

gestions on where to take your snowshoes for a day of fun.

## SANTA FE MOUNTAIN SPORTS
**607 Cerrillos Rd. #A**
**(505) 988-3337**
**www.santafemountainsports.com**
Outdoor sports enthusiasts of all varieties will find something to their liking at Santa Fe Mountain Sports. In addition to a fully stocked retail store, Mountain Sports has rentals galore—downhill ski equipment including high-performance super side-cut skis, snowboards by Volkl, Heelside, and Rosignol, snowshoes, and cross-country skis. The shop will even do rentals for children for an entire ski season. You can get binding adjustments, ski repair, and tune-ups in its full-service shop. If you ask, the staff will give you tips on where to snowshoe or ski. In the summer, look for bike rentals.

## SKI TECH SKI RENTALS
**905 South St. Francis Dr.**
**(505) 983-5512**
**www.ski-tech.com**
This family-owned business specializes in service and has been serving Santa Fe skiers for more than a dozen years. You can rent all the ski equipment you need as well as adult-size jackets, pants, and bibs. In addition to an assortment of downhill skis, you'll find snowboards and cross-country equipment. The full-service shop offers ski repair, tune-ups, binding adjustments, and overnight service.

# RELOCATION

**A**sk most residents why they moved to Santa Fe, and the reply is likely to be "quality of life." To the outdoors enthusiast, this catch-all phrase may mean close proximity to many miles of trails through evergreen forest and alpine wilderness. To the culture buff, it's the opera and the numerous theatrical stages and art film houses around town. To the gourmet, it's the more than 375 restaurants of all shapes and sizes, many of them world-class. To the creative soul, it's the supportive atmosphere of one of America's most active arts communities. Just about everybody agrees that the mild climate, averaging 350 sunny days a year, ranks high among Santa Fe's attractions.

## SANTA FE LIFE

Since the 1970s, Santa Fe has billed itself as "the City Different." It takes living here once around the calendar to realize just how different Santa Fe life really is. Dietary horizons broaden with the realization that the tastiest corn is blue and that green chile is one of the five basic food groups. The deceptive sameness of the brown stucco buildings gives way to a keen eye for the nuances of Spanish Pueblo and Territorial Revival architecture. The rough beauty of yards creatively xeriscaped with cactus, chamisa, juniper, and native plants makes it seem okay that the city's water rationing policy prevents all but hardy native-grass lawns from surviving. Newcomers quickly join in uniquely local concerns both small ("Should prairie dogs be allowed to live in city parks?") and large ("Are we running out of water?").

One factor that certainly does not rank high among most people's reasons for moving to Santa Fe is work. Paradoxically, although unemployment consistently runs well below the state and national averages, finding a well-paid, satisfying job can be a challenge. Since Santa Fe is the state capital, more than 27 percent of the workforce is employed by federal, state, and local government, and the majority of other workers work in the low-paid service industry; in the private sector, the largest employers in Santa Fe County include the opera and Indian casinos.

An extraordinarily high percentage of the workforce is made up of self-employed people, many of whom operate businesses out of their homes, and of telecommuters. Besides hotels and restaurants, growing industries in the city include publishing, filmmaking, new media, information technology, and interior design. Except for arts and crafts—1 in 6 Santa Feans describe themselves as artists—the city has virtually no manufacturing industry or professional-level jobs beyond lawyers, of which there are many.

The median household income in metropolitan Santa Fe is approximately $40,392 per year, $25,454 for individuals—low, but higher than any other county in New Mexico except Los Alamos. Yet 12.3 percent of Santa Feans live below the poverty line. Average wages in Santa Fe are 23 percent below the national average, while the cost of living in Santa Fe is 18 percent higher than the national average. The main factors pushing the cost of living up are housing and health care. Housing costs are 40 percent above the national average. The disparity between incomes and living costs has inspired the city council to pass a "living wage ordinance" that currently sets the minimum wage of $10.50 per hour. The living wage applies only to companies with 25 or more employees. Although this is a huge step, in reality a single minimum-wage job does not pay enough to cover living expenses, and it is quite common for people to have two or three different part-time jobs or to live with others. Various aspects of life as a Santa Fe resident—retirement, education and child care, health care and wellness, media, and worship and spirituality—are covered in detail in separate chapters. The focus of the rest of this chapter is on real estate.

## BUYING REAL ESTATE

The early 1990s brought a flood of buyers to Santa Fe's real estate market. Demand was high, and prices skyrocketed. Houses sold quickly, and customers had to act fast, often at full listing price, to get the home they wanted. Then the market slumped in the mid-90s, but it has enjoyed a strong showing since then, despite the recession. The latest figures from the Santa Fe Association of Realtors indicate a median home price in the city of $350,000, with condos at $307,500; the median sales price in the county, where larger homes usually occupy bigger lots is $427,500. In 2008 a total of 1,350 homes were reported sold in the city and county of Santa Fe, down from previous years as the recession has taken a toll even on comfortable second-homers. Realtors often say that the Santa Fe area is still considered a bargain for many homebuyers from urban areas in other parts of the United States, particularly around major cities. The influx of out-of-state buyers has slowly increased the overall cost of housing here, to the chagrin of local wage earners who are priced out of the market by their relatively small incomes. Nevertheless, if you can get on the property ladder in Santa Fe, your home is a pretty safe bet in this ever-popular city. Even during the 2008–09 recession, long-range forecasts in mid-2009 cited Santa Fe as one of the top-10 housing markets for real estate appreciation in the next decade, with a 3.6 percent projected gain.

The city council has taken a number of steps to address affordable housing in Santa Fe in recent years. A spate of new home construction continues to take place on Santa Fe's fastest-growing area on the south side of town. A 2006 city ordinance requires developers to offer 30 percent of all new-built units as affordable housing priced at or below $200,000. The nonprofit

advocacy organization Homewise works with low-income people and local bank programs to educate and assist first-time homeowners in qualifying for new homes in Santa Fe. Among the qualifying subdivisions are Oshara Village, a mixed-use greenbuilt development of townhomes and single family homes near Santa Fe Community College, and Tierra Contenta, a public-private partnership development on Airport Road, made up primarily of single-family homes on small lots. Both are in the city's most affordable area: the Southwest Side.

Santa Fe was the first city to adopt the 2030 Challenge to lower greenhouse emissions from buildings to zero by 2030 and has developed a Green Building Code. With the increase in construction in the city itself, at developments such as the Railyard, a number of developers have had the opportunity to put green-building ideas into practice. The new Santa Fe Farmers' Market building, for example, which opened in September 2008, is Santa Fe's first Silver Leadership in Energy and Environmental Design (LEED) certified building. The warehouse-style building is powered by solar energy, harvests water from its roof, used up to 50 percent locally recycled materials in its construction, employed nontoxic interior materials and paints, and makes effective use of ambient lighting to cut down on electric use. Other buildings in Santa Fe are following suit. An annual Greenbuilt Tour of homes and buildings that satisfy LEED requirements is sponsored by the U.S. Green Building Council New Mexico Chapter takes place in Santa Fe and neighboring areas during Sustainability Week in May. For more information, log on to www.greenbuilttour.com or call (505) 227-0474.

## AN OVERVIEW

In Santa Fe, location probably has the single biggest impact on a property's price. Whereas in many communities proximity to downtown is a negative factor, in Santa Fe it's a strong selling point.

"Values in Santa Fe are relative to the distance a home is from the Plaza," Realtor Merrily

Pierson added. "The closer to the Plaza, the more a home is worth. For resale appreciation, a buyer is smarter to purchase a house that needs work in a good location rather than a better house farther from the Plaza."

But figuring out a property's value involves more than a home's location and size. Views, open space, lack of highway noise, architectural integrity, landscaping, and "Santa Fe style"—smooth plaster walls, vigas, *bancos,* tile floors, and other amenities are important factors, Kelly said. (See our Close-up in this chapter for more on Santa Fe style.) Santa Fe style isn't just for the wealthy; it can be found in homes of every price range.

For many buyers the biggest surprise is what their money will buy. The real estate dollar doesn't stretch far here. Most Realtors can tell stories of newcomers who see the east side, one of the city's most prestigious areas, and think they've discovered it. Surely, they think, we'll find a bargain here, a little fixer-upper. And they're more than surprised at the $300 to $400 per square foot price these homes sell for.

Some newcomers are surprised to learn that Santa Fe has no industrial section where they can find a building to remodel into lofts. Santa Fe's "lofts" are all purpose-built structures, not converted buildings. Still others find it odd to discover homes worth a half-million dollars or more down dusty dirt roads, where the lack of paving is considered distinctly upmarket and desirable. Some expect that property a few miles out of the city will be available for a huge drop in price. Sorry, partners. This is not necessarily the case. In fact, probably the opposite.

As discussed above, in recent years, thanks to initiatives involving the city of Santa Fe, Santa Fe County, and private agencies, more housing is available for Santa Fe's working families of average income. Many of these subdivisions are on the sprawling southwest side, where the median price in 2009 was $273,000—the lowest in the city. In Tierra Contenta, one of the city's newest neighborhoods, three-bedroom, two-bath homes initially sold for between $120,000 and $160,000 in 1997. Builders in this neighborhood use the latest techniques to come up with a high-quality home at lower per-square-foot cost. Since it was organized in 1995, Tierra Contenta has seen the construction and sale of nearly 2,300 homes. The next phase of construction, on 32 acres of the subdivisions' west side, is due to begin shortly. Subdivisions off Richards Avenue—Rancho Viejo, Nava Adé, and Oshara Village sell new homes relatively quickly. Eldorado is a popular choice for the buyer who wants a house at a moderate price out of town on an acre of land with expansive views. The subdivision is large and self-contained, with its own school, fire department, library, shops, and other services. It is about 15 minutes southeast of Santa Fe via I–25.

What are Santa Fe's desirable areas? Well, it depends on what you want and how much you can spend. A buyer for whom money is no object might select a golf course home at Las Campanas or a historic east-side adobe. Buyers looking for homes on larger acreage have begun exploring Galisteo, Lamy, Nambé, and La Cienega.

## SOME THINGS TO CONSIDER

In her book, *Understanding and Buying Santa Fe Real Estate,* Realtor Karen Walker offers some advice for potential buyers. Here are a few of her observations:

Before you make a commitment, ask to see and take time to read any restrictive covenants from neighborhood associations. Educate yourself about zoning and building regulations from the city and county that apply to the area you're considering. Don't assume that you can build a guesthouse, put up outside lights, or paint your window frames green. Get the facts.

**i** Some designers get carried away in their interpretation of Santa Fe style. If you notice vigas protruding from all sides of a building, you can be sure they're fakes—the support beams simply don't work that way. Builders who use real vigas may leave the ends visible on a front-facing wall for a decorative effect.

Examples of city restrictions are the escarpment ordinance, which restricts building on hillsides and ridgetops; terrain management requirements, which govern the building of roads and structures on steep terrain; and historic-district requirements that dictate what kinds of changes can be made to the exteriors of vintage buildings. Building code and zoning restraints may require setbacks of construction from lot lines and might limit the percentage of your building site you can cover with "improvements." Both the city and the county have archaeological ordinances that require excavation prior to construction if the property is in an archeological zone. Within Santa Fe's famous downtown historic district, restrictions on remodeling are legendarily perverse and far-reaching.

Santa Fe's City Hall takes its zoning regulations seriously. A few years ago a homeowner was required to remove a third story he'd added because the construction violated the city's escarpment ordinances.

Buyers looking at property should make sure that they'll have access to it. Don't assume that because you drove there, the road will be yours along with the land. Also, ask if the area has plans for any new roads, which could have an impact on your property in terms of noise, dust, or access.

Views, a strong selling point for some Santa Fe properties, can come with a down side—wind and noise. Often the same lot placement that gives a home a nice look at the mountains or the lights of the city leaves the place exposed to the wind. With Santa Fe's prevailing westerly winds, traffic sounds will travel to the east and dust will be a particular problem. On the other hand, traffic in modest-sized Santa Fe is hardly a huge problem and you'll never be able to keep a home in the desert free of dust anyway. Don't even try.

If land near the home or lot you're considering is vacant, ask what the owner plans for it and what kind of structure could be built. Your neighbor could one day build a convenience store there, or, more particularly, decide to keep chickens, goats, and other animals, grow corn, or

house several relatives in trailers on the property, quite common in this rural, self-contained community.

Find out if the lot has city water and sewer service. Much of the property in the northern quadrants of the city is not connected to city sewer even though it is inside the city limits. Instead, septic systems serve these homes. Some of the land in the eastern and southeastern parts of the city has neither city sewer nor city water; you'll need a well and a septic system here. Speaking of water, you won't find many homes with pools in the Santa Fe area, partly because the climate only allows a few months of outdoor swimming and partly because of the region's concerns about water availability and focus on water conservation.

Most important of all, don't assume that water rights come with the home at all, a major issue in a state that has historically fought its biggest legal and physical battles over access to limited water via the system of irrigation ditches known as acequias (the subject of John Nichols' famous novel *The Milagro Bean Field War*). Even if an irrigation ditch passes directly through the property, you may not have the right to irrigate using the water. Water rights have to be used to remain in effect, and in a number of areas, such as Tesuque, first rights go to the area's first residents, the local pueblo, and/or those holding Spanish land grants, with all other rights adjudicated on historic usage. In other words, use it or lose it. Irrigation rights are taken seriously, particularly in historic districts of Santa Fe, where homeowners will be expected to participate in meetings, provide the labor to clear out ditches, and participate in all the other wonderful historic but arcane rituals involved in using water in a desert.

The higher in elevation your home is, the more snow you'll encounter. Notice the number of four-wheel-drive vehicles on Santa Fe's streets? Many of these aren't just for show—the drivers need them to get home after a storm. If you're looking at property in the summer, be sure to ask what the roads are like in the winter.

# RENTALS

A few years ago, just finding a place to rent in Santa Fe was a challenge. But recent construction of apartment complexes has made the situation bearable.

According to the Santa Fe Public Housing Authority, which keeps tabs on the situation, renters in 2009 could find a two-bedroom apartment in an apartment complex for about $900 a month and could locate a three-bedroom place for $1,200 to $1,500 per month.

Santa Fe has roughly 35 apartment and condominium complexes with 30 units or more and about 9 complexes with more than 200 rental units. Apartments are scattered around the city, but the largest concentration of apartment complexes can be found on Zia Road, Airport Road, St. Francis Drive, Rodeo Road, and in the southern part of town. Among the choices are Shadowridge, 941 Calle Mejia; Dos Santos Condominiums, 2210 San Miguel Chavez Road; Rancho Vizcaya Apartments, 2500 Sawmill Rd.; Zia Vista Condominiums at 2501 West Zia Rd.; Los Pueblos, 2095 South Pacheco; and San Mateo of Santa Fe, 601 West San Mateo Rd.

Of course, as with the rest of the real estate market, location is everything. The closer to the Plaza, the better the views and amenities, the nicer the neighborhood, the more square feet the property has, the more you'll pay for an apartment or a rental home. Places that take pets are harder to find and usually more costly. Low market price for a three-bedroom house is around $1,400; homes for rent in the $1,000 to $1,400 price range will go quickly.

The Santa Fe Association of Realtors publishes a list of its members' available rental property each week and includes vacation rentals as well as long-term situations. A 2009 "Weekly Rental Sheet" illustrated the range of possibilities and prices. These are also listed on the SFAR Web site. Properties listed included a furnished "Santa Fe charmer" within walking distance of the downtown Plaza, with one bedroom plus additional living space and no pets allowed, for $975 (including utilities). A three-bedroom, two-bath home in a southside neighborhood was renting for $1,800, with amenities that included a fireplace, fenced yard, and *saltillo* tile. About 45 minutes north, in Abiquiú, a two-bedroom, two-bath adobe fronting the Chama River on 20 acres was available for $1,100 a month.

In Santa Fe, incidentally, the market is its own rent control. When there's plenty of property for rent, the owners or their agents may be inclined to lower the cost although many landlords are single women who got into the market purchasing properties as investment income and may rely on the income for living costs, leaving little room for maneuver. If there's more demand than units available, landlords won't be in the mood to dicker on price.

Sometimes people may find that it's difficult to get what they're looking for in the rental market here, but agents say that may be because they're looking for something that isn't realistic in terms of price for the location. If you need a rental, the best plan is to cover all bases, and begin by getting the newspaper early or checking classifieds online at the *Santa Fe New Mexican* or Craigslist. Running your own "wanted to rent" ad offers another option. The Santa Fe Association of Realtors (505-982-8385; www.sfar.com) can give you a list of members who are property managers and can assist you in your search for a place to rent. Don't forget to check the phone book for apartment listings. Bulletin boards at natural food stores such as La Montanita Coop are tried-and-true local resources that often yield leads.

And be forewarned: When the Santa Fe Opera and the Chamber Music Festival bring their artists, support crews, and audiences to town in the summer, rents increase and availability drops. In fact, many homeowners in Santa Fe vacate their homes for that month and rent them out for an exorbitant fee while they go traveling. If you have a choice, rent in May, with a lease, or wait until the middle of August. Expect to pay first and last month's rent and a damage deposit. According to the 2000 census, 31.4 percent of Santa Feans were renters, facing a 5.6 percent vacancy rate.

# SANTA FE NEIGHBORHOODS

Let's assume, for a happy moment, that not only have you decided to move to Santa Fe but that you can also spend as much or as little as you decide on your housing. Among the options:

You can buy a quaint old adobe within walking distance of the Plaza.

You can live in a house with property that gives you access to the Santa Fe River or a historic acequia (irrigation ditch).

You can settle into a neighborhood with sidewalks, paved streets, and potential friends for your children right next door.

You can buy in an area with hiking trails, parks, and other amenities.

You might purchase a 10-acre lot, hire an architect, and use a custom builder to create the best of Santa Fe style.

You could fall in love with a new, energy-efficient house at the end of a bumpy dirt road with gorgeous views and plenty of privacy.

You could relocate to a condominium development complete with full-time security, a health club, and community room.

You might live in a mobile home park or an apartment complex.

Or you could choose to move to a ranch with horses or maybe even llamas and buffalo.

Like Santa Fe itself, the real estate market here is eclectic, diversified, sophisticated, and, compared to many other places in the country, expensive. Real estate is big business in Santa Fe and—because of Santa Fe's impact as the state capital and a trendsetter—throughout much of northern New Mexico.

Look in the Santa Fe phone book and you'll find 11 pages of advertising listings for real estate agents and companies. The Santa Fe Association of Realtors has 900 members, all of whom are sincerely interested in making a living in the profession.

Santa Fe was born around the Plaza and along the Santa Fe River, and the city's oldest neighborhoods are downtown. People have been living in the Barrio de Analco area, for example, since the city's founding in 1610. Although this area and many of the 12 other neighborhoods included in the City of Santa Fe's Historic Neighborhood Study are now largely commercial, special zoning encourages residential uses downtown. As you move away from the Plaza in all directions, you'll encounter newer residential areas with their own flavor.

**i** **Building with straw bale construction is a popular alternative in Santa Fe. It's economical and viable. The plastered bales are secured together with rebar and surrounded by wood or steel for support. For more information, log on to www.straw houses.com.**

Unlike many communities, Santa Fe generally defines its neighborhoods in terms of geographical locations rather than specific streets, parks, the names of builders, or subway stops. The developers of newer subdivisions name their projects, but these "neighborhoods" are the exception. Because of Santa Fe's long history of Catholicism, many people were more likely to identify themselves in terms of the parish where they went to church rather than the neighborhood, and parish boundaries included many different neighborhoods.

In Santa Fe, more so than in many communities in the country, the housing tends to look similar in many sections of town. This is Santa Fe style in its variations. (Please see our Close-up in this chapter.) You will, however, find some differences. Generally, more expensive neighborhoods offer more acreage with your home. But this isn't necessarily true on the east side, where a home worth a half-million dollars or more may have little accompanying land. One of the charming quirks of the city's older neighborhoods, and a part of Santa Fe that is disappearing with its growth, is that a million-dollar home may be next to a less expensive house, built by its owners and their children. This economic mix has been replicated in some of the city's newer developments, which advertise the diversity of single-family homes at a variety of prices, with town houses and apartments as one of their drawing cards.

Both Tierra Contenta, Santa Fe's affordable housing development, and the upper-end Aldea de Santa Fe advertise a return to diversity as part of their attraction.

Some of Santa Fe's residential areas have sidewalks, paved streets, parks, and other amenities. Other homes—including million-dollar estates—lie off dirt roads with no curbs or gutters, no parks, and no bus service.

Here's a brief guide to Santa Fe's residential areas:

## Downtown/East Side

Unlike many cities, Santa Fe's downtown, which includes the areas closest to the Plaza, is a prestigious place to live. This historic area, surrounded by winding streets, galleries, and towering old trees, is a mixture of historic homes that have been restored and modest houses that haven't been prettied up. The boundaries overlap with the east side, South Capitol area, and Guadalupe Street, but to the north, East Palace Avenue, with its big cottonwoods and Spanish Pueblo- and Territorial-style homes set back from the street, is one of the area's trademarks and boundaries. Guadalupe Street defines the downtown area to the west.

Styles tend to be more eclectic downtown than on the adjoining east side. You'll find stone houses as well as vintage hybrids that blend Santa Fe style and western ranch design. Because the downtown area is largely commercial, residential property here is at a premium.

If you live downtown, you can take your morning jog along the Santa Fe River, stop in a cafe for coffee and a muffin, and do gourmet grocery shopping at Kaune Food Town, 511 Old Santa Fe Trail. You can walk to the Plaza. You'll have easy access to the Santa Fe River Park along Alameda Street (from Palace Avenue to Agua Fria/Guadalupe Streets), with its picnic tables and walking path, and to quiet Tommy Macaione Park, 301 East Marcy St., with its statue of the late Santa Fe artist. If you work at City Hall, the main post office, or for the state in any of its downtown offices, you can stroll home for lunch.

The city keeps a close eye on construction, remodeling, and renovation in this area to preserve Santa Fe's historic feel. Don't buy a home in any of the city's historic neighborhoods and plan on major new construction, demolition, or extensive renovation unless you have the time, money, and inclination to follow all the rules.

The east side is marked by real adobe houses on narrow, twisting streets. It's one of Santa Fe's most expensive areas with prices rising to $400 per square foot or higher. But not everyone who lives here is rich. Families who bought or built them before Santa Fe became chic own many of the homes. The boundaries here are nebulous, but Old Santa Fe Trail to the west and Camino Cabra to the east are the general markers. Camino San Acacio, Camino Don Miguel, Canyon Road, Acequia Madre, Garcia Street, and Camino del Monte Sol are among the neighborhood's defining streets.

You don't get earth-shaking views or huge estates in the heart of the east side, but, as some people see it, you get something better: an old Santa Fe neighborhood and genuine charm. The classic adobe look of the east side has influenced much of contemporary Santa Fe's construction. The city's oldest and best preserved Pueblo and Territorial architecture is within this and the downtown district. Earth-tone walls predominate, although you may find some white walls and decorative murals beneath *portals*. Buildings here tend to be true adobe with mud-plaster finish. The historic district ordinance requires that the walls be at least 8 inches thick and specifies that "geometrically straight facade lines shall be avoided" to emphasize the organically flowing nature of the adobe look. The characteristic effect is that of long and low. Setbacks, *portals*, and a second-floor balcony to visually reduce the height and mass of the structure accompany the two-story construction you'll see. Roofs tend to be flat with a slight slope and gutters, or *canales*, diverting water straight off the roof. Wooden lintels and other artistic finishing touches enhance many east-side homes.

The lower section of Canyon Road is a mixture of businesses and residential buildings and

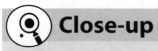 **Close-up**

## Santa Fe Style: Simple Beauty

As you look at Santa Fe's neighborhoods or shop for a home or apartment here, you'll notice numerous variations of the phenomenon known as "Santa Fe Style."

Santa Fe style is deceptively simple. Start with a building that blends into its surroundings because it's the same color as the earth around it and because its contours match those of the landscape in which it is built. Typically, Santa Fe style means modified Pueblo or Territorial style—a thick-walled adobe look, with windows to capture the mountains and the sunsets and patios and *portals* for outdoor living. The doors are likely to be carved wood with a natural finish or perhaps a whimsical painted trim.

In 1918, when an influx of American influences threatened to make Santa Fe look remarkably like Anytown, U.S.A., within a generation, artist Carlos Vierra spearheaded the revival of old styles of building. Vierra, and others who joined him in his work to preserve and contemporize Santa Fe's traditional Pueblo and Territorial look, based Santa Fe style on a combination of the long-standing regional architecture with modifications essential for comfortable contemporary living. Vierra concentrated on the appreciation and development of the great advantages Santa Fe had from its adobe roots. He coined the term "Pueblo Revival" for this updated traditional style. Santa Fe architect John Gaw Meem became one of its finest practitioners.

Santa Fe-style homes may look unimposing from the outside—perhaps just a simple adobe wall with an attractive gate—and that's part of their understated charm. Inside you may find a lovely courtyard leading to the house itself. Santa Fe style has evolved in the hands of contemporary builders and designers. It often includes passive solar energy features such as orienting a house to the south with windows to capture the sun's heat in winter and floors and walls to absorb that warmth and hold it into the evening.

The smooth plastered or sand-textured walls tend to be neutral colors—a variation on the adobe plaster used outside—or white or off-white. Exterior doors may be hand-hewn panels of pine, antiques garnered from older homes, or even imported from Mexico, or original creations crafted from *latillas* or hand-adzed planks. Floors are normally of tile—again in earth tones— or natural stone, brick, or wood. American Indian rugs are common finishing touches. More color usually comes in the accents, in the artwork on the walls, the brightly painted folk-art carvings in the *nichos*, the fresh flowers on the tables, and the textiles on the throw pillows.

When tin came to New Mexico in the form of large storage containers used by the United States Army in the mid-19th century, residents quickly adapted this versatile material to a variety of practical and decorative uses. Tin switchplates with cut and stamped designs, mirrors perhaps with fabric or painted decorative touches, and other tincraft are subtle parts of Santa Fe style.

Exterior adobe walls around the house or garden serve many uses. In some cases they shield homes from the noise and closeness of the street; in a different setting they carve a secure enclosure from the vast landscape, frame the views, and offer a haven for plants, pets, and family use.

For definitive information and beautiful pictures, take a look at *Santa Fe Style*, a wonderful book by Christine Mather and Sharon Woods, published by Rizzoli, New York.

### GLOSSARY

**Adobe:** A brick made of mud and straw, dried in the sun and used as a building material. Adobe is the heart of Santa Fe style because of its sculptural quality. Building with this labor-intensive material tends to be expensive unless you can do it yourself. Many Santa Fe homes that have an adobelike appearance are built of less expensive cinderblock or frame and stuccoed in earth tones to resemble adobe. "Adobe" is also used to mean "earth-colored."

**Banco:** These plastered built-in benches, often found near a fireplace, are either crafted of adobe or framed of wood and stuccoed over.

**Canale:** An open-gutter outlet to allow water to run off flat roofs, *canales* are a distinctive feature of Santa Fe style. Trouble with *canales* can lead to leaky roofs.

**Casita:** This term, meaning a small house, is sometimes used to describe a guesthouse, town house, or upscale condo.

**Corbel:** Usually found atop posts or larger support beams, this decorative feature is usually carved and may also be painted.

**Coyote fence:** Traditionally crafted from juniper branches wired together vertically, coyote fences are used decoratively, for privacy, and as wind breaks. The posts ought to be so close together that a coyote can't squeeze through.

**Horno:** An outdoor beehive-shape oven seen extensively on Indian pueblos.

**Kiva fireplace:** A rounded sculptural fireplace usually crafted from adobe. You'll normally find these in the corner of a room. In Spanish they are called a *fogón.* Kiva fireplaces are often raised from the floor and surrounded with *bancos.*

**Latillas:** These small branches (approximately 3 inches in diameter), usually of juniper or aspen, are placed above the vigas to form the ceiling. They can be laid in various patterns such as herringbone or straight rows.

**Lintel:** An exposed beam placed over a window or door, lintels are sometimes carved or painted.

**Nicho:** A small niche or indentation in a wall, usually rounded at the top, *nichos* are designed to display a work of art or family keepsakes. They could be described as traditional built-in shelving.

**Pen Tile:** A specific variety of hollow clay building block commonly used to construct walls in Santa Fe houses during the early part of the 20th century. The blocks acquired their name because they resemble squarish, four-dimensional tiles and were produced by inmates at the New Mexico State Penitentiary, south of Santa Fe, and sold to local contractors.

**Portal:** A covered porch that is also used as an outdoor walkway, *portals* can stretch across both the back and the front of a building and may be furnished with benches. In their book *Santa Fe Style,* Mather and Woods say the *portal* is the Southwest's most profound contribution to architecture. Santa Fe's best-known *portal* is the porch in front of the Palace of the Governors, 105 East Palace Ave.

**Pueblo style:** This classic design is typified by the homes of the Pueblo Indians and the early Spanish. People interested in the subtleties may differentiate later construction using this theme as Spanish Pueblo style, Pueblo Revival style, and Spanish Pueblo Revival style. Construction is of adobe or other materials with stucco to resemble the adobe look. Small windows and doorways accent the thick sculptural walls. The oldest of these homes grew organically rather than by floor plan, with more rooms added as the family expanded. Low ceilings, flat roofs, vigas, *latillas, bancos,* and *nichos* mark this style, but these features also may be found in Territorial style and in contemporary variations.

**Saltillo tile:** This fired tile from Mexico, available in a variety of earth tones and usually square, is a popular and practical floor covering.

**Territorial style:** Stuccoed walls finished with brick coping, decorative trim over windows and door frames, and sharper corners characterize this traditional architecture. With the opening of the Santa Fe Trail and the coming of the railroad, new materials, such as plate glass for windows, flooded into Santa Fe. The result was a happy marriage of sensuous adobe walls with brick and wood trim for a more formal look.

**Vigas:** Peeled logs used either decoratively or as a ceiling support, vigas are the first part of the ceiling to be installed. These massive timbers may span the house or be found in only a few rooms. In Territorial style, the vigas are often squared-off and finished with a decorated edging.

has become increasingly commercial over the past decade. Canyon Road (see our Attractions chapter) offers galleries, shops, and restaurants as well as wonderful ambience. Garcia Street, Delgado Street, and Camino del Monte Sol also mix businesses and residences. Acequia Madre is residential except for Acequia Madre Elementary School, 700 Acequia Madre. Patrick Smith Park, 1001 Canyon Rd., offers a pleasant expanse of grass for soccer and baseball, picnic spots, swings, and basketball courts along the Santa Fe River east of the junction of Canyon Road and Acequia Madre.

> **i** The Albuquerque-based New Mexico Solar Energy Association offers a solar home tour of northern New Mexico homes each October. The self-guided tour features owner- and contractor-built homes, including the unusual strawbale and rammed earth tire construction "Earthship" houses as well as traditional adobe passive solar designs. The homes use solar energy to create their electricity or heat their water. For more information call (888) 886-6765 or visit www.nmsea.org.

As you move away from the heart of the east side, the terrain becomes more hilly. Cerro Gordo and Upper Canyon Roads are long-established areas where new mansions abut ancient adobe homes. St. John's College, 1160 Camino Cruz Blanca, and Cristo Rey Church, 1120 Canyon Rd., are among this area's landmarks. The Wilderness Gate development in the foothills behind St. John's College offers exclusive homes, many with exquisite views of Santa Fe, on multiacre lots secluded amid the ponderosa pines.

Another relatively definable section of the east side is known as Museum Hill because the Wheelwright Museum of the American Indian, the Museum of International Folk Arts, the Museum of Spanish Colonial Arts, and the Museum of Indian Arts and Culture are all here just off Camino Lejo. (Please see our Attractions chapter.) As late as 1950 much of this rolling, piñon-covered land remained undeveloped. City

planners consider the area "visually important" due to its proximity to the east-side neighborhoods—and many buyers like it for the same reason. Some lots here may include ruts created by heavy wagons that traveled the historic Santa Fe Trail.

Heading north along the Old Taos Highway, Bishop's Lodge Road, or Hyde Park Road, you get a sense of the countryside. This area, which is also known as the northeast or the near north side, is more sparsely populated. You're likely to see jackrabbits and coyotes along the dirt roads. Many of the homes sit on large lots with fine views of the mountains. Town houses tend to be hidden among piñon and juniper trees or positioned to capture the views. Some of the properties border arroyos, or sandy washes, areas that can be great places for walking as long as it isn't during a rainstorm! You won't find many sidewalks in this part of town. The city's Fort Marcy Complex, 490 Washington Ave., is the closest place for kids to swim or play baseball or soccer.

## Southeast

This area includes the South Capitol neighborhood, one of Santa Fe's most architecturally diverse areas, with lots of seasoned homes and some quaint old apartment buildings. Some residents live in California bungalows, a rarity in Santa Fe. You'll also discover brick homes, shade trees, and even a lawn or two. Old Santa Fe Trail provides the border to the east, and Galisteo Street frames it to the west. Paseo de Peralta and Cordova Road are, roughly, the north and south boundaries.

This predominantly residential area includes the Don Gaspar Historic District, which was subdivided as a residential development during the 1890s. For the first time in Santa Fe's history, people here were able to build with materials other than stone, wood, and adobe, thanks to the railroad. Santa Fe families got to experiment with materials and styles popular in the East, West, and Midwest, including Italianate, Mansard, Queen Anne, and Craftsman Bungalow. You'll find gabled and hipped roofs here, gracefully intermixed among small Santa Fe-style, flat-roofed adobes. The city leaders' strong negative reaction to this imported look sparked renewed interest in preserving Santa Fe's historic adobe architecture.

Chinese elms shade the streets here, and the ground is good for gardens. Wood Gormley Elementary School, 141 East Booth St., serves the area. You'll find paved streets, concrete driveways, and sidewalks. Continue out Old Santa Fe Trail to the southeast, and you'll come upon homes in a semirural area in the piñon and juniper forests of the Sangre de Cristo foothills. Many people who live here have tremendous views of the Sandía and Ortíz Mountains. Much of this land is regulated by strict requirements that limit building on slopes, protect the views of the foothills from town (including limits on glare from windows), and restrict the construction of new roads.

Among the more established residential areas in the southeast section is the Sol y Lomas neighborhood, just across Old Pecos Trail and accessed by Sol y Lomas Road. The neighborhood has a country feeling and expansive homes. Old Santa Fe Trail, St. Francis Drive, Galisteo Street, and Cordova Road border the residential area commonly known as the Hospital/E. J. Martinez neighborhood. It includes three- and four-bedroom homes, most surrounded by native landscaping with some sidewalks and some paved streets. Homes here are graciously set back from the road, and neighbors have an easier opportunity to get to know each other. E. J. Martinez School, 401 West San Mateo Rd.; St. Vincent Hospital, which borders the neighborhood at 455 St. Michael's Dr.; and the lovely Harvey Cornell Rose Garden, 1203 Galisteo Parkway, are among this area's landmarks.

Farther out Old Pecos Trail is Quail Run, a gated condominium development of 265 units from studios up to four-bedroom homes, complete with a health club, restaurant, and nine-hole golf course.

## Northwest

The oldest of these neighborhoods began as clusters of Hispanic ranches on the outskirts of Santa Fe's more densely developed Plaza area. The land was plotted in long, narrow parcels so the maximum number of owners could have access to the water in the acequias and from the Santa Fe River for their farms and gardens. The earliest houses were constructed of adobe in the traditional Pueblo style and fronted directly onto the narrow dirt streets.

With the coming of the railroad and construction of its depot and railyards in the area, the near west side and Guadalupe districts became a core of economic and social activity. As Santa Fe grew during the 20th century, families continued the long-established practice of subdividing their property among descendants. This created the west side's large number of small, oddly shaped lots. You'll notice many owner-built homes here, adding to the eclectic look.

### The Guadalupe Street Neighborhood

The Guadalupe area continues as a commercial center with retail shops and restaurants designed to attract both local and visitor business (see our Shopping chapter). It roughly borders both sides of Guadalupe Street from Don Diego Avenue to Agua Fria Street. In addition to old Pueblo-style homes, the Guadalupe area includes bungalows such as those you see in the South Capitol district. The Santuario de Guadalupe, 100 Guadalupe St., is one of the area's—and Santa Fe's—landmarks.

### The Near West Side

In the 1970s, the construction of St. Francis Drive separated the Guadalupe/near west side district from the west side, also known as Barrio del Río. Agua Fria Street from Guadalupe Street to St. Francis Drive is the heart of the near west side. The near west side is probably as close as Santa Fe gets to America's perception of "inner city." Because this area contains the least expensive property in what is still considered the downtown area, it has undergone tremendous change in the last decade.

A gentrified adobe, newly replastered and remodeled to include expensive wooden casement windows, may sit next to a home that looks much the same as it did 50 years ago. The Santa

Fe Boys and Girls Club, 730 Alto St., is one of the landmarks of this area.

## The West Side

From St. Francis Drive south, the area between Alameda and Agua Fria Streets roughly to Hickox Street and Camino Cristóbal Colón is known as the West Side. It's an eclectic, nonglitzy family area, characterized by the remnants of its agricultural days. St. Anne's Church, 511 Alicia St., and Larragoite Elementary School, 1604 Agua Fria St., are among its landmarks. There's some commercial development mixed with the residential here.

You'll find mid-priced houses along with a scattering of apartments and rental units. Because of the casual zoning, values don't increase as fast on the west side as they do elsewhere. Many Santa Fe natives who grew up here hold fond memories of these neighborhoods.

## Casa Solana/Michelle Drive

Just north of Alameda Street bordered by Solana Drive to the south and St. Francis Drive to the west is Casa Solana, a family area with sidewalks, paved streets, and mature landscaping, including some beautiful big trees. Here you'll see kids riding their bikes, parents pushing strollers, and gray-haired gardeners hard at work. You'll find a real sense of neighborhood here.

Developer Allen Stamm built these affordable homes for Santa Feans in the 1960s, on what was once a former Japanese internment camp during World War II, a little-known episode in Santa Fe's history. Stamm homes, though small, are beloved for their vigas, hardwood floors, fireplaces, and solid construction. They are among the most affordable homes for first-time buyers and renters wanting an older single-family home rather than an apartment in an attractive walkable neighborhood. Gonzales Elementary School, 851 West Alameda St., serves this area. For many decades, until the new landfill opened in 1997, Casa Solana did its civic duty by offering a thoroughfare to garbage trucks and people who hauled their own trash up Camino de las Crucitas to the city dump at the intersection of Buck-

man Road. From the old dump the views soar to 360-degree vistas that encompass the Jémez, Sangre de Cristo, Sandía, and Ortíz Mountains.

## Casa Alegre

Bordered by Agua Fria Street to the west, Cerrillos Road to the east, San José Avenue to the north, and Maes Road to the south, Casa Alegre, also an Allen Stamm project, was built in the 1950s as Stamm's first development. Although the houses are smaller than those in Casa Solana, they have the same nice amenities. After World War II, the area provided homes to GIs and their families, some of whom still live in the same homes today. Frenchy's Field at Osage and Agua Fria and Gregory Lopez Park, 1230 San Felipe Rd., gives kids a place to play. The area's landmarks are Salazar Elementary School, 1300 Osage Ave., and St. John the Baptist Catholic Church, 1301 Osage Ave., just across the street from the school.

## Kaune Neighborhood

Another Stamm family area with parks, schools, and churches, Kaune is accessed primarily from Monterey Drive just off Cerrillos Road. The neighborhood is officially known as the Casa Linda neighborhood, but most folks call it the Kaune area because of Kaune Elementary School, 1409 Monterey Dr., which serves the families here. The school, planned by famed Santa Fe architect John Gaw Meem, was named for Alfred Kaune, a past president of the Santa Fe School Board and part of the family that owned the Kaune gourmet grocery store.

The homes here include hardwood floors, vigas, and other Santa Fe-style amenities. Buyers can choose between Spanish Pueblo, Territorial, or California flat-roof styles for their homes. The 128 units originally sold for between $9,000 and $14,000—today you'll easily pay more than 15 times that price.

## West Alameda

From Solano Drive south, West Alameda Street serves as an access road to mixed housing areas. You'll find older, small handmade adobes, manufactured housing, and expensive newer construction. As you continue south you'll discover some designer masterpieces whose very existence bumps the whole area up a notch or two in price. The farther you get from the Plaza, the more rural the area becomes; you'll see horses out here along with some boarding stables. The upscale Puesta del Sol and Piñon Hills developments offer big lots, big views, an openness to variations of Santa Fe style, and a country feel. This area connects directly to NM 599, the Santa Fe Bypass.

## Southwest

This is the section of Santa Fe where you're most likely to find family-affordable homes and apartments. Most of the construction here is newer, and this part of Santa Fe provides easiest access to Santa Fe Place Mall (4250 Cerrillos Rd.), the Santa Fe Auto Park (4450 Cerrillos Rd.), and to Capital High School (4851 Paseo del Sol). Average home price here was $275,000 in the second quarter of 2009, up from $235,000 during the same period in 2005.

### La Tierra Contenta

The Tierra Contenta neighborhood, part of the city's fast-growing Southwest sector, began in 1995, ushering in a hopeful new day for Santa Fe's average working family. Located just off Airport Road west of Cerrillos Road, the neighborhood offers parks and open space and works to cultivate a sense of neighborliness among the home owners. When complete, Tierra Contenta will feature 5,500 units, of which 3,700 will be single-family residences and the rest multifamily town houses, duplexes, and apartments. In 2009, a four-bedroom, four full-bath home was on the market for an astounding $245,000, making this by far the most affordable area of Santa Fe to buy in. The development will also have convenient commercial areas and hundreds of acres of open space with pedestrian walkways and bike trails. Schools and churches are part of the plan. Tierra Contenta was one of the reasons the Ford Foundation awarded the Santa Fe Affordable Housing Roundtable a $100,000 prize in 1996 for success in helping people find affordable housing. For information check www.tierracontenta.com or call (505) 471-4546.

**i** Don't worry if your home doesn't look like a page from *House and Garden* magazine. Santa Fe is not the place for manicured lawns, prim gardens, or perfectly clean homes. Authentic adobe walls shed authentic brown dust. And dirt roads generate dust with every passing vehicle.

### Bellamah

Named after builder Dale Bellamah, this southside neighborhood features houses designed to suit young families. The neighborhood is characterized by square one-story suburban-style homes with touches of Santa Fe-style. These homes are noted for their logical floor plans, garages, and flat or slightly pitched roofs. Bellamah is largely defined by Siringo Road to the west, Richards Avenue to the south, and Yucca Street to the north. The area has several parks, including the city's popular Arroyo Chamisa walking/bike trail that runs from Rodeo Road past the Monica Lucero Park on Avenida de las Campanas, crosses Camino Carlos Rey, and ends at Yucca Street.

General Franklin E. Miles Park, 1027 Camino Carlos Rey, one of the city's largest parks, offers baseball fields, lit basketball courts, playgrounds for the little guys, a skateboarders' section, and grass to roll on for picnics. Francis X. Nava Elementary School, 2655 Siringo Rd., sits at the edge of the park. The Herb Martinez/La Resolana Park, 2240 Camino Carlos Rey, has tennis courts and grass, which is often filled with young soccer players.

**i** The "adobe" look of Santa Fe-style buildings may not be real adobe at all. Most new homes and commercial buildings are constructed of wood framing or concrete blocks. Then the exteriors are covered with mesh, which serves as a base for brown stucco plaster, which looks like the adobe structures Spanish colonists built. As a building material, real adobe bricks and plaster are expensive today.

## Rodeo Road Area

Santa Fe residents jokingly refer to this as "the suburbs." Houses are newer and larger than in Bellamah, but the neighborhood feeling is much the same. Your housing dollar goes further here than in the historic areas, and the number of housing choices is increasing rapidly. You'll find clusters of town houses and apartments, and even a loft development, as well as commercial centers along Rodeo Road, and easy access to I-25. The Park Plaza development of town houses and some single homes is a popular spot because of its walking trails and common-land construction, which consolidates housing to allow for greenbelts and open space. A city/county biking and hiking trail that will ultimately connect Santa Fe from the Guadalupe Street area to the Eldorado subdivision runs through here, offering a fine place for exercise.

## Rancho Viejo

This newer development sits on 2,500 acres about a mile south of I-25 off of Richards Avenue. The area's master plan includes a mix of commercial and residential uses. Homesites focus around a central plaza with shops, delis, small businesses, a school, and public bus service. Homes here start at $159,000 and go all the way up to $428,000. Now doing business as SunCor New Mexico, the Rancho Viejo developer has built more than 550 units at the original master-planned village, constructed a further 761 units in a second village, and is presently constructing a new village of 1,200 homes at La Entrada de Rancho Viejo. For information visit www.ranchoviejo.com.

## Oshara Village

This sustainably built, planned development near the community college completed phase one of construction with 40 greenbuilt townhomes and single-family dwellings around a central community plaza. Homes are superinsulated and oriented for passive solar, there is on-site water reclamation for irrigation of native landscaping, and energy-efficient appliances. The new Rabbit Road extension provides a quick connection to St. Francis Drive and access to I-25 and downtown. Although still in a very early phase of construction, with only 20 homes sold to date, the developer has big plans for Oshara, and even with the slowdown in the economy, this seems to be a development that, once it begins to take fuller shape, will eventually be very attractive to environmentally conscious Santa Feans. Prices start in the $270,000s for townhomes.

## Northwest of Town

US 84/285 serves as the boundary for this area to the east, and Camino La Tierra and Tano Road off NM 599 provide the main access to these properties. The Tano Road neighborhood, La Tierra, La Tierra Nueva, and Salva Tierra are among the residential areas here. All are similar—multiacre lots with expansive views and homes by some of Santa Fe's finest designers and builders. You're likely to find more established homes in the Tano Road area. Dirt roads are the rule, and you won't find any schools, gas stations, churches, or shopping opportunities; they're all in Santa Fe. The trade-off for what some consider inconvenience: plenty of space, the chance to hear coyotes howl at the moon, and breathtaking views.

## Las Campanas

This exclusive development includes the 18-hole Jack Nicklaus signature Sunrise Golf Course on 160 landscaped acres, a beautifully appointed clubhouse with a first-rate restaurant for members and guests, and view lots that range from one to 10 acres. All homesites on this 4,700-acre development include gated entries, paved roads, and underground utilities. The development (online at www.lascampanas.com) has strict covenants that dictate construction and style of homes. Average home price is just over $1.3 million. Of 1,700 zoned homesites, about 1,000 had been sold. Home owners include celebrities like country music singer Randy Travis who enjoy the quiet and relative privacy of this development.

## Aldea de Santa Fe

A peaceful, spacious, new development in this section of Santa Fe, formerly a traditional Hispanic area called Frijoles Village, Aldea began construction in 2003 and is just getting underway, with limited services to date, including a state-of-the-art private holistic health center, coffeeshop, and community plaza and meeting rooms, and WiFi throughout. Described as a "neo-traditional community," the project is south of Las Campanas and 5 miles northwest of the Santa Fe Plaza in a beautiful open area with 365-degree views of the surrounding country. The community has 430 to 470 lots of various sizes, averaging one-quarter acre and costing between $94,000 and $185,000 per lot. The project's homes, built by several Santa Fe builders in an attractive Santa Fe style, currently range in price from $495,000 to $729,000, with some less expensive subsidized housing below $200,000 as required by the City of Santa Fe. The community features narrow, curving roads and a conformity of exterior color, heights, and styles to provide visual unity. Trees have been planted to line the paved streets. An extensive system of foot and bike paths links the village to a regional trail network and 200 acres of open space. The development plan also includes parks and a commercial plaza. Sixty percent of the development is platted as open space, and the village restricts building on its escarpments. For information, go to www.aldeasantafe.com or call (505) 438-2525.

## Southeast of Santa Fe

### Eldorado and Vicinity

This family-friendly area is Santa Fe's rural suburbia. When the Eldorado development was first announced, many Santa Fe residents scoffed. Who, they asked, would drive 15 minutes to get to work? Today Eldorado is a community unto itself, and newer housing developments have sprouted up nearby along Highway 285 in the Galisteo Basin. Thousands of people live here, enjoying the panorama of open plains and distant mountains and the quiet neighborly feeling. In addition to humans, many kinds of critters, including hawks, coyotes, and rabbits, still call this country home.

Unlike much of Santa Fe County, the land here is relatively flat and lower in elevation, which makes for easier construction and lower costs. The

older homes are arranged in a traditional neighborhood style with several to a block. The newer houses tend to be larger and sit on sprawling lots in this world of sand, sage, and piñon. Amenities include a community clubhouse with meeting rooms and a swimming pool and one of Santa Fe's better elementary schools, Eldorado Elementary, 2 Avenida Torreon. The Agora marketplace has a large grocery store, restaurants, and other amenities at 7 Avenida Vista Grande. Across the road is an extensive new commercial center with offices, a gym, and Brumby's Restaurant. There is a gas station opposite the entrance to Eldorado, off Highway 285, with a small restaurant.

The great 20th-century architect Frank Lloyd Wright designed only one adobe house, the Pottery House, which was eventually built on a hillside overlooking Santa Fe. The owner purchased the plans from the Frank Lloyd Wright Foundation and construction began in 1984. The home is shaped like a football.

## REAL ESTATE AGENCIES

### BRANCH REALTY
228 South St. Francis Dr.
(505) 984-8100
www.branchrealty.com
The nine agents in this office focus on commercial real estate. They can help with investment property, exchanges, leases, and consultants as well as sales. The firm, established in 1982, prides itself on its "knowledge and effort." Among the company's projects were Whole Foods Grocery Store, Home Depot, and Phase II of Plaza Santa Fe, which includes many well-known retail stores.

### CITY DIFFERENT REALTY
518 Old Santa Fe Trail
(505) 983-1557
This office features seven agents, all of whom are brokers with experience from 15 to 27 years in Santa Fe. City Different is by design a small firm, owned and run by four brokers and based on a philosophy of bringing together a select group of

experienced, top-producing people who wish to work cooperatively. The office deals mainly with upper-end properties, but since most business comes through personal referrals, it also works in other price ranges.

### COLDWELL BANKER
Trails West Realty Ltd.
2000 Old Pecos Trail
(505) 988-7285, (800) 775-5550
www.cbsantafe.com
With 34 full-time agents, Coldwell Banker represents both buyers and sellers in residential transactions. In business for 24 years, the firm makes extensive use of the Coldwell Banker national Web site and national sales programs, such as Blue Ribbon & Previews Properties. The office provides ongoing training for its agents.

### FRENCH & FRENCH SOTHEBY'S INTERNATIONAL REALTY
231 Washington Ave.
(505) 988-8088, (800) 409-7325
www.french-french.com
French & French continues to lead the Santa Fe-area real estate market in residential sales in all price ranges. In addition to 15 agents, four full-time-staff-supported offices, and an extensive advertising marketing strategy, the agency has a 500-page Web site. British-based Sotheby's global connections complement French & French's local expertise in representing buyers and sellers of premiere properties in and around Santa Fe. French & French has been in business since 1984.

### KAREN WALKER REAL ESTATE
205 Delgado
(505) 982-0118, (800) 982-0118
www.karenwalkerrealestate.com
In business since 1973, this small firm prides itself on its knowledge of land-use codes, building regulations, and restrictions. It has an intimate acquaintance with neighborhoods, historic uses, and districts. Karen Walker is the author of Understanding and Buying Santa Fe Real Estate, illustrated by professional cartoonist Pat Oliphant.

### PRUDENTIAL REAL ESTATE
505 Don Gaspar Ave.
(505) 988-3700, (800) 418-1221
www.prudentialsantafe.com
The Town and Ranch agency is now part of Prudential Insurance. Buyers throughout the country can learn about Santa Fe homes before they visit. This full-service brokerage has 50 licensed agents and includes specialists in ranches and commercial property.

### ROBERT DUNN REAL ESTATE INC./SANTA FE
300 Catron Street #B
(505) 988-2200, (800) 444-9887
www.RobertDunnRealEstate.com
Owners Robert Dunn and Pam Wickiser combined have nearly 45 years experience in the Santa Fe market. In addition to residences, land, and commercial property, they represent Quail Run luxury resort condominium living. Visit their Web site for more information.

**i** Because of the requirements of the Fair Housing Act, Realtors can't steer clients to a certain neighborhood. They also have to decline to answer questions about crime and schools. They can suggest that clients look at police records, watch the crime reports in the newspapers, and talk to the public school systems about programs and achievement in different school zones.

### SANTA FE PROPERTIES
60 E. San Francisco
(505) 982-4466
www.santafeproperties.com
Founded in 1986 by Wally Sargent, this firm has become one of the more successful independently owned brokerages in Santa Fe. Team spirit and a capable staff add to the strength of the company. With an in-depth knowledge of real estate in the Santa Fe area, 85 sales associates provide personal service. More than 60 percent of their sales are from repeat customers. Just a short walk from the downtown Plaza, their attractive office is in the historic 100-year-old José Alarid adobe.

## VARELA REAL ESTATE INC.
1526 Cerrillos Rd.
(505) 982-2525
www.varelarealestate.com

Varela Real Estate, previously known as the Frank Gomez Agency, has been in business since 1949. President Susan Varela, Gomez's daughter, has worked in the office since 1973. The office offers residential and commercial sales and management and leasing services for residential and commercial property.

# RESOURCES

## ADC REFERRAL
5 Bucking Horse Ct.
(505) 474-8388
www.adcreferral.com

Ready to build or remodel in Santa Fe? Let this free service help you find the architect, design staff, and builders you'll need. The process begins with an in-depth interview to help you understand and define your tastes and vision for your home or office. ADC will then assist you in clarifying design needs, establishing a working budget, and identifying the scope of service you'll need to get the job done. The initials, incidentally, stand for architects, designers, and contractors.

## HOMEWISE NEIGHBORHOOD HOUSING SERVICES
1301 Siler Rd., Building D
(505) 983-9473
www.homewise.org

This private, nonprofit organization helps low- and moderate-income families maintain their homes and provides opportunities for new affordable housing. The agency offers below-market mortgages and assistance with down payments. Their home-repair program helps families keep property they already own and home-buyer workshops teach potential buyers much of what they need to know to be successful home owners. The agency also builds new and affordable homes that it makes available to first-time home buyers.

## SANTA FE AREA HOME BUILDERS ASSOCIATION
1409 Luisa St., Suite A
(505) 982-1774
www.sfahba.com

The Santa Fe Area Home Builders Association is a trade organization representing more than 750 firms in the seven-county area in northern New Mexico. This nonprofit association is dedicated to promoting safe, quality, attractive, cost-effective, and affordable housing. The association sponsors several community-based events each year. The Home and Garden Show, which gives you a look at some of Santa Fe's nicest homes, is held in early spring. Haciendas—A Parade of Homes is a self-guided tour held throughout the Santa Fe area each August. The tour features homes representing many varieties of building products as well as new styles. The builders compete for recognition of their craftsmanship and, as a sidelight, may attract new clients based on the opportunity to see the builder's work firsthand. The association also engages in many community service projects.

## SANTA FE ASSOCIATION OF REALTORS
510 North Guadalupe St., Suite E
(505) 982-8385
www.sfar.com

The Santa Fe Association of Realtors is the local affiliate of the National Association of Realtors. This organization compiles the Multiple Listing Service, provides ongoing education for all licensees, and works for legislation to protect property owners. With 900 local members, the association participates in many community service projects. The group's Web site has detailed information about the local real estate market, plus specific listings of sales and rentals.

## SANTA FE CIVIC HOUSING AUTHORITY
664 Alta Vista St.
(505) 988-2859

The authority works with the city's low-income families to help them find a decent place to rent. The program includes a low-rent public-housing program, rental assistance, and other projects to help families become more self-sufficient and eventually purchase their own homes. Funding comes from public and private sources.

### SANTA FE COUNTY HOUSING AUTHORITY
664 Alta Vista St.
(505) 988-2859
The county provides housing services for low-income and elderly people through this program. Included are vouchers that help with the rent and a popular rent-to-buy program in three sites around the county. The elderly, disabled, or families with many dependents may be eligible for help; the waiting list is six to 12 months.

## CHAMBERS OF COMMERCE & BUSINESS ASSOCIATIONS

### SANTA FE CHAMBER OF COMMERCE
8380 Cerrillos Rd., Suite 302
(505) 988-3279
www.santafechamber.com

### SANTA FE CONVENTION & VISITORS BUREAU
Santa Fe Community Convention Center
201 West Marcy St.
(505) 955-6200, (800) 777-2489
www.santafe.org

### SANTA FE ECONOMIC DEVELOPMENT CORPORATION
(505) 955-6915

### NEW MEXICO MUNICIPAL LEAGUE
1229 Paseo de Peralta
(800) 432-2036
www.nmml.org

### REALTORS ASSOCIATION OF NEW MEXICO
2201 Brothers Rd.
(505) 982-2442
www.nmrealtor.com

# RETIREMENT

I t's not in the Sun Belt and it's certainly not cheap. So why is Santa Fe rated among the top spots to retire in the United States? For the same reasons it's attractive to so many other segments of the American population. It's beautiful. It has a healthy, highly livable, four-season climate. Its history is as fascinating as its mixture of cultures. And it has culture—the other kind—in spades: world-class opera, chamber music, symphony and chorale; flamenco and other live dance; theater; repertory cinema; art markets year-round, galleries, and museums; many film venues; excellent bookstores and libraries; and dozens of classes and seminars on any number of topics in the city's public and private institutions of higher learning. The food here is superb, with internationally acclaimed restaurants offering creative fare for the discerning palate and dozens of lower-priced eateries with good, down-home cookin'. Active seniors can burn off the extra calories skiing, hiking, golfing, kayaking, swimming, or enjoying any number of other outdoor endeavors in an environment that begs to be enjoyed.

But there's something else in Santa Fe, a je ne sais quoi, that makes it just a little more attractive for an older population than other cities with similar qualities—the relaxed atmosphere, perhaps, and a cordiality toward older people unmatched in many other cities. Indeed, a number of national publications have rated Santa Fe among the top places in the United States to retire. It even beats out retirement communities in Arizona, California, Florida, and other states because of the city's lack of congestion. As one local senior citizen succinctly put it, "You can grow old here."

The number of residents age 65 and older in the city of Santa Fe was 8,648, or 13.9 percent of the total population, according to the 2000 U.S. Census. The number of older residents continues to increase and officials of Santa Fe County expect those 65 and older will comprise 27 percent of the county's population by 2020.

In this chapter, we tell you about the services and housing options available for the growing senior population in the Santa Fe area. For more news and information by, about, and for seniors, pick up a copy of *Prime Time: For New Mexicans 50 Plus* (see our Media chapter), a free, Albuquerque-based monthly tabloid found at newsstands throughout Santa Fe.

## AGENCIES, SERVICES, AND SOCIAL/SUPPORT GROUPS

### AARP
535 Cerrillos Rd.
(505) 820-2277
www.aarp.org
AARP is a nonprofit, nonpartisan organization dedicated to helping older Americans live independent, dignified, and useful lives. Its Santa Fe chapter has been disbanded due to declining participation and replaced by a countywide council of volunteers who work on community

projects, such as the Safe Kids/Safe Seniors Program and Foster Grandparents (see entries under City of Santa Fe Division of Senior Services in this chapter); and Vials for Life program, which alerts emergency medical technicians that an individual is on medication.

### ADULT PROTECTIVE SERVICES
2001 Vivigen Way
(505) 827-7450
www.newmexico.gov
New Mexico law requires anyone who suspects an adult is being abused, neglected, or exploited

to report it. That's where Adult Protective Services steps in. A branch of the New Mexico Children, Youth, and Families Department, the agency investigates allegations of abuse, neglect, or exploitation of people age 18 and older who are unable to protect themselves. The majority of its clients are seniors. In some cases, Adult Protective Services will provide housecleaning, shopping, transportation, and other services to keep an individual from being institutionalized prematurely. Other cases involve family members or acquaintances who are taking advantage of a vulnerable adult, especially his or her checkbook. The agency has no punitive powers but may refer cases either to other community services or, if it suspects criminal activity, to the police or district attorney.

## ALZHEIMER'S ASSOCIATION SUPPORT GROUPS
(505) 266-4473,
(800) 272-3900 (New Mexico chapter)
(800) 272-3900 (twenty-four-hour national hotline)
www.alz.org/newmexico/in_my_
community_support.asp
Support groups for caregivers of people with Alzheimer's disease are held several times weekly at these Santa Fe care homes with dementia units—Sierra Vista, Kingston Residence, The Rosemont—and at Open Hands, a nonprofit benefiting the elderly, and First Presbyterian Church. Check out the Web site listing above for exact details or call the toll-free phone numbers.

## CITY OF SANTA FE DIVISION OF SENIOR SERVICES
1121 Alto St.
(505) 955-4721, (866) 824-8714
www.nm-santafe.civicplus.com
Part of the city's Community Services Department, the Division of Senior Services is a "one-stop shop" for a wide variety of programs and services at minimal cost for adults age 60 and older throughout the city and county. The division provides

transportation for a suggested donation of 50 cents per trip with 24 hours notice, before 4 p.m. the previous day; $1 meals at designated senior centers or delivered to a person's home via Meals on Wheels; preventive health education and services including blood pressure testing, blood sugar and cholesterol screening, hearing and eye tests, breast cancer screening, and flu shots; recreation and activities such as Senior Olympics, dancing, travel, ceramics, sculpture, woodcarving, and weaving; case management; outreach, information, and referrals. The Senior Services Division sponsors numerous volunteer programs, including Retired and Senior Volunteer Program (RSVP), where seniors act as Medicare-Medigap counselors, peer counselors, nutrition counselors, ombudsmen, craft instructors, etc.; Safe Kids/Safe Seniors to prevent accidental injuries; and the USDA Commodities Distribution, which gets food to low-income seniors and disabled clients. It also offers several paying programs for low-income seniors in conjunction with the State Agency on Aging (see subsequent entry), including Foster Grandparents, which provides a stipend for serving as classroom "grandparents," and Senior Companions, in which individuals age 60 and older can supplement their income by providing companionship to frail, homebound elderly clients. The division's Respite Program provides R&R for primary caregivers of people with Alzheimer's disease and dementia.

The division has 11 senior centers within the surrounding area, eight of them in or near Santa Fe: Casa Rufina Community Center, 2323 Casa Rufina Rd., (505) 988-1116; Eldorado Senior Center, 16 Avenida Torreon, (505) 466-1039; Mary Esther Gonzales Center, 1121 Alto St., (505) 984-6731; Pasatiempo Center, 668 Alta Vista St., (505) 984-9859; Luisa Center, 1510 Luisa St., (505) 984-8091; Villa Consuelo Center, 1200 Camino Consuelo, (505) 474-5431; Ventana de Vida Senior Center, 1500 Pacheco St., (505) 955-6731; El Rancho Senior Center, 334 County Rd. 84, El Rancho, (505) 455-2195. Check the Web site for more information.

i Twice each year, volunteers from the Santa Fe-based Living Treasures Program choose three northern New Mexicans age 70 or older to be "Living Treasure Elders" in recognition of their spirit, energy, and community service. Many of those recognized have been captured in a book of photo essays called *Living Treasures: Celebration of the Human Spirit,* published in 1997 by Western Edge Press of Santa Fe. The book is widely available in local bookstores and public libraries.

## GUARDIAN ANGELS
3 Chamisa Dr. North, Suite 5
(505) 995-8333
www.guardianangelsllc.com
Based near Eldorado, this new family-run company provides guardianship services (making health-care and placement decisions) and conservatorship services (making financial decisions) for mentally incapacitated people in Santa Fe, Albuquerque, Los Alamos, and Las Vegas. It also manages trusts too small for a bank to handle and can serve as durable power of attorney, in which you assign someone to make health-care decisions for you, and other advanced directives, including living wills. Many of its clients are senior citizens who are unable to make life decisions for themselves. The company also offers workshops and seminars on guardianship and related issues through the Guardian Angels Foundation. The company's executive manager, Janice Ladnier, has more than 20 years' experience as a paralegal and is an experienced care manager and patient advocate. She is a professional licensed clinical counselor, a certified grief counselor, an experienced Master National Guardian, conservator, and court visitor. Her daughter, Angela Melton, serves as operations manager and is a National Certified Guardian, office manager, bookkeeper, notary public, and associate care manager. Guardian Angels also offers hands-on care management services for clients who need assistance in the home following a hospital stay or more long-term assistance. For care management, call the sister company Guardian Angels Personal Care (see entry under Home Health Care and Hospice).

## ELDERHOSTEL
(800) 454-5768
www.elderhostel.org
Elderhostel, a Boston-based international travel and education program for people older than age 55, offers short-term education and adventure. It has programs in all 50 states, Canada, and 80 other countries around the world. Northern New Mexico Elderhostel features camping, hiking, climbing, or skiing programs; service programs in which volunteers restore trails in the national forest or adobe structures; theme weeks focusing on the state museums, for example, or perhaps the Santa Fe Opera or the Santa Fe Trail; classes on American Indian or Hispanic culture or any number of other offerings. Recent courses have included such topics as "Spanish Colonial Traditions and Customs," "Cultural Encounters: Examining History through Native Eyes," "African Americans in the Southwest," "Legendary Women of the Southwest," "Artistic Traditions in Northern New Mexico: From the Stone Age to the Present," and "The River of Lost Souls: Aztec, New Mexico, and the San Juan River." Elderhostel courses run in the neighborhood of $155 a night, including housing, meals, and all field-trip and course fees. Housing ranges from dormitories to hotels. Elderhostel participants may take a companion or spouse of any age older than 21. In 2009, Elderhostel programs are being offered through the national organization and in cooperation with Ghost Ranch at Santa Fe, (505) 982-8539, and Ghost Ranch Abiquiú Conference Center, (505) 685-4333, located near Abiquiú in the heart of Georgia O'Keeffe country. Call for details.

ℹ️ Many stores, theaters, and restaurants in Santa Fe, including some national chains, offer senior discounts. Some establishments set aside a particular day or specified hours for seniors to receive the discount. Others offer a discount every day, including Wild Oats Community Market, a natural foods supermarket that gives a 10 percent discount to seniors, and the La Montanita Coop in Casa Solana Center which also takes off 5 percent. While most places advertise their senior discounts prominently, a few prefer to play it low-key. Don't be shy about asking.

## NEW MEXICO AGING AND LONG TERM SERVICES DIVISION
Toney Anaya Building
2550 Cerrillos Rd.
(505) 476-4799, (866) 451-2901
www.nmaging.state.nm.us
The State Agency on Aging oversees the delivery of services for the elderly in New Mexico to help older people and their families achieve a high quality of life. Created to carry out the mandates of the federal Older Americans Act, the agency's mission is to ensure the physical, mental, and economic well-being of aging New Mexicans. In addition to distributing federal and state funds to senior centers for meals, activities, in-home support, and health education, the agency provides job training and placement for low-income seniors; helps seniors find health and other benefits they've earned; advocates for residents of long-term care facilities; and offers volunteer opportunities for seniors and those who want to work with them. It also sponsors an annual statewide conference on aging. The agency contracts with outside organizations for a variety of other services and activities, including free or reduced-cost legal services, Senior Olympics, and the Foster Grandparents and Senior Companions programs (see the City of Santa Fe Division of Senior Services section in this chapter).

## OPEN HANDS
2976 Rodeo Park Dr. East
(505) 428-2320
www.openhands.org
Established in 1977, Open Hands is a nonprofit agency providing essential services to help elderly, disabled, and poor people live independently and with dignity. The organization offers a wide variety of services such as adult day care for up to 50 people, including those with Alzheimer's or other dementia; group support for caregivers; a home safety program that retrofits homes with wheelchair ramps and grab bars; weatherizing homes by replacing leaky windows and doors, testing for carbon monoxide and radon, and helping clients get funds for necessary renovations; a Youth Services Corps in which student volunteers do yard work and other chores for elderly and disabled clients; a medical equipment loan bank; emergency financial assistance; and home visits during a crisis or simply for companionship. Open Hands charges for its services based on a client's ability to pay. The agency operates several thrift stores that not only help support its programs but also employ the disabled. Based in Santa Fe, Open Hands serves 11 counties and 12 pueblos in northern New Mexico.

## SENIORS REACHING OUT
Armory for the Arts Complex
1050 Old Pecos Trail
(505) 428-2352
Seniors Reaching Out is a nonprofit group that celebrates aging through literary and performing arts. SRO produces and stages plays, readings, musical numbers, and conferences and sponsors oral history and storytelling dialogues among some of Santa Fe's "living treasures" in the arts and humanities. The group performs variety shows and reminiscence theater—called "Elders Entertain Elders"—at nursing and retirement homes and senior centers throughout Santa Fe and northern New Mexico and entertains children with its "Kids and Kin" storytelling performances at Santa Fe public schools, Native American headstart programs, libraries, and summer camps.

## TAX AID
**Division of Senior Services**
**(505) 955-4721**
Sponsored by AARP and Santa Fe Community College, this is a free, walk-in, first-come, first-served clinic designed to help low-income seniors filing income tax returns. The clinics are open Monday through Thursday from 9 a.m. to 2 p.m. beginning the first Monday in February through April 15. Clinic volunteers are laypeople certified by the Internal Revenue Service. Call for locations.

## WOMEN IN TRANSITION
**Santa Fe Community College**
**6401 Richards Ave.**
**(505) 428-1736**
Women in Transition is a series of free workshops designed to give widows and other women going through major life changes a better self-image. Part of Santa Fe Community College's Institute for Intercultural Community Leadership, the workshops provide education, information, support, and referrals in the community. Academic credit for the workshops is offered to enrolled students.

# HOME HEALTH CARE AND HOSPICE

## GUARDIAN ANGELS PERSONAL CARE LLC
**3 Chamisa Dr. North, Suite 4**
**(505) 466-3500**
**www.ga-personalcare.com**
This friendly family-owned new home health services agency provides health care to people who want to live at home but need help with daily activities in Santa Fe, Albuquerque, Rio Rancho, and Las Vegas. Three levels of care—companion/homemaker, personal care attendant, and home health aide—are offered, depending on need. Clients include the elderly, people with Alzheimer's disease, or other long-term disabilities, and patients recovering from stroke, heart attack, surgery, or other serious illness. Caregivers are available up to 24 hours a day, seven days a week to assist with personal care, dressing and bathing, prepare meals, help clients walk and get

into and out of bed, monitor medication, provide transportation, run errands, do light housekeeping, and offer companionship. Guardian Angels charges an hourly rate depending on level of care and accepts Medicare or Medicaid and other insurance (see also Agencies, Services, and Social-Support Groups entry above).

## UPAYA INSTITUTE
**1404 Cerro Gordo Rd.**
**(505) 986-8518**
**www.upaya.org**
This Buddhist contemplative retreat and study center (see Worship and Spirituality chapter) offers the well-established Being With Dying: Professional Training Program in Contemplative End-of-Life Care for those wishing to care for people who are terminally ill. Founded and taught by Upaya spiritual director Joan Halifax, the program addresses the need for health care providers to develop knowledge and skills in the psycho-social, ethical, and spiritual aspects of dying: an approach to caregiving that is relationship-centered, including community development and cross-cultural issues; the development of skills related to care of the caregiver; and the means to implement these skills in traditional medical settings. Halifax teaches nonsectarian, contemplative practices based in Zen Buddhism to help bring peace and acceptance to individuals at any stage of illness or grieving. The caregiver helps nurture a calm, sacred space that emphasizes prayer, deep listening, and mindful silence or meditation. The one-week trainings cost $1,590 per person and take place twice a year at Upaya. Places are limited. Preregistration and an application fee are required.

## PRESBYTERIAN MEDICAL SERVICES
**1422 Paseo de Peralta**
**(505) 988-2121, (800) 477-7633**
**www.quasar.pmsnet.org**
Presbyterian Medical Services is a nonprofit corporation that provides medical and dental health care, education, and human services primarily to under-served populations in the Southwest. Its Santa Fe programs include PMS Home Care and

The Hospice Center, both based out of the downtown area. The Home Care Program, (505) 988-4156, offers skilled nursing; home health aides for personal hygiene; physical, occupational, and speech therapy; and medical social services. The Hospice Center, 1400 Chama Ave., Santa Fe, (505) 988-4156, provides medicine, medical supplies, and equipment; on-call registered nurses specializing in pain and symptom control; home health aides; physical, occupational, and speech therapists; volunteers to support both patients and caregivers; social workers and pastors for emotional and spiritual counseling and referral; and bereavement services. The Hospice Center also operates a support and counseling service for groups, including schools and businesses, and a thrift store whose revenues support the center. PMS is Medicare/Medicaid certified, and also involved in long-term care and retirement housing.

## PROFESSIONAL HOME HEALTH CARE
### 10 Calle Medico
### (505) 982-8581
### www.professionalhomehealthcare.com
In operation since the 1980s, Professional Home Health Care is a private, nonprofit agency whose mission is to keep individuals—from the elderly, who comprise the majority of its clients, to infants—out of hospitals, nursing homes, and other institutions. The agency provides skilled nursing, home health aides, hospice, and other complementary or physician-ordered services in clients' homes. The agency covers a large territory in New Mexico, from Sandoval County north of Albuquerque to the Colorado border. It accepts Medicare, Medicaid, and private-pay clients.

# RETIREMENT COMMUNITIES

## EL CASTILLO RETIREMENT RESIDENCES
### 250 East Alameda St.
### (505) 988-2877
### www.elcastilloretirement.com
Located just a few blocks east of the Plaza and west of chic Canyon Road, El Castillo Retirement Residences offer what it calls "Life Care" for retir-

ees 62 or older and their spouses of any age. A popular retirement community in a complex that was expanded and upgraded in 1999, El Castillo has a long waiting list for its 150 apartments, each with a private outside entrance. Upon acceptance, residents pay a one-time, partially tax-deductible entrance fee, a significant sum that varies with the size of the apartment and how many will live there. They also pay a monthly service fee that covers one meal a day in the dining room, scheduled transportation, maintenance, security, a library, an outdoor pool, a pool room, and organized activities such as exercise, arts and crafts, and tours. Together these fees constitute a lifetime contract that assures residents they will have all their needs met—including nursing care and assisted living, should either be necessary. For those in need of temporary assisted living or nursing care, El Castillo has set aside a number of its residences as "rentals," available only to guests of residents or to prospective buyers.

## KINGSTON RESIDENCE OF SANTA FE
### 2400 Legacy Ct.
### (505) 471-2400, (800) 906-9020
### www.kingstonhealthcare.com/santafe
Kingston Residence of Santa Fe is a rental retirement community for the 55 and older set, located on 5½ landscaped acres. It offers 70 large, sunny independent-living apartments, each with either a patio or balcony, some overlooking open courtyards, and another 12 rooms each for assisted-living and Alzheimer's residents. Independent-living rates include breakfast, lunch, and dinner; local transportation in the house Cadillac; all utilities; indoor and outdoor maintenance, including housekeeping every two weeks; social services; and a wide variety of activities from casino excursions, museum visits, and movies to exercise, dancing, and meditation. Assisted-care residents enjoy all the services listed above plus twenty-four-hour care by licensed nurses, medication control, physical therapy, and personal hygiene care. Independent residents may receive any of these services for an additional cost. Kingston Residence of Santa Fe provides on-site banking, a notary public, and free office facilities, includ-

ing copying, faxing, and computer and Internet access. The complex is located a few blocks east of Santa Fe Place Mall (see our Shopping chapter) and immediately west of Sam's Club. The property is adjacent to the city of Santa Fe's Arroyo Chamisa Bike Trail, a 4.5-mile path for walkers, joggers, skaters, and bicyclists.

**i** For information about nursing homes in Santa Fe and throughout the state, contact the New Mexico State Agency on Aging for its *Guide to New Mexico's Nursing Homes,* published for the first time in 1997 by the agency's Long Term Care Ombudsman Program. The guide is a good starting point in a search for a nursing home in New Mexico. It gives a brief description of the facility, Medicare/Medicaid reimbursement rates, inspection scores, and a brief rundown of the medical characteristics of its residents.

## PLAZA DEL MONTE RETIREMENT COMMUNITY
**P.O. Box 2267, Santa Fe 87504**
**(505) 982-5565**
**www.quasar.pmsnet.org**
This facility, operated since 1990 by Presbyterian Medical Services (see listing in this chapter), offers a close-knit independent-living community of 27 small houses and one- or two-bedroom apartments. Originally designed as a retirement center for Presbyterian ministers, it is now open to retirees of any faith or background. Some education and support services (i.e. weekly nurse visits) are available, along with movie screenings, field trips, and other social activities. It's centrally located just north of downtown Santa Fe, within walking distance from the Plaza and Ghost Ranch Santa Fe, a retreat and education center run by the Presbyterian Church.

## PONCE DE LEON RETIREMENT COMMUNITY
**640 Alta Vista St.**
**(505) 984-8422**

Ponce de Leon is a full-service rental retirement community for independent and assisted living. Its 150 apartments include studios, one- and two-bedroom units, each with an electronic emergency call system. Located just five minutes by car from downtown Santa Fe, Ponce de Leon has a distinct Spanish feel with plenty of wrought iron and a lovely interior courtyard with a reflecting pool, shrubbery, flowers, and trees. Independent-living rentals include a continental breakfast and either lunch or dinner; transportation; weekly housekeeping; and flat linen service. These residents enjoy a full activity calendar featuring art exhibits, concerts and other live entertainment, dances, Friday social hours, seminars, art classes, exercise classes, and day trips to Albuquerque, casinos, museums, Indian and Spanish markets, and other events and attractions. Assisted living includes three meals a day, daily housekeeping, help with personal hygiene, dispensing and monitoring medication, regular house checks, and a separate activity calendar with field trips close to home. Ponce de Leon offers on-site banking, a country store, and a large city park across the street with an indoor swimming pool, tennis courts, benches, and picnic tables.

## ROSEMONT OF SANTA FE
**2961 Galisteo St.**
**(505) 438-8464**
**www.therosemont.com/santafe**
This pleasant, family-owned and operated assisted-living retirement community is located on Santa Fe's southeast side, with shopping and other services a few minutes' drive away. Rosemont offers comfortable Southwest-style suites, meals, group activities, and other amenities to seniors who wish to maintain their independence. It also has a separate Memory Care (Alzheimer's unit) and full nursing services. The staff here are friendly and supportive, and the atmosphere is upbeat and professional.

# EDUCATION AND CHILD CARE

I f you want to learn massage therapy or acupuncture, Santa Fe is the right place.

If you're interested in a class in photography, a workshop in flamenco dancing, an intensive experience in cross-cultural awareness, or an afternoon of bird identification, you're in luck.

If you want your child to do well enough in high school to get a scholarship to Harvard, your choices are more limited—yet don't despair.

But if you need a Mary Poppins to take care of your toddler, Santa Fe presents a challenge. It's the same story here as in most cities around the United States. Unless Grandma lives close by and delights in caring for the little ones, securing high-quality child care at a reasonable price is as tough as finding a downtown parking place during Indian Market weekend.

In this chapter, we'll take a look at colleges and special post-secondary programs, the Santa Fe Public Schools, private secondary schools, and options for child care and babysitters. (You'll find special programs and camps for kids in our Kidstuff chapter.)

## COLLEGES AND UNIVERSITIES

### INSTITUTE OF AMERICAN INDIAN ARTS
83 Avan Nu Po Rd.
(505) 424-2300
www.iaia.edu/college

Some of America's leading American Indian artists—among them Dan Namingha, David Bradley, Estella Loretto, Denise Wallace, Allan Houser, T. C. Cannon, and Darren Vigil-Gray—have taught and/or studied at this unique institution. Established in 1962, the IAIA stands alone as the only two-year fine-arts college devoted solely to the study and contemporary practice of the arts and cultures of American Indians and Alaska Natives. The federal government, on which the IAIA depends for most of its support, has reduced the school budget dramatically since 1995. However, the IAIA has managed to move forward, raising needed funds for core operations from alumni and supporters throughout the country. Enrollment is now around 230 at a new campus on the south side of Santa Fe, near Santa Fe Community College. In its new home, the school has expanded its two-year associate degree program

to offer a four-year bachelor's degree with a curriculum encompassing visual art and design, creative writing, performing arts, cultural studies, and liberal arts incorporating Native American perspectives. The new programs also include business courses to help artists become entrepreneurs.

The superb IAIA Museum houses The National Collection of Contemporary Indian Art, the largest curated by American Indians in the world. The museum, with a collection of more than 6,500 pieces, is located in a historic Santa Fe-style building in downtown Santa Fe and features student and alumni work (see our Attractions chapter).

i Santa Fe has five colleges, a total enrollment of about 8,000 students. The largest is Santa Fe Community College. More than 13 percent of the city's population goes to this attractive, modern college—and that's not counting workshops, seminars, and SFCC's popular continuing-education programs.

## NEW MEXICO HIGHLANDS UNIVERSITY— SANTA FE
Santa Fe Community College campus
6401 Richards Ave.
(505) 428-1742
www.nmhu.edu
New Mexico Highlands University programs are intended for students who want to earn a Bachelor of Arts degree in social work, criminal justice, business, or education. Most of the students are working people who have associate's degrees and want to continue their education at a four-year institution. Full-time or adjunct professors do most of the teaching and classes are small. Highlands normally enrolls more than 80 students each semester in Santa Fe. The main campus is in Las Vegas, New Mexico, an hour east.

## ST. JOHN'S COLLEGE
1160 Camino de la Cruz Blanca
(505) 984-6000
www.sjcsf.edu
You won't find any big lecture classes on this campus, and students don't chew their nails over which electives to pick. Most of the course of study for a Bachelor's of Arts is required and most of the work is done in small seminars. The student to faculty ratio here is 8–1. Instead of textbooks, students read the original writing of more than 100 philosophers, scientists, poets, mathematicians, storytellers, and composers. Over their four years of study, students take language and math, three years of laboratory science, a year of music, and seminars in philosophy, political science, literature, history, economics, and psychology.

Established in 1964 in a lovely location near the eastern foothills, Santa Fe's St. John's is an extension of the school's historic Maryland campus, founded as King William's School in Annapolis in 1696. Only Harvard and the College of William and Mary have existed in the United States longer.

St. John's ranks in the nation's top 30 colleges for producing graduates who go on to work on higher degrees, with those who earn Ph.D.s evenly split between the sciences and humanities. The campus offers intensive eight-week summer graduate programs in liberal arts and Eastern Studies. That unusual course includes the classical Chinese and Sanskrit languages and uses texts from India, China, and Japan to prompt student discussions. In the summer St. John's offers its Classics Series, which brings a variety of nontraditional students to Santa Fe to discuss literature, philosophy, and opera.

St. John's invites the public to sample its approach during Community Seminar Day, held twice a year. Tutors, as faculty members are called, lead discussions on topics such as "Scientific and Religious Skepticism," which used Shakespeare's *Hamlet* and *Othello* and Descartes' *Meditation* as its texts. The campus hosts numerous public events and performances. Readings and book signings, arts shows, lectures, concerts, and other events bring town and gown together here.

## SANTA FE COMMUNITY COLLEGE
6401 Richards Ave.
(505) 428-1000
(505) 428-1777 (twenty-four-hour recorded InfoLine)
www.santa-fe.cc.nm.us
Located on 366 acres in southern Santa Fe, the attractive Santa Fe Community College campus opened in 1983. It consists of a main classroom/administrative center, the 122,000-square-foot Witter Fitness Center (see our Parks and Recreation chapter), the Early Childhood Development center, and the Visual Arts Center—55,800 square feet of classrooms, exhibit space, and studios for printmaking, photography, jewelry, drawing, painting, sculpture, and more. Facilities for the performing arts and instructional technology are planned in the coming years.

SFCC offers associate's degrees in more than 30 subjects, along with certificates. Some degrees are designed to transfer to four-year colleges and universities, while others are technical/vocational in nature. In spring 1998, SFCC completed a milestone when it conferred a degree on its 1,000th graduate. Enrollment in credit courses usually ranges around 5,000. SFCC's tuition is among the lowest in the state.

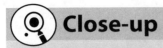 **Close-up**

## A Legacy of Learning

If a sense of astonishment goes with you to Heaven, the Christian Brothers who established St. Michael's High School must be amazed and delighted.

What they started in 1859 has undergone some remarkable changes. But the high school they began, the oldest educational institution in New Mexico, continues to thrive 150 years later.

Archbishop Jean Baptiste Lamy, the energetic French cleric who supervised the construction of St. Francis Cathedral, Loretto Chapel, and Santa Fe's first hospital and orphanage, sent for Brothers of the Christian Schools to help bring Catholic education to the territory. Four Brothers, chosen because they were skilled teachers, left for their American adventure from Clermont, France, on an old steamer. They traveled across the ocean for 14 days, then went by train from New York to St. Louis. They continued by wagon to Kansas City, where they set out for the plains and mountains beyond. They arrived in Santa Fe on October 27, 1859, after 71 days of travel.

Only two weeks later, the hard-working Brothers opened St. Michael's, named in honor of St. Michael the Archangel. Boarding students began to arrive on November 9, 1859, and the school has served Santa Fe families continually ever since. For many years it was the only source of education beyond an elementary level in the Territory. The school quickly had 30 boarders and more than 150 day scholars. By the time the Territory of New Mexico granted a charter to the College of the Christian Brothers of New Mexico in 1874, St. Michael's curriculum had expanded to include college courses.

When New Mexico achieved statehood in 1912, St. Michael's was a well-respected religious and academic institution. As the Brothers and Lamy hoped, many of their graduates had contributed to the Territory's achievement. Under Brother Botulph Schneider's 36 years of leadership, the original school gave way to an impressive two-story building with a third story incorporated in a mansard roof. A tall central cupola rose at the center, distinguishing the school as the first building of its type in Santa Fe. The walls were adobe, and the college quickly became famous as the Southwest's tallest adobe structure.

The Brothers discontinued the college after World War I to focus on the high school but didn't let the dream die. Brother Benildus of Mary began the arduous work of raising the money needed to re-establish the college. In 1947, the Brothers bought land that had been used as an Army hospital and re-opened St. Michael's College with a campus of 51 barracks. Scoffers said the venture was doomed because the college sat too far from the center of town. In 1966 St. Michael's College became The College of Santa Fe to more closely reflect its long ties with the community. That same year, the college admitted women for the first time. In December 1967, the high school moved from its downtown location to a large modern campus on the corner of Botulph and Siringo streets.

In 2009, the college was forced to close its doors due to financial problems. Meanwhile, the Christian Brothers' presence continues strongly at St. Michael's High School, the oldest high school in New Mexico.

The vast majority of SFCC students are adults who have jobs and attend college part time. Flexible scheduling—including short-term, evening, and weekend classes and Flex Labs—gives students the options they need. Contract courses can also be customized for area businesses, offered on campus or at their work place.

Through its Adult Basic Education programs, SFCC provides free instruction in reading, writing, math, GED preparation, English as a second language, and job-readiness skills. Literacy Volunteers of Santa Fe is also headquartered at SFCC.

Santa Fe residents also flock to the community college for its extensive Continuing Education program. Each year, more than 8,500 people of all ages enroll in noncredit classes from professional development and leadership skills to sports, Southwest adventures, cooking, and other leisure and cultural activities. Continuing Education also operates the Planetarium at Santa Fe Community College, which offers low-cost shows for the public and free programs for school groups under its skylit dome.

## UNIVERSITY OF NEW MEXICO—SANTA FE CAMPUS
**Santa Fe Community College campus**
**6401 Richards Ave., Room 309**
**(505) 428-1234, (800) 345-1807**
**www.eunm.unm.edu**
For 25 years, the University of New Mexico, based in Albuquerque, has offered graduate and upper-division programs in Santa Fe. UNM began its program at the request of the governor to fill the educational advancement needs of state employees. Until it found a home on the SFCC campus, UNM rented space from various agencies. Beginning with 50 students, UNM–Santa Fe enrollment now is near 1,000 annually.

Students at UNM–Santa Fe tend to be working professionals returning to school to complete their bachelor's degree or study toward their master's. For student convenience, most courses are scheduled in the evening. Bachelor's degree programs include nursing, speech and hearing, and University Studies, a nontraditional program in which students design their own course of study. Master's-degree programs include counseling, communications, and educational administration. In addition, UNM offers upper-level and graduate classes in multicultural education, Southwestern studies, and more. About half the courses are taught via television from the main campus in Albuquerque. Santa Fe students use the telephone to call in questions or answers.

The UNM office at Santa Fe Community College can provide information to students about main campus programs. They have applications, financial aid information, and UNM's undergraduate catalog and graduate bulletins.

## UNIVERSITY OF PHOENIX SANTA FE LEARNING CENTER
**131 Siringo Rd.**
**(505) 984-2188, (800) 333-8671**
**www.phoenix.edu**
The University of Phoenix offers Bachelor of Science degrees in business administration, accounting, management, and business information systems and a Master of Science in computer information systems, nursing, and education. Its program, intended for working adults, has been available in Santa Fe since 1989, and now occupies its own building off South St. Francis Drive. The Santa Fe programs enroll up to 200 students and are popular for the flexibility and the concentration of academic material they offer their students.

Founded nationally in 1976, University of Phoenix structures its classes to build on the professional experience of working adults. Nationwide, the college enrolls more students than any other private university in the United States and has served more than 400,000 students. In addition to classroom programs, the university offers computer-based education and distance learning, using the Internet and other high-tech tools. In addition to Santa Fe, the university has a main campus in Albuquerque and offers classes in several locations throughout the state. Class enrollment is held in the fall and again in January.

# SPECIAL SCHOOLS AND PROGRAMS

In this section, you'll find schools that offer a variety of programs, some unique to Santa Fe. Included here is a selected sampling of education ranging from advanced science to weekend seminars that can teach you how to shoot a great photograph or cook up the chile verde (green chile pepper sauce) of your dreams. Santa Fe has a wealth of health-care programs leading to various certifications. The city's acupuncture school is among the best in the country. Santa Fe is also home to an educational research center, The Santa Fe Institute, where professors in residence explore the frontier where science meets philosophy.

## ECOVERSITY
**2639 Agua Fria**
**(505) 424-9797**
**www.ecoversity.org**
Located on an old family farm along the Santa Fe River, Ecoversity's courses are focused on "learning and designing from nature," with an emphasis on experiential learning. Workshops and classes deal with such topics as beekeeping, greenhouse building, composting, chicken-and-egg production, farming, ecopsychology, and herbs of the Southwest. There are even some offerings beyond the realm of land-related skills, such as qi'gong, poetry, and Native American history. Registration is available online.

## GHOST RANCH IN SANTA FE
**401 Old Taos Hwy.**
**(505) 982-8539**
**www.ghostranch.org**
Ghost Ranch in Santa Fe, located only 3 blocks from the downtown Plaza, is a nonprofit educational center that presents a wide variety of workshops, classes, conferences, and special programs for the general public, as well as for seniors in association with the international Elderhostel organization. It is affiliated with the Ghost Ranch Foundation's educational center in Abiquiú, about 45 miles north of Santa Fe, which offers similar learning opportunities to individuals and groups. Both centers also work closely with other nonprofit organizations, along with schools, churches, and corporations, in devising or hosting custom programs and specialized retreats. Typical classes at Ghost Ranch focus on making art, writing, regional history, Native American culture, spirituality, photography, gender studies, creative aging, music appreciation, art history, and personal growth. Course catalogs are available by mail or online. Guest rooms are also available for nightly rental at reasonable cost.

## SANTA FE INSTITUTE
**1399 Hyde Park Rd.**
**(505) 984-8800**
**www.santafe.edu**
The Santa Fe Institute is a private, nonprofit, multidisciplinary research and education center, founded in Santa Fe in 1984. The mission of the Santa Fe Institute is to conduct and foster scientific research that has four dominant traits: transdisciplinary, excellent, fresh, and catalytic.

SFI has devoted itself to creating a new kind of scientific research community pursuing emerging science. SFI supports scientific research by providing an environment for multidisciplinary collaborations among visiting and resident scientists from the physical, biological, computational, and social science fields. Over the course of a year, SFI houses more than 100 scientists with about 35 in residence at any one time. Researchers-in-residence could stay for weeks, months, or years. They might be postdoctoral fellows, graduate students, or scientists predominantly from universities in the United States and Europe.

The Institute's research agenda is overseen by a Science Advisory Board that includes Nobel Laureates, MacArthur Foundation Fellows, members of the National Academy of Sciences, and several dozen distinguished scientists from leading universities. They come from a wide variety of fields to guide the general direction, integration, and quality of the Institute's work.

Students are important at SFI. Although it does not grant degrees, the Santa Fe Institute has a strong commitment to training the next generation of scientists. SFI programs include a highly competitive Postdoctoral Fellows program, long- and short-term interdisciplinary research opportunities for graduate students and undergraduates, the Complex Systems Summer School, and the Graduate Workshop for Computational Economics. In 2000, the institute began its advanced physics program, supported by the physics division of the National Science Foundation. For high-school students in the Santa Fe area, SFI offers a program in simulations of complex systems. SFI also presents a free monthly public lecture series at the James A. Little Theater on the New Mexico School for the Deaf campus.

## SANTA FE PHOTOGRAPHY AND DIGITAL WORKSHOPS
P.O. Box 9916, Santa Fe 87504
(505) 983-1400
www.santafeworkshops.com
This prestigious program teams amateur and professional photographers with nationally and internationally known photographers who share their insights both technically and artistically. The weeklong workshops, which run virtually year-round, attract more than 1,000 photographers to Santa Fe and guide them to appropriate sites for shooting assignments. Classes for beginners include aesthetics, technique, and an overview of equipment. Professionals can choose from portraits, lighting techniques, fashion and beauty, hand-colored photos, landscape, color work, and more. The school also features a free summer lecture series, open to anyone interested, which gives the instructors an opportunity to discuss and show their work. Fees for workshops vary widely.

## SANTA FE SCHOOL OF COOKING
116 West San Francisco St.
(505) 983-4511, (800) 982-4688
www.santafeschoolofcooking.com
That great green chile enchilada doesn't have to become just a Santa Fe memory. At Santa Fe School of Cooking, you can learn the secrets of Santa Fe cuisine in programs that take only a morning or an afternoon. During the summer the school offers classes as often as six days a week. Conveniently located downtown in the Plaza Mercado building, the teachers/chefs use indigenous southwestern ingredients to prepare both traditional and contemporary meals. Afterward, the students eat their creations and take home the recipes. Classes range from two to five hours. An on-site store sells cooking utensils and specialized ingredients.

Santa Fe School of Cooking also offers extended programs that include field trips to explore the farms and food of northern New Mexican villages and exciting dinners that take you behind adobe walls for meals in charming private homes. The school happily arranges classes and food tours for groups on request.

## SCHOOL OF ADVANCED RESEARCH
660 Garcia St.
(505) 954-7200
www.sarweb.org
If Santa Fe gave an award for the most beautiful and historic campus, the School of Advanced Research would win, hands down. The shaded, beautifully landscaped grounds and historic adobe headquarters speak of Santa Fe's early days as a magnet for the great minds in archaeology. This nonprofit center has supported innovative scholarship and American Indian artists since its founding in 1905. SAR presents six fellowships to outstanding scholars, giving them nine-month residencies devoted to writing projects related to anthropology, the humanities, and the arts. The school shares their work as part of its publication division. The SAR Press also publishes books designed for a popular audience on topics such as the peoples and cultures of the American Southwest. Three times a year the School of American Research invites 10 scholars to campus for a week of discussion and debate on issues on the frontier of anthropological research. (These meetings are closed to the public and the media.)

As another part of its educational mission, the SAR produces periodic newsletters, hosts traveling seminars to notable sites in the Southwest and around the world, and offers illustrated lectures. The Indian Arts Research Center, with its extensive collection of art and artifacts, is open to the public through special tours (see our Attractions chapter). A Contemporary Issues Initiative was launched in 1999 to apply anthropological research to current global concerns through special seminars. The School recently changed its name from the School of American Research to the School of Advanced Research, denoting its expanded focus.

## SOUTHWEST LEARNING CENTER
P.O. Box 8627, Santa Fe 87504
(505) 989-8898

Southwest Learning Center was established in 1972 as an educational resource to serve the multicultural population of the Southwest. The nonprofit organization presents interdisciplinary classes, research projects, conferences, workshops, apprenticeship programs, community-service projects, and special events. SWLC cultural programs promote a deeper understanding of native traditions. Recent programs include the Center for Indigenous Arts & Cultures, Mountain Light Center/Adopt a Grandparent Program, the Sustainable Native Agriculture Center, Native Roots & Rhythms, and Xochimoki. Programs are funded by tuition for classes, foundation grants, and corporate and private contributions.

## PUBLIC SCHOOLS

### SANTA FE PUBLIC SCHOOLS
610 Alta Vista St.
(505) 982-2631
www.sfps.info

For its first public schoolhouse, which served the community beginning in 1891, Santa Fe paid rent on a home at 352 Palace Ave. The little one-room school, which sat on the edge of an empty field, welcomed students from 1st grade through high school.

Today, Santa Fe Public Schools serve the city of Santa Fe and much of Santa Fe County—1,016 square miles—with a wide assortment of buildings, programs, and opportunities. The district includes a bilingual early-childhood center, 21 elementary schools, four middle schools, and two high schools. The district has also opened four new primary and secondary alternative "charter schools" since 2000. As part of the school system's 2010 Turnaround program, a holistic approach to reenvisioning public schools, three elementary schools have recently changed status to Community Schools, designed to serve the whole community, and more intend to do so. In addition, Turnaround aims to increase the number of Magnet Schools (public schools similar to charter schools that operate by consensus and accept students by lottery, but with a specific theme). The school system enrolls approximately 16,000

students and operates an open-enrollment system, allowing students to attend schools in different districts. SFPS also provides educational services to registered homeschool students and to students at the New Mexico School for the Deaf, the Santa Fe County Juvenile Detention Center, and the New Mexico Girls Ranch.

**i** **To enroll your child in the Santa Fe Public Schools, you must provide a current record of immunization, a birth certificate, and proof that your family lives within the district boundaries—a document with your address such as a utility bill or driver's license. If possible, provide a copy of your child's last report card or a school transcript and his or her Social Security number. If your child is going into 1st grade, he or she must be five years old by September 1 of the current school year. For more information, call the district's central office, (505) 982-2631. They can also tell you which school your children should attend. The cutoff is February each year.**

Enrollment in Santa Fe public schools reflects the racial makeup of the city. In the 2008–09 school year, the number of students enrolled included 10,256 Hispanics, 2,797 Caucasians, 369 American Indian, 210 Asian/Pacific Islander, and 134 African American for a total of 13,766 students. Santa Fe High, with about 2,000 students, is the largest school in the system. Next to state government, the schools are the biggest employer in Santa Fe County, with about 1,850 employees on the payroll. In 2009, the district was operating on a reduced annual budget of some $86 million from all sources. Santa Fe ranks among the worst school districts in the state for graduation rates—and New Mexico tends to place in the bottom quartile when it come to the percentage of students who graduate from high school (50 percent). The reasons for the Santa Fe public schools' poor performance and high dropout rate depend on who's doing the talking, but inadequate funding, children's lack of preparation for school, family stress, and teacher salaries lower than the national average are usually mentioned. Fully 75 percent of students attending schools qualify for free school lunches.

One of the strongest hopes for improving the public schools lies with school-community partnerships. Through an emphasis on volunteers as mentors, tutors, and guests in the classroom, the district wants to give the children in its care more opportunities for success. The nonprofit Santa Fe Partners in Education (505-474-0240) builds links between the community and the public schools to help teachers do their work better. The group underwrites those things beyond the district budget: field trips, special programs in the classroom, and supplies beyond the normal allotment. Partners also honors innovative teachers.

The Santa Fe Public Schools do some things well. In addition to the state-approved curriculum, the Santa Fe Public Schools offer a wide variety of special programs, including art immersion, bilingual education, culinary arts, peer mediation, and after-school care. A Foster Grandparents program matches elementary-school children who need extra attention with senior citizens for tutoring and conversation. The district has been busy building new schools in recent years, a task long overdue.

Santa Fe's first two public secondary charter schools were The Academy for Technology and the Classics, at 74 Avan Nu Po Rd. (505-473-4282), and Monte del Sol School, located in the Nava Adé subdivision (505-982-5225). A third, Tierra Encantada (505-983-3337) is located on the Santa Fe Indian School campus and has 142 students and nine teachers. Although part of the public system, charter schools are responsible for developing their own philosophy and curriculum as well as managing their own personnel and budget. Because they have proven to be very popular, admission is usually by lottery.

During the 2008-2009 school year, The Academy for Technology and the Classics, now located in a beautiful new building near the Institute of Indian Arts, enrolled 75 students in grades 7 through 12, with, as the name implies, an emphasis on modern science combined with classical sources of knowledge. Monte del Sol, enrolling 360 students in grades 7 through 12, stressed a mentorship approach incorporating "art, sustainability, leadership, and community." An elementary charter school (the oldest in the area) is Turquoise Trail Elementary, beyond the city limits south of Santa Fe on Highway 14, near Cerrillos. It enrolls 495 students. The SER/Career Academy, the alternative high school within the public system, works with students who are pregnant, have dropped out and want to return to school, or who need attention not available at the other two public high schools. And, of course, we have sports: Students can try close to 30 different sports in grades 7 through 12.

## OTHER PUBLICLY FUNDED SCHOOLS

Santa Fe is home to the state-funded New Mexico School for the Deaf, 1060 Cerrillos Rd., (505) 476-6311, which serves deaf and hard-of-hearing children from throughout New Mexico. NMSD offers preschool through 12th-grade education to about 135 students. The residential Santa Fe campus is also home to the James A. Little Theater, a popular venue for lectures and performances. (See our The Arts chapter.) NMSD has outreach programs in Albuquerque, Las Cruces, and Shiprock. Students pay no fees or tuition.

Another publicly funded school, Santa Fe Indian School, 1501 Cerrillos Rd., (505) 989-6300, is a boarding school for American Indian children that enrolls about 500 students in grades 7 through 12. To attend, students must be at least one-quarter Indian. Many students come from the nearby pueblos, but 25 other tribes also fill the roster. The Bureau of Indian Affairs established the school in 1890. The All-Indian Pueblo Council, made up of governors from all 19 New Mexico pueblos, now runs it. The school received approval from Congress and the U.S. Interior Department and an authorization of $20 million to begin construction of a new campus and has already razed a number of historic but dilapidated buildings along Cerrillos Road. Despite the ongoing struggle for funding, the school received an

Excellence in Education Award in 1987. Some 90 percent of seniors plan on attending college.

# PRIVATE SCHOOLS

Almost 25 percent of the city's middle- and high-school students attend private schools, according to statistics compiled by the New Mexico Department of Education. (The national average is around 14 percent.) Santa Fe has an abundance of private schools from preschool through secondary. For younger students, choices include church-affiliated elementaries, Waldorf and Montessori schools, informal schools, and those with a structured academic focus. High-school students have several interesting options.

Not all of Santa Fe's private schools are accredited. The State Department of Education, 300 Don Gaspar, (505) 827-6555, can give you a list of all private schools in the Santa Fe area. We have listed some of our private secondary schools to give you an idea of the range of options available in Santa Fe.

## DESERT ACADEMY
**313 Camino Alire**
**(505) 992-8284**
**www.desertacademy.org**
With its inception in 1994, Desert Academy filled a niche in Santa Fe's private school galaxy. The school welcomes children with learning differences among its 160-student enrollment and is the only high school in New Mexico to offer the International Baccalaureate diploma. Desert Academy offers a college preparatory program combined with classes in grades 7 through 12 designed to encourage both creativity and critical thinking. School culture fosters genuine civility, appreciation for learning, and a commitment to character. Student-teacher ratio is 8–1, with a maximum class size of 15. The school is fully accredited. Scholarships and financial aid are available.

## NIZHONI SCHOOL FOR GLOBAL CONSCIOUSNESS
**HC75, Box 72, Galisteo 87540**
**(505) 466-1975**
**www.nizhonischool.com**

As you'd guess from the name, this isn't your little red schoolhouse. Founded by spiritual teacher and author Chris Griscom, Nizhoni's "soul-centered" education focuses on what is described as "the integration of the student's spiritual essence." The class list includes cosmology, peace studies, herbology, astrology, exercises in consciousness, and global communication, as well as such traditional courses as English, math, social studies, and science. The high school accepts both boarders and day students and recruits internationally. The middle school begins at age 14. It promotes itself as "a school without violence, fear, or drugs." Nizhoni also teaches younger children and adults, who can sign up for intensives and short courses, including "Spirituality and Life."

## SANTA FE GIRLS' SCHOOL
**301 West Zia Rd.**
**(505) 820-3188**
The only junior high in New Mexico just for girls, Santa Fe Girls' School opened in September 1999 with its first 7th-grade class. The school added 8th grade in the 2000–01 school year. It now has an enrollment of 45 students for grades 6–8. Class size is limited to 15. The school grew from the philosophy that during early adolescence girls thrive in an all-girl environment, where they feel safe to balance personal, academic, and social concerns. The school's mission is to foster intellectual growth and emotional strength in adolescent girls, preparing them for the demands of high school and beyond. In terms of curriculum, the school focuses on building and refining skills needed for success in high school, with an emphasis on multicultural social studies that includes Spanish as a second language. Scholarships are available.

## SANTA FE PREPARATORY SCHOOL
**1101 Camino de la Cruz Blanca**
**(505) 982-1829**
**www.santafeprep.org**
Santa Fe Prep is an independent, nonprofit, coeducational college preparatory day school. It serves 350 students in grades 7 through 12. Established in 1961, the school's 13-acre campus is located

in the eastside historic district in the foothills of the Sangre de Cristo Mountains. The campus was donated by famed architect John Gaw Meem, and what was once his atelier is now the school's outstanding arts facility. Prep offers a rigorous academic program that emphasizes critical reading and writing, while seeking to inspire in students a love of learning. The school offers further opportunities for growth through athletics (including soccer and lacrosse), the arts, and an award-winning community-service program. With a faculty-student ratio of 1–10, students get personalized attention from the faculty, 70 percent of whom hold advanced degrees. An active financial-aid program makes this school increasingly accessible to children from all economic levels. Prep has a full-time college counselor who helps students choose the right school for them. About one-third of graduating seniors are accepted to the top 2 percent of colleges in the country.

Santa Fe has a large network of private schools. At last count, according to the Santa Fe Chamber of Commerce, there were 25 preschools, 19 elementaries, and 14 high schools. Private school enrollment in Santa Fe, and New Mexico, nearly doubles the national average in terms of percentage of children who attend these schools instead of public schools.

## SANTA FE SCHOOL FOR THE ARTS AND SCIENCES
5912 Jaguar Dr.
(505) 438-8585
www.santafeschool.org
This small school (112 students) serves students K–12 and emphasizes involvement in the community through expeditionary learning and a constructively challenging environment. Student–teacher ratio is 5–1. The school is located in Santa Fe's growing southwest side.

## ST. MICHAEL'S HIGH SCHOOL
100 Siringo Rd.
(505) 983-7353
www.stmichaelssf.org

This Catholic school, founded in 1859, offers a traditional college preparatory program and attracts students with an interest in athletics—more than 40 teams compete in 15 separate sports. St. Mike's regularly wins district sports titles and often takes its teams to the state championships. The school also promotes and encourages service projects, a tradition of the international network of Christian Brothers schools. (Please see our Close-up in this chapter for more information.) The high school enrolls about 850 students with a student ratio of 20–1. St. Mike's also offers grades 7 and 8. The academic program is challenging: 98 percent of students go on to higher education. There's usually a waiting list to attend, especially for 7th graders. Adherence to Catholicism is not required.

## THE TUTORIAL SCHOOL
400 Brunn School Rd.
(505) 988-1859
With an enrollment of just 15 students, aged seven to 19, this school is based on a belief that the pursuit of knowledge thrives in an environment "that is free of fear and authority and whatever else interferes with creativity." That means the school also steers away from coercion, reward and punishments, competition, comparison, and unsolicited criticism or evaluation. The school has no hierarchical structures and students and staff members run the school together. Students are not required to attend formal classes or follow a set curriculum. The school advises parents to send their children here only "if you have absolute trust in the ability of children to take charge of their lives and make their own decisions or if you are at least willing to learn to develop that trust." The student-teacher ratio is 6–1.

# CHILD CARE

When it comes to child care, Santa Fe isn't much different from the rest of the country. Especially for infants and the age-three-and-younger crowd, finding high-quality, affordable child care can be harder than finding opening-night seats to the opera. Of course, some families hire nannies to stay with children in their own homes. Some have relatives who care for their kids. But most moms and dads have to look for outside help.

Santa Fe has a wonderful resource, the Division of Early Childhood, Family Studies, and Teacher Education at Santa Fe Community College, which make parents' plight easier. You can reach them at 6401 Richards Ave., (505) 428-1354. The center offers a variety of services and programs, including information and referrals, fact sheets to help parents select good child care, and training programs for people who wish to go into the child-care field (call 505-428-1344 for information). The Center will not recommend one provider over another, but they give parents a place to start.

The regulations for licensing are complex and confusing. Still, licensing offers parents some assurance of quality care. The average rate per child for child care in Santa Fe is roughly $125 a week. Many home day-care providers have waiting lists and do not accept infants.

Besides in-home day care, most parents have two other basic options: commercial child-care centers and preschools. There are a few excellent facilities here, several good ones, and many that are adequate. The Santa Fe Public Schools have a preschool for children with special needs that enrolls a limited number of other children. Some tribal governments offer their own programs, as well. In 2009, the Santa Fe telephone book listed some 40 child-care centers and preschools. Many programs have waiting lists. The National Association for the Education of Young Children accredits high-quality child-care centers and preschools throughout the country. Here's a list of accredited centers in Santa Fe and a few others Santa Fe parents have recommended. Unless otherwise noted, these facilities are open from 7:30 a.m. to 5:30 p.m. five days a week.

# DAY CARE AND PRESCHOOLS

## GARCIA STREET CLUB
569 Garcia St.
(505) 983-9512
The Garcia Street Club offers child care, preschool, and kindergarten for ages three through

six and has served Santa Fe families for more than 50 years. The former residence that houses the school is on the National Register of Historic Places. The year-round operation appeals to parents who work downtown but also attracts children from around the city. The nationally accredited program offers appropriate activities designed to help the child develop as a whole person. Unlike many preschools, Garcia Street Club does not follow the public-schools schedule and does not cancel when the Santa Fe Public Schools declare a snow day. The school is closed only 10 days a year.

## HEAD START
### Flores del Sol–PMS
**5600 Agua Fria St. and other locations**
**(505) 982-4484**
The federal government specifically designed this long-established program to give kids a boost before they start 1st grade. Families who meet low-income requirements can enroll their three-, four-, and five-year-olds, and there is no fee. Ten percent of the children served are kids with special needs. In addition to the programs' educational and developmental activities, children receive a meal and a snack and medical and dental screening. Besides the Agua Fria school, Head Start offers eight other centers in Santa Fe County. The program encourages family involvement, and at least half the Head Start staff are parents of former Head Start children. The staff holds Child Development Associate credentials.

## LA CASA FELIZ
1519 Fifth St.
(505) 982-4896
Santa Fe's weekly newspaper, *Santa Fe Reporter*, voted this as Santa Fe's best child care based on comments from its readers. The school also received the Piñon Award for its work from the nonprofit Santa Fe Community Foundation. It was founded in 1984 and is NAEYC accredited.

La Casa Feliz serves an enrollment of 75, toddlers through age six, with a child-to-staff ratio of 7–1. The school caters to children by observing what each child needs to learn at his or her own pace. The school's organization gives children choices while also offering consistency. Students have an opportunity to learn sign language and Spanish. Special-needs students are integrated into the classrooms. La Casa Feliz is closed for a week during the Christmas holidays and only a week during the summer. Otherwise, the school follows the Santa Fe Public School schedule.

## LA CASITA PRESCHOOL AND KINDERGARTEN
438 Alamo Dr.
(505) 983-2803
www.lacasita.edu

A nonprofit parent co-op school, based on the philosophy of Reggio Emilia in Italy, La Casita caters to children between the ages of three and six. Parents commit time as well as tuition here. They make up the school's board of directors, serve on committees, and get together twice a year to give the building a thorough cleaning. Once a month parents work in the school along with teachers and bring a snack for the class.

For kids, play is essential here and a wide range of opportunities is available. Established in 1971, La Casita serves about 30 children with two teachers and two parents assigned to the morning preschool class and one parent and one teacher in the accredited afternoon kindergarten class. Preschool enrollment is limited to 21, and a maximum of nine children in the kindergarten. Morning and afternoon programs are available; some children are eligible for all-day school, but La Casita is not a day-care center. It has NAEYC accreditation.

## LA COMUNIDAD DE LOS NIÑOS
1121 Alto St.
(505) 820-1604

A collaboration between the city of Santa Fe and Presbyterian Medical Services, this center accepts children ages two through five. With a maximum enrollment of 87, the center offers a 1–4 adult-to-child ratio in its two-year-old program and a 1–6 ratio in the preschool. Besides enjoying a building specifically designed for the child care, La Comunidad offers access to the play yard

from each classroom and gives kids a choice of indoor or outdoor activities throughout the day. Some spaces are reserved for the children of city employees and for low-income families; fees are on a sliding scale. The play-based program incorporates developmentally appropriate early-childhood theory.

## SANTA FE COMMUNITY COLLEGE CHILDCARE
Center and Preschool
6401 Richards Ave.
(505) 438-1344

The college offers infant/toddler care beginning with infants eight weeks old, a program for two-year-olds, and a preschool program, all designed to suit a child's level of development. Each group has its own bright spacious room and access to its own area in a large outdoor play yard. Preference in enrollment goes to SFCC students, and the college reserves about 75 percent of the slots for these kids. The other places are roughly divided between staff/faculty and the general public. There's always a waiting list for infant care. Kindergartners and pre-schoolers thrive at this clean, sunny center on the south side of the campus. Adult-to-child ratio is high here, and the staff is well trained and professional. The college also offers several day-camp options during summer months.

# SPECIAL CHILD-CARE SERVICES

## EARLY CHILDHOOD RESOURCE CENTER AND TOY LENDING CENTER
Santa Fe Community College
6401 Richards Ave.
(505) 428-1612

You'll find a wealth of goodies here! The Toy Lending Center, affectionately known as TLC, has more than 2,000 toys and playthings for infants and children up to kindergarten age and a small selection of toys for school-age children. Families, teachers, and child-care workers may borrow from the collection for free. The resource center offers books, videotapes, films, and slide/tape presentations for teachers and caregivers who work with children. The phone number above will also connect you to the Warm Line, where child development specialists will answer questions about children's behaviors and attitudes and suggest ways to solve problems. All these services are free. The center is open each Wednesday 1 to 5 p.m. It's also open the second Wednesday of each month to 8 p.m. and the second Saturday, 9 a.m. to 1 p.m.

## EMERGENCY CHILD CARE
Santa Fe Community College
6401 Richards Ave.
(505) 428-1610
Students attending Santa Fe Community College and community members with children ages 12 and younger who are in temporary crisis can receive short-term help of up to 100 hours of child care, in some cases twenty-four hours a day, through this program staffed by trained professionals at SFCC. It also offers consultations with child-care specialists and referrals to other agencies to help families dealing with hospitalization, financial crises, and other types of stress.

## LITTLE BODY CHILD CARE
333 Cordova Rd.
(505) 986-0362
www.bodyofsantafe.com/body_lbchildcare
.htm
BODY day spa offers on-site child care in an attractive purpose-built classroom filled with toys and activities next to the bodywork studio. It is professionally staffed with infant-care employees with certification or degrees in Early Childhood Development and nannying experience. BODY offers kids a variety of toys and learning materials drawing on Montessori philosophy. Materials in the classroom focus on body esteem and awareness topics, and activities are movement- and spatially oriented. BODY also offers scheduled child movement classes in the main studio, including yoga and dance (see Kidstuff chapter). Little Body Child Care is open Monday, Wednesday, and Friday 8:30 a.m. to 7:30 p.m., Tuesday and Thursday 8:30 a.m. to 5:30 p.m., Saturday 8:30

a.m. to 1:30 p.m., and Sunday 8:30 a.m. to 1:00 p.m. The center offers specialized infant care for infants of nine months and up, and afterschool programs. You will be required to sign a liability release form. Staff do not administer medications or feed children; however, they will be happy to change your baby with disposable diapers and offer food you leave for your child. Only parents using BODY facilities may take advantage of Little Body Child Care. Parties can be arranged.

## NEW VISTAS EARLY CHILDHOOD SERVICES
1121 Alto St.
(505) 988-3803
www.newvistas.org
This long-established nonprofit agency provides a full scope of services for children from birth to age three who have, or are at risk for, developmental delays. In addition to direct work with some fragile little ones, the program helps their parents, teaching them how to work with children to promote optimal development. Services include parental support; speech, physical, occupational, and family therapy; home-based assistance; therapeutic programs for toddlers; a lending library; and consultation and coordination of other professional services.

## NOSOTROS PROGRAM
at the Early Childhood Development Center
Santa Fe Community College
6401 Richards Ave.
(505) 428-1697
Nosotros helps strengthen the bonds between Moms and Dads and children from birth to age five by teaching the adults skills they need to parent successfully. Using play as a tool for learning, child-development specialists work with families individually or in small groups to help parents learn how to better care for their children physically, psychologically, and emotionally. A licensed therapist may consult with the parents and children if necessary. The city of Santa Fe provides some of the program's funding; Santa Fe Community College offers the space and staff. Participation is free.

# BABYSITTERS AND BABYSITTING SERVICES

For a come-to-the-house teen to watch your little ones, the informal parent-sitter referral network may be your ticket to freedom. Your six-year-old's best friend's oldest sister might be the babysitter of your dreams. Nieces and nephews might know classmates who babysit. Your child's teacher may have some ideas. If your favorite sitter can't come when you need her, ask if she or he has any friends who might be interested. Some parents trade kids with families of friends so Mom and Dad get an occasional break and then return the favor. Ask, ask, and ask again. Take names and phone numbers. Keep notes. Be generous with your help to other parents.

If you run out of leads, consider the youth group at your church as a resource. They might have a list of recommended sitters. Or call Girls Inc., (505) 982-2042, the YMCA, (505) 983-8821, or Santa Fe Community College, (505) 471-8200, and ask if they've done any babysitter training lately. (YMCA memberships are valid from other cities; although the Santa Fe program has no facility of its own, it offers year-round programs and may have drop-in space for children.) Employment services at the local colleges can sometimes give you the names and numbers of college kids who like to babysit.

If you're in Santa Fe on a family trip and need a vacation from the kids, there are resources to help. And don't feel guilty. After all, it's your vacation, too!

Santa Fe has several commercial services that provide babysitters so Mom and Dad can take a break. (Locals can use these services, too.) They include:

## MAGICAL HAPPENINGS BABYSITTING SERVICE AND CHILDREN'S TOURS
**1124 Don Juan**
**(505) 982-9327**
This special babysitting service, which has been in business since 1990, provides child care for guests in hotels or vacation units and to Santa Fe residents. In the summer months they happily arrange day trips and explorations for their young clients and will put together a custom tour for your children. Sometimes you can find a sitter with this agency on short notice, but it's best to make reservations. Fees start at $17 per hour with a four-hour minimum; group rates available.

## SANTA FE KID CONNECTION INC.
**1023 Dunlap**
**(505) 983-6831**
Founded in 1983, Kid Connection offers care for infants and children of all ages. It screens and requires references from all employees and provides sitters for days, evenings, weekends, holidays, and overnight. Advance reservations are strongly recommended. Kid Connection charges for a required minimum number of hours and increases the rate depending on the number of children. They offer an annual membership for residents or frequent visitors, which lowers the hourly rate. Among their clientele are many return visitors who appreciate being able to request a sitter their child knows.

# HEALTH CARE AND WELLNESS

Long before the term "alternative medicine" came into vogue—and we're talking about centuries, not merely decades—New Mexicans were using herbs, potions, massage, and incantations to cure what ailed them. They came not from acupuncturists, aromatherapists, or biofeedback, but from Hispanic *curanderas*, medicine men, and other native healers who have long been an integral part of New Mexican society.

Some of their therapies—Echinacea and goldenseal for colds, for example, or St. John's Wort for depression—have been "discovered" in recent years by traditional Western medicine, much as Columbus "discovered" an America that had been home to Indians for centuries. Those particular remedies are so common these days that you can usually find them in your local Walgreens.

At last count Santa Fe was home to six licensed schools of alternative/natural/holistic healing and massage, many of them with international reputations. Northern New Mexicans seem comfortable with foregoing the customary white coat, black bag, and medical degree of European medicine for less institutionalized healing methods such as acupuncture, Ayurvedics, herbs, and bodywork—no doubt because non-Western doctoring has a formidable history here. Of course, Santa Fe has always been a beacon for alternative lifestyles and ideologies; hence, its nickname, "The City Different." But long before some smart marketing person came up with that sound bite, both the ailing and the healers made northern New Mexico a destination to fulfill their medical destinies.

For some, fulfillment may come in more conventional settings such as hospitals and doctors' offices. While Santa Fe has only one hospital—Christus St. Vincent Regional Medical Center—there are a number of medical centers and clinics in town as well as a healthy list of M.D.s from which to choose, whether you're looking for a general practitioner or a specialist. And choice is certainly the operative word. St. Vincent has a number of publications that rate New Mexico physicians, including one put out by Ralph Nader's Public Citizen called *Questionable Doctors: State Listing for New Mexico* and *The Best Doctors in America: Central Region,* by Steven W. Naifeh. (For more information about St. Vincent's medical library, see the entry for Christus St. Vincent Regional Medical Center.) Or you can pick your doctor the old-fashioned way—by word of mouth. If you can't wait for an appointment, you can get same-day medical care at a number of locations, including Christus St. Vincent, Lovelace Health Systems, and La Familia Medical Center; see the write-ups in this chapter for more information. In the meantime, here are a few places to start:

## ALTERNATIVE HEALTH CARE

**BODY**
333 Cordova Rd.
(505) 986-0362
www.bodyofsantafe.com

This Santa Fe day spa opened in July 2004. The vision of owner Lorin Parrish, who founded and directed Santa Fe's top-rated New Mexico Academy of Healing Arts, BODY is a completely new kind of bodywork center. Its aim? To be an affordable community gathering place for those interested in wellness. BODYSpa offers Swedish massage, Craniosacral Therapy, Somatic Polarity, Orthobionomy, Thai Massage, Rolfing, Chair Massage, and Acupuncture, as well as facials and body scrubs using BODY's own formulations. BODY also features a state-of-the-art movement studio with several unique offerings, including yoga classes for all ages. Other classes and workshops include Nia dance and meditation weekend intensives. Evening events have included kirtan chanting by award-winning musicians such as Jai Uttal and Shantala, as well as multi-instrument Gong Baths. Showers are available for an extra fee. Child-care specialists in early childhood education staff the Little Body Child Care center (see entry in our Education and Child Care chapter) six days a week. BODY carries a full line of organic cotton workout clothing; CDs; natural candles; books on health care; massage lotions and potions; and bodywork tables, linens, and accessories. Recently, BODY cafe, the best place in Santa Fe to find raw food meals, sweets, and hors d'oeuvres, has expanded into an attractive space and offers entertainment in the evenings.

## GRD HEALTH CLINIC
1505 Llano St.
(505) 984-3034
GRD is a holistic healing clinic, which means it considers the whole system rather than just the part that hurts. Run by members of Espanola's huge Sikh community, it is primarily a chiropractic clinic but also offers therapeutic massage, colonics, raw food diets, and other regimes. All practitioners are licensed or board certified. GRD is open Monday, Wednesday, and Friday 9 a.m. to 6 p.m. and Saturday 9 a.m. to noon.

## HYPNOTHERAPY ACADEMY OF AMERICA
509 Camino de los Marquez, Suite 1
(505) 983-1515, (877) 983-1515
www.hypnosisacademy.com
This school, state approved and nationally certified by the American Council of Hypnotist Examiners, offers classes for hypnotism certification and continuing-education programs. Among the classes are fundamentals of hypnotism, healing

and pain management, preparation for childbirth with hypnotherapy, and how to cure insomnia with hypnotherapy. Classes are offered from beginning levels to master classes. The school, established in 1988, hosts free introductory seminars for people who are curious about hypnosis or interested in hypnotism as a career, which makes a good way of learning how the treatment works. Marriage and family therapists, counselors, and others may receive continuing-education credits for classes in hypnosis and related areas.

## OJO CALIENTE MINERAL SPRINGS
50 Los Baños Rd. (Highway 285)
(505) 583-2233, (800) 222-9162
www.ojocalientespa.com
Though located about 50 miles north of Santa Fe, where it straddles the Río Arriba and Taos County lines, Ojo Caliente Mineral Springs are close enough—and special enough—to warrant a mention in this chapter.

Named by 16th-century explorer Cabeza de Vaca, Ojo Caliente ("Hot Spring") is the only spa in the world with its particular combination of five naturally hot, bubbling mineral springs, flowing from geothermal wells deep beneath the earth. Many people "take the waters" for their purported therapeutic value, others for the sheer pleasure and relaxation.

Ojo Caliente's 113-degree arsenic spring is thought to be the only one outside of Baden-Baden, Germany. In trace amounts, arsenic is supposed to relieve arthritis, rheumatism, stomach ulcers, burns, eczema, and a host of other complaints. The spa also has an iron spring, which comes out of the ground at 109 degrees Fahrenheit into a large pool used for a hot plunge that reportedly rejuvenates the blood. The lithia, soda, and sodium springs are primarily for drinking to heal a variety of symptoms, from depression and sluggish kidneys to excess gas.

One of the oldest health spas in North America, Ojo Caliente was once considered a sacred spot by ancient Tewa Pueblo Indians who lived on a mesa above the present village. (You can visit the old Pueblo on special Sunday tours in summer.) Today the spa is spread out over approximately 1,000 hilly, river-lined acres in the Española Valley. The waters are piped into various pools and tubs, public and private. The spa offers other services, such as therapeutic massage, herbal wraps, facials, and salt rubs. The grounds support a quaint old adobe hotel and cottages whose rooms have no showers; guests use the public bathhouse. Two luxury houses now have showers and tubs. Ojo Caliente is open year-round, seven days a week—from 8 a.m. to 9 p.m. Sunday through Thursday and to 10 p.m. on Friday and Saturday.

## TEN THOUSAND WAVES JAPANESE HEALTH SPA

3451 Hyde Park Rd.
(505) 982-9304
www.tenthousandwaves.com

Located in the mountains, Ten Thousand Waves is not just a spa, it's an experience that bathes your every sense. To get to the tubs, you pass rock sculptures and copious hanging plants and climb a few steps that form a bridge over an indoor stream where you might catch sight of a large orange koi or two. In the lobby you collect your kimono and keys and head to the dressing rooms, pleasantly fragrant with the citrus scent of Yuzu, a vegetable-based lotion the spa puts out for clients to use after a soak, a massage, or both. Beforehand, however, you're expected to be clean and lotion free. Be sure to grab one of the towels you'll find stacked neatly next to a bin of rubber zori on your way to the shower. Freshly showered and kimono-clad, you'll make your way to one of nine chlorine-free tubs. You can spend the entire day in the outdoor, coed public tub, which is clothing optional until 8:15 p.m., or the women's tub, which is fenced but open to the skies. Some are outfitted with a sauna, others with a steam room, and one even has a waterfall.

Ten Thousand Waves has more than 100 bodyworkers on its roster, all of them trained in Swedish and deep-tissue massage. Many are also skilled in shiatsu, reflexology, acupressure, Trager, Reiki, Thai, Alexander Technique, craniosacral therapy, Watsu . . . the list goes on. Or you might want to indulge in a "spa treatment," such as an herbal wrap, salt glow, aromatherapy massage, or Japanese hot stone massage. It's best to schedule weekday massages a couple of days in advance. Call at least a week ahead if you want your massage on the weekend. Ten Thousand Waves opens at 10:15 a.m. every day except Thursday, when it doesn't open until 4 p.m. In the summer, it opens at 9:15 a.m. and closes at 10:30 p.m. In winter the spa closes an hour earlier. Except during the peak season, from mid-July to mid-September, locals get an across-the-board discount of 20 percent. They must present a New Mexico driver's license or other state identification.

# STUDENT CLINICS

## NEW MEXICO ACADEMY OF HEALING ARTS

501 Franklin Ave.
(505) 982-6271 (office)
(505) 982-1001 (clinic)
www.nmhealingarts.org

Founded in 1981, the New Mexico Academy of Healing Arts offers certification programs in both massage and polarity. The academy takes a holistic approach to education and uses energy and conscious touch as a foundation. About 70 percent of the enrollment comes from outside New Mexico. For their massage therapy certification, students choose programs up to 10 months in length, learning anatomy and physiology, aromatherapy, and communication skills and ethics. The academy's foundation is Swedish massage and intuitive touch, though it also teaches other forms of bodywork, including sports massage; craniosacral therapy, which aids circulation of cerebrospinal fluid along the spinal pathway; orthobionomy, which relies on movement to re-align the body for relief of acute or chronic pain, and shiatsu, a form of Oriental body work working with the body's energetic meridians through focused touch. Polarity therapy, a comprehensive health-care system created by Dr. Randolph Stone, draws upon Ayurvedic and Chinese traditions as well as modern physics. Students study to become Registered Polarity Practitioners or Associated Polarity Practitioners and can enroll in dual massage and Polarity certification programs. The public may sample the school's "wares" at a student clinic open Thursday through Sunday. Hours will vary depending on the time of year. Call ahead for an appointment.

## SCHERER INSTITUTE OF NATURAL HEALING
1091 A Siler Rd.
(505) 982-8398
www.shererinstitute.com
Scherer Institute of Natural Healing opened in 1979 as Dr. Jay Scherer's Academy of Natural Healing. In addition to Swedish massage, the school incorporates aromatherapy, herbology, homeopathy, shiatsu (Japanese pressure-point massage), and massage for people with cancer into its curriculum. Founder Jay Scherer was a naturopathic doctor who died at age 83 in 1990, six years after being named one of Santa Fe's "Living Treasures." The Scherer Institute holds a couple of two-month student clinics a year where the public can get an hourlong nurturing Swedish massage—the school's specialty. The massage clinic is part of the institute's internship program, which requires students halfway through the six-month program to perform 30 massages under supervision. The clinics are ongoing. Call for an appointment.

## SOUTHWEST ACUPUNCTURE COLLEGE
1622 Galisteo
(505) 438-8880
www.acupuncturecollege.edu
Operating from Santa Fe, Albuquerque, and Boulder, Colorado, campuses, Southwest Acupuncture College offers a Master's of Science in Oriental Medicine with extensive national accreditation. Enrollment is open to students age 20 and older who have successfully completed two years of general education at the college level. According to the school's guidelines, they must also possess the "personal credentials and intellectual skills" to obtain admission. The academic program consists of more than 2,800 hours of training in the five branches of classical Oriental medicine: acupuncture, herbal medicine, physical therapy, nutrition, and exercise/breathing therapy.

Since its inception in 1980, the for-profit college reports that its graduates have achieved an unsurpassed passage rate on all state and national exams. The preponderance of the curriculum takes a hands-on and clinical approach. Students locate acupuncture points, practice techniques, develop diagnoses and treatment plans, prepare herbal formulas, and observe and treat patients. In addition to the master's program, the college offers continuing-education classes in specialty topics, seminars with international experts, and externships in China. To help students become proficient, the school operates an active low-cost teaching clinic by appointment. Call for hours and other details.

## SOUTHWESTERN COUNSELING CENTER AT SOUTHWESTERN COLLEGE
1628 St. Michael's Dr.
(505) 471-8575
www.swc.edu
Class offerings in counseling and art therapy bring students to this renowned small college on the southwest side of Santa Fe. The college has an accredited two-year residential program as well as other options for full-time, part-time, evening, and weekend study. In its literature the college describes its "transformational approach" to education and a style of teaching that is person-centered, holistic, experiential, reflective, and ecological. The school traces the roots of the transformational approach to Ralph Waldo Emerson, John Dewey, and Carl Jung. The college was dedicated in 1976 and began its programs in 1979. Certificate programs are offered in grief counseling, school counseling, action methods, and art therapy. A low-cost counseling center is available to the public.

Southwestern Counseling Center is a student clinic under the auspices of Southwestern College. Founded in 1976, the college is an accredited institution that offers master's degrees in spiritually oriented counseling and art therapy. It is located near Airport Road on Santa Fe's south side. The clinic, located off-campus on St. Michael's Drive, has served the community here for 18 years with low-cost and free counseling services for individuals, couples, families, and groups. Clinicians are second-year students working under the supervision of licensed professionals. The clinic charges on a sliding-fee scale. Call ahead for an appointment.

## TRADITIONAL WESTERN MEDICINE

### CHRISTUS ST. VINCENT'S REGIONAL MEDICAL CENTER
St. Michael's Drive
(505) 983-3361
www.stvin.org

Christus St. Vincent is the regional medical center for northern New Mexico and the largest medical facility between Albuquerque and Pueblo, Colorado. It's a nonprofit, nonsectarian hospital with 268 beds, around 300 staff physicians representing 22 medical specialties, and a nursing staff of more than 400. With close to 1,300 employees, the hospital is also Santa Fe's largest private employer.

Established in 1865 by Sisters of Charity of Cincinnati, Ohio, St. Vincent was New Mexico's first hospital. It began its days in an old adobe building next to St. Francis Cathedral in downtown Santa Fe. The Sisters ran the hospital for more than a century, moving it three times before turning it over to a community-based board of trustees in 1973. In 1977 it moved to its current location on St. Michael's Drive. Today, aside from the Indian Health Hospital, St. Vincent remains the only hospital in Santa Fe, and while four smaller local hospitals also serve this region, many residents and physicians from those areas come to St. Vincent for more specialized care. In addition to the usual departments, St. Vincent has a pain clinic, a sleep disorders clinic, comprehensive cancer services, and the second-busiest Level III trauma center in the state.

The emergency room and adjacent FirstCARE unit treat more than 52,000 patients annually, making it the second-busiest acute-care facility in New Mexico after University Hospital in Albuquerque. FirstCARE is open for walk-ins from 9 a.m. to 9 p.m. The emergency room is open

twenty-four hours. In addition, more than 5,500 scheduled outpatient surgeries are performed annually. St. Vincent offers a number of support groups. It is particularly well known for its cancer care. Classes, such as yoga, meditation and contemplative care, and breast cancer support for cancer patients and caregiver support for careers, are held in the Cancer Support Center.

ⓘ One out of every 26 Santa Feans does healing work. But an estimated 20 to 25 percent of Santa Fe County's population is uninsured and 17 percent of Santa Fe's children live in poverty. A Community Access Program strives to improve healthcare availability for the uninsured. Santa Fe Project Access was started by local physicians to organize and improve low-cost care.

### LA FAMILIA MEDICAL CENTER
1035 Alto St. (downtown)
(505) 982-4425 ext. 2145
Caja del Oro Grant Rd. (southside)
(505) 438-3195
www.lafamiliasf.org

La Familia truly is a community health center. The clinics provide primary medical care from obstetrics to geriatrics. The nonprofit medical center is the primary deliverer of babies in the community. Both locations have dental clinics that take Medicaid patients. Between them, the two clinics employ 41 medical personnel, including doctors, family nurse practitioners, nurses, and lab personnel; nine are on the dental staff. La Familia's health providers recognize the validity of alternative medicine and respect its cultural importance, particularly to Hispanic and Native American patients. They often incorporate alternative therapies into patients' health-care plans, referring them outside if La Familia doesn't offer a particular treatment.

La Familia started in 1972 as a little neighborhood clinic in a building it shared with a day-care center on Santa Fe's west side. Today it operates two full-time, stand-alone medical centers. It leases each building from the city of Santa Fe for

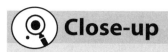 **Close-up**

## Santa Fe Stands Out in AIDS/HIV Care

For a city of only 63,000 people, Santa Fe has an extensive network of AIDS/HIV health services and support groups. That's largely due to efforts by, and in response to, the city's sizable gay population—a segment of the community that in Santa Fe, as elsewhere, has been hit particularly hard by the AIDS epidemic.

Many gays and lesbians move to Santa Fe because of its reputation for welcoming people who, whatever their orientation, might not be welcome elsewhere. This isn't a new phenomenon; homosexuals have been coming here since the 1920s, during the city's heyday as an art colony. Indeed, Santa Fe is a gay-friendly town. Its city council has an openly gay member; its mayors have offered a supportive voice for the city's homosexual population, many of them speaking at the annual Santa Fe Lesbian, Gay & Bi Pride Parade; and the general population has traditionally been nonjudgmental and accepting.

Starting in the 1980s, however, gay men began coming to Santa Fe in droves for another reason—to die. They made the pilgrimage so that they could succumb to AIDS in a beautiful, mystical place that didn't condemn them for who they were or for the illness they contracted. In a small town like Santa Fe, AIDS touches everybody—with horror, at first, then fear, and finally compassion, especially for those who've died alone because no support systems existed.

Even before people understood that AIDS was an equal-opportunity killer—when the disease appeared to be uniquely the scourge of gay men, who have been a significant and visible presence in Santa Fe—both the city and state rallied with aggressive treatment and substantial public funding to provide a host of public services. As AIDS widened its net, so did Santa Fe's health community, creating an enviable network of publicly funded support and cutting-edge AIDS treatment, which has turned Santa Fe into a Lourdes for those afflicted with AIDS or HIV-related illnesses. Lots of support comes from Santa Fe's private sector, too—particularly from the arts community, which has lost so much talent and friendship to AIDS.

Much of the private funding comes from Santa Fe's numerous fund-raisers throughout the year, including the AID and Comfort Gala, an annual party at the elegant Eldorado Hotel with proceeds helping to cover HIV-related bills. These fund-raisers are organized by Southwest CAR. (Comprehensive AIDS Treatment, Research and Education) Center, a specialty AIDS/HIV clinic providing some of the most comprehensive care in New Mexico. Located at 649 Harkle Rd., Suite E, the clinic offers under one roof virtually every service someone with AIDS or an HIV-related illness might need. In addition to state-of-the-art medical care, including access to clinical trials, Southwest CARE. Center works with the state to provide a full range of practical and emotional support services for its clients. That might include finding a dentist who will treat an HIV-infected person; making referrals for alternative medical treatment; coordinating home or hospice care; finding insurance or emergency funding for patients in need; or matching up trained volunteers to visit isolated AIDS patients or drive them to doctor's appointments. Southwest CARE. offers medical treatment on a sliding scale. Free anonymous HIV testing is offered on Monday nights between 5:30 and 7 p.m. The nonprofit center is open Monday through Friday from 8 a.m. to 5 p.m. but there are staffers on call 24 hours a day, 7 days a week for emergencies. Locally, call (505) 989-8200. For out-of-town callers, Southwest C.A.R.E. Center also has a toll-free line at (888) 320-8200. You can also find them online at www.southwestcare.org.

It's precisely these sorts of comprehensive and compassionate services that draw people with AIDS or the HIV infection to Santa Fe. But unlike in the recent past, they're arriving with some hope. Combination therapy, used aggressively in Santa Fe long before it became de rigueur throughout the nation, has prolonged the lives of many an AIDS sufferer, some of whom are returning to the large urban areas they fled a few years earlier.

$1 a year. At last count the center had 9,800 registered patients. The majority—53 percent—is uninsured, relying either on the county indigent fund or La Familia's sliding-fee scale. A number of patients who can afford to go elsewhere choose La Familia for its quality comprehensive health care. The clinics ask for a minimum payment, though they will provide services to anyone who walks in their doors, regardless of ability to pay. They accept all forms of insurance and contract with HMOs to provide medical care for their patients. La Familia also operates a number of outstanding community outreach programs, including "Promotoras," which promotes community health education through lay advisors. Promotoras provide information on such topics as prenatal care, diabetes, child immunization, asthma, and breast-feeding, including teaching working mothers how to pump their breast milk to leave with their children's caregiver.

Both clinics are open from 8 a.m. to 5 p.m. Monday to Friday, until 6 p.m. on the South Side; closed the first Wednesday morning of each month. The centers accept walk-in patients but ask that you try to call ahead so the staff can fit you into the best available appointment slot or, if one isn't available, send you to Christus St. Vincent Regional Medical Center.

## PRESBYTERIAN MEDICAL SERVICES
1422 Paseo de Peralta
(505) 986-8299
www.quasar.pmsnet.org

Presbyterian Medical Services is the primary provider of mental health and counseling services in Santa Fe County. A nonprofit corporation, its mission is to furnish high-quality, affordable medical, dental, mental health, hospice, retirement, and other human services throughout the Southwest, particularly to Hispanic and Native American communities. PMS is the successor to the Presbyterian Church's medical mission to the Southwest, which began in 1901. When the church could no longer provide financial support, PMS incorporated in 1969 to carry on the work. Although it's an independent organization, it maintains its ties to the church through

a covenant with the Presbytery of Santa Fe and the Synod of the Southwest. PMS employs about 1,000 people in 82 program sites in 38 communities, including primary health-care centers and agencies; comprehensive mental health-care programs; home health-care and hospice programs; nursing homes; developmental disabilities programs for children and adults; substance abuse treatment; Head Start programs; AIDS and other health education and counseling; and a pharmacy consulting service. PMS also offers the following services:

Traumatic Brain Injury Program, 2960 Rodeo Park Dr. West, (505) 986-9633, provides case management for individuals with traumatic brain injury by assisting clients and their families in reintegrating into the community. At the same address, Crisis Response of Santa Fe, (505) 820-1440 (office), (505) 820-6333 (hotline), is a suicide prevention program with a telephone hotline and mobile crisis team, both available twenty-four hours a day, seven days a week in Santa Fe County. Volunteers trained in short-term telephone crisis intervention operate the hotline to offer immediate suicide counseling as well as information and referrals. The mobile crisis team comprises professionals who respond to suicide, drug/alcohol abuse, and psychiatric emergencies.

The Hospice Center, 1400 Chama St., (505) 988-1477, (800) 880-8001, established in 1991, provides at-home care for people with terminal illnesses and their families. Its registered nurses are specialists in pain and symptom control and are on call twenty-four hours a day. The center offers regularly scheduled nursing visits; volunteer support services for patients and their families; home health aide services for personal care; social work visits for counseling; pastoral counseling and referral; physical, occupational, and speech therapy; bereavement services; medication; and medical treatment, equipment, and supplies. The center offers support for individuals and groups, including schools or businesses, facing life-threatening illness or experiencing grief or loss.

Ortíz Mountain Health Center, 06B Main St., Cerrillos, (505) 471-6266, open since 1995, is

## Emergency Numbers

**Local**

| | |
|---|---|
| AIDS Hotline | (800) 545–AIDS (2437) |
| Domestic Violence Twenty-Four-Hour Hotline | (800) 773-3645 |
| Environmental Emergency (after hours) | (505) 827-9329 |
| Esperanza Shelter for Battered Families | (505) 473-5200 or (505) 474-5536 |
| Hantavirus Hotline | (800) 879-3421 |
| Police, Fire, Ambulance | 911 |
| Rape Crisis Center Hotline | (800) 721-RAPE or (505) 988-1951 |
| Christus St. Vincent Regional Medical Center | (505) 983-3361 |
| Suicide Intervention Project | (505) 820-1066 |
| Youth Shelter and Family Services | (505) 983-0586 |

**National**

| | |
|---|---|
| Alcohol and Drug Abuse Hotline | (800) 390-4056 |
| Cancer Information | (800) 422-6237 |
| Depression and Anxiety Hotline | (800) 422-HOPE |
| Missing Children Hotline | (800) 843-5678 |
| National Runaway Switchboard | (800) 621-4000 |
| National Youth Crisis Hotline | (800) 442-4673 |
| Poison Control | (800) 662-9866 |
| Suicide Intervention Project | (800) 273-8255 |

a three-day-a-week primary health-care clinic located in Cerrillos, New Mexico, about 20 miles southwest of Santa Fe. The center provides diagnostic and treatment services, limited pharmacy and laboratory services, and prenatal and perinatal care and treatment of minor emergencies. It coordinates with health-care providers in Santa Fe for referral and specialty care.

PMS Home Care, 1400 Chama St., (505) 988-4156, (800) 880-8001, provides comprehensive home-care services to residents of Santa Fe County with an emphasis on rehabilitation. Licensed by both Medicaid and Medicare, it provides skilled nursing, home health aides, physical therapy, occupational therapy, speech pathology, and medical social services. The staff works with physicians, hospitals, rehabilitation centers, nursing homes, and medical equipment suppliers to make a smooth transition to home health care.

Santa Fe Community Guidance Center, 2960 Rodeo Park Dr. West, (505) 986-9633, is a mental-health outpatient facility for day treatment; case management; and supported living and employment. The program provides rehabilitation for the long-term mentally ill through its Spirit Club, (505) 986-8827, which focuses on social, recreational, and vocational skills. Santa Fe Community Guidance Center, (505) 982-8899, founded as a community coalition of organizations and individuals, is primarily an educational organization that aims to increase community awareness about substance abuse and prevention and ensure the existence of treatment and recovery options. Among the programs it has initiated are life-skills training, including parenting; special training for clergy; and a free/low-cost small business employee assistance program to help workers cope with marriage and family issues, alcohol and drug abuse, gambling, depression, or financial troubles.

## WOMEN'S HEALTH SERVICES FAMILY CARE AND COUNSELING CENTER
901 West Alameda
(505) 988-8869
www.womenshealthsantafe.org

Located in Solana Center just west of St. Francis Drive, Women's Health Services is a primary-care health facility with an extensive family practice that includes obstetric, gynecological, and family-planning services; mental-health care; therapeutic massage; acupuncture; and limited laboratory work. Its staff includes physicians, nurse practitioners, and master's level mental-health practitioners, all of whom provide services on a sliding-fee scale. The center also has several grant programs to lessen the financial burden on low-income and uninsured patients. Although Women's Health Services has no pediatricians on staff, a good many of its patients are children, while 10 to 15 percent are men, the center's name notwithstanding. Women's Health Services opened in 1973 as a self-health education resource center for women. A progeny of the feminist self-help movement, the clinic's initial raison d'être was to give women more information to take better care of themselves. Within a couple of years, it began to provide services and, by the late 1970s, became a full-fledged medical clinic staffed by volunteers. It's only in the last decade that staff doctors, nurses, and therapists have been on full salary. Although the clinic is geared toward low-income and uninsured patients, its waiting room is a true cross-section of Santa Fe. Many women who could afford to go elsewhere choose Women's Health Services because of its reputation for excellent health care and for providing patients with information and suggestions about complementary therapies, including such alternatives as acupuncture, herbology, and homeopathy. Open Monday through Friday from 8 a.m. to 5:30 p.m., the center operates by appointment only. Walk-ins will be sent to St. Vincent or Lovelace.

# MEDIA

S anta Fe might be small in population, but it's huge in diversity. One need only spend a few hours nursing a latte at Downtown Subscription, 376 Garcia St., (505) 983-3085 (see our Restaurants chapter) to witness firsthand the fascinating mix of residents—and visitors, too—that makes Santa Fe "The City Different."

It's not just what the habitués are drinking or wearing that gives them away; it's also whatever magazine or newspaper they happen to be thumbing through—and there are plenty to choose from at Downtown Subscription. The newsstand/cafe offers up to 1,000 periodical titles from around the world and around the corner.

It's what comes from around the corner that interests us here. For such a small metropolis—remember, only 72,000 people call this city home—Santa Fe offers a surprisingly wide variety of homegrown publications to suit almost any taste, lifestyle, or political persuasion. Many of them, of course, continue to be hard hit by plummeting circulation as readers increasingly get up-to-date news from electronic media and advertisers follow them. After nine decades, the Albuquerque *Tribune* ceased publication in 2008, and both the Santa Fe *New Mexican* and Albuquerque *Journal* have gone through layoffs and reduced special sections of their newspapers. Also included in this chapter are several Albuquerque publications that have enough of a following in Santa Fe to merit mention.

## DAILIES

### ALBUQUERQUE *JOURNAL*
**7777 Jefferson St. NE, Albuquerque**
**(505) 823-7777**
**www.abqjournal.com**
Founded in 1880, the Albuquerque *Journal* takes great pride in being part of an ever-shrinking pool of independently owned American dailies. The front page proclaims in bold white-on-blue that the paper is "home-owned and home-operated." Home is Journal Center, an industrial park owned by Journal publisher Thompson H. Lang. Lang rose to the helm of the family-owned *Journal* in 1971 with the death of his father, C. Thompson Lang. As a seven-day-a-week morning paper with statewide circulation, the *Journal* considers itself New Mexico's newspaper of record and concentrates heavily on state and local government. While stories are generally accurate and balanced, they tend to be rather dry and heavily edited. The Albuquerque *Journal* is unquestionably the dominant news voice in its hometown

and throughout New Mexico, with a daily circulation of 102,902.

*Journal* subscribers get a variety of special sections throughout the week including Thursday's "Go!" for outdoors and recreation, a Friday entertainment section called "Venue," "Wheels" on Saturday, and a Sunday paper fat with ads.

### JOURNAL NORTH
**328 Galisteo St.**
**(505) 988-8881**
**www.journalnorth.com**
*Journal North*—a zoned edition of New Mexico's largest and most widely read newspaper, the Albuquerque Journal—is the primary competitor for daily news coverage in Santa Fe and northern New Mexico against the hometown paper, the Santa Fe *New Mexican*. While parochial Santa Feans will always consider it "the other paper," *Journal North* certainly gives the *New Mexican* a run for its money with even-handed, tightly edited, if somewhat dry, coverage of local government and breaking news.

In contrast to the *New Mexican* and especially to the heretofore unapologetically liberal weekly, the Santa Fe *Reporter* (see the entry under our Weeklies section), Journal North tends to be conservative in its editorial policy as well as its style, though somewhat less so on both counts than its parent publication, the Albuquerque Journal.

Journal North appears seven days a week wrapped around the Albuquerque *Journal.* Its northern New Mexico circulation hovers around 14,000 during the week. Just six to eight pages long, *Journal North* often prompts readers to wonder why they seem to get so much news from such a small section. It's because Journal North is wall-to-wall news stories with only a smattering of display ads in between. Santa Fe classified ads appear in the main paper. Despite being a fixture in Santa Fe since the early 1980s, *Journal North* can't shake its reputation as an interloper. That's due, in part, to the section's relative youth compared to the *New Mexican.* Not only can't the Journal North claim to be a hometown paper but its deadlines are far earlier than the *New Mexican's*—sometimes by as much as two-and-a-half hours. This puts *Journal North* at a distinct disadvantage in the Santa Fe news war. It loses nearly every time to the *New Mexican* on late-breaking stories. As a relative newcomer, *Journal North* is also often left in the dust on insider news. For local political gossip, the inside scoop, the "Hey, Martha" stories, most Santa Feans will tell you they rely on the *New Mexican.*

### THE SANTA FE NEW MEXICAN
**202 East Marcy St.**
**(505) 983-3303**
**www.sfnewmexican.com**
Founded in 1849, Santa Fe's only local daily boasts on its masthead that it's "The West's Oldest Newspaper." But the *New Mexican,* as Santa Feans call it, stands out for another reason: It's one of a steadily declining number of American newspapers that have remained independently owned and operated—though only by the skin of its journalistic teeth.

In 1975, then-publisher Robert McKinney sold the Santa Fe *New Mexican* to Gannett, the largest newspaper chain in the United States. Less than three years later, however, McKinney sued Gannett for breach of contract. McKinney, a Virginia resident who maintained a hacienda in northern Santa Fe County until his death in 2001, claimed Gannett reneged on its agreement to let him retain editorial and operational control of the *New Mexican.* A jury agreed and, in July 1980, a federal judge ordered Gannett to return the newspaper to McKinney, a one-time assistant secretary of the interior and a former ambassador to Switzerland.

Although it took several years for the *New Mexican* to gain back readership it lost during Gannett's brief reign, the newspaper has once again become a staple—and a favorite target—of locals. Indeed, Santa Feans have a love-hate relationship with the *New Mexican.* Readers, especially local politicians, love to hate the newspaper for its "gotcha" articles, its no-holds-barred editorials, and its frequent editing errors. But—and it's a big "but"—the *New Mexican* is widely read in Santa Fe, whose slightly left-of-center politics and ideology jibe with the newspaper's editorial leaning. The daily circulation rate—which includes paid subscriptions and street sales—is 25,249. It's easy to find the paper, just look for the *New Mexican's* colorful street vendors at intersections throughout the city between the early morning hours and noon.

Pasatiempo, the newspaper's Friday arts and entertainment section, alone is worth the subscription price. Pasatiempo ("pastime" in Spanish) contains comprehensive, informative, and entertaining sections on movies, music, theater, art, dance, and all other manner of diversion in and around Santa Fe for the upcoming week. It features primarily local reviewers who are knowledgeable in their fields and give the skinny on what's good and what's not.

Other weekly sections include Monday's "El Nuevo Mexicano," an all-Spanish news feature page; "Taste," the Wednesday food section; "Outdoors" on Thursday; Saturday's "Teen Page"; and "¿Que Pasa?," a day-by-day calendar of free and nonprofit events and meetings that accompanies the usual array of Sunday sections. The *Sunday*

*New Mexican* is a must-have for jobs and rentals in the Santa Fe area. *NOTE:* these can also be viewed online, albeit less easily.

# WEEKLIES

## SANTA FE REPORTER
**132 East Marcy St.**
**(505) 988-5541**
**www.sfreporter.com**

No doubt, the first issue of the Santa Fe *Reporter* on June 26, 1974, gave the local hometown daily, the Santa Fe *New Mexican,* the willies. Grown fat and lazy from lack of any real competition, the *Reporter*'s predecessor, the Santa Fe *News,* was primarily a "shopper" and didn't pose much of a threat. Now, the *New Mexican* had to deal with the new kid on the block, who was lean and hungry. Founding publishers Dick McCord, a former *Newsday* reporter, and Laurel Knowles, a writer for *Women's Wear Daily,* were ready to kick butt. And kick butt they did, in the very first issue, with a scoop on commercial flights between Santa Fe and Denver. A mere weekly, and a free one at that, over the next 15 years, the *Reporter* would beat the *New Mexican* on other occasions on local news and investigative stories, garnering journalism awards in the process.

Under its second publisher—Rockefeller heiress Hope Aldrich, a former *Newsday* reporter and a staff writer for the *Reporter* who bought the paper in 1988—the alternative weekly focused on issue reporting, publishing the occasional investigative pieces.

In 1997 Aldrich sold the newspaper to the owners of an alternative weekly in the Willamette Valley of Oregon. For the first time in its 24-year history, the *Reporter* was in the hands of absentee owners. The new publishers lived up to their promise to put greater emphasis on art coverage. The current staff is young and smart and in your face. The paper is not adverse to shocking readers with its subject matter, language, and graphics as well as down-and-dirty investigative journalism. It provokes engagement, not a bad thing in a city that is so accepting it easily becomes apathetic. The paper is a popular advertising vehicle for

businesses, both mainstream and alternative. It has an estimated circulation of 60,000 a week.

## THRIFTY NICKEL
**2641½ Cerrillos Rd.**
**(505) 473-4111, (800) 382-6330**

This free weekly is a favorite among Santa Fe's workday lunch crowd, especially lone diners who thumb through it while downing green chile cheeseburgers at neighborhood joints all over town. The *Thrifty Nickel* is a hefty little tabloid with 24 to 32 pages chock-full of mostly local ads trying to sell everything from cockatiels to used equipment from nearby Los Alamos National Laboratory (the folks who brought you "The Bomb"). Every once in a while, you'll happen across an ad praising St. Jude or one of the other saints—just another reminder of Santa Fe's Catholic roots.

In addition to merchandise and garage sales, the *Thrifty Nickel* advertises real estate, both sales and rentals; local and national jobs; and, of course, vehicles—lots of them. It also contains a one-page listing of local businesses and services. *Thrifty Nickel* distributes 20,000 copies a week to racks throughout Santa Fe County and parts of neighboring Río Arriba and San Miguel Counties.

## WEEKLY ALIBI
**2118 Central Ave. SE, #151**
**Albuquerque**
**(505) 346-0660**
**www.alibi.com**

The *Weekly Alibi,* formerly *NuCity,* is a free alternative weekly that emphasizes Albuquerque politics, culture, and entertainment but isn't afraid to venture into Santa Fe, too. The tabloid appeals to Santa Feans because of its irreverence and strong counterculture voice as well as its in-depth coverage of art and music. It also contains an extensive "personals" section toward the back with some truly off-the-wall ads that make for great reading even if you're not in the market. The freebie has a circulation of 46,492 and is available at newsstands, news racks, coffee shops, bookstores, and other locations throughout metro Albuquerque and Santa Fe.

# MONTHLIES

## LOCALFLAVOR
535 Cerrillos Rd.
(505) 988-7560
www.localflavormagazine.com

In a town as obsessed with food as Santa Fe, it's appropriate that there be intelligent, well-written newspapers here devoted to New Mexican fare and other types of cuisine. localflavor fills that niche, "explor(ing) the world of food and wine from farm to plate." The oversized color newspaper publishes 10 times a year and is filled with articles and photos profiling chefs throughout New Mexico, though it tends to focus on Santa Fe and Albuquerque. localflavor also features first-person prose on food and cooking, recipes, cooking techniques, a wine section, and dispatches from around the state. localflavor distributes 30,000 copies free at newsstands and street boxes.

## SANTA FE MONTHLY
11 Bonito Ct.
(505) 466-4661
www.sunmonthly.com

Although it is produced in Eldorado, a semirural development southeast of Santa Fe, this free black-and-white monthly is distributed widely throughout the area. Founded in 1986 as the Eldorado Sun by editor/copublisher Gershon Siegel (who sold it in January 2008 and now teaches media literacy at St. Michael's High School), the paper is known for its a broad, progressive view of issues. Many of the paper's columns and features are not exclusively local in their outlook. A typical edition might tackle such subjects as New Mexico film, gender issues, nuclear weapons research, national politics, and water scarcity, for example, using a combination of specially written articles and columns. Regular contributors include Siegel; Dick McCord, founder of Santa Fe Reporter; photographer Jennifer Esparanza; Kendra Arnold; Gail Snyder; and new publishers Richard H. Rogers and Alena Hart.

## ROUND THE ROUNDHOUSE
1339 Cerrillos Rd., Suite 3
(505) 988-1135
www.roundtheroundhouse.com

Round the Roundhouse, not to be confused with the Roundhouse Roundup political blog by New Mexican columnist Steve Terrell, calls itself a "New Mexico state employees' newspaper," even though it is privately owned and mainly circulates among state workers based in Santa Fe. Here you will find lots of insider news about politics, state worker benefits, noteworthy employees, and changes in bureaucracy. It's chock-full of ads for Santa Fe businesses, including many that extend special discounts to the paper's readers. Distribution is 14,000 copies monthly. Copies are distributed free in various locations throughout Santa Fe, but the easiest place to find it is in the lobby of various state government office buildings.

# BIMONTHLIES

## NEW MEXICO KIDS! MAGAZINE
P.O. Box 93385, Albuquerque 87199
(505) 797-2708, (888) 466-5189
www.newmexico-kids.com

With both children and parents in mind, this free bimonthly "magaloid" is geared toward local and visiting families in search of children's activities from Tijeras to Taos—an area that includes Santa Fe, Los Alamos, Albuquerque, and points in between. New Mexico Kids! got its start in 1992 when publisher Alexis Sabin of Santa Fe discovered that her four-year-old was one of 25,000 children, including babies and high-schoolers, growing up in a town perceived primarily as an adult playground. It's not that kidstuff doesn't exist here. On the contrary, says Sabin, there's plenty for kids to do in Santa Fe. At that time, however, there wasn't a whole lot of information about what was available and where. So Sabin decided to fill in the void. She compiled what turned out to be a tremendous number of youth activities and published it in a newspaper she called Santa Fe Kids! The concept met with so much enthusiasm that she expanded to Albuquerque the following year with a sister publication called, you guessed it, *Albuquerque Kids!* The two papers merged in 1997 to become *New Mexico Kids!* with separate Albuquerque and Santa Fe events calendars. The paper has now been sold to Nina Plevin and is based in Albuquerque. A 3-D flip digital version is published online.

Each issue usually contains at least two feature stories about seasonal events or activities such as fairs and festivals, hiking or camping, or family day trips. It also includes a seasonal calendar of events as well as seasonal directories of camps in the summer issue, schools in the fall, and winter's "It's Party Time!" with places to throw a child's party, buy party supplies, or locate storytellers, puppeteers, magicians, photographers, etc. A collection of short articles and announcements called "KIDBITS" appears regularly, as do book reviews, community resources, and nonprofit organizations. *New Mexico Kids!* has a healthy circulation of 75,000 readers in Santa Fe, Albuquerque, and northern New Mexico.

## QUARTERLIES

### TUMBLEWEEDS
**369 Montezuma Ave. #191**
**(505) 984-3171**
**www.sftumbleweeds.com**
*Tumbleweeds* started out in 1991 as a four-page photocopied newsletter called Tot's Hot News. In the intervening years, it has matured to a full-grown tabloid of 30 or more pages offering support, information, and resources for parents with kids in their low teens or younger and professionals who work with children. Its advisory board includes an impressive assemblage of child welfare specialists from health, education, legal, and other relevant arenas. *Tumbleweeds* includes news and feature articles written for children and includes a comprehensive calendar of child- and parent-oriented events. You can pick up *Tumbleweeds* free throughout Santa Fe and nearby Española and Los Alamos.

**i** You can have your own personal e-mail account—even if you don't have a computer—courtesy of the Santa Fe Public Library. All you have to do is show up at any of the library's three branches and sign up for a 30- to 45-minute time slot (depending on the library) and wait your turn. It's absolutely free and you don't even have to have a library card. If you already have e-mail but your computer's not handy, you can use the library computers to access your account or browse the Internet for up to 45 minutes.

## MAGAZINES

### DESIGNER/BUILDER
**2405 Maclovia Lane**
**(505) 471-4549**
**www.designerbuildermagazine.com**
Officially subtitled "A Journal of the Human Environment"—and, unofficially, "Architecture's More Than a Pretty Face"—*DESIGNER/builder* started locally in 1994 with an emphasis on Santa Fe. The bimonthly has since gone international, raising design and building issues around the globe, from the Third World to the First World, and describing all manner of architecture, from mud floors to high-rise buildings. Among the topics *DESIGNER/builder* discusses are cultural issues affecting architecture (and vice versa); urban landscapes; social spaces (i.e., malls, parks, streets, and other places where people congregate); alternative building materials and technologies; affordable housing; architectural history; and criticism.

Never shy of controversy, *DESIGNER/builder* has run stories deconstructing Nazi architecture, including concentration camps; describing a "vertical village" in Manhattan of Senegalese nationals trying to preserve their culture in a completely foreign landscape by taking over a high-rise and living in it as they would in their villages back home; and discussing a program in which prison convicts create city gardens in San Francisco that supply produce to local restaurants.

Many of the articles featured in *DESIGNER/ builder* come from other magazines. The husband and wife team of Kingsley and Jerilou Hammett, publisher and managing editor, respectively, write the rest.

## EDIBLE SANTA FE

**551 West Cordova Rd. #511**
**(505) 212-0791**
**www.ediblecommunities.com/santafe**
This lovely quarterly magazine, edited by Kate Manchester, promotes and celebrates seasonal, local, and sustainably grown foods in northern New Mexico. Articles highlight fresh seasonal ingredients at the Santa Fe Farmers' Market, chefs and growers at the farmers' market, recipes and profiles of locals by famed local chef/writer and Slow Food Santa Fe organizer Deborah Madison, and elegant photography and design. It's available free at Santa Fe Farmers' Market booths.

## EL PALACIO

**113 Lincoln Ave.**
**(505) 476-5055**
**www.elpalacio.org**
*El Palacio: The Museum of New Mexico Magazine* is the oldest museum publication in the United States. What started out as a weekly pamphlet about the size of one's hand is today published under the auspices of the Office of Cultural Affairs as a quarterly glossy showpiece for the Museum of New Mexico museum system: the New Mexico History Museum/Palace of the Governors, Museum of Indian Arts & Culture, Laboratory of Anthropology, Museum of International Folk Art, New Mexico Museum of Art—all in Santa Fe, six state monuments, and the Office of Archeological Studies, which collects and shares information about New Mexico's prehistoric and historic sites.

Taking its lead from the museums it represents, *El Palacio* (The Palace) covers New Mexico history, culture, art, and anthropology with lively articles accompanied by striking photos and graphics. It's also a darned good substitute, both visually and textually, for those who can't attend museum exhibits or events in person. Articles are posted online. The 2009 summer issue celebrating Santa Fe's 400th birthday was particularly rich, with articles on 100 years of the Museum of New Mexico, its founder Edgar Lee Hewett, and a reprint of an article by the early-20th century artist and puppeteer Gustave Baumann.

Handsome *El Palacio* practically jumps out at you on the newsstand. But it was originally a staid, black-and-white scholarly journal read almost exclusively by museum members and a few hundred academics and professionals. After suspending publication for about eight months, the magazine re-appeared in the spring of 1991 with a cleaner, slightly more colorful format. By the very next issue—the first in its history to incorporate outside advertising—*El Palacio* had evolved into a full-color magazine on the art and culture, history, and lore of the Southwest, winning an honorary mention for design from the American Association of Museums (AAM). Since that time the magazine has once again narrowed its focus to New Mexico rather than the entire southwestern region, garnering a 1995 AAM honorary mention in the process.

*El Palacio* publishes quarterly with an average run of 10,000 issues. Subscriptions are free for the Museum of New Mexico's approximately 6,100 members.

## MOTHERING

**P.O. Box 1690, Santa Fe 87504**
**(505) 984-8116, (800) 984-8116**
**www.mothering.com**
Read in more than 65 countries, this 30-year-old bimonthly, founded by Peggy O'Mara, is a progressive parenting magazine that addresses contemporary health, personal, environmental, medical, and lifestyle issues affecting today's families. Articles range in tone from practical to philosophical on such topics as circumcision, midwifery, home birth, home schooling, organic food, alternative and traditional health care, and home businesses, to name just a few. It also features reviews of books, music, films, and videos.

## NEW MEXICO MAGAZINE
**Lew Wallace Building,**
**495 Old Santa Fe Trail**
**(505) 827-7447**
**www.nmmagazine.com**

First published in 1923 as the *Highway Journal,* *New Mexico Magazine* started out as a high-quality, internal newsletter of the state Highway Department to promote "interest in good roads through the state" and "advertise to the people of the United States the attractions of New Mexico as a playground, and its possibilities as a place of location and business."

Little did editor Ray W. Bennett realize to what extent New Mexico would indeed turn into a playground, nor could he have imagined at the time the beautiful and highly popular magazine his little newsletter would become. The first metamorphosis occurred in 1931, when *Highway Journal* merged with the Game and Fish Department's magazine, *The Conservationist,* to become *New Mexico: The Sunshine State's Recreational and Highway Magazine.* Six years later the publication took on its current name and style, becoming the first official state magazine in the nation with a format that would be emulated many times over.

*New Mexico Magazine* operates under the auspices of New Mexico's tourism department and specializes in travel and historical features with regular sections on regional cuisine, literature, art, and culture and high-quality color photographs, essays, and illustrations. The magazine's list of contributing authors, photographers, and illustrators reads like a "Who's Who" of major *New Mexican* writers and artists. *New Mexico Magazine* has a paid circulation of more than 117,000 with an estimated readership of 500,000. About 70 percent of the readership comes from outside New Mexico, in 75 countries worldwide.

## SANTA FEAN
**466 West San Francisco St.**
**(505) 983-1444, (800) 770-6326**
**www.santafean.com**

After a brief hiatus covering politics and local personalities, and several ownerships, the *Santa Fean* has returned to its roots as a lifestyle magazine. The magazine focuses on art, first and foremost, as well as entertainment, home design, fashion, dining, and always some of Santa Fe's fascinating history. The *Santa Fean* also features regular columns by hooked-in locals like chef John Vollertson and editor Marin Sardy. Ubiquitous in hotel rooms in northern New Mexico and art galleries throughout the state, the glossy monthly has attracted a sizable out-of-state readership with 80 percent of its subscriptions outside New Mexico. The *Santa Fean* has received several national awards for its design and editorial content. The *Santa Fean* publishes six times a year and has a circulation of 28,000.

## THE MAGAZINE
**1208-A Mercantile Rd.**
**(505) 424-7641**
**www.themagazineonline.com**

When Judith Wolf and Guy Cross moved to Santa Fe in 1988, they were amazed to discover that what is reputedly the third-largest art market in the country had no local magazine dedicated to the arts. Sure, there was good old Pasatiempo, a Friday insert in the *Santa Fe New Mexican* that serves as Santa Fe's what's-happening bible. But they considered Pasatiempo primarily a preview vehicle. What Santa Fe needed, they felt, was a critical voice.

As Cross puts it, "We saw a niche and we sold it." Since then, *THE magazine* has taken off like a rocket with readership all over the United States. It even has a handful of international subscribers in places as far-flung as Thailand, Japan, South America, Australia, and London. Total circulation runs 20,000 a month.

Unlike most art magazines, *THE* is neither glossy nor usually published in color. Yet its matte black-and-white format lends it an air of simple sophistication—not unlike a basic black dress with pearls. At 10¾ by 13¼, it's also a large magazine—one that stands out on a coffee table. But *THE* is more than just a pretty face. It covers the Santa Fe art scene with articles, reviews, and a listing of exhibits and openings. Free on newsstands.

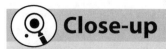

# Close-up

## KUNM-FM

Go into anyone's home or car in Santa Fe and check the pretuned stations on their stereo. Chances are pretty good they'll have their first or second button set to 89.9 FM. That's the home in Santa Fe for KUNM, the state's largest volunteer-operated public radio station and certainly the most diverse.

Broadcasting from the campus of the University of New Mexico in Albuquerque, KUNM provides news, talk, and every kind of music imaginable. Its goal is to satisfy a broad spectrum of listeners in a state that's home to New Agers and rednecks, liberals and reactionaries, sophisticates and simple folk, and everything in between.

Even a cursory glance at the program listings makes it clear that KUNM offers something for everyone. News hounds can tune in Monday through Friday from 5 to 8:30 a.m., to hear in-depth news and features on "Morning Edition" and again from 5:30 to 7 p.m., for "All Things Considered"—both award-winning news magazines from National Public Radio. For local news, tune in at 5 p.m., Monday through Friday, for the 30-minute "KUNM Evening Report." The station also gives news junkies a weekend fix with NPR's "Weekend Edition," airing at 7 a.m. on Saturday and Sunday at 9 a.m.

Musically, KUNM has the widest offering of any station in New Mexico. Its repertoire includes blues, bluegrass, Cajun, classical, country music, folk, gospel, heavy metal, hip-hop, jazz, Native American music, new rock, oldies, reggae, salsa, Tejano, and world beat—whew!—to give just a partial list. You can tune in 24 hours a day, 7 days a week and rarely, if ever, hear the same thing twice—except, of course, the news. Deejays for the local music programs—which includes all but NPR's weekday 9 to 11 a.m. classical music show, "Performance Today"—are volunteers who truly know and love the music they play. As nonprofessionals, few affect the classic, smooth radio voice that commercial stations require.

KUNM features a variety of Hispanic programs, including a Latin-American "free-form" show called "Raices," which plays all genres of Hispanic music at 2 p.m. on Saturday and 7 p.m. on Monday; and Friday night's "Salsa Sabrosa," three hours of Afro-Caribbean music primarily from Puerto Rico, Cuba, the Dominican Republic, etc., starts at 7 p.m.

The station also airs a number of programs for and about Native Americans, such as "National Native News," weekdays at 5:25 p.m., five minutes of news and issues affecting American Indians; "Native America Calling," a live call-in show weekdays at 11 a.m.; and "Singing Wire," a Sunday afternoon program featuring Native American music from the traditional to country and western, rock and roll to folk.

Twice a year KUNM holds a weeklong, on-the-air fund-raising drive to raise enough money to keep up its eclectic programming. Members get KUNM's monthly program guide, "Zounds," which includes a day-by-day listing of on-air events as well as a detailed description of its regularly scheduled programs and times.

The programs mentioned here are only a partial listing of KUNM's offerings. For more information, call the business office at (505) 277-4806. After hours, call the request line at (505) 277-5615 for information about whatever program is airing at that time. The station streams its programming on the Internet at www.kunm.edu.

# RADIO

For a state with only about 2 million residents and a radio market ranked 235 out of a possible 276, New Mexico's airwaves carry a surprisingly eclectic collection of sounds that come to Santa Fe via 30 or so radio stations, depending on the area, most of them from Albuquerque.

On the music front, listeners can tune in to anything from rap to rock, jazz to Jewish Klezmer music, oldies to opera, classical to Christian music—the list goes on and on. If news/talk is your preference, you can choose among a wide spectrum of offerings. Like elsewhere in the country, however, New Mexico's radio options are becoming increasingly limited as chains buy out independent stations and homogenize the musical mix. Still, many stations have managed to avoid the Top 40 abyss that seems to be sucking in the larger markets.

Family-owned Hutton Broadcasting purchased several popular Santa Fe radio stations from giant Clear Channel Communications in 2007. It has aimed to preserve unique formats and DJ formats, such as eclectic community-oriented KBAC-FM (98.1 FM, "Radio Free Santa Fe") and BLU, which plays laid-back jazz, world, rhythm, and chill music, while offering broad radio coverage for the outdoors (Project 101.5 and Outlaw Country) and sports and talk am formats KVSF 1400 and 1260 KTRC.

## Christian

KDAZ 730 AM, Christian music/talk. (Albuquerque)
KFLQ 91.5 FM, Christian music, news/talk. (Albuquerque)
KKIM 1000 AM, Christian news/talk. (Albuquerque)
KLYT 88.3 FM, Christian hit radio—all rock, some news. (Albuquerque)
KNKT 107.1 FM, Christian music, rock. (Albuquerque)
KSVA 920 AM, Christian talk. (Albuquerque)
KXKS 1190 AM, Christian talk. (Albuquerque)

## Classical

KANW 89.1 FM, bilingual variety programming includes classical. (Albuquerque)
KHFM 95.5 FM, all classical music. (Santa Fe)
KSFR 101.1 FM, variable programming includes classical. (Santa Fe)
KUNM 89.9 FM, variable programming includes classical. (Albuquerque) (See our Close-up in this chapter.)

## Community

KRSN 1490 AM, syndicated and local news/talk/information, plus some jazz, classical, Big Band, and radio drama. (Los Alamos)
KSFR 101.1 FM, local community radio, alternative programming includes blues, classical, jazz, opera, Spanish music, news, talk, and information. (Santa Fe)
KUNM 89.9 FM, public radio includes community programming. (Albuquerque)

## Country

KBQI 107.9 FM, modern country. (Albuquerque)
KRST 92.3 FM, new country, morning and evening drive-time news, weather, traffic. (Albuquerque)

## Jazz

KANW 89.1 FM, bilingual variety programming includes jazz. (Albuquerque)
KSFR 101.1 FM, variable programming includes jazz. (Santa Fe)
KUNM 89.9 FM, variable programming includes jazz. (Albuquerque)

## News/talk

KANW 89.1 FM, Spanish language variety programming includes Public Radio International and National Public Radio. (Albuquerque)
KKOB 770 AM, news/talk—local and syndicated programs. (Albuquerque)
KRSN 1490 AM, news/talk, plus some varied music. (Los Alamos)

KTRC 1260 AM, news/talk, religion. (Santa Fe)

KUNM 89.9 FM, variable programming includes National Public Radio, Pacifica News, and Public Radio International. (Albuquerque)

## Public Radio

KANW 89.1 FM, bilingual variety programming including Public Radio International, National Public Radio, variable programming includes classical music, jazz, New Mexico music, Native American programming, news, and talk shows. (Albuquerque)

KSFR 101.1 FM, local public radio, alternative format includes blues, classical, jazz, opera, Spanish music, and news/talk/information. (Santa Fe)

KUNM 89.9 FM, National Public Radio, Public Radio International, Pacifica Radio, alternative programming. (Albuquerque)

## Rock

KABG 98.5 FM, oldies—'60s and '70s. (Los Alamos)

KBAC 98.1 FM, Radio Free Santa Fe, progressive music format includes alternative rock, reggae, world beat, local music and live studio appearances by visiting musicians. (Santa Fe)

KKOB 93.3 FM, Top 40 adult contemporary and oldies. (Albuquerque)

KKSS 97.3 FM, rhythmic contemporary hits, urban. (Albuquerque)

KLBU 102.9 FM, chill-out music with a cool vibe. (Pecos/Santa Fe)

KMGA 99.5 FM, light rock. (Albuquerque)

KPEK 100.3 FM, adult contemporary. (Albuquerque)

KUNM 89.9 FM, alternative programming includes rock. (Albuquerque)

KZRR 94.1 FM, classic rock. (Albuquerque)

## Spanish

KANW 89.1 FM, bilingual variety programming includes New Mexico music, classical, jazz, NPR, Native American programming, news/talk. (Albuquerque)

KARS 860 AM, country/Spanish music, bilingual news/talk. (Belen/Albuquerque)

KDCE 950 AM, Spanish language, music, news, talk. (Española)

KLVO 106. FM, Spanish language regional Mexican music. (Los Alamos)

KRZY 1450 AM, Spanish language, music, news, traffic. (Albuquerque)

KSWV 810 AM, bilingual, music, news, weather, sports. (Santa Fe)

KYBR 92.9 FM, all Spanish regional Mexican music. (Española)

## Sports

KVSF 1400 AM, twenty-four-hour ESPN sports. (Santa Fe)

KNML 610 AM, twenty-four-hour sports (Albuquerque)

KQTM 101.7 FM, twenty-four-hour sports (Rio Rancho/Albuquerque)

# TELEVISION

Santa Fe has no television stations of its own. Most television stations are based in Albuquerque, the state's largest city. Combining network television with cable, Santa Fe has an enviable choice of stations—50 in all, including premium and Pay-Per-View stations. Comcast of Santa Fe, 2534 Camino Entrada, (505) 438-2600, is the primary cable provider for Santa Fe County. Surrounding areas—Eldorado, Tesuque, and South Santa Fe, for example—have their own cable systems with different channels. Check the *Santa Fe New Mexican* for details.

Over-the-air TV reception is difficult for many Santa Fe-area residents because of rugged terrain that interferes with signals. Cable TV service is not always available in outlying areas. These factors have contributed to the growing popularity of satellite TV service in the region, available from DirecTV and Dish Network listed in the phone directory. Public-access channel six is programmed by Santa Fe Community College on local cable systems, with a community-oriented schedule that is largely produced by local residents.

## Network Channels:

Ch. 2 –KASA (Fox)
Ch. 4 –KOB (NBC)
Ch. 5 –KNME (PBS)
Ch. 7 –KOAT (ABC)
Ch. 8 –KLUZ (Univision–Spanish variety)
Ch. 11 –KCHF (Christian)

Ch. 13 –KRQE (CBS)
Ch. 14 –KAPX (Pax)
Ch. 19 –KWBQ (Warner Bros.)
Ch. 23 –KNAT (Christian)
Ch. 32 –KAZQ (Independent)
Ch. 41 –KLUZ (Univision)
Ch. 50 –KASY (UPN)

# WORSHIP AND SPIRITUALITY

I t's no accident that this high-desert land of magnificent natural beauty, crystal-clean air, and spectacular sunshine has for centuries drawn spiritual seekers and inspired religious awe among followers of all faiths. From the Ancestral Pueblo and Athapascan—respective forebears of the region's Pueblo Indians and Navajo and Apache tribes, for whom the land they call "ground of the dancing sun" remains sacred—to today's New Age adherents, who combine ancient mysticism with modern thought, northern New Mexico beckons. For what is religion if not the spiritual cement that binds humankind to nature and supernature—what some call "God" and others call "Yahweh," "Allah," "Krishna" or simply "higher power."

## OVERVIEW

The late Fray Angélico Chávez—a Franciscan priest, poet, and author from northern New Mexico who wrote some two dozen books about his homeland and the anima hispanica (Hispanic soul)—understood this clearly when he likened New Mexico to Palestine in both topography and climate. "The New Mexican landscape . . . is the holy land," Chávez wrote in his compelling 1974 book, *My Penitente Land*. He called the Río Grande New Mexico's Jordan River and Santa Fe its Jerusalem. He similarly compared Palestine to Spain, the land from which the first European settlers in what would become New Mexico arrived nearly 450 years ago. "Grazing lands all and most alike in their physical aspects," Chávez wrote, adding that they "share a distinctive underlying human mystique born of that very type of arid landscape." Thus both the pobladores (settlers) sanctioned by the Spanish Crown, whose Catholicism was as much a part of their anima hispanica as their Spanish roots, and the conversos (crypto Jews who fled the Spanish Inquisition to the New World in search of religious freedom) sensed a comfortable familiarity in this strange new land they called "Nuevomejico." Its appearance and clime approximated not only the home they recently left but also the ancient biblical soil of their common ancestors.

The Catholic Church vigorously opposed the Protestant incursion that arrived in the form of missionaries from points east on the Santa Fe Trail after New Mexico became a U.S. territory in 1846. While hostilities rarely erupted in violence, they came out in other ways. It was not unheard of for Catholic clergymen to drown out Protestant sermons by ringing their church bells as loudly as possible. Relations between Catholics and Protestants became still more strained with the arrival in 1850 of Jean Baptiste Lamy, a French priest whom the pope named as Santa Fe's first bishop. Lamy attempted to suppress the Protestant movement by subtle means, including wedding local government to the Catholic Church; replacing Hispanic clergy with less tolerant French and Italian priests; sheltering the local Hispanic and Indian population from the Protestant influence of Americans, who were arriving in wagonloads on the Santa Fe Trail; and by making outcasts of Protestant preachers and their converts.

New Mexico's first Protestant missionary, a Northern Baptist preacher named Hiram Walter Read, arrived in 1849—three years after the end of the Mexican-American War (see our History chapter) and one year before it became an American territory. Methodist, Presbyterian, and Episcopalian missionaries arrived on the heels of the Baptists. Meanwhile American Jews, many of them German immigrants, predated the Baptists by six years. Documents place Albert Speyers, a Jewish trader from New York, on the Santa Fe Trail as early as 1843. Unlike the Protestants, however, the Jews came not on a religious mission but an economic one. In fact, Santa Fe had no synagogue until 1952, 76 years after New Mexico's first recorded bar mitzvah.

It wasn't until early in the 20th century that the next wave of pilgrims came to northern New Mexico. But they differed dramatically from their predecessors in that they came not to spread religion but to find it. These were the artists, writers, and thinkers of the East Coast who left the decadence and materialism of their own culture for what they felt was the purity and mysticism of New Mexico. It's largely the legacy of this generation—one that included the likes of Georgia O'Keeffe, D. H. Lawrence, and Mabel Dodge Luhan—which lends Santa Fe a mystique that has since achieved mythological proportions. However patronizing, they idealized the place, inadvertently advertising it through their artwork and their prose and luring others—artists and free thinkers in the early part of the century, hippies and New Age practitioners in recent generations.

Today Santa Fe is home to more than 50 active Christian churches; two synagogues, and five Jewish congregations; three Buddhist temples and several meditation centers; and dozens of other nondenominational and unaffiliated spiritual centers of every bent. Just open the Yellow Pages to "religion" and you'll find a mind-boggling array of choices. Or look in the Religion page of Saturday's *New Mexican* for a large listing of spiritual groups along with addresses and phone numbers.

## ROMAN CATHOLIC

There's no doubt that Santa Fe is first and foremost a Catholic town, an identity so profound that it pervades every aspect of daily life here. Public prayers open government meetings at City Hall, the County Courthouse, and the state Legislature. Prayers even preceded sporting events at public schools until a 1997 legal challenge put an end to the practice, causing an uproar among students and parents. You'll still hear religion taught in some classrooms, though it's not an official part of the curriculum. It might be, however, were it left up to the New Mexico Board of Education, which in 1996 attracted national attention after voting to remove evolution as a school requirement to make way for teaching creationism as described in the Bible.

**i** **Catholicism arrived in New Mexico in 1598 with Don Juan de Oñate, who colonized the region for Spain, making it the first European settlement west of the Mississippi River.**

The two main historic Catholic churches in Santa Fe—the Cathedral Basilica of St. Francis de Assisi and the Cristo Rey Church on Canyon Road—are covered in the Attractions chapter. St. John's Church, on Osage Road in the Casa Alegre neighborhood off Cerrillos Road, is known for its outreach, particularly the daily soup kitchen program.

The only post-Vatican II Catholic congregation in Santa Fe, Santa María de la Paz is without doubt the most progressive of the area's Catholic communities. Its founding pastor, Father Jerome Martínez y Alire, once described the parish as "catholic in the best sense of the word"—i.e., liberal and universal in scope. Formed in 1990, Santa María de la Paz has grown 10-fold from some 200 families that met in the gymnasium of nearby Piñon Elementary School to more than 2,200 registered households from Santa Fe's fast-growing, suburban South Side. Today Santa María de la Paz's parishioners—a mixture of natives and newcomers of many races, languages, and ways of life—meet in a church they designed and built themselves and of which they're rightfully proud. Everything about and in the structure was crafted from native materials by New Mexican artists. Works by some of the finest *santeros* in the world—among them Charles Carrillo, Marie Romero Cash, Victor Goler, Felix Lopez, and David

Nabor Lucero—as well as a bronze by renowned Native American sculptor Allan Houser, have found a home in the church.

# BUDDHIST

Santa Fe Buddhists are numerous: some follow Japanese Zen lineage, others Vietnamese, and still others Tibetan Buddhism. The county is home to a number of beautiful Buddhist centers, each as unique as the individuals they attract. Upaya Institute's campus, located in Santa Fe's scenic eastern foothills, has five traditional adobe buildings that reflect both its southwestern and Asian roots. Cerro Gordo ("Fat Hill") Temple, once the site of the first Tibetan stupa (temple) in the United States, hosts several Buddhist groups. The largest and most well established is Upaya itself—Sanskrit for "skillful means" or "the craft of compassion." Founded in 1990 by renowned Soto priest, teacher, and author Joan Halifax Roshi, Upaya offers Zen training and meditation retreats. It also gives courses and retreats on "engaged spirituality" and contemplative care of the dying (see the Retirement chapter).

On Santa Fe's south side, the 69-foot-tall stupa of Kagyu Shenpen Kunchab (KSK) Dharma Center, and especially its 12-foot bronzed spire, provide a stunning contrast to Santa Fe's primarily single-story adobe or adobe-colored architecture. Founded in 1975 by the late meditation master Kalu Rinpoche, KSK is a Tibetan Buddhist center under the guidance of resident lama (teacher) Karma Dorje, who oversees a similar center in nearby Taos. Its form is that of an ancient architectural structure called a caitya, which dates from 1000 B.C. The blessing post in the Santa Fe spire contains a pearllike crystal said to have been recovered from the Buddha's cremation. The center regularly sponsors visits by Tibetan Buddhist teachers of all lineages and offers classes in Tibetan art, music, and language. Behind the center is Noble Truth Bookstore, which sells literature and other items related to primarily Tibetan Buddhism.

Mountain Cloud Zen Center is a beautiful Buddhist retreat tucked away on 43 acres in the foothills of the Sangre de Cristo Mountains off Old Santa Fe Trail. Its members follow a combination of the Rinzai and Soto schools of Zen Buddhism as practiced by their teacher, Robert Aitken Roshi, who founded the Diamond Sangha in Hawaii. The center's small, sunny zendo (meditation room) has windows on three sides and raised wooden platforms upon which sit 24 flat cushions (zabwons) topped by plump round meditation cushions (zafus). Vipassana or Insight Meditation students, who practice a form of Theravada Buddhism found primarily in Southeast Asia, rent space at Mountain Cloud for regularly scheduled meditation sessions and retreats.

# CHARISMATIC CHRISTIAN

Calvary Chapel de Santa Fe describes itself as "conservative charismatic"—a fundamentalist, evangelical congregation that takes the word of the Bible literally, but with a minimum of display, such as speaking in tongues or the laying on of hands. At the other end of the charismatic spectrum is the Potter's House Christian Center, an evangelical Pentecostal church that does indeed practice spontaneous displays of faith. Services at Potter House are exuberant affairs during which people sing, clap, shout, weep, speak in tongues, and perform the "laying on of hands." The church also conducts adult baptisms from time to time at either of two municipal swimming pools. Services are conducted in a simple, prefabricated metal building with rows of padded metal chairs in front of a raised platform. Templo Betel is a Spanish Assembly of God church that attracts native Spanish speakers, many of them from Mexico and Central America. This is a fundamentalist Pentecostal church that believes in the "manifestation of the Holy Spirit" whether it arrives in the form of speaking in tongues or divine healing. Located on a busy residential street on Santa Fe's west side, Templo Betel offers services with lots of music and singing that reflect the various Latino cultures the congregation represents.

## Penitentes

Driving along the back roads of northern New Mexico, you're likely to pass many a simple, one-room adobe structure with no windows and little external evidence of life. What you're looking at is probably a *morada*—a house of worship used by *penitentes* and that, despite appearances, is teeming with life, but of a spiritual nature.

*Penitentes* are members of the centuries-old "Hermandad de Nuestro Padre Jesus Nazareno"—Brotherhood of Our Father Jesus of Nazarene—a religious fraternity that traces its roots back to a 16th-century nobleman from Seville who was so moved to see pilgrims in Jerusalem carrying heavy crosses along the Vía Dolorosa—the route Jesus walked to his crucifixion—that he founded a society to carry on the tradition in Spain.

Present-day New Mexican *penitentes* keep the tradition alive while keeping a low profile, as evidenced by their humble *moradas*. While not precisely a secret society, they are certainly a reserved one. Their reasons are both reverent and pragmatic. The practice of the *penitente* is one of humility; of subservience to, and demonstrative empathy for, a suffering Christ expressed in prayer, meditation, and physical penance; of community service, whether by feeding the hungry or comforting the dying; of preserving their culture. They wish also to avoid the prurient gaze of the curious and the sensation-seekers, the voyeurs who want to witness the rituals of self-flagellation and the rigors of Holy Week, when *penitentes* reenact Christ's march to Calvary. Better to rent *The Penitent,* a 1988 movie starring Raul Julia and Armand Assante, which provides an admittedly melodramatic glimpse of the *penitente* society.

## EASTERN ORTHODOX

Holy Trinity Orthodox Church is an Eastern Rite church whose diocese was founded in Antioch, the birthplace of Paul and the place where Christians were first called by that name. Orthodox Catholic churches broke from the Roman Catholic Church in the 11th century, when the Roman church insisted on the infallibility of the pope and maintained the supremacy in the Trinity of the Father and Son over the Holy Spirit—in other words, that Jesus is purely divine. Orthodox churches believe what's called the Holy Paradox—that Jesus is both human and divine. Holy Trinity parish formed in 1996 when its priest, Father John Bethancourt, defected from a local Episcopalian church, taking a quarter of the congregation with him. At first the new parish comprised only 22 people, but their numbers quickly grew to 35 households. They eventually bought a ranch-style house in Santa Fe's South Capitol neighborhood, near a number of other houses of worship, and converted it into a church with a couple of bell towers and an interior richly decorated with the ubiquitous icons of Orthodox Catholicism. Mass at Holy Trinity is very ornate and sung and chanted from start to finish.

St. Elias the Prophet Greek Orthodox Church is a beautiful white Byzantine structure, built in 1992 in the Dos Griegos (Two Greeks) development adjoining the Eldorado subdivision some 15 miles southeast of downtown Santa Fe. The "Two Greeks"—Alex Constantaras and Frank Carras—donated the land for the church as well as much of the 4,000-square-foot building. About 70 families belong to the parish, which worshipped at churches in town before building its own church. At 7,200 feet, St. Elias is reputedly the highest Greek Orthodox church in the nation—at least according to a Santa Fe mayor, who made a proclamation to that effect.

## JEWISH

Until just a few years ago, Temple Beth Shalom was the only central place of worship for Jews in Santa Fe and was almost certainly the only synagogue in the country shared by reform, conservative, and orthodox Jews. Today a Reformed and a lay-led conservative congregation share the temple, which is located in a largely residential area shared by a number of houses of worship as well as two museums and a repertory cinema. An orthodox minion still meets in what was the original sanctuary. Although practicing Jews have been in Santa Fe at least since the mid-19th century, they didn't build a synagogue until 1953. During World War II, laymen conducted Sabbath services in the chapel of Bruns General Hospital, a military facility that stood where the College of Santa Fe (now closed) stands today. (No one's quite sure where Jews met for Sabbath services before that time.) After the war, however, the Santa Fe Jewish Temple and Community Center collected $100 from 18 families toward the purchase of land. It hired nationally renowned local architect John Gaw Meem, whose signature is on a number of Santa Fe churches, to design a synagogue. The temple was dedicated in 1953, but there was no money left to furnish it. The congregation of 40 families sold raffle tickets for $100 each to pay for seats, carpeting, drapes, and paving. By 1980 the congregation—now called Temple Beth Shalom—was well established with a full-time rabbi and a congregation that had quintupled in size from 27 years earlier to 200 families. It commissioned a new sanctuary from solar architect Ed Mazria. Judging by the temple's growth—its membership currently numbers more than 350 families—another expansion is likely.

## NEW THOUGHT

The New Thought movement began in the late-19th century on the heels of New England Transcendentalism—a literary and philosophical movement popularized by Ralph Waldo Emerson, Margaret Fuller, Henry David Thoreau, and others who believed that God is inherent in humans and in nature and that individual intuition is the highest source of knowledge. New Thought encourages individuals to have a personal relationship with God instead of one whose parameters are defined by a particular organization. Many New Thought religions have strong overtones of mysticism and/or the occult and might be considered a bridge between traditional and New Age religions.

Among the New Thought groups in Santa Fe is the Church of Religious Science, an alternative religion serving those who strive for a personal relationship with God. Founded in the early 20th century by Ernest Holmes, the religion has a strong existential and humanistic base while touching on the metaphysical. Its core belief is that God is alive through an individual's thoughts and beliefs; that the spirit moves in each person's mind and heart. The church is a teaching and healing denomination that, like its distant cousin Christian Science, believes in healing the body through prayer. Unlike its cousin, however, it does not eschew doctors, medicine, or science. The Church of Religious Science has a worldwide following, including 300 members in Santa Fe whose minister, the Rev. Bernardo Monserrat, leads Sunday services at 9:30 and 11 a.m.

Unity Church of Santa Fe is part of the Unity School of Christianity, founded in 1889 by Charles and Myrtle Fillmore of Kansas City, Missouri. Unity, whose roots lie in the New Thought movement, believes in Christian principles, spiritual values, and the healing power of prayer, though not to the exclusion of medical care. Its message is a little untraditional in that it focuses on the teachings of Jesus, not on the man himself. Members believe that if they follow the teachings of Christ, they will experience peace and joy and love right here on earth. About 150 members belong to the

Santa Fe church, whose Sunday services attract up to 120 people. Services focus on applying spiritual principles to daily life. About an hour long, they are filled with song and a few minutes of silent meditation.

# PROTESTANT

## Episcopalian

Episcopalians made their first official appearance in Santa Fe in 1863 with the arrival from the Pacific Northwest of the Right Rev. Josiah C. Talbot. On July 5 of that year, he administered to seven people the Holy Communion according to the Anglican rite—the first ever in the Spanish-speaking Roman Catholic town. Four years later Good Shepherd Mission was born. It became a parish in 1868 and 10 years later, at the urging of then-Governor Bradford Prince, it changed its name to Church of the Holy Faith—the literal translation for "Santa Fe."

In 1927, famed architect John Gaw Meem designed Palen Hall. He also designed a chancel and a sanctuary at the back of the main church in 1954. Its centerpiece is a carved reredos (altar screen), completed in 1945 by world-renowned Santa Fe artist Gustave Baumann. Over the church's main doors is a small window with a Star of David in recognition of the Jewish merchants who donated generously to the church's building fund in 1879. Holy Faith has experienced a number of other alterations since that time, including Conkey House, completed in 1966. As a "medium-high" church, Holy Faith follows ceremonies and liturgies that are extremely formal, with much ritual and spectacular vestments.

Among the newest and most liberal of Santa Fe's churches, St. Bede's was founded in 1962 as a mission of the Church of the Holy Faith (see entry above). A few dozen families composed the congregation, which met in a rented building on Cerrillos Road for two years before moving into its own newly built church on San Mateo Road. At that time San Mateo was a dusty dirt road on the outskirts of town. Today it's a bustling residential commuter street that meets with St. Francis Drive

directly in front of St. Bede's to create one of the busiest intersections of the city. The city's growth is clearly reflected at St. Bede's, a thriving church with 210 households and a 10,000-square-foot building on four and a half acres. Worship centers on the Eucharist and Rite II, a less formal ritual than the older, more traditional Rite I. The atmosphere at St. Bede's tends to be informal, or what one parishioner describes as "relaxed spirituality."

## Lutheran

Among the last of the mainstream Protestant faiths to send missionaries to Santa Fe were the Lutherans, who arrived in 1914 when Pastor Carl F. Schmid of Albuquerque began coming to the state capital for monthly services. That lasted about two years, followed by a 12-year dormant period when Santa Fe had little, if any, Lutheran activity. But in the late 1920s, Santa Fe enjoyed a period of growth that brought more Lutherans to the small city. Services resumed irregularly but with increased frequency until 1938, when the church inaugurated regular Sunday services and officially became Immanuel Lutheran Church. With 240 baptized members, Immanuel Lutheran (Lutheran Church-Missouri Synod) is the largest Lutheran church in Santa Fe as well as being its oldest and most conservative. It worships in a simple, Spanish-style adobe structure that architect John Gaw Meem designed in 1948. Once past the open *portal* and inside the church, visitors are greeted with a beautiful collection of banners depicting biblical themes handmade by members. The altarware—candlesticks, offering plates, missal stand, etc.—are all Nambéware, a special silver-colored metal manufactured near Nambé Pueblo, about 20 minutes north of Santa Fe.

## Methodist

With about 1,000 members, St. John's United Methodist Church is the largest Protestant congregation in Santa Fe. Its beginnings date from 1850, when the Rev. E. G. Nicholson set out from his home in Independence, Missouri—not coincidentally the beginning of the Santa Fe Trail—to establish the first Methodist church in the frontier

Territory of New Mexico. Nicholson managed to achieve his goal in 1853, but not without vigorous opposition by the Catholic Church. Still, the congregation grew and the church flourished until 1866, when the U.S. Army withdrew from the Territory, taking much of the area's Methodists with it. Those who remained persevered, slowly building up their congregation once again until, in 1881—the year after the first railroad steamed into northern New Mexico—they built their first church on West San Francisco Street. They moved twice more before 1954, when they settled into their present location on Old Pecos Trail.

i President Lyndon Baines Johnson married Claudia "Lady Bird" Taylor at St. John's United Methodist Church in Santa Fe, where Lady Bird's brother was a member.

## Presbyterian

Presbyterians weren't the first Protestants in New Mexico—Baptists and Methodists preceded them by a number of years—but theirs was the first Protestant congregation to survive the 1866 departure of the U.S. Army, whose members accounted for the majority of the area's Protestants. It was in November 1866—more than a year after the Civil War ended—that the Rev. David McFarland of Mattoon, Illinois, held the first Presbyterian service in Santa Fe at the Palace of the Governors. Within a few months he established the First Presbyterian Church. Shortly thereafter the new congregation bought the ruins of an adobe chapel built in 1853–54 by Baptists, who had abandoned their mission in Santa Fe. The First Presbyterian Church restored the building—located at what is now the corner of Grant Avenue and Griffin Street—to a useful, if not terribly comfortable, condition and held its first service there in 1867. First Presbyterian would rebuild its church twice more on the same site, consecrating its present structure— a grand Pueblo-style church whose sanctuary was designed by renowned architect John Gaw

Meem—in 1939. The building was expanded and renovated in 2008.

## Quakers (Religious Society of Friends)

The Santa Fe Monthly Meeting of Friends gathers every Sunday at 630 Canyon Rd. in what was once the home and studio of the late Olive Rush. A Quaker reputed to be the first female artist to move to Santa Fe, Rush left her beautiful, earthy 150-year-old house to the Friends when she died in the mid-1960s. The group had only formed some 10 years earlier when a handful of people met in different homes. Today about 75 people belong to the Santa Fe Monthly Meeting of Friends.

Established in 1647 as a reaction to the extreme Puritan formalism of the Presbyterian Church, the Religious Society of Friends places a high value on conscience, self-examination, and social responsibility, embracing pacifism and left-leaning political activism. In Santa Fe that translates into such affiliations as Concerned Citizens for Nuclear Safety, which opposes the opening of the Waste Isolation Pilot Plant—an underground nuclear waste dump near Carlsbad, New Mexico; Los Alamos Study Group, a grassroots watchdog organization that keeps tabs on Los Alamos National Laboratory and the U.S. Department of Energy; and other progressive organizations and causes. Meetings are generally distinguished by their silent, meditational atmosphere, broken only when members share thoughts and feelings with others.

## Southern Baptist

Baptists not only established New Mexico's first Protestant congregation but also built the territory's first Protestant house of worship. It was a little adobe chapel at the corner of Grant Avenue and Griffin Street, completed in 1854 and purchased 13 years later by the Presbyterian Church (see entry above). The chapel followed by five years the arrival of the area's first Protestant missionary, a Northern Baptist named Hiram Walter Read, who stayed in the territory for two years before taking his mission to other parts. Baptists survived

Read's departure, maintaining an official presence in Santa Fe until 1866 when the American Baptist Home Mission Society—the governing board for Northern Baptists—thought its money and time would be better spent back East, where newly freed slaves were trying to make a life for themselves and their families. The Baptists that remained, most of whom were Hispanic, turned to the Presbyterian and Methodist missionaries just arriving in the territory to spread their style of Christianity. It would be another 13 years before the American Baptist Home Mission Society would resume its work in Santa Fe. In 1912 it turned its mission over to the Southern Baptist convention, which, five years later, established the First Baptist Church of Santa Fe. First Baptist originally operated out of a small adobe chapel at the corner of Manhattan and Don Gaspar Avenues, very close to what is now downtown Santa Fe. Later it moved to its present location on Old Pecos Trail to accommodate a growing congregation. Today First Baptist is the largest Southern Baptist church in Santa Fe with more than 600 members.

## United Church of Christ

The United Church of Santa Fe is part of the United Church of Christ (U.C.C.), a denomination that dates from the Protestant Reformation and the pilgrims of New England. Like its parent organization, United Church of Santa Fe believes spirituality is inextricably tied to social justice. It's an activist church that has been involved in community projects such as Habitat for Humanity, Esperanza Shelter for Battered Women, the hospitality center at the Penitentiary of New Mexico, St. Elizabeth's Shelter for the needy, and the Inter-Faith Council. United Church of Santa Fe's liberal bent hearkens back to the United Church of Christ, the first Protestant church to allow women clergy and to ordain an openly gay man.

United Church of Santa Fe opened a new church building in 2003. The interior is quite remarkable. Built into the "gathering room" (sanctuary) is an indoor acequia (irrigation channel), there to irrigate not the soil but the soul. It wraps like the letter "J" around the entire south wall to form a complete set of elements—earth, wind, fire, and water—within and around the church. While its presence is primarily symbolic, the acequia also serves a practical function: It's part of the solar gain system that heats the building. The church's music program is very popular, featuring everything from classical to gospel to South African freedom songs.

## SIKH

Some 25 miles north of Santa Fe, off the main drag that goes through Española—a small, but bustling village nestled between the Jémez Mountains and Truchas Peaks—a large golden dome marks the entrance to Hacienda de Guru Ram Dass, the gudwara, where the American Sikh community attends services Sundays at 11 a.m. Inside, worshippers sit with bare feet and covered heads on the floor, singing and chanting and praising God to music. After the service, which usually lasts a couple of hours, they share a free vegetarian meal. Visitors are welcome at both the service and the meal.

Española, a small city that sits both in Santa Fe and Río Arriba Counties, is headquarters for the Sikh Dharma of the Western Hemisphere. The Sikh presence in northern New Mexico began in the early 1970s, when the late Yogi Bhajan, the chief religious authority for Sikhs in the Western Hemisphere, moved to Santa Fe from Los Angeles, bought land in Española, and began teaching Kundalini yoga, a form that works closely with the body's natural energy centers to create wellbeing and abundant energy. Yogi Bhajan soon attracted a following of converts that over the past years has evolved into a community of 300 people.

Members of the Sikh community have a high profile in northern New Mexico not only because of their distinctive white garb and turbans but also because of their involvement in such arenas as politics, business, and especially health. Following the tenets of health, happy, holy organizations (3HO), Sikh Dharma in the West places holistic health high up on its list of religious virtues, and some of its members operate a number of successful alternative health-care clinics and yoga centers in northern New Mexico.

Other tenets of the Sikh religion, which began in India, include belief in one god who created all humans equally; eating no flesh—meat, fish, fowl, or eggs; abstinence from alcohol and drugs; not cutting or removing any body hair, hence the turbans; and wearing white as a sign to each other and the rest of the world that they are of service.

## UNITARIAN/UNIVERSALIST

The Unitarian Church of Santa Fe on West Barcelona Road got started in 1952 as a lay-led fellowship of about two dozen liberal-minded families from Santa Fe and Los Alamos. They were attracted to the church's doctrine of no doctrine. Rather, the Unitarian/Universalist Church, once part of the Congregationalist movement, functions by a consensus that is constantly in flux because its "eternal truths" are still emerging.

For two years after its founding, the Santa Fe Fellowship met at a private club on Garcia Street near downtown Santa Fe. In 1954 they began meeting at Temple Beth Shalom—Santa Fe's first synagogue, completed only a year earlier. There

they conducted an active Sunday school that attracted so many children that the youngsters reportedly outnumbered the adults—perhaps because they learned "social graces" in addition to the usual Sunday school subjects.

This forced another move—and another and another, including one to the local Church of Jesus Christ of Latter-day Saints, or Mormon Church, whose rules against coffee, tea, and smoking, even outside, proved difficult. Finally, in 1968, the 35-member fellowship bought a house it could barely afford, one that allegedly came with a ghost. None except a live-in caretaker family ever heard or saw him, however.

By 1979 the congregation once again outgrew its quarters and bought the Mormon church it had rented two decades earlier, its current base of operations. It hired a full-time minister in 1981 and has since renovated and enlarged its church, located in Santa Fe's upscale South Capitol area. Today the Unitarian Church of Santa Fe has 300 members from a variety of religious backgrounds. They're a relatively well-educated and well-heeled group whose members, like their church, tend to be activists with politics that lie somewhere left of center.

# INDEX

# ABOUT THE AUTHOR

Nicky Leach was born near Cambridge, England, and moved to the United States nearly 30 years ago. Trained as an educator, she embarked on a second career in 1982 as a book editor in Santa Barbara, California, and went on to become executive editor of Sequoia Communications, a company specializing in high-quality, four-color visitor guides and coffee-table books for clients all over the country. She began working as a freelance editor, project manager, and writer in 1989. Her first book, *The Guide to National Parks of the Southwest,* published by Southwest Parks and Monuments Association, won the National Park Service Cooperating Association Interpretive Excellence competition in 1994. Since then Nicky has authored or contributed to more than 45 guidebooks focusing on the natural and cultural history of the United States, from the U.S. West to Florida and Hawaii. In addition to writing and editing, Nicky is a trained bodyworker, specializing in biodynamic craniosacral therapy and stress management. She lives in Santa Fe with her tabby cat, Molly.

# Travel Like a Pro

The Cheap Bastard's Guide to
NEW YORK CITY
MORE THAN 1,000 **FREE** LISTINGS

100 BEST
Resorts of the Caribbean

OFF THE BEATEN PAT
VIRGINIA A GUIDE TO UNIQUE PLACES

*The Luxury Guide to*
Walt Disney World® Resort
*Second Edition*
How to Get the Most Out of the
Best Disney Has to Offer

shifra stein's
day trips®
from kansas city
*fifteenth edition*

NINTH EDITION
JOHN HOW
CHOOSE COSTA R
FOR RETIREMEN

FUN WITH THE FAMILY
Hundreds of Ideas for Day Trips with the Kids
Connecticut

INSIDERS'® GUIDE
Florida Keys
and Key West

SCENIC DRIVING
COLORADO
STEWART M. GREEN
THIRD EDITION